STEINBERG'S DICTIONARY
OF
BRITISH HISTORY

Steinberg's Dictionary

of

British History

Second Edition

EDITED BY

S. H. STEINBERG and I. H. EVANS

P. M. BARNES   B. W. FAGAN
R. B. GRASSBY   M. L. HENRY
SIR PATRICK KINGSLEY   M. ROPER
C. F. SLADE   SIR ROBERT SOMERVILLE
R. F. WALKER   GLANMOR WILLIAMS

BOOK CLUB ASSOCIATES
LONDON

© EDWARD ARNOLD (PUBLISHERS) LTD. 1970
First published 1963
Reprinted with corrections 1964
Second Edition 1970

This edition published 1973 by
Book Club Associates
By arrangement with Edward Arnold (Publishers) Ltd.

Reproduced photolitho in Great Britain by
J. W. Arrowsmith Ltd. Bristol

PREFACE

The predecessor of the present book was *A Dictionary of British History* edited by J. A. Brendon, B.A., F.R.Hist.S. It appeared in 1937 and went quickly out of print, but war-time conditions prevented its re-issue so that it failed to 'establish itself as the true and trusted friend of many teachers and students', as the editor had hoped.

When the publishers approached the present editor in December 1958 with a view to producing a revised edition, it was decided at once that this revision should become a completely new book.

Certain principles were laid down for the guidance of the contributors and a summary of the main points they contained may serve as 'advice to the user', who will thus see at a glance what he may legitimately expect to find.

1. The present book is the co-operative effort of a dozen contributors. They have co-operated in drawing-up the list of entries and seen, at least in the proofs, all entries; they have suggested numerous amendments which have recommended themselves to their fellow-authors and therefore been embodied in the final text. While each one bears the main responsibility for the articles signed by him or her, a number of entries include the work of other contributors. They are therefore reasonably hopeful that no serious mistakes have been allowed to pass uncorrected.

2. All purely biographical entries, which in Brendon's Dictionary took up more than half of the book have been excluded. For these the student should refer to the *Dictionary of National Biography*, its twentieth-century continuations and concise editions, and the *Dictionary of Welsh Biography*. The space thus gained has been used for increasing the scope as well as the number of individual headings.

3. The scope of the present book has been extended to comprise:

(a) The countries which are, or at some time were, part of England and her overseas possessions, the British Empire, or the Commonwealth of Nations. Their history, however, is carried on only as long as their British connexion lasted: that of Calais, for instance, terminates in 1564, that of the United States of America in 1783, that of Burma in 1947.

(b) Political, constitutional, administrative, legal, ecclesiastical and economic events have received varying stress in different periods, but the aim has been to strike a fair balance between their claims to the historian's attention. The histories of literature, music, the arts and architecture, philosophy and science have been excluded, except in a few cases when they have direct bearing on other aspects of history, as for instance CASTLES.

(c) The internal history of Scotland and Ireland, although not neglected, has been treated less fully than that of Wales. Rather than accord superficial treatment to all three, the first two have been treated mainly, although not exclusively, from the point of view of their relations with England; the close association of Wales, from Roman times onward, with England made it the obvious subject for fuller treatment.

4. Contributors have generally used as headings such terms as come most readily to mind when looking for information, even if they are not strictly

accurate: e.g. BEVERIDGE REPORT rather than *Social Insurance and Allied Services: Report*. Items such as King's Bench/Queen's Bench have been given under King's. The liberal insertion of CROSS-REFERENCES (printed in SMALL CAPS) will lead the student to cognate and supplementary entries. Obvious alternatives, such as 'Duchy of Cornwall' and 'Cornwall, Duchy of', have not been cross-referred, the second form of such entries being used.

5. Bibliographical titles have been added only in those rare cases where there is available a book that can fairly be described as a definitive monograph unlikely to be superseded in the foreseeable future. For general bibliographies the student should refer to the *Bibliography of British History*, issued by the American Historical Association and the Royal Historical Society of Great Britain, the *Writings on British History*, ed. A. Taylor Milne, and the *Annual Bulletin of Historical Literature* published by the Historical Association.

6. The work has been divided among the contributors as follows—although, as mentioned above, there has been much overlapping and collaboration:

Dr Patricia M. Barnes, F.R.Hist.S., Assistant Keeper, Public Record Office; General Editor, The Pipe Roll Society: administrative terms and institutions (PMB)

I. H. Evans, B.A. (London), A.K.C., Editor, Brewer's *Dictionary of Phrase and Fable*: 1485 to 1785 (IHE)

B. W. Fagan, C.B.E., M.C., sometime Director of Edward Arnold (Publishers) Ltd: Printing and Publishing (BWF)

R. B. Grassby, M.A. (Oxon), Fellow and Tutor of Jesus College, Oxford: 1603–1688 (RBG)

M. L. Henry, M.A. (Oxon), Assistant Librarian, The Queen's University, Belfast. 1785 to date (MLH)

Sir Patrick Kingsley, K.C.V.O., Secretary of the Duchy of Cornwall: Cornwall (PK)

M. Roper, M.A. (Manchester), F.R.Hist.S., Assistant Keeper, Public Record Office: administrative terms and institutions (MR)

Dr C. F. Slade, F.S.A., F.R.Hist.S. Reader in History, Reading University: Prehistory, Roman Britain, Anglo-Saxon England (CFS)

Sir Robert Somerville, K.C.V.O., M.A., Clerk of Council and Keeper of Records, The Duchy of Lancaster: Lancaster (RS)

Dr S. H. Steinberg, F.R.Hist.S., late Editor, *The Statesman's Year-Book*: Colonial, Imperial and Commonwealth affairs (SHS)

Dr R. F. Walker, Lecturer in History, University College of Wales, Aberystwyth: 1066–1485 (RFW)

Professor Glanmor Williams, F.R.Hist.S., Professor of History, University College of Swansea: Wales (GW)

It is the editor's privilege to end this preface on a personal note. I wish to thank all contributors for their co-operation and, in addition, Dr Barnes, Mr Evans and Dr Slade for help in general editorial work that went well beyond their responsibilities as contributors. Finally, it is with very great pleasure that I record the friendly interest shown by Sir Frank and Lady Stenton and Professor Treharne in the preparation of this book.

S. H. STEINBERG

PREFACE TO THE SECOND EDITION

This revised edition has been renamed as a tribute to its late editor, Sigfrid Henry Steinberg, who died while it was in the early stages of preparation. As his successor I have sought to maintain the standards he set and I have been helped in this by the continued co-operation of all but one of the original contributors. Unfortunately Dr Barnes was unable to assist and her assignment has been taken over by Mr Roper.

A number of new articles have been introduced and existing entries brought up to date or amended where improvements could be made. Entries on the Commonwealth countries and government departments have been especially affected by recent change and particular attention has been give to this; where Commonwealth countries have undergone a change of name their history is given under the old name until the date of change, thereafter under the new. Dr Steinberg's articles now carry his initials, but I have accepted responsibility by adding my own to those which have been amended, although the credit for such entries must remain his. I have also amended the list of contributors given in the original preface.

I wish to thank sincerely all the contributors for their efforts and friendly collaboration, as well as for many helpful suggestions. Lastly I must record my gratitude to Mrs Christine Steinberg for her generous co-operation and for very practical assistance with the Commonwealth entries.

I. H. EVANS

STEINBERG'S DICTIONARY
OF
BRITISH HISTORY

Aachen, peace of (18 Oct. 1748), ended the AUSTRIAN SUCCESSION WAR. It was signed by England, the Netherlands, France, and subsequently by Spain, Austria and Sardinia. Conquests were restored, Holland regained the Barrier fortresses, the PRAGMATIC SANCTION was guaranteed, Francis I was recognized as emperor, but Prussia retained Silesia and Glatz. Parma and Piacenza went to Don Philip of Spain, Savoy and Nice to Sardinia. France was to expel the Young Pretender and restore MADRAS. England returned Louisbourg.   IHE

Abbeville, treaty of (1259), see PARIS, TREATY OF.

Abdication. Edward II and Richard II, see DEPOSITION.

JAMES II. The birth of a son to James II (10 June 1688) created the threat of a permanent Catholic dynasty. Tory leaders allied with Whigs and Dissenters against him and seven prominent statesmen sent an invitation to William of Orange for assistance (30 June). William landed at Brixham (15 Nov.) and marched on London. James II was rapidly deserted on all sides. The Queen and her son were sent to France and James fled to Sheerness (21 Dec.) but was brought back to Whitehall and finally allowed to escape to France. A CONVENTION PARLIAMENT declared that James had broken the original contract between king and people, violated the fundamental laws and, by running away, had abdicated, and the throne was declared vacant (Feb. 1689).   IHE

EDWARD VIII. During the summer of 1936 the foreign press commented freely on the friendship of Edward VIII (succeeded 20 Jan.) with the American Mrs Wallis Warfield Simpson. On 20 Oct. the Prime Minister, Baldwin, learning that Mrs Simpson was seeking a decree nisi from her husband (granted 27 Oct.), sought an audience of the king. In the next 6 weeks a struggle developed between Edward VIII (who informed Baldwin, 16 Nov., of his intention to marry Mrs Simpson) and his senior ministers who, backed by all the dominion governments, objected to a marriage with a twice divorced woman. A morganatic marriage was proposed and rejected. English newspapers broke their self-imposed silence, 3 Dec., following a supposed reference to the matter by the bishop of Bradford. Baldwin made a full statement in Parliament, 10 Dec., and the next day an A. Bill (with the consent of the Dominions under the Statute of WESTMINSTER) was quickly passed.   MLH

Abernethy, treaty of (1072). After the NORMAN CONQUEST of England King Malcolm III of Scots harboured important English fugitives and married Margaret, sister of Edgar Atheling. Following a series of border raids, William I invaded Scotland in the summer of 1072, supported by a fleet. Malcolm attempted little resistance, and at A. (Perthshire) on the Tay, he did homage to William and gave him his son, Duncan, as a hostage. Edgar was later expelled from Scotland. Malcolm renewed his homage to William II in 1091, but although he recognized the theoretical superiority of the King of England, the practical independence of Scotland was not prejudiced.   RFW

Abhorrers, see PETITIONERS.

Abjuration Oath. An oath to abjure the realm imposed until 1531 upon law-breakers who claimed privilege of SANCTUARY was occasionally used as an indirect method of deportation by Elizabeth I against Protestant and Catholic RECUSANTS. The same name was given to a different oath in 1662, requiring the Scots to abjure the SOLEMN LEAGUE AND COVENANT, and to an oath abjuring the exiled Stewarts imposed by Parliament in 1701. Used intermittently as an alternative to the oath of ALLEGIANCE, and in 1778 as a condition prior to the removal of certain catholic disabilities, it was eventually amalgamated with the customary oath of allegiance in 1858. RBG

Abjuration of the Realm, an alternative to OUTLAWRY for criminals unwilling to stand trial or already convicted, was apparently introduced by the Normans. When the criminal in SANCTUARY decided to abjure, the CORONER (earlier the king's serjeant) was called: in the neighbourhood's presence he heard the criminal's confession and abjuration, then assigned a port of exit, commonly Dover, though some abjurors went to Scotland. Wearing sackcloth and carrying a cross, the abjuror had to travel to the port by main roads, staying one night only at each stop, and leave by the first available ship. A royal pardon was his only hope of return. PMB

Aboukir Bay, battles; see NILE; ALEXANDRIA.

Acadia (French: Acadie), the present Canadian provinces of NOVA SCOTIA and NEW BRUNSWICK, was discovered by John Cabot in 1497 and colonized by French Huguenots in 1604. These were expelled by a British expedition from Virginia in 1614, and the territory was granted to Sir William Alexander and renamed NOVA SCOTIA in 1621. The settlement failed, however, and A. was restored to the French in 1632. Reconquered by a Cromwellian expedition in 1654, it was again ceded to France in 1667: and the same happened after the third British occupation (1689) in 1697. A. was finally captured in 1710 and formally ceded to Britain by the treaty of

UTRECHT. In 1755 the French were deported to English colonies for their active disloyalty, an event portrayed in Longfellow's *Evangeline.* SHS

Ackling Dyke, see PORT WAY.

Aclea, battle of (851), fought at an unknown site (probably represented by a modern Oakley) between the men of WESSEX under king Ethelwulf and a large army of DANES. It was the one major English victory over the Danes during this period and a step in the rise of WESSEX to supremacy in England. CFS

Acre (modern Akka, near Haifa in Israel), siege of (1) (1189–91). The recovery of A., which had fallen to Saladin in 1187, was the first objective of the Third CRUSADE. The crusaders maintained the siege for two years from June 1189. Richard Lionheart, who had left England in Dec. 1189, arrived on 8 June 1191, after long delays in Sicily and Cyprus. Under Richard's leadership the crusaders finally took A. on 12 July, and for a century it remained the chief city and port of the remnants of the kingdom of Jerusalem. RFW

(2) (March–May 1799), by Napoleon's Egyptian army. The Turkish defenders were assisted by the English ships *Theseus* and *Tigre* under Sir Sidney Smith, who captured siege artillery and gunboats, thus delaying the final assault until 7 May. British seamen helped to hold the breach until Turkish reinforcements arrived. Napoleon was forced to raise the siege and retreat to Egypt (ALEXANDRIA). MLH

Acre, bombardment of (3 Nov. 1840), by a British, Austrian and Turkish fleet under Sir R. Stopford in an attempt to force the withdrawal of Mehemed Ali of Egypt, who had held Syria since 1831 and had defeated the Sultan Mahmud at the battle of Nezib (June 1839). The town was reduced and taken. Syria was restored to the Porte by the Convention of London (13 July 1841). MLH

Acton Burnell, statute of (12 Oct. 1283), part of the legislation of Edward I which sought to enable merchants, particularly foreign merchants, to obtain payment of debts. The statute provided that the mayor of London, York or Bristol should witness acknowledgements of debt, and should seal bonds as well as the debtors. If a debtor failed to pay, the creditor might appeal to the mayor, who would secure the distraint of the debtor's chattels. The procedure was clarified and revised by the statute of merchants in 1285.   RFW

Addled Parliament (5 Apr.–7 June 1614) was summoned by James I to obtain supplies. Although he denied making use of the UNDERTAKERS, the Commons refused to make a grant unless the king abandoned IMPOSITIONS and reinstated those clergy deprived in 1604. It was derisively called 'Addled', being dissolved before passing a single Act.   IHE

Aden, first mentioned in Ezekiel xxvii, 23 as a city of merchants, was unsuccessfully attacked by the Portuguese from Goa in 1513 and captured by the Turks in 1538. Under their misrule the flourishing port was reduced to a poor village when the Indian navy in 1839 took possession of it by treaty with the sultan of Lahej. Its importance as a coaling station and entrepôt increased especially after the opening of the SUEZ CANAL (1869). The settlement was separated from India in 1935 and was organized as a colony in 1937. It had a legislative council with (since 1957) an elected majority.

The governor of A. also controlled the Kuria-Muria islands (ceded by the sultan of MUSCAT in 1854), Perim island (occupied in 1857), Kamaran island (taken from the Turks in 1915) and the Western and Eastern A. protectorates. These consisted of respectively 17 and 5 sultanates, amirates and shaikdoms, which from 1839 onward entered into treaty relations with Britain. In 1959 a 'federation of Arab amirates of the south' was formed in the Western protectorate. Aden joined it on 1 March 1963. From Aug. 1967 the country was overrun by forces of the National Liberation Front, the last British troops left A. on 29 Nov., and the Southern Yemen Peoples' Republic was proclaimed (30 Nov.).
                                                              SHS ; IHE

Admiral, a title of Arab origin first used in England in the late-13th century. It was applied first to administrators of naval affairs, from which the office of Lord High Admiral developed (the duke of Buckingham was the first so styled, in 1618). From the mid-17th century the title was applied to commanders at sea. This post became a rank during the 18th century. First within the fleet then, as England gained control of the narrow seas, outside it, the a. acquired a court over maritime matters. Founded c. 1340, it was regulated by statutes of 1391 and 1393: as commerce and colonies developed, overseas courts of vice-admiralty were established. The a.'s jurisdiction, founded on the laws of OLÉRON, was both civil, in the prize and instance court, and criminal, in Oyer and Terminer. The court was merged with other special jurisdictions under the 1873 Judicature Act.   PMB

From 1625 the fleet was divided into Red, Blue and White squadrons under an a., vice a. and rear a., in that order of precedence. The order was changed in 1653 to Red, White, Blue. Each squadron was then formed into three divisions, each under an a., vice a. and rear a., the A. of the Red being A. of the Fleet. These nine flag posts were steadily increased by reduplication from 1743. From 1747 suitable captains were promoted for whom there was no employment and were nicknamed Yellow A. (from the quarantine flag). In 1805 a tenth rank of A. of the Red was created as distinct from A. of the Fleet. Squadronal colours were abolished in 1864 and the White flag which had been surcharged with the cross of St George in 1702, to distinguish it from the French flag, became the White Ensign of the Royal Navy.   IHE

Admiralty, Board of. Early medieval navies were formed of merchant shipping under temporary commanders, but from the 13th century warships were built and maintained as an increasingly large part of the naval force by clerks or keepers of the king's ships and, from the late 14th century, the office of the Lord ADMIRAL (from the 17th century: Lord High Admiral) developed. The first step to modern organization was taken in 1546, when principal officers of marine causes, later the Navy Board, were appointed to provide shipping and civil administration, maintain dockyards etc., with specialists in various branches. The office of Lord High Admiral was, frequently between 1628 and 1689 and almost continuously thereafter, entrusted to commissioners, the B. of A., responsible for strategy, naval personnel and allied matters. In 1832 the Navy Board was merged into the B. of A. On 1 Apr. 1964 the B. of A. was abolished and replaced by a new A. Board of the DEFENCE Council. At the same time the office of Lord High Admiral was vested in the crown.

PMB; MR

Admonitions to Parliament (1572), two Puritan indictments of the established church, especially attacking episcopacy and advocating a Presbyterian system. They were suppressed by the government but produced a vigorous pamphlet warfare and marked the growing militancy of the Presbyterian party.   IHE

Adulterine Castles. During the ANARCHY royal control of private castle-building temporarily lapsed and hundreds of new castles, many as yet unidentified, were built without Stephen's permission (hence 'a.c.'). Though many were slightly constructed, they served the barons, whether of Stephen's party or Maud's, as centres from which they commanded or terrorized their immediate neighbourhoods, and made the restoration of order and royal authority more difficult. In a period when the defensive enjoyed a temporary advantage over the offensive their reduction often involved lengthy operations, but Stephen, a specialist in sieges,

destroyed many or forced their abandonment. Systematic destruction of most of the surviving a.c. was begun by Stephen after the treaty of WINCHESTER (1153) and was rapidly completed by Henry II in 1154–5.   RFW

Adventurers (1642). To raise money to meet the expenses of the IRISH REBELLION (1641) Parliament, with the consent of Charles I, confiscated some 2,500,000 acres from the rebels. Debenture bonds totalling £1,000,000 were issued to A. payable in Irish land. More lands were set aside to meet their claims under the Cromwellian Act of SETTLEMENT (1652). Charles II confirmed their titles by the Act of SETTLEMENT (1662), but the grants were modified by the Act of SETTLEMENT AND EXPLANATION (1665). (PLANTATION OF IRELAND.)   IHE

Advertisements, Book of (1566), was issued by Matthew Parker, archbishop of Canterbury, to secure stricter observance of the Act of UNIFORMITY in worship and to check the VESTIARIAN CONTROVERSY.   IHE

Advocate, Lord, see SCOTTISH OFFICE.

Advowson, the right of presentation to a church benefice by patrons clerical or lay. Lay PATRONAGE is known from the 8th century, when churches came to be built and endowed by lay landowners. After the constitutions of CLARENDON (1164) a. was recognized as a right of property which could be bequeathed and sold like other forms of property. It thereby became open to many abuses. Their transfer is now subject to controls.   IHE

Adwalton Moor (or Atherton Moor, near Bradford), battle of (30 June 1643), left the ROYALISTS supreme in Yorkshire with the exception of Hull.   IHE

Afghan wars. (1) (1839–42). Russia's increasing influence in central Asia and her ascendancy over Turkey and Persia (coupled with the latter's siege of Herat, 1837) seemed to presage an attempt to dominate Afghanistan and thus endanger the security of the PUNJAB. Lord Auckland, governor-general of India, determined with the help of the SIKH leader Ranjit Singh to replace Dost Muhammad, the amir at Kabul, with his own nominee, Shah Shuja. In spite of serious doubts in England and India, Kandahar, Ghazni and Kabul were occupied (Aug. 1839), and for 18 months Shuja was upheld by a British garrison against incipient unrest which culminated in concerted revolt and the murder of two political agents. Under Maj.-Gen. W. G. K. Elphinstone about 4,500 Anglo-Indian troops (with 12,000 followers) left Kabul (6 Jan. 1842). The weather and Pathan horsemen accounted for the whole force; one survivor reached Jalalabad. The new governor-general, Lord Ellenborough, decided that the country should be evacuated, but he first permitted Maj.-Gen. (later F.-M. Sir) G. Pollock (at Jalalabad) and Maj.-Gen. Sir W. Nott (Kandahar) to advance on Kabul where the Pathan leader Akbar Kahn was defeated. Dost Muhammad returned and ruled for a further 20 years.

(2) (1878-80). Russia, in occupation of Turkistan and victorious over the Turks (1877-8), again became the object of serious British suspicion. Lord Lytton, governor-general (1876-80), took matters into his own hands. On the amir Sher Ali's refusal to receive a British agent (though a Russian had been accepted), 3 British armies marched through the passes and Yakub Khan (Sher Ali's son) by the treaty of Gandamak (May 1879) accepted a British resident, Sir L. Cavagnari. But Cavagnari was murdered (3 Sept.) and Maj.-Gen. F. (later F.-M. Lord) Roberts occupied Kabul (7 Oct.). In July 1880 the Gladstone ministry, having replaced Lytton by Ripon, recognized Abdur Rahman (a nephew of Sher Ali) as amir in Kabul with a British subsidy. Meanwhile Ayub Khan, who had been recognized in Herat, overwhelmed the British southern force at Maiwand west of Kandahar (July 1880), and this necessitated Roberts's famous march (313 miles in 22 days) from

Kabul. Roberts defeated Ayub (Sept.), the British were able to withdraw, and Abdur Rahman quickly consolidated his power.

(3) (1919). Amir Amanullah (who had succeeded on the murder (1919) of Abdur Rahman's son Habibullah) incited the Pathan tribes to invade India through the Khyber Pass. Their main force was defeated at Bagh Springs (11 May) and, after the occupation of Dakka and Baldak and the bombing of Kabul and Jalalabad, Amanullah signed the treaty of Rawalpindi (8 Aug.) by which he lost the subsidy.   MLH

African Company (the Company of Royal Adventurers Trading to Africa), chartered in 1660, acquired the EAST INDIA COMPANY's forts on the GAMBIA and GOLD COAST and after 1662 the slaving monopoly was its main concern. Bankrupted by losses in the DUTCH WARS it was taken over by the Royal A.C. (1672), but interlopers caused financial difficulties by the 1690s. The trade was thrown open in 1698 and the company's ASIENTO contract (1713) failed to restore its fortunes. In 1750 a new regulated company was set up to manage the forts, which reverted to the crown (1827) after the abolition of the SLAVE-TRADE.
                                              IHE

Agen, process of (1331–4). In 1325, at the end of the war of ST SARDOS, King Charles IV of France retained the Agenais as a war indemnity. The p. of A., like those of MONTREUIL (1306) and Périgueux (1311), was an examination by English and French diplomats of outstanding disputes concerning the duchy of GUIENNE, and on this occasion of the future of the Agenais in particular. The problems proved insoluble by peaceful means, and the p. was the last attempt at a negotiated settlement in Guienne before the outbreak of the HUNDRED YEARS' WAR in 1338.   RFW

Agincourt, battle of (25 Oct. 1415). After the surrender of HARFLEUR Henry V garrisoned the town and determined to lead the remainder of his army, perhaps 6,000 strong, northwards to CALAIS. Unable to cross the flooded and well-guarded lower Somme, the army had to make a long detour before getting over the river near Béthencourt on 19 Oct. A large French army nominally commanded by the constable D'Albret and the marshal Boucicault was in a position to dispute Henry's progress. The battle was fought on ground which favoured traditional English tactics and which prevented the French from taking full advantage of their superior numbers. The English first advanced and provoked a French cavalry attack, then halted and repelled the attack largely by archery. A heavy assault by dismounted French men-at-arms followed immediately, and was only broken after prolonged hand-to-hand fighting. The English then attacked and defeated a second division of French infantry. Many of the cavalry of the French rearguard never came into effective action, and its attack in the last stage of the battle was beaten off without difficulty. Estimates of the size of the French army vary widely, but it is likely to have numbered 20,000, of whom about 7,000 were killed or captured. The highest contemporary estimate of English losses was 1,600. After the battle Henry V resumed his march to Calais, which he reached on 16 Nov. The dramatic victory of A., however, could not be followed up immediately: systematic conquest began only with Henry's renewed attack on NORMANDY in 1417. On the other hand, A. recovered the military prestige which the English had enjoyed in the mid-14th century, and secured popular support in England for further military ventures in France.   RFW

Agitators. Angered by Parliament's proposals to disband the army after the first CIVIL WAR without settling their arrears of pay, each regiment elected two A. or Agents (Apr.–May 1647). They were the instigators of the removal of the king from Holmby House to Newmarket, but after the PUTNEY DEBATES and a mutiny in the army (15 Nov.) control of opinion reverted to the council of officers.   IHE

Agra, see BENGAL; UTTAR PRADESH.

Agreement of the People was presented to the army council at the PUTNEY DEBATES (28 Oct. 1647) by the AGITATORS under the influence of the LEVELLERS, summarizing their demands for a more democratic constitution than the HEADS OF THE PROPOSALS, e.g., constituencies based on population, biennial parliaments, religious freedom, legal equality, no compulsory military service. The army redrafted it (Jan. 1649) and presented it to the RUMP (20 Jan.). It was not acted upon.   IHE

Agricultural Revolution, a term, no longer accepted by some historians, used to describe the intensification of the transition from the open-field system and the technical progress made in farming during the 18th century. INCLOSURES, especially in the midlands and north, and the consolidation of holdings elsewhere increased the area under cultivation and facilitated improvements in land use, drainage, soils, crops, etc. Pioneer experiments in the 17th century, such as the use of turnips and clover as fodder crops, found general acceptance in the 18th under improving landlords. A critical and more scientific approach to stock breeding, crop rotation, the use of fertilizers, etc., was stimulated by increasing demands for meat and wheat. Especially notable contributions were made by Jethro Tull (1674–1740) in arable farming, Viscount ('Turnip') Townshend (1674–1738), Robert Bakewell (1725–95) in breeding sheep for meat, and Arthur Young (1741–1820) as a propagandist. A Board of Agriculture was established in 1793, and George III took a keen interest in farming progress. The use of the seed drill and horse hoe and the replacement of oxen by horses for ploughing led to more intensive farming. The whole process was accelerated by the high prices during the REVOLUTIONARY and NAPOLEONIC WARS (1793–1815).   IHE

Agriculture, Fisheries and Food, Ministry of. A Board of Agriculture

1793–1822 and its successor the Royal Agricultural Society of England, incorporated in 1840, encouraged professional and lay interest in agricultural improvement. The Board of Agriculture, founded in 1889, combined government interest with the cattle-plague department of the PRIVY COUNCIL and certain administrative duties of the tithe, inclosure and copyhold commissions established 1836–54. In 1903 oversight of sea and fresh-water fisheries was transferred to the Board from the Board of TRADE, and in 1919, losing forestry affairs to the FORESTRY COMMISSION, the Board was renamed the Ministry of Agriculture and Fisheries, to which Food was added in 1955, when it was amalgamated with the Ministry of Food (established in 1939, on the model of the Ministry of 1916–21, to administer the nation's wartime food supplies). The Ministry's work now covers the whole field of national agricultural and fishery policy, assisted locally by county agricultural advisory committees. PMB

Aids, taxes falling into two groups, feudal and gracious. MAGNA CARTA, following earlier practice, allowed feudal aids to be taken on three occasions: to redeem the lord's body (e.g. the RANSOM of Richard I), to knight his first son and marry his first daughter. Gracious aids, though scarcely voluntary, were taken on other special occasions, e.g. for a war or payment of the lord's debts. When imposed by kings such aids fell heavily on his ancient DEMESNE, notably the towns, who preferred the term to that of TALLAGE, since it implied a free gift, not the stigma of villein tenure associated with tallage. Aids declined in the 13th century as new forms of taxation were devised. In the medieval period a sheriff's aid was levied in each shire to reward the officer. PMB

Air Ministry. The invention of the aeroplane and its adoption as a weapon by both army and navy during the first world war led to friction, waste, lack of co-ordination and a failure to develop new and separate air tactics,

arousing popular indignation. An Air Board, with little power, was appointed in 1916; then in 1917–18 an Air Council, headed by a Secretary of State, and the A.M. were set up to administer the Royal Air Force, founded in 1918. On 1 Apr. 1964 the A.M. ceased to exist and the Air Council became the Air Force Board of the DEFENCE Council. PMB; MR

Aix-la-Chapelle, see AACHEN.

Ajmer. An agency of the EAST INDIA COMPANY, subordinate to the factory at Surat, was established in A. early in the 17th century. In 1818 the maharaja of GWALIOR ceded to the Company what became the province of A.-Merwara, which was administered by a chief commissioner, from 1950 as a C-State, until its merger (1 Nov. 1956) with RAJASTHAN. SHS

Akeman Street, a ROMAN ROAD on the line St Albans–Alchester–Cirencester. Another with this name lay on the line Arrington–Cambridge–Ely and beyond. The origin of the name is not known, but *Acemannes ceaster* was a name for Bath in the 10th century. CFS

Alabama Case. In March and July 1862, 2 ships (subsequently named *Florida* and *Alabama*), being built on the Mersey, were allowed to leave their berths although it was known that they would be used as privateers in the service of the southern states in the American Civil War. Both ships did serious damage to commerce of the northern states. During and after the war claims for reparations were made but refused. Finally Britain and the U.S. agreed (Washington, 8 May 1871) to submit to arbitration (U.S., Britain, Italy, Switzerland and Brazil). The decision (14 Sept. 1872) that Britain was liable in the sum of $15.5m. was accepted. MLH

Alamein, battle of El (23 Oct.–4 Nov. 1942), 60 miles west of Alexandria, a decisive victory for the British 8th Army (Gen. B. L. (later F.-M. Lord) Montgomery) over the Desert Axis Army (F.-M. E. Rommel) during

WORLD WAR II. XXX Corps advanced south of Tel-el-eisa ridge behind a barrage followed by the armour of X Corps; a regrouping was made, 29–31 Oct., in preparation for a second attack, 2 Nov., when armour successfully broke through. Rommel started to withdraw German units, 3 Nov., and was in full retreat by 4 Nov. In the first phase, containing attacks were made to the south of the main battle area, whilst before and during the final phase there was a diversionary attack in the coastal area to the north. 8th Army casualties were 8,000; Axis losses, 60,000 (including 30,000 prisoners).   MLH

Alberta, originally part of RUPERT'S LAND, was after 1763 opened up by the North-West Company, organized as a district of the NORTH-WEST TERRITORIES in 1875 and became a province of CANADA on 1 Sept. 1905.   SHS

Albuera, battle of (16 May 1811), a sharp conflict of the PENINSULAR WAR, lacking in strategic significance. Soult, marching to the relief of Badajoz with about 24,000 French, was met by Gen. Sir W. (later Lord) Beresford in command of about 35,000 allied troops (9,000 British). Soult attacked and gained an important height; Beresford was saved by the arrival of 2 brigades of the 4th Division. A resolute attack at the instance of Col. H. (later F.-M. Lord) Hardinge by the 7th and 23rd Fusiliers was decisive. Casualties were heavy: French, 8,000; allies, 6,000 (including 4,000 British).   MLH

Alderman, see COUNTY COURT, EALDORMAN.

Alexandria, battle of (21 Mar. 1801). Gen. Sir R. Abercrombie, ordered to EGYPT to destroy the French army left there by Napoleon after his defeat at ACRE, landed under heavy fire at Aboukir Bay (8 Mar. 1801) with 14,000 men. Fighting the action of Mandora (13 Mar.) he advanced west along the narrow peninsula between lake Aboukir and the sea. The French under Gen. Menou attacked 4 miles east of Alexandria. The attack was beaten off after about 4 hours fighting, the British right and reserves (Maj.-Gen. John Moore) being heavily engaged. French casualties were about 3,000; British, 1,400, including Abercrombie (died 28 Mar.). The army, now under Lt.-Gen. Sir J. H. Hutchinson, forced the capitulation of the French at Cairo (June) and Alexandria (Aug.).   MLH

Alexandria, bombardment of (11 July 1882), by a British squadron under Adm. Sir. B. Seymour (later Lord Alcester) in an endeavour to quell Arabi Pasha who had assumed control of EGYPT (1881). Arabi was defeated by an expedition under Sir G. Wolseley at TEL-EL-KEBIR.   MLH

Alienation Office. Lands held feudally in chief of the king could not, at least from Edward I's reign, be alienated without licence: otherwise they were forfeit or, after 1327, subject to a pardon. Revenue from licences and pardons, paid into CHANCERY, was leased at farm to the earl of Leicester in 1576; his deputies, appointed to value lands and assess and collect fines, became the A.O. After Leicester's death the lease was granted to the Lord TREASURER and the office was subsequently administered by the TREASURY. Feudal incidents were abolished at the RESTORATION, and in 1834 revenues from fines and recoveries also ceased. The A.O. was abolished in 1835.   PMB

Aliens. Medieval a., outside the feudal and customary bonds of English society were, by the mid-13th century, at a considerable disadvantage, e.g. they could not hold land nor inherit it. Kings, however, found it advantageous to grant favours to a. such as merchant bankers and mercenaries; and letters patent of denization were devised, allowing land holding, etc., but leaving other disadvantages removable only by private Act. Modern laws, notably the Naturalization Act 1870, have further mitigated the position of a. in society. The Home Office now receives applications for denization, requiring a 5 years' residence qualification. In English law a child born within any British jurisdiction, and in some places outside, is of British nationality, whatever its parents' citizenship. PMB

Aljubarrota, battle of (14 Aug. 1385). About 8 miles south of Leiria, on the road to Lisbon, king João I of Portugal (John of Aviz) with some 7,000 men, including some hundreds of English and Gascons, decisively defeated king Juan I of Castile and his army of c. 18,000, which included a French contingent. The victory, which ensured the continued independence of Portugal under a native dynasty, was commemorated by João's foundation of the great abbey of Batalha nearby. The help given to the Portuguese by English and Gascon men-at-arms and archers was not as considerable as was once thought, but victory was due to the tactics developed by the English in the HUNDRED YEARS' WAR and adopted by their allies. RFW

Allegiance, the bond of a man to his lord, the subject to the crown. It was secured in the medieval period by liege HOMAGE, and in more modern times by bonds of national sentiment, precise legal definition of nationality and, for officers of state etc., the taking of an oath of a. To gain a favourable interest, less formal than a., medieval kings granted money–fees, payable at the EXCHEQUER, to innumerable foreign allies, great and small. PMB

Allegiance, Oath of. A feudal o. of a. was exacted by medieval kings, but the first statutory oath on civil and ecclesiastical office-holders, foreshadowed by Henry VIII's second Act of Succession (1534), was imposed by the Act of SUPREMACY (1559) and on M.P.s by an Act of 1563. Special oaths were required of Catholic RECUSANTS by Acts of 1606 and 1610. In 1678 renunciation of Roman Catholicism was added to the Parliamentary oaths, and in 1689 new oaths were instituted to abrogate allegiance to the Stewarts (NON-JURORS). The Relief Act of 1829 included a special oath for Roman Catholics. The o. of

a., supremacy and ABJURATION were combined in 1858, and the form further simplified in 1866 and 1868. Affirmation was permitted in 1888. IHE

All the Talents, Ministry of (1806–7), the inappropriate name given to the administration of Lord Grenville which took office on the death of the younger Pitt (23 Jan.). The main element came from the followers of Charles James Fox. Addington (Lord Sidmouth) as lord privy seal was a necessary link with George III, whilst an innovation was the inclusion of the lord chief justice, Addington's friend Lord Ellenborough. Fox, who took the foreign office, tried, but failed, to make peace with Napoleon. On his death (13 Sept.) the ministry's incohesion was evident. It fell (Mar. 1807) on the king's refusal to open the higher ranks of the army to Roman Catholics and his demand that no other emancipatory bill be introduced. The one act of importance passed by the ministry was that abolishing the SLAVE TRADE (Mar. 1807). MLH

Alma, battle of the (20 Sept. 1854), the first engagement of the CRIMEAN WAR. The Russians were established on high ground on the south bank of the river Alma. Owing to lack of liaison the French attack was delayed but the British force took the heights and the Russians retreated. MLH

Almanza, battle of (25 April 1707). The defeat of the British army under the earl of Galway (of French Huguenot extraction) by the French under the duke of Berwick (English-born bastard of James II) decided the ascendancy of the French pretender (Philip V) over his Austrian rival (Charles III) in the SPANISH SUCCESSION WAR. SHS

Alnwick, battles of. (1) (13 Nov. 1092). Provoked by the seizure of Cumberland and Westmorland by William II of England in the spring of 1092, and failing to obtain redress by peaceful means, Malcolm III (Canmore) of Scots invaded Northumberland. The invasion collapsed when

Malcolm was ambushed near A. and killed, together with his eldest son, Edward.

(2) (13 June 1174). In 1173 William I (the Lion) of Scots allied with Henry 'the young king', eldest son of Henry II of England, in his rebellion against his father. William invaded England, but in 1174, while besieging A. castle with part of his forces, he was surprised and captured by an English relieving army. Subsequently imprisoned in Normandy, William secured his release only by agreement to humiliating terms, which included his recognition of Henry II's feudal overlordship of the kingdom of Scotland (FALAISE). By agreement with Richard I in 1189, however, William regained his independence.   RFW

Ambassador, the representative of one sovereign power in the country of another. Most medieval a.s were appointed for specific, short-term embassies: permanent representation, originating with late-13th-century Aragonese kings, was accelerated by the Italian states at the renaissance. Continuing English interests in France and Rome had already led to periods of almost continuous representation at Paris and Rome. Early a.s were councillors, nobles, clergy and professional civil servants; this system long persisted, though some men became specialists in particular countries; the professional diplomatic service is of late development (see VIENNA CONGRESS). Each a. has letters of credence to the head of state; instructions were first given orally, then also written.
      PMB

Amboina, massacre of (1623). Ten English settlers on the Molucca island of A. were put to death by the Dutch governor on a trumped-up charge of conspiracy with the Japanese. The EAST INDIA COMPANY thereupon abandoned the competition for the spice islands and concentrated on India. After the first DUTCH WAR Cromwell exacted a heavy indemnity for the m. of A. (1654).   SHS

Amercement. In Anglo-Saxon and Norman times a person convicted of an offence against the king or KING'S PEACE was 'in the king's mercy'. Forfeiture could ensue, but after the NORMAN CONQUEST money payments were imposed for lesser offences. The system was widespread by the 13th century, and MAGNA CARTA sought to relate the sum demanded to a man's resources. A.s have gradually been replaced by statutory penalties.   PMB

American Import Duties Act (1767) was the ill-conceived work of Townshend, Chancellor of the Exchequer, imposing duties on paint, paper, lead, glass and tea, to be collected in America. As with the STAMP ACT, rioting and protest resulted in their repeal (1770) except for the small duty on tea.   IHE

American Revolution (war of independence) was the work of a group of determined men who used grievances caused by such measures as the STAMP ACT (1765) and the AMERICAN IMPORT DUTIES ACT (1767) to resist the British Parliament's claim to legislate for the colonies. Growing antagonism was revealed by the BOSTON MASSACRE (1770) and the GASPEE AFFAIR (1772), and the INTOLERABLE ACTS (1774) consequent upon the BOSTON TEA PARTY (1773) marked the British failure to appreciate the need for conciliation. Decisions of the Continental Congress (1774) led to open rebellion, and fighting began at LEXINGTON and BUNKER HILL (1775). Between 1775 and 1777 the British failed to make proper use of their military and naval strength. The DECLARATION OF INDEPENDENCE (1776) and Burgoyne's surrender at SARATOGA (1777) brought France in openly on the side of the rebels (6 Feb.), giving them naval, financial and military support. Failure in the north, except at NEW YORK, led the British to concentrate in the south, where they made good progress (1778–80) in Georgia and South Carolina but met with reverses in 1781. The British surrender at YORKTOWN (1781) virtually ended the war, which was concluded by the treaty of VERSAILLES (1783). American success owed much to British ministerial incompetence, French help and Washington's leadership. Moreover, Britain was engaged in a desperate maritime struggle with France (1778), Spain (1779) and Holland (1780), as well as being confronted with the ARMED NEUTRALITY.

IHE

American war of 1812 (1812–5). The harsh treatment of American ships in pursuance of the British blockade (intensified by the ORDERS IN COUNCIL) of Napoleon's ports, together with IMPRESSMENT of Americans, were the main reasons given for the American declaration of war on Britain (18 June 1812). But the maritime states on whose behalf the war was ostensibly declared were against it. A more potent cause can be seen in hostility to Britain engendered by her presence in CANADA, which seemed a promising field for U.S. expansion; there was also a belief, to some extent well-founded, that the British were assisting Indian resistance to western advance.

Until the temporary defeat of Napoleon (1813) Britain was unable to spare sufficient ships or men for North America. At sea, U.S. frigates had successes until they were driven off the seas and the blockade of the American coast became effective (1813). On land, the various attacks against Canada and America were characterized on both sides by inefficient command. In 1812 a grandiose 4-pronged attack on Canada was withstood at QUEENSTON HEIGHTS. In 1813 the Americans captured and burnt York (Toronto) and launched an unsuccessful land and sea expedition against Montreal. A stalemate ensued, broken by the arrival of troops after the end of the PENINSULAR WAR. Sir G. Prevost led a badly coordinated attack on Plattsburg (Sept. 1814) and was forced to withdraw by the defeat of his fleet on Lake Champlain. Meanwhile the British fleet under Adm. Sir A. Cochrane transported Maj. Gen. J. Ross's force of 4,500 men into Chesapeake Bay and up the river Patuxent; Ross defeated the

Americans at Bladensburg (24 Aug.) and captured Washington, burning the public buildings. Following an abortive advance on Baltimore (where Ross was killed) the expedition, reinforced in Jamaica and led by Gen. Sir E. Pakenham, made an ill-conceived attack on New Orleans (Dec. 1814–Jan. 1815), defended by Gen. Andrew Jackson. Pakenham was killed and his force was with difficulty extricated. By this time peace had already been signed at GHENT (24 Dec. 1814). The treaty merely established the *status quo*; some of the outstanding differences between the U.S. and Canada were, however, settled by agreements in 1817–8.   MLH

Amicable Loan (1525). Wolsey's expensive foreign policy and futile war with France (1522–5) caused the exaction of a FORCED LOAN in 1522. The failure to obtain adequate subsidies from Parliament (1523) and the impracticable scheme for an invasion of France led to the a.l. This arbitrary and excessive forced loan from laity and clergy met with such resistance that the king abandoned it.   IHE

Amiens, Mise of (23 Jan. 1264). In July 1263 Simon de Montfort and his party regained control of the government, and attempted to stabilize the position by reaching some agreement with King Henry III on the basis of the PROVISIONS OF OXFORD. As long as the essentials of the Provisions were retained, De Montfort was willing to submit to arbitration any disputes arising out of them, and he remained willing despite the deterioration of his political and military position later in the year. Louis IX of France was invited to act as arbiter, and after the failure of a conference at Louis' court at Boulogne at Michaelmas, Henry III and the MONTFORTIANS in December formally agreed to submit the Provisions of Oxford and all disputes arising from them to Louis' arbitration. King Louis' award or Mise, pronounced at Amiens, was an adverse judgement rather than an arbitration; the Provisions were annulled and Henry was released from any obligation to observe them. The award was completely unacceptable to De Montfort, and caused many waverers to join his party: so far from producing a settlement, the M. of A. led almost immediately to the outbreak of civil war. RFW

Amiens, peace of (27 Mar. 1802), which separated the FRENCH REVOLUTIONARY AND NAPOLEONIC WARS, was signed by Lord Cornwallis and Joseph Bonaparte, preliminary articles having been signed on 1 Oct. 1801. Both sides were ready for a rest; the British were supreme at sea, the second ARMED NEUTRALITY having been broken at COPENHAGEN, whilst Pitt's second coalition had been ended by the treaty of Lunéville (Feb. 1801) and economic considerations were pressing at home. Britain agreed to surrender all her conquests except TRINIDAD (from Spain) and CEYLON (from Holland): Cochin, the CAPE and the Spice Islands were returned to Holland (Batavian Republic); MINORCA to Spain; Indian and African territories and ST LUCIA, TOBAGO, MARTINIQUE, ST PIERRE AND MIQUELON to France. France relinquished Naples and the papal states; Egypt was returned to the Porte and the integrity of Portugal recognized. MALTA was to be returned to the Knights of St John, its independence guaranteed by the great powers. Finally, the British crown dropped its anachronistic title to France. The peace lasted until 17 May 1803, by which time Napoleon had broken the terms of Lunéville (which Britain considered concomitant to Amiens) as regards the independence of the Cisalpine, Helvetian and Batavian Republics and had annexed Piedmont; Britain in turn had delayed returning the Indian conquests and Malta. MLH

Amiens, treaty of (23 May 1279). Eleanor of Castile inherited the county of Ponthieu from her mother Joan, and her husband, Edward I, added it to his continental possessions in right of his wife. Philip III of France admitted Edward's rights by the t. of A., which also attempted to deal with

problems arising from the execution of the treaty of PARIS (1259). Despite the readiness of both kings to make concessions—Philip, for example, agreed to the return of the Agenais to the duchy of Guienne—many points remained unsettled and were to be the cause of future dissension. RFW

Amritsar 'massacre' (13 Apr. 1919) occurred during riots protesting against the ROWLATT ACTS. Troops under Brig.-Gen. R. E. H. Dyer fired into a prohibited assembly in an enclosed area; 379 people were killed and 1,208 wounded. Feeling engendered by this incident (which was followed by drastic punitive measures) did much to undo the goodwill resulting from the MONTAGU–CHELMSFORD REPORT. Dyer was censured in the Hunter Committee Report. MLH

Amritsar, treaty of (April 1809), signed by (Sir) Charles Metcalfe for the EAST INDIA COMPANY and the SIKH ruler Ranjit Singh, allowed the latter's influence to prevail to the west of river Sutlej so long as he did not interfere to the east. Stability was brought to the PUNJAB until the first SIKH WAR (1845). MLH

Anabaptists (re-baptizers), extremist religious reformers appearing on the continent in the early 16th century. Vigorously denounced by more orthodox reformers for their religious, political and social radicalism, they were persecuted in England as early as 1534, though few in number and mainly continental refugees. Further suppression followed under Edward VI and Elizabeth I. Advocating complete religious independence, they probably influenced the BROWNISTS and early separatists. BAPTISTS of the 17th century were often miscalled a., which became a term of abuse. IHE

Anarchy is the name frequently applied to the whole reign of King Stephen (1135–54), a period of confusion and weak rule falling between the strong government of the Norman kings (1066–1135) and of Henry II (1154–89). On the death of Henry I the succession to the throne was disputed between his daughter Maud 'the empress' (widow of the Emperor Henry V) and his nephew Stephen of Blois. In the absence of any accepted constitutional rule governing the succession, Stephen's initial success was due to his greater personal popularity, the support of the church and the speed with which he secured his election and coronation. Stephen was brave, generous and courteous, but suspicious and guileful. He lacked both the ruthlessness and the ability to govern of his Norman predecessors, and his position, already insecure because of Maud's claim to the throne, was further weakened by the uncertainty of the support of prelates and barons who were far from satisfied by his CHARTERS OF LIBERTIES.

The civil war which followed a rebellion on Maud's behalf in 1138 was partly a baronial reaction after the harsh rule of Henry I. Family feuds, especially over the inheritance of lands, and old grievances against the crown frequently determined baronial choice of sides. Both Stephen and Maud purchased support by grants of titles, lands and offices. There were many changes of sides— the bishops, alienated by Stephen in 1139, supported Maud in 1141 but later swung back to the king—but the instability of baronial loyalties has probably been exaggerated.

Neither side was strong enough to gain a decisive advantage in the civil war, in which most of the fighting took place on the borders of the south-west, where Maud's support was strongest. The capture of Stephen at the battle of LINCOLN in 1141 nearly ruined his cause. Maud was elected 'lady of the English' on 8 Apr. by an assembly of bishops at Winchester, but she was never crowned queen. She rapidly lost ground through her own high-handed conduct, which alienated the all-important city of London, and the vigorous military activity of Stephen's party, led by his queen, Maud (of Boulogne). The rout of WINCHESTER restored the balance in favour of Stephen's supporters, and eventually secured the release of the king himself.

Although Stephen came near to complete success in 1142 and 1145, he was never able to reduce the south-west. His failure to secure decisive victory in England prevented his giving adequate backing to his supporters in Normandy, which was finally conquered by Maud's husband, Geoffrey of Anjou, in 1144. In the north, although the invading Scots were defeated at the battle of the STANDARD in 1138, Stephen had to cede Northumberland and Carlisle in 1139, and the Scots later extended their temporary hold to County Durham.

Despite the civil war, royal government continued to function, at least in the south-east: the CHANCERY and EXCHEQUER remained at work, and sheriffs and royal justices held their courts in counties controlled by the king, and some of the judicial reforms of Henry II were anticipated. While the extreme north was held by the Scots, and the English hold on the MARCHES OF WALES slipped, the south-west was governed more or less peacefully for Maud by Robert of Gloucester. Outside these areas the real rulers were great magnates. A local reign of terror, like that of Geoffrey de Mandeville in the Fen country in 1143-4, seems to have been exceptional, and though it was in the magnates' interests to preserve order in their spheres of influence, many lesser barons and knights, whatever their nominal allegiance, took advantage of the impotence of the central government to impose a tyrannical rule in their immediate neighbourhoods (ADULTERINE CASTLES).

Maud's chief supporter, Robert of Gloucester, died in 1147, her son Henry's expedition in England failed miserably in the same year, and in 1148 Maud retired to the continent. Henry failed again in 1149, and the years 1149–53 were comparatively peaceful. By 1153, however, Stephen's position had been weakened by a new quarrel with the church, many of his chief supporters had died and he had failed to get his son, Eustace, crowned as his successor. Henry's campaign of 1153 was successful, and the treaty of WINCHESTER finally ended the civil war, and secured Henry's succession to the throne on Stephen's death in 1154. Henry's victory determined that the English monarchy should be hereditary, not elective, while the principal baronial gain was that tenure of estates held of the crown should be hereditary and not at the King's will.

RFW

Andaman and Nicobar Islands. The A. group was annexed by the Indian government in 1858 and used until 1945 as a penal settlement for long-term convicts. It was occupied by the Japanese from 23 Mar. 1942 to Aug. 1945. The N. group was annexed in 1869. It was occupied by the Japanese from 13 June 1942 to 9 Oct. 1945. Since 1950 the A. and N. I. form a centrally administered territory of INDIA.

SHS

Andhra Pradesh was on 1 Oct. 1953 constituted an 'A State' of India, comprising the Telugu-speaking area of MADRAS. It was greatly enlarged on the partition of HYDERABAD (1 Nov. 1956).

SHS

Angel, an English gold coin first minted in 1465, and worth 6s. 8d., the original value of the NOBLE, which it helped to replace. The coin imitated the *ange* of Louis XI of France, and took its name from the design of the obverse—the Archangel Michael standing on a dragon. The minting of a.s and half-a.s (3s. 4d.) continued into the early Stewart period.

RFW

Angevin Empire, modern description of the territories accumulated by Henry II and subsequently held by his sons, Richard I and John, which should not be regarded as an 'English' continental empire. Though England, wealthy and well organized, was a specially important possession, Henry and Richard spent a great part of their time on the continent, and in as far as their dominions had a centre it was on the Loire rather than the Thames. From his father Geoffrey, Henry received the duchy of NORMANDY (conquered by 1144) in 1150, and on Geoffrey's death in 1151 inherited the counties of Anjou, Maine and Touraine. In 1152 Henry married Eleanor, divorced wife of Louis VII of France, and received her inheritance of the duchy of AQUITAINE. In 1154 Henry succeeded Stephen as king of England, and by 1173 he had added Brittany, Auvergne and Toulouse to his continental 'empire'—which remained a collection of separate duchies and counties with their own laws and administrations and which its rulers never attempted to make into a single state. The breaking up of the A. e. was mainly the work of King Philip II of France. By 1204 King John had lost Normandy, Maine, Anjou, Touraine and parts of Aquitaine to Philip, and a new line of dukes was established in Brittany. Thereafter the continental possessions of John and his son Henry III were limited to the remnants of AQUITAINE, though Henry's claims to his ancestral lands north of the Loire were not given up until the treaty of PARIS in 1259. After 1204 King John and his successors spent most of their time in England, but both Henry III and Edward I paid prolonged visits to Gascony. By the 14th century, however, there was a tendency for Englishmen to regard the dominions of their kings as falling into two distinct parts, i.e. England, and the 'overseas posesions'.

RFW

Angevins. Henry II, king of England 1154–89, was the son of Geoffrey 'Plantagenet', count of Anjou, by Maud, daughter of King Henry I. Henry II and his lineal successors in the 12th and 13th centuries are frequently referred to as the A. as an alternative to PLANTAGENETS. The term is not usually applied to the kings of the 14th century despite their direct descent from Henry II.

RFW

Angles, one of the groups that took part in the TEUTONIC CONQUEST of Britain in the late 5th and early 6th centuries and eventually gave their name to the whole country and its language. The centre of their power in pre-conquest times was Angeln, at the base of the Danish peninsula.

Archaeology indicates that they were the most primitive of the invaders. Anglian kingdoms were eventually established in the midland and northern areas of England: MERCIA, NORTHUMBRIA, and those of the EAST and MIDDLE ANGLES. CFS

Anglo-Saxon Chronicle, the primary authority for the history of Anglo-Saxon England (c. 450–1066). It is written in Old English, and seven manuscripts, of which one is a Latin translation, survive. They contain basically the same information for the period 55 B.C. to A.D. 891, have much in common for the years 892–915, but thereafter have no common element. The manuscripts end at different times, the longest-lived being MS. E, the so-called Peterborough Chronicle, that ends in 1154. The A.-S.C. was composed in 891, information for events outside the author's life-time coming from various sources, including tradition, Bede's *Ecclesiastical History* (finished 731) and sets of annals now lost. After 891 copies of the A.-S.C. were kept up to date in various religious houses. It seems to have been compiled in south-western England. The original compiler is unknown, although historians have at times attributed the authorship to king Alfred (871–99). CFS

Annates were payments to the pope of the first-fruits (or part of a year's income) of a benefice by bishops on appointment. In 1532 Henry VIII secured the passing of the first Act of A. providing for their suspension, subject to royal confirmation. This was an unsuccessful attempt to induce the pope to grant his divorce. The Act was confirmed (July 1533) and a second Act was passed (1534) renewing the prohibition of a. and of papal nominations to bishoprics. FIRST-FRUITS AND TENTHS of all benefices were annexed to the crown, but later given to QUEEN ANNE'S BOUNTY. IHE

Anti-Corn-Law League, see CORN LAWS.

Antigua, was discovered by Columbus in 1493 and occupied by English settlers from ST KITTS in 1632. It remained royalist during the COMMONWEALTH and, after a temporary seizure by the French (1666), was finally ceded by the treaty of BREDA (1667). It formed part of the LEEWARD ISLANDS federation from 1871 to 1960. Barbuda and Redonda are dependencies of A. which became a WEST INDIES Associated State on 27 Feb. 1967. SHS; IHE

Antiquaries of London, Society of. There had been a S. of A. from c. 1584 to 1608, but there is no connection between this and the present S. of A. which was started in 1707, reconstituted in 1717 and granted a royal charter in 1751. It is the second oldest of the royal societies. Its headquarters are now at Burlington House and its membership consists of some 1,200 Fellows elected by ballot. It publishes (*Antiquaries Journal, Archaeologia,* Excavation reports, etc.), supports archaeological excavation, holds weekly meetings during the winter months, and has an excellent historical and archaeological library. CFS

Antonine Wall (*Vallum Antonini*), built 140–2 while Antoninus Pius (138–61) was emperor, it reoccupied the positions established by Agricola along the Clyde–Forth line during the earlier phase of the ROMAN CONQUEST. It consisted of a turf wall c. 36 miles long: on its south side a military road and 19 forts: on its north a ditch c. 12 feet deep and 40 feet wide, with a bank on the north edge of the ditch. Militarily it was unsatisfactory, as its flanks could be turned, although recent excavation has shown defence and signal stations extending south down the coast. It was abandoned c. 185 or soon after. CFS

Anzac, the Australian and New Zealand Army Corps, which took part in the GALLIPOLI expedition. The corps under Lt.-Gen. (later F.-M. Lord) Birdwood landed at Anzac Cove (as it quickly became known), 25 Apr. 1915, a day of remembrance in both Dominions. MLH

Apology of the Commons (1604). Having asserted their rights in the cases of SHIRLEY and GOODWIN, the Commons outlined their privileges, holding them to be not of grace but of right. They claimed freedom of election and of speech, and from arrest during session; also the right to deal with the proposed Anglo-Scottish union and the settlement of revenues from PURVEYANCE, WARDSHIP and feudal incidents. Nor was the crown to legislate in ecclesiastical matters without consent. Although it was never presented, James I was aware of it. IHE

Appeal, the review of a judgement by a higher court, was not a COMMON LAW term: it belonged to canon and civil law. Under canon law appeals from England to Rome were made in spiritual cases until the Reformation: in civil and French customary law appeals from Gascon courts to the PARIS PARLEMENT vexed Anglo-French relations. In common law a. meant a personal accusation of felony leading to a first trial, e.g. the kin of a murdered man could appeal his murderer. The procedure declined in importance with the advent of the presenting JURY and other new criminal procedures. Review of cases under common law, except by petition to the crown, was slow to develop. From the 12th century a jury's verdict could be upset by a second jury of attaint and, later, actions in error could be brought in KING'S BENCH from COMMON PLEAS and in Exchequer Chamber from EXCHEQUER, but full chains of a., civil and criminal, were not set up until the courts of a. were established.

A CHANCERY a. court was set up in 1851, but complete re-organization was achieved only by the JUDICATURE Act 1873, which set up the court of a. within the supreme court. Second a. to PARLIAMENT was abolished in 1873, revived in 1875 and amended in 1876 by the creation of Lords of A. in Ordinary sitting either in the House of Lords or as the Judicial Committee of the PRIVY COUNCIL.

Although bills were introduced into Parliament from 1844 onwards, attempts to establish a full criminal appellate jurisdiction were abortive until the proof, in 1907, that Adolf Beck had twice been wrongly convicted. An Act of the same year set up the Court of CRIMINAL APPEAL, consisting of the Lord Chief JUSTICE and eight other judges. PMB

Appeals, Act in Restraint of, see RESTRAINT.

Appeals to Rome, see PRAEMUNIRE.

Appellant, Lords. On 14 Nov. 1387 Thomas of Woodstock, duke of Gloucester, Richard II's uncle, Richard, earl of Arundel, and Thomas, earl of Warwick, brought a formal 'appeal of treason' against a group of the king's friends. Richard II referred the appeal to the next parliament. In the meantime the original appellants were joined by Henry Bolingbroke, earl of Derby, and Thomas Mowbray, earl of Nottingham, and attempts to take military action against them collapsed at RADCOTE BRIDGE. The appellants gained control of the government, and in the MERCILESS PARLIAMENT of Feb. 1388 proceeded with their appeal of treason —a new procedure of doubtful legality. The lords attending parliament finally condemned the earls of Oxford and Suffolk, the archbishop of York, chief justice Tresilian and Nicholas Brembre. The last two were executed, the others having escaped overseas.

Richard II, who had been a helpless spectator of the destruction of his friends, in Sept. 1397 employed the same procedure against his enemies. Eight of his kinsmen and friends brought an appeal of treason in parliament against Gloucester, Arundel and Warwick. Arundel was condemned and executed; Warwick confessed his guilt and was exiled; Gloucester was reported to have died in prison at Calais but had almost certainly been murdered. RFW

Apprentices, Statute of (1563), a comprehensive act for artificers, labourers and a., attempted to stabilize industry and agriculture. It insisted on 7-year apprenticeships for crafts-men; men between the ages of 12 and 60 not otherwise lawfully employed were to work on the land; unmarried women between the ages of 12 and 40 might be compelled to enter service. Hours of work were fixed and wages were to be assessed annually by the magistrates. Workpeople were not to leave their districts without official permission, nor were employers to dismiss their servants before their agreements expired. The wages clauses were repealed in 1813 and the apprenticeship regulations in 1814.

                                                    IHE

Approvers, self-confessed criminals who, as common informers and for hope of a pardon, undertook appeals of felony and the consequent TRIALS BY BATTLE. In the 13th century a. were required to fight five battles before ob-taining a pardon: in return they were maintained and equipped by the crown, but if an appeal failed or a battle was lost the a. were hanged. A., always regarded with distaste, disappear in the 15th century.   PMB

Aquitaine, Duchy of, part of the 'ANGEVIN EMPIRE', held by the English kings from 1154 to 1453. In 1224 Louis VIII of France conquered Poitou, the northern part of A., and repeated attempts of Henry III to re-cover lost ground (1225, 1229–31, 1242) resulted only in the additional loss of Saintonge. By the treaty of PARIS (1259) Louis IX restored some of the eastern lordships of the duchy and was recognized as Henry's feudal overlord in his French possessions. The treaty's provisions for further cessions were only partially fulfilled by Edward I's agreements with Philip III at AMIENS in 1279 and with Philip IV at PARIS in 1286. Philip IV con-fiscated A. in 1294, and the French occupied most of it until the peace of PARIS in 1303. Despite the negotia-tions conducted at MONTREUIL in 1306, at PÉRIGUEUX in 1311 and at AGEN in 1331–4, the boundaries of the duchy remained ill-defined, and while the French kings were deter-mined to exercise to the full their

rights as overlords, the English kings found their position as vassals increasingly irksome. Strained rela-tions in the duchy were one of the major causes of the HUNDRED YEARS' WAR, and one of Edward III's main war-aims was to free himself from French overlordship. The area ruled by the English kings, reduced by 1327 to a coastal strip some 50 miles wide between the Charente and the Pyre-nees, expanded and contracted with the varying success of the war. By the treaty of BRÉTIGNY (1360) Edward III received the duchy in full sove-reignty, almost to its extent under Henry II. After the resumption of the war in 1369 the English quickly lost these recent gains, and by 1375 they held less than in 1337. Despite their temporary advance in the 1420s and the repulse of a French invasion in 1438–9, Charles VII of France even-tually overran the whole duchy in 1451. A last English expedition gained some success in 1452, but after its defeat at CASTILLON in 1453 A. finally passed to the French.

                                                    RFW

Arcot, principality in the Carnatic whose nawab in 1750 sided with the French. Its capture by Robert Clive and successful defence against the besiegers (1751) shattered French prestige in INDIA.   SHS

Argyll's rebellion (May–June 1685) was planned in Holland to coincide with MONMOUTH'S REBELLION in Eng-land. With some 300 supporters, in-cluding former RYE HOUSE con-spirators, the 9th earl of A. unsuccess-fully attempted to raise the Campbells of Argyllshire and finally invaded the Lowlands to march on Glasgow. Followed by a stronger royalist force, his disorganized followers deserted. Argyll was caught (18 June) and executed without trial.   IHE

Armada, this Spanish invasion fleet of 130 ships prepared by Philip II was delayed by Drake's attack on CADIZ (1587) and finally left Lisbon under Medina Sidonia's command in May 1588. Its aim was to win command of the Channel and safeguard the transport of Parma's troops from Flanders. The A. was sighted off the Lizard 19/29 July and the English under Howard worked out of Plymouth securing the windward position. Proceeding at an average speed of 2 knots, indecisive actions were fought off Portland and the Isle of Wight, and the Armada anchored off Calais 27 July/6 Aug. English fireships dispersed the Spaniards in confusion during the night, and the final action was fought off GRAVELINES 29 July/ 8 Aug. With great skill Medina brought two-thirds of the A. back to Spain, through the North Sea and round Scotland and Ireland, suffering further losses from gales, reefs and shortage of food and water; but unmolested by the English who had to maintain precautionary measures against Parma. The moral impact rather than the actual losses (44 ships) made the defeat of the A. decisive.   IHE

Armagnacs and Burgundians, two factions of the princes and nobility of France struggling to control the state under the mad king, Charles VI (1380–1422). One was led originally by the king's brother, Louis of Orleans, and after his murder by the B. in 1407 leadership passed to Bernard, count of Armagnac. Successive dukes of Burgundy, Philip the Bold (†1404) John the Fearless and Philip the Good led the opposing faction. Civil war, in which both sides in turn employed English troops, preceded Henry V's invasion of France in 1415, and the feud gravely weakened French resistance to the invader. Armagnac was murdered when the B. seized Paris in 1418. The murder of John the Fearless, at a meeting with the Dauphin Charles (later VII) on the bridge of Montereau in 1419, brought about the alliance of his successor, Philip, with Henry V, and led directly to the treaty of TROYES. The dauphin, backed by the A., maintained his position south of the Loire, but his reconciliation with Philip and the B. was only effected in 1435, by the treaty of ARRAS.   RFW

Armed Neutrality. (1) (Mar. 1780), a league formed by Russia, Sweden and Denmark, while Great Britain was at war with her American colonies, France and Spain, to resist the British claim to right of search of neutral vessels. It was later joined by the Netherlands, Prussia, the Empire, and in 1782 by Portugal, Naples and even Turkey, and led to war with the Netherlands (20 Nov. 1780).

(2) (16 Dec. 1800), formed during the war against revolutionary France by Russia, Sweden, Denmark and Prussia, but was abandoned in 1801 after the British attack on the Danish fleet at COPENHAGEN (2 Apr. 1801).
                                    IHE

Arminians were those churchmen who reacted against the rigid Calvinism of the early 17th century, their name being derived from the Dutch theologian Jacob Arminius (1560–1609), who led a similar revolt on the continent. Rejecting predestination, they emphasized the doctrine and worship of the early church, and Bishop Andrewes (1555–1626) began the revival of ceremonial afterwards enforced by the LAUDIANS. The crown and court became Arminian, but Parliament remained essentially Puritan and Calvinist. Occupying a position midway between Geneva and Rome, the A. were suspected of trying to reintroduce Roman Catholicism and were denounced by the Parliament of 1629. Their ascendency ended in 1640.   IHE

Arms, Assize of (probably 1176), reorganized the non-feudal military service owed to the crown by all free men. The assize laid down scales of armour and weapons to be kept by men, ranging from the full equipment of a knight to the doublet, iron cap and spear of a burgess. Juries of towns and hundreds were to assess and declare the wealth of inhabitants on oath before royal justices. Individuals (from 1225 VILLEINS as well as free men) were in turn 'sworn to arms', i.e. they undertook to maintain arms according to their assessment and to bear them in the king's service when required. Henry III's regulations of 1242 increased the number of classes of assessment and introduced a wider range of equipment: the poorest men were to have at least bows and arrows if possible. Mayors and bailiffs of towns, constables of vills and head constables of hundreds were responsible for calling out the *jurati ad arma*. Further modifications were introduced by the statute of WINCHESTER, 1285. Scales of equipment were belatedly brought up to date by an act of 1558, repealed in 1603. The assize of a. was eventually replaced by the statutory scales of equipment of the MILITIA.

RFW

Army Council. Though political direction of the army lay, after 1794, with the Secretary of State for WAR, military direction remained with the commander-in-chief. This arrangement, producing conflict and inefficiency, and made more difficult by the custom of royal commanders-in-chief, lasted until 1895. Then the duke of Cambridge was persuaded to resign after nearly 40 years of office; the commander-in-chief's powers were cut; a war office council under the secretary was set up to advise on general policy and an army board, under the commander-in-chief, to advise on purely military matters. Unity of civil and military direction was attained in 1904 with the establishment of the A. C. under the Secretary of State, comparable with the Board of ADMIRALTY. On 1 Apr. 1964 the A.C. was abolished, being replaced by a new Army Board of the DEFENCE Council.

PMB; MR

Arnhem, battle of (Sept. 1944). Montgomery's plan (*Market Garden*) for an outflanking movement from Belgium to the Zuider Zee and thence into the Ruhr, involved dropping airborne troops ahead to secure bridges over canals and rivers. Units of 1st Airborne Division (Maj.-Gen. R. E. Urquhart) landed furthest north (17 Sept.), 8 miles west of A., and a battalion captured the Neder Rijn bridge in A. which it held for 3 days. Ground forces could not break

through till 25 Sept. and then only in strength sufficient to evacuate the remnants of Urquhart's hard-pressed force. There were tactical errors, and supreme command can be held responsible for insufficient logistic aid. But bad weather (preventing air reinforcement and support) and breakdown of wireless communication were vital causes of the failure.   MLH

Arras, Congress and Treaty of (1435). Popes Martin V (†1431) and Eugenius IV (1431–47) and the Council of Basle in 1431 undertook the negotiation of a peace between France and England or, failing that, between Charles VII of France and England's ally, Philip the Good of Burgundy. Although an attempt to arrange a peace conference at Auxerre in 1432 failed, there was growing coolness between Philip and the English, while France and Burgundy were moving towards an understanding. In Jan. 1435, at Nevers, peace preliminaries were agreed upon by France and Burgundy, and arrangements were made for a general peace congress. This congress, presided over by the cardinals Albergati (papal) and de Lusignan (conciliar), opened at A. on 5 Aug. The English refused any substantial concessions and in particular maintained Henry VI's claim to the lands he still held in France. By 6 Sept. Anglo-French negotiations had broken down, and the English delegates left. There followed on 21 Sept. the treaty of A. between France and Burgundy, on the lines agreed on at Nevers. For the English, the defection of a valuable ally marked a decisive turning-point in the HUNDRED YEARS' WAR. For the French, the treaty restored unity in the war against England, at the price of the virtual independence of an enlarged duchy of Burgundy.   RFW

Array, commissions of. The ancient obligation of all free men to assist in the defence of the country was extended to the unfree in the 13th century, and successive assizes of ARMS laid down what weapons they were to keep ready. From the 13th century onwards, commissioners, usually experienced soldiers, were appointed by the crown to 'array' the able-bodied men of each shire between the ages of 15 (16 in the 14th century) and 60, and to select the best men for the king's service. Sub-arrayers conducted the musters in HUNDREDS, towns and LIBERTIES. Each shire was responsible for the initial expenses of mustering and equipping the men, who then passed into the king's pay. These conscript levies were frequently employed in the Welsh, Scottish and French wars, but during the HUNDRED YEARS' WAR became much less important than forces raised by contract (INDENTURE). From the mid-16th century a. became one of the principal functions of the LORD LIEUTENANT, and the shire levies, themselves the descendants of the FYRD, were the direct ancestors of the MILITIA. RFW

Arthurian Legend. The earliest definite mention of Arthur (late Latin, *Artorius*) occurs in the *Historia Brittonum* (late 7th century), where it is stated that he was the British leader at the battle of Mons BADONICUS, fought 12 major battles and was not king but *Dux Bellorum*. This title is similar to that of *Dux Britanniarum* in later ROMAN BRITAIN, the commander of all military forces except those of the SAXON SHORE. Later a strategic reserve was established under the command of the *Comes Britanniarum*: and from the late 4th century cavalry became the *corps d'élite*. It is likely that British rulers, to check the TEUTONIC CONQUEST, revived the concept of this late-Roman organization but muddled the title of its commander. Nothing more is known with certainty concerning Arthur. Legends concerning him soon developed in the Celtic west, and he was mentioned in some Welsh poems. He was also mentioned by William of Malmesbury, the leading English historian of the early 12th century. The real author of the A. l. was Geoffrey of Monmouth, who in 1136 produced the HISTORIA REGUM BRITANNIAE, a major historical fantasy in which Merlin first appeared and where Arthur's cavalry became knights. From the work of Geoffrey and others Wace, writing in Normandy, produced a metrical version in Norman French that first mentioned the Round Table. The A. l. became a major subject of European literature, attracting to itself many previously unrelated romances concerning Gawain, Lancelot, etc. The major English contributions have been: Layamon's *Brut* (13th century); Malory's *Mort d'Arthur* (15th century); Tennyson's *Idylls of the King* (19th century). CFS

Articles of Religion. Henry VIII's breach with Rome and the spread of Protestant opinion resulted in 1536 in the issuing of ten articles, under the king's authority, on Church of England doctrine (five dealt with the faith and five with ceremony). Mainly conservative, baptism, the eucharist and penance were held to be the essential sacraments, but on prayers to the saints and for the dead the articles were cautiously Lutheran. The statute of six articles (1539) was passed to establish uniformity and was firmly Catholic, emphasizing transubstantiation, communion of one kind for the laity, celibacy for the priesthood, auricular confession, etc. It made heresy a felony, was a severe blow to protestantism, but was never rigidly applied. This 'whip with six strings' was repealed after the accession of Edward VI (1547). The 42 articles, published by royal authority in 1553, were of a markedly protestant character, having been prepared by Cranmer and Ridley. Baptism and the eucharist were held to be the only sacraments, and transubstantiation was rejected. To confirm the Elizabethan settlement 39 articles were approved in the Convocation of 1563, being Parker's revision of Cranmer's 42, and issued under royal authority. Though they did not satisfy the Puritans, they were ratified by Convocation in 1571 and are still valid. IHE

Articuli super Cartas, the modern name for a statute of Edward I's Parliament of March 1300, which supplemented MAGNA CARTA and the charter of the FOREST, both of which were reissued in full. The articles provided, *inter alia*, for the appointment of special justices to deal with breaches of Magna Carta, the election by shires of their own sheriffs and the regulation of PRISAGE. Deepening suspicion that Edward was going back on his CONFIRMATION OF THE CHARTERS (1297) had led to renewed opposition. Edward's concessions of 1300, however, were made with the express reservation of the rights of the crown, and although the charters were reissued, the additional articles of 1297 were dropped. On the whole, in the last decade of his reign Edward successfully avoided limitation of his powers, and in 1305 he was released by Pope Clement V from his obligations of 1297. The observance by the king of the charters gradually ceased to be the principal objective of constitutional opposition, which turned to new ways of restricting the royal prerogative, such as the ORDINANCES of 1311.   RFW

Ashanti, an inland province of GHANA, formed in the 18th and 19th centuries as a military and economic confederation under a paramount chief (Asantehene). Contact (from 1806) with the A. tribes was made during their frequent invasions of the coastal areas controlled by the Fanti, who accepted protection from the British at Cape Coast. Several treaties (all soon broken) were made in an endeavour to keep the trade routes to the interior open and to extinguish the SLAVE TRADE. At last (1873) the home government sent Sir G. Wolseley with 2,500 British troops to deal with the Asantehene Kofi Karikari who laid claim to Elmina on the withdrawal of the Dutch and had defeated the coastal tribes. Wolseley defeated the A. at Amoafo (31 Jan. 1874) and reached Kumasi (4 Feb.). By the treaty of Fomena (14 Mar.) Kofi agreed to pay an indemnity, keep trade routes open and try to prevent human sacrifice.

None of these promises were kept, whilst the temporary diminution of A. power led to more rather than less intertribal warfare. A second expedition, under Sir F. Scott, entered Kumasi (17 Jan. 1896) and Asantehene Prempeh was deported. In 1900–1 a revolt was put down with some difficulty by native troops; A. was annexed to GOLD COAST under a chief commissioner (1 Jan. 1902). The Asantehene (Sir Osei Agyeman Prempeh II) was restored in 1935, when the Ashanti Confederacy Council (later known as the Asanteman Council) was formed (abolished in 1958).   MLH

Ashby v. White, see AYLESBURY ELECTION.

Ashdown, battle of (*c.* 8 Jan. 871). The exact site is unknown, A. being the old name for the Berkshire Downs. The men of WESSEX under king Ethelred and his brother Alfred won a major victory over a large force of DANES that had emerged from their camp at Reading, but subsequent Danish victories in the same year reduced its influence on the course of the war.   CFS

Ashingdon, battle of, in Essex (18 Oct. 1016). The English under king Edmund Ironside were decisively defeated by the DANES under king Cnut, aided by the treachery of some of the English leaders. An agreement made soon after the battle gave Cnut all England except WESSEX, and after the death of Edmund in Nov. 1016 Wessex also accepted him as king.   CFS

Asiento, a 33-year monopoly of selling negro slaves to the Spanish colonies obtained by Great Britain by the peace of UTRECHT (1713). At the same time the right was gained to send one ship annually to trade with the Spanish Indies (JENKINS' EAR). The A. was renewed for 4 years by the treaty of AACHEN (1748) and finally surrendered for a lump sum in 1750. These concessions were managed by the SOUTH SEA COMPANY, which obtained the slaves first from the Royal AFRICAN COMPANY and later from JAMAICA.   IHE

Assam. The country, split in numerous tribes and principalities, was in 1816 conquered by BURMA and became a British protectorate after the first Burmese war (1826); further annexations took place in 1832 and 1835. A. was part of BENGAL from 1839 to 1874, when it became a separate chief commissionership. On the partition of Bengal in 1905 A. was included in the Eastern Bengal and A. province, was again made a separate chief commissionership in 1912, a governorship in 1921 and an autonomous province with a bicameral legislature in 1937. The only major feudatory state within the A. administration was MANIPUR, which in 1947 was detached from A. A. became an 'A State' of India, without the district of Sylhet which in 1947 was amalgamated with the Pakistani province of East Bengal. On 26 Sept. 1957 some hill districts of A. and the North-East Frontier Agency were put under central control but administered by the governor of A.   SHS

Assize, a term of widespread medieval usage, derived either from the decision of a seated assembly, 'session', or from a thing established, fixed. Assized rents were those firmly fixed, in cash or in kind. Certain royal declarations of statutory force were called a.s, e.g. of CLARENDON 1166, of ARMS 1181, as were judicial processes, the GRAND ASSIZE and the POSSESSORY ASSIZES. These gave their name first to the judges who heard them, then to the sessions where they were heard. In the 13th century commissions, outside EYRES, were issued to judges and laymen to hear one case or all cases within one or more counties. The issue of commissions NISI PRIUS to professional judges after 1285 transformed the system, producing the modern system of professional judges on circuit with united commissions of the PEACE, OYER AND TERMINER, general GAOL DELIVERY, A. and *Nisi Prius*. The six circuits formally established in 1293, to which a Welsh circuit was later added, have under subsequent reorganization become the modern seven circuits.   PMB; MR

Athelney, Isle of, in Somerset at the junction of the rivers Parrett and Tone. It was a desolate site, surrounded by water and marshes, where Alfred king of WESSEX (871–99) at Easter 878 established a base from which to continue his resistance to the DANES under Guthrum. These, by a surprise attack in the winter of 877/8, had forced Alfred to flee and had occupied much of Wessex. After seven weeks Alfred abandoned this base and embarked on the campaign that culminated in the battle of EDINGTON and Guthrum's baptism at WEDMORE. Writers of the 12th and later centuries embroidered the outline story of Alfred's stay here with various tales, including that of the burning of the cakes.   CFS

Atrebates, a powerful group of the BELGAE, occupying the area of Berkshire and Hampshire from *c.* 50 B.C. They were ruled by kings who issued coins and who, during the earlier part of the 1st century A.D., extended their power to the west. In the years immediately before the ROMAN CONQUEST the CATUVELLAUNI encroached on their kingdom, forcing a king on them, and this may have facilitated their submission to the Romans soon after A.D. 43. Their territories to the west became a separate CIVITAS, that of the A. being limited to the areas of original settlement and having its capital at Calleva Atrebatum (Silchester).   CFS

Attachment, in medieval and later periods the means of compelling a reluctant defendant in a civil case to appear in court. In the first instance he was attached by pledges, then by better pledges or gage and pledge. In international mercantile disputes a similar practice was followed; to obtain redress in a foreign court reprisals from the goods of the defendant's fellow countrymen were seized in the plaintiff's own country.   PMB

Attainder. In the medieval period felons sentenced to death, outlaws, etc., as well as juries convicted of false verdicts were subject to attaint, the forfeiture of goods and lands and disinheritance of their heirs; in succeeding centuries these rigours were mitigated. Bills of a. producing like penalties were devised in the 15th century, the first in 1459, to allow Parliament to act both as judge and jury: to some defendants counsel and witnesses were allowed, from others they were withheld. Much used for state trials in the Tudor and Stewart periods, the last bill was introduced in 1798.   PMB

Atterbury's Plot (1722), a Jacobite conspiracy, included seizure of the Bank of England, an insurrection and an invasion by Ormonde and Dillon. The government was warned by the French minister Dubois, and Atterbury, bishop of Rochester, leader of the High Church JACOBITES, was arrested, as were a number of others. Atterbury was condemned by a Bill of Pains and Penalties and banished (1723), and a special tax was imposed on Roman CATHOLICS and NON-JURORS.   IHE

Attorney. The a.-in-fact, lay or professional, medieval or modern, acts in his principal's business affairs for short periods or long, according to the terms of his letters of a. The a.-in-law has a more complex history. Early king's courts required the personal attendance of suitors, but from the 12th century onwards, as courts became busier and law more complex, appointment of a.s 'to win or to lose' was permitted, first as a mark of royal favour, then, in the 13th century, as general practice, though personal conduct of an action has never been forbidden. A.s frequently appointed became professionals; then in the later 13th century conduct of an action was divided between narrators, later SERJEANTS, who dealt with oral proceedings, and a.s, who drew up written proceedings. With the growth of importance of the serjeants, their apprentices and barristers trained in the INNS OF COURT, the a., excluded from the Inns in the later middle ages, became a lesser member of the legal profession, akin to the equity SOLICITORS. The professions were merged in 1873 as solicitors

of the supreme court, though they have remained separate in the United States of America.   PMB

Attorney-General, the senior law officer of the crown. From early times kings appointed several regular attorneys to appear for them, and by the 15th century only one attorney acted. As the A.-G. was not a SERJEANT, the office was unimportant until in the later 16th century outstanding men were appointed and subsequently promoted to CHANCELLOR. The A.-G. was not allowed to sit in the Commons until the GLORIOUS REVOLUTION, then becoming the chief link between government, politics and the law. PMB

Audit Office, see EXCHEQUER AND A.O.

Augmentations, Court of, was created by statute in 1535 as the C. of A. of the Revenues of the Crown to administer the lands etc. of dissolved religious houses, those acquired by purchase, etc., and later from CHANTRIES and similar foundations, paying the revenues into the CHAMBER. The court, consisting of a chancellor, treasurer and others, had power to make grants, leases etc. under its seal. In 1547 it was merged with the Court of General Surveyors as the C. of A. and Revenues of the King's Crown. It was abolished in 1554, and its functions transferred to the EXCHEQUER.   PMB

Augmentations Office was established in 1554 to keep the records of the court of AUGMENTATIONS, both official and those of religious houses, etc., before the DISSOLUTION. The keeper was appointed by the Clerk of the Pipe: the clerkship was abolished in 1833, and the keepership lapsed on the death of the then keeper. The king's REMEMBRANCER took over the rich collection of records, which passed into the control of the Master of the ROLLS under the PUBLIC RECORD OFFICE Act 1838.   PMB

Augsburg, League of (9 July 1686), was a defensive alliance between the Emperor, Spain, Sweden, the Netherlands and lesser German states against the aggressive designs of Louis XIV of France and ostensibly to uphold the treaties of Westphalia (1648) and Nymegen (1678). Louis XIV used the existence of the league as an excuse to invade the Palatinate (Sept. 1688) and to declare war on the Netherlands (Nov.). The ensuing struggle, known as the war of the L. of A. or war of the GRAND ALLIANCE, was ended by the treaty of RYSWICK (1697).   IHE

Aulnage (alnage, ulnage), crown supervision of the size and quality of woollen cloth. Though standards for cloth were first laid down in 1196, only in Edward I's reign were royal officers, aulnagers, appointed to enforce them, measuring cloth and stamping it: faulty cloth forfeited to the crown. Size regulations were repealed in 1381, but standards continued to be enforced, to be revised in 1665 and finally abolished in 1699.   PMB

Auray, battle of (29 Sept. 1364). Despite the Anglo-French peace of BRÉTIGNY (1360), the struggle for the duchy of Brittany continued between candidates backed by England and France respectively. At A. Bertrand Duguesclin was defeated by Sir John Chandos, and the French candidate, Charles of Blois, was killed. The pro-English John de Montfort IV gained possession of the duchy but, after obtaining the recognition of King Charles V of France in 1365, established Brittany as an independent neutral rather than an English 'protectorate'.   RFW

Australia, Commonwealth of, came nto being on 1 Jan. 1901 by the federation of NEW SOUTH WALES, VICTORIA, QUEENSLAND, SOUTH AUSTRALIA, WESTERN AUSTRALIA and TASMANIA, after a referendum in all six colonies (1899) had brought to fruition the discussions begun in 1888; the first suggestion of a federal union, broached by Earl Grey in 1849, had been turned down by the colonies. The federal government consists of the governor-general, a house of representatives and a senate (in which each state has ten senators); voting was made

compulsory in 1925; the cabinet was reorganized on the British model in 1956. As in CANADA, the state rights are considerable.

Until the first gold-rush in the 1850s the majority of the population consisted of convicts and ex-convicts. The aborigines, never numerous, now number some 50,000, divided into c. 400 tribes; half-castes account for some 30,000. The 'white A.' policy, pursued from 1860, has prevented the influx of Asians and placed many restrictions on non-English white immigration. Labour shortage has therefore often been a serious problem and resulted in an early ascendancy of the trades unions (from 1838) and the Labour party (from 1910). Compulsory labour and arbitration courts, introduced in the 1890s, exercise wide powers; minimum wages were established as early as 1907. The advantages of (probably) the highest wages in the world are, however, largely nullified by the traditional high tariff policy, which started in 1861 and 1865 with the protective tariffs of Victoria. The main export commodities of the C. of A. are wool (one-quarter of world production), wheat and gold.

The C. of A. administers the Australian Capital Territory of CANBERRA, the NORTHERN TERRITORY, NORFOLK ISLAND, PAPUA, the trusteeship territory of NEW GUINEA (see NAURU), the Australian Antarctic Territory (7 Feb. 1933, effective 24 Aug. 1936), the Heard and MacDonald Islands (transferred from Great Britain 26 Dec. 1947), the COCOS ISLANDS and CHRISTMAS ISLAND.   SHS

Austrian Succession War (1740–48) was caused by Prussia's rejection of the PRAGMATIC SANCTION and her invasion of Silesia (Dec. 1740). In 1741 France, Spain, Saxony and Sardinia supported the Bavarian claim to the imperial title, each coveting part of the Habsburg dominions. Britain persuaded Austria to make peace with Prussia (1742), and after DETTINGEN (1743) the French withdrew from Germany. In 1743 the alliance of Britain, Austria and Sardinia to drive the Bourbons from Italy led to a renewed compact between France and Spain and Prussia's re-entry into the war in 1744. In 1745 France gained control of Flanders after FONTENOY and Prussia withdrew, retaining Silesia. In 1746 the French and Spaniards were driven out of north Italy. Although France did not declare war on Britain until 1744 (FORTY-FIVE REBELLION), it became as much an Anglo-Bourbon maritime and colonial struggle (JENKINS' EAR) as a complexity of European rivalries. British sea supremacy was established, but the capture of Louisbourg (1745) was followed by the loss of MADRAS (1746). War ended by the treaty of AACHEN (1748).   IHE

Authorized Version (1611). This translation of the BIBLE, resulting from the HAMPTON COURT CONFERENCE (1604), the work of 47 scholars, was based on the Bishops' Bible (1568). They made use of their English and continental predecessors and the A.V. superseded other editions by its merits. The increase of biblical knowledge led to the production of the Revised Version (1881–5), the American Standard Version (1901), the Revised Standard Version (1952) and the New English Bible (1961–70).
                                                    IHE

Avebury (near Marlborough, Wilts.), the largest stone circle monument in Europe, the boundary ditches enclosing almost 30 acres. It was, in its surviving form, constructed by people of the BEAKER CULTURE, together with an avenue marked by standing stones. Considerable destruction took place during the middle ages, probably for religious reasons, and in the 17th and 18th centuries many stones were broken up to provide building material. Excavation and restoration took place during the 1930s, and in 1942 it was presented to the National Trust.   CFS

Aviation, Ministry of. On 21 Oct. 1959 the M. of SUPPLY changed its title to M. of A. and took over the civil aviation functions formerly exercised by the M. of TRANSPORT and Civil Aviation. At the same time it returned certain supply functions to the service departments but continued to be responsible for research, development and supply of guided missiles, radar and other electronic equipment. During 1966 its civil aviation functions were transferred in stages to the Board of TRADE. The M. of A. was wound up and its remaining functions transferred to the M. of TECHNOLOGY in Feb. 1967.   MR

Avranches, compromise of (21 May 1172). The murder of Archbishop Thomas Becket at Canterbury (29 Dec. 1170), for which Henry II admitted indirect responsibility, obliged the king to make some concessions to the church. In May 1172 Henry met the papal legates at A. and was absolved of blame. In return Henry promised to go on crusade, to maintain knights in the Holy Land, to effect a reconciliation with Becket's supporters and the see of Canterbury, and to abolish all new customs hurtful to the church introduced during his reign. Although the 'new customs' clearly referred to the constitutions of CLARENDON, the only article of the constitutions explicitly renounced at A. was the prohibition of appeals to Rome. In 1176, however, Henry II made one more major concession to Pope Alexander III, viz. that CRIMINOUS CLERKS should no longer be brought before secular courts, except for FOREST offences. In practice, Henry surrendered very little of the crown's authority over the church.
                                                    RFW

Axholme, Isle of (1265). After the defeat and death of Simon de Montfort at EVESHAM, a body of MONTFORTIANS took refuge in the I. of A., in the fen country of northern Lincolnshire, where the younger Simon de Montfort became their leader. Resistance was speedily ended by Edward, son of King Henry III, who in December, by the convention of Bycarrs Dyke, forced Simon and his followers to submit to the king's judgement, on the understanding that

B

they should not forfeit their lives or liberty. Some of the Montfortians later broke the convention and joined the rebels in the Isle of ELY, while Simon himself fled overseas in 1266.

RFW

Aylesbury Election (1702–5). Matthew Ashby, a whig, brought a successful action against William White, tory mayor of Aylesbury, for refusing his vote at the parliamentary election of 1700. The decision was reversed by Queen's Bench (1704) as affecting Parliamentary privilege and therefore outside common law jurisdiction. When reversed again by the Lords, a conflict with the Commons ensued, which encouraged five more Aylesbury men to bring similar actions, and the Commons imprisoned them for contempt. Unsuccessfully seeking release by HABEAS CORPUS in Queen's Bench, one of them (Paty) sought to bring his case before the Lords. This appeared to make the Lords judges of the privileges of the Commons and created a further crisis, which the queen overcame by proroguing and dissolving Parliament (1705). The Aylesbury men were freed and obtained verdicts against the returning officers.

IHE

Babington Conspiracy (1586) was organized by Ballard, a Jesuit, in concert with Mendoza, Philip II's ambassador in Paris. There was to be a Catholic rising in favour of Mary Queen of Scots, and Elizabeth I was to be murdered. Anthony B. agreed to lead the assassins, but his communications with Mary were known to the government and the conspirators were executed (Sept.). Mary was found guilty by a special court and beheaded at Fotheringay (8 Feb. 1587). IHE

Bachelors, a term applied in the 13th century to young knights and squires attached to the households of great nobles—the forerunners of the military retainers of 'BASTARD FEUDALISM'. 'The B.' refers in particular to a group of knights and lesser gentry who, at

the October Parliament of 1259, voiced their fears that the PROVISIONS OF OXFORD were not being implemented for the good of their class. The PROVISIONS OF WESTMINSTER, published soon afterwards and probably prepared before the b. made their protest, went far towards meeting their grievance. RFW

Badonicus, Mons, battle of, was fought at an unidentified place in Southern Britain some time in the years 493–516 between the Britons and the Teutonic invaders. The Britons were victorious, and for nearly two generations there was no major Teutonic advance towards the west. There are many unsolved problems connected with this battle. Gildas, writing in the 6th century, calls it a siege, but gives no details, and names Ambrosius Aurelianus, a Roman, as the overall commander of the Britons at this time. The work preserved by Nennius some two centuries later makes Arthur commander of the Britons at this battle (ARTHURIAN LEGEND). What Teutonic invaders were involved is a matter of speculation; possibly all those of the south, and if so, it is likely that they fought as a united force under a supreme commander (BRETWALDA). But British pride may have exaggerated the importance of the battle (TEUTONIC CONQUEST). CFS

Bagdad Pact, see CENTO.

Bahamas, discovered by Columbus in 1492 and ruthlessly depopulated by the Spaniards as a source of slave labour for Hispaniola. English settlements on New Providence (1629–41, 1666–1703) and Eleuthera (1646) suffered from frequent Spanish and French attacks and were abandoned in 1703. The B. became a hide-out of pirates until in 1718 the merchants of London and Bristol persuaded the British government to annex the islands. Representative government was granted in 1728. New Providence was taken by the Spaniards in 1781 but regained in 1783. After the

AMERICAN REVOLUTION many loyalists from Georgia settled in the B. About 85% of the population are descended from African ex-slaves. The B. were given internal self-government on 7 Jan. 1964.   SHS; IHE

Bahrain, see PERSIAN GULF.

Bail, see MAINPRISE.

Balaclava, battle of (25 Oct. 1854), in the CRIMEAN WAR, developed from a Russian attack on the port of B., the base of the British forces which under Lord Raglan were besieging Sevastopol. The scene was a plateau surrounded by hills and bisected by a causeway carrying the metalled Woronzoff road. Raglan, who had ignored a report of the Russian advance, directed the battle from the heights, ½-hour's ride away. The Russians quickly occupied the causeway and advanced on the 93rd Highlanders ('the thin red line') under Sir C. Campbell (later F.-M. Lord Clyde); these, with Lord Lucan's cavalry division, were the only men available for the defence of the gorge leading down to the port. The Heavy Brigade (Brig. Gen. (Sir) J. Scarlett) then charged uphill against about 3,000 horsemen and put them to flight. There was no follow-up at this decisive moment as Lucan misread Raglan's orders; the Russians were able to reform. Raglan sent another, perhaps imprecise, order which Lucan again misinterpreted; instead of directing the Light Brigade (Lord Cardigan) to the causeway he ordered it up the heavily defended valley to the north. The brigade, supported by the Chasseurs d'Afrique, got through to the guns at the head of the valley and returned; of 673 horsemen, 113 were killed and 134 wounded. This ended the battle, the Russians being left in possession of the Woronzoff road.   MLH

Balfour declaration (2 Nov. 1917), was drafted by A. J. Balfour as foreign secretary and issued on behalf of the British government, and on 10 Aug. 1920 endorsed by the allied powers. The B.D. was concerted with Chaim

Weizmann (1874–1952, from 1948 president of Israel) and aimed at enlisting Jewish support for the allied cause by expressing favourable consideration of 'the establishment in PALESTINE of a national home for the Jewish people' without 'prejudice [to] the civil and religious rights of existing non-Jewish communities in Palestine'. The clash between Jewish and Arab aspirations, however, proved irreconcilable, especially as the Zionists interpreted the B.D. as a promise to make Palestine the Jewish state.   SHS

Ballot Act (1872). Secret parliamentary and municipal voting as a means of overcoming bribery and corruption had long been advocated by the RADICALS and formed an essential part of the CHARTISTS' programme. The report of a select committee convinced Gladstone's ministry and a bill (also containing detailed rules for the conduct of elections) was introduced (1871), defeated in the Lords, reintroduced and finally passed (18 July 1872). A necessary supplement to the REFORM ACTS, the B.A.'s effect, everywhere important, was immediately noticeable in Ireland where it enabled a strong Irish HOME RULE party to be formed in the Commons.   MLH

Baltic Expeditions (1854–5). During the CRIMEAN WAR 2 Anglo-French naval expeditions were sent to the Baltic to bombard coastal fortresses and blockade the Russian fleet. In Aug. 1854 Vice-Adm. Sir C. Napier with a mixed squadron of sail of the line, screw- and paddle steamers took Bomarsund (Aland Islands) with the aid of 10,000 French troops. In Aug. 1855 an all-steam British fleet and a French fleet bombarded Sveaborg (near Helsinki). Hopes were high of both expeditions but they proved ineffective and did not influence the course of the war.   MLH

Baluchistan was in Nov. 1887 constituted a chief commissionership out of the districts ceded by Afghanistan after the second Afghan war under the treaty of Gandamak (24 May 1879); further tracts were ceded or leased by native rulers between 1883 and 1903. Until 1947, when B. became a province of PAKISTAN, the country consisted of B. proper, the leased and tribal areas, and three princely states, of which Kalát was the most important. The exclave of Gwadur was ceded by the sultan of MUSCAT on 8 Sept. 1958.   SHS

Bamburgh, 'Bebba's fortress', first built by Ida, King of BERNICIA (547–59) and named after a late-6th-century queen, long remained one of the principal castles of northern England and was the last castle save Harlech to hold out for Henry VI during the wars of the ROSES. LANCASTRIANS from Scotland captured B. in Oct. 1462, and it served as the queen's base in Northumberland until its recapture by Warwick late in December. A fresh Lancastrian invasion secured B. and other castles in the spring of 1463, and after the dispersal of the Lancastrian army in July B. sheltered Henry and Margaret. After the final Lancastrian defeats at HEDGELEY MOOR and HEXHAM, B. was captured about 10 July 1464.   RFW

Banbury, battle of (26 July 1469). The years 1468–9 saw not only a series of LANCASTRIAN risings against Edward IV but also a split within the Yorkists between the factions of the Woodvilles and of Warwick and Clarence. William Herbert, earl of Pembroke, on his way to join the king with an army from Wales and the Marches, was defeated at Edgcott, six miles north-east of B., by Warwick's men. Pembroke was captured and executed, and his defeat left the king at the mercy of Warwick, who swiftly secured the judicial murder of the surviving Woodville leaders. RFW

Bangorian Controversy was caused by the publication of a pamphlet by Hoadly, bishop of Bangor, attacking the NON-JURORS and defending ERASTIANISM (1716), and his subsequent sermons preached before George I (1717), in which he denied the existence of any visible church authority. Convocations were prorogued by the

government to silence the attacks on Hoadly. The B.C. produced a vigorous pamphlet warfare, and the convocation of Canterbury did not meet effectively again until 1852, and York not until 1861.   IHE

Bank Holidays. The B.H. Act, 1871, scheduled Easter Monday, Whit Monday, the 1st Monday in Aug. and 26 Dec. (if a weekday) as B.H.; and in Scotland, New Year's Day, Christmas Day, Good Friday and the 1st Mondays in May and Aug. A proclamation (1967) varied the Spring (Whit) and Aug. B.H.s to the last Mondays in May and Aug. The Holidays Extension Act, 1875, added 27 Dec. if 26 Dec. be a Sunday. St Patrick's Day (17 Mar.) was made a B.H. for Ireland in 1903. The Acts apply only to banks but B.H. soon became general public holidays. The 12 July (BOYNE) is a B.H. (by proclamation) in Northern Ireland.   MLH

Bank of England, the first English joint-stock bank established in 1694 to help finance the war with France. It survived the opposition of the GOLDSMITHS, and as the government's bank steadily gained a key position in national finance. Note issue became a main function. The Act of 1708 confirming its monopoly forbade the establishment of banks with more than six partners, thus preventing the growth of other joint-stock banks until 1826, when they were permitted outside a 65-mile radius of London, and inside after 1833. B. of E. notes were made legal tender in 1833, and the Bank Charter Act (1844) fixed the fiduciary issue and began the process of securing a note-issue monopoly which was complete by 1921. It was established as the bankers' bank by the end of the 18th century, and was highly developed as the central bank by the end of the 19th, becoming a nationalized institution in 1946, having already shed its ordinary banking business. It acts as government agent of financial policy.   IHE

Bank of Ireland was established in 1783 with a charter modelled on that of the BANK OF ENGLAND. After 1821 other joint-stock banks were permitted outside a 50-mile range of Dublin, but these restrictions were removed in 1845. It never fully attained the status of a central bank, as it ultimately relied on the Bank of England, and in 1943 the Central Bank was established with the sole right to issue legal-tender notes. IHE

Bank of Scotland, the first Scottish joint-stock bank, was established in 1695 with a 21-year monopoly. Scotland was not affected by the BANK OF ENGLAND's monopoly, and Scottish joint-stock banks had free scope to develop after 1716, the most important being the Royal Bank of Scotland (1727) and the British Linen Company (1746). The B. of S. was the first to issue £1 notes (1704). It established a London office in 1867, and with other Scottish banks still retains the right of note issue. IHE

Banneret. Knight b. was originally a military rank only. From the second half of the 13th century b.s were knights placed in command of troops of other knights and men-at-arms, receiving higher pay than ordinary knights (who came to be called knights bachelor) and bearing a distinctive banner, from which they took their name. When a knight became a b. he cut off the tail of his pennon, converting it into a rectangular banner like those carried by barons. In the 14th century b. became a title of honour, often conferred by the king on the battlefield for good service in action, but it was not an hereditary dignity. By the early 17th century b. and baronet were often used synonymously. After James I's creation of the BARONETCY, there do not appear to have been any further creations of knights b. RFW

Bannockburn, battle of (24 June 1314). Between 1307 and 1314 Robert Bruce both imposed unity upon the Scots and captured all the castles held by the English except BERWICK and Stirling. Edward II organized a full-scale invasion of Scotland with about 20,000 men. He reached Falkirk on 22 June and thence advanced along the Stirling road as far as its crossing of the B. where Bruce with perhaps 10,000 men blocked further progress. The movements of the English and the site of the battle have not been determined beyond doubt, but it is likely that Edward's army was caught on the marshy ground in the angle of the Bannock and the Forth. The English cavalry failed to halt the advance of the 'schiltroms' of Scottish spearmen. Owing to their cramped position much of the English infantry could not be deployed, and the archers were not brought into effective action. When the English finally broke many of them were drowned in the Forth; Edward himself narrowly escaped capture. Bruce's victory ensured the independence of Scotland. RFW

Baptists descended from the more restrained ANABAPTISTS. The first English B. church was founded by John Smyth in Amsterdam (1609) among refugee separatists, from where a group under Thomas Helwys returned to London (1612) and founded the General B. Their ARMINIANISM did not suit the Calvinists, hence the growth of the Strict, Particular or Calvinistic B. (1633–8). The latter flourished in the 18th century, but many General B. became UNITARIANS, causing the more orthodox to form the New Connexion (1770). The formation of the Baptist Union (1813) eventually promoted closer co-operation, and the merger of the Particular Baptists and New Connexion was completed in 1891. IHE

Barbados was discovered by the Spaniards in 1519, annexed by Britain in 1625 and settled in 1627. After the introduction of sugar cane (1640), B. became the richest island in the West Indies. From 1642 it was a haven of refuge for royalists until Cromwell forced them to surrender in 1652. A Dutch attack in April 1665 was beaten off. In 1663 B. was taken over by the crown, and in 1885 made a separate colony. It joined the federation of the WEST INDIES in 1958, was given full internal self-government in 1961 and became an independent sovereign state within the COMMONWEALTH on 30 Nov. 1966. SHS; IHE

Barbary Corsairs, Moslem pirates from ports of the Barbary States, were a menace to Mediterranean shipping throughout the 16th century. Helped by English and Dutch renegades, they began operating in the Atlantic early in the 17th century. The naval decay under James I made them a constant threat to the Channel ports, which was only partially checked by Charles I's SHIP-MONEY navy. The Cromwellian fleet drove them out of the Channel and destroyed the Algerine fleet in its stronghold (1655). The menace ended with the British navy's expedition to Tunis, Tripoli and Algiers in 1816. IHE

Barebone's Parliament (4 July–11 Dec. 1653). The army, having dismissed the RUMP and established a new council of state, sought to strengthen the civil power by a 'parliament of saints'. Independent congregations nominated godly men, from whom the council of officers chose 129 English members, 5 Scottish and 6 Irish. The Nominated or Little Parliament was derisively nicknamed after a member called Praise-God Barebon. It instituted civil marriage and appointed a committee to codify the law and voted for the abolition of the Court of CHANCERY. Their attack on ecclesiastical PATRONAGE and tithes encouraged the moderates to secure a majority and resign their powers to Cromwell by the INSTRUMENT OF GOVERNMENT. IHE

Barham Down (1264). Although by their victory of LEWES the MONTFORTIANS had gained control of King Henry III and the government of England, they faced a serious threat of an invasion from France organized by royalist exiles. Both feudal forces and shire levies were summoned and posted at strategic points on or near the south and east coasts. The largest camp was on B.D., near Canterbury, where King John had mustered

troops to oppose a possible French invasion in 1213. Peace negotiations with the exiles came to nothing, and the camp was maintained through the summer and autumn of 1264, until it was clear that there would be no landing that year. The considerable military effort involved was an impressive demonstration of the support enjoyed by Simon de Montfort. RFW

Barnet, battle of (14 April 1471). Edward IV, driven into exile in 1470, secured financial and military assistance from Charles the Bold of Burgundy and landed at RAVENSPUR in March 1471. Joined by his brother Clarence, who deserted the LANCASTRIANS, Edward occupied London and captured Henry VI, then met the Lancastrians led by Warwick. The complete Yorkist victory at B. owed much to the mutual suspicion of the Lancastrian leaders and the confusion caused by thick fog. Although Warwick was killed and his army destroyed, Edward IV was not securely back on his throne until his victory at TEWKESBURY. RFW

Baroda formed, as the province of Gujarat, part of the Mogul empire, but early in the 18th century the MARATHAS gained independence under the Gaekwar dynasty, who allied themselves with the EAST INDIA COMPANY in 1779 and put themselves under British protection in 1817. B. was one of the most important princely states in India until it was merged in BOMBAY on 1 May 1949. On 1 May 1960 B. joined the newly formed State of Gujarat. SHS; IHE

Baronage (from Old French *barnage,* Med. Latin *baronagium*), in medieval English history most often used as a general name embracing the earls, the tenants of feudal baronies and other important feudal tenants-in-chief: i.e. the whole of the titled and landed nobility, not merely those peers entitled barons. RFW

Baronetcy. The order of Baronets in England was established by James I in 1611, originally to provide money for the defence of the English settlement of Ulster. Each knight was to pay £1,095 (enough to maintain 30 foot soldiers for 3 years). It was part of the attempt to raise money by the sale of titles and offices, and the original limitation of numbers to 200 was subsequently abandoned. Baronets of Ireland were established in 1619 and of Scotland and NOVA SCOTIA in 1625. Baronetcies of Great Britain replaced those of England and Scotland consequent upon the Act of Union of 1707 and after the Union with Ireland (1800) all baronetcies were of the United Kingdom.   IHE

Barons' Wars (1) (1215–7). By Aug. 1215 it was clear that the granting of MAGNA CARTA was not going to avert civil war. The barons offered the crown to Louis, son of Philip II of France. Although the barons retained London, King John captured Rochester in Nov., campaigned successfully in the midlands and north, and was getting the upper hand when Prince Louis landed in Kent in May 1216. Many of John's supporters now deserted him, and he lost south-east England except for the castles of Dover and Windsor. However, after raising forces in the south-west, John was able to relieve Lincoln in the autumn, but died at Newark on 18 Oct. 1216. A group of loyal barons had John's young son crowned as Henry III at Gloucester on 28 Oct., and William Marshal, earl of Pembroke, became regent. While Louis and the barons held most of the south and east and were allied with Alexander II of Scots and Llywelyn the Great of GWYNEDD, the royalists held the west midlands, the south-west and isolated strongholds in the east. Among their ranks were many of the most powerful magnates, such as the earls of Chester and Pembroke and a strong group of MARCHERS; they commanded the services of John's capable mercenary captains; and they enjoyed the full support of the papacy, represented in England by the legate Guala. John's death had removed the source of many baronial grievances, and on 12 Nov., at Bristol, the royalists

reissued Magna Carta with modifications. A drift from the baronial to the royalist side set in. The royalists regained Rye and Winchelsea and began to threaten Louis's communications with the continent. In Apr. 1217 Louis determined to press the siege of Dover, ably defended by the justiciar, Hubert de Burgh, while a second baronial army undertook to relieve Mountsorel and assist in the siege of Lincoln. The complete defeat of the latter force at LINCOLN (20 May) caused Louis to raise the siege of Dover and was followed by further defections. The royalist victory off SANDWICH stopped reinforcements from France, and on 12 Sept. Louis agreed to the treaty of KINGSTON. Peace was quickly followed by a reissue of the modified Magna Carta, and a separate charter of the FOREST.

(2) (1264–7). The civil war which followed the Mise of AMIENS went at first against the MONTFORTIANS. They failed to secure the Severn valley, and Henry III and his son, Edward, joined forces at Oxford and captured NORTHAMPTON. The king's advance into the south-east to secure the CINQUE PORTS compelled De Montfort to raise the siege of ROCHESTER and retire to London. Despite the defeat of the royalists at LEWES and the capture of Henry III and although a royalist invasion from France failed to materialize (BARHAM DOWN), De Montfort's position was precarious. He failed to secure the co-operation or obedience of the northern barons or of the Marchers, although he twice forced the latter to come to terms. In the spring of 1265 De Montfort was weakened by the desertion of some of his supporters, especially Gilbert de Clare, earl of Gloucester; and on 28 May Prince Edward escaped from custody and joined Gloucester and the Marchers. De Montfort secured the aid of Llywelyn ap Gruffydd by the treaty of Pipton, but the royalist capture of Gloucester penned his forces west of the Severn. Eventually De Montfort crossed the Severn at Kempsey and marched for Evesham to effect a junction with the forces which his son, Simon, was bringing from the south-east. The younger Simon got no further than KENIL-WORTH, where he was surprised by Edward. De Montfort was finally defeated and killed at EVESHAM on 4 Aug. 1265. Although Henry III quickly recovered control of most of England, groups of Montfortians—the DISIN-HERITED—held out in Kenilworth castle and the Isle of AXHOLME. In 1266 resistance in the Cinque Ports was brought to an end, a Montfortian concentration at CHESTERFIELD was routed, and the garrison of Kenilworth eventually accepted the terms of the Dictum of KENILWORTH. The earl of Gloucester secured further concessions which brought over most of the more intransigent Montfortians (June 1267). Organized resistance came to an end with Edward's capture of the Isle of ELY, but small bands of the Disinherited remained as outlaws in the forests. (ROBIN HOOD LEGEND). RFW

Barotseland, see NORTHERN RHODE-SIA, ZAMBIA.

Barrier Treaties. The GRAND AL-LIANCE treaty of 1701 recognized the Dutch demand for a barrier against France and by the first B.T. (1709) Great Britain undertook to secure the Dutch up to 19 fortresses in order to keep them in the SPANISH SUCCESSION WAR. The second B.T. (1713) greatly reduced their number, and the arrangement was substantially confirmed by the third B.T. (1715) with the emperor, now in possession of the southern Netherlands. It remained a source of friction with Austria and was a factor in the DIPLOMATIC REVOLUTION. It was cancelled by the treaty of Fontainebleau (1785). IHE

Barrowists, a Puritan sect in the reign of Queen Elizabeth I, named after their leader Henry Barrow, holding a congregatioralist position similar to the BROWNISTS. Barrow was executed (6 Apr. 1593) with John Greenwood for writing 'sundry seditious books, tending to the slander of queen and state'. After the CON-VENTICLE ACT of 1593, punishing with exile or death those refusing to attend church, many went to Holland and afterwards to NEW ENGLAND. IHE

Bastard Feudalism. The pattern of society designed by William I was centripetal, the king at its centre: the pattern of society called b. (or new) f. was centrifugal, taking shape in the 14th century and surviving into the Tudor period. Behind this change lay factors working over several centuries. William's barons and knights became country gentlemen, with no place on the battlefield, little conception of service in return for land, but with vested interests in their lands, buttressed by the development of primogeniture etc. By marriage, grant etc., many lands were grouped into a family's hands, and the ties of such units strengthened by the grant of liberties, which Edward I's legislation rationalized but did not break. Such large estates needed officers and councillors to administer them, to hold courts, etc., and these were appointed for money fees, not land; lesser servants were given LIVERY AND MAINTENANCE, becoming, on occasion, private armies. The influence which such estates and dependants, seas of independence, allowed their lord to wield over sheriffs, local officers, juries etc., was enhanced by numbers of country gentlemen seeking patrons, and extended to Parliament: it was in no way harnessed to the king and his interests, except at the will of the lord. The disruption that could arise from disputes between lord and lord, and lords and the king, was demonstrated in the wars of the ROSES, but did not conform to the pattern of strong, centralized monarchy favoured by the Tudors. By legislation against LIVERY AND MAINTENANCE, by resuming royal rights from LIBERTIES and, indirectly, by creating a new class of landed gentry, the Tudors broke first the power and then the pattern of b.f. PMB

Basutoland was founded in the 1820s by the chief Moshesh out of the remains of many Bantu tribes whom the Zulu had destroyed. Harried by the Boers, Moshesh in 1868 placed B. under British protection. After his death (1870) B. was annexed to CAPE COLONY, but the protectorate was re-established in 1884 at the request of the Basuto. Together with BECHUANALAND and SWAZILAND, B. was 1906–60 administered by the High Commissioner; under its new constitution B. enjoys complete internal self-government, prepared for by the establishment of district councils (1944) and a national council (1959). On 4 Oct. 1966 B. became an independent and sovereign member of the COMMONWEALTH as the Kingdom of LESOTHO.   SHS; IHE

Bate's Case (1606). A merchant named Bate challenged James I's right to levy an imposition on currants. The courts of the EXCHEQUER decided that the king had the right to levy impositions of duties at the ports in control of trade, but this did not extend to levying for purposes of taxation. This led to the issue of a revised Book of Rates (1608), levying new impositions to increase the royal revenue. The Commons, realizing that with increasing trade they would lose financial control, unsuccessfully contested this issue in 1610 (GREAT CONTRACT).   IHE

Bath, Order of the, was founded by George I in 1725 and remodelled by George IV in 1815, though it was once thought to have been founded by Henry IV in 1399. The term 'knights of the bath' was, however, applied to those knights who were created knights on ceremonial occasions after observing the ritual of the night vigil followed by the symbolic purifying bath.   RFW

Bats, Parliament of, the Northampton parliament of 1426, to which the retainers of Humphrey, duke of Gloucester, and Henry Beaufort, bishop of Winchester, forbidden to appear bearing arms by the regent

Bedford, came carrying 'bats' or clubs. Beaufort was unsuccessfully accused of treason by Gloucester. A formal but insincere reconciliation of the rivals followed, and their quarrel was eventually appeased by Beaufort's surrender of the chancellorship.   RFW

Battle-axe Culture, a pre- and early BRONZE-AGE culture so called from the polished stone axes used; sometimes called the Corded-ware from its typical pottery decoration. In conjunction with people of the BEAKER CULTURE, they invaded Britain from c. 1800 B.C., and probably formed the dominant element in the WESSEX CULTURE. It is possible that they introduced an early form of the Celtic language (CELTS).   CFS

Baugé, battle of (21 March 1421). Thomas, duke of Clarence, brother of King Henry V, led a hurried pursuit of a Franco-Scottish army which had been raiding southern Normandy and Maine. Leaving his infantry behind, Clarence caught up his opponents and committed his cavalry to an attack on superior forces. At B. in Anjou Clarence was killed and his force completely destroyed by John Stewart, earl of Buchan and constable of France.   RFW

Bayeux Tapestry, an embroidery in coloured wool on plain linen, some 230 feet long by 20 inches wide, probably commissioned by Bishop Odo of B. between 1066 and 1077. The design and workmanship are authoritatively considered to be English, of the school of Canterbury. The B.T. forms a pictorial narrative of events from 1064 to 1066, with Harold Godwinson and Duke William of Normandy as the central figures. The sequence starts with Harold's mission to France in 1064 and closes with the battle of HASTINGS. Two scenes have been lost at the end of the work, which probably finished with the coronation of William as king of England. The B.T. is a unique survival. Beside its great artistic merits, it is a most valuable contemporary narrative of the events leading to the

NORMAN CONQUEST, and an unrivalled source of information on the costume, arms and armour of the 11th century. In 1803 the tapestry was used as invasion propaganda by Napoleon. It is still in B. cathedral.
The B.T., ed. Sir Frank Stenton (1957). RFW

Bay Islands, off the coast of Honduras, were occupied by Britain in 1839, annexed in 1852, but, at the insistence of the U.S.A., ceded, together with the northern part of the MOSQUITO COAST, to Honduras in 1859. SHS

Beachy Head, battle of (10 July 1690). At the outset of the war of the GRAND ALLIANCE (1689–97) part of the English fleet was being used to cover William III in Ireland. The reduced Channel fleet, reinforced by a Dutch contingent, was defeated by the numerically superior French force off B.H. The English admiral failed to press the attack, and the Dutch bore the heaviest fighting. The French made little use of their victory and contented themselves with burning Teignmouth. IHE

Beaker Culture, an early BRONZE AGE culture, so called from the shape of the drinking-vessels constructed. It probably originated in central Spain. Some of its practitioners mingled with the BATTLE-AXE people of central Europe, and mixed groups invaded Britain from *c.* 1800 B.C. Other Beaker people may have come by sea from the Iberian peninsula. They spread over much of the British Isles, but their main concentration was in the south where, influenced by native NEOLITHIC cultures, variant forms of B.c. developed. Their needs for copper, then bronze, implements and weapons stimulated manufacture in Ireland. They were essentially nomadic stock-raisers; had an effective pottery; imported luxury goods in gold, jet, etc.; and introduced the practice of individual burial in round barrows. They built stone circles as religious centres, the best known being AVEBURY and

STONEHENGE II, a practice that continued late Neolithic religious ideas. The B.c. was an essential ingredient of the succeeding WESSEX CULTURE.
CFS

Beaufort family, the descendants of John of Gaunt, duke of Lancaster, third son of King Edward III, and his third wife, Katharine Swynford, who had been his mistress since 1371 or 1372. Their children, John, Henry, Thomas and Joan, born between 1373 and 1379, took the name of B. from a castle between Châlons and Troyes which belonged to the earls and dukes of Lancaster. After their parents' marriage these children were legitimized by the pope in 1396, and by Parliament and royal letters patent in 1397. Their half-brother, King Henry IV, while confirming their legitimacy in 1407, expressly excluded them from the succession to the throne. From John B. descended the earls and dukes of Somerset, who were staunch adherents of the house of Lancaster in the wars of the ROSES. The battle of TEWKESBURY in 1471 ended both the legitimate line of Lancaster, by the death of Edward, Prince of Wales, and the male line of B., by the deaths of Edmund, duke of Somerset, and his brother John. It was through Margaret B., a granddaughter of the first John B. that Henry TUDOR derived whatever hereditary claim to the throne he may have had. RFW

Bechuanaland. The history of the Bechuana tribes up to 1870 consists mainly of inter-tribal anarchy and merciless wars with Zulu, Matabele and Boer raiders. Order and stability were created by the Bamangwato chiefs, Sekgoma I and his outstanding son Khama III, a strict Christian, great administrator and successful military leader. Shortly after his accession (1872) Khama, supported by Cecil Rhodes, asked to be taken under British protection, but the British government procrastinated and only in 1885, with the concurrence of Khama and the other chiefs, proclaimed a protectorate. The southern part, with Mafeking (until 1962 the seat of the administration) and Kuruman (where Robert Moffat had established the first Christian mission in 1820), was constituted a crown colony and later incorporated in CAPE PROVINCE. When in 1895 the British government wanted to transfer the protectorate to the British South Africa Company, Khama and the chiefs of the Bangwaketse and Bakwena went to London and obtained their wish to remain under the crown. Central advisory councils of Africans and Europeans were set up in 1920, a joint advisory council in 1950 and local African councils in 1957. Representative government was introduced in 1960 and B. was made fully self-governing internally in 1965. On 4 Oct. 1966 it became an independent member of the COMMONWEALTH as the Republic of Botswana.   SHS; IHE

Bedchamber Crisis (7–13 May 1839). On her accession Queen Victoria had identified herself completely with the Prime Minister, Melbourne, and his insecure Whig administration. When Melbourne resigned (7 May 1839, his majority being reduced to 5), Peel, attempting to form a minority Tory government, requested that certain Ladies of the Household whose husbands were strongly connected with the previous government should vacate their posts; this was a logical extension (the sovereign being female) of the custom that Gentlemen of the Household who were M.P.s retired on a change of government. Victoria, however, refused. Peel then withdrew and Melbourne, being led to believe by Victoria that the resignation of all the Household had been required, consented to remain in office. No one but Peel came out of the incident with credit; Melbourne and his cabinet acted unconstitutionally in giving advice to the queen (10 May) after their resignation, whilst Victoria was both impetuous and stubborn. When the government finally fell (Aug. 1841), the prior resignation of 3 Ladies was agreed at the instigation of the prince consort.   MLH

Bedford, siege of (1224). Conspicuous among the trusted servants of King John who had lost their posts by 1224 was Fawkes de Bréauté, a loyal and capable but ruthless and high-handed mercenary captain and local administrator. Numerous legal actions were brought against Fawkes by victims of past oppression, some of which had been decided against him in June 1224, when he was outlawed, having failed to answer an accusation of felony. On the day of Fawkes' outlawry his brother William kidnapped a royal justice and imprisoned him in B. castle, a royal fortress which Fawkes had been allowed to retain. The justiciar, Hubert de Burgh, besieged B. and forced it to surrender on 14 Aug. William and most of his garrison were hanged the following day. After unsuccessful attempts to persuade the earl of Chester and Llywelyn of Wales to support him in rebellion, Fawkes surrendered to the king and was sent into exile; he died in Rome in 1226.   RFW

Beefeaters, see YEOMEN OF THE GUARD.

Belgae, Celtic-speaking tribes of north-east Gaul that contained a strong Germanic element. Their civilization was IRON AGE; and they possessed the technique of working heavy soils, produced efficient wheel-made pottery, struck coins, had some embryonic concept of towns as distinct from hill-forts, and their isolated farms foreshadowed the later VILLAS. They first invaded Britain soon after the mid-2nd century B.C., settling in the area of Essex, Herts. and Kent, but remained an essential part of the Gaulish B. This official connexion was lost when Caesar conquered Gaul, and the Belgic invasion of c. 50 B.C. into the area of Hampshire was due to Belgic exiles from Roman Gaul. Support by the British for the Gaulish B. was one reason for the ROMAN CONQUEST. In Britain itself the technical superiority of the B. influenced many tribes in the south; but territorial expansion by the ATRE-

BATES and especially the CATUVEL-LAUNI made them unpopular, and thus helped the Romans. After the conquest the Romans created a CIVITAS of the B. from the west part of the former kingdom of the Atrebates. It lay in the area of Wiltshire, south Hampshire and east Somerset, and its capital was Venta Belgarum (Winchester).   CFS

Benefit of Clergy arose from the 12th-century dispute between church and lay courts. By the Constitutions of CLARENDON (1164) CRIMINOUS CLERKS were to be handed to the church courts for trial and punishment. As the conflict died down the importance of benefit declined. By the 14th century clerks were tried in lay courts, then sent to the church for punishment. By the 15th century b. could be claimed only once, and the claimant was branded. Under Henry VIII and Edward VI the number of beneficiaries was reduced and the number of offences without b. was increased: but in 1547 b. was extended to peers and in 1692 to women. In 1707 tests were abolished and b. was available to all; it was abolished in 1825. In the early period tests of clergy were stringent, but by the 14th century ability to read, later only to read the 'neck verse' (Ps. li, 1) was sufficient proof.   PMB

Benevolences. Payments 'to have the king's benevolence' were known from the early middle ages, but in 1473–4 Edward IV requested individual lords and the city of London to make voluntary contributions towards the expenses of his forthcoming French expedition: gifts were to be made as an expression of the donors' 'good will and benevolence'. The experiment was repeated, notably in 1481–2, when county and borough assemblies were induced to make grants for a Scottish war. B. contributed to the unusual financial prosperity of the crown under Edward IV, but were regarded with suspicion as a form of taxation uncontrolled by Parliament. In 1484 Richard III's Parliament declared the 'newe and unlawfull invencion' of b.

to be illegal, but the Tudors professed to regard the act as invalid, since Richard was a usurper. In practice, b. were often distinguished from FORCED LOANS only in that they were not repayable. B. were last raised by James I in 1614 and 1622. Charles I affirmed their illegality by his consent to the PETITION OF RIGHT, but abortive proposals for another levy were made in 1633.   RFW

Bengal, in 1576 annexed to the Mogul empire, had the first British factories established in 1633; their administrative centre was in 1690 fixed at Fort William, Calcutta. The reconquest of Calcutta by the nawab of B. in 1756 was offset by Clive's victory at PLASSEY, and on 12 Aug. 1765 the Great Mogul ceded B., BIHAR and ORISSA to the EAST INDIA COMPANY. From 1699 to 1774 the presidency of B. was under separate governors (the last of whom was Warren Hastings), from 1774 to 1854 under governors-general (from 1833 designated governors-general of India) who also controlled MADRAS and BOMBAY. In 1854 B., Bihar, Orissa and ASSAM were each placed in charge of a lieutenant-governor. The presidency of B. was in 1834 divided into Agra (corresponding roughly to the later UNITED and CENTRAL PROVINCES) and Fort William. In 1874 the province was reconstituted, consisting of B. proper with Bihar and Orissa. Lord Curzon's partition of B. in 1905, with the creation of a Moslem province of 'Eastern B. and Assam', caused great dissatisfaction and had to be repealed in 1912 when all Bengali-speaking districts were combined under a governor (with, from 1921, an Indian majority in his executive council). Made into an autonomous province with a bicameral legislature in 1937, B. was in 1947 divided between India and PAKISTAN, the latter obtaining about two-thirds of the territory (renamed East Pakistan) and population (of which 75% are Moslems). West B. in 1950 became an 'A State' with a unicameral legislature.   SHS

Berar, see CENTRAL PROVINCES.

Berkeley. In Apr. 1327, after his DEPOSITION, Edward II was moved from Kenilworth to B. castle (Glos.) and placed in the custody of Thomas Berkeley son-in-law of Roger Mortimer. Sympathizers were already plotting his release, and he was rescued from B. in July, only to be recaptured and eventually returned to that prison. In Aug. there is evidence of a Welsh conspiracy to rescue Edward, and Roger Mortimer dropped a clear hint to the King's gaolers, who apparently murdered him about mid-Sept. Edward was buried in Gloucester Abbey, where his tomb became a place of pilgrimage.   RFW

Berlin Congress (13 June–13 July 1878), convened by Bismarck to settle Balkan affairs after the Russo-Turkish war of 1877–8. The participants were the powers which had concluded the treaty of PARIS after the CRIMEAN WAR (1856) and its modification at the London conference of 1871: Russia, Great Britain (represented by Beaconsfield and Salisbury), France, Germany, Austria, Italy and Turkey. The peace of San Stefano (3 March 1878), which had created a Greater Bulgaria as a Russian satellite, was set aside at the instigation of Britain and Austria. Instead the Berlin treaty (signed 13 July) recognized Bulgaria as an autonomous principality tributary to the sultan and enlarged by Eastern Rumelia which nominally remained an autonomous Turkish province; declared Rumania, Serbia (enlarged by the district of Nish) and Montenegro (nearly doubled in size) sovereign and independent principalities; authorized Austria to occupy and administer Bosnia, Hercegovina and Novibazar which remained under Turkish suzerainty; while Russia obtained Batum and Kars and regained Bessarabia, and Great Britain occupied CYPRUS in return for an annual tribute to Turkey. While Disraeli brought home 'peace with honour' and Bismarck, the self-styled 'honest broker', boasted he had 'driven Europe four-in-hand', the B.C. in fact contained the seeds of the first world war: it left the Balkan countries dissatisfied, Turkey seriously weakened, and Russia and Germany permanently estranged; it sharpened the rivalry between Russia and Austria, and provided no long-term solution of any Near Eastern problem.
                                                                    SHS

Berlin Decrees, see CONTINENTAL SYSTEM.

Bermuda, discovered by Juan Bermudez in 1522, settled by Sir George Somers who was shipwrecked there in 1609, and from Virginia in 1612. From the Somers Islands Company (formed in 1615) the crown took over the colony in 1684. A partly elected assembly met from 1620. A more extensive franchise was introduced in 1962 and a new constitution providing a form of responsible internal self-government on 8 June 1968. Two square miles were leased for 99 years to the U.S.A. in 1941 as a naval and air base.   SHS; IHE

Bernicia, a kingdom of the ANGLES, extended from northern Yorkshire into the Lowlands of Scotland and westward into Cumberland. It appears to have been settled late. Its first recorded king, Ida, is mentioned in 547; and for a generation after this the invaders could do no more than hold strong-points, of which BAMBURGH was the chief, on the east coast. It existed as a separate kingdom until near the end of the 6th century, and from 632 to 633 and 641 to 654, but was otherwise joined with DEIRA to make the kingdom of NORTHUMBRIA.
                                                                    CFS

Berwick-on-Tweed on the Scottish border, was captured by Edward I on 28 Mar. 1296, was refortified and largely rebuilt, and was an important English base in the wars of Scottish independence. After an unsuccessful attack in 1312, Robert Bruce retook B. in 1318, and it withstood Edward II's siege in 1319. Edward III received the surrender of B. after his victory at HALIDON HILL in 1333, and speedily retook the town when the Scots captured it with French assistance in 1356. On two further occasions in the 14th century, in 1378 and 1384, B. was briefly in Scottish hands. Henry VI ceded B. to the Scots in 1461 in order to purchase their assistance against Edward IV, and it was held by them until 1482, when Richard, Duke of Gloucester, took the castle on 24 Aug. B. was formally retroceded by the treaty of EDINBURGH (1560), thereafter remaining in English possession. In 1604 James I made B., which had now lost its importance as a military outpost against the Scots, a 'free burgh'; but it was never formally incorporated in England and until 1747 was always specifically mentioned in statutes etc. applying to 'England and B.'   RFW

Berwick, treaty of. **(1)** (Jan. 1560), an alliance between England and the Scottish Lords of the Congregation to expel the French, who were helping the regent, Mary of Guise, against the Calvinists. Mary Stewart was to remain queen, although she had insulted Elizabeth I by assuming her English title. The French, driven into Leith, surrendered and agreed to the treaty of EDINBURGH (July).

(2) (July 1586), marked the establishment of English influence over James VI of Scotland by a defensive alliance against Roman Catholic invasion. Both sides undertook to maintain their respective established religions, and James accepted an English pension of £4,000 per annum.

(3) (June 1639), ended the first BISHOPS' WAR. The Scots were to disband their army, all ecclesiastical matters were to be settled by the General Assembly and civil matters by a parliament at Edinburgh.   IHE

Betagh, see VILLEIN.

Beveridge Report on *Social Insurance and Allied Services* (Cmd 6404) by Sir William (later Lord) Beveridge (signed 20 Nov. 1942) recommended a 'plan for social security' based mainly on an integrated scheme of insurance covering every member of the community. Benefits according to class of insurer would be payable in case of unemployment, disability, old age, widowhood and separation; they would be available without means test and they would be linked to a recognized subsistence level. There would be grants for marriage, childbirth and death. Beveridge advised Exchequer financing of children's allowances, of national assistance and, most important, of a comprehensive health service (which would receive an insurance fund grant). The whole scheme, except the health service, was to be administered by one government department to which certain functions of local authorities (national assistance) and FRIENDLY SOCIETIES (industrial assurance) were to be transferred. The proposals were accepted with modifications (e.g. a subsistence level of benefit was considered impractical; marriage grants and separation allowances were dropped) and given effect in 6 Acts (1944–8).   MLH

Bezant, see GOLD PENNY.

Bhopal, from the middle of the 16th century a vassal state of the Mogul empire, was the most important of the 88 feudatory states administered by the Central India Agency through a political agent. During the mutiny the begum of B. remained loyal. In 1927 a legislative council was established. B. became a centrally administered area on 1 June 1949 and was merged in MADHYA PRADESH on 1 Nov. 1956.   SHS

Bhutan entered into treaty relations with the EAST INDIA COMPANY in 1774, but guerilla warfare with the hill tribes continued until 1865 when, in return for a subsidy from the British government, the frontier passes came under British control. Since 1907 B. has been ruled by a hereditary maharaja, who in Jan. 1910 agreed to be guided by British advice in external relations in exchange for British non-interference in internal affairs. The subsidy was increased in 1910, 1942 and 1949. On 8 Aug. 1949 the Indian government took over the British commitments.   SHS

Bible, English. In late O.E. times and in the earlier 14th century certain books of the Bible had been translated from Latin, but Wyclif's translation (1384) was the first complete E.B. Tyndale's translation of the New Testament was printed at Worms (1525), but the old Testament was incomplete at his death (1536). Coverdale's Bible (1535) was based on the German and Latin Bibles, with some use of Tyndale. The first officially permitted version (1537), essentially a combination of Tyndale and Coverdale, was by John Rogers (alias Thomas Matthew). The Great Bible (1539) was by Coverdale, largely based on Rogers; Cranmer wrote the preface to the second edition. Marian exiles produced the Geneva Bible (1557–60), which by its merits and Calvinistic leanings soon became popular; consequently Archbishop Parker commissioned the Bishops' Bible of 1568. These were superseded by the AUTHORIZED VERSION (1611).

Roman Catholic exiles produced the Reims New Testament (1582) and the Douai Old Testament (1609–10). A new translation prepared by Roman Catholic scholars, the Jerusalem Bible, appeared in 1966.   IHE

Bible, Welsh. Progress towards a W.B. was slow: there were no printing-presses in Wales; English was the official language after 1536; literary difficulties were formidable, and translators scarce. William Salesbury in 1551 published a translation of the epistles and gospels of the Prayer Book. In 1563 an Act of Parliament authorized a W.B., and in 1567 appeared a translation of the New Testament, Psalter and Prayer Book— mainly Salesbury's work. The whole B. was translated in 1588 by William Morgan, an achievement as pregnant with consequence for Welsh history and literature as Luther's B. for Germany. A Welsh translation of the AUTHORIZED VERSION was published in 1620.   GW

Bihar is the cradle of the Jain and Buddhist religions and was the centre of the Nanda, Maurya (324–187 B.C.) and Gupta (A.D. 320–530) empires. It came under Moslem rule in 1190

and formed part of BENGAL under the Mogul empire. An English trading settlement in B. was in 1658 placed under the factory at Fort St George, Madras. By treaty of 12 Aug. 1765 Clive obtained the formal cession of Bengal, B. and ORISSA, which remained united until 1912 when the separate province of B. and Orissa was constituted; in turn this was divided into two provinces on 1 Apr. 1936. On 28 Jan. 1950 B. became an 'A State'; on the reorganization of states on 1 Nov. 1956 B. lost some districts to West Bengal.   SHS

Bill. Legislation by Parliament in in the form of b.s was founded on petition, and laws originating in this form were frequently altered by the crown before becoming statutes. This was overcome in the 15th century with the development of legislation by b., and in Tudor times most b.s originated from the king and council. B.s are classified as public or private, and today most public b.s are government-sponsored. Except money b.s and certain others, they can originate in either House and pass through similar stages in both. After passing both Houses, or else in accordance with the terms of the Parliament Acts of 1911 and 1949, they receive the royal assent (*La Reine remercie ses bons sujets, accepte leur benevolence, et ainsi le veult*, to supply and taxation; *La Reine le veult*, to PUBLIC and PRIVATE BILLS; *Soit fait comme il est désiré*, to personal bills), which has not been refused (*La Reine s'avisera*) since 1707.
IHE

Billericay (28 June 1381) marked the end of serious resistance in the PEASANTS' REVOLT in Essex. The rebels, demanding the ratification of Richard II's promises made at Mile End, met with an abrupt refusal on 23 June. They therefore entrenched themselves near B., but, after a tough resistance, were scattered by Sir Thomas Percy and Thomas of Woodstock.   RFW

Billeting, the practice of compelling householders to provide billets for soldiers and sailors. The term derives from the *billet* or ticket directing the addressee to provide board and lodging. B. became a major abuse under Charles I and provoked the clause against it in the PETITION OF RIGHT (1628). Although b. without consent was forbidden by law (1679), it was employed by Charles II and increasingly by James II, hence the provision in the BILL OF RIGHTS (1689) against quartering troops contrary to law. B. on inn-keepers was authorized from 1690, but when Parliament at last permitted the building of barracks (1792) it soon ceased to be a nuisance. IHE

Bill of Rights (Oct. 1689), was passed by the second session of the CONVENTION PARLIAMENT embodying the DECLARATION OF RIGHTS with some additions. It summarized the illegal acts of James II and stated that by abdicating the government he had left the throne vacant. It then asserted the ancient rights and liberties of the nation, declaring illegal the use of the SUSPENDING POWER, the DISPENSING POWER (as exercised of late), the ECCLESIASTICAL COMMISSION and similar courts, the levying of money without consent of Parliament, the maintenance of a standing army in time of peace, etc. Parliament was to be freely elected, have the right of free debate and meet frequently. William and Mary were declared king and queen, and the succession was settled on the children of Queen Mary, and in default of issue on those of Anne, and then on those of William. Roman Catholics or those marrying same were excluded from the throne. The oaths of SUPREMACY and ALLEGIANCE were replaced by oaths requiring allegiance to the new sovereigns and renunciation of papal jurisdiction. The constitutional settlement of the GLORIOUS REVOLUTION was further consolidated by the TRIENNIAL ACT (1694) and the Act of SETTLEMENT (1701). IHE

Birgham, treaty of (1290). To secure the succession of Margaret, granddaughter of Alexander III (d. 1286), to the Scottish throne, the Guardians of Scotland obtained the assistance of Edward I of England. After preliminary negotiations at Salisbury, English and Scottish representatives met at B., near Berwick-on-Tweed, on 14 Mar. 1290. A treaty drawn up in July was ratified by Edward at Northampton on 28 Aug. The price of Edward's assistance was the promise of the marriage of Margaret to his heir, Edward of Carnarvon. Although a union of the crowns was anticipated, the treaty carefully provided for the continued separation and independence of Scotland. The death of Margaret on 26 Sept. 1290 reopened the problem of the Scottish succession. RFW

Birmingham Riots (14–17 July 1791) were a sign of the growing alarm in England at the French Revolution. There was a long-standing feud in B. between members of the established Church and Unitarians whose support of the Revolution made popular enthusiasm for 'church and king' easy to kindle. A mob collected outside a hotel where supporters of 'the ideas of 1789' were celebrating the anniversary of the fall of the Bastille and soon got out of hand. It ransacked the house and laboratory of Joseph Priestley, the Radical Unitarian theologian and scientist. About 20 chapels and homes of dissenters were burned or damaged. Dragoons from Nottingham eventually restored order. Four men were hanged and the city ordered to pay £35,000 damages. MLH

Bishops' Wars (1639–40). After the Scottish General Assembly abolished EPISCOPACY (see COVENANT) Charles I resorted to war. Lacking men and money, and not wishing to summon the English Parliament, he soon realized his raw levies were no match for the Scots. There was no fighting, and the treaty of BERWICK ended the first war (18 June). Again the General Assembly and Parliament renounced episcopacy and the king resolved to assert his authority. He obtained supplies from the Irish Parliament, but none from the SHORT PARLIAMENT, and began the second B.W. (1640).

He was defeated at Newburn on Tyne (28 Aug.), the Scots occupied Northumberland and Durham, and Charles was forced to agree to the treaty of RIPON.   IHE

Black Death, the plague, in pneumonic and bubonic forms, which first broke out in England in the mid-14th century. The first outbreaks occurred in the western counties in the summer of 1348, and by the end of 1349 the plague had swept the entire country. Further outbreaks occurred in 1361–2, when mortality among children was particularly high, in 1369 and again in 1379. Recovery from its recurrent onslaughts was more difficult than from a single great catastrophe. The population of England, the increase of which had already been halted by the severe famines of the early 14th century, has been variously estimated at between 2.5m. and 4m. before the B.D. Mortality varied greatly from place to place, being generally heaviest where rats were most numerous, i.e. in the towns and corn-growing areas, but contrary to traditional exaggerations, probably never exceeded 10–12% in the worst years. Certain professions, such as textile workers and bakers, suffered more than others, and a shortage of clergy was a chronic problem of the later 14th century. Among the immediate economic consequences of the B.D. were a shortage of labour and a continued fall in prices, which in turn accelerated the leasing of DEMESNE lands. The more prosperous peasants were able to take up additional holdings, but peasants who still owed customary labour services found their lords more determined to retain these services because of the labour shortage and the rise of wages, which almost doubled between 1340 and 1360 despite the attempts of the government to keep them down (Statute of LABOURERS). Hostility to the labour legislation, together with growing resentment of the restrictions imposed by villeinage, contributed to the PEASANTS' REVOLT of 1381. England, particularly its large towns, continued to suffer periodic visitations of the PLAGUE throughout the later middle ages and into the 17th century.   RFW

Blackheath, the encampment of the Kentish rebels under Wat Tyler during the PEASANTS' REVOLT of 1381. Richard II's attempt to discuss terms with the rebels from a boat on the river at Greenwich, on 13 June, failed and was immediately followed by the peasants' assault on London.   RFW

Black Hole of Calcutta. After the surrender of Fort William (20 June 1756) to Siraj-ud-daulah, the nawab of BENGAL, 146 English prisoners are said to have been imprisoned in a small room of 18 by 15 feet, where 123 died of suffocation. The only source of this story is John Holwell (1711–98), who had good reasons for glossing over the incompetence and cowardice of the British governor and council, of which he was a member.   SHS

Blacklow Hill. On 19 May 1312, at Scarborough, Piers Gaveston, Edward II's favourite, was forced to surrender to the earls of Pembroke and Surrey, who guaranteed his personal safety. However, Gaveston was seized by Guy Beauchamp, earl of Warwick, and carried off to Warwick castle. Despite Pembroke's attempts to redeem his promise, other ORDAINERS joined Warwick and on 19 June had him beheaded at B.H. between Warwick and Kenilworth. The execution of Gaveston indirectly strengthened Edward II by causing a serious rift in the ranks of the Ordainers.   RFW

Blenheim, battle of (13 Aug. 1704). After the battle of SCHELLENBERG the Franco-Bavarian armies retired to Augsburg and were joined by further French forces under Tallard. The allies under Marlborough and Eugene of Savoy found them encamped at B. (12 Aug.) and decided to attack. Advancing at night, they opened battle in the early afternoon, but the enemy held their ground until Marlborough's cavalry swept away the French centre. This was decisive. The divided enemy forces were driven from their positions, Tallard and his infantry were taken, Vienna was saved and the French remnant driven back to the Rhine. IHE

Bloemfontein Convention, see SAND RIVER.

Bloody Assizes (Sept. 1685). After MONMOUTH'S REBELLION many insurgents were hanged by the military, and Judge Jeffreys and 4 other judges toured the western circuit to try offenders. The B.A. earned their name from the brutality and unfairness of the proceedings and the barbarity of the sentences. Estimates of the hangings vary between 150 and 320. Over 800 were transported to the West Indies in addition to the infliction of fines, floggings and imprisonments. Jeffreys was rewarded by James II with the office of Lord Chancellor. IHE

Blore Heath, battle of (22 Sept. 1459), a defeat of the LANCASTRIANS by the YORKIST earl of Salisbury, who, coming with a small northern army to join the duke of York at Ludlow, was pursued by one Lancastrian force and intercepted by another at B.H., near Market Drayton, Staffs. RFW

'Blue Books, Treachery of the' (*Brad y llyfrau gleision*), the label given by Welsh critics to a report published in 1847. Its authors—Lingen, Symons and Vaughan Johnson—were required by the government to 'enquire into the state of education . . . especially into the means afforded . . . of acquiring a knowledge of the English tongue'. Able, painstaking and industrious, the inexperienced commissioners, with no intention of being unjust, were misled by the bias of mainly Anglican informants about a predominantly Nonconformist population. Their factual account of deplorable educational facilities was incontestable; their strictures on popular immorality and the alleged connexion between it and Nonconformity and the Welsh language were a travesty. Hotly resented, their findings exacerbated religious controversy and strengthened patriotic sentiment and educational voluntaryism. GW

Boer War, see SOUTH AFRICAN WAR.

Bombay was acquired by the Portuguese in 1534 and ceded to Charles II in 1661 as part of the dowry of Catherine of Braganza. He granted it in 1668 to the EAST INDIA COMPANY for an annual rent of £10, and it was placed under the presidency of Surat, where a British factory had been established by a firman of the emperor Jahangir in 1613. The seat of the governor was transferred to B. in 1708, and the area of the presidency was increased by cessions and conquests from the MARATHAS (from 1773) and the occupation of SIND (1843), which became part of B. province until its separation in 1936. On 1 Apr. 1937 B. was constituted an autonomous province with bicameral legislature, and on 28 Jan. 1950 became an 'A State'. It was completely reorganized on 1 Nov. 1956 as the largest of the 14 Indian states, but in 1960 divided into the Marathi-speaking state of Maharashtra and the Gujarati-speaking state of Gujarat. SHS

Bond, a document of early development, generally of two sections: first the b. proper, frequently in Latin, wherein A is bound to B in a sum of money which does not change hands; second, a condition, generally in the vernacular, which, if ignored, will cause the stated sum to pass. As a means of compulsion as well as security b.s have many uses, e.g. to ensure good behaviour, to enforce commercial contracts etc. PMB

Bondman, see COMMOTE, VILLEIN.

Bond of Association (1584) was drawn up by the council after THROCKMORTON'S PLOT (1583) and the murder of William of Orange (10 July 1584). It pledged its thousands of signatories to protect Elizabeth I from assassination or to revenge her death, also to exclude from the throne any person in whose cause the attempt was made. It was substantially legalized by act of Parliament. IHE

Bookland (Old English *bocland*), became, during the 9th century, the normal description for land granted by royal CHARTER or *boc*. This privileged form of grant exempted the holder from the majority of public services due from FOLKLAND, although the three duties of BURH and bridge building and FYRD service were normally still required. In the modern form Buckland, the word survives in numerous place-names in south and south-west England, where the Anglo-Saxon kings had most authority.   CFS

Book of Common Prayer, the official liturgy of the Church of England. The first B. (1549) drawn up under Cranmer was largely a condensation and simplification in English of the former Latin service books. It both failed to satisfy the reformers and provoked the WESTERN REBELLION (1549). The second more Protestant B. (1552) ordered the use of the surplice instead of vestments, omitted prayers for the dead and remodelled the Communion Service. Elizabeth I's B. (1559) was substantially that of 1552 with the ornaments rubric added, and was soon objected to by the PURITANS. Some minor modifications were made after the HAMPTON COURT CONFERENCE (1604). The B. was superseded by the Presbyterian Directory for Public Worship (1645–61), but a revised B. was reintroduced (1662) after the SAVOY CONFERENCE. The Books of 1549, 1552, 1559, 1662 were accompanied by Acts of UNIFORMITY to ensure their use. Convocation approved revised Prayer Books in 1927 and 1928, but they were rejected by Parliament, although the 1928 version is used in some churches.   IHE

Book of Common Prayer, Welsh, see BIBLE, WELSH.

Book of Rates, see BATE'S CASE.

Booth's Rising (Aug. 1659). After the resignation of Richard Cromwell from the Protectorship dissensions among the leaders of the army encouraged Cavalier and Presbyterian ROYALISTS to prepare risings. Support was to be given by Mountagu and the fleet, and James, duke of York, was to effect a landing with French support. The main force rose under Sir George B. in Cheshire, but was easily suppressed by Lambert at Winnington Bridge, and the plan collapsed.   IHE

Bordeaux, the chief city and port of the remaining French possessions of the English kings in the 13th century, the headquarters of the seneschal of Gascony, and the seat of one of the four chief courts of the duchy of GUIENNE. In 1294 the city was surrendered to Philip IV of France as part of Edward I's security for making amends for recent breaches of the peace, and Edward recovered B. only after the treaty of PARIS, 1303. B., with its important trading links with England, remained loyal to the English kings throughout the HUNDRED YEARS' WAR, despite the devastation of much of the duchy and a great decline in the wine trade. B. was the Black Prince's base in his expeditions of 1355–7, and the seat of his court after 1362 when he received the duchy as an appanage of the English crown. In the final phase of the war B. was taken by the French on 30 June 1451, but was recovered by the earl of Shrewsbury in 1452. B. held out after Shrewsbury's defeat at CASTILLON and finally surrendered on 19 Oct. 1453.
                                      RFW

Borneo, was in 1518 claimed by the Portuguese, whom the Dutch ejected in 1598. During the NAPOLEONIC WARS it was occupied by the British from 1809 to 1816. SARAWAK was in 1842 ceded to Sir James Brooke. The sultan of BRUNEI ceded LABUAN to Britain in 1846 and placed himself under British protection in 1888. NORTH B. was ceded by the sultan of Sulu to a British syndicate in 1878. The 3 colonies were joined to MALAYSIA in 1963.   SHS

Borough, Old English, combined the characteristics of a trading centre (PORT) and a defended area (BURH).

Normally it was defended by walls or earthworks, had a market, was a minting place, contained houses belonging to rural manors and had open fields around the town that were shared among the inhabitants. Local affairs and justice were regulated by its MOOT. Most b.s were on royal land, and the king's interests were represented by a REEVE. The Danish invasions of the later 9th century stressed their military functions, as shown in the BURGHAL HIDAGE, but this emphasis was reduced after the 10th-century reconquest of the areas settled by the DANES. CFS

Boroughbridge, battle of (16 Mar. 1322). Late in 1321 Edward II recalled the Despensers from exile and prepared military action against Thomas earl of Lancaster. Most of Lancaster's following among the MARCHER LORDS submitted, but others rallied to him at Pontefract early in 1322. Lancaster attempted to link up with his Scottish allies, but on 16 Mar. failed to force a crossing of the river Ure at B. The arrival of a pursuing royalist force from the south next day forced Lancaster to surrender, and he was executed at Pontefract. The royal victory ensured the final failure of the ORDAINERS and placed the Despensers firmly in control of the government. In military history the battle is an early example of the successful use of dismounted men-at-arms and archers in a defensive position. RFW

Borough English, a customary tenure whereby a man's land was inherited by his youngest son. It was followed in some boroughs, but as a manorial custom it was widespread; like other special tenures, it was abolished by the 1922 and 1924 Property Acts. The name originated after the Norman conquest from the existence of a new French town beside the old English borough of Nottingham. The custom of the old borough was called B.E. to distinguish it from the Borough French of the new town. PMB

Boston Massacre (5 Mar. 1770). A mob of Boston rowdies pelted and provoked a British patrol knowing they had orders not to fire. In the ensuing scuffle four or five of the mob were killed. It provided propaganda for American extremists. IHE

Boston Port Act (1774), one of the INTOLERABLE ACTS consequent upon the B. TEA PARTY closed the port of B., except to firewood and provisions, and removed the customs house to Salem until the wasted tea had been paid for. IHE

Boston Tea Party (16 Dec. 1773). To help the EAST INDIA COMPANY out of financial difficulties and to dispose of its surplus stocks of tea, a Tea Act (1773) was passed enabling the Company to send tea from London to America, avoiding the middlemen and with a complete refund of the usual British duties. This cheap tea was also designed to make smuggling unprofitable. After the AMERICAN IMPORT DUTIES ACT tea was already regarded as an unpatriotic drink, and the tea ships were boycotted all along the coast. At B. radical leaders disguised as Indians boarded the ships and threw the tea into the harbour. This was the B.T.P., and B. was punished by the INTOLERABLE ACTS. IHE

Bosworth, battle of (22 Aug. 1485), ended the wars of the ROSES. Henry Tudor, with some exiled LANCASTRIANS and former YORKISTS, sailed with 2,500 men from Harfleur on 1 Aug., landed in Milford Haven, probably near Dale, on 7 Aug., and reached Shrewsbury by the 13th. Richard III heard of the invasion on 11 Aug., at Nottingham, and ordered his forces to muster at Leicester. There was no general rising in Henry's favour in Wales, but some influential leaders such as Rhys ap Thomas joined him, and his force now numbered 5,000. Although Thomas Lord Stanley and his brother Sir William sent assurances of their support to Henry at Shrewsbury, they and their 6,000 men retired as Henry advanced through Stafford and Lichfield; despite Henry's secret meeting with the

Stanleys at Atherstone on 20 Aug. their attitude remained in doubt until the last moment. Richard III left Leicester with 9,000 men on 21 Aug. and early the following day posted himself on Ambien Hill, two miles south of Market Bosworth, with the Stanleys in striking distance of either army. Henry's main attack on Ambien Hill was being held and Richard and a small body of cavalry attacked. At the crucial moment the Stanleys came in on Henry's side, and the issue was quickly decided. Richard himself was killed, and the earl of Northumberland, who with his division of Richard's army had taken no part in the action, did homage to Henry, whom the battle made king by right of conquest.   RFW

Bothwell Bridge, battle of (2 July 1679). After the RESTORATION, EPISCOPACY was reintroduced in Scotland (1661), and some third of the clergy were ejected and in 1663 banned within 20 miles of their former parishes. Persecution led to the abortive Pentland rising (1666), but conventicles increased and the Covenanters rose in the Western Lowlands (June 1679). After an initial success at Drumclog they were routed by Monmouth at B.B.   IHE

Botswana. The name under which BECHUANALAND became an independent republic in 1966.

Bounty, Mutiny on the (28 Apr. 1789), occurred during a scientific voyage under Lieut. (later Vice-Adm.) W. Bligh which was to introduce the breadfruit tree of Tahiti to the British West Indies. Under the leadership of an officer, Fletcher Christian, members of the 45-man crew mutinied. They preferred the women and other comforts of Tahiti to rounding the Horn in the company of 1,015 breadfruit plants. The ship was then near Tofua Island (N. of Tonga). Bligh and 18 men were cast adrift in a 23-ft boat in which they reached Timor (14 June). The mutineers returned in the *Bounty* to Tahiti from where Christian and 8 others set sail for PIT-

CAIRN. The Admiralty (Aug. 1790) commissioned the *Pandora* to bring the mutineers to justice and 14 were captured in Tahiti. Four were drowned when the *Pandora* was wrecked and the remaining 10 were court-martialled at Portsmouth (Sept.–Oct. 1792); 3 were hanged.   MLH

Bouvet Island, about 1,800 miles S.W. of Cape Town, was discovered (1739) by a Frenchman, Capt. Lozier Bouvet, and claimed for Britain (1825) by Capt. Norris. A Norwegian whaling expedition occupied B.I. (1927) and it was ceded to Norway by Britain (Nov. 1928).   MLH

Bouvines, battle of (27 July 1214). King John planned to follow up the naval victory of DAMME by an invasion of France on two fronts in the summer of 1214. After long delays, John himself led a diversionary attack on Poitou. This petered out after the king's failure to take La Roche-aux-Moines, and failed to draw Philip II of France southwards. The main attack, directed on northern France, was conducted by John's allies, the emperor Otto IV, the count of Flanders and other princes of the Low Countries, accompanied by an English contingent under the earl of Salisbury. The decisive defeat of the allied army by Philip II at B., between Lille and Tournai, completely wrecked John's schemes and postponed indefinitely the recovery of the lost Angevin provinces. Resistance in England to demands for military service on the continent, and to the king's financial exactions to meet war expenditure, had already begun: the utter failure of the campaigns of 1214 brought open hostilities between John and his barons measurably nearer.
                                         RFW

Bovate, or oxgang; an eighth of a HIDE or carucate.   CFS

Bow Street Runners, the name applied by the end of the 18th century to the first regular police and detective force in London organized by Henry Fielding, chief magistrate at Bow Street (1748), and his brother,

Sir John, who succeeded in 1753. A government grant was given in 1757 and they became available for use outside their own district. Bow Street became the police centre of London to combat highwaymen and thieves. The foot patrols were merged with the Metropolitan Police under the Home Secretary (1829) and the horse patrols abolished in 1839.

IHE

Boycott, was used during the agrarian unrest in Ireland of 1880. Parnell suggested (19 Sept.) that anyone taking land from an evicted person should be 'isolated from his kind as if he were a leper'. The idea was adopted by agitators of the LAND LEAGUE and first applied to Capt. C. C. Boycott, Lord Erne's agent in Co. Mayo. The term has since passed into the English language to mean 'social and commercial ostracism'.

MLH

Boyne, battle of the (1/12 July 1690), marked the defeat of the STEWART cause in Ireland. William III landed at Carrickfergus (June 1690) and with Schomberg advanced against James II's forces holding the line of the river Boyne, and drove them into retreat. James fled to Kinsale and thence to France and William entered Dublin. Checked at Limerick (Aug.), he left his subordinates to complete the conquest.

IHE

Bracton, *De Legibus et Consuetudinibus Anglie,* was written *c.* 1250-56 by Henry of Bratton, a Devonshire man, formerly clerk to the distinguished judge William of Raleigh and a judge himself. His book, made up of an introduction and commentaries on various actions and procedures, is a monumental study, partly based on cases, collected in his extant notebook, heard by Raleigh, his predecessors and contemporaries. In part B. wrote of, and wished to recall, the golden days of Raleigh, in part he discussed the procedure and underlying problems of English law. His view-point was occasionally that of Roman lawyers. The importance of the book is immense: it shows English law at work 60 years after GLANVILL; it is based, for the first time, on cases cited as examples though not precedents; it was widely circulated and imitated as a model for legal literature until the present day, and its opinions could still be profitably cited in 18th-century courts.

PMB

Bradlaugh's Case arose out of the claim of Charles B. (1833-91), an atheist and free-thinker who was elected M.P. for Northampton (1880), to affirm rather than take the oath. Speaker Brand failed to act with decision, a select committee decided against allowing affirmation and B. was arbitrarily prohibited from either affirming or taking the oath. He was re-elected and excluded 4 times before Speaker Peel allowed him to take the oath and his seat (1886). B. was then instrumental in passing the Oaths Act, 1888, by which anyone objecting to an oath could affirm.

MLH

Bramham Moor, battle of (19 Feb. 1408). After the collapse of the northern rebellion of 1405, Henry Percy, earl of Northumberland, had sought assistance, without much success, from King Henry IV's enemies in Wales, France and Scotland. Early in 1408 Northumberland and Lord Bardolph, with some Scots troops, crossed the border and attempted to raise the north. The response was poor, and on B.M., near Tadcaster, the rebels were defeated by Sir Thomas Rokeby, sheriff of Yorkshire. The death of Northumberland in the battle finally brought to an end the series of rebellions against Henry IV led by the Percy family.

RFW

Breda, Declaration of (Apr. 1660), was sent by Charles II to the CONVENTION PARLIAMENT as a basis for the RESTORATION of the monarchy. On Monck's advice it promised amnesty to all (other than those excepted by Parliament), safeguards for the purchasers of the estates of DELINQUENTS, religious toleration and payment of arrears to the army. On Hyde's advice these points were to be subject to

Parliament's decisions, which in the event did not accept them as binding.   IHE

Breda, Treaty of (31 July 1667), ended the second DUTCH WAR (1665–7). England retained NEW YORK, NEW JERSEY and DELAWARE, and the Netherlands kept SURINAM and Polaroon. The NAVIGATION laws were modified, allowing the Dutch to transport goods to England from Germany and the Spanish Netherlands. England regained her part of ST. KITTS, ANTIGUA and MONTSERRAT, restoring ACADIA to France, which kept TOBAGO and St Eustatius.   IHE

Brémule, battle of (Aug. 1119), a decisive victory won by Henry I of England over Louis VI of France, brought to an end the attempts of Louis, in alliance with the counts of Flanders and Anjou and with the support of a faction within Normandy, to oust Henry from the duchy in favour of William Clito, son of Robert, the former duke. William survived until 1128, but although Louis continued to foster his cause by diplomatic means, Henry's possession of Normandy was never seriously threatened again.   RFW

Breteuil, customs or laws of (*Leges Britolii*), the customs of B. in Normandy, were introduced into England soon after the NORMAN CONQUEST and formed the basis of the customs granted to the 'French borough' in Hereford by William Fitz Osbern (d. 1071), earl of Hereford and lord of B. His kinsman, Roger de Montgomery, earl of Shrewsbury, introduced the customs to Shrewsbury, and in amended forms, often incorporating native English customs, they spread to other boroughs along the Welsh border. Thence they were carried by the MARCHER LORDS to boroughs founded by them in Wales, in south-west England and, late in the 12th century, in Ireland. The customs of Hereford eventually provided a model for the boroughs founded in North Wales by Edward I.   RFW

Brétigny, treaty of (1360), alternatively called the treaty of Calais. Edward III's campaign of 1359–60 having failed, peace negotiations were opened at B., near Chartres, on 1 May. Under the terms agreed between the Black Prince and the dauphin Charles, Edward III was to receive a greatly enlarged duchy of GUIENNE, CALAIS and Ponthieu, all in full sovereignty. King John of France, captured at POITIERS, was to be ransomed for £500,000. Edward III was to surrender his claims to the French throne and to any overlordship outside his dominions as defined by the treaty, and was to give up lands held by his forces outside their boundaries. Edward and John ratified a modified treaty at Calais in October, when a separate agreement provided that Edward should formally renounce the French throne and that the transfer of territory should be completed by Nov. 1361. The cessions were delayed, and although Edward dropped the title of king of France he did not make his renunciation. Nevertheless the treaty brought a break of nine years in the HUNDRED YEARS' WAR.   RFW

Bretwalda, the term applied by the compiler of the earlier part of the ANGLO-SAXON CHRONICLE to certain early kings who were also overlords of England south of the Humber. It would seem to mean 'Britain-ruler' and thus to be identical with the style *Rex Britanniae* used in the 8th century. The term itself was probably an epithet of praise. But the reality behind it, the overlordship, was an accepted political concept in the earlier Old English period; and possibly arose during the TEUTONIC CONQUEST when overall leadership was at times necessary. The rulers named as having this title were Ælle of SUSSEX in the late 5th century; Ceawlin of WESSEX, Ethelbert of KENT, Raedwald of EAST ANGLIA, Edwin, Oswald and Oswiu of NORTHUMBRIA, who together cover the century from *c.* 570; Egbert of Wessex (802–39). Not named but also exercising lordship were kings Ethelbert and Offa of MERCIA (8th century). The character of this overlordship changed with time from general military leadership to strict control of subject rulers. This overlordship was an important force working towards the unity of England. CFS

Brice's Day, Massacre of St (13 Nov. 1002). On the orders of king Ethelred II, who feared a plot against his life, all DANES within his power were murdered. According to tradition, the victims included the sister of Swein king of Denmark. CFS

Brigantes, a tribal group in northern England, controlling the area from south Lincolnshire to the Scottish border. They consisted of a Celtic (CELTS) aristocracy ruling over various pre-Celtic peoples. Although not attacked in the early days of the ROMAN CONQUEST, their queen, Cartimandua, favoured the Romans and in or soon after A.D. 43 made her territories a client kingdom of Rome. The rise to supremacy among the B. of an anti-Roman party eventually forced Rome to conquer the area (71–9); but sporadic revolts continued during the 2nd century. The B. became a CIVITAS with their capital at Isurium (Aldborough), but with much reduced territory; that in the neighbourhood of HADRIAN'S WALL came under military government, and other land was lost to the COLONIA at Lindum (Lincoln) and to that at Eburacum (York). CFS

Britain. The British Isles were known in the 4th century B.C. as the Pritanic Isles. The inhabitants appear to have described themselves as Pritani or Priteni, which may mean 'tattooed men'. Latinized, and possibly confused with a tribal name on the Gallic side of the Channel, this became Britanni and the name of the province Britannia. During the period of ROMAN BRITAIN the inhabitants called themselves Britones, leaving the name Priteni for those living in the north of the island and subsequently known as PICTS. CFS

Britain, Battle of (Aug.–Oct. 1940), the unsuccessful attempt of the German air force to prepare for invasion by decisively defeating R.A.F. Fighter Command (A.C.M. Sir H. C. T. (later Lord) Dowding); so called after Churchill's reference (18 June): 'the battle of France is over. I expect the B. of B. is about to begin.' The Luftwaffe had about 2,500 aircraft available; Fighter Command an average of 650–750, mostly Hurricanes and Spitfires. The all-out German attack on airfields and aircraft factories in S.E. England lasted from 12 Aug. to 7 Sept. when it was switched to London. Defence was initially dependent upon warning given by radar. Against great odds the British squadrons were often able to break up with disproportionate loss the German formations before they reached their objectives. Plans for invasion had to be postponed from 15 to 25 Sept. and then to spring of 1941. During Oct. the Germans confined themselves to night bombing and the B. of B. was over. The crucial period was the fortnight before 7 Sept. when British reserves of aircraft and trained pilots were diminishing dangerously. But the decision to direct the attack on London relieved the pressure; from this moment the survival and recovery of Fighter Command was certain. During the period 10 July–31 Oct. the R.A.F. lost 915 and the Luftwaffe 1,733 aircraft; casualties in Fighter Command were: killed, prisoner, missing, 481; wounded, injured, 422. MLH

British Antarctic Territory. Formed March 1962 largely from the area formerly known as the FALKLAND ISLANDS Dependencies (Graham's Land, S. Orkneys, S. Shetlands, etc.). It includes all lands and islands south of lat. 60° S. between 20° and 80° W. long. IHE

British Church. Christianity spread in Britain as in other parts of the Roman empire, and by the 5th century was the religion of the majority of the inhabitants. It was organized by bishoprics, although details are unknown. Its best-known members are the martyr, St Alban, and the heretic, Pelagius. It was in full communion with the main body of the church at least until the council of Arles (453), the decrees of which it received. It attempted conversion work, the most successful being that by St Ninian among the southern PICTS around the beginning of the 5th century. After the TEUTONIC CONQUEST it was confined to the western areas of the island (see CELTIC CHURCH IN WALES) and in this later period lacked the missionary zeal of the somewhat similar IRISH CHURCH.

                               CFS

British Columbia was explored by Capt. Cook in 1778, surveyed by Capt. George Vancouver in 1792–94 and mapped by David Thompson in 1811. John Jacob Astor had to give up to the British his trading post Astoria on the north of the Columbia river in 1812, and the territory, called New Caledonia, became part first of the North-West Company's and in 1838 of the HUDSON'S BAY COMPANY'S concession. To meet the situation created by the gold-rush immigration, Vancouver Island (1849) and B.C. (1858) were constituted as crown colonies and in 1866 combined. The colony entered the Canadian Confederation on 20 July 1871. Its boundary dispute with the U.S.A. was settled in 1871 by the German emperor, whose arbitration deprived CANADA of a satisfactory outlet to the Pacific. The Canadian Pacific Railway, the construction of which was one of B.C.'s conditions in joining Canada, reached Vancouver in 1886.

                               SHS

British Commonwealth, see COMMONWEALTH.

British Guiana grew out of the Dutch settlements of Berbice, Demerara and Essequibo, which the Dutch West India Company had occupied from 1620. They were captured by the British in 1796, formally ceded in 1814 and united under the name of B.G. in 1831. Previous English attempts to found a colony (e.g. Sir

Walter Raleigh, 1595; SURINAM, 1651) were unsuccessful. The boundaries with Venezuela and Brazil were settled by arbitration in 1899 and 1904 respectively. Self-government was introduced in 1953, but the constitution had to be suspended owing to Communist intrigues; full self-government, except for defence and foreign affairs, was granted in 1961. It became an independent member of the Commonwealth on 26 May 1966 under the name of GUYANA.   SHS; IHE

British Honduras was first settled in 1638 by shipwrecked British sailors, later reinforced by woodcutters from JAMAICA, and from 1670 considered a British possession. Spanish attempts at conquest were finally beaten off in the battle of St George's Cay (10 Sept. 1798). The first constitution was granted in 1765; in 1862 the settlement was designated a colony subordinate to the governor of Jamaica, from which it was detached in 1884. The constitution of 1964 introduced a system of internal responsible self-government.

The Republic of Guatemala claims B.H. as Guatemalan territory, but refuses to submit the dispute to the International Court of Justice.

                           SHS; IHE

British Museum, resulted from an act of 1753 providing for the purchase, from the proceeds of a public lottery, of the books, manuscripts and museum collection of Sir Hans Sloane (bequeathed to the nation for £20,000) and the Harleian manuscripts of the 1st and 2nd earls of Oxford. These were to be permanently housed with the Sir Robert Cotton (1571–1631) manuscripts acquired in 1707. Montagu House, Great Russell Street, was bought and opened in 1759. George II transferred the royal library to the B.M. in 1757 and the privilege of obtaining a free copy of every book entered at Stationer's Hall. George III's library was acquired in 1823. The present building was designed by Sir Robert Smirke in 1823. The B.M. contains the largest collection of historical source material next to that of the PUBLIC RECORD OFFICE as well as a priceless store of prints, drawings, coins, medals, Oriental, Asiatic, Egyptian, Greek, Roman and British antiquities. Part of the collection was transferred to the Natural History Museum at South Kensington (1881), and a newspaper repository was established at Colindale in 1902. IHE

Broad-bottom Administration, defined by Horace Walpole in 1742 as 'the taking of all parties or people indifferently into the ministry' and applied particularly to Henry Pelham's administration of 1743–54 when reconstituted after Carteret's resignation in 1744. Pelham and his brother, the duke of Newcastle, sought to strengthen the ministry by including members of the different opposition cliques, even the Jacobite Sir John Cotton. George II secured the exclusion of the elder Pitt until 1746.

IHE

Bronze Age, the period, characterized by bronze implements and weapons, that followed the NEOLITHIC, although there were some centuries of overlap. Ireland became one of the main centres of bronze manufacture in Europe, native copper and Cornish tin being used. Copper implements were in use from c. 1900 B.C., but the B.A. proper in Britain began a century or more later. In the early B.A., to c. 1400, bronze objects were comparatively rare, flint, stone and bone still predominating; but by the late B.A. they were common-place. Development was accelerated by a series of invasions from mainland Europe, starting c. 1800. The newcomers were a mixture of the BEAKER and BATTLE-AXE cultures. They spread over much of the British Isles, influencing and being influenced by the native Neolithic cultures. Their main strength was in the south, where the early B.A. was marked by the emergence of the wealthy WESSEX CULTURE, during the period of which considerable advances in bronze working were made. The parallel development north of the Thames was the FOOD-VESSEL CULTURE, an insular development where Beaker techniques were grafted on to existing Neolithic cultures. Both these early B.A. cultures gave way after c. 1400 to an insular development, the URN CULTURE, whose main new features were the use of barley as a cereal crop and the production of spear-heads and stabbing swords. About 1000 bronze manufacture and trade were radically reorganized, much more being done in England. The first invasion of Britain by CELTS occurred in this period of the middle B.A., pressure becoming heavy after c. 900. These invaders established in the south the DEVEREL-RIMBURY and other cultures that eventually extended through the lowland area. The late B.A., c. 800– c. 600 in the south, later in the north, saw a great increase in the number and variety of bronze objects, improvements in spinning and weaving, and the introduction of the plough. During the 6th century Britain was invaded from mainland Europe by the first representatives of IRON-AGE cultures. CFS

Brownists. About 1580 Robert Browne established a congregational society at Norwich rejecting EPISCOPACY and PRESBYTERIANISM, holding connexion between church and state unscriptural. Worship was non-ritualistic, and both pastor and congregation derived their authority from God. They formed the vanguard of Elizabethan separatism and were soon in conflict with authority (MARPRELATE TRACTS). Browne eventually left his own society and was rector of Achurch, Northants, at his death (1633). (BARROWISTS, CONGREGATIONALISTS, PURITANS.) IHE

Brunanburh, battle of (937), was fought at an unidentified site (probably in the southern midlands) between the men of WESSEX and English and Danish MERCIA under king Athelstan and a composite northern force that included Irish VIKINGS under Olaf king of Dublin, PICTS and SCOTS under their king, and Britons under the king of STRATHCLYDE. The lands of the last two kings had been ravaged by Athelstan in 934, and the first wished to regain the Norse kingdom of YORK, lost in 927. After a very hard-fought battle king Athelstan's army won a crushing victory, celebrated in an O.E. poem.   CFS

Brunei, in BORNEO, entered into treaty relations with Great Britain in 1847, and the sultan placed himself under British protection in 1888. From 1906 he acted on the advice of a British resident, who was replaced by a high commissioner in 1959, when the sultan introduced a constitution, amended in 1965 to include elected members. B. was occupied by the Japanese from 16 Dec. 1941 to 10 June 1945. In 1963 B. did not join MALAYSIA.   SHS ; IHE

Brut. Of the Welsh chronicle known as *Brut y Tywysogyon* ('Chronicle of Princes'), the primary native source for the history of medieval Wales, there are three main recensions: the version contained in the Red Book of Hergest and comparable texts; the version contained in Peniarth MS. 20; and the composite version known as *Brenhinedd y Saeson* ('Kings of the Saxons'), made up of the *Brut* together with the translation of an English chronicle. The Welsh chronicles are independent translations of a Latin original, of which the texts in the *Annales Cambriae* (Harl. MS. 3859, Domesday Breviate and Cott. MS. Dom. A.i) were probably the skeleton outlines, and the *Cronica de Wallia* (Exeter Cath. MS. 3514) the nearest extant version. The Latin archetype seems to have originated at St David's in the 8th century. The connexion between the chronicle and the cathedral was probably maintained until the removal of the family of Bishop Sulien to Llanbadarn in 1099. The *Brut* was then linked with the Llanbadarn area until 1175. Thereafter, until it ended in 1332, it was unmistakably a Strata Florida chronicle, to which many other Welsh Cistercian houses made contributions. Other so-called Bruts, including Brut Aberpergwm, Brut Ieuan Brechfa

and Brut y Saeson, are either spurious or worthless.

Thomas Jones, *Brut y Tywysogyon, or the Chronicle of Princes* (Cardiff, 1954).   GW

Brut, the English, a medieval chronicle of the history of Britain from its legendary beginnings, which took its name from its account of the mythical conquest of the island by Brutus, a Trojan prince, after the fall of Troy (HISTORIA REGUM BRITANNIAE). As in Welsh, b. came to have the general meaning of 'a chronicle'. Thought to have been originally written in French in the early 14th century, the b. was later translated into English and brought up to 1377. Successive 15th-century extensions carried the history up to 1461, while one late-15th-century version has brief notices of events up to 1475. The b. finally represented the cumulative labour of many hands, and though it has close links with the city chronicles of London, it is rich in unique information from personal observation, news letters and contemporary ballads. Its wide popularity is evidenced by the large number of surviving MSS., by the translation of versions into Latin and by the demand for printed editions, of which Caxton's *Chronicles of England* (1480) was the first. Much used by 16th- and 17th-century historians, and influential in forming Tudor views of the 15th century, the B. remains a most valuable source for late medieval history.

The Brut or the Chronicle of England, ed. F. W. D. Brie, Early English Text Society, original series 131 (1906) and 136 (1905).   RFW

Bulls, Papal. Formal letters issued by popes containing exhortations, commands, grants, etc., classified by their purpose, e.g. privileges, letters of grace etc. The name is derived from the double-sided lead seal on silk or hemp strings, the *bulla,* used from the 6th century onwards; parchment was substituted for papyrus at the beginning of the 11th century. Bulls are generally described by the first word or phrase of the text proper, e.g. *Regnans in excelsis*, which in 1570 declared Elizabeth I excommunicate.   PMB

Bunker Hill, battle of (17 June 1775). After LEXINGTON the New England militia besieged Boston and sent a force to fortify B.H. overlooking Boston from the north. (They fortified Breed's Hill by mistake.) The British under Howe made a frontal attack and took it on the third assault, largely because the Americans had run out of powder. British losses were twice those of the Americans, who regarded B.H. as a moral victory.   IHE

Burgage, the burgess' tenement, and thus his form of tenure. A burgess' land was free, heritable and alienable according to the custom óf his BOROUGH. The distinguishing mark of b. tenure in Anglo-Saxon times was the payment of a rent, *land-* or *hawgable*. After the NORMAN CONQUEST the tenure and attendant privileges were more closely defined, to be used first to exclude incomers from borough commerce and government and, in more modern times, for the manipulation of parliamentary elections (see SCOT AND LOT). The burgess' special franchise was ended by the MUNICIPAL CORPORATIONS ACT 1835.   PMB

Burghal Hidage, a record, dating from the early 10th century, of the number of HIDES attached to each of the BURHS of WESSEX. The origin of the scheme should be placed in the reign of Alfred (871–99), its aim being to protect Wessex against the DANES by establishing a number of fortified positions there. These were manned and maintained by garrisons made up of one man from each hide.   CFS

Burgh-by-Sands (pron. *bruff*). In Feb. 1307 Robert Bruce resumed campaigning in south-west Scotland while Edward I was lying ill at Lanercost Priory. Edward was well enough to move to Carlisle in March, and after Bruce's defeat of the earl of Pembroke at Loudun in May Edward left Carlisle at the beginning of July, but on 7 July died in his camp on Burgh

marsh, where he was preparing to cross the Solway Firth.   RFW

Burgundians, see ARMAGNACS.

Burh, a fortified area in old English times. It could describe a fortified dwelling, but also a defended town, the defences consisting of either a wall or a bank and ditch. *Burhs,* in the sense of large fortified camps, were used by Edward the Elder (899–924) as bases for the reconquest of the areas occupied by the DANES. See BOROUGH.   CFS

Burma. In 1612 the EAST INDIA COMPANY established factories at Syriam (near Rangoon), Prome and Ava, but the conquest of B. began only after the repulse of the Burmese attack on BENGAL in 1824. The first Burmese war ended with the treaty of Yandaboo (24 Feb. 1826), by which B. ceded Arakan and Tenasserim and gave up her claims to ASSAM and MANIPUR. The second Burmese war (1852) was provoked by a naval commander whose precipitate action was upheld by the governor-general, Lord Dalhousie. Lower B. or Pegu was annexed by proclamation on 20 Dec. 1852. The Burmese provinces were amalgamated under a chief commissioner in 1862. Relations with Upper B., never satisfactory, deteriorated when King Thibaw sought the support of the French in Cochin-China and Tonkin (1885) and simultaneously provoked the English trade interests and humanitarian sentiments. He rejected a peremptory ultimatum of the Indian government, but was overthrown and deposed within 20 days. Upper and Lower B. were combined in a single Indian province, which was raised to a lieutenant-governorship in 1897 and a governorship in 1923, and separated from India on 1 Apr. 1937.

The tribes of the interior—Shan, Kachin, Karenni—carried on guerilla warfare for many years, but afterwards became loyal adherents of the British, who administered them through their own chiefs under the supervision of a commissioner. The 34 Shan states were federated in 1922, and a council of chiefs was set up in 1923.

After the liberation from Japanese occupation (Mar. 1942 to Aug. 1945) the country chose to leave the British COMMONWEALTH (treaty of London, 17 Oct. 1947) and to become the independent republic of the Union of B. (4 Jan. 1948), in which the Shan, Kachin and Karenni states have been granted a measure of self-government.   SHS

Bushell's Case (1670). When two Quakers were acquitted on an indictment of holding an unlawful assembly the Recorder of London fined each of the jury 40 marks. Juryman Bushell was imprisoned for non-payment, and the return to his writ of HABEAS CORPUS stated that he had been committed for finding a verdict contrary to full and manifest evidence. Chief Justice Vaughan discharged Bushell, finding the return insufficient, thereby establishing the immunity of juries from fines for their verdicts.   IHE

Butler, a leading member of the CURIA REGIS at the time of the NORMAN CONQUEST, serving the king with wine at special feasts; later the duty was restricted to coronations. Henry I gave the office to William Daubeney of Belvoir, later earl of Arundel. Subsequent earls, later dukes of Norfolk, of successive creations performed the office to which they had but dubious title, as it is uncertain whether the office was a Grand SERJEANTY attached to lands in Norfolk or whether it was granted to Daubeney and his heirs. The under-butler, however, was a serjeant with lands at Sheen in Surrey. The Belet family held the office in the 12th and 13th centuries, but the serjeanty was challenged and the office finally usurped by the mayors of London.   PMB

Bycarrs Dyke, see AXHOLME.

Bye Plot (1603) was organized by William Watson, a Roman Catholic priest, to kidnap James I and force him to grant toleration. Some PURI-

TANS were also involved, but the plot was revealed by a Jesuit and Watson was executed. In 1604 a proclamation banished priests and Jesuits alike and the fines for RECUSANTS were enforced. (MAIN PLOT, GUNPOWDER PLOT.)
                                                IHE

Byland, battle of (14 Oct. 1322). The Anglo-Scottish truce after the battle of MYTON (1319) having expired, the Scots again invaded England in 1322. Edward II retaliated by invading Lothian, but on withdrawing was pursued by Robert Bruce deep into England, and in a skirmish between B. and Rievaulx Edward was defeated and nearly captured. After this latest demonstration of Edward's inability to defend England, let alone conquer Scotland, many northerners were prepared to make their own terms with the Scots and even to change their allegiance. Edward was compelled to conclude a 13 years' truce, and although formal English recognition of Bruce as king of Scots did not follow until the treaty of NORTHAMPTON (1328), the independence of Scotland was an accomplished fact.   RFW

Bytham, siege of (1220). A difficult problem facing the conciliar government during the minority of Henry III was the recovery of castles, both royal and private, from barons and mercenary captains who had held them for King John and his son during the BARONS' WAR (1215-17). Open opposition to the government's programme of resumption came in 1220 from William de Forz, earl of Aumâle, who refused to surrender two royal castles and the private castle of B., Lincs. The justiciar, Hubert de Burgh, besieged and quickly took B. and compelled the earl's obedience. Although disappointed loyalists still opposed the surrender of their charges to the crown, there was no more serious armed resistance.   RFW

Cabal (1667-73) was the name given to the group of five ministers chosen by Charles II after the fall of Clarendon (Clifford, Arlington, Buckingham, Ashley-Cooper, Lauderdale) whose initials by coincidence spelt the word cabal, a name commonly applied in the 17th century to the king's inner group of councillors. Their personal and religious differences gave Charles closer control of policy, and none upheld the Anglican interest. They supported religious toleration and sought to encourage commerce. They abandoned the TRIPLE ALLIANCE of 1668 in favour of the treaty of DOVER (1670) with France, and a third DUTCH WAR (1672-4). Parliamentary opposition to this foreign policy, condemnation of the DECLARATION OF INDULGENCE (1672) and the passing of the TEST ACT (1673) broke up the C.   IHE

Cabinet, see PRIME MINISTER.

Cádiz, the most important port on the Atlantic coast of Spain and the frequent target of English raids.

(1) (29 Apr.-1 May 1587). Sir Francis Drake sank or captured about 30 vessels in C. harbour and defied the duke of Medina Sidonia's shore artillery and fire-ships without loss of a ship or a man. After thus 'singeing the king of Spain's beard', he harassed the Portuguese coast, captured a carrack with East Indian goods worth £114,000, destroyed the casks and staves assembled for provisioning the ARMADA and thereby delayed its sailing by a year.

(2) (6-7 June 1596). Lord Howard of Effingham and the earl of Essex took and sacked C., destroyed some 40 vessels and made a huge booty worth about 12m. ducats. But indiscipline and greed of leaders and men hastened the English back to Plymouth instead of going after the Spanish treasure-fleet.

(3) (Oct. 1625). The duke of Buckingham, through negligence and incompetence, failed either to take C. or to intercept the treasure-fleet.

(4) (Aug. 1702). During the SPANISH SUCCESSION WAR an Anglo-Dutch expedition against C. under Admiral Sir George Rooke and the duke of Ormonde miscarried, but destroyed a Spanish-French fleet off Vigo.

(5) (3 and 5 July 1797). Nelson ineffectively bombarded C. after the battle of ST VINCENT.   SHS

Calais, from 1347 to 1558 the 'brightest jewel in the English crown', the king's principal gateway to France and possibly the French throne. After his victory at CRÉCY Edward III began the siege of C. on 4 Sept 1346. Half-hearted attempts at relief failed and C. was finally starved into surrender on 4 Aug. 1347. Edward was incensed at the stout resistance of the town, and the story of the Burghers of Calais may well be true. The French population was evacuated and the town was resettled with English. Thereafter C. formed an important commercial bridgehead on the continent, the wool STAPLE being established there in 1363. Its military importance was greater, however; by the treaty of BRÉTIGNY C. and its small March or Pale, enlarged by the county of Guines, were ceded to Edward III in full sovereignty, and C. itself came to be protected by an outer ring of castles, of which Guines and Hammes were the most important. English determination to keep C. at all costs prevented the conclusion of peace with France under Richard II; though John of Gaunt held that the expense of its maintenance outweighed its value. C. indeed proved the most expensive of English fortresses in the late middle ages; building materials were difficult to obtain locally, and while water defences rendered it virtually impregnable, the sea and the Hammes river constantly threatened the stability of walls and towers, and the safety of the vital harbour. Successive kings had extreme difficulty in raising sufficient money to maintain C., and in 1466 Edward IV handed over its financial administration to the Staple. Unsuccessfully besieged by the Burgundians in 1406 and 1436, almost destroyed by the sea in 1439, C. was the sole remaining English possession in France after 1453, and was Edward IV's base in the campaign of 1475 (PICQUIGNY). In the wars of the ROSES the ships and garrison of C. played a notable part, particularly in 1459–60 (SANDWICH).

The early Tudor kings improved the defences and C. was the advanced base of Henry VIII's French expeditions. Maintaining its English character to the last, C. was represented in parliament by two burgesses from 1536 to 1558. It was lost to England as a result of Mary I's subservience to her husband, Philip II of Spain. Spanish interests forced England into war with France (7 June 1557), Mary refused to send either men or money, and the garrison had to capitulate after a siege of 5 days (6 Jan. 1558). The neighbouring fortress of Guines held out until 20 Jan. By the treaty of CATEAU-CAMBRÉSIS (1559) the French promised to return C. after 8 years, but by the treaty of Troyes (11 Apr. 1564), which terminated Queen Elizabeth I's unsuccessful intervention in the French religious wars, she abandoned her claim in return for 120,000 écus.   RFW

Caledonia, a name frequently used in Roman times for the Highland area of Scotland, in which lived the Caledones or Caledonii. The name was more precisely applied to a single group in Perthshire, but its more general usage suggests that this group was extending its power. From the 3rd century Caledonians was replaced by PICTS as the general name for the inhabitants of that area. The name was revived in more recent times, e.g. Caledonian Canal. Its origin is unknown, but is probably pre-Celtic.   CFS

Calendar. Until 31 Dec. 1751 the Julian c. or old style was used in England and Ireland. Instituted by Julius Caesar in 45 B.C., it was replaced first in Catholic, later also in Protestant countries by the more accurately calculated Gregorian or new style c. introduced by Pope Gregory XIII in 1582. As a result, in the 17th century the English c. was 10 days behind those of other countries and 11 in the 18th. Moreover, from the late 12th century the year of grace in England began on Lady Day, 25 Mar. (*mos Anglicanus*), not on 25 Dec. or 1 Jan. as in Europe; although in Anglo-Saxon times the beginning of the year had usually been taken as 25 Dec., sometimes (e.g. late 9th century) as 24 Sept. By Chesterfield's Act (Mar. 1751) the new style was adopted and the day after 31 Dec. 1751 began the New Year as 1 Jan. 1752 (not 1751). To correct the discrepancy between the calendars 11 days were omitted, 2 Sept. 1752 being followed by 14 Sept. In Scotland 1 Jan. was adopted as the beginning of the year 1600, thus only the days 3–13 Sept. were dropped in 1752. See also EASTER; EASTER TABLES; REGNAL YEAR.   IHE

Calvin's Case see POSTNATI.

Cambridge Conspiracy. On 1 Aug. 1415, while at Southampton preparing to invade France, Henry V learned of a plot against his life. The leading conspirator, Richard, earl of C., himself a grandson of Edward III, intended to secure the throne for his brother-in-law, Edmund, earl of March, as the true heir of Richard II. C.'s supporters Henry lord Scrope of Masham and Sir Thomas Grey were kinsmen of unsuccessful rebels against Henry IV. March himself revealed the plot to the king, and the three leaders were beheaded.   RFW

Cambridge Parliament (Sept. 1388), the only parliament to meet at C. An ordinance provided for the confiscation of the property of clergy who sought papal PROVISIONS, and a statute regulated labourers' wages and forbade them to seek employment without the written permission of the justices. Within two years it was found that the statute could not be enforced.   RFW

Cameroons (Portuguese *camarões*, prawns), from 1835 visited by English coastal traders and from 1848 by Baptist missionaries. Hamburg merchants from 1874 ousted the British and caused Bismarck on 14 July 1884

to declare C. a German protectorate a few days before the British government acceded to the repeated requests by African chiefs for a British protectorate. In return, Germany relinquished her claims to NIGERIA and in 1887 bought out the British missionaries. During the first world war C. was conquered by Nigerian and French troops; German resistance ceased in Feb. 1916. On 10 July 1919 C. was divided between Britain and France, both parts in 1922 being placed under LEAGUE OF NATIONS mandate, which in 1947 was superseded by UNITED NATIONS trusteeship. The British portion was administered by Nigeria. By plebiscites in Feb. 1961 the northern part decided to join Nigeria, the southern to join the ex-French C. (independent 1960).   SHS

Camperdown, battle of (11 Oct. 1797), was fought off the Dutch coast between the English under Adm. (Lord) Duncan and the Dutch under Adm. de Winter. In hard and close fighting the British captured 9 of the 16 Dutch ships without loss, casualties on both sides being heavy. C. prevented any but small-scale intervention in the IRISH REBELLION (1798).
                                        MLH

Canada was first explored by Jacques Cartier of St Malo on several voyages between 1524 and 1542; in 1535 he sailed up the St Lawrence as far as modern Montreal. He claimed 'New France' as a French possession and realized the importance of furs as the base of trade. The first settlers were Huguenots, but they disappeared after the murder of Henri IV (1610) and were expressly excluded in 1627. By this time, Samuel de Champlain, one of the greatest French colonial pioneers, had founded Port Royal in NOVA SCOTIA (1604) and Quebec (1608) and discovered Lake Champlain (1609). The administration of New France was in the hands of the Compagnie de la France Nouvelle (1627–63) and the Compagnie des Indes Orientales (1664–74) until it was taken over by the crown in 1674. Robert de la Salle, between 1666 and his murder in 1687, discovered the Great Lakes and sailed down the Ohio and Mississippi, claiming (1682) 'Louisiana' for France. Under the governorship of Count Frontenac (1672–82, 1689–98) the power of the Iroquois, the strongest Indian tribe, was broken and New France reached its zenith.

Between 1688 and 1763 the French were ousted from North America by the British. Their rivalry in the fur trade began in the early 17th century: the cheaper English cloth and rum outbade French cloth and brandy, and the passage from English New York to Europe was shorter than from French Quebec. By the peace of UTRECHT (1713) France lost ACADIA, NEWFOUNDLAND and the HUDSON'S BAY TERRITORIES; by the peace of PARIS (1763) France lost the whole of C. to Great Britain and LOUISIANA to Spain.

C. was acquired against the wishes of powerful City groups, who would have preferred the sugar island of Guadeloupe. The new colony was organized as the province of QUEBEC by proclamation on 7 Oct. 1763. Its southern frontiers were delimitated after the defection of the 13 colonies in 1783, extended westwards by Jay's treaty in 1794 and finally along the 49th parallel in 1818—every time to the advantage of the U.S.A. The continent was first crossed by Alexander Mackenzie, who in 1793 reached the Pacific coast opposite Vancouver Island.

Relations with the U.S.A. remained somewhat strained throughout the 19th century. The attempt to conquer Upper C. by force of arms in 1812 was frustrated by military incompetence (Canadian victory at QUEENS-TON HEIGHTS) and senseless savagery (burning of Newark and York (Toronto)). The U.S. government, it is true, agreed to the demilitarization of the lakes (1817) and later the whole frontier, but made repeated and partly successful efforts to restrict Canadian access to the Pacific (Alaska purchase, 1867; Vancouver boundary dispute, 1871; Alaska boundary dispute, 1903).

Efforts of U.S. big business to dominate Canadian economy continue.

C.'s economy, originally based on the fur trade, underwent several decisive changes. From 1780 to 1790 and especially after 1810 when Napoleon's CONTINENTAL SYSTEM blocked the Baltic timber trade, the vast Canadian forests supplied the most valuable export commodity. From 1830 wheat became the most important cash crop, and when in 1846 Peel's free-trade policy endangered the timber and wheat exports, the reciprocity treaty of 1854 (terminated 1866) between C. and the U.S.A. opened a new market. Wheat was superseded from 1865 by dairying as the leading industry, until the discovery of extensive iron-ore, uranium and oil fields made mining the foremost industry of modern C. The economic development was much helped by a transcontinental network of railways which, beginning in 1837, reached the Pacific coast in 1886.

In the political and constitutional field C. has on five occasions vitally influenced the development of the British COMMONWEALTH and Empire. The Quebec Act of 1774 established the precedent that colonial rule should be regulated by Act of Parliament rather than royal prerogative. The Constitutional Act of 1791, designed to pacify C. after the secession of the 13 American colonies, determined the shape of government in all white British colonies by basing it upon the co-operation of a governor appointed by the crown, a council appointed by the governor and an assembly elected by popular vote. The 'Report on the Affairs of British North America', submitted on 31 Jan. 1839 to the Colonial Office by the Earl of Durham (1792–1840), inaugurated the policy of responsible self-government based on elected majorities. The 'British North America Act', passed on 29 Mar. 1867, brought into being the Dominion of C. (1 July 1867), marking a completely new relationship between motherland and overseas countries. In 1919 C., by independently signing the treaty of Ver-

c

sailles and joining the LEAGUE OF NATIONS—followed by instituting separate diplomatic representation abroad in 1927—paved the way for the statute of WESTMINSTER, 1931, which granted full sovereignty to all dominions.

The significant stages of this development inside C. were the Act of Union (1840), which combined Upper and Lower C. in the single province of C. on the basis of equal representation; the meeting of the first Canadian parliament with a parliamentary executive (1841); the formation of the first responsible ministry under Robert Baldwin and Louis Lafontaine (1848); the movement towards confederation, mooted from 1858 (the year when the capital, originally Montreal and from 1849 alternating between Quebec and Toronto, was moved to Ottawa), worked out in detail by Alexander T. Galt in 1864, and consummated 1867, when the four provinces of ONTARIO, QUEBEC, NEW BRUNSWICK and Nova Scotia combined in the Dominion of C.

The Dominion purchased the NORTHWEST TERRITORIES from the HUDSON'S BAY COMPANY in 1869, out of which the provinces of MANITOBA (1870), ALBERTA and SASKATCHEWAN (1905) and the YUKON TERRITORY (1898) were formed. The former colonies of BRITISH COLUMBIA (1871) and PRINCE EDWARD ISLAND (1873) and the former Dominion of NEWFOUNDLAND (1949) joined C.

Two features are characteristic of Canadian home politics: the bitterness of racial and religious strife, which, contrary to popular belief, does not go back to the English–French rivalries of the 18th century but was introduced by the Irish immigrants of the 1820–50 period; and, secondly, the longevity of provincial and federal governments, for which the premierships of Oliver Mowat (Ontario, 1872–96), Wilfrid Laurier (1896–1911) and Mackenzie King (1921–30, 1935–48) may be cited.

The ten Canadian provinces have each a separate parliament and administration under a lieutenant-governor appointed by the governor-general-in-council. The governor-general(now alternately an English- and a French-speaking Canadian) is assisted by a privy council, composed of cabinet ministers; a senate, nominated for life by the governor-general -in-council; a house of commons, giving the provinces a proportionate representation according to their population. Appeals to the British Privy Council were terminated in 1949 and the right to amend the British North America Act was granted to the Canadian Parliament with certain reservations.   SHS; IHE

Canals developed rapidly in Britain after the opening of the canal linking the duke of Bridgewater's collieries at Worsley to Manchester (1759–64). Although not the first, it was a spectacular achievement and halved the price of coal in Manchester. Like the Grand Trunk Canal (1765–77) linking the Trent and Mersey, it was planned by James Brindley, who envisaged a complete system. Between 1780 and 1800 a network of c. was built, which was especially important in furthering the INDUSTRIAL REVOLUTION in the mining and manufacturing areas. No serious competition was felt from the RAILWAYS until 1840, when steady decline of traffic set in, although the Ship Canal opened in 1894 has made Manchester a major port. The C. were nationalized under the British Transport Commission (1947) and since 1962 controlled by the British Waterways Board; under 2,000 miles are now open to traffic.
IHE

Canberra was settled in 1824 and on 1 Jan. 1911 ceded by NEW SOUTH WALES to the Commonwealth of AUSTRALIA, which had chosen the site as the seat of the federal government; the transfer took place in 1927. Since 1948 C. has one elected, non-voting member of the Australian house of representatives.   SHS

Canterbury, peace of (12 Aug. 1264), an attempt by Simon de Montfort to reach agreement with the royalists after LEWES. The terms accepted by Henry III and his eldest son, Edward, provided for the maintenance of the FORMA REGIMINIS during Henry's reign and into Edward's; aliens were to be excluded from royal offices; MAGNA CARTA and the PROVISIONS OF WESTMINSTER were to be observed. The terms proved unacceptable to the royalist exiles in France.   RFW

Cantiaci or **Cantii,** one of the four tribal groups of the BELGAE in Kent north of the Weald, who, during the earlier part of the 1st century A.D., were under the control of the CATUVELLAUNI. Conquered by the Romans in 43 they were formed into a CIVITAS with their capital at Durovernum Cantiacorum (Canterbury).   CFS

Cantref (Welsh 'hundred townships') was probably the historical successor to the older Welsh *gwlad* ('country') or *tud* ('tribe'), the body of independent tribesmen settled within territorial limits marking them off from their neighbours. The larger *gwlads*, e.g. Anglesey or Brycheiniog, became divided into c.s, the smaller ones, e.g. Dyffryn Clwyd or Builth, became c.s themselves. The c. was the administrative, judicial and fiscal unit of early Wales. With the growth of population and settlement, however, the c. was usually divided up into two, three or more COMMOTES. In South Wales such a subdivision does not seem to have taken place until as late as the appearance of the Normans at the end of the 11th century.   GW

Cape Breton Island (Isle Royale), from the 16th century became the centre for French fishermen fishing the St Lawrence estuary and, during Anglo-French wars of the 18th century, a permanent threat to NEWFOUNDLAND and NOVA SCOTIA, especially after the building of the great fortress of Louisbourg in the 1720s. It was captured by the British in 1745 but exchanged for MADRAS in 1748, recaptured in 1758 and retained by the Treaty of PARIS, 1763. Louisbourg was destroyed. Made part of Nova Scotia, it had a separate existence from 1784 to 1819, consequent upon the influx of American Loyalists (UNITED EMPIRE LOYALISTS). IHE

Cape Matapan, see MATAPAN.

Cape of Good Hope. The annexation of Saldanha Bay (west of the C.) by English sailors in 1620 was repudiated by James I. In 1652 the Dutch East India Company occupied the site as a refreshment station on the way to India and founded Cape Town. The Company showed no interest in a permanent settlement or the production of exportable commodities, and the immigrants—Dutch, Germans and (1688–90) 200 French Huguenots—reverted from settled urban and agricultural pursuits to a restless nomadic life. In 1701 the use of French was forbidden in church and school, and stern Dutch Calvinism became the hallmark of the colony where the church was a government organ. When Bantu tribes, fleeing from the East African slave-raiders, reached South Africa about 1700, continuous warfare ensued, during which the mobile 'commando' system was developed. After the invasion of the Netherlands by the French revolutionary armies (1793) and the bankruptcy of the Dutch East India Company (1794), the stadholder William V asked Britain to protect the Dutch colonies. Cape Town was therefore occupied in 1795, restored to the Batavian Republic in 1803 after the peace of AMIENS, re-taken on the renewal of hostilities in 1806 and finally ceded to Britain on 13 Aug. 1814. At this time C. colony contained about 25,000 burghers, 30,000 slaves and 20,000 Bushmen, Hottentots and Coloured.

Resentment of control from Cape Town first broke into revolt on the eastern frontier where a short-lived republic was set up in 1795–99. It was aggravated by the influx of English missionaries (from 1799, London MISSIONARY SOCIETY) and English settlers (from 1820); the missionary-inspired Ordinance 50 (1828), which placed the Africans on an equal footing with Europeans; and the introduction of English institutions: freedom of press, land survey, independent judiciary (1828), abolition of slavery (1833), executive and legislative councils (1834), elected municipal councils (1836); with English as the only official language (1828–82). At the same time the burghers looked to government for protection against the Bantu tribes with whom they were involved in the first six Kaffir wars (1779–1834), fought mainly on the eastern frontier along the Great Fish river, which in 1812 was fixed as the boundary. Dissatisfaction with British rule culminated in the GREAT TREK (migration) of 1835–48; the most unruly and adventurous tenth of the C. burghers left the colony and, after feats of endurance and heroism, in 1852–4 established the ORANGE and TRANSVAAL republics.

The Trek had far-reaching consequences. It opened up the whole of South Africa to white settlement; it separated the British and Boer communities politically while preserving their economic interdependence; it made impossible the geographical segregation of whites and Bantu; it made all but certain the eventual overthrow of white rule by the huge black majority.

The C. Punishment Act (1836), which declared the Trekkers to be still British subjects, remained a dead letter, as was the claim (1848) to the Vaal river as northern boundary; finally, in 1880 the Orange river was fixed as the northern frontier of C. colony. After the 7th and 8th Kaffir wars (1846, 1850–3) and the national suicide of the Xhosa at the instigation of their witch-doctors (1857) Kaffraria, i.e. the land between the Great Fish and Kei rivers, was annexed in 1865. After the 9th and last Kaffir war (1877) Trans-Kei, East Griqualand and, in 1894, Pondoland were annexed, fixing the final frontier with NATAL.

In 1853 representative government was introduced with an appointed executive council and elected legislative council and house of assembly (property qualification, regardless of colour). This system was in 1872 changed to responsible cabinet government, of which Cecil Rhodes was prime minister in 1890-6. As the C. province in 1910 the colony joined the UNION OF SOUTH AFRICA. SHS

Cape Passaro, battle of (11 Aug. 1718). At the time when Spain rejected the terms of the QUADRUPLE ALLIANCE a Spanish army landed in Sicily. Most of the escorting fleet of 22 ships was subsequently destroyed by Admiral Sir George Byng off C.P. IHE

Cape St Vincent, battle of, see ST VINCENT.

Carham, battle of (probably 1016), was fought in Northumberland on the river Tweed between the NORTHUM-BRIANS under earl Uhtred and a combined force of SCOTS under king Malcolm and STRATHCLYDE Britons under king Owain the Bald. The Northumbrians were heavily defeated. The battle was once regarded as gaining for Scotland the area between the Tweed and Forth. This is not so, but it did confirm Scottish possession of the Lowlands. CFS

Carlisle, parliament and statute of (1307). Though the parliament which met at C. from Jan. to March was largely concerned with the Scottish war, it was most notable for the statute prohibiting alien priories from sending revenues to their mother-houses overseas, and for the strong expression of opposition to papal PROVISIONS. A petition presented in the C. parliament formed the basis of the first statute of PROVISORS (1351). RFW

Carte Baronum, replies of tenants-in-chief to Henry II's inquiry in 1166 for the numbers and names of knights enfeoffed before Henry I's death (1135) and thereafter, and for the service due to him, the *servitium debitum.* Copied into the Red Book of the EXCHEQUER, the c.b. show the arrangements for military service in England a century after the NORMAN CONQUEST: many honours had more enfeoffed knights than their *servitium debitum,* a few retained some in DEMESNE. The inquiry had two pur-

poses: political, for Henry was leaving England and wanted all knights in his allegiance; financial, as a basis for more efficient taxation. The c.b. reveal that the process of enfeoffment was virtually complete by 1135. PMB

Cartulary, Coucher or Leiger book, a landowner's register of the title deeds of his lands, liberties and privileges. Occasionally in rolls, most are in book form, often elaborately decorated. The earliest surviving English c., of Worcester Cathedral priory, was written shortly before the NORMAN CONQUEST. Though most early c.s belonged to religious foundations, the practice of making them was later adopted by lay men and institutions, and the documents entered form an important source for early medieval history.

G. R. C. Davis, *Medieval Cartularies of Great Britain* (1958). PMB

Carucage or hidage, a short-lived, non-feudal tax, based on the appropriate local land unit of carucate or HIDE, first levied in 1194, on the basis of the DOMESDAY assessment, for Richard I's RANSOM. Opposition to a new levy in 1198 produced a new assessment. The last c. was taken from the clergy in 1224 to put down Fawkes de Bréauté's rebellion (BED-FORD). PMB

Carucate, see BOVATE; PLOUGHLAND.

Casket Letters. After LANGSIDE (May 1568) Mary Queen of Scots placed herself under Elizabeth I's protection. English commissioners met at York (Oct.) to hear evidence on the charges against her in connexion with Darnley's murder. Regent Moray of Scotland produced letters and sonnets from a casket of Bothwell's. If written by Mary they proved her complicity, but the originals disappeared in 1584 and their authenticity has never been proven. The evidence against her is circumstantial, but most of her subjects were convinced of her guilt at the time. The commission's findings (Jan. 1569) were inconclusive, and Mary was retained as a prisoner at Tutbury. IHE

Castile, kingdom of, was claimed in 1371 by John of Gaunt, third son of Edward III, in right of his wife Constance, daughter of Pedro the Cruel whom Henry of Trastámara had ousted despite his defeat at NÁJERA. John enjoyed the support of Castilian exiles, of legitimists in C. and of the adherents of the Roman pope Urban VI, since C. recognized the Avignonese, Clement VII. Plans for an invasion of C. from Gascony came to nothing, and attacks by way of, and in alliance with, PORTUGAL did little to further John's claims. After the failure of his invasion of León, John eventually came to terms with John I of C. in 1388. He married his daughter Catalina to Henry, the heir of C., and in return for abandoning his claims received an indemnity and a pension. John's activities drew England and Portugal closer together, but failed to break the alliance of C. with France against England.   RFW

Castillon, battle of (17 July 1453), the last battle of the HUNDRED YEARS' WAR. John Talbot, earl of Shrewsbury, temporarily recovered BORDEAUX and part of Gascony from the French in 1452. Attempting to raise the siege of C., on the Dordogne, Talbot attacked the French camp outside the town and was completely defeated, largely because of his opponents' effective use of artillery. Talbot himself was killed, and the destruction of his army spelled the end of English rule in Gascony.   RFW

Castlery (*castellaria*), the district organized feudally for the defence of a particular castle.   CFS

Castles. The art of fortification was largely neglected from the collapse of ROMAN BRITAIN until the 11th century. Although the Anglo-Saxons enclosed their towns with ditches, earthen ramparts and wooden palisades, they did not develop the castle, unless that name can be given to those earthworks, smaller than the BURH, which were built, e.g. at Nottingham, as part of the 10th-century defences against the DANES. C. were introduced to England from Normandy about 1050, but few were built before 1066, e.g. one at Dover by Harold Godwinson and a group in Herefordshire by Norman settlers. The scarcity of c. undoubtedly facilitated the NORMAN CONQUEST, while the building of 50–60 c. by William I gave him a firm grip on his newly-won kingdom. Comparatively few stone c., e.g. the Tower and Colchester, were built in the Conqueror's reign; most c. were of the motte and bailey type, earthen mounds and ramparts, surrounded by ditches and carrying timber defences, on the continental model illustrated in the BAYEUX TAPESTRY. Earth-and-timber c. had a long active history largely because of the speed and cheapness with which they could be erected by unskilled labour. Hence their widespread employment by William I and, for example, by the MARCHER LORDS to secure their conquests in Wales. The type soon spread into Scotland and was used in the 12th-century conquest of IRELAND. In Wales it remained in use, sometimes in a subordinate role to new stone castles, up to the mid-13th century. Probably most of the ADULTERINE c. of the ANARCHY were of the motte and bailey type, soon thrown up by forced labour, but easily made untenable when Henry II restored royal authority.

The replacement in stone of timber defences was well under way in the 12th century. Where building stone was readily available, e.g. Ludlow, Richmond (Yorks), stone towers and walls formed part of the earliest defences of 11th-century c. Typical of the 12th century were the great rectangular keeps, e.g. at Dover and Rochester, combined with walled enclosures which might be strengthened by rectangular wall-towers. Their height and solidity gave the great keeps considerable powers of resistance, and their reduction was almost impossible save by surprise, treachery or starvation. It was therefore imperative for 12th-century kings to retain firm control of the building and ownership of c., and by the destruction or acquisition of many baronial castles together with his own vigorous building-programme, Henry II significantly strengthened the royal position. By 1200, however, the defensive had lost its advantage, owing to the development of siege engines and the technique of battering and mining, and new defences had to be devised.

The characteristic developments of the 13th century were (1) the abandonment of the great keeps in favour of enclosures bounded by high curtain walls, defended at intervals by round, half-round or polygonal towers from which archery could sweep the walls and their approaches, and with gateways defended by pairs of towers; (2) the increasing use and elaboration of water defences to thwart the operations of miners, e.g. Caerphilly; (3) the multiplication of lines of defence—anticipated in the late 12th century, e.g. at CHATEAU GAILLARD—either by constructing a series of fortified enclosures on a narrow site, such as a ridge, e.g. Chepstow, Montgomery, or by adopting the concentric plan best illustrated by Beaumaris. The great series of c. built by Edward I to hold his conquest in Wales shows all these features. Edward took particular care that most of his Welsh castles should be accessible by water, e.g. Rhuddlan, while some of them were further strengthened by the attachment of a strongly fortified borough, e.g. Conway, whose defences may be rated as the greatest single achievement of military architecture in medieval Britain. Edward I carried this type into Scotland where, however, it proved less effective than in Wales.

The mid- and late-14th century was a period of comparative peace in England: there was a marked decline in the number of new c. built, while old ones entered a long period of decay. The Welsh c. shared in the general neglect until the rude awakening of the GLYN DŴR REBELLION. During the HUNDRED YEARS' WAR the defence of the southern and south-eastern coasts against the French and Castilians necessitated the building of a few new c., e.g. Bodiam and Queenborough (the latter representing the ultimate in concentricity) and the strengthening of existing town and castle defences, particularly from about 1360, to enable them to mount cannon. The elaboration of gatehouses and their approaches continued, and increasing provision was made for the use of hand-guns. Whereas the civil wars of the 12th and 13th centuries had largely revolved around the siege or relief of c., they and fortified towns played a comparatively small part in the wars of the ROSES. Artillery occasionally proved its increasing power, e.g. in reducing BAMBURGH; but a resolutely defended castle was still capable of prolonged resistance, e.g. Harlech. Fifteenth-century castle building produced some highly original work, e.g. Raglan, but on the whole there was less solidity of construction and more concessions to domestic convenience and comfort. Except in the north, especially on the Scottish border, c. tended to become grander relations of the fortified manors, castellated houses of no great defensive strength, whose gatehouses and towers were to remain salient features of the great Tudor houses. The development of the true castle was not resumed until Henry VIII built fortresses capable of carrying the improved artillery of the 16th century: his citadels, e.g. Carlisle, and his coastal c., e.g. Camber, Calshot, St Mawes.

With the notable exception of BERWICK-ON-TWEED English towns were not re-fortified in the revolutionary Continental manner in the 16th century, but in the CIVIL WARS of the 17th century their medieval defences were supplemented by elaborate earthworks, e.g. Oxford. Medieval c. still played a part in these wars, when some put up a surprisingly stout resistance, e.g. Pembroke and Raglan, while Carlisle castle stood its last siege during the FORTY-FIVE REBELLION. Since the 16th century most new fortifications in Britain have been erected for coastal defence—the MARTELLO TOWERS of the Napoleonic period, the pill-boxes of 1940–, for the seaward and landward defence of naval bases, notably Portsmouth, and the defence of the approaches to London, but all these belong to the era of the fort rather than of the castle.

RFW

Cateau-Cambrésis, treaty of (3 Apr. 1559) between England, France and Spain, ended the Habsburg–Valois struggle in Europe. CALAIS was left in French hands, ostensibly for eight years, and England and France were to abstain from intervention in Scotland. The boundaries of the Netherlands were restored with modifications, and Spanish supremacy in Italy was accepted. France restored Savoy and Piedmont but kept Saluzzo.

IHE

Cathay Company. In 1576 Michael Lok, a London merchant and NORTH-WEST PASSAGE enthusiast, in collaboration with Martin Frobisher equipped two ships to search for a north-west route to Asia. The discovery of Frobisher Sound, claimed to be a strait, led to the formation of the C.C. Ore believed to contain gold had been brought home, and the voyage of 1577 was used to bring more. The Company's stocks rose to £20,000, but after the voyage of 1578 the ore was found to be worthless. The C.C. went bankrupt.

IHE

Catholic Apostolic Church grew from a discussion circle started in 1826 at Albury Park, Surrey, home of Henry Drummond, M.P. The group soon came under the influence of Edward Irving, the Scottish revivalist minister of Regent Sq.; members of the C.A.C. are sometimes called Irvingites, though most of Irving's congregation did not join. They believed that the Second Coming was at hand and that it was necessary to re-establish the primitive church; hence the appointment of 'apostles' who alone could interpret 'prophetic utterances'. The C.A.C.'s influence was past before the end of the 19th century. The last apostle died in 1901.

MLH

Catholic Association, founded (5 May 1823) by Daniel O'Connell, developed into a national movement (1824–5) aided by parish priests; 1d per month subscription (the 'Catholic rent') raised more than £1,000 per week. The C.A. dissolved itself before it could be legally suppressed (1825), was re-formed within the law and became almost a rival to the government. In 1826 it started the promotion of Catholic parliamentary candidates (including O'Connell himself who won Co. Clare). By the end of 1828 Wellington and Peel were convinced that CATHOLIC EMANCIPATION was inevitable if civil war was to be avoided. Emancipation being achieved (1829), the C.A. again dissolved itself before a suppression act was passed.   MLH

Catholic Emancipation. In England during the 18th century Roman CATHOLICS received a large measure of illegal toleration; they were in any case a small minority (about 60,000 in 1780). In Ireland, however, the great bulk of the population was Catholic and it felt the full rigour of the PENAL CODE. C.E. was therefore essentially an Irish problem, albeit in the forefront of English politics for over 30 years.

By the first relief act (1778)—there had been inconsiderable Irish measures (1771/74)—English Catholics were enabled to acquire real property; prosecution of priests on the evidence of an informer and life imprisonment for keeping a Catholic school were abolished. Two years later occurred the GORDON RIOTS. Greater relief was given to English Catholics by the act of 1791: those who took a prescribed oath were freed from penalties for exercising their faith; they were able to teach and take certain posts in the legal and military professions.

An act of 1778 and two more passed (1782) by GRATTAN'S PARLIAMENT, following the repeal of POYNING'S LAW, gave relief in Ireland similar to that given in England in 1778 except that Catholics were still prevented from acquiring land freehold. Langrishe's act (1792) admitted Catholics to the bar and to teaching; it also permitted mixed marriages. The Catholic Committee, led by John Teogh, formed a convention ('Back Lane Parliament') which petitioned George III for complete C.E. (2 Jan. 1793). Pitt, seeking a permanent solution to the Irish problem, pressed the Irish Parliament to pass the relief act of 1793 which gave Catholics the vote and the right to sit on juries; they were admitted to the universities and to all but the higher civil and military posts; but not to Parliament.

The king refused further measures of C.E. following the Act of UNION (1800) and Pitt resigned; the Ministry of ALL THE TALENTS resigned (1807) when the king did not allow a bill opening the upper ranks of the Services to Catholics, though this was passed in 1817. The final jolt was administered by the CATHOLIC ASSOCIATION led by O'Connell and other members of the professional class which was arising in Ireland as a result of the act of 1793. Wellington and Peel realized that drastic conciliation in Ireland was necessary. The C.E. Act, 1829, received the reluctant assent of George IV (13 Apr.), the Irish 40s.-freeholder losing his vote by an accompanying act. Almost all disabilities of Catholics were removed; they were admitted to Parliament (1830 saw 16 Catholic M.P.s) and to all offices except those of Regent, Lord Chancellor and Lord Lieutenant of Ireland; all restrictions on the ownership of property were ended.

Subsequent legislation included the opening of universities (Oxford, Cambridge and Durham) by the Universities Tests Act, 1871, and the total abolition of the already restricted declaration against transubstantiation (1867). A minor relief act was passed in 1926. A few disabilities remain (e.g. exercise of Church of England patronage).   MLH

Catholics, Roman, those who still adhered to the church of Rome after the ELIZABETHAN SETTLEMENT. Most of the clergy conformed after the Act of SUPREMACY (1559), but a large part of the laity in the north and west remained RECUSANTS. After the NORTHERN REBELLION (1569), the RIDOLFI, THROCKMORTON and BABINGTON conspiracies and the political intrigues of the JESUITS, the PENAL LAWS were intensified. They were further discredited by the GUNPOWDER PLOT (1605), but James I was not unduly hostile. Charles I showed more sympathy, MARYLAND was founded under an R.C. proprietor and R.C.s became royalists during the CIVIL WARS. They were not persecuted under the COMMONWEALTH and PROTECTORATE. Charles II favoured them, but they were excluded from office and from Parliament by the TEST ACTS and suffered severely from Protestant frenzy during the POPISH PLOT. James II's tactless attempts to promote their religion resulted in the GLORIOUS REVOLUTION (1688) and some further slight restrictions. Numbers declined in the 18th century when they enjoyed substantial practical toleration. The Relief Act (1778) led to the GORDON RIOTS, but CATHOLIC EMANCIPATION was finally achieved in 1829. From 1598 their clergy were organized under an archpriest, the first bishop was appointed in 1623, and from 1685 control was exercised by vicars apostolic. In 1850 the hierarchy was restored under the archbishop of Westminster, causing the passing of the abortive ECCLESIASTICAL TITLES ACT. The mass of the Irish population remained R.C., suffering severe hardships under the PENAL CODE until 1782, obtaining final emancipation in 1829.   IHE

Cato Street Conspiracy (1820) was devised by Arthur Thistlewood and others to assassinate the Cabinet, seize various vantage points in London and form a government. Most of the plotters were arrested in Cato St., Marylebone (23 Feb.), when about to execute their plans, one of their number being an *agent provocateur*; 5 including Thistlewood were hanged, 5 transported for life. The C.S.C. had little political significance except that it seemed to justify the SIX ACTS. MLH

Catuvellauni, the main group of the BELGAE in Britain, their original settlement being in the area of Hertfordshire. Under their ruler Cassivellaunus they put up considerable resistance to Julius Caesar in 54 B.C. Before the end of the 1st century B.C. they had expanded into the area of Beds., Bucks. and Oxon. Their king Cunobelinus, Shakespeare's Cymbeline, controlled the ATREBATES and CANTIACI, conquered the TRINOVANTES, extended his power to the north-west, issued coins in considerable quantity and established a new capital for his kingdom at Colchester. The anti-Roman policy of his sons was an important factor in producing the ROMAN CONQUEST, and fear of the C. led other tribes to submit to Rome. Conquered by the Romans in A.D. 43, they became a CIVITAS; and their original tribal capital at Verulamium (St Albans) was rebuilt, becoming possibly a MUNICIPIUM.   CFS

Cavalier Parliament (1661–79), so called from its royalist majority, also known as the Pensionary (owing to the acceptance of bribes by its members) or Long Parliament of Charles II. It confirmed the work of the CONVENTION PARLIAMENT of 1660, passed the CLARENDON CODE and the LICENSING ACT (1662), reconstituted the militia but refused to authorize a standing army or agree to the DECLARATION OF INDULGENCE. It secured the appropriation of supplies (1665) and the dismissal of Clarendon because of his opposition to this policy and the failures of the DUTCH WAR (1665–7). The TEST ACT (1673) resulted in the disruption of the CABAL, and a second Test Act (1678) was passed at the time of the POPISH PLOT. Parliament was dissolved when it impeached Danby for his connivance at the secret dealings between Charles II and Louis XIV of France. Notable for the growth of party politics, it extended its control in domestic and foreign issues.   IHE

Cavaliers, see ROYALISTS.

Cayman Islands, were discovered by Columbus in 1503, but never occupied by the Spaniards. British settlers from JAMAICA arrived from 1734. The C.I. was a dependency of Jamaica until 1962.   SHS

Celtic Church (in Wales). During Roman times Wales was in the sphere of the BRITISH CHURCH, but Christianity had made insignificant progress there by the beginning of the 5th century. The CONVERSION of the greater part of the population was carried out in the 5th and 6th centuries by Celtic monk-missionaries who derived their inspiration from Egyptian monasticism. These 'saints', of whom the most notable Welsh representatives were Dyfrig, Cadog and Illtud in the south-east, David and Teilo in the south-west, Padarn in mid-Wales and Deiniol in the north, successfully established centres of worship and learning along characteristically Celtic non-territorial and monastic lines. The monastery's endowment became the patrimony of the founder's family and was held in common by a *clas* (chapter), only one of whom might be in priestly orders. Where an abbot was also a bishop, he exercised no territorial jurisdiction, though the authority of his church might be filially acknowledged by daughter-churches. Following the conversion of the Anglo-Saxons, differences between the Celtic and Roman churches, notably over the date of EASTER, clerical tonsure and forms of baptism, led to serious difficulties, and Welsh asceticism and organization were not acceptable to those of the Roman persuasion. Conferences to resolve them, held with Augustine of Canterbury, proved abortive. In 768, however, the Welsh church, following the lead of Elfodd, bishop of Bangor, submitted to Roman authority. Even so, it retained until the NORMAN CONQUEST and long after many of the distinguishing marks of its Celtic origins.   GW

Celtic Fields, the small fields once cultivated on lighter upland soils, especially in chalk areas. First used in the later BRONZE AGE, they continued in use until the TEUTONIC CONQUEST.

Their boundaries can in many cases be detected by air photography or as surface marks. CFS

Celts, people who spoke the Celtic language and who first invaded Britain from mainland Europe in the late BRONZE AGE. Racially mixed, they appear to have been similar to peoples already in the island. During the 5th and 3rd centuries B.C. they again invaded, on these occasions bringing IRON-AGE cultures. Celtic replaced all earlier languages spoken in Britain, and has, in WALES, continued to the present day. CFS

Celts, prehistoric stone or metal tools of chisel form. CFS

Cely Papers, the family and commercial correspondence of the C. family, merchants of the staple, of Aveley, Essex, 1475–88. The C.P. throw much light on the contemporary wool trade in England, Calais and Flanders, and on the difficulties, political, from piracy etc., of those engaged in it. The C.P. are now in the PUBLIC RECORD OFFICE. PMB

Census. In classical usage a registration of population for taxation: part of this usage was retained by the medieval church in describing its estimates and receipts from international ecclesiastical taxation; part was revived in the 19th century to describe returns of population. Clergymen's returns of baptisms, marriages and deaths in England and Wales 1821–30 were collected in 1831. The first nationwide c., renewed every 10 years, was taken in 1801. The medieval EXCHEQUER also described the casual profits of crown woodlands as c. PMB

CENTO, the Central Treaty Organization, comprising Turkey, Iran, PAKISTAN and the United Kingdom, is the successor of the 'Bagdad pact' of mutual defence and economic cooperation, signed by Turkey and Iraq on 24 Feb. 1955 and subsequently joined by the other partners; the United States is represented in various committees (since 1956–7) and has concluded bilateral agreements with Turkey, Iran and Pakistan (1959). Iraq ceased to participate after the revolution of July 1958 and formally withdrew on 24 March 1959. The headquarters of C. was therefore transferred from Bagdad to Ankara in Oct. 1958, and the name was adopted on 21 Aug. 1959. SHS

Central Provinces and Berar. On the death in 1853 of the last, childless Maratha raja of Nagpur, Lord Dalhousie declared Nagpur lapsed to the EAST INDIA COMPANY, which had maintained a resident in Nagpur from 1803 and brought the state under its control in 1816–18. In 1861 Nagpur was combined with Saugor and Nerbudda as C.P. under a chief commissioner. In 1902 the district of Berar, assigned to the British by the nizam of HYDERABAD in 1853, was perpetually leased to the government of India and transferred to the chief commissioner of the C.P., who was replaced by a governor in 1920. Under recognition of the nizam's sovereignty over Berar, the C.P. and B. was constituted a governor's province on 24 Oct. 1936 and an autonomous province with unicameral legislature on 1 Apr. 1937. Renamed Madhya Pradesh, the province became an 'A State' on 28 Jan. 1950. It was completely reorganized on 1 Nov. 1956, absorbing the former states of MADHYA BHARAT, VINDHYA PRADESH and BHOPAL. SHS

Ceorl, the general O.E. term for a free peasant. Men of this class inevitably varied in economic standing, but all were personally free with, in much of England, a WERGILD of 200s. The c. of KENT was wealthier than those elsewhere and had the large wergild of 100 gold shillings. C.s were liable to military service (FYRD); church dues (PARISH); public service such as bridge and BURH building and attendance at their local court (MOOT); royal dues and taxes. The weight of these burdens joined with the general unrest of the period in depressing them economically, and by 1066 many held land from nobles in return for work done on their lord's DEMESNE.

The assumed holding of a c. in early days was one HIDE, but by the late O.E. period the majority held considerably less. The class was subdivided on economic lines (GENEAT, GEBUR, KOTSETLA). In post-Norman times the majority lost their personal freedom, becoming the VILLEINS, bordars and cottars of the middle ages; and the word, as 'churl', survived as a disdainful epithet.   CFS

Ceylon attracted the Europeans as the main source of cinnamon, which (growing wild in the Kandy highlands) from the 13th to the mid-19th centuries was the island's chief export. The Portuguese from 1505 settled on the west and south coasts, founded a fort at Colombo in 1517 and conquered Jaffna in 1593. They were expelled by the Dutch between 1609 and 1656, when Colombo fell to them. The Dutch started cinnamon plantations in 1769 to make themselves independent of Kandy. In 1796 the British captured the maritime provinces, which were attached to MADRAS presidency. They were not restored at the peace of AMIENS, but organized as a crown colony (1802). The kingdom of Kandy was conquered in 1815 and, after a rebellion in 1818, secured first by a line of forts, then (1820–32) by building roads between all important places.

On the strength of the reports of two commissions of inquiry (1829–30), of which Sir William Colebrooke (1787–1870) was the leading spirit, thorough-going reforms were carried out in 1833. The ancient kingdoms of Kotte and Jaffna, where the Dutch colonial system continued, and Kandy, where after the deposition of the last king in 1815 the feudal structure was preserved, were amalgamated under a single administration and redivided into five provinces. Legislative and executive councils were set up, the judiciary was made independent, forced labour was abolished, as was the cinnamon trade monopoly which the government had taken over in 1821 from the EAST INDIA COMPANY. English schools were established for the training of Sinhalese civil servants.

The first effect of the Colebrooke reforms was a rapid deterioration of the social and economic conditions of the peasantry, who felt neglected and oppressed by the bureaucracy of the far too large and ill-assorted provinces run by an underpaid and inefficient civil service; by the official encouragement of plantations owned by the same civil servants and other Europeans and worked by Indian immigrant labour; and by the reduction to insignificance of the cinnamon trade owing to Javanese and Indian competition. To counteract these justified grievances which eventually exploded in serious riots (1848), the government fostered the cultivation of coffee (first planted in 1827), which from 1837 became competitive in international markets; reformed the civil service by making appointment dependent on examination and forbidding participation in trade and agriculture (1845); created a new, the North-Western, province (1845); later augmented by the North-Central (1873), Uva (1886) and Saboragawuma (1889) provinces); restored the rule of the local headmen and chiefs (1848); and constructed a network of railways (from 1858).

By the time coffee lost its importance as a result of a fungus disease (1889) the cultivation of cinchona, tea (1867) and rubber (1876) had supplied C. with fresh and stable commodities; and the setting-up of an irrigation department (1896) further improved Sinhalese economy.

Constitutional reforms began in 1910 with the introduction of elections to the legislative council on a communal basis. This was changed to a mainly territorial basis in 1921, and to universal franchise on a wholly territorial basis in 1931 (retaining a state council elected on a territorial basis). The constitution of 15 May 1946 was modelled on those of Great Britain and the dominions, with a governor-general, a senate and a house of representatives. On 4 Feb. 1948 C. became an independent member of the COMMONWEALTH.   SHS

Chalgrove, battle of (18 June 1643). Prince Rupert, with royalist cavalry, returning to Oxford from a raid on Chinnor, was pursued by Stapleton and Hampden, but took them at a disadvantage in C. cornfield and won the skirmish. Hampden was wounded and died at Thame, and Essex abandoned the idea of blockading Oxford.

IHE

Chamber, a financial department of the royal household which, in the years preceding and immediately following the NORMAN CONQUEST, was probably also the centre of finance, soon giving way to the EXCHEQUER. As a department of the CURIA REGIS, providing ready cash and freedom from control, it served Henry II and John well. In the 13th century it gave way before the WARDROBE; but as that department's activities widened it became less flexible, more open to opposition attacks, and in Edward II's reign the C. was revived. It freed the king from financial and administrative controls, was endowed with revenues from forfeited estates, e.g. the Templars', and received a new seal, the SIGNET. Escaping the ORDAINERS' attention, its political importance was dimmed first by the transfer of many of its lands to the Exchequer in 1322, then by the political confusion at the end of the reign. It survived as a household office, to regain importance under the strong, personal government of the early Tudors, endowed with revenues from new bodies like the Court of AUGMENTATIONS. With the incorporation of such bodies in the revived EXCHEQUER in 1554, the C. lapsed into obscurity. PMB

Chamberlain, a financial officer. Both before and for a short period after the NORMAN CONQUEST c.s were associated both with the king's household and his treasury at Winchester; but as the EXCHEQUER developed, with charge over the treasury, so the various lay c.s, holding by SERJEANTY, withdrew from the household. Two of these offices, one held by the Mauduit family, the other created for Geoffrey de Clinton by Henry I and later held by the FitzGeralds, were later known as c.s of the Exchequer, and discharged by deputy. Within the household there were other c.s and when, in Henry II's reign, the CHAMBER became an important office, two lay c.s of the household, holding in serjeanty, gained supremacy: their duties too were later performed by deputy. On the Chamber's revival under Edward II one active c. was appointed, and his successors, with altered responsibilities, became the modern Lord CHAMBERLAINS OF THE HOUSEHOLD. PMB

Chamberlain of the Household, Lord, responsible for the administration of the royal household, honorary appointments, entertainments and the royal palaces, including Westminster. He had a long association with the theatre, deriving partly from the players retained by chamberlains in Elizabethan and Stewart times for court entertainments, and partly from the licensing of theatres in Westminster, from about the time of the RESTORATION, and, from 1737, of plays for public performance. His responsibilities for licensing plays ended on 26 Sept. 1968. PMB; MR

Chancellor, Latin *cancellarius*, the man behind a screen. Following their late Anglo-Saxon predecessors, c.s after the Norman conquest were custodians of the GREAT SEAL and heads of the CHANCERY, preparing and issuing documents for the strong and developing central government. By the early 12th century the C. was the chief officer of the CURIA REGIS, sitting also in the EXCHEQUER, travelling with the king through his realm, advising him at all times. Though the chancery separated from the household, the C. maintained his political eminence, a member of the council, president of the Lords when separated from the Commons and, as some legal matters were delegated to him, judge of a developing EQUITY court, which in time overshadowed his former departmental duties. To this court, as well as to his continuing importance and his preparation of judges' commissions, he owes his position as senior judge. Occasionally one or more keepers of the Great seal have been appointed, medievally between c.s' appointments, and in Tudor times with the title Lord Keeper and discharging for considerable periods all the C.'s duties. The practice was, however, discontinued, and alone among the officers of the Norman kings' household, the C. has retained his importance.

C.s of bishoprics etc. were medievally responsible for the education of clerks etc., later presiding over courts of audience etc.; bishops' secretarial work was discharged by their registrars, an office now held by lay solicitors.   PMB

Chancellor of the Exchequer. 12th-century CHANCELLORS sat in the EXCHEQUER, assisted by a clerk: after their withdrawal custody of the Exchequer seal and other of their duties fell to the clerk who, by the mid-13th century, was called C. of the E. The office's transition from administration to politics was slow. Chancellors, appointed to the TREASURY board, increased their control over financial policy as the first lords became premiers, but even in the 19th century the C. was not always included in the cabinet. Still attending the ceremony of 'pricking' SHERIFFS, formerly held in the Exchequer, C.s have, from 1870, been appointed Masters of the MINT.
                                                  PMB

Chancellor's Rolls, see PIPE ROLLS.

Chancery, in origin the writing office of the CURIA REGIS, presided over by the CHANCELLOR. As business increased, the staff became too numerous and the records too bulky to travel: C. settled in permanent quarters, slowly passing, with the GREAT SEAL, out of court. By this 13th-century development C., remote from the king, lost its political importance, but retained its administrative work, carried out by specialists, e.g. the Clerk of the HANAPER, the Clerk of the CROWN, the MASTERS etc. For much of the middle ages the staff

lived together, in the Chancellor's or Master of the ROLLS' household, or in the Inns of C. With the growth of modern government departments, its work quickly diminished, and the clerks discharged their trivial tasks, for which they received considerable fees, by deputies. Such sinecures were attacked and abolished in the late 18th and early 19th centuries, and the remaining clerical work of the C. was transferred to the CROWN OFFICE, the central office of the Supreme Court of JUDICATURE and the Patent Office.

As C. declined in political importance, so it assumed new, legal duties. Legal documents had been regularly prepared and returned into C., and some clerks became legal experts. From the late 13th century onwards petitions to king and council were sent to the Chancellor, sometimes together with the keeper of the PRIVY SEAL, for settlement, and by the mid-14th century C. had become a flourishing and popular EQUITY court. At the same period it began to hear COMMON LAW cases, though little is known of this side of its work. The C. court survived the attacks of the 16th- and 17th-century common lawyers to form, by the Judicature Act 1873, the Chancery Division of the High Court. The Chancellor had ceased to be the king's senior clerical officer: instead he had become senior judge, and his clerks Chancery Masters.   PMB

Chandigarh. A Union Territory of INDIA which serves as the joint capital of HARYANA and PUNJAB.   IHE

Channel Islands, formed part of the duchy of NORMANDY from 933 to 1204 and have remained attached to the English crown since 1066; 1940–5 under German occupation. The C.I., which are not part of the United Kingdom, consist of the autonomous bailiwicks of Jersey and Guernsey (with the dependencies of Alderney and Sark), under royal lords, wardens, captains (16th century), governors (17th century to 1835 in Guernsey, to 1854 in Jersey) and lieutenant-governors, with elected assemblies (States of Deliberation); the constitution of Sark is semi-feudal, under the *Seigneur* (or *Dame*) *de Sercq* and the elected Chief Pleas. The law is based in Jersey on the *Grand Coutumier de Normandie* (1539) and in Guernsey on the *Approbation des Lois* (1580/1).

SHS

Chantries were the many endowments made for religious, charitable and educational purposes usually connected with chantry chapels (often part of the parish church). Their main religious purpose was to offer masses for the repose of the souls of the dead. Their spoliation was begun by an act of 1545, but the survey was not completed at Henry VIII's death. By a new act of 1547 confiscation of chantry property was completed. Pensions were provided for dispossessed chantry priests, but little appears to have been done for education or charity.

IHE

Charity Commission. Control over the administration, abuse etc., of charitable trusts was exercised by the CHANCERY court until 1853, when commissioners were appointed to inquire into the administration of trusts and the production of proper accounts. Their powers have since been extended to cover the control of investments as well as schemes for varying the object of trusts, but judicial work still devolves on the Chancery division.

PMB

Charter (Latin *carta*), a document recording a grant, normally in perpetuity, of land, privileges etc. The solemn LATIN c., based on the Roman diploma, was brought to England under archbishop Theodore to provide written title to church estates, and was also adopted by laymen. At first simple, it became ponderous, laden with anathemas against transgressors, and unsuitable for the increasing complexity of land tenure. From the 9th century onwards VERNACULAR was used, first to record the settlements of disputes which lay behind many c.s, then to translate the

c.s themselves. WRIT–charters, flexible and brief, superseded even these translations and became, with their formulae translated into Latin by the Normans, the normal form for grants in perpetuity. C.s addressed to all persons present and future, generally couched in the past tense recording a transaction already completed, in theory, in a court, attested by WITNESSES and authenticated by SEAL, gave birth to many types of conveyance, though many modern documents, e.g. c.s of incorporation, are in fact letters patent.

PMB

Charter Acts, renewing the original charter of the EAST INDIA COMPANY (1600), were passed at 20-year intervals from 1773 (REGULATING ACT) to 1853 (INDIA ACTS).

SHS

Charter of Liberties. (1) On the death of King William Rufus in the NEW FOREST, his younger brother Henry lost no time in making himself king *de facto* by securing his formal election and coronation. At his coronation (5 Aug. 1100) Henry issued a c. of l. to win the support of church and baronage against the claims of his elder brother, Robert, duke of Normandy. The c., while proclaiming the accomplished fact of Henry's accession, promised the abolition of the evil customs of Rufus' reign, a return to the good laws of King Edward the Confessor's day, and the redress of specified grievances. In effect, the c. was an 'election manifesto': Henry broke his promises when they had served their immediate purpose. Nevertheless, the c., by which the king had subordinated himself to the law, had a long-term constitutional importance. Its terms furnished King John's barons with a precedent for the limitation of the powers of the king.

(2) Like Henry I, King Stephen secured the throne by prompt action, before his rival, Maud, could press her claims. He similarly attempted to consolidate his initial success by issuing c.s of l. By a first c., issued about the time of his coronation (22 Dec. 1135), Stephen confirmed in vague terms the laws and liberties enjoyed

under Henry I, and the laws of Edward the Confessor. At Oxford in early Apr. 1136 the king issued a second c., clearly stating his title as lawfully elected and consecrated king, and promising in particular to respect the liberties of the church, to whose support Stephen largely owed his election (see ANARCHY). RFW

Charter of Liberties, the 'Unknown', has survived only in a rough draft, of uncertain date but is evidently connected with the negotiations between King John and the barons preceding the grant of MAGNA CARTA. It may have been drawn up in the autumn of 1214 when the barons demanded the confirmation of Henry I's C. of L. More probably, it belongs to May 1215. Most of its clauses foreshadow John's concessions in Magna Carta. RFW

Chartism (1838–58), a working-class movement in which persons with widely divergent social aims were temporarily united by a 'Charter' embodying specified political reforms; it depended for mass support on economic depression.

In 1837 leading members, including W. Lovett, of the newly formed London Working Men's Association listed 6 political demands (manhood suffrage, the ballot, payment of M.P.s, abolition of the property qualification for M.P.s, equal constituencies, annual elections). Associations were formed in the provinces and support was given by the Birmingham Political Union led by the banker, T. Attwood. The demands were incorporated in a parliamentary bill (drafted by Lovett), published as *The People's Charter* (8 May 1838). Mass meetings, in the North dominated by F. O'Connor's agitation against the POOR LAW and everywhere augmented by economic distress, elected representatives to a convention; this met (Feb. 1839) and presented to Parliament a national petition (May) which was duly rejected (July). The government had prepared for trouble, but the convention broke up in disunity after ordering and then countermanding a 'sacred

month' (general strike). The only insurrection was at Newport, Mon., where an armed body was easily dispersed (Nov.). Leaders were imprisoned throughout the country and only continued economic depression kept C. in being. In 1840 the National Charter Association was formed and quickly became controlled by O'Connor who organized a second petition to Parliament (May 1842); its rejection was followed by strikes and riots inspired more by physical distress than by C. From this moment the movement declined. Lovett became interested in education, Attwood in currency reform, O'Connor in land settlement. During 1842–6 the Anti-CORN LAW League, led by merchants and manufacturers who were the economic enemies of the Chartists, outrivalled C. in anti-government agitation. A recurrence of C. in 1848, the background to which was revolutionary spirit abroad and another economic crisis at home, led to a mass demonstration on Kennington Common (10 Apr.) and to the presentation of the third petition. This was the end of C. as a movement of national importance, though it continued in name for a further 10 years. MLH

Château Gaillard, a castle at Andeli in the Seine valley, built by Richard I to block the French advance towards ROUEN after the treaty of LOUVIERS. Constructed at great expense under Richard's personal supervision, the castle was as strong as contemporary military science could make it. After the treaty of LE GOULET, C.G. was a small enclave in French territory. When Philip II launched his final attack on NORMANDY, C.G., defended by Roger de Lacy, was one of the few fortresses to make a resolute resistance. It fell after a siege lasting from Sept. 1203 to March 1204. RFW

Cheshire archers, famous from the time of Edward I. Cheshire had a strong connexion with kings and their eldest sons as earls of Chester, and a royal bodyguard was recruited from there at least as early as 1334. Richard II from 1395 created a small standing army of his own retainers, of which his C. a. formed part. These wore the famous badge of the white hart. After Richard's DEPOSITION some of the C. a. took part in the rebellions against Henry IV.   RFW

Chester, battle of, fought sometime in the years 613–16, was a decisive victory of the NORTHUMBRIANS under king Æthelfrith over the Britons under Solomon king of Powys. Before the battle the Northumbrians slaughtered a large number of monks from the monastery of Bangor Is-coed who had come to pray for British success. This victory was the final step in their advance towards the Irish sea, thereby driving a wedge between the Britons of STRATHCLYDE and those of WALES, which was made permanent by the battle of WINWAED (654).   CFS

Chesterfield, battle of (15 May 1266), the last pitched battle in the BARONS' WARS. The MONTFORTIANS under the earl of Derby were routed by the royalists under Henry III's nephew Henry of Almain. Derby was captured, but others escaped to continue their resistance with the DISINHERITED garrisons in KENILWORTH and the Isle of ELY.   RFW

Chiltern Hundreds. As a result of the Succession to the Crown Act (1707) and subsequent PLACE ACTS, the holding of most non-political offices of profit under the crown involved disqualification of members of the House of Commons without the opportunity of re-election. Thus from about 1750 application for the office of steward of the C.H. of Stoke, Desborough and Burnham (whose original function was to suppress robbers in the thickly wooded Chiltern Hills) came to be used as the means of resignation since members cannot directly resign their seats. Other stewardships were similarly used, e.g. Old Shoreham, East Hendred, Hempholme, Poynings, Northstead. The stewardship of the C.H. and the Manor of Northstead (Yorks) were preserved for this purpose by the House of Commons Disqualification Act (1957); their gift lies with the Chancellor of the Exchequer.   IHE

Chinon, truce of (18 Sept. 1214), brought hostilities between King John and Philip II of France to an end, after the decisive French victory at BOUVINES. The truce was renewed after the wars of 1224, 1230 and 1242 (SAINTES) and was not replaced by a definitive peace until the treaty of PARIS, 1259.   RFW

Christmas Island (1), south of Java, was annexed by Great Britain on 6 June 1888, placed under the administration of the STRAITS SETTLEMENTS in 1889, incorporated with SINGAPORE in 1900 and transferred to AUSTRALIA on 1 Oct. 1958.

(2), the largest atoll in the Pacific, was discovered by Cook in 1777, annexed by Great Britain in 1888 and included in the GILBERT AND ELLICE ISLANDS colony in 1919.   SHS

Chronology, see CALENDAR; EASTER; EASTER TABLES; REGNAL YEAR.

Church Assembly, or National Assembly of the Church of England, was established in 1919. It consisted of a House of Bishops, a House of Clergy composed of the members of the 2 Lower Houses of Convocation, and a House of Laity elected 5-yearly by representatives of Diocesan Conferences. The C.A.'s chief function was to prepare measures to be laid before Parliament; on a 'resolution passing both Houses of Parliament, a measure had the force of an Act of Parliament. It was renamed and reconstituted as the General Synod in 1970.   MLH

Church Commissioners. Ecclesiastical Commissioners were first appointed in 1836 to manage the civil affairs of the Church of England, superseding, in 1856, the Church Building Commissioners established in 1818 for building the 'Waterloo' and other new churches. In certain of the commissioners, Church Estate Commissioners, were vested the lands, etc., of ecclesiastical corporations as they fell vacant after 1860: they returned sufficient to produce a pre-determined sum for the corporation's expenses, retaining the remainder for general church purposes, e.g. augmentation of benefices. In 1948 the Commissioners, with modified powers and united with those of QUEEN ANNE'S BOUNTY, were renamed the C.C.   PMB

Church of England, severed its connexion with the Church of Rome by the Henrician REFORMATION, but there were few doctrinal changes until the Edwardian REFORMATION. The MARIAN REACTION temporarily restored papal authority until the ELIZABETHAN SETTLEMENT. The opposition of Roman CATHOLICS, separatists and of those seeking to establish PRESBYTERIANISM from within was met by PENAL LAWS and the activities of the HIGH COMMISSION. After the HAMPTON COURT CONFERENCE (1604) the PURITANS acquired growing political importance, while ARMINIANS gained control of the C. of E. under Charles I. Suppressed as a result of the CIVIL WARS, it was re-established at the RESTORATION, and Presbyterianism failed to secure comprehension at the SAVOY CONFERENCE (1661). The CLARENDON CODE and TEST ACTS secured its religious, social and political dominance, and its resistance to James II's attempts to further Roman Catholicism helped to bring about the GLORIOUS REVOLUTION (see SEVEN BISHOPS). The Whig ascendancy after the HANOVERIAN SUCCESSION encouraged ERASTIANISM and the LATITUDINARIANS at the expense of C. of E. Tories. Religious decline in the 18th century was arrested by the METHODISTS and EVANGELICALS, who were largely responsible for the growth of the MISSIONARY SOCIETIES. In the 19th century further stimulus came from the OXFORD MOVEMENT, although it led to bitter controversy with the Evangelicals and in 1874 to an Erastian Public Worship Regulation Act to check ritualism. The ancient abuse of NON-RESIDENCE was dealt with in 1836, Convocation (suspended after the BANGORIAN CONTRO-VERSY) was revived by 1861 and a national CHURCH ASSEMBLY established in 1919. The C. of E. played a full part in the development of education with its SUNDAY SCHOOLS and National Society (1811) and in other humanitarian activities. Attempts to secure revision of the BOOK OF COMMON PRAYER were defeated by Parliament in 1927 and 1928.   IHE

Church of Ireland became Protestant consequent upon the Henrician and Edwardian REFORMATIONS and the ELIZABETHAN SETTLEMENT, but the vast majority of the Irish remained Roman CATHOLIC, although in the 17th century PRESBYTERIANISM became dominant in Ulster. Largely the church of an upper class minority, it steadily declined, and NON-RESIDENCE and other abuses became widespread. The number of bishops was reduced in 1833, and it was disestablished and largely disendowed in 1869.   IHE

Church of Scotland became Presbyterian as a result of the Scottish REFORMATION, but James I cautiously restored EPISCOPACY from 1599, and this was ratified by the Scottish Parliament in 1612. In 1618, supported by bishops and nobles, he secured the General Assembly's acceptance of the FIVE ARTICLES OF PERTH. Charles I's introduction of an Anglican–type prayer book led to the National COVENANT of 1638 and the rejection of episcopacy. In 1643 the Covenanters effected the SOLEMN LEAGUE AND COVENANT with the LONG PARLIAMENT and through the WESTMINSTER ASSEMBLY aimed at enforcing PRESBYTERIANISM throughout Britain. Episcopacy was re-introduced (1661) by Charles II, and the resentful Covenanters were later defeated at BOTHWELL BRIDGE (1679). Presbyterianism was finally re-established (1690) after the GLORIOUS REVOLUTION of 1688, the dissentients forming the Episcopal C. of S. The C. of S. was weakened by secessions, largely over questions of church patronage, in 1733 and 1761 and in 1843 when nearly one-third of its members left to form the Free C. of S. Patronage was abolished in 1874, and in 1900 the secessionist groups formed the United Free C. of S., which apart from irreconcilables joined the C. of S. in 1929.

IHE

Church of Wales, see WELSH DISESTABLISHMENT.

Church Scot, originally known as food-rent, and the main source of income for parish priests in the earlier post-CONVERSION period. It was paid to the original PARISH churches, the old MINSTERS, and arrangements had to be made for payment to priests of churches built later. It was a payment of grain and hens levied on all free men in proportion to their holdings. Its incidence varied, but it was generally a heavy burden on the peasantry. It continued after the development of TITHE, becoming eventually a modest payment of hens and eggs.

CFS

Cinque Ports. From late Anglo-Saxon times certain south-eastern ports were granted the profits of justice in their courts in return for providing ships for the king's service, and by 1100 the chief ports of Kent and Sussex performing ship service were known collectively as the C.P. Hastings—which later claimed to be the premier port—Romney, Hythe, Dover and Sandwich were the original five. The service owed in the 13th century was 57 ships, each with a crew of 21, for 15 days in the year, or for longer periods at the king's expense. Each head port had lesser ports as its 'members' or 'limbs', contributing to its service and sharing its liberties. There were 24 members by the end of the 13th century, and 32 in the mid-16th—from Seaford in Sussex to Brightlingsea, the only Essex member. Winchelsea and Rye, members of Hastings, outstripped their head in importance and by 1224 were called the 'nobler members': in the 14th century, under the title of 'ancient towns', they were regarded in practice as head ports. The members were either 'corporate', with their own municipal government and liberties, or 'non-

corporate', governed by their own head port. While the liberties enjoyed by the ports were not exceptional, they formed a confederation of towns, with common duties and privileges, unique in England.

The title of 'Barons of the C.P' for the burgesses may first have arisen in connexion with their coronation service of holding a canopy over the monarch, performed at Richard I's coronation and perhaps earlier. With the loss of NORMANDY the ports became vital for the defence of the realm. Although they performed useful service to the crown, their seamen won their reputation as ruthless fighters as much at the expense of their fellow countrymen as of foreign enemies. Their indiscriminate piracy and their private wars with other English ports—notably Yarmouth—frequently hindered the naval operations of the crown. From 1268 onwards the king appointed a warden of the C.P. who combined his office with that of constable of Dover castle. The warden became president of Shepway, the royal court common to the ports established by 1150, held near Hythe; it became the court of appeal from the ports' individual courts and the only external court to which portsmen could normally be summoned. In the 14th century Shepway lost much of its business to the warden's court held in St James' church, Dover, which developed as a court of equity for the ports. By the 15th century the warden had acquired admiralty jurisdiction over the ports and neighbouring seas to the exclusion of the Lord High ADMIRAL. The title of lord warden survives as an honorary office.

The decline of the C.P. was partly due to natural causes, erosion at Hastings and Old Winchelsea (finally destroyed in the great storm of 1287), silting-up of harbours, the withdrawal of the sea at Romney, Hythe and Sandwich, and Edward I's foundation of New Winchelsea. Dover harbour has only been kept open by a long series of engineering works. Other south-coast ports grew in comparative importance—Southampton, for example, eventually replacing Sandwich as the port of call of Italian vessels. During the HUNDRED YEARS' WAR the king came to place more reliance on other ports for the larger fleets, while the larger ships needed larger crews than the 21 men of the ancient service. From the early 14th century the C.P. provided fewer ships, but with the same total number of men. To the fleet which opposed the Spanish ARMADA of 1588 the C.P. contributed only 5 ships and a pinnace. The C.P. surrendered their charters in 1685 and lost their remaining privileges by the REFORM ACT of 1832 and the Municipal Corporation Act of 1835.   RFW

Circulating Schools, founded c. 1734 by Griffith Jones, vicar of Llanddowror (1683–1761), they carried forward with extraordinary success the work of the WELSH TRUST and the S.P.C.K. in Wales. Impelled by religious motives and aiming only at teaching as many as possible to read, Jones sent an itinerant teacher to a parish for about three months, usually in the slack winter season. His genius for organizing and raising charitable support enabled him to arrange 3,324 classes between 1737 and 1761, through which 153,835 registered child-pupils, together with many unregistered adults, passed. His work was continued after 1761 by his associate Bridget Bevan (d. 1779).   GW

Circumspecte agatis (June 1286), a royal WRIT, directing the justices to 'deal circumspectly' with the bishop of Norwich and his clergy, and to allow them to hear certain pleas, e.g. tithe disputes up to a certain value, moral offences, and cases of defamation of the clergy where a money penalty was not involved. C.A. was Edward I's concession to complaints voiced by the clergy in the Westminster Parliament of 1285 against the royal courts dealing with matters proper to the ecclesiastical courts, and to specific complaints against the itinerant judges who in 1286 had proceeded against ecclesiastical judges in the diocese of Norwich. The writ made a much-

needed definition of the sphere of jurisdiction of the church courts, was taken as a general ruling, and was soon regarded as a statute.   RFW

Civil Aviation, Ministry of, see TRANSPORT.

Civil List, the annual payment to the crown (fixed at £475,000 in 1952) for royal expenditure from the CONSOLIDATED FUND. The names derives from the fact that the salaries of judges, civil servants, etc., were charged upon it until 1831, giving the crown a fruitful source of political PATRONAGE. It originated from a Parliamentary grant made to William III (1698) to supplement the remaining hereditary revenues for personal and governmental expenses, excluding naval and military, and became known as the C.L. early in the 18th century. It was modified from time to time, as the crown was frequently in debt, and in 1760 George III surrendered most of the hereditary revenues in return for a fixed annual payment (see CROWN ESTATE COMMISSIONERS). Debt remained a constant problem until 1831, when the last governmental expenses were removed from the C.L.   IHE

Civil Service Department. The home civil service, recruited in the medieval period from clerks in minor orders and then from laymen, pruned of many archaic offices in the late 18th and early 19th centuries, was in the grip of patronage when in 1853 Sir Stafford Northcote and Sir Charles Trevelyan proposed recruitment by open competition and promotion by merit, recently introduced into the Indian service by Lord Macaulay. Although their recommendations were ill-received, a C.S. Commission was first appointed in 1855 to examine candidates. Candidates and standards were, however, put forward by departments until 1870, when PATRONAGE was abolished by the introduction of open competition. Since then the C. has been responsible for testing candidates' qualifications for most posts, a few, e.g. crown appointments, inspectors of schools etc., excepted.

Pay and conditions of service were, however, a TREASURY responsibility until 1 Nov. 1968 when a C.S.D., under the PRIME MINISTER as Minister for the C.S., was established to have responsibility for the pay and management of the c.s. The C.S. Commission also passed under the new D., subject to arrangements designed to ensure continuing independence and political impartiality in recruitment to the c.s.

PMB; MR

Civil Wars (1642–8) resulted from the constant friction between crown and Parliament since the reign of James I over their respective prerogative and privileges. The king was supported by upholders of Anglican EPISCOPACY and opposed by Presbyterians and sectaries and groups of social reformers. Parliament was strong in the south and east, and largely supported by the mercantile classes and townsfolk. After the attempt on the FIVE MEMBERS and the king's rejection of the NINETEEN PROPOSITIONS the first civil war (1642–6) began. The king's objective was to enter London. The first battle at EDGEHILL (1642) was indecisive, but the campaigns of 1643 left the royalists successful in Yorkshire and the West. Parliament's forces were strengthened by the formation of the EASTERN ASSOCIATION (1642), and the SOLEMN LEAGUE AND COVENANT (1643) paved the way for their victory at MARSTON MOOR (1644) which gave them control of the North. Royalist success in the West and the surrender at LOSTWITHIEL (1644) allowed Charles to march on London, but he was checked at the second battle of NEWBURY. The failure of the UXBRIDGE NEGOTIATIONS and the formation of the NEW MODEL ARMY led to the defeat of the royalist cause at NASEBY (1645), and Charles surrendered to the Scots at Newark (1646). Refusing to take the COVENANT, he was handed over to Parliament (Jan. 1647) and then seized by the army. Rejecting their HEADS OF THE PROPOSALS, he escaped to the Isle of Wight and made the ENGAGEMENT with the Scots. The second civil war

resulted (1648) and consisted of royalist risings in Wales, Kent and Essex, and a Scottish invasion which was defeated by Cromwell at Preston. (CHALGROVE, CROPREDY BRIDGE, ADWALTON MOOR, LANGPORT, PHILIPHAUGH).

IHE

Civitas (Latin, citizens as a corporate body, the state), in ROMAN BRITAIN gained the meaning of a tribal group organized as a corporate entity for purposes of local government. The basis was pre-Roman tribal organization, but many smaller tribes lost their separate identity, and there were a few artificial groupings. Each c. covered a defined territory; possessed a capital town where the tribal aristocracy provided annual magistrates and something resembling a senate; and was responsible for its own taxation and local administration. They were capable of concerted action as in A.D. 410 and 446, when they appealed to Rome for help. They disappeared during the period of the TEUTONIC CONQUEST, although there is a rough correlation in the east between their areas and those of later Teutonic kingdoms that may be more than the result of geography. The civitates identified are: ATREBATES; BELGAE; BRIGANTES; CATUVELLAUNI; CANTIACI; CORITANI; CORNOVII; DOBUNI; DUMNONII; DUROTRIGES; ICENI; PARISI; REGNENSES; SILURES. Tribes not known to form civitates are: DEGEANGLI; DEMETAE; ORDOVICES; TRINOVANTES.

CFS

Clacton-on-Sea, Essex, has the type site that since 1929 has given its name to the earliest known stoneworking industry in Britain, the Clactonian, which flourished in the lower PALAEOLITHIC. Its main products were heavy flakes and the corresponding cores.

CFS

Claim of Rights, see DECLARATION OF RIGHTS.

Clapham Sect (c. 1785–c. 1830), a small group of influential EVANGELICALS within the CHURCH OF ENGLAND, most of whom lived in Clapham; 'sect' is a misnomer popularized by

Sir J. Stephen. Besides their faith, they had in common social position, wealth, intellect and a sense of moral responsibility. Among members of the C.S. were William Wilberforce, Henry Thornton, Granville Sharp, Zachary Macaulay, John Shore (Lord Teignmouth), James Stephen, Charles Grant and John Venn. Their share in the restriction of SLAVERY was perhaps their greatest achievement; they were also active in the colonization of SIERRA LEONE, the foundation of the Church MISSIONARY SOCIETY (1799), the opening of India to missionary activity (1813) and various projects for improving the moral and physical conditions, but not the political status, of the lower classes in this country.

MLH

Clarendon, Assize of (early 1166), is specially notable for its extension of the use of the jury of presentment. Hundred-juries of 12 men, and township-juries of 4 were to declare what men were robbers, murderers or thieves or were receivers of these criminals. The sheriffs were to arrest the accused and imprison them until they could be brought for trial before the king's justices. Trial was to be by ORDEAL, and mutilation and banishment were to be the penalties. Notorious criminals, however, were to be banished even if they succeeded at the ordeal. The assize was imitated by William I of Scots, and was developed by the assize of NORTHAMPTON (1176).

RFW

Clarendon, Constitutions of (30 Jan. 1164), laid down by Henry II at a council held at C. (Wilts.), purported to represent established customs governing the relations of church and state, but in fact incorporated some new regulations. Cases concerning debts, ADVOWSONS and lay fees were reserved to the secular courts, which should also determine whether disputed lands were lay fees or lands held in free alms (UTRUM). Appeals to Rome might not be made and clergy might not leave the realm without the king's consent. Restrictions were laid on the imposition of excommunication and interdict on the king's tenants-in-chief and his officers. Ecclesiastical tenants-in-chief were to act as judges in the king's court, save in judgments involving the shedding of blood; the king was to enjoy the revenues of vacant sees and abbacies; the election of prelates was to be conducted with the king's assent at the king's court, and those elected were to do HOMAGE and swear FEALTY to the king before their consecration. A procedure for dealing with CRIMINOUS CLERKS met strong clerical opposition. At first the bishops, led by Thomas Becket, refused to agree to the C. but gave way when their leader did so—an action he bitterly regretted later. The majority of the C. were condemned by pope Alexander III, but few of them were withdrawn by Henry II after his reconciliation with the church at AVRANCHES.

RFW

Clarendon Code. The failure of the CONVENTION PARLIAMENT (1660–1) and of the SAVOY CONFERENCE (1661–2) to settle the religious problems of the RESTORATION on a basis of comprehension or toleration led to the CAVALIER PARLIAMENT passing this 'code' of four acts named after the king's minister Clarendon (although he was not their instigator). The CORPORATION ACT (1661) was primarily political, and the Act of UNIFORMITY (1662) drove out Presbyterians and CONGREGATIONALISTS from church benefices. Venner's rising and other conspiracies led to the CONVENTICLE ACT (1664), which was defined and supplemented by the FIVE MILE ACT (1665). The religious persecution was less important than the social, cultural and political divisions created between 'church' and 'chapel'. Dissent, though lawful and strengthened in isolated areas, was weakened, and the English Presbyterians dwindled away (UNITARIANS). Some relief came with the royal use of the DISPENSING and SUSPENDING POWERS, but the first permanent relief to NONCONFORMISTS came from the TOLERATION ACT (1689).

IHE

Classes, Act of (1649), was passed by the Scottish Estates to exclude four classes of men from all public offices and military commands—enemies of the COVENANT, MALIGNANTS, those who had entered into the ENGAGEMENT with Charles I, and immoral persons. After the coronation of Charles II at Scone (1 Jan. 1651) the act was repealed and the authority of the strict Covenanters, the REMONSTRANTS, was broken. IHE

Clayton–Bulwer Treaty, was signed (19 Apr. 1850) by J. M. Clayton, U.S. secretary of state, and Sir H. Bulwer, British ambassador in Washington. It guaranteed the neutrality of any canal or 'other practicable communications' between Atlantic and Pacific. Neither party would assume dominion over any part of Central America; provision was made for fixing the frontier between BRITISH HONDURAS and Guatemala. Britain subsequently renounced her settlement in the BAY ISLANDS and the protectorate over the MOSQUITO COAST. The C.–B.T. was superseded by the HAY–PAUNCEFOTE TREATY (1901). MLH

Clericis Laicos (Feb. 1296), Pope Boniface VIII's bull ('laymen are notoriously hostile to the clergy') forbidding the clergy to grant taxes without papal consent, on pain of excommunication. It may have been published by Archbishop Winchelsey during the parliament at Bury St Edmunds in Nov. 1296. The refusal of the English clergy to grant a tax to Edward I was answered on 30 Jan. 1297 by the 'outlawry of the clergy', if they did not pay the fifth on MOVABLES asked for at Bury. Winchelsey's opposition was resolute—though the clergy were divided—but the situation was eased by the pope's grant to Philip IV of France of the right to tax his clergy in an emergency (*Etsi de Statu*, July 1297) and the Scots' victory at STIRLING BRIDGE. The English clergy finally granted a subsidy—to be used only against the Scots—and Edward abandoned his attempt to tax them without papal consent. RFW

Close Rolls, CHANCERY enrolments of royal letters close, i.e. letters of transitory importance closed with the GREAT SEAL, the first roll dating from 1204–5. Early C.R. cover most government business, but their scope gradually narrowed as new series of rolls for special documents were devised. From the late 14th century private deeds were copied on to the dorse of the C.R., and from 1533 such deeds, enclosure awards, deeds poll, etc., form the sole contents of the rolls. The series ended in 1903, to be replaced by the ENROLMENT books of the Supreme Court of Judicature. PMB

Cloth Industry, see WOOLLEN INDUSTRY.

Clubmen, bands of country folk formed in 1645 in the southern and western counties to protect themselves against the exactions of both Cavaliers and ROUNDHEADS. IHE

Cniht (Old English: servant) was a retainer of some greater man, attached to his household and performed military and administrative duties. The GILDS of *cnihtas* in certain towns probably owed their origin to associations of those *cnihtas* who were responsible for their lords' town houses. The word was applied by the English to the followers of their Norman conquerors (KNIGHT). CFS

Coburg, German duchy in southern Thuringia, from 1572 to 1918 ruled by a branch of the house of Wettin, which in the 19th century supplied sovereigns to Belgium (Leopold I, 1831; in 1816–17 consort of Charlotte, heir presumptive to George IV), Portugal (Ferdinand, 1836 consort of Queen Maria; monarchy abolished in 1910), Great Britain (Albert, 1840 consort of Queen Victoria; family name changed to WINDSOR in 1917) and Bulgaria (Ferdinand, 1887; monarchy abolished in 1946). SHS

Cocos or **Keeling Islands,** discovered by Capt. William Keeling of the East India Company in 1609, were first settled in 1826 and, from *c.* 1830, by Malays under the Scottish adventurer John Clunies Ross, to whom in 1886 all land was granted in perpetuity. The C.I. were annexed to the crown in 1857, transferred to CEYLON in 1878, to the STRAITS SETTLEMENTS in 1882, to SINGAPORE in 1903 (to Ceylon, 1942–6) and to the Commonwealth of AUSTRALIA on 23 Nov. 1955.   SHS

Coif, see SERGEANTS-AT-LAW.

Coinage, see ANGEL, CROWN, DOLLAR, FARTHING, FLORIN, GOLD PENNY, GROAT, GUINEA, HALFPENNY, MARK, MINT, NOBLE, ORA, PENNY, POUND, ROYAL, SHILLING, UNITE.

Colenso Controversy, arose from the publication by J. W. Colenso, first bishop of Natal, of commentaries on *Romans* (1861) and the *Pentateuch and Joshua* (1862–3); the former questioned the accepted meaning of the atonement; the latter disputed both the authorship and veracity of the books. Orthodox opinion, already disquieted by Darwin's *Origin of Species* (1859) and *Essays and Reviews* (1860), reacted violently. 41 bishops asked C. to resign (Feb. 1863) and he was deposed by Robert Gray, bishop of Cape Town (Dec.). C. appealed to the Privy Council which pronounced invalid Gray's letters patent (Mar. 1865); but Gray excommunicated C. (Dec.) and consecrated W. K. Macrorie as rival 'bishop of Maritzburg' (Jan. 1869). But C. was able by legal action to maintain his position in which he remained a champion of native rights until his death (June 1883). Schism was virtually healed when Archbishop Benson of Canterbury consecrated his domestic chaplain, A. H. Baynes, bishop of Natal (Sept. 1893). The constitutional issue decided in Colenso v. Gray was important in shaping the relationship of the Church of England to Anglican churches in the self-governing colonies.   MLH

College of Arms. Heralds, employed as announcers of, and criers and marshals at, tournaments, are first mentioned in the late 12th century.

In their employment they acquired detailed knowledge of the heraldic devices borne, from the early 12th century onwards, by the combatants, a knowledge subsequently extended to the design and authentication of such devices. Some heralds were private retainers, others itinerant: the royal heralds were the foremost, the chief among them the 'kings of arms', with special control over sections of the king's domains, e.g. Norroy over northern England. Apart from their duties at tournaments and ceremonies, the king's heralds acted as envoys and lent their technical knowledge to the CONSTABLE and MARSHAL in the court of chivalry on heraldic matters. First incorporated in 1484, the C.'s present charter and the site of its building in Queen Victoria St. in the City of London, date from 1555.

From 1417 onwards the kings granted patents of arms: later visitations, to register and check claimants to arms were instituted, involving the heralds in genealogical research, some worthless, some accurate. The heralds were at their busiest in the 16th and 17th centuries; thereafter the C. declined to its modern business of attending ceremonies and issuing patents of arms.

The earl marshal is head of the present C. Of the kings, Garter principal king was created in 1417 and attached to the order of the GARTER without regional responsibility; Norroy king north of the Trent may date from 1277, and his title is now joined to Ulster created by Edward IV; Clarenceux, the southern king, was created c. 1417 to honour the duke of Clarence, a reformer of the heralds. The 6 heralds' titles commemorate favourite royal children's titles or royal residences: Windsor, Chester, York and Lancaster were created by Edward III, Richmond by Edward IV, Somerset by Henry VIII. The pursuivants, followers and junior officers, recall royal emblems: Rouge Croix the red cross of St George; Blue Mantle the blue field of the French arms quartered with England by Edward III; Rouge Dragon the Welsh emblem and supporter of the Tudor arms; Portcullis the Tudor badge.

In Scotland Lyon herald first appears in the late 14th century, later becoming a king of arms appointed by letters patent. No c. for Scotland exists: instead the Lord Lyon is assisted by 3 heralds, Rothesay, Albany and Marchmont, and 3 pursuivants, Unicorn, Kintyre and Carrick, whom he appoints. As in England attempts to register arms by visitations were made; from 1672 however all arms claimed in Scotland have, by statute, to be entered in the register of the Lyon office.   PMB

Colombo Plan for co-operative economic development in south and south-east Asia, was published (Nov. 1950) after consultation between Commonwealth countries: Australia, Canada, Ceylon, India, New Zealand, Pakistan and the U.K., with Malaya, Singapore, North Borneo and Sarawak (MALAYSIA). By 1968 membership also included Afghanistan, Bhutan, Burma, Cambodia, Indonesia, Iran, Japan, Korea, Laos, Maldive Islands, Nepal, Philippines, Singapore, Thailand, U.S.A. and Vietnam. The U.K. contributed (1950–67) £500m. by loans, grants etc.; British private investment was considerably larger. The U.K. also trained technologists and provided experts to assist specific projects.   MLH

Coloni, semi-free peasants who worked the land of VILLAS in later ROMAN BRITAIN.   CFS

Colonia, an urban settlement of time-expired Roman soldiers. They were Roman citizens, lived in the town but held agricultural land outside and possessed a considerable degree of self-government in local affairs. Surrounding land was 'attributed' to it. In later ROMAN BRITAIN a c. and its territory seem to have differed little from a CIVITAS, especially as the British element there steadily increased. Britain had four *coloniae*: Camulodunum (Colchester); Eburacum (York); Glevum (Gloucester); Lindum (Lincoln).   CFS

Colonial Office. From 1634 special commissions on colonies were issued, but the ˌCOUNCILS OF TRADE AND PLANTATIÒNS (1672–5 and 1695–1781) formed the nucleus of the modern office. A special SECRETARY OF STATE for Colonies was appointed 1768–82, but his duties were thereafter discharged first by the home department and then, from 1801 onwards, jointly with the war department. The C.O. finally achieved independence in 1854, administering all aspects of government in the expanding empire. With the extension of self-government in modern times its work contracted and in 1966 it merged with the Commonwealth Relations Office to form the COMMONWEALTH OFFICE.   PMB; MR

Combination Acts (1799, 1800), part of the repressive legislation which followed the naval mutinies and the IRISH REBELLION, illegalized TRADE UNIONS and other forms of industrial combination by reinforcing the existing common law of conspiracy in order to impede political agitation. Not used against employers, its application to the embryonic unions varied according to trade and locality. The C.A., 1800, was repealed in 1824; an amendment act (1825) was restrictive but did not reimpose criminality of combination for advancement of wages or alteration of hours of work.   MLH

Comitatus, the term used by Tacitus (1st century A.D.) to describe the bodyguard of a Germanic chief, and adopted into modern historical usage. This bodyguard consisted of chosen men of good birth or reputation who, coming from any part of the Teutonic world, attached themselves to the leader of their choice. They were expected to serve their chief with unswerving loyalty, and he in return was expected to reward them generously. These men formed the leading element in a chief's warband during the period of the TEUTONIC CONQUEST, and are found as late as the end of the 10th century (MALDON). The Old English term for an individual of this body was GESITH, who would likewise have his own band of sworn companions.   CFS

Commission—an instrument delegating part or all of the grantor's powers to specified persons, the commissioners. Royal c.s under the GREAT SEAL may be special, for distinctly defined purposes, e.g. judicial inquiry, HISTORICAL MANUSCRIPTS C., etc., or general, e.g. for a regency during the absence or disability of the sovereign.   PMB

Committee of Both Kingdoms was established (16 Feb. 1644), after the SOLEMN LEAGUE AND COVENANT, to carry on joint military operations. It consisted of 7 English peers, 14 M.P.s and 4 Scottish commissioners. Their report on the parliamentary armies led to the creation of the NEW MODEL ARMY (1645). Its powers were taken over by the DERBY HOUSE COMMITTEE (Jan. 1648).   IHE

Common Land, waste land, roadside strips etc., within a manor upon which all tenants of arable land have the right to pasture their beasts. With growth of population and in times of great agricultural activity, commons were encroached on and inclosed. Such encroachments, with safeguards, were allowed by the statute of MERTON 1236 and subsequent legislation; nevertheless, in the great eras of IN-CLOSURE the commons were strongly defended and some survive, though shrunken in extent.   PMB

Common Law, the unwritten custom of the king's courts, other than those of EQUITY. These courts, fusing parts of Anglo-Saxon and feudal law, deferring to local custom, produced a body of law pre-occupied, in its early stages, with land. Forms of action devised for land were adopted for legal fictions, adapted and amplified, with some influence from criminal law, to suit other types of case. C.l. has on occasion been amended or improved by statutes, themselves becoming part of it; it has been influenced by civil and canon law, mitigated by equity and, under Lord Mansfield, it embraced the custom of merchants. The use of precedent developed as the law grew more rigid and exclusive. In early stages certain procedures led to foreseeable results, and, as for convenience one judge followed another's decision, some custom developed; in the late 15th century precedent began to be accepted; in the 16th and 17th centuries local custom was rejected unless proved to the limit of legal memory (1189, fixed in 1275), but only in the 19th century was the full rigour of precedent and leading cases accepted. By then C.l., beginning as an alternative to feudal and other courts, providing a sound basis for good government, had become a check on the prerogative of the descendants of sovereigns who created it, and the guarantee of a subject's liberty. C.l was taken to colonies by the settlers but its unity with the continuing law of England was reiterated and safeguarded by Blackstone, giving a community of C.l. history and precedent within the Empire, Commonwealth and United States of America. See BRACTON; GLANVILL; JUDICATURE, SUPREME COURT OF; PROHIBITION, WRITS OF; SERJEANTS-AT-LAW; STATUTE; VILLEINS; WAGER OF LAW; WESTMINSTER, SECOND STATUTE OF; WILLS; WITNESS; YEAR BOOKS.   PMB

Common Pleas, Court of, arose from two main causes, firstly, the need to transact at least routine judicial business in the king's absence, secondly, the need to review decisions and judges' behaviour, complained of in 1178. The court seems to date from this period, and came to be known as *de Banco,* of the bench of judges, to distinguish it from KING'S BENCH. In the 13th century it dealt with routine and simpler cases, sitting, from MAGNA CARTA onwards, normally at Westminster. As the legal system developed and law and procedure became more complex, rivalry arose between King's Bench and C.P.: beginning in the late 14th century, with a brief unity in opposition to the EQUITY courts, this rivalry persisted until 1832, when the two courts' spheres, now vastly different from their inception, were exactly defined. The C. of C.P. survived the JUDICATURE Act 1873 as a division of the High Court, but in 1881 was united with its ancient rival in the Queen's Bench division.   PMB

Commons, House of, see PARLIAMENT.

Common Seal. The seal of a corporation in law, i.e. a self-perpetuating body such as a religious house or the governing body of a borough. C.s.s are one-sided, but are frequently counter-sealed by the heads of religious bodies or the mayors of boroughs, etc.   PMB

Commonwealth, a term sometimes used to cover the period between Charles I's execution and the RESTORATION but more specifically applied to the republic set up in 1649 until the establishment of the PROTECTORATE in 1653. After abolishing the House of Lords and the monarchy and establishing the COUNCIL OF STATE, the RUMP declared England a C. and Free State (19 May 1649). In danger from ROYALISTS and LEVELLERS alike, it became treasonable to print attacks on the C. A censorship was instituted, also a high court of justice, to try, without jury, cases of treason and mutiny in the army, and all men had to take an ENGAGEMENT of loyalty (1650). Its revenues were derived from taxation, sale of church and crown lands, and the victimization of royalists. Its navy drove Rupert's royalist fleet off the seas and established the republic's authority in the West Indian and American colonies (1650–2). The NAVIGATION ACT of 1651 led to war with the Dutch. The Army secured the survival of the C. by its ruthless suppression of the Irish (1649–52) and the defeat of the Scottish invasion at WORCESTER (1651). It then quarrelled with Parliament, which had become an irresponsible oligarchy. Cromwell dismissed the RUMP (Apr. 1653) and the new BAREBONES PARLIAMENT adopted the INSTRUMENT OF GOVERNMENT and

established the Protectorate (16 Dec. 1653).   IHE

Commonwealth (British), the association of independent nations, Associated States and dependencies sprang from units of the former British Empire. The independent members are: Great Britain, CANADA, AUSTRALIA, NEW ZEALAND, INDIA, PAKISTAN, CEYLON, GHANA, MALAYSIA, NIGERIA, CYPRUS, SIERRA LEONE, TANZANIA, JAMAICA, TRINIDAD and TOBAGO, UGANDA, KENYA, MALAWI, MALTA, ZAMBIA, THE GAMBIA, SINGAPORE, GUYANA, BOTSWANA, LESOTHO, BARBADOS, MAURITIUS and SWAZILAND.

In 1925 a Dominions Office was established to deal with the self-governing Dominions (Canada, Australia, New Zealand, South Africa), which were recognized at the Imperial Conference of 1926 as autonomous nations 'freely associated as members of the British Commonwealth of Nations', and their legal independence was underlined by the Statute of WESTMINSTER (1931). The Dominions Office duly gave way in 1947 to the C. Relations Office (FOREIGN AND C. OFFICE, 1968).

Since World War II most of the remaining countries administered by Britain gained independence, the first being India and Pakistan in 1947, and the C. became predominantly Afro-Asian. Burma left the C. in 1947, Eire in 1949 and the UNION OF SOUTH AFRICA in 1961. All members recognize the Queen as Head of the C.
                                            IHE

Commonwealth Office. Though CANADA became a Dominion in the mid-19th century and other Dominions followed, no Secretary of State for Dominion affairs was appointed until 1925, and until 1930 the office was held jointly with the Colonial Secretaryship. The title of the Secretary and his office was changed to C. Relations in 1947 and, with the growth of self-government, the office's business, partly inherited from the COLONIAL OFFICE, steadily increased, covering all relations between the United Kingdom and the Commonwealth countries and the Irish Republic. Both offices were placed under one secretary of state in 1962 and were united in a single C.O. in 1966. On 17 Oct. 1968 the C.O. merged with the Foreign Office to form the Foreign and C.O.   PMB; MR

Common Wealth Party, a socialist party formed (July 1942) and largely financed by Sir Richard Acland; its policy included nationalization of all land, banks, building societies etc. The C.W.P. owed its temporary importance to the wartime electoral truce observed by the other parties; in 1944 it had 3 M.P.s. At the 1945 election 23 candidates polled 110, 634 votes but only one was returned, who, with Acland and many others, soon joined the Labour Party.   MLH

Commote (Welsh *cwmwd*) came into existence as a subdivision of the CANTREF, in which the functions formerly exercised via the latter became centred. Each c. had its court of justice, its machinery and officials for the supervision of the unfree in *maerdrefi* (bond villages) and for the collection of tribal dues from bondmen and from free tribesmen in *gwestfas*. Each was sufficient unto itself for all civil relations and, within its bounds, a hereditary chief might maintain the status of a ruling prince. Such arrangements, detrimental though they were to centralized political authority, arose of necessity from the Welsh custom of partition of the inheritance among all the sons.   GW

Communist Party, see MARXIST PARTIES.

Compurgation, see WAGER OF LAW.

Confirmation of the Charters (*Confirmatio Cartarum*), 1297, Edward I's expedient in meeting the crisis caused by wars in Scotland, Wales and France, and English opposition to his military and financial demands. Opposition came to a head with the earl of Norfolk's refusal to serve in GASCONY and his condemnation of Edward's proposed Flemish expedition (Mar.

1297). Edward continued his preparations and imposed a new tax, not granted in Parliament. The earls of Norfolk and Hereford, in a declaration of grievances, denied liability for service overseas, condemned the king's financial exactions and alleged that MAGNA CARTA and the charter of the FOREST were being infringed. Before sailing for Flanders on 20 Aug. Edward promised to confirm the charters, and news of the Scottish victory at STIRLING BRIDGE (11 Sept.) underlined the need to restore unity. On 10 Oct. Edward, the king's eldest son, confirmed the charters and made additional undertakings; Edward I reissued the C. at Ghent on 5 Nov. The additional articles provided for the regular publication of Magna Carta and its observance; the MALETOLT was abolished, and extraordinary taxation was to be enacted only with the consent of the whole realm.   RFW

Congé d'Élire, a royal writ directed to a chapter to elect the person named therein to a vacant see. It was introduced by Parliament in 1533 and represents the end of the crown's successful struggle first with chapters and then with popes to control episcopal elections.   PMB

Congregationalists, independent separatists with a continuous history since the BROWNISTS and BARROWISTS of Elizabeth I's reign. Persecution sent many of them to Holland and NEW ENGLAND until the civil wars, when they became the main opponents of Presbyterian domination during the COMMONWEALTH. They secured full freedom under Cromwell until the Act of UNIFORMITY 1662, and they were freed from persecution by the TOLERATION ACT (1689). The Congregational Union formed in 1832 also strengthened the NONCONFORMISTS in their agitation against remaining disabilities.   IHE

Connaught, see IRELAND, CONQUEST OF; O'NEILL'S REVOLT; PLANTATION OF IRELAND.

Connecticut, a NEW ENGLAND colony developing from a number of settlements in the fertile C. valley. Before 1633 Dutch settled around Hartford, followed by English from PLYMOUTH (1633) and MASSACHUSETTS (1635–6). The latter established their own government in 1639 on a democratic basis and were joined (1644) by other PURITANS established at Saybrook (1635–6). Another group founded NEW HAVEN (1638), which was merged with C. by royal charter in 1662. C. and New Haven joined the New England Confederation in 1643. C. was temporarily absorbed in the Dominion of New England (1687–9), regaining its charter in 1691. Congregational church government was replaced by a Presbyterian system in 1708, when dissent was allowed. C. supported the campaign against the STAMP ACT (1765) and the AMERICAN REVOLUTION (1775). IHE

Conscience, Court of, see REQUESTS, COURT OF.

Conservative Party, as a description of the parliamentary groups known as the TORIES, was suggested by J. W. Croker (*Quarterly Review*, Jan. 1830) and generally adopted after the REFORM ACT (1832) when Peel realized that the Tories must bid for middle-class support by a reorientation of policy towards further moderate reform (TAMWORTH MANIFESTO, 1834). The C.P. was successful in the 1841 elections but having passed useful social and administrative measures, broke up on Peel's forcing the abolition of the CORN LAWS (1846)—the 'Peelites' later joining the LIBERAL PARTY.

During the next 20 years Disraeli reorganized the C.P. and it evolved a coherent philosophy. Disraeli was responsible for the second REFORM ACT (1867), and during his administration (1874–80, the first since 1841 in which the C.P. had a clear majority) important social legislation was passed. On Gladstone's declaring for HOME RULE (1886) the Liberal Unionists under Joseph Chamberlain allied with the C.P. From 1886 to 1905 the C.P. was almost continually in office under Salisbury and Balfour; ultimate defeat was aggravated by dissension over

Chamberlain's plans for IMPERIAL PREFERENCE. The C.P. recovered sufficiently to join the coalition of 1915–22. There followed another period of C. predominance under Bonar Law, Baldwin, Neville Chamberlain and Churchill which lasted (with the exception of the two intervals of LABOUR PARTY government) until 1945; the C.P. was the major partner in the two coalition governments (1931–5; 1940–5).

Churchill's wartime services could not outweigh a desire for change; the years after the severe defeat of 1945 were formative of a revitalized policy. The 1951 election gave the C.P. a majority of 17 in the House of Commons, increased to 58 in 1955, and to 100 in 1959. The C.P. were in office under Churchill (1951–5), Eden (1955–7), Macmillan (1957–63) and Douglas-Home (1963–4). After defeat in the 1964 election Home was replaced by Heath, chosen by a new procedure of ballot by the parliamentary party. The C.P. regained office in 1970.

Since 1886 the C.P. has also been called the Unionist Party, its official title (since 1909) being the C. and Unionist P.; 'Tory' is still used, in denigration or pride—or for short. MLH

Consolidated Fund, consists of the national revenue from all sources paid into the Exchequer account at the BANK OF ENGLAND, the main expenditure being the interest on and management costs of the NATIONAL DEBT. The CIVIL LIST is also met from the C.F. It dates from 1787 when the younger Pitt consolidated the customs and excise duties into a single fund and secured public liabilities upon it. IHE

Constable, the chief military officer of the royal household. Walter of Gloucester is the first identifiable c., in Henry I's reign. From his son, later earl of Hereford, the office passed to the Bohun earls of Hereford and Essex and thence to the dukes of Buckingham. Other lesser c.s mentioned in the 12th century were short-lived appointments, probably political expedients. Since Tudor times the Lord High Constable has been appointed by the sovereign for coronation day alone. The title c. has been widely used for lesser officers, e.g. commanders of castles, N.C.O.s in medieval armies, parish officers in Tudor times and in modern times for policemen.   PMB

Constance, Council of (1414–18), was attended by an English delegation, led by Robert Hallam, bishop of Salisbury, who took part in the deposition of pope John XXIII in 1415. The renewal of the HUNDRED YEARS' WAR made the English and French delegations take opposite sides, the English, along with the Germans, demanding that church reform should precede the election of a pope. After Hallam's death, however, and the arrival of Henry Beaufort, bishop of Winchester, in 1417, the English changed their plans, and their votes secured the election of Martin V. But the concordat negotiated between Martin and the English made poor provision for reform in England and was never effective, while Martin failed to change the English attitude towards papal PROVISIONS.   RFW

Constitucio Domus Regis, a list of pay and allowances for the CURIA REGIS, compiled c. 1136, ranging from the CHANCELLOR to the wolf-hunter and archers, and showing Henry I's household in all its various branches.   PMB

Continental System (1806–13), the name given to the economic warfare used by Napoleon against Britain after TRAFALGAR had destroyed hope of conquest by invasion; it involved the isolation of Britain from trade through all European ports under his control. In accordance with MERCANTILIST thought British goods had been theoretically banned at earlier stages of the FRENCH REVOLUTIONARY AND NAPOLEONIC WARS, but the C.S. was established in earnest when the North German ports were closed to British ships (1 Apr. 1806). There followed the treaty of Tilsit (7 July 1807) and a series of decrees of increasing severity (Berlin, 21 Nov. 1806; Warsaw, 25 Jan. 1807; Milan, 23 Nov., 17

Dec. 1807; Fontainebleau, 18, 25 Oct. 1810), aimed at crippling British trade and thus her ability to wage war by denying an outlet for her manufactured goods and colonial produce. Britain answered with a total of 24 orders-in-council imposing control and taxation on neutral trade with Europe. Napoleon found it necessary to annex Tuscany and the Papal States, Holland, Oldenburg and the Hanseatic republics; his invasions of Portugal and Spain were partly occasioned by his desire to stop British commerce with the Peninsula; and one of the reasons for his attack on Russia was that the tsar had opened ports to British goods. The issue of licences and large-scale evasion as well as increased exports to Spain, Portugal and South America in part offset the decline of traditional markets. Nevertheless the effect of the C.S. on Britain's economy was severe; 1808 was a difficult year, but a period of danger came in 1811 when the C.S. heightened an already serious economic and monetary crisis. The position would have been critical had not Napoleon allowed grain to be shipped to Britain, thus further draining her gold reserves but enabling her continuance of the war. The C.S. broke down (1812–3) on Napoleon's losing power in Europe.   MLH

Controller, an officer, originally subordinate to the head of a department, keeping a counter-roll, i.e. a duplicate record, of financial business for checking purposes. The title is now used for heads of departments, e.g. c.-general.   PMB

Conventicle Act (1) (1593), was directed against the Puritans. Those disputing the queen's ecclesiastical authority, abstaining from church, or attending religious conventicles were to be imprisoned until they conformed. Otherwise after three months they were to abjure the realm or be hanged on return. A similar act was passed against popish RECUSANTS.

(2) (1664), the third act of the CLARENDON CODE, largely designed to prevent the clergy ejected by the Act of

UNIFORMITY (1662) from forming their own congregations. It forbade conventicles of more than five persons (other than meetings for family worship), except in accordance with the BOOK OF COMMON PRAYER. Penalties were imposed by magistrates. It expired in 1667, but was renewed in 1670 with some reduction of penalties but wider in scope. It was repealed in 1812.   IHE

Convention Parliament. (1) (1660), was called after the final dissolution of the LONG PARLIAMENT. It approved the Declaration of BREDA and effected the RESTORATION of Charles II. It passed 37 bills, including an act legalizing its own existence, an Act of INDEMNITY AND OBLIVION and a NAVIGATION ACT. It provided a fixed revenue for the crown, restored alienated church and crown lands but left individual claims to land to the ordinary processes of law. The religious settlement was effected by the CAVALIER PARLIAMENT which confirmed the legislation of the C.P.

(2) (1689), was authorized by William of Orange and met on 22 Jan. The throne was declared vacant and offered to William and Mary together with the accompanying DECLARATION OF RIGHTS (12 Feb.). On their acceptance the C.P., as in 1660, legalized its existence. Its legislation, which was confirmed by the next Parliament (1690), included the MUTINY ACT, the Coronation Oath Act, the TOLERATION ACT and the BILL OF RIGHTS. Its enactment of new oaths of SUPREMACY and ALLEGIANCE led to the growth of the NON-JURORS.   IHE

Conversion of England from HEATHENISM occupied the first half of the 7th century, although the kingdom of SUSSEX was not converted for another generation and isolated heathen practices continued long after. It was accomplished basically by the ROMAN MISSION entering through KENT, and by the Scottish mission entering through NORTHUMBRIA. The success of the Roman mission was limited, probably due to the strength of heathenism and the lack of outstanding personalities. The archbishopric of Canterbury was set up, and bishops were established at Rochester and London, and in LINDSEY and Northumbria. But heathen reaction temporarily destroyed the work done in London and Northumbria, and even put Christianity in Kent on the defensive. Other representatives of Roman practices, although not members of the mission, set up bishoprics in EAST ANGLIA and WESSEX. The SCOTTISH CHURCH entered Northumbria, establishing its headquarters at LINDISFARNE, and quickly converted most of England north of the Thames. Its success was probably due to constant royal support, the weakness of heathenism in those parts and the evangelizing fervour of the missionaries. Differences between Roman and Scottish practices made it imperative that one or other should be recognized as standard. This was accomplished at the synod of WHITBY and during the years following.

The part played by lay rulers in the conversion is very important. Ethics of the time made leading men support the ideas of their superiors; and missions invariably entered kingdoms on royal invitation or with royal permission. In addition to Christianity, both the Scottish and, especially, the Roman churches brought higher standards of civilization and culture to England. The Scottish church came from Ireland, which had escaped devastation by Teutonic invaders, the Roman from the centre of civilization in the west. Of special importance are the Roman alphabet and the late Roman land deed, the forerunner of the CHARTER.   CFS

Convocation, see CHURCH ASSEMBLY.

Cooch Behar, a powerful kingdom under a Mongol dynasty in the 16th century, was incorporated in the Mogul empire in 1639 and remained one of the 42 feudatory states administered by the Eastern States Agency until its merger with West BENGAL on 1 Jan. 1950.   SHS

Cook Islands, discovered by Cook in 1777, were christianized by John Williams (1796–1839) of the London MISSIONARY SOCIETY, proclaimed a British protectorate in 1888 and attached to NEW ZEALAND on 11 June 1901.   SHS

Cooperative Movement, inspired by Robert Owen, was successfully established by the ROCHDALE PIONEERS (1844); among the many earlier societies was that at Brighton (1827–32) founded by William King. The 'Rochdale principles', in the favourable circumstances of the 1850s, were widely adopted, particularly in the North, and have remained the basis of consumers' cooperation. The Industrial and Provident Societies Act (1852), passed at the instance of the Christian Socialists, legalized the movement's position. An amendment (1862) allowed the formation of the (North of England) C. Wholesale Society (1863) and the Scottish C.W.S. (1867); their expansion was to parallel that of the affiliated retail societies, which by 1881 numbered 971 with a membership of 547,000. The C. Congress, which first met in 1869, instituted a C. Union; this guided the c.m. during its period of rapid growth and remains the coordinator of its non-trading activities. In 1967, 727 retail societies had 12·7m. members and sales were £1,048m. Producers' cooperation has not played an important part in the c.m.; there were (1967) 438 agricultural trading societies. Housing societies increased largely in the 1960s, in 1967 numbering 2,373, with assets of £118m. The C. Party was formed in 1917. It is closely allied to the LABOUR PARTY. Its parliamentary candidates (limited to 30 since 1959) have since 1946 been chosen jointly with the Labour Party. C. Party M.P.s numbered 9 in 1935, 23 in 1945 and 19 in 1966.   MLH

Coorg was placed under British protection on 7 May 1834 at 'the unanimous wish of the inhabitants' after the removal of its insane and tyrannic ruler. It was administered by the commissioner of MYSORE, but on 1 July 1940 became a separate chief commissionership and on 20 Jan. 1950 a 'C State'. On 1 Nov. 1956 C. was merged in Mysore.   SHS

Copenhagen, battle of (2 Apr. 1801), broke the ARMED NEUTRALITY, which would in any case have been weakened by the coincidental murder of tsar Paul. Nelson, as second to Adm. Sir Hyde Parker, sailed a detachment into a narrow channel before C. guarded by the anchored Danish fleet and shore batteries. After heavy fighting during which Nelson acknowledged but otherwise ignored Parker's signal to withdraw, the Danes agreed to a truce; this was followed by an armistice (9 Apr.). The Danes lost 17 first-line ships, taken or destroyed.   MLH

Copenhagen, bombardment of (2–5 Sept. 1807), led to the capture of the Danish fleet before it could fall into the hands of Napoleon, as provided by the secret clauses of the treaty of Tilsit. A British fleet landed 18,000 English and Hanoverian troops on Zealand (16–18 Aug.) and invested C., a relieving force being defeated by Wellesley (Wellington) at Kjöge (29 Aug.). A heavy bombardment of town by land and sea resulted in capitulation (7 Sept.); the Danes surrendered their fleet and war ensued, 1807–14.   MLH

Copyhold. After the BLACK DEATH and PEASANTS' REVOLT, VILLEIN tenements were gradually changed into c. tenements. The copyholder became more of a freeman, though not protected by law until the 17th century. He was subject to the steadily diminishing manorial customs, but had a written title to his land, a copy of the record of his admission on the manorial COURT ROLL. C. tenure was abolished in 1926.   PMB

Copyright developed with increasing use of PRINTING and the law of libel, originally subject to the PREROGATIVE and PREROGATIVE COURTS. From the 16th century printers were occasionally granted a monopoly of printing a work; their special interest came, by the 17th century, to be regarded as property, producing the idea of c. Its subsequent history lies in the definition of the period of protection and its extension to items other than printed books, the latest legislation, 1956 and 1958, giving greater protection to artists, musicians, correspondence, etc. From 1849 to 1912 the STATIONERS' COMPANY kept c. registers; other means of establishing c. include the use of the symbol ©.   PMB

Coritani, a British tribe occupying the eastern midlands. Conquered by the Romans before A.D. 47 they became a CIVITAS with their capital at Ratae (Leicester).   CFS

Cornage, a rent from pasture paid by free men, most common in northern England where beasts were grazed on the hills. In Cumberland the rent was called *notegeld*, neat (cattle) rent. PMB

Corn Laws. From 1360 laws regulating the export and import of wheat and other grains were passed periodically, according to the needs of the time. Rates of duties were fixed and Tudor legislation also sought to prevent 'engrossing' (buying for resale). An act of 1689 granted bounties on exportation. In 1796 bounties were given on imported corn and in 1814 corn exports were no longer to be subject to duty or bounty. After the FRENCH REVOLUTIONARY WARS the c.l. became a significant political factor, producing sharp clashes between different classes and interests. The act of 1815 aimed at keeping the price of corn at a level which would ensure a reasonable return for the landed classes; foreign wheat was prohibited until the home price reached 80s. a quarter (import of colonial wheat being allowed at 67s.). Such a rigid system proved ineffective. In 1828 therefore William Huskisson and Wellington introduced a sliding scale of import duties. Since the grievance was most marked in bad seasons, agitation for abolition of the c.l. tended to be seasonal also. The demand for repeal, evidenced in the 1820s and argued by the free-traders

on economic grounds, did not revive until the bad harvests of the late 1830s. In 1839 the Anti-Corn Law League was formed in Manchester. Well organized, it was essentially a middle class movement led by free-trade industrialists. Cobden and Bright turned it into a moral crusade against 'the bread-taxing oligarchy'. Its able leadership, middle class character and clear-cut purpose helped it to succeed where CHARTISM failed.

Meanwhile Peel, who led the Conservative government of 1841, had carried on the gradual movement towards free trade and an improved sliding scale was introduced in 1842. He became convinced that the agricultural interest which dominated his party, could not claim a special treatment detrimental to the interests of the country as a whole. His hand was forced by the bad harvest of 1845 and by the Irish famine. Failing to carry the cabinet, he resigned (5 Dec.) but withdrew his resignation on the failure of the Whig Lord John Russell to form a government. Peel's bill, providing for a small fixed duty for 3 years only, passed the Commons in May 1846, 231 protectionist Conservatives, led by Disraeli, voting against. A nominal duty of 1s. per quarter was retained until 1869. Abolition of the c.l. had decisively split the CONSERVATIVE PARTY.

The economic arguments in favour of repeal were certainly exaggerated; mid-Victorian prosperity depended on factors little related to it. The main significance of the battle for repeal was social and political.

A small 'registration duty' on corn was introduced in 1902 but abolished in 1903.   IHE; MLH

Cornovii, a British tribe occupying the area of Staffordshire, Cheshire and Shropshire. Conquered by the Romans before A.D. 47, they became a CIVITAS with their capital at Viroconium (Wroxeter).   CFS

Cornwall, Duchy of. On 17 March 1337 in Parliament at Westminster Edward III created his eldest son Edward (the Black Prince) duke of

C. by charter and granted him a number of HONORS, MANORS, FRANCHISES, rights etc. in the counties of C. and Devon and elsewhere. These were to belong to the duke and the first-begotten sons of him and his heirs, kings of England and dukes of C.; in default of a duke, the duchy to revert to the crown until a proper son should appear. The eldest living son of the sovereign is automatically duke of C.

The Black Prince was the first DUKE created as such. His estates comprised also several castles (e.g. Lydford, Berkhamsted, Launceston), the forest and chase of Dartmoor, the STANNARIES (until 1838) and profits of the coinages of tin, the shrievalty of C., wreck of the sea and royal fish in C. and a number of ADVOWSONS. There have been many sales and purchases from time to time in the interests of good management; there were notable additions under Henry V, mostly in Somerset, and Henry VIII, mostly in C., and considerable sales to pay the land tax imposed in 1798.

On the initiative of the Prince Consort an Act of Parliament in 1863 put the management of the affairs of the duchy on a modern basis. This private estate, made up of various properties in the south-west of England and in Kennington, is administered under the direction of the council of the duchy, headed by the lord warden of the stannaries; and the sheriff of C. is appointed by the possessor of the duchy.   PK

Coronation. The English c. ceremony comprises four main parts: the anointing, the oath, the recognition and the c. itself. The first English king to be anointed, probably in imitation of the Frankish kings, was Ecgferth of Mercia in 785. In the middle ages the anointing was perhaps the most important part of the ceremony, signifying that the king received divine sanction to rule. After the Reformation the anointing, although retained, received less emphasis. At his c. in 973 King Edgar took an oath to maintain peace, to repress wrong-doing and to do justice

D

with mercy. Subsequent kings took similar oaths, and their form was not materially changed until 1308, when Edward II promised to maintain such laws as might be made in future. Under the TUDORS and STEWARTS modifications safeguarding the royal PREROGATIVE were introduced, but in 1689 William and Mary took an oath which acknowledged the supremacy of the law and of Parliament, and which included the promise to maintain 'the Protestant Reformed Religion established by law'. William III and subsequent sovereigns have made a declaration of their Protestantism before their c. More recent changes in the wording of the oath have reflected the growth of, and constitutional changes in, the Empire and COMMONWEALTH.

Anglo-Saxon kings succeeded to the throne by the WITAN's choice as well as by hereditary right, and a formal assent by the people to his succession was included in the c. ceremony of William I. The dangers to the monarchy inherent in an admission that the right to rule might be conferred by election was underlined when pretenders such as the Empress Maud and Prince Louis of France were elected by the clergy or baronage. Election in the c. ceremony was, however, revived in the 14th century in the form of the 'elevation' of the king before the ceremony—symbolical of election by the nobles—and the 'recognition' of the sovereign in the ceremony itself. The elevation gradually lost its significance and was finally dropped in 1831. In 1377 the recognition included the people's promise to obey Richard II as well as their acceptance of him. A recognition without such a promise found favour under the LANCASTRIANS and YORKISTS, while Henry VII was presented at his c. as elected by the estates of the realm. Under the later Tudors and the Stewarts the recognition amounted to an acceptance of the rightful sovereign. The convenient formula 'your undoubted king and queen', devised for the recognition of William and Mary in the special circumstances of 1689, has been retained.

The crown, replacing the Teutonic helmet, became the principal emblem of sovereignty at the c. of Edgar in 973, which was strongly influenced by Frankish practice. At the same time the ring, sword and sceptre took their place among the regalia. Solemn enthronement of the sovereign after the crowning has been regularly practised since the 12th century, and the chair of St Edward, embodying the Stone of SCONE, has been used since the 14th century. The chair was also used for the installation of Cromwell as Lord Protector. Since the Reformation the actual crowning and enthronement have come to be the climax of the ceremony. The doing of homage to the new monarch after the crowning appeared surprisingly late, in the 14th century. The c. banquet, probably of very early origin, and the challenge by the sovereign's champion, introduced in the 14th century, were both abandoned in the economical c. of William IV (1831) and have not been revived.

Anglo-Saxon c.s took place in various towns, notably Kingston-on-Thames in the 10th century: since the Norman conquest Westminster Abbey has been the usual place, and the right of the archbishop of Canterbury to perform the crowning has been unchallenged since the 12th century. Richard I and John were separately installed as dukes of Normandy, while Henry VI was crowned king of France in Paris. Despite Henry VIII's assumption of the title of king of Ireland, no separate Irish c. of an English monarch was ever held, though the three crowns used at the c. of Elizabeth I, for example, may have signified her (nominal) rule over three realms. Charles I, Charles II and James II received separate Scottish c.s, that of Charles II in 1651 being the last to be held at Scone.

P. E. Schramm, *A History of the English Coronation* (1937). RFW

Coronel, battle of (1 Nov. 1914), a British naval defeat in WORLD WAR I. Rear-Admiral Cradock's squadron of three cruisers and one armed merchant cruiser encountered Admiral von Spee's superior German force composed of two powerful and three light cruisers off C. on the coast of Chile. The British flagship *Good Hope* and the cruiser *Monmouth* were sunk with little damage to the Germans. This misfortune was reversed at the battle of the FALKLAND ISLANDS. IHE

Coroners or keepers of the PLEAS OF THE CROWN, appear first in 1194, replacing the king's serjeants of WAPENTAKE or HUNDRED, performing additional duties and marking a new stage in the administration of criminal justice by providing a check on SHERIFFS' powers. They were not justices, but carried out the preliminaries of criminal justice: sitting in the SHIRE court, they heard criminal matters, appeals of felony and of APPROVERS; they heard ABJURATIONS of the realm and held inquests on all who died suddenly, on treasure trove and wreck. They enrolled such matters and presented the rolls at the next judicial EYRE for the cases to be heard. The c.' importance declined with new methods of criminal justice, and their duties are now restricted to holding inquests. Originally there were four elected c. in each COUNTY, in Wales one in each COMMOTE, but the numbers increased as liberties, boroughs etc. were granted election of their own c. PMB

Corporation Act (1661), the first act of the CLARENDON CODE. All municipal office holders were to take the oaths of ALLEGIANCE, supremacy and NON-RESISTANCE, renounce the COVENANT and take Communion according to Church of England rite (Act of UNIFORMITY). It was primarily designed to destroy the political power of Dissenters in the towns and in Parliament. Repeal was attempted in 1718 and subsequently but without success until 1828. Annual Indemnity Acts were passed from 1727. IHE

Coruña campaign (1808–9), a grim and nearly disastrous phase of the PENINSULAR WAR. In support of the then victorious Spanish armies Sir John Moore advanced into Spain from Lisbon (11 Oct. 1808); at Salamanca he learned of sweeping Spanish defeats by the French and of Napoleon's approach to Madrid. Although greatly outnumbered and hampered by bad intelligence, insufficient supplies and lack of liaison with the Spanish, Moore struck north at Napoleon's communications. Joined by Sir David Baird's force (landed at Coruña, 26 Oct.) he advanced to Sahagun against the detached army of Soult. When this manoeuvre made Napoleon concentrate his armies against himself instead of subjugating southern Spain, Moore withdrew his 29,000 men by the mountainous route to C., the light brigades making for Vigo to protect the southern flank. During the 300-mile retreat (25 Dec.–11 Jan.) Moore's army suffered from an almost complete breakdown of discipline—the result of difficult terrain, bitter weather, forced marches and lack of provisions; only the rearguard remained firm. On 16 Jan. 1809 Soult with 16,000 troops attacked Moore's 14,000 infantry (the cavalry and most of the artillery already being embarked) holding an inner ring of low hills around C. By a judicious use of his reserve Moore ensured victory before being mortally wounded; Maj-Gen. John Hope completed the evacuation by 18 Jan.   MLH

Cotton Industry. Cotton imported by the LEVANT COMPANY was used with flax to make fustian from the late 16th century, but all-cotton cloths were not produced on any scale until the 18th century, when manufacture became centred in Lancashire and Cheshire, especially in the Manchester area. In its early days the c.i. was opposed by the WOOLLEN INDUSTRY. It was organized under capitalist control by the mid-18th century. The INDUSTRIAL REVOLUTION was most marked in the c.i. and it became a factory industry from the 1780s. The inventions of the fly shuttle (1733) and spinning jenny (1770) did not depend on power, but the water frame (1769) involved the use of water power and the factory system. Crompton's mule (1779), at first a hand machine, led to

the production of finer threads, and water power was applied after 1790. Cartwright's power loom (1785) gave further impetus to the factory system. Steam power superseded water power between 1820 and 1850. Pauper apprentices were early used as a source of labour in the cotton mills, and the first Factory Act (1802) was designed for their protection, but local labour was soon found to be cheaper. After 1800 cotton goods took the place of woollens and the spectacular growth of the c.i. continued throughout the 19th century, with temporary setbacks from the shortage of American cotton during the AMERICAN WAR of 1812–14 and the civil war (1861–5). Largely dependent on exports, the c.i. suffered severely through the loss of the Indian and Far Eastern markets between the two world wars, due to the growth of their own domestic production. Since World War II further severe contraction took place, increased by the growing use of synthetic fibres, and in 1967 imports exceeded home production.   IHE

Council for New England (1620–35) was a reconstituted form of the PLYMOUTH COMPANY operating between latitudes 40° and 48° N. It relied on its trading and fishing rights and on the granting of licences to intending settlers, notably to the PILGRIM FATHERS (1621) and to the promoters of MASSACHUSETTS (1628–9). It made numerous conflicting grants and was dissolved in 1635, its members dividing the remaining lands among themselves.   IHE

Council of State was elected by the RUMP (14 Feb. 1649) to act as the executive. Of its 41 members 31 were M.P.s. After the expulsion of the Rump (29 Apr. 1653) a new council of 13 was appointed to which BAREBONES PARLIAMENT added 18 of their members. The INSTRUMENT OF GOVERNMENT created a council of 22 life members with substantial control over the Protector. By the HUMBLE PETITION AND ADVICE it became a less important Privy Council (21 members). In 1660 the LONG PARLIA-

MENT appointed a new council at Monck's request. IHE

Council of the Marches, first established for the PRINCE OF WALES in 1471, disappears from view after 1478. It may have come into existence again as Prince Arthur's council in 1493, and was certainly constituted in 1501. Substantially strengthened by Wolsey in 1525, it was galvanized into activity by the appointment of Rowland Lee as its president (1534–43) and was given a statutory basis for its existence by the Act of UNION in 1543. Thereafter it carried out a wide miscellany of responsibilities as the chief court of justice in Wales and the March and, under the privy council, the highest administrative authority there. Despite the handicaps of long-standing opposition from English border counties, unsuitable presidents, officials on the make, a growing breadth and burden of litigation, tight finances and the need to pay judges out of fines imposed by them, it functioned tolerably well until its abolition in 1641. Re-established at the RESTORATION, it enjoyed scant prestige or authority until it finally disappeared in 1689.

Penry Williams, *The Council in the Marches of Wales* (Cardiff, 1958). GW

Council of the North (1537–1641) became a permanent body after the PILGRIMAGE OF GRACE, replacing earlier experiments made since the time of Edward IV (1461–83) to deal with the special problems of this remote border area. Dominated by royal officials, including clerics and lawyers and using STAR CHAMBER methods, it became the judicial and administrative authority for the counties of York, Durham, Northumberland, Cumberland and Westmorland. It acted as a COURT OF REQUESTS, and after 1559 virtually as a Court of HIGH COMMISSION of the North. It was unpopular for its enforcement of government policy and effective work of centralization, and successfully dealt with the NORTHERN REBELLION (1569). It was attacked by the common lawyers early in the 17th century, and internal scandals weakened its im-

portance. Wentworth became its last president (1628), enforcing his policy of THOROUGH. It was abolished with the other PREROGATIVE COURTS (1641). IHE

Council of the West (12 Apr. 1539–18 June 1540) was established as a judicial and administrative body under the presidency of Lord Russell, with jurisdiction over Cornwall, Devon, Somerset and Dorset. Russell was granted most of the Tavistock abbey lands (4 July 1539) to help sustain his position. This council, created when disaffection was rife after the Henrician Reformation and modelled on the COUNCILS OF THE NORTH and Wales, was to hold four sessions per year at Dorchester, Wells, Exeter and Tavistock. It was to give swift justice, deal with riots and sedition, attend the needs of poor suitors, enforce religious conformity and investigate INCLOSURES. It lapsed when Thomas Cromwell, its originator, fell in June 1540. Little is known about it, as its records have disappeared. IHE

Councils for Trade and Plantations. Special committees of the PRIVY COUNCIL were appointed during the 17th century to deal with the colonies and plantations. Mostly short-lived, similar C. T. P. were established in 1660. A new C. for T. (1668–72) had its functions transferred to the C. for Foreign P. (formed 1670), which from 1672–4 was known as the C. T. P. This gave way in 1675 to a committee known as the Lords of Trade, replaced in 1696 by the Board of T. and P., which lasted till 1782, promoting close regulation by the mother country but losing most control over colonial policy after 1704 (except between 1748 and 1757), when colonial affairs were put under the SECRETARY OF STATE for the Southern Department. In 1786 a new Committee for T. and P. was set up, which was absorbed by the Board of TRADE by 1861. IHE

Country Party, a term chiefly used from 1673 for the Parliamentary opposition to the Court Party led by Danby, which was dependent on crown patronage. It included Shaftesbury, Cavendish and Russell. They supported the liberties and privileges of the subject free from dependence on the court and drew support from dissenters and conformists of puritan origin. They opposed Charles II's pro-French policy, secured rejection of the Non-Resistance Bill (1675) and supported the anti-Catholic policy of the TEST ACTS and EXCLUSION BILLS. They became labelled PETITIONERS, then Whigs, their opponents being Abhorrers or Tories.   IHE

County (Norman-French *comté*), the term applied by the Norman conquerors to the existing SHIRE. The sixth and last c. created since 1066, the c. of London, was formed in 1888 from parts of Kent, Surrey and Middlesex. In addition, the Local Government Act (1888) gave c. status to many large towns (c. boroughs). C. administration continued after 1066 to be the responsibility of the SHERIFF, but his powers were lost to JUSTICES OF THE PEACE in QUARTER SESSIONS; and these, by the Act of 1888, were superseded by elected c. councils, c.s being subdivided into districts (rural and urban) and civil PARISHES (1894).

The Welsh c.s were organized in their present form by the Acts of Henry VIII (1509–47) which accomplished the UNION of England and Wales.

The Scottish c.s were created in the Lowlands by Malcolm III Canmore (1057–93) and his sons who copied the English system. The Highlands were divided into c.s between the 16th and 18th centuries, during which period c. organization also came into being in Ireland.

In England, Wales and Ireland the c. is called 'administrative c.', in Scotland 'civil c.'   CFS

County Court, descended from the SHIRE court of Anglo-Saxon times. At this all free men of the shire attended under the presidency of the bishop of the diocese and the leading lay official, originally the EALDORMAN, later the SHERIFF. These officials merely declared the law, those attending being both suitors and judges. The c.c. dealt with civil and criminal cases, settled ecclesiastical matters, arranged GELD payments and FYRD service for the shire and heard royal WRITS. After the Norman conquest ecclesiastical matters were removed to church courts and the sheriff came regularly to preside over the court's generally monthly meetings: through the increasing duties laid on sheriffs, c.c.s were harnessed to central government, with safeguards against sheriffs' abuses by the CORONERS' presence after 1194. The courts dealt with many PLEAS, civil and criminal, preliminary business for cases in higher courts, OUTLAWRY of convicted persons, as also with general business, proclamation of ordinances, treaties etc. and election of officers. Attendance was regarded as burdensome: first after 1236 suit was allowed by ATTORNEY, thereafter becoming attached to particular pieces of land. From the later 13th century the c.c., superseded by new local jurisdictions, e.g. JUSTICES OF THE PEACE, and new social and governmental organizations, began to wane in importance. By the 18th century it had almost lapsed but legal experiments, culminating in the C.C. Act 1846, revived it, by appointing paid magistrates in place of the sheriff to hold courts with jurisdiction over recovery of small debts, within the county. The usefulness of the system has led to a constantly expanding jurisdiction. PMB

Coupon election (14 Dec. 1918) was so named because each candidate of the Liberal–Conservative coalition received an endorsing letter, or 'c.' as Asquith contemptuously called it, signed by the two leaders, Lloyd George and Bonar Law. The 106 Liberals who had voted with Asquith in the 'Maurice debate' (9 May) did not get the c. Thus the split in the LIBERAL PARTY was made final. 484 candidates holding the c. were elected and Lloyd George continued as prime minister.   MLH

Court Baron. Every MANOR had a c.b. to deal with matters relating to services and duties pertaining to the manor and with personal actions under 40 shillings. Freeholders were subject to the COMMON LAW; COPYHOLD and other customary tenants were subject to the customs of the manor. C.s b. have never been formally abolished, but they were virtually superseded by the COUNTY COURT Act 1867. MR

Court Leet. A court of record granted by royal charter to a HUNDRED, lordship or MANOR, etc., which took view of FRANKPLEDGE and had jurisdiction in minor criminal cases. C.s l. have fallen into disuse since the Summary Jurisdiction Act 1848. MR

Court Martial, see MILITARY LAW.

Court of Arches, see ECCLESIASTICAL COURTS.

Court Roll, the written record of proceedings in court, generally applied to manorial records. Such rolls include proceedings for breach of customs, regulations of COMMON LAND, the surrenders and admissions of tenants and similar local affairs (COPYHOLD). PMB

Covenant. In 1557 the Scottish Protestant leaders, the Lords of the Congregation, entered into a bond or C. to advance their cause. In 1581 another C. was drawn up in defence of the Protestant religion and signed by James VI. The National C. (1638) was provoked by Charles I's attempt to Anglicize the Scottish church. A Book of Canons was issued (1636) requiring the use of a new prayerbook of an anti-Puritan character, and its first use in Edinburgh (23 July 1637) ended in a riot. The TABLES denounced the book and drew up the National C. (Feb. 1638) 'to recover the purity and liberty of the Gospel'. The book was revoked (2 Sep.), but the General Assembly abolished episcopacy and re-established the Presbyterian system (21 Nov.). (REFORMATION, SCOTTISH; BISHOPS' WARS; SOLEMN LEAGUE AND COVENANT.) IHE

Coventry, the lists at (16 Sept. 1398), an attempt to decide by TRIAL BY BATTLE the accusation of treason brought against Thomas Mowbray, duke of Norfolk, by Henry Bolingbroke at the SHREWSBURY parliament. Both duly appeared in the lists at C., but at the very last moment Richard II forbade the combat and exiled Norfolk for life and Bolingbroke for ten years, ridding himself of two dangerous potential enemies at one stroke (DEPOSITION of Richard II). RFW

Cowick Ordinances (1323), together with ordinances of 1324 and 1326, put into effect the reforms of the treasurer Walter Stapleton, bishop of Exeter. They were particularly concerned with the system of keeping records in the EXCHEQUER—especially with the PIPE ROLLS—and the allocation of duties to its officers, who were increased in number. More lasting administrative reforms were in fact accomplished in the reign of Edward II under the Despenser regime than by the Lords ORDAINERS. RFW

Cravant, battle of (1 Aug. 1423), the defeat of a Franco-Scottish army by the Anglo-Burgundian forces led by John, duke of Bedford, regent of France for the infant Henry VI. It secured the Burgundian hold on east-central France. RFW

Crécy, battle of (26 Aug. 1346), like AGINCOURT a surprising English victory in unfavourable circumstances. Edward III had invaded Normandy with the probable objects of relieving French pressure on Gascony and of joining up with his allies in Flanders. He eluded Philip VI and forded the Somme at Blanche Tache just ahead of his pursuers. With an army that was by now tired and short of supplies Edward turned at C. in Ponthieu and awaited the attack of Philip's superior forces. The French army arrived in haste and some confusion in the late afternoon, was committed piecemeal to a series of cavalry attacks and by nightfall had been bloodily repulsed. The victory was the first large-scale demonstration in the HUNDRED YEARS' WAR of the tactical superiority of the English, based mainly on the use of large numbers of archers in combination with dismounted men-at-arms, which proved particularly effective in defensive actions against mounted assailants. The immediate advantage gained was that Edward was able to embark upon the long siege of CALAIS.   RFW

Creswellian Culture, see PALAEO-LITHIC.

Crewe's Act (1782), the last of the PLACE ACTS, 'for better securing the freedom of elections' was mainly the work of John Crewe, M.P. for Cheshire (1748–1829). It aimed at reducing government and court influence over certain borough elections where local voters held offices under the Boards of Customs and Excise. Revenue officers were disfranchised.   IHE

Crimean War (1854–56) between Russia on the one hand and Turkey, Britain, France and, later, Sardinia on the other, broke out ostensibly because of Russia's claims to the guardianship of the Holy Places and the protection of the Greek Christians in the Turkish empire. Its underlying cause was the fear of Russia's expansion in the Balkans and Mediterranean, at the expense of the decaying Turkish power. Traditional British policy was to preserve Turkish integrity; thus tsar Nicholas I's suggestion (Jan. 1853) for the partition of the 'sick bear' (as he called the Turkish empire) between Russia and Britain merely awakened suspicions. Turkey's refusal of the tsar's demand for a protectorate over Christian Slavs was followed by Russian occupation of the principalities of Moldavia and Wallachia (July 1853). Diplomatic efforts (not least those of Lord Stratford de Redcliffe, British ambassador in Constantinople) were unavailing; Turkey declared war on Russia (4 Oct.). The destruction of a Turkish flotilla at Sinope (30 Nov.) exacerbated anti-Russian feeling in Britain. A Franco-British fleet sailed into the Black Sea (Jan. 1854) with the intention of confining the Russian fleet to its Crimean base at Sebastopol, and

Britain and France declared war in March. No participant had wanted this result; a series of badly calculated actions had produced a situation from which neither side felt able to withdraw.

Attacks against Russia could take place only in the Black Sea and the Baltic. Two BALTIC EXPEDITIONS were made, both ineffective. For operations in the Black Sea an expeditionary force under Lord Raglan and St. Arnaud arrived at Varna to find that the Russians, at the instance of Austria, had withdrawn from the principalities (June 1854). Raglan was thereupon ordered to attack Sebastopol although ill-prepared to do so; cholera had already broken out, little information was available, there was serious lack of transport, artillery and cavalry; above all, the expedition was not equipped for a winter campaign if the attack was not immediately successful. The armies landed in Calamita Bay (14/15 Sept.) and marched towards Sebastopol defeating the Russians at the river ALMA. A quick advance might then have taken the city, but St. Arnaud insisted on a detour, thus giving time for the defences to be prepared. In October and November Russian attacks at BALACLAVA and INKERMAN were beaten off. The besieging forces, encamped on unsheltered heights, were then faced with the full rigours of the winter. Disease, cold and lack of supplies took a severe toll. The British had only the tiny harbour of Balaclava as their base. The appalling conditions (somewhat alleviated at the Scutari base hospital by the devotion of Florence Nightingale) led to an outcry at home and to the resignation of the prime minister, Lord Aberdeen.

In June 1855 the assault on Sebastopol was begun. The attack of 18 June failed largely because Pélissier, St. Arnaud's successor, did not wait for adequate artillery support. On 28 June Raglan died and was succeeded by (Sir) J. Simpson. After a lengthy bombardment the final onslaught was launched on 8 Sept.; the British failed to take the Redan fort but the French occupied the commanding Malakoff redoubt and the Russians evacuated the city. Although their field army had not been defeated, the fall of Sebastopol virtually ended the war. The death of Nicholas I in March had removed an obstacle in British eyes, and France, who had a preponderance of troops in the field, wished for peace. Tsar Alexander II signed the preliminaries of peace (Feb. 1856) and the treaty of PARIS was concluded on 30 March. The 'eastern question' was postponed, but the war had maintained the integrity of Turkey and checked Russian influence in southern Europe.

MLH

Criminal Appeal, Court of, see APPEAL.

Criminous Clerks. In the mid-12th century the ecclesiastical courts claimed the exclusive right to try and punish clergy, including those accused of criminal offences. Although c.c.s found guilty in the church courts might be unfrocked and imprisoned, they were often punished less severely than laymen would have been by the king's courts. In 1163 Henry II claimed the right to punish c.c.s convicted by the church courts, but the bishops, led by Thomas Becket, refused to agree. A provision of the constitutions of CLARENDON (1164) seems to have intended that c.c.s should be seized and punished like laymen, if found guilty and degraded by church courts. In 1176, after his reconciliation with the church at AVRANCHES, Henry conceded that clergy should not henceforth be tried by a secular court except for forest offences—though in practice the king's courts also dealt with clerks accused of treason. From the late 12th century the rights of the church courts to try clergy were not disputed, provided the accused proved BENEFIT OF CLERGY. A degraded clerk was treated like a layman and might therefore be tried by a secular court for a second offence.

RFW

Cromwell's Case (1572) was an enforcement by the House of Lords of the privilege of its members of freedom from arrest in civil actions. Lord Cromwell was arrested for contempt of an injunction of the Court of Chancery and was freed by the Lords. They claimed that his arrest was contrary to the ancient privilege and immunity of their house.

IHE

Cropredy Bridge, battle of (29 June 1644), Charles I's defeat of Waller near Banbury, enabling him to march into the West country in pursuit of the Earl of Essex.

IHE

Crown, a gold coin first minted in 1526 valued at 4s. 6d. but superseded in the same year by one worth 5s. Gold c. and half-c. were made until the reign of Charles II. Silver c. and half-c. were struck from 1551, but c. were infrequently minted and are now restricted to special issues. Owing to impending decimalization the half-c. was withdrawn at the end of 1969.

IHE

Crown colonies, legally 'colonies not possessing responsible government' and formerly administered by the COLONIAL OFFICE, now by the FOREIGN AND COMMONWEALTH OFFICE. Originally all executive and legislative powers were vested in the governor; gradually legislative and executive councils, first with an official, later an elected majority, were introduced and paved the way to representative government and finally self-governing status. C.c. proper are now only those dependencies which, like HONG KONG, BAHAMAS, GIBRALTAR, are unable to bear the burden of independence.

SHS; IHE

Crown Estate Commissioners. The crown's land revenues, vast after the Norman conquest, diminished by alienation, extended in the 15th century and again diminished under the Tudors and Stewarts, were temporarily surrendered by William III in 1698 as security for part of the new CIVIL LIST. George III surrendered them for life in 1760, a practice followed by subsequent sovereigns. In the later 18th century Burke and others advocated their sale, but Commissioners of

Woods, Forests and Land Revenue were not appointed until 1810 to sell some and manage other of the crown's English and Welsh estates, to which Irish, Isle of Man, Alderney and Scottish revenues were subsequently added. Joined by the Surveyor-General of Works 1832–51, the commissioners' title was altered to Commissioners of Crown Lands in 1924 and C.E.C. in 1956 after the Crichel Down inquiry. Though much concerned with sale in the early period, the commissioners also protected crown rights, were responsible for purchases and development, e.g. Regent's Park, and for the development of forest remaining in their hands, transferred to the FORESTRY COMMISSION in 1919.   PMB

Crown in Chancery, Clerk of the, originally one of the CHANCERY clerks who became skilled in drafting documents of special interest to the crown and was known by this title from the early 14th century at least. In the late 14th century an assistant was appointed, and these officers, together with their staff in the CROWN OFFICE, received PRIVY SEAL warrants and drafted grants of honours, commissions to judges and justices of the peace etc. Later they received Speakers' warrants for parliamentary elections and returns, attending Parliament for the royal assent. Almost abolished in 1832, the office survived, acquiring the residuary duties of many abolished offices, e.g. the compilation of PATENT ROLLS. Modern clerks are normally the Permanent Secretaries to the Lord CHANCELLOR.   PMB; MR

Crown Office. Both modern c.o.s may once have been subordinate to the Clerk of the CROWN IN CHANCERY: one remained with him, now forming part of the Lord Chancellor's department; the other had, by the early 14th century, become attached to the crown, i.e. criminal, side of KING'S BENCH, its head being known as the Clerk of the Crown, copying documents for the court, assisting judges, attorneys and suitors, entering cases etc. Joined to the Central Office of

the Supreme Court in 1879, acquiring the residuary duties of the Clerk of the PETTY BAG in 1889, its modern work is to enter and list cases from London and Middlesex in the Queen's Bench division and perform routine duties for that division and the court of APPEAL in Queen's Bench and COUNTY COURT matters.   PMB

Crown Wearings. William I introduced the practice of appearing in full regal splendour, wearing his crown, on the three great feasts if he was in England: at Christmas at Gloucester, at Easter at Winchester and at Whitsun at Westminster. The presence of all the magnates of England on these state occasions facilitated the holding of great councils and enabled the king to maintain personal contact with his barons, to redress grievances and to keep a check on their loyalty. C.w. continued to be held by William's successors, though not with the same regularity nor at the original places. They were certainly held as late as the reign of Henry III (1216–72), when the majesty of the divine institution of kingship was particularly stressed by a solemn ritual.   RFW

Crusades, English share in the.
(1) Robert, duke of Normandy, eldest son of William I, took the cross, pledged his duchy to his brother, William Rufus, to raise money, and set out for the Holy Land in 1096 with a following of Normans, Bretons, Scots and English. Robert reached Constantinople in May 1097 and took part in the capture of Nicaea, the victory of Dorylaeum, the siege of Antioch, the capture of Jerusalem (15 July 1099) and the defeat of the Egyptians at Ascalon. English mercenaries in the service of the Byzantine emperor, Alexius Comnenus, also contributed to the success of the first crusade.

(2) The English played a minor role in Syria for most of the 12th century, although bands of armed pilgrims carried in English vessels occasionally provided much-needed reinforcements for the kingdom of Jerusalem. In Oct.

1147 an English fleet carrying crusaders who intended to take part in the second crusade sailed only as far as Portugal and there took part in the capture of Lisbon from the Moors.

(3) After the crushing defeat by Saladin at Hattin and the fall of Jerusalem in 1187 plans were made for a joint crusade by French, Flemish and English forces, and special taxation (SALADIN TITHE) was imposed. Anglo-French hostilities delayed the start, but Richard I finally set off in July 1190. Some English crusaders preceded their king: a fleet of Londoners stopped on their way to fight the Moors in Portugal and then went on to join in the siege of ACRE. Richard's tardy arrival brought the siege to a successful conclusion and, after the departure of Philip II, Richard remained in general command of the third crusade. He defeated Saladin at Arsuf (2 Sept. 1191) and secured Jaffa as a base for operations against Jerusalem. On two occasions Richard advanced to within 12 miles of Jerusalem, but he was never strong enough to undertake its siege. After the loss and recapture of Jaffa, Richard defeated Saladin again (5 Aug. 1192) and, by the peace concluded on 2 Sept. 1192, secured Christian possession of a coastal strip from Tyre to Jaffa and right of access for pilgrims to Jerusalem.

(4) A party of English crusaders led by the earls of Chester, Arundel, Derby and Winchester joined the fifth crusade in 1218. The crusaders took Damietta (5 Nov. 1219), but refused to surrender it in exchange for Jerusalem, and the enterprise ended in complete failure when the Moslems retook Damietta (8 Sept. 1221).

(5) In 1228-9 an English party including the bishops of Exeter and Winchester accompanied the emperor Frederick II—despite his excommunication by pope Gregory IX—on his crusade: the bishops were witnesses to the treaty whereby Frederick recovered Jerusalem, Bethlehem and Nazareth for the Christians. In Oct. 1240 Richard, earl of Cornwall, brother of Henry III, and Simon de Montfort, earl of Leicester, arrived with a small force, at a time when the kingdom of Jerusalem was distracted by feuds between the Templars and the Hospitallers and between the supporters and opponents of Frederick II. Although he only remained until May 1241, Richard restored some measure of unity and secured the cession of eastern Galilee by the Sultan Ayub.

(6) William Longespée, earl of Salisbury, joined the crusade of Louis IX of France in 1248-9 with a small force and took part in the second capture of Damietta and the subsequent advance up the Nile to Mansourah. In February 1250 Salisbury was killed with most of his followers in an attempt to rush the defences of Mansourah.

(7) Although he took the cross, Henry III never went on crusade. After the pacification which followed the BARONS' WARS, however, the fall of Antioch (1268) prompted his eldest son, Edward, to organize an expedition. Edward, who was followed later by his brother, Edmund of Lancaster, arrived at Acre in May 1271. He received little support from the knights of the crusader states, and his own forces were too small to undertake more than a few minor raids into Moslem territory. His presence and activity were, however, partly responsible for obtaining a ten-year peace for the Christians. Edward sailed for England in Sept. 1272, and later sent some reinforcements. His Swiss follower and friend Otto von Grandson 'took part in the last heroic defence of Acre, which finally fell in May 1291.

(8) An English and Scottish force joined in King Peter of Cyprus' crusade of 1365, in which Alexandria was captured, only to be hastily abandoned after it had been looted and its inhabitants massacred.

(9) John Holland, earl of Huntingdon, led 1,000 men on the crusade against the Ottoman Turks which ended with the disastrous defeat of the Christians at Nicopolis (25 Sept. 1396).

(10) The bishop of Norfolk's 'crusade': see FLANDERS, WAY OF. RFW

Cuba was conquered from the Spaniards by the British in 1762 (siege of Havana, 5 June–14 Aug.) but exchanged for FLORIDA at the peace of PARIS (1763).   SHS

Culloden, battle of (16 Apr. 1746), the final defeat of the JACOBITES. After FALKIRK Prince Charles Edward retreated northwards, taking Inverness and Fort Augustus. Cumberland reached Aberdeen (27 Feb.) and eventually met the rebels at C. Moor. With twice the Highlanders' forces and with well-placed artillery Cumberland withstood the charges of the Jacobites, and his cavalry completed the victory.   IHE

Cumbria, see STRATHCLYDE.

Curaçao was taken from the Spaniards by the Dutch in 1634 and occupied by the British in 1800–2 and 1807–16.   SHS

Curia Regis. From the Norman conquest until comparatively recent times all political, governmental and legal power stemmed from the c.r., the king's household and court. All the older government departments came from it: in early days the EXCHEQUER was the king's counting house, the CHANCERY his writing office: as business increased first one then the other separated from the household, being replaced successively by the WARDROBE and the PRIVY SEAL, the CHAMBER and the SIGNET. From the conquest to the Tudors English history is characterized by the growth of new household departments which pass into the public sphere. In this flexible instrument lay much of the sovereign's powers, as successive oppositions realized, calling for a return to older ways.

William I's officers and fellow conquerors soon became too settled on their lands to travel through the country with him. Nevertheless, they formed his great court, giving him council at the three CROWN WEARINGS. This duty, later claimed as a right, had a profound influence on baronial opposition and the development of the king's council in PARLIAMENT assembled. Meanwhile the business of the household and thereby the country was carried out, from Henry I's reign at least, by men of ability if little background. Generally these were clerics, partly because of their education, partly because they could be provided for, and rewarded, by ecclesiastical preferment; the lay element gradually increased, but did not predominate until the Reformation. The use of men wholly dependent on the king was, from time to time, unpopular: e.g. John's preference for foreigners was strongly opposed. Such officers could have much influence with the king, reflected in the 13th- and 14th-century charges of evil councillors and, as late as 1839, in the BEDCHAMBER CRISIS.

As the crown's power grew, so did the influence of the c.r.: nowhere is this clearer than in the growth of the law courts. The magnates of the Conqueror and his successors formed his courts where, among other business, their cases could be tried. As the king moved through the country other cases were brought to him, which he and those of his court with him would hear. Henry I and Henry II threw their courts open to all, and the system reached out to embrace the older communal courts of SHIRE and HUNDRED. As business increased, new methods and professional judges were required: certain cases were kept for consideration before the king in his itinerant court, which became KING'S BENCH; others were heard by travelling bands of judges, drawn at first from the household, in general EYRE or sent to take ASSIZES, and as the king was constantly travelling a fixed court was required, becoming the COMMON PLEAS. A somewhat similar proliferation of courts is to be seen in the later middle ages and Tudor period in the conciliar courts, e.g. STAR CHAMBER, REQUESTS, etc. In sum the continued unity of England, governmental and legal, from the Norman conquest onwards is due, in no small measure, to the infinitely varied c.r.   PMB

Curragh 'mutiny' (March 1914) arose from the possibility that the British army might be used to coerce Ulster into accepting the HOME RULE bill. The C.-in-C., Ireland, Sir A. Paget, acting on ambiguous directions from the secretary for war, J. E. B. Seely (Lord Mottistone), told his officers that whilst those who were Ulster-domiciled could 'disappear' the rest must carry out orders or be dismissed; the C.O. (Brig.-Gen. (Sir) H. Gough) and 56 officers of the 3rd Cavalry Brigade, stationed at the Curragh, outside Dublin, were among those who preferred 'to accept dismissal if ordered north'. Gough reported to the war office and was given an assurance drafted in cabinet that there had been a 'misunderstanding'; this document was, however, amended by Seely and the C.I.G.S., Sir J. French, to the effect that the officers would not be required to act against Ulster. This was unacceptable to Asquith's government and Seely, French and Sir S. Ewart (adjutant-general) resigned. The incident lent colour to the belief in a Liberal 'plot' to provoke the Conservative-supported Ulster Volunteers.   MLH

Cursitors, junior clerks of the CHANCERY, proficient in the formal court hands, who were appointed to write out the formal, common-form writs. By the 14th century their number was fixed at 24 celibates living in the Inns of Chancery, each assigned to one or more county's business, though the celibacy rule was thereafter gradually relaxed. The c. were incorporated in 1573, and their office and adjoining hall stood in Chancery Lane, London, at its junction with the present Cursitor Street. With the increasing use of printed forms, the c. steadily declined in importance. They were abolished in 1835 and their remaining work transferred to the PETTY BAG OFFICE.   PMB

Curtesy of England. The right of a husband to hold his deceased wife's land if a live child had been born to them, until the child came of age. A similar practice was followed in Nor-

mandy, but English c. was distinctive in allowing a husband to remarry without losing his right. See also GAVELKIND.   PMB

Customs and Excise. Customs, duties on goods passing to and from foreign countries, derived from early local taxes at fairs and certain seaports, which the crown adopted as models for taxation. Though a nationwide custom, the fifteenth levied on merchants at ports, was imposed from 1203, the modern system of collection on fixed scales by royal officers at every royal port began with the MALETOLT imposed on wool and skins from 1275 onwards. This regular revenue, gradually encompassing other commodities (PRISAGE), was used by Edward I and his successors to guarantee loans from LOMBARD and other bankers. The customs, occasionally farmed, were administered by the EXCHEQUER until 1605, when all were farmed. When they were resumed in 1671, Commissioners of Customs were appointed, administering Scots revenue after 1723 and renamed the Board of Customs, with control over Ireland also, in 1823.

Excise duties, on goods for domestic consumption, were first levied in 1643: commissioners to administer them were appointed in 1660, to be amalgamated with the Board of Stamps, etc., in 1849. Excise was separated in 1909 and united with the customs administration under a new Board of C. and E.   PMB

Custos Rotulorum, an office of obscure history. Charged with keeping the records of courts in a county, such officers, members of the commissions of the PEACE, were appointed by the CHANCELLOR before 1545, thereafter by the crown. Always persons of rank, the office is now generally combined with that of the LORD LIEUTENANT and the records kept by the Clerk of the Peace, technically the c.r.'s deputy.   PMB

Custumal, a statement of the incidents of tenure and of services owed by free and unfree tenants of a MANOR or similar organization to their lord, or the duties and rights of burgesses in their town etc., containing much information on the conditions of medieval life.   PMB

Cymmrodorion, Honourable Society of. The first society (1751–87) was founded among London Welshmen primarily for social and philanthropic purposes and only incidentally for patriotic ends. The second (1820–37) tried to foster and co-ordinate Welsh cultural activities by means of EISTEDDFODAU, prizes and publications. The third (1873–), essentially a London-Welsh society, has been a patron of Welsh literature, art and antiquities, sponsoring a national university, library and museum, and publishing its journals and individual volumes, the most notable of which is its *Dictionary of Welsh Biography* (1959).
R. T. Jenkins and H. M. Ramage, *History of the Hon. Soc. of Cymmrodorion* (1951).   GW

Cyprus was from *c.* 1500 B.C., subject to one or another great power temporarily supreme in the eastern Mediterranean, often ruled by its native princelings. One of these, who styled himself emperor of C., was treacherously deposed by Richard Lionheart in 1191. Richard celebrated in Limasol his wedding with Berengaria of Navarre, who was there crowned queen of the English. He organized C. on the English model under two sheriffs, but soon afterwards sold it to the Knights Templar and in 1192 enfeoffed Guy de Lusignan, ex-king of Jerusalem. King Peter I in 1363 went to London to solicit Edward III's help for the reconquest of the Holy Land, but was not prepared to surrender C. In 1489 the widow of the last Lusignan was forced to cede C. to Venice, her native city. One Venetian officer, Francesco da Sessa called Il Moro (dismissed the service in 1545), is the prototype of Shakespeare's Othello. The last Latin outpost in the eastern Mediterranean was conquered by the Turks in 1570–1.

The Orthodox church of C., autocephalous since 478, was suppressed by the pope in 1260, and the French barons and Italian merchants lorded it over the inhabitants. Church and people therefore welcomed the Turks as liberators. The Orthodox archbishopric was restored and the archbishop was recognized as 'ethnarch', i.e. the political and national representative of the people. Turkish soldiers were settled in C., but there was no intermarriage with the Greek-speaking population, and C. became an unimportant province of the Ottoman empire.

During the BERLIN CONGRESS Disraeli concluded a 'convention of defensive alliance' with Turkey (4 June 1878) which included the occupation and administration of C. by Britain (effected 12 July). When Turkey entered the FIRST WORLD WAR on Germany's side, Britain annexed C. on 5 Nov. 1914. In Nov. 1915 C. was promised to Greece if she would declare war on the central powers; the offer was refused. C. was declared a crown colony on 1 May 1925.

Agitation for *hénosis*, i.e. union with Greece, flamed up sporadically, especially in 1931, when the constitution granted in 1882 had to be suspended; after the SECOND WORLD WAR it was exploited by Communist agents and led to the terrorism of 1955–8. In Feb. 1959 agreement was reached between the British, Greek and Turkish governments and the Greek and Turkish Cypriots that C. should become an independent republic with safeguards for the rights of the Turkish minority (about 20%). On 13 Mar. 1961 C. was admitted as a member of the COMMONWEALTH. Constitutional reforms proposed by President Makarios in 1963 led to further conflict between Greek and Turkish Cypriots and in 1965 a U.N. force assumed the task of maintaining order.   SHS ; IHE

Dadra and Nagar Haveli. Former Portuguese colonial territory which became a Union Territory of INDIA on 11 Aug. 1961.   IHE

Dalriada, a Scottish kingdom, originally in Antrim in Northern Ireland. During the 5th century SCOTS from here established another kingdom of D. in Argyll and the adjacent islands, including IONA. From the end of the 6th century the kingdoms were virtually independent of one another, and historical usage distinguishes them as Irish and Scottish D. Scottish D. attained its greatest importance under king Aedan (c. 574–608), but the territory he gained from the PICTS was soon lost, and he and his successors were defeated by the ANGLES of NORTHUMBRIA. Between the mid-7th and early 9th centuries the kingdom was normally disunited and played a subordinate part in northern affairs. In the mid-9th century its king, Kenneth mac Alpin, became also king of the Picts. D. thereafter lost its separate identity, the united kingdom becoming known as Scotland.   CFS

Dammaree, case of (1710). At the time of the SACHEVERELL affair Daniel D., a waterman, led a group of rioters to destroy a Presbyterian meetinghouse in Drury Lane. He was found guilty of high treason on the ground of intent to destroy all such meeting-houses, this amounting to raising rebellion and insurrection against the queen. He was sentenced to death but later pardoned.   IHE

Damme, battle of (late March 1213). As a preliminary step to the projected invasion of England, Philip II Augustus of France invaded Flanders by land and sea. The count of Flanders appealed to his ally, King John, for help, and an English fleet under the earl of Salisbury sailed on 28 Mar. from Portsmouth, where it had been assembled to guard against invasion. The French fleet was caught at anchor, seriously undermanned, off D. in the Zwyn estuary, and was completely destroyed or captured. Philip II had to withdraw from Flanders and to postpone the attack on England, whereas John was encouraged to launch the campaign of BOUVINES.
          RFW

Damnonii, a British tribe that during the time of ROMAN BRITAIN occupied the area inland and south from the Firth of Clyde. After some time of intermittent Roman control or influence they became, in the later 4th century, FOEDERATI, continuing after the fall of Roman power as the kingdom of STRATHCLYDE.   CFS

Danegeld, see GELD.

Danelaw. The term, first used in the reign of king Cnut (1017–35), indicates the area in which Danish law as opposed to West Saxon or Mercian law was current. It occupied about half of England, extending north-south from the Tees to the Thames, and lying east of a line running along the eastern borders of Oxfordshire, Warwickshire, Staffordshire and Cheshire. Although the term occurs late, the area was occupied by the DANES in the 9th century. Danish law differed from the others in various ways: details of procedure, amount of fines for various offences, the concept that a man of bad standing could 'buy law', i.e. the right to appear in a MOOT, an embryonic JURY of presentment, etc. Danish settlement within this area varied in intensity, being greatest in the area of the FIVE BOROUGHS, EAST ANGLIA, northern Northamptonshire and Yorkshire; and being shown in place-names, in the substitution of the PLOUGHLAND for the HIDE and in the large numbers of SOKEMEN.   CFS

Danes. The first recorded raid on England by VIKINGS occurred in 835. Raids increased in scope and intensity during the next 30 years, despite major Danish defeats at the battles of HINGSTON DOWN (838) and ACLEA (851); and from 865 a great Danish army remained continuously in England. By 874 it had conquered all English kingdoms except WESSEX. In this year it split, part occupying and settling southern NORTHUMBRIA, part remaining in the south. The greatest success of this southern group was attained in 878, when Alfred, king of Wessex, was forced to flee to ATHELNEY; but in the same year he decisively defeated the Danes at EDDING-TON. As a result the D. abandoned the attack on Wessex. Some settled in eastern MERCIA, others in EAST ANGLIA, where their leader Guthrum established a kingdom. He and Alfred, probably in 886, made the treaty that defined its boundaries. But intermittent fighting took place between 879 and 892, and in the latter year a fresh Danish force from the continent attacked Wessex. It received help from the Danes of East Anglia and Northumbria, but the military reorganization by king Alfred proved effective in preserving Wessex and western Mercia from serious damage; and this Danish army dispersed in 896. At the end of the 9th century Danish power in England was based on the kingdoms of YORK and East Anglia and the area of the FIVE BOROUGHS, all of which were later known as the DANELAW. Fighting took place between D. and English during the earlier years of Edward the Elder, king of Wessex (899–924), but the decisive defeat of the Northumbrian D. at the battle of TETTENHALL (910) opened the way for the English reconquest of the midlands and East Anglia between 911 and 918, and of the Norse kingdom of York in 954. Danes who submitted retained their lands and customs. In the reign of Ethelred II (978–1016) the weakness of England encouraged a resumption of Danish attacks. The first raids took place in 980, and in 991 a tax, the first of five such in this reign, was imposed to buy off the invaders (GELD). In 994 Swein, king of Denmark, led a large-scale raid, and from this time the main Danish attacks, now directed by him, increased in scope and intensity. In 1003 he personally led an expedition, probably in revenge for the massacre of St BRICE'S day; he ravaged much of southern England 1003–4 and again 1006–7. Between 1009 and 1012 Danish ravaging in the south and midlands under Swein's representatives, together with the obvious ineffectiveness of the English king, severely weakened English powers of resistance, and when Swein in 1013 led an extremely powerful force to England king Ethelred fled. On Swein's death in 1014 his English schemes were continued by his second son Cnut, whom, on the death of Ethelred and his son in 1016, the English recognized as king. The dynasty of Danish rulers of England died out in 1042, but the last Saxon king, Harold II (1066), was, through his mother, half-Danish by blood.

CFS

Darien Scheme. The Scots, excluded by the NAVIGATION ACTS from the trade of the English empire, established the Company of Scotland for trade with Africa and the Indies (1695), but it was handicapped by the withdrawal of English capital secured by the EAST INDIA COMPANY'S assertion of its own monopoly. Three expeditions were sent (1698–9) to establish a colony on the Darien coast of the isthmus of Panama with the idea of controlling the trade route between the Atlantic and Pacific. Disavowed by William III, the colonists were expelled by Spain in 1700. Losses in men and money were disastrous. IHE

Dark Ages, the term conventionally applied to the period c. 450 to c. 600. The 'darkness' refers mainly to the lack of contemporary written evidence, for in the eastern half of England writing disappeared between the TEUTONIC CONQUEST and the CONVERSION. Archaeological evidence is also limited, being largely confined to grave-goods and weapons.

CFS

Darnel's Case, see FIVE KNIGHTS.

Darrein Presentment, Assize of (*de ultima presentatione*). In the Constitutions of CLARENDON (1164) Henry II claimed for his lay court disputes on ADVOWSONS, regarded as valuable possesssions in the middle ages. A quick action was necessary, lest the diocesan should present to a vacant church: the 3rd Lateran Council (1179) allowed the bishops to present after a lapse of three months. This assize was devised as remedy. The jurors were asked: which advocate presented the last parson, now dead, to the church which is said to be vacant. Sale of the land to which the church belonged or other change in tenure during a parson's lifetime could obscure the simple issue, and slightly later the action *quare impedit*, why A impedes B from presenting, was devised as remedy. See POSSESSORY ASSIZES.   PMB

'Daylight Saving', first advocated in 1907 by W. Willett, a London builder, was adopted (1916) as a wartime fuel economy measure, clocks being put forward by 1 hour in spring and summer; the arrangement was made permanent in 1925. During certain periods of the Second World War double summer time was in force. British Standard Time (1 hour in advance of Greenwich Mean Time) was instituted in 1968 for an experimental period of 3 years.   MLH

Debenture, a sealed negotiable instrument acknowledging a debt, so called because of the opening word *Debentur*, there are owed. From the 13th century onwards d.s were issued by the itinerant WARDROBE redeemable at the fixed EXCHEQUER, and later by the Exchequer and commercial enterprises to postpone payment or levy capital.   PMB

Declaration of Independence (4 July 1776). After LEXINGTON and BUNKER HILL (1775) prospects of peaceful settlement between Britain and the American colonists rapidly receded. Ideas of independence were stimulated by Tom Paine's pamphlet *Common Sense* (Jan. 1776) and news that German mercenaries were to be used against the colonists. The Continental Congress passed a resolution in favour of independence (2 July) and two days later adopted Jefferson's formal D. of I. In propagandist language it began by appealing to Locke's theory of natural rights 'that all men are created equal . . . with certain unalienable rights, that among these are life, liberty and the pursuit of happiness', and then asserted their right to dissolve the

existing form of government. Then followed a list of the 'repeated injuries and usurpations' perpetrated by George III designed to reduce them 'under absolute despotism'. This was a concrete statement of their grievances in the manner of the DECLARATION OF RIGHTS. Finally, it asserted the sovereign independence of the United States of America.   IHE

Declaration of Indulgence (1662), was an undertaking by Charles II to dispense with the laws against Dissenters subject to Parliament's approval. The Commons refused to consent.

The second d. of i. (1672) of Charles II, designed to promote national unity against the Dutch, was issued under royal prerogative. It suspended all penal laws against NONCONFORMISTS and RECUSANTS, but was withdrawn after condemnation by Parliament, which replied by passing the TEST ACT (1673).

The third d. of i. (1687), by James II, suspended all penal laws against Roman Catholics and Dissenters, allowing freedom of public worship. The main motive was to promote Roman Catholicism.

The fourth d. of i. (1688) was ordered to be read in churches and resulted in the trial of the SEVEN BISHOPS. (DISPENSING POWER, SUSPENDING POWER.)   IHE

Declaration of Rights (Feb. 1689) was adopted by the CONVENTION PARLIAMENT and presented to William and Mary and accepted by them. They were then formally proclaimed as king and queen (23 Feb.). The D. of R. consisted of a list of what were considered to be the arbitrary and illegal acts and practices of James II, safeguards for the future and the SETTLEMENT of the succession. The Convention then declared itself a parliament and embodied the D. of R. in a BILL OF RIGHTS. The Scottish Estates accompanied their acceptance of William and Mary (11 Apr.) by a somewhat more extensive Claim of Right.   IHE

Declaration of the Army (15 June 1647). Having possession of the king at Newmarket, the army had the advantage over the LONG PARLIAMENT and put forward this declaration of its demands. It claimed the right to speak on behalf of the people whose liberties it was defending, demanded an early dissolution and frequent parliaments together with an act of oblivion and toleration of the sects, and suggested Parliament should be purged of its corrupt members. The army then advanced on London and enforced the withdrawal of 11 Presbyterian M.P.s. Reaching no conclusions with the Parliamentary oligarchy, it put forward the HEADS OF THE PROPOSALS to the king.   IHE

Declaratory Act. (1) (Ireland, 1719), reaffirmed the right of the British Parliament to legislate for Ireland (POYNINGS' LAW) and abolished the appellate jurisdiction of the Irish House of Lords. It was repealed in 1782.
(2) (America, 1766), followed the repeal of the STAMP ACT. It asserted British sovereignty and the full rights of the British Parliament to legislate for the American colonies.   IHE

De donis conditionalibus, see WESTMINSTER, 2nd STATUTE.

Deed Poll, literally a deed with a straight upper edge, used for transactions where no duplicate is required, e.g. grants in perpetuity; most CHARTERS are deeds poll. The term is restricted in modern usage notably to instruments for changing names. PMB

De Facto Act, the popular description of the Act passed by the Parliament of 1495 to protect the property and persons of supporters of the *de facto* king from retribution should he be overthrown. Neither the words *de facto* nor *de jure* occur in the Act, and its importance has been exaggerated. Had Henry VII been overthrown, his supporters would not have secured much protection. Its significance lies in the limited but practical intention of Henry to declare that the wars of the ROSES, with their conflicting pretenders and summary executions, were finally over.   RBG

Defence, Ministry of. Between 1936 and Apr. 1940 there was a Minister for the Co-ordination of D. whose duties were strictly limited to coordination, mainly in the field of supply, with no executive powers. In Apr. 1940 the PRIME MINISTER assumed the additional title of Minister of D. In 1947 a separate Minister of D. was appointed with a Ministry, to be responsible to PARLIAMENT for the inter-relations of the three services and their supply. On 1 Apr. 1964, a unified M. of D., under a single SECRETARY OF STATE advised by a D. Council, absorbed the ADMIRALTY, WAR OFFICE and AIR MINISTRY.   MR

Defender of the Faith (*fidei defensor*), the title awarded to Henry VIII by Pope Leo X (11 Oct. 1521) for his pamphlet *Assertio Septem Sacramentorum* attacking Luther's doctrines. 'F.D.' was permanently put on the coinage by George I.   IHE

Degeangli, a primitive tribe occupying north and north-west Wales. Overrun by the Romans c. A.D. 48, they never became a CIVITAS, probably remaining under military government. CFS

Degsastan, battle of (603), was fought at an unidentified site in the kingdom of NORTHUMBRIA between the Northumbrians under king Æthelfrith and the SCOTS of DALRIADA under king Aedan, assisted by Scots from Ireland. The Northumbrians were victorious, and the Scots did not obtain possession of the Lowlands between Tweed and Forth until the early 11th century (CARHAM).   CFS

De heretico comburendo, an act of the parliament of 1401, responded to urgent appeals by Thomas Arundel, Archbishop of Canterbury, backed by convocation, for stern measures against the LOLLARDS. The act forbade preaching without licence from a bishop and aimed at the suppression of Lollard conventicles, schools and literature. Suspected heretics were to be arrested, tried by the diocesan courts and imprisoned if convicted. If the heretic refused to abjure his errors or if, having once abjured, he relapsed into heresy, he might be handed over to the local sheriff or mayor to be publicly burned. The first Lollard martyr, William Sawtrey, was burned at Smithfield on 2 March 1401, on the order of the strictly orthodox Henry IV before the act had received his royal assent. Retained by Henry VIII, the act was repealed under Protector Somerset in 1547, revived under Queen Mary in 1554 (MARIAN REACTION), and finally repealed by the Elizabethan Act of SUPREMACY in 1559.   RFW

Deheubarth, 'D. Cymru', or *dextralis pars Britanniae* (Asser), may originally have referred to the whole of south Wales. Later it became restricted to that kingdom which embraced all south Wales excluding the provinces of Morgannwg and Gwent (roughly, modern Glamorgan and Monmouthshire). The core of the future kingdom was formed in the 8th century, when Seisyll, ruler of Ceredigion (Cardiganshire), annexed Ystrad Tywi (roughly Carmarthenshire) to create Seisyllwg. To this, Hywel the Good (*c.* 910–50) added the old south-western kingdom of Dyfed (Dimetia) by his marriage. Under Hywel's grandson, Maredudd (986–99), Brycheiniog (Brecknock) probably first acknowledged the overlordship of D. Subjected to extensive Norman encroachments on all sides from the end of the 11th century, and almost extinguished during the reign of Henry I, D., in close co-operation with GWYNEDD, nevertheless recovered most of its losses between 1135 and 1154. Under its outstanding ruler, the Lord Rhys (1155–97), it gained recognition of its independence from Henry II, entered upon a period of prosperity and influence, and firmly drew the line against further MARCHER encroachment in south Wales. Following Rhys's death, the partition of his inheritance and dissensions among his descendants led to D.'s playing a weak and divided role in the 13th century, with some of its princes supporting Gwynedd and others the kings of England.   GW

Deira, a kingdom of the ANGLES in central and eastern Yorkshire, expansion to the west being prevented by the British kingdom of ELMET. The name D. is of British origin, and archaeology shows that the area was settled early, but nothing more is known of the relations between natives and invaders. Its first recorded king, Ælle, is not mentioned until 560. He figures in the reputed puns of pope Gregory I (ROMAN MISSION), but otherwise little is known of Deiran history. It existed as a separate kingdom until near the end of the 6th century, and from 632 to 633 and 641 to 654, but was otherwise joined with BERNICIA to make the kingdom of NORTHUMBRIA.   CFS

Delaware, one of the original 13 states of the U.S.A. taking its name from Lord de la Warr, governor of Virginia (1609–18), who entered the bay one year after Hudson. The first Dutch West India Company's settlement of 1631 was destroyed by Indians. Swedes settled from 1624 and Germans in 1633, and the Dutch established Fort Christina (Wilmington) in 1638, absorbing New Sweden in 1655. Captured by the English (1664) with NEW AMSTERDAM, it was conveyed to William Penn (1682) and remained part of PENNSYLVANIA until 1702 when it became a separate colony.   IHE

Delegates, High Court of, a civil and canon law appellate court established in 1534 to hear appeals from church courts hitherto sent to Rome, which later acquired an appellate jurisdiction from the Instance court of the High Court of Admiralty. There was no permanent court: on the ecclesiastical model judges were appointed to each case by special commission. The court, which fell into disrepute, was abolished in 1832; its powers are now exercised by the Judicial Committee of the PRIVY COUNCIL.   PMB

Delhi, the ancient capital of the Hindu and Mogul empires, was taken by the British in 1803 and incorporated in the PUNJAB. In 1911–12, however, the capital was transferred from Calcutta to D., a new city (New D.) inaugurated and a separate province created (enlarged by additions from the UNITED PROVINCES in 1915), which was designated a Union territory in 1956. D. was the scene of fighting in the second Maratha war (1803–5) and the mutiny (1857).   SHS

Delinquents. Parliament issued a declaration (6 Sept. 1642) that it would not discharge its forces until the king should abandon to it all 'delinquents' and other 'malignant and disaffected persons'. The term was applied to royalists in general, and by 1648 the king was named the 'chief delinquent'. After NASEBY royalists had to pay crippling fines to 'compound for their delinquency'. (MALIGNANTS; HEADS OF THE PROPOSALS; MAJOR-GENERALS; PENRUDDOCK.) IHE

Demerara, see BRITISH GUIANA.

Demesne, land etc. kept in the lord's hand. In HONORS the d. represented that part of the due military service not allocated to sub-tenants but discharged by household knights, a practice almost dead in 1166. In manors the d., worked principally by VILLEINS, supplied the lord's arable etc. requirements. Varying d. administration, whether by intensive farming, leasing as a whole or granting in sections, is a guide to the agricultural policies and pressures of a period.

Ancient d. in England was land, including boroughs, vested in the crown in 1066 and recorded in DOMESDAY, even if subsequently granted away. Villeins on ancient d., freer than their fellows elsewhere, paid national not manorial TALLAGES and taxes on MOVABLES, and had special privileges, probably derived from the freer pre-Norman conquest villeinage, notably the right to sue at COMMON LAW.   PMB

Demetae, a primitive tribe occupying the area of Pembrokeshire. Conquered by the Romans in the later 1st century A.D., they either became a CIVITAS or remained under military government.   CFS

Deodand. The object, whether an animal or inanimate, which brought about a human being's death and which, in the early middle ages, was believed to share the guilt for the death. The object itself or its value was received by the king to be applied to charitable purposes, as a gift to God, *Deodandum*. D.s were abolished in 1846.   PMB

Deorham, see DYRHAM.

Deposition of Kings. (1) Edward II. In Sept. 1326 Queen Isabella, her lover, Roger Mortimer, and a group of exiled nobles were in open opposition to her husband. Isabella and her followers, with a band of mercenaries, sailed from Holland to Suffolk, and quickly found support in East Anglia against Edward II and his favourites, the Despensers. The king and the Despensers fled from London to the west: the city promptly declared for Isabella. The queen advanced to Bristol, where Hugh Despenser the elder, earl of Winchester, surrendered, to be sentenced to death on 27 Oct. Edward II and Hugh Despenser the younger, lord of Glamorgan, were captured in Neath Abbey by the earl of Lancaster on 16 Nov. Despenser was sentenced to death at Hereford on 24 Nov., while the king was imprisoned in Kenilworth castle. Meanwhile the king's son, Edward, then nearly fourteen, had been proclaimed keeper of the realm. The victorious rebels summoned a parliament for Jan. 1327, at first in the prince's and then in the king's name. Lords, clergy and commons quickly assented to a proposal from the city of London that Edward II should be deposed and replaced by his son. On 15 Jan. Walter Reynolds, archbishop of Canterbury, proclaimed Edward II deposed by the will of the nobles, clergy and people. The king, informed of this decision by a deputation representing the estates of the realm, was finally induced to abdicate by the threat that his son might be passed over if he refused. It was evidently felt, in the absence of any clear constitutional means of deposing a king, that a declaration of deposition needed to be backed up by Edward's 'voluntary' surrender of the throne. The reign of Edward III was dated from 25 Jan. 1327. Edward II was murdered in BERKELEY castle in September.

(2) Richard II. After the death of John of Gaunt, duke of Lancaster (3 Feb. 1399), Richard, through the committee of eighteen, appointed at the SHREWSBURY parliament, extended the sentence imposed on Gaunt's heir, Henry Bolingbroke, at the lists at COVENTRY, to banishment for life and seized the greater part of Gaunt's vast estates. In May Richard set out for Ireland, leaving as keeper of the realm his uncle Edmund, duke of York. Early in July Henry landed at RAVENSPUR; by the end of the month Richard's caretaker government had collapsed, York had submitted and Richard's most unpopular servants had been executed. Sending the earl of Salisbury to raise forces in North Wales, Richard himself sailed from Ireland on 27 July and, while his forces either deserted or were disbanded, reached Conway by 11 Aug., to find that Salisbury's army had already broken up. A deputation led by Henry Percy, earl of Northumberland, went to Conway, and by treacherous assurances that he should remain king induced Richard to leave the castle. Between Conway and Flint Richard was ambushed and delivered to Henry, who imprisoned him in the Tower of London, and summoned Parliament—in Richard's name—to meet at Westminster on 30 September. The estates received Richard's 'voluntary' abdication, heard articles of accusation against him and, backed by a concourse of Londoners, declared that Richard should be deposed. So far the revolution of 1399 had followed closely the precedents of 1327. Henry

Bolingbroke, before the assembled estates and people, 'challenged the crown', on the grounds of his direct descent from Henry III and by the right given him by the grace of God—inferring that victory over Richard was a clear demonstration of divine favour. The assembly accepted the claim, Henry was enthroned, and his reign was officially dated from that day, 30 Sept. 1399. Richard remained a prisoner until his death early in 1400 in PONTEFRACT.

(3) Henry VI. At the parliament of Oct. 1460 Richard, duke of York, formally claimed the throne as the heir of Richard II, but on 25 Oct. it was decided that Henry VI, a prisoner of the YORKISTS since the battle of NORTHAMPTON, should remain king for his lifetime, while Richard should be recognized as his heir. Richard, however, was killed by the LANCASTRIANS at WAKEFIELD on 30 Dec. After his victory at MORTIMER'S CROSS (2 Feb. 1461) Richard's eldest son Edward, earl of March, entered London on 26 Feb. and was acclaimed as king on 1 March by an assembly of soldiers and Londoners; on 3 March a council of Yorkist lords asked him to assume the crown; and on 4 March, after a crowd had heard a sermon at Paul's Cross reiterating Edward's claim and had manifested their approval, Edward took a form of the coronation oath and was seated on the king's bench in Westminster hall and sat enthroned in Westminster abbey. His reign was deemed to start on 4 March, and on 28 June, after his decisive victory at TOWTON, he was crowned at Westminster. Henry VI, rescued at the second battle of ST ALBANS, had found refuge in Scotland, but, when Edward made peace with the Scots in 1464, wandered about the north of England. In 1465 he was captured at Bungerley Hippingstones (Lancs.) and imprisoned in the Tower. Briefly restored during the 'READEPTION' of 1470–1, Henry VI was finally put to death on 21 May 1471.

(4) Edward V. Edward IV died on 9 April 1483, leaving as his heir his elder son Edward, aged 12, and appointing his brother Richard, duke of Gloucester, protector. On 30 April Richard gained control of the young king at Stony Stratford and was acknowledged as protector in London on 4 May. Edward was lodged in the Tower, and his coronation was planned for 24 June. On 13 June a group of Edward IV's councillors was arrested and Hastings was immediately executed on charges of plotting against the protector. A week of rumour and uncertainty followed. On 22 June, in a sermon at Paul's Cross, a friar, Ralph Shaw, asserted that Edward IV's children were illegitimate, because before his marriage to Elizabeth Woodville he had been contracted to Lady Eleanor Talbot; since the children of George, duke of Clarence (executed in 1478), were barred by their father's attainder, Richard was the true heir to the throne. Other preachers soon declared Edward IV himself to have been illegitimate. On 23 June the duke of Buckingham laid Richard's claim before a council of lords, and on the following day the harangue he delivered to the corporation of London was followed by a somewhat half-hearted acclamation of Richard as king. Parliament assembled on the 25th, heard a full recital of Richard's claim and approved it. On the same day Richard's Woodville prisoners were executed at Pontefract. Finally, on the 26th, the estates petitioned Richard to assume the crown, and, closely following the precedent established by Edward IV in 1461, he was enthroned at Westminster, his coronation following on 6 July. Edward V and his younger brother Richard, the PRINCES IN THE TOWER, may have been murdered soon after the coronation.   RFW

Derby House Committee. After the ENGAGEMENT Parliament replaced the COMMITTEE OF BOTH KINGDOMS by an all-English military committee which first met in Derby House, London (Jan. 1648). It acted with promptitude and vigour during the second CIVIL WAR.   IHE

Dere Street, see ERMINE STREET.

Desmond Revolt, (1) (1569–73). After Gerald earl of D.'s misgovernment in Munster he was detained in England. His cousin, Sir James Fitzmaurice, became leader of his clan, the Geraldines, and led a Roman Catholic rising, which was joined by those resisting the English PLANTATION OF IRELAND. Foreign help did not materialize, and the revolt was suppressed.
(2) (1579–83). Sir James Fitzmaurice left Lisbon (July 1579) with a motley force to promote a Roman Catholic revolt of the Geraldines of Munster. Landing in Kerry, he was soon killed in an affray. Philip II of Spain and Pope Gregory XIII sent a small contingent which was destroyed by the English at Smerwick (Nov. 1580). The earl of D. joined the rising, but was killed in 1583. Munster was devastated, and further plantation by English undertakers followed in 1586.
    IHE

Despard's Plot (1802). E. M. Despard, an engineer officer who had held a number of colonial appointments but had been unfairly dismissed, planned to seize the Tower and Bank of England and to assassinate the king. Arrested (16 Nov. 1802), he was tried (7–8 Feb. 1803), Nelson speaking in his defence, and executed (21 Feb.).
    MLH

De tallagio non concedendo, a list of articles thought to be a STATUTE in the 17th century, but probably a draft of concessions demanded from Edward I by the baronial opposition and prepared for discussion in Parliament in the autumn of 1297. The name is derived from the first provision—that no TALLAGE or AIDS shall be imposed without the consent of the whole realm. The baronial demands were largely met by the CONFIRMATION OF THE CHARTERS.   RFW

Dettingen, battle of (27 June 1743), was fought during the AUSTRIAN SUCCESSION WAR. The Anglo-German forces, under George II, marching to Hanau were in danger of being cut off between D. and Aschaffenburg by the French. George II halted before D., where the French lost their advantage by a rash attack and were driven in flight across the Main. No use was made of this victory, but the French withdrew beyond the Rhine. This was the last battle in which an English monarch was present.   IHE

Devaluation of sterling. After WORLD WAR II the £ was fixed at $4·03, the pre-war parity, an over-valuation which remained until d. (Sept. 1949) to $2·80. A further d. occurred (Nov. 1967) to $2·40.   MLH

Deverel-Rimbury Culture, a culture of the middle and late BRONZE AGE, so called from two type-sites in Dorset. It was due to an invasion of CELTS, and it and similar cultures eventually spread over the lowland zone. It revolutionized agriculture by introducing into Britain a light two-ox plough. This, although coulterless, was capable of breaking light soil, and men for the first time became concerned with the cultivation of crops, previously a subsidiary task carried out by women with hoes, etc. Textile manufacture was facilitated by the introduction of spindle whorls for spinning and loom weights for weaving. Bronze tools and vessels increased in efficiency and variety; gold and other luxuries were imported. The people appear to have lived in small farming communities, cultivation of crops (CELTIC FIELDS) being as important as animal husbandry. Cremation burials continued (URN CULTURE), the ashes being placed in urns, but with extremely few grave-goods, and buried in large cemeteries. From the 6th century B.C. this and similar cultures gave way in the lowlands to those of the IRON AGE.   CFS

Devil's Highway, see PORT WAY. The Devil was also associated with other sections of ROMAN ROADS.   CFS

Dialogus de Scaccario. The D. was written 1176–9 by Richard fitzNigel, TREASURER of Henry II and later bishop of London, son of Nigel bishop of Ely, treasurer of Henry I.

In the form of question and answer between a pupil and his master, it covers the whole of EXCHEQUER organization and procedure. Richard wrote with clarity and accuracy of the department in which he worked and which affected the lives of almost everyone in the country; his historical passages are, however, less reliable. The D. is fundamental to an understanding of 12th- and 13th-century English history and stands beside GLANVILL as a monument to the strong efficient government of Henry II.

PMB

Diggers, a small group of extreme radicals founded by Winstanley, who began digging the common at St George's Hill, Surrey (1649). Opposed to physical force, they were easily suppressed by the army leaders. They held that the political revolution must be based on a social revolution, and wished to restore the land to the people.   IHE

Digges' Case (1584) was a case of the privilege claimed by Parliament of freedom from arrest of members' servants. The archbishop of Canterbury asserted this claim on behalf of James Digges, a gentleman in his service, committed to the Fleet during session. The House of Lords ordered his release. This privilege ceased in 1770.   IHE

Dingaan's day. During the GREAT TREK Piet Retief, leader of the trekkers into NATAL, visited the Zulu chief Dingaan to secure a grant of territory. He gained a written title to the land between the Umzimvubu and Tugela rivers but was treacherously murdered with his 100 followers while being entertained in Dingaan's kraal (6 Feb. 1838). Further Zulu attacks made the trekkers' position precarious until Andries Pretorius with about 500 men slew some 3,000 Zulus on the banks of the Blood River (16 Dec. 1838). The anniversary was celebrated as D.D. until 1952 when it came to be called the Day of the Covenant (the trekkers had vowed to build a church if God granted them victory).   IHE

Diplomatic Revolution (1756) was a reversal of the long-standing alliances under which Great Britain, Austria, France and Prussia had fought the AUSTRIAN SUCCESSION WAR. The treaty of AACHEN (1748) was an uneasy peace, Austria was not reconciled to the loss of Silesia, Prussia became convinced that her ruin was planned and Anglo-French rivalry in India and North America produced a critical situation by 1755. Continued co-operation of Britain, the Netherlands and Austria was hampered by Austro-Dutch disputes over the BARRIER fortresses and Austrian dissatisfaction with the British alliance. Austria sought closer relations with France after 1750. Royal concern for Hanover led to a British pact with Russia (1755), causing Prussia immediate alarm and resulting in the defensive convention of Westminster between Britain and Prussia (16 Jan. 1756). This caused France and Austria to make the defensive treaty of Versailles (1 May 1756) which was joined by Russia (Dec.). This was the D.R., confirmed by the offensive treaty of Versailles (May 1757), aligning the powers for the ensuing SEVEN YEARS' WAR. The Netherlands remained neutral throughout, Spain until 1762.   IHE

Disestablishment, see WELSH DIS-ESTABLISHMENT; CHURCH OF IRELAND.

Disinherited, the. (1) 1265. After the defeat of the MONTFORTIANS at EVESHAM (4 Aug.), the victorious royalists proceeded to penalize their opponents. By an ordinance made at Winchester on 17 Sept. the lands of all supporters of Simon de Montfort were to be seized for the king. Many such lands were then—or had already been—distributed among the king's supporters. This harsh measure increased the resistance of those Montfortians who were still in rebellion and whom the ordinance had 'disinherited'. (Dictum of KENILWORTH.)

(2) 1332. Although after the treaty of NORTHAMPTON (1328) Robert Bruce had agreed to restore the Scottish lands

of certain English lords, no restoration was made either by Bruce (†1329) or the earl of Moray, regent for David II. In 1332 the 'disinherited' lords, led by Edward Balliol, son of the former king John Balliol (NORHAM, ARBITRATION OF), landed in Fife, defeated the Scots at Dupplin Muir (11 Aug. 1332) and had Balliol crowned king at SCONE. Edward III, though denying any knowledge of the expedition, was certainly aware of it. Balliol acknowledged the overlordship of Edward III and promised substantial cessions of territory to England, thereby strengthening the nationalist reaction which speedily swept him out of Scotland. (See HALIDON HILL.)   RFW

Dispenser, a secondary officer of the household responsible for apportioning food and drink. The office, mentioned in DOMESDAY, was a Grand SERJEANTY with land at Great Rollright, Oxfordshire. In the late 13th century the D. family sold the land to Robert Burnel, bishop of Bath and Wells, to whom the office passed. The D. family prominent in the reigns of Henry III and Edward II descended from the d.s of the Anglo-Norman earls of Chester.   PMB

Dispensing Power, the PREROGATIVE right of the crown to exempt from the operation of laws in individual instances, was a discretionary power necessary to the medieval monarchy. It came to be used to protect royal officials and give licence to worship, trade, etc., contrary to statute. The growth of Parliament led to protests against these dispensations, especially by the LONG PARLIAMENT against Charles I's use of the D.P. during the ELEVEN YEARS' TYRANNY. Charles II failed to get approval for its use in his DECLARATION OF INDULGENCE, but made some use of it in matters of trade and against the TEST ACT. James II's use of the D.P. to promote Roman Catholics (HALES'S CASE) resulted in its being declared illegal by the BILL OF RIGHTS (1689), 'as it hath been assumed and exercised of late'.   IHE

Dissenters, see NONCONFORMISTS.

Dissolution, Right of, to end a Parliament by exercise of the royal PREROGATIVE. It was particularly used by the Stewarts to terminate Parliamentary opposition and to govern by prerogative and remained a valuable royal instrument as long as the crown actively intervened in politics. The decision to consent to or withhold a d. was for all practical purposes finally abandoned during the reign of Queen Victoria as an inevitable consequence of the REFORM ACT of 1832. Parliament is now dissolved on ministerial advice by a royal proclamation which also fixes the date of meeting of the new Parliament.   IHE

Dissolution of the Monasteries. In 1535 Thomas Cromwell, vicar-general, and his agents began their visitation of the religious houses, issued INJUNCTIONS for their better conduct and collected the required information and evidence. In 1536 Parliament approved the suppression of all houses valued at less than £200 per annum, largely on the pretext of the scandalous lives of their inmates. This was partly responsible for the PILGRIMAGE OF GRACE, which again led to further attacks on the abbeys. The greater houses were dissolved (1537–40) mainly by 'voluntary' surrender, and Parliament authorized complete suppression in 1539. A special court of AUGMENTATIONS was set up to deal with the lands and properties which yielded enormous profit to the crown. The nobility and gentry profited as a class, some of the wealth was spent on the navy and coastal fortifications, and six new bishoprics were created. This revolution was effected comparatively quietly. Monasticism was a spent force and held in little regard by the mass of the laity who resented the wealth of the monasteries. Only a small part of their income was devoted to charity and hospitality, and most houses contained fewer than ten monks. An indirect result was to give the laity a majority in the House of Lords. The monks were pensioned or found employment as secular clergy, although some fared badly.   IHE

Distraint of Knighthood, the compulsion of persons with lands of stated value (£20, later £40) and tenants of knight's fees to assume knighthood. It was introduced in Henry III's reign and periodically revived to obtain further receipts from feudal incidents (notably RELIEF, WARDSHIP and SCUTAGE), to provide for the legal and administrative business discharged by knights. It was continued by the Tudors and James I, and the fines levied by Charles I on those who neglected this obligation alienated many of the gentry. It was declared illegal by the LONG PARLIAMENT (1641) and was not revived after the RESTORATION.   PMB; IHE

Distress, a means of compelling a tenant to perform services. The d., generally livestock, was seized by the lord; the tenant could recover it either by performing his services or, if he wished to contest the lord's claim, by a writ of replevin. The procedure was open to much abuse, and from the statute of MARLBOROUGH (1267) onwards many attempts were made to regulate it.   PMB

Divine Right of Kings to unquestioned control over their subjects was put forward by Richard II at the end of the 14th century, but was first explicitly formulated in England by James I. This theory with medieval origins enhanced the ultimate power of European monarchies at a time when they were threatened by the activities of Protestant and Catholic zealots and other disruptive forces. Monarchy based on primogeniture was held to be divinely ordained, and rulers were answerable to God alone. It was expounded in an extreme form by James I in his *True Law of Free Monarchies* (1598) and in subsequent works and speeches. A free monarchy was one free from control which could make and suspend laws, and no tyranny justified resistance. The theory was more rationally expressed in Sir Robert Filmer's

Patriarcha, written in 1642 and published posthumously in 1680 as an argument against the EXCLUSION BILL. D.R. was supported by ARMINIANS and LAUDIANS but disputed vigorously by Parliamentarians and Puritans (PROTESTATION). Anglican canons of 1640 provided a definition of D.R. to be read quarterly at morning prayer, stating that armed resistance involved damnation. It was still supported by Tories and Anglicans after the Restoration, but as the absolutist tendencies of Charles II and James II developed the emphasis was on NON-RESISTANCE. D.R. in England was extinguished by the GLORIOUS REVOLUTION and demolished as a theory by the first of John Locke's *Two Treatises on Civil Government* (1690). Thenceforward only JACOBITES and NON-JURORS upheld it.   IHE

Dobuni or **Dobunni,** a powerful British tribe occupying the Cotswold area. During the earlier part of the 1st century A.D. they were ruled by kings who issued coins. Conquered by the Romans before A.D. 47, they became a CIVITAS with their capital at Corinium (Cirencester).   CFS

Dollars were issued in 1797 countermarked with the head of George III, to overcome the acute shortage of Spanish silver d. (valued at 4s. 9d. and 5s. in 1800). Bank of England d. were overstruck in 1804 with a new design, the first instance of Britannia appearing on a silver coin. D. were bank tokens and not a legal issue.   IHE

Dolly's Brae, Co. Down (12 July 1849), the scene of an affray between Orangemen and Ribandmen on the anniversary of the battle of the BOYNE.   MLH

Domesday Book. This most famous and controversial of all English public records, now in the PUBLIC RECORD OFFICE, was begun at Christmas 1085. Thereafter commissioners were sent through England asking jurors: the name of the manor, town etc.; the tenant in Edward the Confessor's time and now; how many hides in it; how many ploughs and men on demesne; how many KOTSETLAS, slaves, freemen and sokemen; how much woodland, meadow and pasture; how many mills and fishpools; how much land added or subtracted since Edward's time; the value then and now; the tenement of each freeman and sokeman. How the commissioners worked and how long the two volumes took to compile is not exactly known. Vol. 1 contains most of England, vol. 2 Essex, Suffolk and Norfolk only, but in greater detail: remote counties, e.g. Cumberland and Northumberland, are omitted. In each volume and county the king's land is described first, then that of his various tenants. D. has been called simply a geld- or tax-book, but it is easier to suppose that William I wanted a complete description of all his conquered land. It has always been a reference book, borne about with the king or kept in his treasury, frequently cited in court. Together with the *Inquisitio Eliensis, Exon Domesday* and the *Inquisitio comitatus Cantabrigiensis*, smaller works produced from the same materials, D. is a magnificent source for late Anglo-Saxon and early post-Norman conquest history, with no parallel elsewhere.   PMB

Dominica was discovered by Columbus on 'Sunday' 3 Nov. 1493. Charles I granted it to the earl of Carlisle in 1627, but the French settled it from 1632. It was captured by the British in 1761 and formally ceded in 1763; the French retook it in 1778, but lost it after the battle of the SAINTS in 1782. D. was federated with the WINDWARD ISLANDS in 1763, became a separate colony in 1767, was federated with the LEEWARD ISLANDS in 1871 and rejoined to the Windward Islands in 1940. On 1 Mar. 1967 D. became one of the WEST INDIES Associated States   SHS ; IHE

Domus Conversorum, founded by Henry III for converted JEWS in 1232, on a site in Chancery Lane, London. The numbers in the house varied: in 1280 there were 96, served by a chaplain, maintained and, if possible, taught a trade; others outside were

advanced in royal service or given pensions. After the Jews' expulsion in 1290 the D. remained with steadily diminishing numbers, and in 1377 the offices of Warden and Master of the Rolls were united, remaining linked until the mid-19th century. The D. was demolished in 1717 and the Master of the ROLLS' house built on the site, but pensions to converts were paid at least until 1773. The PUBLIC RECORD OFFICE now occupies the site.
PMB

Don Pacifico incident (1850). David Pacifico, a British subject (by reason of birth in Gibraltar) resident in Athens, had his house burnt by a mob (Easter 1847). His extravagant claim on the Greek government being unsatisfied, Palmerston, the foreign secretary, took this (together with other outstanding debts) as reason for ordering the British fleet into the Piraeus (Jan. 1850) to seize Greek shipping. This action angered France and Russia, guarantors with Britain of Greek independence, and Palmerston's attempted repudiation of an agreement on the matter with France led to the withdrawal of the French ambassador in London. Palmerston's high-handed attitude called in question his general conduct of foreign policy: a motion of censure was carried in the Lords, but a similar motion in the Commons failed, Palmerston defending himself in a brilliant speech (25 June 1850). MLH

Doom, the judgment given by a court (MOOT) in Old English times. CFS

Dover, one of the earliest English CASTLES and one of the original CINQUE PORTS. The castle quickly surrendered to William the Conqueror after the battle of HASTINGS and opposed little resistance to King Stephen at the outset of the ANARCHY. Greatly strengthened by Henry II in the 1180s, D. was the only fortress and port in the south-east to hold out in 1216–17 against Prince Louis of France, who made a most determined effort to reduce it. D. was stoutly defended by the JUSTICIAR, Hubert de Burgh, who fully appreciated its im-

portance as the Key of England: '*clavis enim Anglie est.*' The baronial defeat at LINCOLN eventually caused Louis to raise the siege. In the 1260s Henry III and the MONTFORTIANS contended for the control of D. Placed in baronial control after the PROVISIONS OF OXFORD, D. was recovered by the king in May 1263 but lost again in the summer. During the campaign of LEWES, D. was held for the Montfortians and did not return to royal control until after the battle of EVESHAM (1265) when Simon de Montfort's widow, Eleanor, surrendered to Edward, the king's son, after part of the garrison had mutinied. RFW

Dover, treaty of (1 June 1670), was made between England and France through the medium of Charles II's sister Henrietta, duchess of Orleans. The CABAL abandoned the TRIPLE ALLIANCE of 1668 and agreed to war on Holland in return for Walcheren, Sluys and Kadzand. Louis XIV was to be assisted in his claims to the Spanish dominions and in the event of success England was to gain Ostend, Minorca and territories in South America. Charles was to receive annual subsidies from France. By a secret treaty, known to Clifford and Arlington, Charles was to declare himself a Roman Catholic. It led to the third DUTCH WAR (1672–4), but when Charles issued the DECLARATION OF INDULGENCE (1672) Parliament replied with the TEST ACT of 1673. The anti-Catholic suspicions aroused created lasting opposition. IHE

Dower. The practice of d. was adopted in the 12th century, replacing the earlier custom of a husband's morning gift to his bride. To secure the wife's claim as well as to discourage clandestine marriages, the husband publicly dowered his wife at the church door at their wedding. After the husband's death the widow's d., usually a third of the husband's lands at the time of the marriage but a half in some tenures, was assigned to her for life. Widows' difficulties in obtaining control of their d., mentioned in MAGNA CARTA figure largely in the court records of the 13th century. As time passed the law of d. became first more intricate, then waned as other forms of marriage contract, e.g. jointure, were adopted.   PMB

Drogheda 'massacre' (11 Sept. 1649). Ormonde, the king's lord-lieutenant, having surrendered Dublin to the Parliamentarians (1647) rather than let it fall to the Irish, returned to Ireland (1649), formed a royalist–Catholic alliance and proclaimed Charles II. He was defeated at Rathmines. Cromwell landed at Dublin (May), marched north and took Drogheda. The English garrison were put to the sword as perjured rebels, in accordance with accepted custom. Roman Catholic priests suffered, but there was no 'massacre' of the inhabitants. Similar treatment followed at Wexford (11 Oct.). Cromwell left in 1650, the conquest was completed in 1652, and followed by wholesale land confiscation to reward ROUNDHEADS and ADVENTURERS.   IHE

Druidism, the system of religion, etc., taught by the Druids, a priestly, judicial and scholarly caste among the CELTS of Britain, Gaul and Ireland. It was flourishing c. 200 B.C., but comparatively little is known of it apart from the information given by Julius Caesar. D. taught the immortality of the soul; mistletoe and oak were objects of veneration; human sacrifice and divination played a prominent part; and an aspirant had to spend a long period as a novice. The element of human sacrifice caused its suppression by the Romans, towards whom the Druids showed great hostility. A main centre of D. in the west was in Mona (Anglesey), and the Roman attack on it in A.D. 61 was to wipe out a major centre of resistance to the ROMAN CONQUEST, the Druids there being massacred and the sacred groves destroyed. D. disappeared as an organized system, but some elements survived, certainly in folk-lore and local custom; although the TEUTONIC CONQUEST limited these to the Celtic west. Many antiquaries of the 17th and 18th centuries unjustifiably re-garded stone circles, e.g. STONE-HENGE, as centres of Druidical practices. But this renewed interest helped to produce a reconstructed system, Neo-D., in the early 19th century, and the term Druid has been revived in connexion with EISTEDDFODAU. In 1781 the Order of Druids, a FRIENDLY SOCIETY, was founded.   CFS

Duke (Latin *dux*). Although medieval kings of England were also d.s of NORMANDY and AQUITAINE, d. did not become a style of nobility in England until the 14th century, when Edward III, to give his sons a style of greater dignity than EARL, created them d.s (1337 ff.). It was first extended to those not of royal blood when Richard II created Robert de Vere d. of Ireland (1386). D. has remained the premier title of NOBILITY.   CFS

Dumnonii, a British tribal group occupying the area of Cornwall, Devon and west Somerset. Conquered by the Romans by A.D. 47, they became a CIVITAS with their capital at Isca Dumnoniorum (Exeter).   CFS

Dunbar, battle of (27 April 1296), brought about a temporary collapse of Scottish resistance to Edward I. Since the coronation of John Balliol as king of Scots in 1292 Edward had steadily asserted his rights as superior lord of Scotland; Scottish resentment had grown, and by the end of 1295 Balliol's nobles had swept him into a French alliance and open war with Edward. After the defeat of the Scots at D. by John de Warenne, earl of Surrey, and the capture of many of their leaders, Edward was able to take Edinburgh and to overrun the Lowlands. Balliol abdicated, surrendered his kingdom to Edward on 2 July 1296 and died in exile in 1315. (NORHAM; STIRLING BRIDGE).   RFW

Dunbar, battle of (3 Sept. 1650). When the Scottish Estates proclaimed Charles II king the LONG PARLIAMENT dismissed their envoys. In July Cromwell marched towards Edinburgh but, after fruitless negotiations, was outmanoeuvred by Leslie and hemmed in between the Lammer-muirs and the sea near D. The Scots rashly moved too soon and were trapped between the English under Lambert and Monk, and Cromwell's force in their rear. The victory was complete, there being over 3,000 Scottish casualties and nearly 10,000 prisoners taken.   IHE

Dundalk, battle of (14 Oct. 1318). After the victory of BANNOCKBURN the Scots not only invaded England but Edward Bruce, brother of King Robert, in 1315 also invaded Ireland. Many native Irish chiefs and some English lords allied themselves to Bruce, who gained control of Ulster and Meath, and on 1 May 1316 was crowned king of Ireland at D. Bruce's Irish allies were defeated in Connaught, however, and although Robert Bruce himself came to his brother's assistance they failed to capture Dublin in 1317. Finally Edward Bruce was defeated and killed by John de Bermingham at Faughart, near D. Ireland suffered severely from the devastation by the Scots and the consequent famine. English rule suffered a severe setback, and areas such as northern Thomond, which had been reconquered by the Irish during the invasion, were not recovered. With Bruce's invasion the tide of conquest turned and, from being an asset to the English crown, Ireland became a heavy liability.   RFW

Dunes, battle of the (13 June 1658). The English capture of JAMAICA (1655) led to war with Spain (Feb. 1656) and to an alliance with France (Mar. 1657) for a joint attack on Gravelines, Mardyke and DUNKIRK. Mardyke fell in 1657. The English fleet covered the siege of Dunkirk, begun in May 1658. The Cromwellians and French defeated the English royalists and Spaniards in the battle of the D.   IHE

Dunkirk, in the 16th and throughout the 17th and 18th centuries was the haunt of pirates and privateers preying on British shipping. Captured from Spain in 1658, ceded in 1659 but sold to France in 1662, the menace of D. is reflected in the provisions for the destruction of its fortifications in the treaties of UTRECHT (1713), the TRIPLE ALLIANCE (1717), AACHEN (1748) and PARIS (1763). In the SECOND WORLD WAR it witnessed the evacuation of British troops from the continent (May–June 1940) when the German advance threatened complete disaster.   IHE

Dunkirk evacuation (26 May–4 June 1940), in WORLD WAR II, the heroic operation 'Dynamo' which rescued 338,226 British and allied troops from imminent disaster. The main British expeditionary force, surrounded at D. together with men of the French First Army, were lifted by Vice-Admiral Ramsay's motley force of some 850 destroyers, personnel ships, schuyts, yachts etc., which ran a shuttle service from the harbour and beaches with the vital support of R.A.F. fighter command. Losses included 106 aircraft (against 133 of the enemy) and 235 vessels, including 6 British and 3 French destroyers.   IHE

Dunning's Resolution (6 Apr. 1780), 'that the influence of the crown has increased, is increasing, and ought to be diminished', was passed by the House of Commons by 233 votes to 215. Although not now regarded as historically fair criticism, it expressed the views of the Whig opposition, which aimed at destroying crown influence in Parliament and ending the American War of Independence.   IHE

Dupplin Muir, see DISINHERITED (2).

Duquesne, Fort, one of the key French forts established (1754) on the Mississippi and the Ohio to restrict British westward expansion and link up Canada and Louisiana. It was situated on the forks of the Ohio (now Pittsburg). Washington led an unsuccessful expedition against it, and in 1755 regular troops under Braddock were disastrously ambushed before reaching it. In 1758 General Forbes found it abandoned, the French having retreated to Canada. It was renamed Fort Pitt.   IHE

Durham Report (1839), 'report on the affairs of British North America', was prepared by John George Lambton, earl of Durham (1792–1840), with the help of his private secretary, Charles Buller (1806–48). 'Radical Jack', M.P. from 1813 and a peer from 1830, was an active supporter of the REFORM ACT of 1830 and a co-founder of the Colonization Society to improve colonial government; in 1838 he was appointed governor-general of British North America to deal with the problems resulting from the rebellions in QUEBEC and ONTARIO. His rigorous procedure lost him the confidence of the government and he resigned (1838), but his advocacy of colonial self-government, as expressed in the D.R., served as the foundation of the Dominion of CANADA and indirectly the basis of the modern British COMMONWEALTH.   SHS

Durotriges, a British tribe occupying the area of Dorset and part of Somerset with the great hill-fort of Maiden Castle as their capital. The fort was stormed and the tribe subdued by Roman forces under Vespasian soon after A.D. 43. They became a CIVITAS with, apparently, two capitals, at Durnovaria (Dorchester, Dorset) and Lindinae (Ilchester).   CFS

Dutch Wars. The 1st D.w. (1652–4) was mainly caused by political frictions, the English claim to right of search and to a lesser extent by the damaging effects of the NAVIGATION ACT (1651) on the Dutch carrying trade. The COMMONWEALTH navy ultimately gained ascendancy after hard-fought actions in the Channel and North Sea, and the Dutch with their bigger mercantile marine suffered heavier losses. At the peace the Dutch conceded most of the points at issue, including payment of compensation for the AMBOINA massacre (1623).

The 2nd D.w. (1665–7) was due to commercial and colonial rivalry. The Navigation Act (1660) was a further blow at the Dutch, and their hostility to the AFRICAN COMPANY led to local war in 1663, leaving them in possession of the Gold Coast forts (1664).

The English captured NEW AMSTERDAM (1664) and war was officially declared (Mar. 1665). There was fighting in Guiana, the West Indies and on the Dutch frontier, and the Netherlands was joined by France (1666). At sea the English decisively defeated the Dutch off Lowestoft (1665), had the worst of it in the indecisive Four Days' Battle in the Straits of Dover (1666), but again beat the Dutch off the North Foreland. In 1667 the Dutch entered the Thames and Medway and bombarded Chatham. The war was ended by the treaty of BREDA (1667).

The 3rd D.w. (1672–4) resulted from the treaty of DOVER (1670), when England supported the French attempt to overrun Holland. At sea the Dutch had the advantage in the battle of Southwold Bay (June 1672), and three drawn battles were fought in 1673, the last off Texel (Aug.). The Dutch took NEW YORK (1673), but it was restored by the treaty of Westminster (Feb. 1674), when England and the Netherlands made a separate peace.   IHE

Dyrham, battle of, north of Bath (577). The men of WESSEX under king Ceawlin defeated the Britons, killing three British kings and capturing Bath, Cirencester and Gloucester. The battle marks an important step in the Teutonic advance towards the west, and it broke the land communications between the Britons of the south-west and those of WALES.   CFS

Ealdorman, an Old English official of noble rank (GESITH, THEGN) placed by kings in charge of a SHIRE or *regio*, whose appointment or removal was at royal pleasure. His duties were to keep law and order, to preside at and enforce the judgements of local courts (MOOT) and to lead the local militia (FYRD). He seems to have received the profits of certain manors. From the early 9th century SHERIFFS assumed control of individual shires and ealdormanries became larger, although still being homogeneous administrative areas. During the time of king Cnut

(1017–37) the word was replaced by the Anglo-Scandinavian term EARL and ealdormanries by earldoms whose creation was frequently as much for political as administrative reasons. The term has survived as 'alderman'.   CFS

Earl. The term earl or *eorl* is an anglicization of Norse *jarl*. *Jarls* were leaders, of non-royal blood, in the 9th-century Danish armies; and during the 10th century under the title of e. they performed in the Danish areas the duties that EALDORMEN performed elsewhere. Under the Danish king Cnut (1017–37) e.s replaced ealdormen throughout England; but earldoms were created as much for political as administrative reasons and lacked the local unity of the former ealdormanries. Disputes between the e.s of Mercia, Wessex and Northumbria seriously weakened England under Edward the Confessor (1042–66) and Harold II (1066). Such earldoms were not, in theory, hereditary. The e. shared the presidency of the MOOT (COUNTY COURT) and led the militia (FYRD) of the shires that composed his earldom. He received the THIRD PENNY of the profits of the shire courts and of the payments made by towns, and seems to have drawn profits from certain manors that went with the office. The title continued after the Norman conquest and from the 12th century became one of NOBILITY rather than of office.   CFS

East Africa. In 1698 Arabs from MUSCAT AND OMAN captured the Portuguese fort of Mombasa and subsequently the whole coast, including the islands of ZANZIBAR and Pemba, using the mainland as a huge reservoir of their slave-raiding activities. From 1822, when a treaty terminated the export of slaves from the sultan of Zanzibar's territories, until 1890, when the Church Missionary Society overcame the government's reluctance to declare a protectorate over Uganda, the fight against the SLAVE-TRADE determined British policy in E.A. The British consuls and missionaries as a rule enjoyed the co-operation of successive sultans of Zanzibar, who

facilitated the work of the MISSIONARY SOCIETIES (Mombasa, 1844), outlawed (1873) and abolished (1889) the slave-trade and looked for British support against the Germans, French, Portuguese and Belgians. The E.A. COMPANY was instrumental in opening up KENYA and UGANDA; TANGANYIKA became a British MANDATE after the first world war; the E.A. HIGH COMMISSION (and its successor) is in charge of the services common to the three territories.   SHS

East Africa Company, Imperial British, chartered in 1888, acquired from the sultan of ZANZIBAR the British East Africa Protectorate (later renamed KENYA) and extended its activities to UGANDA in keen rivalry with the German E.A.C. and the Belgian African International Association. After its territories had been taken over by the government, the E.A.C. was wound up in 1896.   SHS

East Africa High Commission, consisting of the governors of KENYA, TANGANYIKA and UGANDA and a central legislative assembly, was set up on 1 Jan. 1948 in Nairobi, to provide and regulate the services common to the three territories. These include a court of appeal (1921), uniform currency (1922), customs union (1927), railways, harbours, posts, etc. From 28 Dec. 1961 the name was changed to East African Common Services Organization, and the three prime ministers took the governor's place. On 1 Dec. 1967 this was replaced by the East African Community formed by treaty between Kenya, TANZANIA and Uganda.   SHS; IHE

East Anglia, the kingdom of the East ANGLES, occupied the area of modern Norfolk and Suffolk and, in its early days, the Isle of Ely and part of Cambridgeshire. Settlement of the area began before the end of the 5th century. The kingdom was thickly populated and affluent, the wealth of its 7th-century rulers being shown by the ship burial at SUTTON HOO. It was converted to Christianity during the earlier 7th century. The majority of its kings are obscure figures and, with the exception of Rædwald (died *c.* 627), played little part outside their own kingdom. For much of its history the kingdom was threatened or dominated by MERCIA: three E.A. kings were killed by Penda of Mercia; one was killed with Penda at the battle of WINWÆD (655); one was executed by Offa of Mercia in 794. After the battle of ELLENDUNE (825) the king of E.A., in revolt against Mercia, sought the protection of Egbert of WESSEX, and in the same year the king of Mercia was killed while attacking E.A. In 841 E.A. was devastated by the DANES, and in 865 the great Danish army landed there. In 869 king Edmund was defeated near Hoxne by the Danes; he seems to have been executed after the battle—tradition has it that he was shot full of arrows—and within a generation had become a very popular saint. In 879 the Danish army under king Guthrum established a Danish kingdom of E.A. that included the land to the east of the rivers Lea, Ouse and Welland. Relations between Wessex and this kingdom were uneasy, and in the fighting of 892–6 the Danish army worked mainly from bases there. In the summer of 917 the last Danish king of E.A. was killed while attacking the invading English; in Nov. 917 the E.A. Danes submitted to the king of Wessex, and E.A. became two SHIRES. During the 11th century E.A. formed an earldom. In 1066 it was held by the brother of king Harold II, this last English holder being killed at the battle of HASTINGS. In the Anglo-Norman period the earls of Norfolk were known alternatively as earls of E.A.   CFS

Easter. The name is derived from *Eosturmonath*, the fourth month of the year of the heathen Anglo-Saxons. Bede (died 735) explains the first part of the name as that of the goddess *Eostre*, for whom festivals were held at that time. Nothing more is known of her.

The date on which E. should be celebrated was to early Christians a matter of great practical importance: it was the supreme Christian festival,

and from it the dates of many other church festivals were established. The calculation of the date was, however, a difficult and technical study. The lunar year of the Jews contained 354 days, and was kept roughly consistent with the solar year of 365 days by the insertion from time to time of an extra month. The Jewish Passover fell on 14 Nisan, the lunar month of which the full moon either fell on the vernal equinox or was the first after that equinox. It was impossible to equate this with a date on the current Julian CALENDAR, a solar calendar, especially as early Christians preferred to maintain the connexion with the Passover rather than select an arbitrary date. After abandoning the Jewish calendar the Christians devised various rules for computing the Easter date. The BRITISH, IRISH and, later, SCOTTISH CHURCHES used the computation in vogue in the west of Europe during the early 5th century (an 84-year cycle); and the TEUTONIC CONQUEST cut them off from knowledge of the computations of a 532-year cycle made, with variations, by Victorius in 457 and Dionysius in 525. The ROMAN MISSION to England used that of Victorius, and the clash between the Roman and Scottish churches concerning E. calculation was settled at the synod of WHITBY (663) in favour of the Roman. The new calculation gradually triumphed throughout the British Isles: S. Ireland had adopted it by the middle, N. Ireland by the end of the 7th century; Pictland and Cornwall by the early and Wales by the late 8th century. From the time of the synod of Whitby the calculations of Dionysius were preferred to those of Victorius.

                                                                    CFS

Eastern Association was the name given to the counties of Norfolk, Suffolk, Essex, Cambridge and Hertford combined in the Parliamentary cause (Dec. 1642). Joined by Huntingdon and Lincoln, their forces were organized by Cromwell. He recruited zealous PURITANS, enforced strict discipline and training, and tried to secure regular pay. His cavalry became famous for efficiency and restraint, and the system formed the basis of the NEW MODEL ARMY. IHE

Easter Rising (1916). Leaders of the SINN FEIN movement were determined to use Britain's pre-occupation with the first World War to gain immediate independence for Ireland by force. The Irish Republican Brotherhood and the Citizen Army planned a large-scale revolt for Easter 1916, to be aided by German arms. But the arms ship was seized (20 Apr.), Sir Roger Casement (landed from a German submarine) was captured (21 Apr.) and Eoin MacNeill, chief of staff of the Irish Volunteers, cancelled the manoeuvres designed to cover the insurrection. Nevertheless the E.R. was begun (24 Apr.), two of the leaders being P. Pearse and J. Connolly. In Dublin the General Post Office and other central buildings were occupied by about 1500 men and a 'provisional government of the Irish Republic' was proclaimed. The military took quick action and after 5 days' fighting the insurgents surrendered (29 Apr.); 15 were court-martialled and immediately shot, and many hundreds imprisoned. Casement was tried for treason and hanged (3 Aug.). Sporadic outbursts in other parts of Ireland were easily controlled. Birrell, the chief secretary, took responsibility for the lax security measures which had enabled the E.R. to take place and resigned (1 May). The harshness with which the E.R. was put down did much to ensure the predominance of Sinn Fein under one of the survivors, de Valera.   MLH

Easter Tables. The technical difficulties of calculating the date of EASTER led to the drawing-up of tables giving the date of Easter year by year. For some time there was no unanimity concerning the era from which dates should be reckoned; but from the early 8th century the year was reckoned from the Incarnation. Once this time scale became generally accepted, the remainder of the lines left blank after the Easter dates could

be used for brief mention of events of importance, thus leading to the development of annals.   CFS

East India Company. On 31 Dec. 1600 Queen Elizabeth I granted a charter to 'the governor and company of merchants of London trading to the East Indies'. The company was originally interested chiefly in the Moluccas, from which the Dutch dislodged them in 1623 (AMBOINA), but from c. 1610 turned to the Indian mainland where William Hawkins (1609–11) and Sir Thomas Roe (1615–18) obtained concessions in BENGAL from the Great Mogul. Further factories were established at Madras, Bombay and Calcutta. A competitor, the 'English company of merchants', founded in 1698, was induced, with some government pressure, to amalgamate with the E.I.C. (1708) under the name of 'the united company of merchants of England trading to the East Indies'. The most dangerous rival, however, was the French 'Compagnie des Indes Orientales', which in 1664 established its first factory at PONDICHERY. Open warfare between the two companies ensued during the SEVEN YEARS' WAR and the AMERICAN REVOLUTION. The victories of ARCOT, PLASSEY and WANDIWASH and the subsequent conquest of Bengal and the Carnatic ensured British supremacy. The structure of the E.I.C. made it unfit, however, to administer a growing empire and wield political power. The REGULATING ACT of 1773 and later CHARTER ACTS and INDIA ACTS therefore gradually transferred authority to the crown. The territory under direct control of the E.I.C. as well as the number of dependent princely states continued to grow, especially under the governorship of Warren Hastings (1774–85), Lord Wellesley (1798–1805) and Lord Dalhousie (1848–56), partly as a result of the MYSORE, MARATHA and SIKH wars, partly through the ruthless application by Dalhousie of the 'doctrine of lapse', which, on the flimsiest of pretexts, led to the wholesale annexation of dependent and protected states. After the loss of its trading monopoly (1813, 1833) the E.I.C. became a purely administrative agency. When the mutiny (1857–8) revealed the incapability of ruling a subcontinent by a private company, the entire administration of India was taken over by the INDIA OFFICE of the crown (1858).   SHS

Eastland Company. By charters of 1404 and 1408 English merchants trading to the Baltic were given organizational powers, but they lost their separate identity before the end of the century. In 1579 they were incorporated as the E.C. to ensure the supply of naval stores and most probably to weaken the HANSE. The main export was dyed and dressed cloth, and the Danish trade was shared with the MERCHANTS ADVENTURERS. Dutch competition and English interlopers led to decline in spite of the confirmation of its monopoly by the NAVIGATION ACTS of 1651 and 1660. The trade was virtually thrown open in 1673, although the E.C. still nominally existed in the reign of George III.
                                                       IHE

Ecclesiastical Commission Act (1661) restored all ecclesiastical jurisdictions abolished by the LONG PARLIAMENT in 1641, except the HIGH COMMISSION Court, and expressly forbade the revival of the clause of the Elizabethan Act of SUPREMACY which gave authority for the erection of such a court. This was disregarded when James II established the Court of Ecclesiastical Commission to coerce the clergy in 1686. It limited the jurisdiction of the ECCLESIASTICAL COURTS to those powers exercised before 1639 and asserted the king's supremacy in ecclesiastical matters.
                                                       IHE

Ecclesiastical Courts, established after the NORMAN CONQUEST with excommunication as a main weapon, dealt with questions of church property, tithes, etc., except cases of ADVOWSON and PATRONAGE. They exercised discipline over the clergy, over the laity for sins, dealt with all

E

marriage and testamentary cases (except over land), heresy, USURY, WITCHCRAFT, etc., by canon law. From the archdeacon's court appeals went to the consistory or diocesan courts (also courts of first instance), presided over by a chancellor as judge, from thence to the consistory courts of the archbishops (Court of Arches for Canterbury, Chancery for York). The archbishops also held a personal court of audience, court of peculiars (Canterbury only—abolished 1847) and a prerogative court for testamentary jurisdiction. Papal influence was limited by PRAEMUNIRE, appeals to Rome were restricted (1533) and abolished (1534) and a court of DELEGATES instituted for special appeals as well as a court of faculties. The judicial committee of the PRIVY COUNCIL took over the work of the court of delegates in 1833. The HIGH COMMISSION existed on a statutory basis from 1559 primarily as an administrative instrument to enforce religious conformity, but it developed wide powers as a court. Abolished in 1641, it was briefly revived in a modified form by James II (1686–8). The jurisdiction of the other courts was restored by the ECCLESIASTICAL COMMISSION ACT (1661), but their coercive powers over the laity steadily disappeared. Their jurisdiction in matrimonial and testamentary causes was removed in 1857, and the principal courts which still function (Bishops' Consistory, Provincial Courts of Arches and Chancery, Court of Faculties) deal essentially with clerical matters, the civil affairs being managed by the CHURCH COMMISSIONERS.   IHE

Ecclesiastical Titles Act (1851), was introduced by Lord John Russell to counter the 'aggression of the pope' (Pius IX) in setting up a Roman Catholic hierarchy in Britain (1850). It was a demonstration of anti-papal feeling which had been encouraged by fear of the effects of CATHOLIC EMANCIPATION, the OXFORD MOVEMENT and the growth of ritualism in the established Church. The Act forbade

R.C. priests to assume titles adopted by the Church of England. No prosecutions followed since R.C. dioceses were not given the same names as Anglican ones. It was repealed in 1871. MLH

Economic Affairs, Department of, was set up in Oct. 1964 to take over from the TREASURY responsibility for economic affairs and planning. The D. was originally under a First SECRETARY OF STATE and Secretary of State for E.A., but in Aug. 1967 the PRIME MINISTER took direct command of the D. with a secretary of state of less seniority, though still in the CABINET, to assist him. In Apr. 1968 responsibility for productivity, prices and incomes was transferred to the Department of EMPLOYMENT AND PRODUCTIVITY. In Oct. 1969 the D. of E.A. was wound up, its responsibilities for regional economic development being transferred to the Ministry of TECHNOLOGY and its responsibilities for medium- and long-term economic assessment returning to the Treasury. MR

Edgecott, see BANBURY.

Edgehill, battle of (23 Oct. 1642), the first engagement in the CIVIL WAR. Charles left Shrewsbury for London, encountering Essex at E. near Banbury. The royalist horse routed the two wings of their opponents, but missed their opportunity by reckless pursuit. The king's infantry were badly mauled and the battle resulted in a draw. The king took Banbury and Oxford and marched on London, but was turned back by Essex and the train-bands at Turnham Green. IHE

Edinburgh, treaty of (6 July 1560). As a result of the treaty of BERWICK (Jan.) the French were defeated and agreed to withdraw from Scotland. Mary Queen of Scots and her French husband, Francis II, were to discontinue using the royal arms of England, and during the queen's absence Scotland was to be governed by a council of 12 (5 appointed by Mary, 7 by the Scottish Parliament). Although not ratified, it saved the REFORMATION

in Scotland and led to a common interest with England. IHE

Edington, battle of, south of Chippenham, Wilts. (May 878). The men of WESSEX under king Alfred gained an overwhelming victory over the DANES under Guthrum. It was followed after three weeks by the baptism of Guthrum (WEDMORE). It is one of the decisive battles of English history, ensuring that Wessex, the last independent surviving English kingdom, should remain so and should provide the base from which, in the 10th century, the areas occupied by the Danes could be reconquered. CFS

Education and Science, Department of. A PRIVY COUNCIL committee was formed (1839) to administer grants to voluntary societies, thus gaining some supervisory powers: to assist it, an E. Department was set up (1856). Its functions were much enlarged by the Elementary E. Act 1870, co-operating with the new school boards, inspecting schools, etc. The committee was replaced by a Board of E. in 1899, whose work, particularly in secondary education, was extended by the 1902 E. Act and subsequent legislation; in turn the Board was replaced by a Ministry of E. under the 1944 E. Act. On 1 Apr. 1964 the functions of the Minister of E. and the Minister of Science (first appointed in Oct. 1959) were combined in a single SECRETARY OF STATE for E. and S. and the department was renamed the D. of E. and S. PMB; MR

Education Acts. For most of the 19th century elementary education in England and Wales was provided only by voluntary (sectarian) schools. Although small grants were made (from 1833) to the National Society and the British and Foreign School Society, these schools became increasingly unable to cope with the needs of an expanding population. Attempts to form a national system of state-aided elementary education were defeated by denominational rivalry and the prevalent dislike of state control. However, interest in child welfare (FACTORY

ACTS) and the advocacy of such persons as J. S. Mill, Carlyle and M. Arnold produced a change in opinion. The report of the Newcastle commission on 'the extension of sound and cheap elementary instruction' (1861) and the REFORM ACT of 1867 made educational reform inevitable. Religious antagonism made a compromise necessary. W. E. Forster's E.A. (1870) provided for a dual system. The voluntary schools remained with increased grants but in areas where they were deemed inadequate locally elected boards were authorized to provide schools by a levy on the rates. School boards were permitted to make attendance compulsory, and also free in cases of need; denominational instruction in board schools was forbidden. Lord Sandon's Act (1876) and A. J. Mundella's Act (1880) made elementary education compulsory; in 1891 it was made virtually free.

The inadequacy of secondary education was shown by the Taunton commission (1868). Minor reforms of endowed schools were effected in 1869; in 1874 these came under the CHARITY COMMISSION. The upper classes were catered for by the growth of the PUBLIC SCHOOLS. The Technical Instruction Act (1889) gave local authorities the power to levy a rate for technical education, but it was left to the more energetic school boards to make provision for higher-grade education generally. The work of the school boards was seriously handicapped by sectarian differences and the voluntary schools were in increasing financial difficulties. Thus a reorganization of the whole educational system was called for (Bryce commission, 1895), and this was accomplished by Balfour's E.A. (1902), largely the work of a civil servant, (Sir) R. Morant. The school boards were abolished, counties and county boroughs becoming the authorities for elementary, secondary and technical education (except that the larger boroughs and urban districts became authorities for elementary education only); the current expenses of voluntary schools were met from the rates;

undenominational teaching in 'provided' (ex-board) schools remained.

H. A. L. Fisher's E.A. (1918) gave greater powers to the Board of Education and to the local authorities; the aim was a comprehensive system from the nursery school to the evening class. Education was made compulsory and free to the age of 14 and thereafter compulsory in 'continuation' schools; central grants were increased to at least 50% of expenditure; authorities were empowered to create recreational facilities and to provide for physically defective children. Owing to the post-war retrenchment not all these provisions came into force; in particular the 'continuation' schools came to nothing.

The latest important E.A., the R. A. Butler Act (1944), envisaged education as a continuing process and enunciated the principle of secondary education for all. The permissive powers of local authorities were replaced by compulsory powers. The new ministry of EDUCATION was given tighter control; the number of authorities was further reduced; the voluntary schools became either 'aided' or 'controlled' according to their financial position; religious undenominational instruction became compulsory in all but 'aided' schools; the leaving age was to be increased to 16; 'county colleges' (the ill-fated 'continuation' schools) were to be established. Although in the post-war period progress was slow, the 1944 E.A. provided a comprehensive framework for future development.   MLH

Edwardian Conquest, Wales. Following the accession of Edward I in 1272 growing friction between him and Llywelyn ap Gruffydd of GWYNEDD led to an English campaign against WALES in 1276–7. Welsh defeat was followed by the Treaty of Aberconway (1277) which stripped Llywelyn of the overlordship accorded him by the Treaty of MONTGOMERY. A Welsh uprising of March 1282 was crushed by Edward in a campaign lasting until the spring of 1283. His victory was made permanent by the extinction of the native ruling line, the construction of formidable CASTLES and the imposition of royal rule by the Statute of RHUDDLAN.

GW

Egypt attracted English attention (apart from the abortive CRUSADES of 1218, 1248 and 1365) when Napoleon invaded it as a stepping-stone to India. The French, defeated in the battle of the NILE (1798), at the siege of ACRE (1799) and at ALEXANDRIA (1801), had to evacuate E. (1801), but their invasion marked a turning-point in the history of E. Turkey (which had conquered E. in 1517) lost her grip on E.; the Mameluk soldiery, the effective rulers of E. from 1261, were exterminated in 1811 by Mohammed Ali, an Albanese officer, who in 1805 had established himself as governor under nominal Turkish overlordship. British awareness of the strategic importance of E. was heightened when naval lieutenant Thomas Waghorn (1800–50) in 1829 established the overland route Alexandria–Cairo–Suez which by 1845 had reduced the passage London–Bombay to 30 days. Mohammed Ali's conquest of the SUDAN (1820) and Syria (1831), his intervention against the Greeks (when the Egyptian navy was annihilated at Navarino, 1827) and advance on Constantinople (1839) aroused English antagonism, and Mohammed Ali (†1849) and his successors Said (†1863) and Ismail (deposed 1879) therefore turned to France for advice and support. The greatest achievement of 19th-century E., the SUEZ CANAL, was therefore an almost exclusively French undertaking.

A corrupt and oppressive administration, aggravated by the extravagance of the Khedive Ismail, increased the misery of the population and the insolvency of the government to such an extent that in 1876 an Anglo-French control of the public finances had to be established. The Egyptians believed—not without reason—that the commissioners of the 'Caisse de la Dette' were only interested in satisfying the European bondholders; the revolu-

tion, started in Sept. 1881 by Arabi Pasha and other army officers, therefore found support throughout the country. An Anglo-French naval demonstration (May 1882) could not prevent frightful massacres of Europeans in Alexandria and elsewhere. France refused military co-operation, but British public opinion forced Gladstone to act: the bombardment of ALEXANDRIA (11 July 1882) and Arabi's defeat at TEL-EL-KEBIR (13 Sept.) preceded the occupation of E., intended to be of short duration. The dual control of the finances was abolished and Evelyn Baring (1841–1917), as 'agent and consul-general', became the sole financial adviser (11 Sept. 1883).

Baring (from 1892 Lord Cromer), an anti-imperialist liberal, established ordered government, created a civil service, achieved financial solvency (from 1889) while reducing taxation, abolished slavery, founded schools, built railways, dams and irrigation canals, and completely regenerated E., in the face of continuous French obstruction and despite the upheaval in the SUDAN. After his retirement (1907) the liberal government immediately undid most of his work by foisting British-made democracy on a totally different society.

On Turkey's entry into the first world war Turkish suzerainty was repudiated (18 Dec. 1914), the pro-Turkish Khedive Abbas Hilmi was deposed and E. was made a British protectorate under a high commissioner, with Hussein Kamil as 'sultan'. Lloyd George's inept handling of the post-war situation resulted in nationalist risings and general chaos (1919–21). On the recommendation of the Milner commission of inquiry (1919–20), the British protectorate was abolished and E. was recognized as a sovereign state under Fuad I as 'king' (28 Feb. 1922), with a small British garrison as security force. The 20-year treaty of alliance of 22 Aug. 1936 terminated the British occupation and completed the independence of E., while recognizing the special British interests in the Suez Canal zone and re-affirming the Anglo-Egyptian condominium of the Sudan. The Montreux convention of 8 May 1937 abolished the foreign jurisdiction of capitulations and, after a transitional 12-year period, of the mixed courts. The demand by E. for a revision of the 1936 treaty in Dec. 1945 was immediately complied with by the British government which unconditionally withdrew all British troops from E. In Oct. 1951 E. denounced the 1936 treaty and the 1899 Sudan convention. While negotiations were in progress, a revolution deposed King Farouk (23 July 1952) and his son, Fuad II (13 June 1953) and declared E. a republic. In Oct. 1954 the complete evacuation of the Suez Canal zone and on 1 Jan. 1956 the abolition of the Sudan condominium were agreed upon. A last attempt to exercise some control over E. ended disastrously; following the Israeli attack upon E. (29 Oct. 1956), France, which was in collusion with Israel, and Britain, which mishandled the matter from start to finish, undertook a combined operation (5 Nov.) which had to be given up the next day because of determined American and Soviet opposition at the United Nations.   SHS

Eikon Basilike or the Royal Likeness appeared in 1649 within a few days of Charles I's execution, purporting to be his own record of his thoughts and feelings. Dr John Gauden, afterwards bishop of Exeter (1605–62), had edited the king's papers, but Charles had approved the final version. It immediately strengthened and revived royalist loyalties and sentiments. Milton was commissioned to write his much less effective counterblast, *Eikonoklastes* or the Image-Breaker.   IHE

Eisteddfod, National. In medieval and early modern Wales the e. met to regulate the bardic order, though a competitive meeting for song and poetry is known to have been held at Cardigan in 1176. The modern e., a product of the romantic revival and the patriotic societies, dates from one held at Corwen in 1789. 19th-century regional *eisteddfodau* culminated in the formation of the N.E. Association in 1880, since when a national festival has been held annually, lasting a week and held alternately in north and south Wales. The 'druidic' bardic rites, an invention of the arch-romantic, Iolo Morganwg (1747–1826), have been associated with *eisteddfodau* since 1819. The e. has done much to foster singing and literature, and is a primary focus of national consciousness.   GW

Eleanor Crosses. Eleanor of Castile, first wife of Edward I, died at Hadby (Notts.) on 28 Nov. 1290. Her body was carried to Westminster Abbey for burial, and at each of the twelve places where it rested on the way Edward had memorial crosses erected (Lincoln, Grantham, Stamford, Geddington, Northampton, Stony Stratford, Woburn, Dunstable, St Albans, Waltham, and West Cheap and Charing Cross in London). Only those at Waltham, Northampton and Geddington survive, differing in design and admirably executed. Philip III of France had commemorated his father, Louis IX, in a similar way.   RFW

Eleven Years' Tyranny (1629–40) denotes Charles I's attempt to govern without Parliament, and is particularly associated with Strafford's and Laud's policy of THOROUGH. The Three Resolutions (1629) against innovations in religion, the advising or levying of TUNNAGE AND POUNDAGE or payment of same without parliamentary consent indicate the issues involved. The king's success largely depended on finance. He made peace with France (1629) and Spain (1630) and levied tunnage and poundage. By economy, proper use of money raised and the revival of old exactions solvency was achieved. DISTRAINT OF KNIGHTHOOD, revival of the forest laws (especially fines for encroachments), MONOPOLIES and SHIP-MONEY were used. A weakness was the lack of subservient sheriffs and J.P.s to enforce the policy locally, but effective support came from Strafford as president of the COUNCIL OF THE NORTH (1628) and lord-deputy in Ireland (1632). Laud's enforcement of church discipline through the courts of

STAR CHAMBER and HIGH COMMISSION and the metropolitan visitations (1634–7), the suppression of lecturers and the censorship of Puritan writings further alienated the PURITANS and stimulated emigration to America. The attempt to enforce a Laudian prayer book on the Scots led to the National COVENANT (1638) and the first BISHOPS' WAR (1639). This drove Charles to summon the SHORT PARLIAMENT (1640). IHE

Elizabethan Settlement. On the accession of Elizabeth I (1558) the MARIAN EXILES returned and the PURITANS in Parliament pressed for a Protestant religious settlement. After hesitation Elizabeth assented to the Act of SUPREMACY (1559) renewing the breach with Rome. The Act of UNIFORMITY authorized the Book of Common Prayer, the book of 1552 slightly modified, and Henry VIII's anti-papal legislation was revived. Most of the lesser clergy accepted the oath of supremacy, but by 1560 all but one of the Marian bishops were deprived and replaced by Marian exiles and those displaced in 1553. The 39 ARTICLES were promulgated in 1563, and this essentially parliamentary settlement was consolidated by the sound administration of Archbishop Parker. IHE

Ellendun, battle of (Wroughton near Swindon, Wilts.). In the later part of 825 king Beornwulf of MERCIA was decisively defeated by king Egbert of WESSEX. The battle marked the end of Mercian ascendancy and was a most important step in the rise of Wessex. CFS

Elmet, a British kingdom that came into being after the Roman period. It occupied the modern West Riding of Yorkshire and land farther west. It was conquered by king Edwin of NORTHUMBRIA in the early 7th century. CFS

Ely, Isle of, was in 1070–1 the centre of resistance to the NORMAN CONQUEST in the East Midlands. The local English leader, Hereward the Wake, was assisted by Danes from the invasion fleet of 1069 and by Northumbrian rebels under Earl Morcar. With the help of the Danes Hereward carried out his most notable exploit, the successful raid on Peterborough in 1070. The Danes withdrew in the spring of 1071 under an agreement between King Swein and King William, and in the following summer William began the difficult siege of the Isle. English resistance eventually collapsed, but Hereward himself made his escape.

In late Aug. 1265 groups of MONTFORTIANS who had escaped from the battles of EVESHAM and CHESTERFIELD established themselves in the Isle under the leadership of John d'Eyvill and refused the terms of the Dictum of KENILWORTH. After the failure of negotiations they were attacked by the Lord Edward who occupied the Isle in the summer of 1267. The surviving rebels made their submission. RFW

Employment and Productivity, Department of. A Ministry of Labour was established in 1916 to carry out industrial conciliation, administer employment exchanges and the unemployment acts, tasks previously assigned to the Board of TRADE and other departments. Its work was subsequently enlarged, e.g. in the youth employment service, the training of the disabled, etc., to cover a wide field of industrial relations, training and placing workers. From 1939 to 1959 it was known as the Ministry of Labour and National Service with responsibility for the registration and call-up of those liable for national service. In Apr. 1968 responsibility for productivity, prices and incomes was transferred from the Department of ECONOMIC AFFAIRS and the title of the expanded D. was changed to the D. of E. and P. under a SECRETARY OF STATE. PMB; MR

Engagement, (1) (26 Dec. 1647), an agreement between Charles I and the Scots. The king, retaining personal freedom of worship, was to establish PRESBYTERIANISM in England for three years and suppress the INDEPENDENTS.

The English Parliament, soon aware that some agreement had been made, passed the VOTE OF NO ADDRESSES and dissolved the COMMITTEE OF BOTH KINGDOMS.

(2) (2 Jan. 1650). All men over 18 were to take an e. of loyalty to the COMMONWEALTH as established 'without a king and House of Lords'. It was annulled by the LONG PARLIAMENT (1660).   IHE

Engagement of the Army (June 1647). Alarmed by Parliament's disbandment proposals, the army met at Newmarket and made the Solemn Engagement not to disband until satisfactory terms were approved by their council.   IHE

Englishry, the distinction between Anglo-Saxons and Normans or Anglo-Normans and Welsh. As early as Henry I's reign the HUNDRED could escape the MURDER FINE by successfully presenting E., i.e. proving that the dead man was English not Norman. See also MARCHES OF WALES.
                                                     PMB

Enrolment. The widespread use of rolls for records, abandoned on the continent in the earlier 13th century, is peculiarly English. The first CHANCERY rolls were 'file copies' of the king's WRITS, but they acquired authority and were in safe-keeping so that, as legal acceptance of written records grew, individuals paid to have private documents entered on them. Following the model of charters enrolled on the earlier PIPE ROLLS, increasing with the growth of trade and commerce, entry on the rolls of KING'S BENCH, EXCHEQUER and particularly Chancery was further stimulated by a statute of 1382 allowing lost titles to be replaced on acceptable evidence. In 1535 Henry VIII made e. of many deeds compulsory, and the CLOSE ROLLS were soon entirely appropriated to private documents: in 1833 they became the only available series. (See also LAND REGISTRY.)
                                                     PMB

Entente Cordiale, the name given to a series of conventions signed 8 Apr. 1904 by Britain and France, settling various outstanding issues—fishing rights off NEWFOUNDLAND and spheres of influence in Siam, Madagascar and the NEW HEBRIDES—but in particular recognizing British and French preponderance in EGYPT and Morocco respectively. French public opinion, seriously disturbed by FASHODA and the SOUTH AFRICAN WAR, was mollified by the visit of Edward VII to Paris (May 1903). France needed an ally to thwart German designs in Morocco and wanted to keep Britain neutral in the impending clash between her ally Russia and Britain's ally Japan (Anglo-Japanese alliance, 1902). The defeat of Russia by Japan (1905), the Algeciras crisis (1906) and the expansion of the German navy moulded the E.C., by virtue of common interests, into a more formal alliance. The Anglo-Russian convention (1907) further involved Britain in the European political situation which produced WORLD WAR I.   MLH

Entry, Writs of. Henry II's POSSESSORY ASSIZES marked an advance in English law but were too inflexible to deal with many of the complexities of land tenure. To provide such remedy and to extend the work of the king's courts, the group of w. of e., of which PRECIPE for DOWER was an early example, was devised from the late 12th century onwards. Such writs demanded that the plaintiff have entry to the land since the tenant's title was defective, e.g. because of an ancestor's disseisin, the expiry of a lease etc., and so extended both the grounds of, and the time allowed to bring, an action. The writs' success in giving flexibility was marked by an increasing flow of business to the courts.   PMB

Eorl, a Kentish noble in the earlier Old English period. This style was peculiar to KENT and may represent an original nobility by birth rather than by service. The equivalent rank elsewhere was GESITH.   CFS

Episcopacy. Church government by bishops, retained at the Elizabethan settlement, distinguished the Anglican church from most other reformed churches. Calvinists sought to introduce a Presbyterian system but were checked by Archbishops Parker and Whitgift. The struggle continued under James I and Charles I when Puritan attacks culminated in the ROOT AND BRANCH PETITION (1641) and Parliament's abolition of e. (1643), which lasted until the RESTORATION. The SAVOY CONFERENCE (1661) rejected any modification of e., which only again became an issue with the rise of METHODISM. The Scottish Reformation created a Presbyterian system, but e. was gradually reintroduced by James I. The Covenanters abolished it in 1638, but were forced to accept it again in 1661. The Scottish church finally rejected e. in 1689.   IHE

Equity, the custom of courts outside the COMMON LAW, notably CHANCERY; its history is the history of those courts. From the late 13th century petitions to the king for remedy where Common law failed were referred to the CHANCELLOR and later addressed to him alone. He developed within the chancery a system, later a court, to deal with such petitions, summoning defendants on writs *sub pœna*, under pain of forfeiting a sum of money, and allowed parties to testify; both practices were unknown at Common law. Though unfettered by fixed rules, the chancellor's work on trusts and uses was fundamental to their 15th-century development, and fraud, accident, breach of contract, etc., were later added to his work. The Tudors, providing new courts both civil and criminal, increased e.'s scope and enraged common lawyers. When these courts, and criminal e., were abolished, chancery again stood alone, now as a settled institution, whose work and rules pre-supposed yet supplemented Common law and whose decisions were made according to conscience and e. So it remained until the JUDICATURE ACT 1873 when e. and Common law jurisdictions were merged, though its former work is still, by

rules of the court, chiefly discharged by the chancery division. As tribute to the merits of e. its processes, e.g. *sub pœna* and injunctions, were adopted by other divisions and it was laid down that, in case of conflict, e. rules should prevail over those of Common law.   PMB

Erastianism implies the dominance of the state in ecclesiastical matters (after the principles of the German theologian Thomas Erastus, 1524–83), and the term was established in England by its use in the WESTMINSTER ASSEMBLY (1643–9). The LAUDIANS were driven to an Erastian position by using the personal interference of the king to realize their aims, and in return they gave him political support. The scheme of a Puritan state church embodied in the ROOT AND BRANCH bill was Erastian, and resulted from disbelief in toleration. The Church of England was never more Erastian than in the 18th century, following the BANGORIAN CONTROVERSY, but in a different way and for different reasons.
                                                 IHE

Ermine Street (Old English *Earningastræt*, the road to Earn's people), a ROMAN ROAD on the line London–Braughing – Huntingdon – Chesterton (near)–Lincoln–Brough on Humber–York, although the name does not extend over the last section. Its continuation York–Aldborough–Scotch Corner–Corbridge–High Rochester–Newstead–Dalkeith (Scotland) is known as Dere Street. E.S. is the name also given to the road on the line Silchester–Cirencester–Gloucester. See KING'S PEACE.   CFS

Escheat, an incident of KNIGHT service and SERJEANTY tenures. The feudal bond of personal service was broken on the tenant's death, and the land returned, 'escheated', to the lord to be regranted. In practice it was kept in his hand until an adult heir paid relief or a minor heir came of age.   PMB

Escheator, a royal officer administering ESCHEATS and forfeited goods and lands. E.s appear first in 1195 as checks on the SHERIFFS; by the mid-

13th century there were two only, for lands north and lands south of the Trent, but e.s were later appointed again for single counties or groups. The office lapsed when feudal tenures were abolished. Feodaries performed similar duties in some LIBERTIES. PMB

Espagnols sur mer, see WINCHELSEA.

Esquire or squire (Old French *esquier*, shield-bearer), the personal attendant of a knight, usually a youth of gentle birth who aspired to become a knight himself. The term is now applied in addressing letters (abbreviated Esq.) to any untitled gentleman, despite the abortive attempts of the COLLEGE OF HERALDS to confine its use to certain circumscribed groups of persons.   SHS

Essex, the kingdom of the East SAXONS, occupied for most of its existence the area of the county of E. It was poor; its dynasty was the only Teutonic line that did not claim descent from Woden; and it was generally under the influence of some more powerful kingdom. By the beginning of the 7th century MIDDLESEX was included in the kingdom, and London was its chief town; but both these seem to have been gained by MERCIA during the reign of Ethelbald of Mercia (murdered 757). Although the East Saxon dynasty survived into the 9th century, the names of its later kings are not known, and for much of the 8th century and part of the 9th it was controlled by Mercia. In 825 the men of E. submitted to Egbert, king of WESSEX. In the later 9th century it became part of the Danish kingdom of EAST ANGLIA, and in the 10th century it became a SHIRE.   CFS

Essoins, excuses for non-appearance in the king's court. The commonest were *de malo veniendi* (mishap *en route*), *de malo lecti* (ill in bed) and *de ultra mare* (abroad on the king's service), securing delays of from three weeks to *sine die*. They had to be proved in court: *de malo lecti* was only accepted after the defaulter had been seen in bed, ungirt,

with his boots off, by four knights. Designed to overcome genuine difficulties, e.s were unscrupulously used to delay actions. They were not allowed in pleas of service and the assize of NOVEL DISSEISIN, and restricted in other POSSESSORY ASSIZES.
                                                        PMB

Etaples, treaty of (Nov. 1492). After the treaty of MEDINA DEL CAMPO (1489) English troops were sent to Brittany, but by the end of 1491 it was under French control. Henry VII maintained the threat of war and besieged Boulogne (Oct. 1492). Charles VIII of France, contemplating the invasion of Italy, agreed to the treaty of E., promising to make good arrears of payment due under the treaty of PICQUIGNY (1475) and to compensate Henry for abandoning the war. A total of 745,000 gold crowns was to be paid by instalments, and the Yorkist pretender was expelled from France.
                                                        IHE

Ethandun, battle of, see EDINGTON.

Evangelicals, emerged as a group within the CHURCH OF ENGLAND at the same time as the METHODISTS, with whom they had much in common. By the end of the 18th century they had notably contributed to religious revival. Emphasizing personal conversion based on faith, they placed more stress on preaching and less on liturgical worship, and their ideas later conflicted sharply with the OXFORD MOVEMENT. Conspicuous for their support of MISSIONARY SOCIETIES and other religious bodies, they championed many humanitarian and social reforms (CLAPHAM SECT).   IHE

Evesham, battle of (4 Aug. 1265), the decisive defeat of the MONTFORTIANS in the BARONS' WARS. Simon de Montfort, after losing vital time penned behind the Severn by the royalists, at last crossed the river at Kempsey on 2 Aug., when his son, Simon, had already been defeated at KENILWORTH. The Montfortians were caught at E. between Henry III's son Edward, who blocked the Kenilworth road, and Roger Mortimer, who held the bridge over the Avon. Simon, his son Henry and many of his leading supporters were killed.   RFW

Exchequer, in origin the financial department of the CURIA REGIS. Later Anglo-Saxon kings seem to have had a central financial organization with a treasury at Winchester, but the Normans subordinated this treasury to the chamberlains and the household financial organization. The E., so called because of the chequered cloth used for calculations, was the result, established by Henry I's reign, presided over by king or TREASURER, dealing with the income and expenditure of most of the crown's ordinary and extraordinary revenue. The E.'s 12th-century work, the attendance of sheriffs and other accountants, its records etc. are described in the DIALOGUS. Though the volume of business first expanded then contracted and more parchment and paper than cash passed through it, its function remained substantially the same throughout its long history. The E. was at various periods challenged by CHAMBER and WARDROBE, but lost its financial supremacy only to the TREASURY. Of diminishing business, the E. was abolished in 1833, but the name is still applied to the nation's public funds. See also AUGMENTATIONS; CHANCELLOR OF THE EXCHEQUER; CUSTOMS AND EXCISE; DEBENTURE; ENROLMENT; FIRST FRUITS AND TENTHS; GREAT SEAL; HANAPER; LAND REVENUE; MARSHAL; PIPE ROLLS; REGNAL YEAR; REMEMBRANCER; SHERIFF; TALLY.   PMB

Exchequer, Red Book of, a reference collection of documents, precedents etc., compiled in the EXCHEQUER by Alexander of Swerford († 1246), with later additions; now in the PUBLIC RECORD OFFICE. The book, whose contents range from the 12th to the 16th centuries, is a treasury of vital documents, among which the *Leges Henrici Primi*, the CONSTITUCIO DOMUS REGIS, the DIALOGUS and the CARTE BARONUM are the most important.   PMB

Exchequer, Stop of (1672), was caused by the disastrous finance of the CABAL and the diversion of funds to war supplies in anticipation of the third DUTCH WAR. The government suspended its payments to the bankers for 12 months, causing a temporary financial crisis. It affected the king's credit and revealed the weaknesses of the system of obtaining advances on the revenue by bankers' loans.   IHE

Exchequer and Audit Office, founded by an Act of 1866 to combine the duties of the Controller-General of the EXCHEQUER, who had survived the Exchequer's abolition, and the Commissioners of Audit, first appointed in 1785 to discharge the work of the Auditors of the Exchequer and the Audit Office. The senior officer, the Controller- and Auditor-General, covers the whole field of government expenditure, issuing annual and sometimes critical reports.   PMB

Exchequer of Pleas grew, in the 13th century, from the debate and decision by the Barons of the EXCHEQUER of legal points arising on accounts or affecting royal revenues. Once established as a court, it heard all manner of pleas, by the legal fiction of *Quo minus*, i.e. that the plaintiff was disabled in paying crown taxes. Its COMMON LAW side became the Exchequer division of the Supreme court of JUDICATURE (1873), to be merged in the Queen's Bench division in 1880. Its EQUITY court, of which little is known, was united with CHANCERY in 1841.   PMB

Excise, see CUSTOMS AND EXCISE.

Excise Bill (1733). Excise, a tax on goods for internal consumption, was first introduced in 1643. In 1733 such taxes existed on malt, beer, soap, candles, tea, etc. Walpole aimed to substitute excise for customs duties on wine and tobacco by collecting the tax when these goods left the bonded warehouse, thereby increasing revenue and checking smuggling. As a result he hoped to abolish the LAND TAX. The E.B. was defeated by mob violence and factious parliamentary opposition. Excise men were intensely unpopular.   IHE

Exclusion Bills were introduced in the reign of Charles II by the opponents of the court party to exclude the heir to the throne, James, duke of York, from the succession. They made use of the militant Protestantism aroused by the POPISH PLOT to introduce an E.B. (May 1679), but the king dissolved Parliament when it passed its second reading. Another bill was introduced (1680) which designedly left the way open for the possibility of Monmouth's succession, but it was rejected by the Lords. Charles cleverly summoned the next Parliament at Oxford to prevent possible intervention of the London mob in favour of the exclusionists. The king, strengthened by the promise of French financial aid, dissolved his last Parliament when the E.B. was reintroduced (Apr. 1681).   IHE

Exclusion Bill, Bishops', the Commons' attempt to weaken royalist influence in the House of Lords by excluding the bishops. Their first e.b. was rejected by the Lords (June 1641). After Charles I's attempted arrest of the FIVE MEMBERS the Lords passed an e.b. which deprived all persons in holy orders of any temporal jurisdiction and authority. It received the royal assent (Feb. 1642).   IHE

Eyre (Latin *iter*, Old French *eire*, a circuit), originated with the travels of the king and his court through the country. Henry II, as government grew stronger and legal business increased, detached judges from his central court and sent them on e. through the country to hear all manner of pleas and perform some general supervisory work, linking local and central government. Sitting generally in the SHIRE court, they heard the presenting juries of HUNDREDS and townships answer the questions in the chapters of the e.: the chapters covered finance, administration and justice, the first known dating from 1194. The justices itinerant also received the records of SHERIFFS and

CORONERS, and proceeded to hear criminal and civil pleas, reserving the more difficult for the king's own court. Occasionally special inquiries were made, e.g. the Inquest of SHERIFFS 1170. At first general e.s were irregular, but became more regular, cumbersome and financially burdensome: by the early 14th century one in seven years was thought reasonable. They lapsed in the mid-14th century. PMB

Fabian Society, a non-Marxist socialist society founded 1883–4 and named after Q. Fabius Maximus ('*Cunctator*'). Its primary object has been to present the results of research into social and political questions, suggesting practical answers on evolutionary socialist lines. Several hundred tracts and research papers have been published, some of real importance, e.g. the typical *Facts for Socialists* (1887), *Facts for Londoners* (1889)—socialism in local government was a cardinal aim—and *The Education Muddle and the Way Out* which anticipated the 1902 EDUCATION ACT. Notable members have included S. and B. Webb, G. B. Shaw, Wallas, H. G. Wells, Tawney, G. D. H. Cole, Ensor, Cripps, Attlee and Gaitskell. The influence of the F.S. on the LABOUR PARTY has been out of all proportion to its size; for instance in 1918 both the new constitution and programme (*Labour and the New Social Order*) of the Party were wholly F. inspired. In 1915 the F. Research Department withdrew from the F.S. and (1921) became Communist-dominated. In 1930 an independent New F. Research Bureau was formed by Cole and others; it was merged with the F.S. in 1939. The F. Colonial (now Commonwealth) Bureau (1930) and the F. International Bureau (1931) are semi-autonomous branches of the F.S.   MLH

Factory Act. In 1802 Parliament first recognized a limited responsibility for the protection of child labour when the elder Peel attempted to regulate the employment of pauper children in cotton mills. The efforts of R. Owen resulted in the F.A. 1819 which dealt with all children; no child under 9 was to be employed, those between 9 and 16 for not more than 12 hours a day and no child was to work at night. Both these Acts were largely evaded since enforcement was the duty of local magistrates. In the early 1830s the 'ten-hour movement' began with agitation from J. Wood and R. Oastler and under the parliamentary leadership of Lord Ashley (Shaftesbury). The F.A. 1833 affected all textile mills (other than silk); children between 9 and 13 were limited to a 48-hour week (not more than 9 hours a day) and those under 18 to a 68-hour week (12 hours). Inspectors were appointed responsible to the central government; the Act was therefore at any rate partially effective. The F.A. 1844 secured a 6½-day week for children between 8 and 13 and a 12-hour day for women; it also included the first regulations for fencing of machinery. A 10-hour day for women and children in the textile industry was achieved by the F.A. 1847. However, it did not automatically lower the hours for all workers, as was expected, since employers used a relay system, it still being legal to employ women and children between the hours of 5.30 a.m. and 8.30 p.m. This led to the F.A.s of 1850 and 1853 which at last effectively limited the hours of all textile workers; factories were to remain open for 12 hours a day only, as a compromise the hours for women and children being slightly extended from 58 to 60 a week (10½ on weekdays, 7½ on Saturdays). The F.A.s of 1847, 1850 and 1853 mark a real victory for the reformers and the principles of factory legislation. Regulation of hours was seen not to have had the deleterious effects on production and costs which employers and economic theorists had prophesied.

Actual conditions of employment in other industries were made known by numerous commissions of inquiry, and by the 1860s there was little opposition to the extension of the F.A.s to these industries. In 1845 calico-printing had been made a protected industry. Bleaching and dyeing was brought under control in 1860 and lace manufacture in 1861. The F.A. 1864 included the pottery and lucifer-match industries. In 1867 the F. Extension A. gave a wider definition of 'factory' to include any building in which more than 50 persons were employed in a manufacturing process for gain; special regulations were made for 'dangerous trades' (e.g. glass-making). The Workshop Regulation Act 1867 applied to establishments in which less than 50 persons were employed. In 1874 and 1875 hours were reduced in the textile industry from 60 to 57 and the minimum age raised to ten. In 1878 a consolidating and amending act was passed; certificates of fitness for children were introduced; another consolidating act (1891) raised the age limit for factories and workshops to twelve. The F.A. (1895) fixed a week of 30 hours for children and of 60 hours for women and young persons; it forbade night-work for children under 14. Further consolidating F.A.s were passed in 1901 and 1937; the latter limited hours of work for women to 48 a week (9 a day) and for young persons to 44. The F.A. 1937 was amended (1948, 1959) and superseded by the consolidating F.A. 1961; provision is made for hours of women and young persons working in factories operating a 5- or 6-day week; overtime for women and children is restricted to 1 or 1½ hours per day, 6 hours per week and 100 hours per year in not more than 25 weeks. The Act includes regulations concerning health (cleanliness, temperature, ventilation, lighting, sanitary accommodation, first aid, seating, etc.) and safety (fencing, use of lifting machinery, etc.). Details are the subject of statutory instruments issued by the Dept. of EMPLOYMENT AND PRODUCTIVITY.   MLH

Falaise, treaty of (1174, ratified at Valognes on 8 Dec.), made William I of Scots, captured at ALNWICK and imprisoned at F., Henry II's vassal; the Scottish barons were to do homage to Henry for their lands and the Scottish prelates for their temporalities. Edinburgh, Roxburgh and Berwick castles were surrendered as securities. The Scottish homages were performed at York in Aug. 1175, and William was not released from his obligations under the treaty until 1189.   RFW

Falkirk, battle of (1) (22 July 1298), a defeat of the Scots under William Wallace by Edward I, attempting to enforce his control over Scotland.

(2) (17 Jan. 1746), the last victory of the JACOBITES in the FORTY-FIVE REBELLION. After entering Derby (Dec. 1745) the Young Pretender retreated, recrossing the border after a successful skirmish against Wade at Clifton. Wade's army was entrusted to Hawley, and the best regiments were sent south against the threat of French invasion. The armies met at F. Muir and the Highlanders decisively routed Hawley, who was replaced by Cumberland.   IHE

Falkland Islands, first sighted by Elizabethan sailors in 1592, named after Lord F., treasurer of the navy, in 1690, and first settled in 1764 by de Bougainville (who named them Les Malouines, after St Malo, his port of departure) and simultaneously by an English expedition under John Byron. In 1767 the French sold their claim to Spain, and the Spaniards in 1770 ejected the English from their Port Egmont. This was restored to Britain in 1771 but abandoned in 1774. Argentina, from 1820, revived the Spanish claims, but in Dec. 1832–Jan. 1833 Britain finally took possession of the F.I. From about 1880 sheep's wool has been the basis of the colony's prosperity.

The F.I. dependencies are mainly whaling and scientific stations: South Georgia and South Sandwich islands, discovered and annexed by Cook in 1775; South Shetlands, 1819; South Orkneys, 1821; Graham Land, 1832.   SHS

Falkland Islands, battle of (8 Dec. 1914). After the disaster of CORONEL two battle cruisers were ordered to the F.I. under Admiral Sturdee (11 Nov.), arriving 24 hours before von Spee's squadron (5 cruisers, 3 supply ships). The British ships were coaling but von Spee sought escape. Immediately giving chase, Sturdee's squadron (2 battle cruisers, 5 cruisers, 1 armed merchant cruiser), with superior speed and gun-range, sunk all but one German auxiliary and one light cruiser, the latter being trapped in March 1915. The outer seas were thus cleared of German surface raiders, allowing concentration of forces in home waters.   IHE

Farthing (Old English *feording* or Old Norse *fiordungr*, a fourth part), began literally as a quarter of the silver PENNY, which from the 8th century until the 13th was the only coin normally minted in England. The cross design characteristic of the reverse of the penny from the Norman conquest to 1489 facilitated cutting it up into f.s or halfpence. Round f.s may have been first coined early in the reign of Henry III (1216–72), but none appears to have survived. The regular minting of round, silver f.s started under Edward I in 1279, and the new coins were called 'Londoners' because at first they were minted only in London. In the late 17th century advocates of decimal coinage suggested, unsuccessfully, that the f. should be made one-fifth of a penny. The f. became a copper coin in 1821, a bronze coin in 1860 and was discontinued in 1961.   RFW

Fashoda incident (1898), the last serious Anglo-French dispute. While Britain was preparing the conquest of the SUDAN, the French tried to forestall them and occupy the upper Nile region, which would have extended their vast west- and central-African empire to the Red Sea, given them control of the waters of the Nile and cut the British Cape–Cairo line. Major (later general) Jean-Baptiste Marchand (1863–1934), started in March 1897 with a small force from Brazzaville and on 10 July 1898 hoisted the tricolour in the village of

F. on the White Nile. Immediately after the victory of OMDURMAN (2 Sept.) Kitchener went to F. and tactfully convinced Marchand of the hopelessness of his position. The French left F. in November. The F. i. caused deep resentment in France, and war seemed imminent. The skilful handling of the situation by Lord Salisbury not only achieved a peaceful settlement (21 March 1899)—in return for giving up F. (renamed Kodak), France obtained the western Sudan (now Mali)—but marked the first step towards the ENTENTE CORDIALE. SHS

Fealty, Oath of, sworn by a man to his lord or employer, promising faithful service against all men. Such oaths were required from feudal tenants when doing liege homage and from other dependants and employees. Though HOMAGE was abolished at the Restoration, o. of f. are still administered. PMB

Federated Malay States. The rulers of Perak, Selangor, Negri Sembilan (itself a federation of small states) and Pahang entered into treaty relations with Great Britain in 1873, 1874, 1876 and 1888 respectively. They formed a federation in July 1895 and joined the Union (Federation) of MALAYA in 1946. SHS

Fee (Latin *feodum*), at first meaning a retainer in cash or kind, later extended to cover many miscellaneous payments. The knight's fee was intended to provide him with maintenance and arms for military service, the foreigner's money fee to retain his adherence to the English cause. The working official's fee constituted his wages, extending thence to the moneys paid for various professional services. The fees charged for fixing the GREAT SEAL etc., partly in payment for wax, partly in payment for officials' time and trouble, extended thence to all manner of fixed payments for governmental and legal processes. PMB

Fee-farm Rents, a miscellaneous group of crown revenues, among which borough rents are historically most important. Farm of the borough revenues for a fixed sum paid at the EXCHEQUER fostered, by excluding the SHERIFF, burghal independence. Lincoln obtained the privilege in 1130: other boroughs received it temporarily in the 12th and 13th centuries, but from Richard I's reign onwards an increasing number were granted perpetual fee-farms. In financial difficulty Charles II agreed to the transfer of f.r. to trustees for sale in 1670: the sale of the majority realized about £700,000. PMB

Fees, Book of, a collection of documents relating to feudal tenures collected and copied for the EXCHEQUER in 1302, and frequently called the *Testa de Neville*. The two volumes contain returns to special inquiries throughout England into serjeanties, knights' fees, aliens etc. as well as extracts from purely financial documents for the period 1198–1293. They are important sources for historians and genealogists alike (ed. Public Record Office, 1920–31); similar materials for the period 1284–1431 are printed in *Feudal Aids* (1899–1920). PMB

Fees, Commissions on. By the early 17th century at least a governmental clerical post was regarded as salable property, and generally performed by deputy. For each routine transaction fees were charged, providing officers' salaries: their poorly paid deputies ingeniously devised new and necessary procedures with appropriate fees. Parliament opposed the expense of legal actions in particular and, from 1622 to 1640, a series of commissions, dominated by the scholar Sir Henry Spelman, were appointed to inquire first into legal fees, then into those of many offices. Their work was largely abortive, for no attempt at radical reform was made for 150 years, but the evidence they received gives a detailed picture of contemporary courts and government departments. PMB

Feodary, see ESCHEATOR.

Fernando Pó, discovered (1469) by the Portuguese, in 1778 ceded to Spain and 1827–34 entrusted to Great Britain as a naval base for suppressing the slave-trade. The last British superintendent, John Beecroft (1790–1854), continued as Spanish governor until his death.   SHS

Ferrers' Case (1543), an important assertion by the Commons of their immunity from arrest. Their serjeant, with only the authority of his mace, freed George F., burgess of Plymouth, consigned for a debt for which he had gone surety. The Commons, supported by the Lords and the judges, imprisoned the civil officers who had arrested their member. Henry VIII upheld their action: Parliament was the king's high court and F. was his page.   IHE

Feudalism took many forms in medieval Europe: English f. was distinctive in its centralization and precision. Before the NORMAN CONQUEST there are signs of the dependence of one man on another, of military or quasi-military obligations on tenants and, in Edward the Confessor's time, of a centralizing movement. Some scholars interpret these as the beginnings of f.; the majority argue that English f. began with the Norman conquest. William I, as conqueror, had a unique opportunity, while rewarding his followers, to build a new society, based on the principle that all land belonged to him; in this he rejected Norman practice, though following it in so many other respects. He granted his land to tenants-in-chief in return for specific services, knight service, FRANKALMOIN or SERJEANTY. The tenant-in-chief, in return for a grant of land, passed on part of his service to his tenant, so that society became a pyramid, each man tied to his superior and ultimately to the king. To enforce the specified services and do justice between his tenants-in-chief, the king compelled them to form his court and they, in their turn, held courts of their tenants.

This structure could not long survive. Within a few years of the conquest the invaders became country gentlemen, more interested in their lands than in war and too old to ride to battle. Then primogeniture was accepted, lands were divided between daughters, tenants-in-chief became tenants of others and the structure became increasingly complex. The greater tenants grew powerful, challenging the king. He in turn successfully extended his authority by his officers and his courts, checking the power of his tenants and intervening between them and their tenants. The delicate balance was destroyed. Great changes had taken place by 1166, and at the beginning of the 13th century feudal society was held together more by financial ties than those of personal service. Some personal performance of knight service survived until the 14th century; attendance at court was inflated by the greater tenants into a claim to be the king's hereditary councillors, a claim reflected in MAGNA CARTA, the PROVISIONS OF OXFORD and the ORDINANCES of 1311, and with considerable influence upon early parliamentary history. But in general the society designed by William I decayed, quickly at first and then more slowly (see BASTARD FEUDALISM). Feudal tenures in England were abolished in 1661, in Scotland in 1914 with the exception of feu duty, but the modern laws of peerage and heraldry embody the feudal principles of descent.   PMB

Fianna Fáil, the Irish political party formed (1927) and led (until 1959) by E. De Valera. With the exception of the years 1948–51 and 1954–7 the F.F. has been in office since 1932.   MLH

Field of Cloth of Gold (June 1520), a ceremonial meeting in Picardy (between Guisnes and Ardres) of Henry VIII and Francis I of France who hoped for English support against the Emperor Charles V. Lavish arrangements were made for jousting and dancing. Henry's ostensible role was that of mediator but his real aim was to enhance the value of the English alliance to the emperor. There were no positive results, and Henry met the emperor at Gravelines and Calais and they effected a treaty in July.   IHE

Fifteen Rebellion. Scottish dissatisfaction with the Act of UNION (1707) and the unpopularity of the Hanoverian monarchy in England encouraged the JACOBITES to organize a rebellion. The death of Louis XIV of France, the Old Pretender's loyalty to Roman Catholicism, dissensions and incompetent leadership spoilt their plans from the outset. Mar's premature rising at Perth (6 Sept.) was undermined by his irresolute leadership and after SHERIFFMUIR (13 Nov.) his disillusioned forces withdrew to Perth to be finally dispersed by Cadogan (Feb. 1716). James, the Old Pretender, having landed at Peterhead (Dec.), left for France with Mar (4 Feb. 1716). Ormonde unsuccessfully tried to raise support in Devonshire, but in Northumberland English Jacobites rose under Squire Forster. Joined by Scottish rebels, they reached Preston, where they were easily defeated (13 Nov. 1715). The government acted with resolution but not with undue severity. The failure to break up the clan system in Scotland helped to make possible the more serious FORTY-FIVE REBELLION.   IHE

Fifth Monarchy Men, an extremist sect of the Cromwellian period believing that the time had come for the rule of Christ and His Saints—the Fifth Monarchy succeeding those of Assyria, Persia, Macedonia and Rome (Daniel, 11). They supported Cromwell until disillusioned by his assumption of power, when they agitated against him. Their leaders were imprisoned and General Harrison was deprived of his command. Venner's futile rising in London (Jan. 1661) was their last attempt to achieve the Fifth Monarchy.   IHE

Fiji, discovered by Tasman in 1643, were visited by Cook in 1774, and first recorded in detail by Capt. Bligh after the BOUNTY mutiny. The islands attracted white adventurers and exploiters throughout the 19th century until the annexation by Britain on 10 Oct. 1874. Previous offers of the native chief to cede F. to Great Britain (1858 ff.) had been turned down by the foreign and colonial offices, as had petitions of the German and American settlers by their respective governments. The Fijians retained a large measure of self-government. A constitution introduced in 1966 enlarged the franchise and emphasised the representative element.   SHS ; IHE

Final Concords, INDENTURES made in the king's courts recording settlements of actions of titles to lands, services etc. Before Richard I the concord was bipartite : thereafter it was tripartite, one section, the foot, remaining in the court. Though concords became legal fictions to establish dubious titles, they provide for the local historian continuous evidence of land ownership until their abolition in 1833.   PMB

Fire of London (2–7 Sept. 1666), originated in a bake-house in Pudding Lane, Thames Street, in the early hours of Sunday morning. Fanned by high winds, it spread rapidly, and all the City from the Tower to the Temple and from the Thames to Smithfield was destroyed, including 89 churches, St Paul's and many public buildings. It covered 373 acres within the walls and 63 without. It increased prejudice against the Roman Catholics, who were blamed for it. It was not the reason for the disappearance of the PLAGUE, as most of the slum districts survived.   IHE

First Fruits and Tenths, Court of. In 1531 Henry VIII appropriated to the crown ANNATES and tenths for the recovery of the Holy Land formerly paid to the pope, and in 1540 the C. of F.F. and T., headed by a chancellor, treasurer etc., was established to administer the revenues, according to the rules of the Court of Duchy Chamber of LANCASTER. The court was abolished in 1554 and its work transferred to the EXCHEQUER : the revenues were later applied to QUEEN ANNE'S BOUNTY, founded in 1704.   PMB

First World War, see WORLD WAR I.

Five Articles of Perth (1618), were imposed on the CHURCH OF SCOTLAND by James I, enforcing kneeling at communion, observance of Christmas and Easter etc., confirmation, communion for the dying and prompt baptism of infants. Ratified by the Scottish Parliament in 1621, they were rejected by the General Assembly of the Church in 1638.   IHE

Five Boroughs, Derby, Leicester, Lincoln, Nottingham, Stamford, the headquarters of Danish armies that settled the territory round each in the later 9th century, being the area of the DANELAW where Danish settlement was thickest. They formed a federation, with the general assembly of the F.B. as the highest court. The first four later gave their names to SHIRES. In 1015 there is a unique reference to the Seven Boroughs. These were the five above with, probably, Torksey and York.   CFS

Five Knights, case of (1627). Among those imprisoned by order of the king and Privy Council for refusing payment of a FORCED LOAN, five knights (Corbet, Darnel, Erle, E. Hampden, Hevingham) appealed to the court of King's Bench. They argued the right to be tried on cause shown or liberated on bail. The crown pleaded the right to imprison without showing cause. The judges sent the knights back to prison but did not decide the point, and they were released early in 1628.   IHE

Five Members. Charles I decided to impeach five of the most active leaders of the Commons—Pym, Hampden, Hazelrig, Holles and Strode (and also Lord Mandeville)—on charges of high treason, knowing that they had been negotiating with the Scots. The Lords refused to order their arrest (3 Jan. 1642). Next day, Charles, with 300–400 armed men arrived at the House to seize the five members, but they had escaped to the City by boat. Failing to obtain their surrender from the citizens, he had them proclaimed traitors. They returned in triumph to Westminster (11 Jan.) escorted by the City TRAIN-BANDS. The king's actions united Lords, Commons and City against him and helped the passage of the bishops' EXCLUSION BILL through the Lords.   IHE

Five Mile Act (1665), the last act of the CLARENDON CODE striking at the ministers who had evaded the CONVENTICLE ACT (especially in London during the Great PLAGUE). Nonconformist clergy were forbidden within 5 miles of a corporate town or place where they had previously ministered unless they would take an oath of NON-RESISTANCE. NONCONFORMISTS were forbidden to teach in any public or private school. The Act was repealed in 1812.   IHE

Flanders, the Way of (1382–3), an alternative to the 'way of PORTUGAL' for attacking France. Parliament favoured the W. of F. which envisaged an attack on northern France in alliance with the Flemings under Philip van Artevelde and was strongly urged by Henry Despenser, bishop of Norwich; the Roman pope, Urban VI, supported it as a 'crusade' against the French adherents of the Avignon pope, Clement VII. Before the expedition could start, the Flemings had been defeated at Rozebeke (27 Nov. 1382), van Artevelde had been killed, Bruges and Ypres had fallen to the French, and the English wool trade with Flanders had been strangled. The 'bishop of Norwich's crusade', largely financed by the sale of indulgences, set out in May 1383 and won some initial successes, taking Gravelines and Dunkirk. Divided counsels hampered further progress: no attack on France was made; the Flemings deserted; and on the approach of a French army the English were evacuated by sea. Despenser had failed to reopen the wool market and had done no harm to France, while the indiscipline of his army had brought discredit on the Urbanist cause.

RFW

Fleet Prison. A royal prison was probably established by the Fleet river near the modern Farringdon Street by the 12th century. Later it housed many STAR CHAMBER prisoners, then became almost exclusively a debtors' prison. Destroyed in the Great FIRE 1666 and twice rebuilt, the Fleet was closed by an Act of 1842. PMB

Flodden, battle of (9 Sept. 1513). While Henry VIII was at war with Louis XII of France, James IV of Scotland renewed the French alliance demanding Henry's withdrawal from France. On refusal the Scots invaded Northumberland and chose the strong position of F. Edge to meet the English under the earl of Surrey. The Scottish defeat was complete and James was slain. IHE

Florida was first occupied by Spain in 1565 and, after the English colonization of Carolina, border friction developed, leading to open attacks on each other's settlements during the SPANISH SUCCESSION WAR. GEORGIA was partly founded in 1733 to contain F., and it was ceded to Great Britain by the treaty of PARIS (1763) in exchange for CUBA. Separate governments were established for East and West F. and a good deal of money was spent on development. F. did not support the American Revolution, but it was reconquered by Spain (1779–81) and retained by the treaty of VERSAILLES. IHE

Florin. After the unsuccessful experiment of Henry III's GOLD PENNY, English production of gold coins in imitation of the famous *fiorino de oro* of Florence was resumed by Edward III. By 1337 Edward was minting for Aquitaine a gold f. which closely copied the design of its original, having on its obverse the lily or *fiore* which gave the coin its name. The Aquitaine f., valued at 3s. sterling, was soon followed by other gold coins, the *écu* and *léopard*, both worth 3s. 4d. At the beginning of 1344 Edward made current three new gold coins for England, the f. or two-leopard piece, the leopard or half-f. and the helm or quarter-f., worth 6s., 3s. and 1s. 6d. respectively. The characteristic flower type was not continued, however. The issue was not a success, and within the year it was replaced by the NOBLE. The f. was reintroduced as a silver coin worth 2s. in 1849—a tentative step towards decimalization. RFW

Floyd's Case (1621) was a questionable assertion of Parliamentary jurisdiction. Floyd, a Roman Catholic barrister, was condemned to heavy punishment by the Commons for malicious speeches against the Elector Palatine and his wife, James I's daughter. The Lords argued that the Commons had no jurisdiction except where their own privileges were involved. The Commons assented, and the Lords proceeded to inflict a savage sentence on Floyd. IHE

Foedera. In 1693 Thomas Rymer, historiographer royal, was appointed to edit for publication a chronological series of treaties and other diplomatic documents. He had free access to the public records and produced from them the first 15 volumes of *F.*, covering the years 1101–1543 (1702 ff.). As he progressed Rymer widened his scope, including many important, non-diplomatic documents. He was uncritical, and his texts are not always reliable; nevertheless he made available vast numbers of documents, some now lost. *F.* has been supplemented and re-printed, with additional inaccuracies, several times. PMB

Foederati (Latin 'allies'), the name given to barbarians who were, in later Roman times, given land within the frontiers of the empire on which to settle and who were expected to defend that part of the frontier against other barbarians. The device seems to have been employed in the late 4th and early 5th century for the defence of parts of ROMAN BRITAIN, and according to tradition, by Vortigern (mid-5th century) when he invited Hengest and his followers to settle in KENT. CFS

Folkland, a rare Anglo-Saxon term describing land owing FOOD-RENTS and customary duties to the king, subject to customary rules of inheritance and regulated by local, communal courts. F. represents an early stage in society when all land bore common burdens, only mitigated if any part became BOOKLAND.   PMB

Fontenoy, battle of (11 May 1745). After DETTINGEN the French made the conquest of Flanders their chief objective in the AUSTRIAN SUCCESSION WAR. The allies under the duke of Cumberland, advancing to the relief of Tournai, were repulsed by the French under Marshal Saxe at F., the British and Hanoverian troops being inadequately supported by the Dutch and Austrians. The French subsequently gained control of Flanders and the British troops were recalled to fight the FORTY-FIVE REBELLION.   IHE

Food-Rent (Old English *feorm*, latinized in DOMESDAY BOOK as *firma unius noctis*), in O.E. times took the form of sufficient provisions to maintain the king and his household for 24 hours, and vills on the royal estates were grouped so that each group rendered it once a year. By later O.E. times many of these f.s had been granted away by kings, and many others had been commuted to money payments. The term continued as *ferm*. A f., later known as CHURCH SCOT, formed the earliest endowment of parish churches.   CFS

Food-vessel culture, the general name for the insular BRONZE-AGE cultures that developed in Britain north of the Thames. It takes its name from a characteristic wide-mouthed pot. Those practising it continued the NEOLITHIC life of nomadic pastoralism, but engaged in the bronze trade. Flint, stone and bone implements, etc., continued to predominate, and pottery was of a poor standard. Bronze objects in general show no advance on those of the BEAKER CULTURE, and the improvements made by the southern WESSEX CULTURE are not found. After *c.* 1400 B.C. it became an element in the URN CULTURE.   CFS

Forced Loans were levied by the crown on wealthier subjects to meet extraordinary financial needs, especially due to war. Henry VII levied small amounts in 1486 and 1489, but repaid promptly (when not repaid they differed little from BENEVOLENCES). Henry VIII met with more resistance, as did Mary. James I used them, but the levies of 1626 and 1627 to support the foreign policy of Charles I and Buckingham aroused strong resistance (FIVE KNIGHTS). Although condemned by the PETITION OF RIGHT, Charles resorted to a f.l. in 1640 to fight the second BISHOPS' WAR. No attempt was made to revive them after the RESTORATION.   IHE

Foreign and Commonwealth Office. Following the Plowden Report of 1964 the overseas services of the FOREIGN OFFICE and Commonwealth Relations Office (see COMMONWEALTH OFFICE) were merged on 1 Jan. 1965 in a single diplomatic service administered by a Diplomatic Service Administration Office, drawing its staff from the diplomatic service and serving both offices equally. With the ultimate merger of the two offices in mind, several other joint departments were set up and on 17th Oct. 1968 the two offices and the Diplomatic Service Administration Office were merged to form a united F. and C.O. under a single SECRETARY OF STATE.   MR

Foreign Office. When in 1782 the Secretary of State for the Northern Department (created 1688) became Secretary of State for Foreign Affairs, his secretariat emerged as the F.O., with the duty of carrying his policies into effect. As the scope and complexity of foreign affairs increased, the office grew. Its staff, though civil servants, were separately recruited, and from 1920 could be called upon to serve at home in the F.O. or abroad in the diplomatic or (from 1943) consular services. On 17th Oct. 1968 the F.O. merged with the COMMONWEALTH OFFICE to form the FOREIGN AND COMMONWEALTH OFFICE.

                                    PMB; MR

Forensic Service, a service which is attached to land etc. and, unlike an INTRINSIC SERVICE, cannot be detached from it or altered by any contract or alienation etc., e.g. liability to GELD and similar land taxes.   PMB

Forest, Charter of the (6 Nov. 1217), developed the forest clauses of MAGNA CARTA. Woods outside the royal demesne afforested between 1154 and 1216 were to be deafforested; fines or imprisonment were to replace death or mutilation for forest offences; the rights of landowners within the forest were defined and safeguarded; certain forest regulations were clarified, and the exactions of forest officials restricted; and outlaws for forest offences were pardoned provided they could find pledges for their good conduct in future. The C. of the F. was confirmed along with Magna Carta by Edward I's CONFIRMATION OF THE CHARTERS.   RFW

Forestry Commission. The first commission was issued in 1919 to promote forestry, afforestation and the timber trade and to advise private owners. Its power to buy land was surrendered to the Ministry of Agriculture and Fisheries in 1945. The F.C. halted the inroads made from time immemorial on the British forests. Acquiring powers over the felling of timber in 1951, its achievements are to be seen in the planting of marginal and unproductive land and in decreasing soil-erosion.   PMB

Forests, areas subject to f. law, irrespective of the type of vegetation. For love of hunting William I designated f. in England: his successors, notably Henry II, extended them. Medieval f. were widespread, e.g. almost all of Essex was f., though some counties, e.g. Kent, contained no f. at all. Those living within or near the f. were subject to special forest laws, whose aim was to protect the game: to this end also grants of warren were made, licensing the hunting of the fox, cat and hare held to be harmful to game. The f. were administered by the chief forester and his sub-ordinate wardens and verderers in each forest, who held regular courts reviewed by special forest eyres; pasture etc. within the forest was regulated by the thrice-yearly swanimote courts. The forest and its laws were unpopular: afforestation and the rigours of forest law were mitigated by MAGNA CARTA; subsequently the forest clauses were abstracted and enlarged in the 1217 Charter of the FOREST, on which later forest history is based. Increasingly f. were encroached on for arable land, but the forest law remained, to be vigorously revived by the early Stewarts and abolished at the RESTORATION.   PMB

Forfeited Estates, Commissioners of. After the FIFTEEN REBELLION an Act vested lands etc. of recusants those attainted of treason, etc. in the crown: C. of F.E. were appointed to list, value and sell them, and adjudge claims to them. Though the work was supposed to be complete by 1719, the C. sat 1716–24 at first in Preston and Newcastle upon Tyne but from 1717 in London, following chancery procedure when hearing claims; estates worth more than £84,000 were sold by them. A separate body of C. sat at Edinburgh to deal with estates in Scotland.   PMB; MR

Forfeiture. The outlawed, those convicted of high treason or specially disinherited, e.g. rebels, forfeited their goods and lands to be divided between the crown and their lords. All possessions of those convicted of high treason went to the crown: felons' goods so passed, while their lands, after the crown's year of waste, went to their lords. Partial f. was elsewhere imposed: usurers' chattels and debts fell to the crown, as did intestates' at various periods; heretics' goods were disputed between kings and popes. Now severely restricted, f.s are governed by an Act of 1870.   PMB

Forgery for gain, glory and other reasons is an age-old occupation: of its many branches documentary f. is the most important for historians, especially when documentary evidence is scarce. In the 12th century, the golden age of such f., respect for written records grew: they were forged in great numbers and presented to the king for confirmation, for a bad title so confirmed was good in English law. Some were wholly spurious, some replaced lost originals, others combined the spurious and genuine. The English CHANCERY, unlike the papal, developed little skill in detection: modern scholars, following Mabillon (1632–1707), have brought palaeography, diplomatic, genealogy etc. to bear. Detected f.s may still contain genuine information.   PMB

Forma Regiminis, 'form of government' (28 June 1264), drawn up by parliament and accepted by Henry III and his son Edward, who had been in the power of the MONTFORTIANS since the battle of LEWES. The F. R. constituted a provisional government which was to last until the Mise of LEWES or a similar agreement had received general assent. Three principal councillors—Simon de Montfort, Gilbert de Clare earl of Gloucester, Stephen Bersted bishop of Chichester —were to elect another nine councillors, of whom three at a time were to be in constant attendance on the king. The Nine, who when chosen included the chancellor and the treasurer, were to appoint all royal officers and direct the administration in the king's name. The Three exercised general supervision of government, but ultimate authority was vested in the 'community of the prelates and barons'. This provisional government lasted until the royalists recovered power after the battle of EVESHAM (1265).   RFW

Formigny, battle of (15 Apr. 1450), the final English defeat, beside CASTILLON, in the HUNDRED YEARS' WAR. Despite the cession of MAINE to Charles VII of France, war was renewed in 1449 largely as the result of an irresponsible English raid into Brittany. Charles VII embarked on a systematic invasion of Normandy and captured ROUEN. English reinforcements brought over by Sir Thomas

Kyriel were inadequate, and they and troops drawn from the surviving English garrisons were crushingly defeated at F. Artillery played an important part in the French victory, which proved that the English had lost their former tactical superiority. With the loss of Caen in June and Cherbourg in August English rule in Normandy came to an end.   RFW

Forty-five Rebellion. The outbreak of war between England and France in 1744 encouraged Prince Charles Edward Stewart, the Young Pretender, to attempt a rising. Landing on Eriskay island (23 July 1745), he raised his standard at Glenfinnan (19 Aug.). The English under Cope left the route to the lowlands open and the JACOBITES proclaimed the Old Pretender king at Perth and entered Edinburgh (16 Sept.). Cope's army was routed at PRESTONPANS (21 Sept.) and the Young Pretender entered Carlisle (17 Nov.). Intent on getting to London, the Highlanders reached Derby (4 Dec.) via Preston, Manchester and Macclesfield. The news caused a run on the banks in London. With only 5,000 men, no help from France or from the English Jacobites and contained by the English navy, Charles reluctantly yielded to his advisers and retreat began (6 Dec.). After the victory at FALKIRK (17 Jan. 1746) the rebels withdrew to Inverness and were finally beaten by Cumberland at CULLODEN (16 Apr.). The Young Pretender escaped to France (20 Sept.) and Cumberland's ruthless reprisals and subsequent legislation destroyed the power of the Highland chiefs. The Jacobite cause ceased to be a serious threat.   IHE

Foss Way (derived from its accompanying ditches, Latin *fossa*), a ROMAN ROAD on the line Axmouth–Ilchester – Bath – Cirencester – Leicester–Lincoln. The major part of it was probably constructed by A.D. 47 as a fortified frontier road (Latin *limes*) that marked the extent of the ROMAN CONQUEST at that time. See KING'S PEACE.   CFS

Fotheringhay, treaty of (10 June 1482), secured the assistance of James III's exiled brother Alexander, duke of Albany, in Edward IV's war against the Scots. Albany promised that, if he dethroned James with Edward's assistance, he would become Edward's vassal, cede the western march of Scotland as well as BERWICK, and break off the Scottish alliance with France. In the event it was the military activity of Richard, duke of Gloucester, that secured the cession of Berwick rather than the assistance of Albany, who soon came to terms with his brother.   RFW

'Foul Raid' (Oct. 1417), an invasion of English-held territory carried out in time of peace by Sir William Douglas. Douglas was an opponent of the Scottish regent Albany—James I was a prisoner in England—and may have been in touch with Sir John Oldcastle, leader of the LOLLARDS. Douglas failed to take Roxburgh castle and quickly retreated when the duke of Bedford moved north with an army.   RFW

Fourth Party (1880–5), the nickname for a small 'ginger group' within the Conservative opposition to Gladstone's second administration. The F.P. was led by Lord Randolph Churchill (1849–95); other members were Sir H. Drummond Wolff, (Sir) J. Gorst and, for a time, A. J. (Lord) Balfour. First drawn together in attack on Gladstone's handling of BRADLAUGH'S CASE, they united both in providing a more vigorous opposition to the government than Sir Stafford Northcote's leadership in the Commons afforded, and in demanding a reformation of CONSERVATIVE PARTY organization.   MLH

Franchise. The MANUMISSION of the unfree was said to enfranchise him, and f. came to be used first to describe the body of freemen in a manor, borough etc. It was then extended to their rights and duties, particularly their right to vote to which, with the growth of universal suffrage, the term is now chiefly applied. It also denotes a liberty (LIBERTIES).   PMB

Frankalmoin, or free alms, a feudal tenure peculiar to the church, wherein land was granted by pious laymen in free and perpetual alms, principally in return for general praying service, an *obit*, or the manning of a chantry, but occasionally for rents etc. also. All ecclesiastical bodies held some at least of their lands in f., but many, notably bishoprics and older abbeys, also held by KNIGHT service. See MORTMAIN; UTRUM.   PMB

Frankpledge. The origins of the system, that each man belonged to a locality, the vill often identical with the manor, and that each should be guaranteed by others who would compel him to answer for his actions, the lord for his man, the *paterfamilias* for his household, lie in Anglo-Saxon times. In the 11th century responsibility shifted from lords to tenants, and the Norman lawyers, calling the system f., insisted that most men over 12, free or unfree, belonged to the small groups of f. and TITHING: the vill had to see that they did. F., enforced by inspection (SHERIFF'S TOURN) and subject to local variation, never covered all England: knights, clerks etc. were exempt and outlying counties, e.g. Westmorland, never adopted it. It decayed with the rise of the PARISH and the decline of the MANOR as an administrative and police unit.
                                              PMB

Free Companies, troops of mercenary soldiers of many nations—English, French (especially Bretons and Gascons), Spaniards, Germans—under professional captains who took service with both sides in the HUNDRED YEARS' WAR. In the French service such companies were called *routes*, hence the name *routiers* for the mercenaries. In periods of peace or truce the F.C. lacked employment and turned to indiscriminate plundering and extortion. The ravages fo unemployed *routiers* in the late 1350s contributed to the outbreak of the Jacquerie, and after the treaty of BRETIGNY they battened upon areas of France that had suffered little in the regular campaigns, e.g. Burgundy,

Languedoc and the Rhône valley. The civil wars in Spain in the 1360s drew off many companies in the service of Bertrand Duguesclin or the Black Prince. The survivors returned to plague France afresh, and their suppression was one of the most beneficial achievements of Charles V (1364–80). Mercenaries were again troublesome during the long Anglo-French truce concluded in 1394 and soon found employment with the ARMAGNACS and Burgundians. Their activities increased with the renewal of war by Henry V, and their atrocities outdid even those of their predecessors. Although the majority of the mercenaries were not English, the misery they caused was blamed on the English and contributed to the growth of French national hatred of the invaders. In the late 1440s Charles VII got rid of most of the mercenary bands, largely by an effective reorganization of the royal forces. Some bands remained in English service until the end of the Hundred Years' War.   RFW

Freehold, see SOCAGE.

Free Speech was claimed by the Speaker of the House of Commons in 1541 as a Parliamentary PRIVILEGE. The debating of matters affecting the PREROGATIVE began to develop in the 14th century, and Henry VIII did not interfere with this freedom. Strode's case (1512) established f.s. against legal proceedings by private individuals, but Elizabeth I resisted full and free discussion on certain matters, especially religion. The Commons reasserted their right to f.s. in their APOLOGY (1604) and the PROTESTATION (1621) against James I's attempts to limit their discussions. The Commons protested in 1641 and 1667 against the imprisonment of Eliot and others after the Three Resolutions of 1629, and the judgement was reversed by the Lords in 1668. F.s. was finally secured by the BILL OF RIGHTS (1689).
                                                              IHE

Free Trade. Although used in other senses in earlier times, the term now implies the removal of protective tariffs and monopolies to allow of natural competition between countries. F.t. theory was therefore opposed to the dying system of MERCANTILISM, the abuses of which Adam Smith attacked in *Wealth of Nations* (1776). F.t., when achieved in mid-19th-century Britain, was well suited to the economic conditions of the time and was readily accepted in the prevalent atmosphere of individualism and *laissez-faire*, of which it was a practical expression.

Some movement towards f.t. formed part of Pitt's financial and commercial reconstruction after the AMERICAN REVOLUTION. A treaty with France (1786) reciprocally lowered tariffs between the two countries. Pitt's policy did not survive the FRENCH REVOLUTIONARY AND NAPOLEONIC WARS; Britain emerged with an unwieldy tariff system built up for revenue purposes. During 1822–7 inroads were made on the system by Robinson (Lord Goderich) and Huskisson. Huskisson lowered the general duty on manufactured goods from 50 to 20% and reduced the special duties on textiles and other goods. The NAVIGATION LAWS and CORN LAWS were modified. Due regard was, however, given to colonial preference and the tariff, though simplified, remained comprehensively protective. The next step was taken by Peel in his budgets of 1842 and 1845. In order to wipe out the annual deficit by an improvement in commerce he abolished almost all export duties and lowered import duties, the accounts being balanced by the reintroduction of the INCOME TAX. Finally the CORN LAWS were repealed. Gladstone, who had been Peel's lieutenant at the Board of Trade, completed the movement towards f.t. as Chancellor of the Exchequer under Aberdeen and Palmerston. His 1853 budget abolished most of the duties on semi-manufactured goods and foodstuffs and halved nearly all duties on manufactured goods. Further progress was hampered by the CRIMEAN WAR, but in

1860, following the reciprocal commercial treaty with France negotiated by Cobden, Gladstone reduced the tariff to such an extent that only 16 articles made a substantial contribution to revenue and no element of protection remained.

Most European countries moved towards f.t. after 1860, but a reaction was marked by the 1880s, e.g. in France and Germany. This produced in Britain the advocacy of 'fair t.' or retaliatory tariff policy and in 1903 Joseph Chamberlain's Tariff Reform Movement on the basis of IMPERIAL PREFERENCE. Chamberlain's policy was, however, decisively repudiated at the 1906 election and Britain remained a f.t. country until the first world war. The McKenna duties on luxury goods (1915) were retained after the war and a movement towards protection started with the Safeguarding of Industries Act, 1921. In the 1920s the Conservative Party came to favour protection for the home market against cheap imports. Fundamental change came finally after economic and political crisis; the Import Duties Act (1932), passed by the National government of MacDonald, imposed duties of 10% on almost all imports, and these duties were increased on the recommendation of an advisory committee; imperial produce was excepted as a result of the Ottawa agreements. A series of bilateral agreements with other countries (1932–9) resulted in some modification in protection and preference. Since the second world war Britain's membership of G.A.T.T. has resulted in substantial reductions in tariffs on imported goods. Reciprocal reductions in tariffs on industrial products were effected (1966) within the European Free Trade Area.   MLH

French language, see VERNACULAR.

French Revolutionary and Napoleonic Wars (1793–1815). Britain's participation in these wars was occasioned by French disregard of treaties affecting Britain's maritime and commercial interests—the annexation of the Austrian Netherlands and the opening of the Scheldt. On 1 Feb. 1793 (10 days after Louis XVI's execution) France declared war on Britain and Holland. The war of the first coalition (1793–6) was characterized by a lavish dispersal of British effort. Pitt mainly used British naval predominance to overrun the French West Indian sugar islands and ruin French trade. TOBAGO and ST PIERRE AND MIQUELON were occupied in 1793; reinforcements captured MARTINIQUE, ST LUCIA and GUADELOUPE (1794) and were established on Haiti; command of the sea was emphasised by the GLORIOUS FIRST OF JUNE (1794). But sickness and negro insurrections produced serious difficulties; in 1794–6 an estimated 80,000 casualties were suffered—more than in the Peninsular campaign. Such dissipation of manpower provided insufficient troops for the strategically decisive area—Europe. A small ill-equipped British and Hanoverian force under the duke of York on the outbreak of war joined the allied armies under the Austrian Frederick of Saxe-Coburg, unsuccessfully attempted Dunkirk, became involved in Austrian defeats and consequently retreated from Flanders into Germany (1794), British troops being finally evacuated, March 1795. An allied force was fortuitously established at Toulon (Aug. 1793) in support of royalist risings in S. France but, ill-reinforced, was driven out in Dec.; in 1794 it occupied Corsica. The rising in La Vendée was defeated before British troops could intervene (Dec. 1793) and a further expedition failed at QUIBERON (June–July 1795). On Holland's transformation into the Batavian Republic (1795) Dutch possessions were occupied—CAPE OF GOOD HOPE, Trincomalee and Colombo on CEYLON, MALACCA, Amboina and Banda. Although in Dec. 1796 a French expedition to Ireland was frustrated by bad weather, the British position was critical as her allies were making peace with France (Tuscany, Prussia and Spain in 1795, Sardinia in 1796, Austria in 1797). A French plan to make invasion possible by uniting the Spanish and Dutch fleets at Brest was frustrated by Jervis's victory off Cape ST VINCENT (Feb. 1797) and that of Duncan off CAMPERDOWN (Oct.)— these in spite of the naval mutinies.

The war of the second coalition (1799–1801) was preceded in 1798 by Britain's re-entry into the Mediterranean; Napoleon's expedition to EGYPT and Nelson's victory at the NILE (Aug.); the capture of MINORCA (Nov.); and the IRISH REBELLION. In 1799 occurred an unsuccessful invasion of North Holland by troops under the duke of York and Abercrombie in collaboration with Russia; the British force returned to England after the convention of Alkmaar (Oct.). The Austrians and Russians drove the French from Italy but Napoleon's return to Europe was followed by Marengo and Hohenlinden. Pitt and Dundas repeated their previous strategic errors in widely dispersing their available forces (by planning descents upon Belle Ile, Ferrol and elsewhere) with the result that they were not able to intervene decisively in Italy. The second coalition came to an end when Austria, Naples and Turkey made peace with France (1801), and Russia with Prussia, Sweden and Denmark formed the anti-British ARMED NEUTRALITY which was, however, broken by the naval action at COPENHAGEN (1801). Britain captured MALTA (Aug. 1800) and the French army in Egypt surrendered after Abercrombie's victory at ALEXANDRIA. There was now deadlock, with France victorious on land and making preparations for invasion of England and Britain commanding the sea thus making invasion impossible. Negotiations for peace, attempted by Pitt (1796–7) and by Napoleon (1798) were re-opened by Addington (Pitt having resigned on the question of CATHOLIC EMANCIPATION) and concluded at AMIENS (27 March 1802).

Napoleon's renewed aggression in Europe led to Britain's refusal to surrender Malta, as agreed at Amiens, and war was resumed (18 May 1803). Napoleon seized HANOVER and made preparations for invasion of England.

His plan depended upon union of the French fleets from Toulon, Rochefort and Brest with the Spanish fleet. But the combined Toulon and Spanish fleets were decisively defeated at TRAFALGAR (21 Oct. 1805). Meanwhile Napoleon defeated the Austrians and Russians at Ulm and Austerlitz (1805), the Prussians and Saxons at Jena (1806) and the Prussians and Russians at Friedland (1807). Pitt, who had succeeded Addington (May 1804), died (Jan. 1806) and Fox, on behalf of the ministry of ALL THE TALENTS, made an abortive effort to come to terms with Napoleon. The latter instituted the CONTINENTAL SYSTEM in an attempt to defeat Britain by economic means. In 1806 British troops from Sicily invaded Calabria in an effort to restore the queen of Naples, won a victory at Maida, but had to withdraw. The same year the Cape of Good Hope was recaptured and an expedition left there for South America; grandiose designs to 'liberate' the Spanish colonies and secure the South American market culminated in surrender at Buenos Aires (July 1807). An expedition to Egypt was as unsuccessful. A combined operation against COPENHAGEN, however, resulted in the surrender of the Danish fleet (Sept. 1807). The large-scale WALCHEREN EXPEDITION (1809) ended in complete failure.

Napoleon's occupation of Portugal (Nov. 1807) and his attempt to gain complete control of Spain (1808) led to the PENINSULAR WAR which for six years engaged some 250,000 French troops and was one of the main causes of Napoleon's eventual defeat. After the CORUNNA CAMPAIGN (1808–9) Wellesley (Wellington) was able to recover Portugal (1809), maintain himself there (1810–11) and advance victoriously into Spain (SALAMANCA, 1812; VITTORIA, 1813) and eventually into France (TOULOUSE, 1814). Meanwhile Napoleon had invaded Russia and retreated (1812); the alliance of Russia, Prussia, Sweden and Austria was subsidized by Britain (1813). Napoleon was defeated at Leipzig (Oct. 1813), the allied armies crossed the Rhine, Paris fell and Napoleon abdicated (April 1814). There followed the first treaty of PARIS and the VIENNA CONGRESS which was in progress when Napoleon returned from Elba (March 1815). After WATERLOO (June) the second treaty of PARIS terminated the F.R. and N.W.   MLH

Fréteval, near Vendôme, scene (July 1170) of the reconciliation of Henry II and Thomas Becket, who had been in exile since 1164. Two previous interviews in 1169 had failed, and even at F. no compromise was reached on the main points at issue, e.g. the question of CRIMINOUS CLERKS: the reconciliation was a purely personal one. Even so, Henry omitted the symbolic kiss of peace. Before Becket returned to England (1 Dec.) he imposed, with papal authority, severe penalties on his ecclesiastical opponents: angered at the news, Henry spoke the fatal words which led to Becket's murder in Canterbury cathedral on 29 Dec. 1170.   RFW

Friendly Societies for mutual insurance against sickness and old age were first formed in the 17th century. In the 18th century local f.s. became a conventional alternative to parish relief, their numbers increasing to 7,200 with a membership of 648,000 by 1797; many were short-lived owing to inadequacy of contributions, misappropriation of funds and lack of legal standing. Some protection and recognition was given by the first F.S. Acts of 1793 and 1795. Thereafter the movement grew rapidly and was the subject of frequent legislation (e.g. 1829, 1850, 1855, 1875 and 1896); the act of 1875 set up a registry and subjected f.s. to annual audits and quinquennial valuations. Distinctive types of f.s. emerged, notably the large centralized societies, the affiliated orders and the collecting (burial) societies; in addition TRADE UNIONS provided similar benefits. By 1899 the number of registered f.s. had increased to 27,592 (excluding collecting societies) with a membership of 5,466,000 (affiliated societies accounting for 2,398,000). The National Insurance Act (1911)

used the framework of the f.s. in the form of 'approved' societies. In the next 30 years their number diminished whilst membership continued to grow (in 1946, 18,293 f.s. had 8,670,000 members). The approved-society system was abolished by the National Insurance Act (1946) since when both the number and membership of f.s. have declined (in 1966, 9,002 had 5,503,000 members).   MLH

Frisians, named by Procopius (6th century) as one of the Teutonic races invading Britain (TEUTONIC CONQUEST). No kingdom was named after them, but the English language is closely related to Frisian. Possibly Procopius confused them with SAXONS. In later centuries F. had a great reputation as sea-farers, and king Alfred (died 899) employed them in his navy.   CFS

Frith (Old English 'peace'), as applied to the situation within kingdoms is best defined as a set of generally accepted conventions, any breach of which was punishable on the judgment of the community as given in its MOOT. It was first supplemented and then replaced by the KING'S PEACE.   CFS

Fulford, battle of (Gate Fulford, 2 miles south of York), was fought on 20 Sept. 1066 between the men of MERCIA and NORTHUMBRIA under their earls Edwin and Morcar and the NORWEGIAN invaders under their king Harold Hardrada and his ally Tostig, formerly earl of Northumbria. The Norwegians won, but their success was transitory (STAMFORDBRIDGE). The losses suffered by the forces of the English earls prevented their participation in the battle of HASTINGS.
CFS

Fyrd, the local MILITIA of Old English times. F.-service was an obligation on all free men, and exemption from it was rarely granted. The main military force was not the f., but consisted of king's THEGNS and their personal retainers who served as an obligation inherent in their rank in society. These overshadowed the f., and details of its composition, organization, military value, etc., are not known. In the later

O.E. period it was unusual for the f. of a SHIRE to serve beyond its borders; but there are indications that at times f.-service was selective rather than universal, and this may indicate more extended service. The ill-equipped peasants who fought at the battle of HASTINGS (1066) were not typical of the f.   CFS

Gallipoli Expedition (1915–16), a major campaign of WORLD WAR I, originated from a Russian request (Jan. 1915) to draw off Turkish pressure in the Caucasus; the object was to force the Dardanelles and open up direct communications with Russia via the Black Sea. Operations were at first envisaged as purely naval; the fleet under (Sir) S. Carden attacked Turkish defences on the G. peninsula (Feb. 1915). Naval bombardment culminated on 18 Mar., but the fleet (now under (Sir) J. De Robeck) withdrew after loss of ships to floating mines. A further naval attack, as advocated by Commodore (later Adm. of the Fleet Lord) Keyes—and Churchill at the Admiralty—, would almost certainly have been successful. Instead military operations were decided upon. A force (including some French troops) under Sir Ian Hamilton landed (25 Apr.) with heavy loss at Cape Helles and ANZAC Cove—the French making a diversion to Kum Kale (on the Asian side). Surprise had been forfeited and under Hamilton's loose leadership little headway was made. Large reinforcements, arriving on 6 Aug., consisted of raw troops under elderly inept commanders. The main attack from Anzac under Lt.-Gen. (later F.M. Lord) Birdwood failed; supporting landings at Suvla Bay under the mediocre command of Sir F. Stopford made no progress. Stalemate again ensued—to be broken by the arrival of Sir C. Monro (replacing Hamilton) who advocated evacuation (Oct.); this recommendation coincided with the government's desire to intervene in Salonika. All troops were withdrawn without loss from Suvla and Anzac by 20 Dec. and from Cape

Helles (6 Jan. 1916). British casualties numbered 205,000 out of 410,000 engaged; French 47,000 out of 79,000; Turkish, 250,000 out of 500,000. At times the G.E. came tantalizingly near to success. Poor planning and leadership ensured its failure.   MLH

Galloglasses (Irish *gall-óglaigh*, 'foreign warriors'), first appeared in the service of a native chief in 1258. Recruited mainly from the Hebrides and north-western Scotland and speaking a mixture of Gaelic and Norse, the g. were redoubtable infantry soldiers, more heavily armoured and better disciplined than the native Irish and fighting Viking-fashion with heavy axes. Large numbers of these mercenaries settled in Ireland, especially in Ulster, where families such as the MacSweenys and the MacDonnells provided an hereditary *corps d'élite* in the chiefs' service. The g. played an important part in halting the English conquest. From Ulster g. spread to the other provinces and in the 15th and 16th centuries were employed in large numbers by the great Anglo-Irish lords and even by the government of the English PALE. Converted to pikemen in the 16th century—when the lightly armed kerns became musketeers—the g. still formed the hard core of Irish armies in the wars of Elizabeth I's reign, when they were reinforced by a new wave of mercenaries from the Isles, nicknamed the Redshanks by the English. Winning their last battles in Tyrone's rebellion, the g. finally disappeared after the English victory at Kinsale (1601) and Tyrone's submission.   RFW

Gambia was discovered by the Portuguese in 1455 and sporadically visited by English traders from 1587. The colony established in 1651 on St Andrew's island by James, duke of Courland (godson of King James I), was taken by the AFRICAN COMPANY on 19 Mar. 1661 and renamed James Island. It was disputed by the Dutch and, from 1667, the French and frequently changed hands until it was finally ceded by France in the treaty of VERSAILLES, 1783. In 1815 James Island was abandoned in favour of Banjol which was renamed St Mary's Island; here Capt. Alexander Grant laid out Bathurst in 1816. On the dissolution of the African Company G. was placed under the administration of SIERRA LEONE (1821) and was settled by liberated slaves. The subordination of the G. under Sierra Leone was repealed in 1843, but resumed 1866–88 in the combination of the 'British West Africa Settlements' ruled from Freetown. From 1869 to 1876 the British government negotiated with France over the exchange of G. for the Ivory Coast; this was resisted by the African chiefs and eventually scotched by Parliament. The frontiers along 300 miles of the river G. were delimitated in 1891 and 1899, with utter disregard of geography, ethnography and economics. Colony and protectorate were placed under a governor in 1901, and were granted responsible government in 1960. It became an independent member of the COMMONWEALTH on 18 Feb. 1965. The chief commodity of the G. is groundnuts; they were introduced from Brazil by the Portuguese, first cultivated by the Wesleyan missionaries in 1823 and first shipped to Europe in 1830.   SHS

Gaol Delivery. In the middle ages imprisonment was mainly used to ensure appearance in court, not to punish. Gaols, often in castles, held prisoners committed on indictment to be delivered by the general EYRE. From the early 13th century onwards this part of the eyre's work was frequently deputed to specially commissioned justices, often serjeants, for the speedier delivery of a gaol. Like other special commissions, g.d. was gradually merged into the commissions of ASSIZE of modern judges on circuit.
                                   PMB

Garter, Order of the, the oldest and most renowned English ORDER OF CHIVALRY, was inspired by the ARTHURIAN LEGEND of the Round Table. Planned by Edward III in 1344, the order was formally inaugurated on St George's day 1348 at Windsor castle, which has remained its home. Membership was limited to the king and 25 other knights: the Black Prince and other famous commanders of the HUNDRED YEARS' WAR were among the original members. Distinguished foreign knights were later admitted when places fell vacant. Recent historians favour the acceptance of the story that the emblem of the order, the blue garter, had its origin in an incident at a ball at Calais, when Joan, the Fair Maid of Kent (then Countess of Salisbury, later the Black Prince's wife), lost her garter when dancing, and Edward III returned it with the words *Honi soit qui mal y pense.* The order was enlarged in the late 18th and early 19th centuries to admit the sovereign's sons and other descendants of George I; dames of the order—queens consort and wives and daughters of K.G.s—have been admitted from 1376 or earlier.   RFW

Gascony. While the official name of the duchy held by the kings of England in south-western France in the middle ages was AQUITAINE, from the 13th century Englishmen most often called it G., the name of one of its parts. The French on the other hand tended to call the duchy after its other major part, Guienne, and French historians have followed suit. Although Guienne was originally synonymous with Aquitaine, by the 13th century it was specially applied to its northern part containing the valleys of the Garonne and Dordogne, while G. was the southern part of the duchy, in the angle of the Bay of Biscay and the Pyrenees. Neither area, however, was defined with any precision, and on the whole modern historians, like 14th-century Englishmen, employ the three names without distinction to indicate the whole duchy after the loss of Poitou by Henry III. When the whole of the ANGEVIN EMPIRE south of the Loire, including POITOU, is referred to, it is usually called Aquitaine.   RFW

Gaspee Affair (June 1772), a symptom of American resistance to British authority. The revenue cutter *Gaspee* ran aground off Providence, Rhode Island, and was plundered and burnt by local smugglers. A royal commission of inquiry was appointed, but failed to secure any evidence as to the culprits.   IHE

Gavelkind, the 'law of Kent', a system of tenure of uncertain, probably post-Norman conquest, origin, peculiar to that county. It was based on humble freemen who owed their lord rent, *gafol*, instead of services. Its principal features were divisible inheritance, the inheritance of felons' property, DOWER of a half instead of a third of the husband's lands and widower's CURTESY of half of the wife's lands.   PMB

Gebur, a free peasant in Old English times (CEORL). Such men normally worked a yardland and owed a heavy burden of dues and services to their lords. Economically their position resembled that of the later VILLEINS. The word, later, as 'boor' became an unflattering description of a peasant.
                                                                  CFS

Geld, the Old English term for an extraordinary tax assessed on land. It may have been foreshadowed in the later 9th century, when various rulers had to raise money to 'buy peace' from the DANES; but it is first seen as a national system of taxation in the time of Ethelred II (978–1016). From 991 to 1012 it was used to buy peace from the Danes; from 1012 to 1051 under the name of *heregeld* (O.E. *here*: army) it was used to maintain a standing military (HOUSECARLE) and naval force. It was later described generally as DANEGELD whatever its purpose. For this tax each SHIRE was assessed at a round number of HIDES, carucates or SULUNGS. These were divided among the HUNDREDS or WAPENTAKES of which the shire was composed; and their share was in turn divided among their constituent villages. Local variations occur in KENT (LATHE) and EAST ANGLIA (LEET). Its incidence varied,

but in later times a g. was normally 2s. per hide or carucate.   CFS

After the Norman conquest g. continued to be levied frequently—at times almost every year. The normal rate remained 2s., but double-gelds (e.g. in 1096) or treble-gelds (e.g. in 1084) were levied on some occasions. DEMESNE lands and the lands of collectors were free from g., and many individual exemptions were granted. By the middle of the 12th century a g. was only producing about £3,000, and the tax was last levied in 1162. Richard I's CARUCAGE of 1194 approximated to a g., but further experiments with this type of tax proved unsuccessful, and it was abandoned in favour of taxes on MOVABLES.   RFW

Geneat (Old English: companion), free men who formed the peasant aristocracy (CEORL). Originally they were probably members of a WARBAND, but of a lower standing than GESITHS. Their services later were those suitable to their standing; but their WERGILD of 200s. sharply distinguished them from the nobility. In the middle ages the class was represented by radknights.   CFS

General Strike (May 1926) resulted from the inability of the coal-mining industry to agree upon terms of employment during an economic crisis. In anticipation of the end (1 May 1926) of a temporary subsidy, forced on the government by T.U.C. action (Red Friday, 31 July 1925), the mine-owners repeated demands for lower wages and longer hours. Baldwin's government, willing to implement the Samuel report (March) but not to continue the subsidy, considered a reduction in wages necessary, but the Miners' Federation refused any compromise. The owners therefore ordered a lock-out for 30 April and this was answered by the T.U.C.'s proposal of a 'national' strike. Final negotiations proved ineffective and the g.s. started, 11.59 p.m., 3 May, when 'first-line' industries (railways, docks, road transport, printing, iron and steel, heavy chemicals, building, electricity and gas) responded to the call. The government's plans, perfected in the previous 9 months, came into operation, and the middle-class public, backed by the police and armed forces, responded quickly to representations of grave constitutional danger. On the other side, the T.U.C. had made no adequate preparations; though the workers were solid locally, the leaders were disorganized and became convinced that they could not succeed. Possibly influenced by declarations of the strike's illegality, the T.U.C. surrendered unconditionally (12 May). The disillusioned men returned to work in the following days, individual unions making what terms they could. Only the miners stood out but, after abortive negotiations, were gradually (July–Dec.) forced by economic necessity to accept longer hours for less pay. The total failure of the g.s. was further emphasized by the vindictive Trades Disputes and TRADE UNION Act, 1927.

MLH

General Surveyors, Court of, a Tudor chamber creation. After an Act of 1512 G.S. were periodically appointed to audit accounts formerly presented at the EXCHEQUER, e.g. HANAPER, Great Wardrobe, and of Crown Lands, e.g. the Principality of Wales. To prevent interference from other departments an Act of 1541 created the C. of G.S. of the king's lands to control lands acquired by FORFEIT, ATTAINDER and ESCHEAT. It was abolished in 1547 and its functions merged with those of the Court of AUGMENTATIONS.

PMB

General Warrants for the arrest of unspecified persons were issued by the court of STAR CHAMBER, but their later use was authorized by the LICENSING ACT (1662) and continued after its lapse (1695). G.W. were used to arrest and search the property of unnamed authors and publishers of allegedly libellous and seditious writings, and their legality was tested by Wilkes' Case and the actions arising therefrom. In No. 45 of the *North Briton* Wilkes offensively criticized the king's speech to Parliament (1763) and a G.W. was issued against the authors, printers and publishers. Wilkes, among the 49 arrested, was released after pleading his privilege as a member of Parliament, but fled abroad when the Commons declared seditious libel outside privilege. He was subsequently outlawed (MIDDLESEX ELECTION). By legal actions Wilkes recovered damages and G.W. were declared illegal (1763–5), a decision reinforced by a resolution of the Commons in 1766. This was an important victory for the liberties of the subject against the executive.

The Incitement to Disaffection Act (1934), designed to prevent communist propaganda in the armed services, allowed the issue of a g.w. by a High Court judge.

IHE

George Cross, a silver cross showing St George and the dragon and inscribed *For Gallantry*, with a dark-blue ribbon, was instituted on 24 Sept. 1940 as an award for acts of conspicuous courage. The G.C. is intended mainly for civilians and ranks next to the VICTORIA CROSS.

SHS

Georgia, the last American colony to be established under British rule, named after George II. In 1732 the land between Carolina and FLORIDA was granted by charter for 21 years to General James Oglethorpe. A philanthropic enterprise to provide a fresh start for debtors, it was supported by Parliamentary grants as an outpost against Florida, and the first settlement was established at Savannah (1733). Slavery was reluctantly permitted in 1749 and rice became a staple crop. Boundary disputes with Florida were a contributory cause of the war of JENKINS' EAR (1739–48). It became a crown colony in 1752 and supported the American Revolution after LEXINGTON (1775), although the strength of the loyalists largely made the revolt a civil war.

IHE

Geraldines, see DESMOND REVOLT.

Gesiths (Old English: companions), composed a king's WARBAND in the days of the TEUTONIC CONQUEST of Britain. They later formed the aristocracy in all Teutonic kingdoms except Kent (EORL). In the 8th century a *gesithcund* man in Wessex had a WERGILD of 1200*s*. as opposed to the GENEAT or CEORL's of 200*s*. During the 9th century the term was replaced by THEGN.   CFS

Ghana, a powerful and highly civilized African empire on the middle Niger, founded *c.* A.D. 300, was overthrown in the 14th century. The name was revived when the GOLD COAST became independent in 1957. A republican constitution was adopted on 29 June 1960 and it became a one-party state under the Convention People's Party on 21 Feb. 1964. In 1966 President Nkrumah was overthrown by an army and police *coup d'état*. The ensuing National Liberation Council suspended the constitution. A democratic constitution was approved in Aug. 1969.   SHS; IHE

Ghent, treaty of (24 Dec. 1814), ended the AMERICAN WAR OF 1812, negotiations having started in Aug. 1814. Outstanding differences were left open, the treaty merely restoring the territorial *status quo*; minor clauses were concerned with the cessation of operations against Indians and condemnation of the SLAVE TRADE. Commissions were, however, appointed to settle the Canadian boundary; their reports resulted in the convention of London (1818), which also settled outstanding fisheries disputes. The demilitarization of the Great Lakes was accomplished by the Rush–Bagot agreement (Apr. 1818).   MLH

Gibraltar ('Djebel Tariq', mountain of Tariq), starting-point of the Moslem conquest of Spain by Tariq (711), conquered by the Castilians in 1462 and captured by an Anglo-Dutch fleet under Sir George Rooke on 4 Aug. 1704. G. was formally ceded to Great Britain by the treaty of UTRECHT (1713). The fortress withstood sieges by the Spaniards (1727) and the combined Spanish and French forces (3 years and 7 months, 1779–83). G. is a crown colony under a governor, who is also commander-in-chief, assisted

by an executive council and (since 1950) a legislative council. Substantial self-government was granted in 1964 and in 1967 a referendum was held, consequent upon a U.N. resolution for the decolonization of G. From a total electorate of 12,762, those supporting the British connexion numbered 12,138.   SHS; IHE

Gilbert and Ellice Islands became a British protectorate in 1892 and were annexed at the request of the native rulers on 10 Nov. 1915 (effective 12 Jan. 1916). The colony, which is under the jurisdiction of the WESTERN PACIFIC HIGH COMMISSION, also includes Ocean Island (annexed 1900), the Phoenix Islands (1937; with the Anglo-American condominium of Canton and Enderbury islands), the Line Islands (1916; including CHRISTMAS ISLAND).   SHS

Gilbert's Act (1782), a permissive measure allowing parishes to combine to build Union poorhouses, allowing the able-bodied to be provided with work outside and permitting outdoor-relief from the rates, thus virtually abolishing the workhouse test of 1723. Guardians of the Poor could be appointed by J.P.s.   IHE

Gilds, as fraternities for religious and social purposes were common in medieval England. The earliest known is a g. of *cnihtas* in Canterbury in the 9th century; the 10th-century peace-g. of London had the additional purpose of maintaining public order. Merchant g. combining these features with the defence of commercial interest arose from the late 11th century, controlling trade within a town's boundaries by monopolistic privileges. Most of the craft g. developed from the 12th century, regulating and protecting particular trades and industries. The apprenticeship system (usually 7 years) was established by the 13th century with an entry fee high enough to be restrictive. Additional labour was provided by day workmen or journeymen (*journée*). By the late 14th century the leading London g. sought incorporation as Livery Companies, many of which still exist. Amalgamations of allied trades took place and journeymen began to develop their own organizations. G. exercised some of the functions of FRIENDLY SOCIETIES, although their religious endowments were largely confiscated by the Chantry Acts of 1545 and 1547. G. were undermined from the time of the Protectorate by the breakdown of the apprenticeship system and the growth of capitalist enterprise, although there were numerous survivals into the 18th century and beyond. IHE

Glamorgan Treaty (25 Aug. 1645) was made between the IRISH REBELLION Confederates and the earl of Glamorgan. In return for 10,000 Irish troops the confederates were to retain control of the churches and the PLANTATION lands were to be returned. The English Parliament became aware of it and the outcry led to its disavowal by Charles I (16 Jan. 1646). IHE

Glanvill, *De Legibus et Consuetudinibus regni Anglie,* the first important manual of COMMON LAW, written 1187–9 and customarily attributed to Ranulf de G., justiciar of Henry II. It briefly classifies criminal and civil pleas and those of the crown and gives, with commentary, the writs and procedures to bring each action to a conclusion, thus showing the early history of the common law in the king's courts. With the DIALOGUS, it is a monument to the good government of Henry II. The book was popular and influential and numerous MSS survive; the *Regiam Majestatem,* a suitably revised version, was current in Scotland. PMB

Glastonbury Legend had as its core the belief that G. had the earliest associations with Christianity in England. William of Malmesbury, writing between 1125 and 1135, cautiously recorded a G. tradition that a Christian church had been founded there in the time of the Apostles, together with an alternative account of a late-2nd-century foundation and stories associating G. with many notable saints—David, Patrick and Columba among them. By the mid-13th century the G.l. had been elaborated: a 1st-century foundation was ascribed to Joseph of Arimathaea, sent to England by the Apostle Philip and bearing with him precious relics—the blood and sweat of Christ. Geoffrey of Monmouth had not connected King ARTHUR with G., but in 1191 the graves of Arthur and Guinevere were found there—a discovery closely linked with the monks' efforts to raise funds for the rebuilding of their abbey after the fire of 1184—and Gerald of Wales duly identified G. as the Isle of Avalon. Arthur and Joseph of Arimathaea became linked in the G.l., and in one version Joseph brought the Holy Grail with him. The G.l. continued to flourish in the later middle ages: Edward III authorized a search for Joseph's tomb in 1345; new stories were tacked on, such as that of Joseph's staff taking root and becoming the famous G. Thorn, and an extreme form of the legend brought Christ in person to G. (reflected long afterwards in Blake's *Jerusalem*). The G.l. survived the Reformation and the dissolution of the abbey and obtained some credence among Tudor antiquaries. As late as 1588 a fresh discovery among the ruins was reported—prophetic verses foretelling the impending doom of empires. Modern historians consider that the G.l. may in its early, simple form contain some grains of truth. The abbey of G. may have been founded as early as the 6th century, and it is not impossible that the site was associated with Christianity during the Roman period and visited by the Celtic saints.

R. F. Treharne, *The Glastonbury Legends* (1967). RFW

Glebe or parson's glebe, the land held by the incumbent of a PARISH church as part of the endowment of that church. It represented the original endowment of a parish church, and in the areas of open-field agriculture the parish priest normally participated in the agricultural life of the community. CFS

Glencoe, massacre of (1692). In order to secure the pacification of Scotland, the Highland chiefs were ordered to take an oath of allegiance to William III and Mary before 1 Jan. 1692. Macdonald of Glencoe, accidentally late, took the oath (6 Jan.), but the Master of Stair secured an order for the extirpation of the Macdonalds for their disobedience. Troops drawn from their enemies, the Campbells, were quartered on the clan (6 Feb.) and treacherously fell upon their hosts (13 Feb.). The majority luckily escaped, but 38 Macdonalds were killed.   IHE

Glorious First of June (1794), a British naval victory in the FRENCH REVOLUTIONARY WARS. The French fleet under Admiral Villaret Joyeuse left Brest (16 May) to meet and escort a fleet of cornships from the United States. The Channel Fleet under Lord Howe made contact some 400 miles west of Ushant (28 May) and after 4 days skirmishing the decisive action was fought by 26 ships of the line on either side. Six French ships were captured and one sunk, but Howe did not give chase and the convoy entered Brest (14 June).   IHE

Glorious Revolution (1688) was the name given to the course of action which led to the flight of James II and the establishment of William and Mary on the throne. James II had alienated Whigs and Tories and the church by his endeavours to promote Roman Catholicism, and his use of the DISPENSING and SUSPENDING POWERS failed to win over the Protestant Dissenters. The appointment of Roman Catholics to the Privy Council, the army and the universities caused widespread apprehension, and the birth of his son destroyed the chance of a Protestant succession. Consequently seven prominent statesmen invited William of Orange to land with an army. James rejected French help, and Louis XIV's invasion of Germany enabled William to land at Brixham (15 Nov.). James made last-minute concessions but was deserted on all sides and at the end of December

F

escaped to France. The so-called ABDICATION of James II was a convenient fiction which enabled the CONVENTION PARLIAMENT of the interregnum to declare the throne vacant. Some Tories favoured a regency, but the Whig policy of excluding James and subjecting the crown to Parliamentary conditions won the support of the majority of the governing class. Their case against James was stated in the DECLARATION OF RIGHTS, which was accepted by William and Mary when they assumed the throne (Feb. 1689), and was subsequently embodied in the BILL OF RIGHTS. Conservative in form, this revolution involved the ending of DIVINE RIGHT, tied the crown to the established church and introduced constitutional monarchy. A similar revolution was effected by the Scottish Estates (Apr.), but the JACOBITES in Ireland had to be suppressed by military action (1689–91).   IHE

Gloucester, statute of (Aug. 1278), resulted from the enquiry into franchises included in the 'RAGMAN' inquest 1274–5. Edward I wanted to recover lost royal rights and to obtain a comprehensive picture of local administration, much of which was in the hands of the lords of franchises. The statute provided *inter alia* for the proving (before the king's justices) of titles to franchises, all of which had originated, in theory, in royal grants. The inability of many lords to produce documentary evidence of title raised problems which were dealt with in the statute of QUO WARRANTO (1290); those lords who successfully proved their titles were confirmed in possession.   RFW

Glyn Dŵr Rebellion. Owain G.D. (c. 1354–?1416), descendant of princes of POWYS and DEHEUBARTH, educated at the Inns of Court and trained in the royal service, began his revolt as a private quarrel with Lord Grey of Ruthin. But depopulation, economic depression, social dislocation and messianic bardic divinations made WALES ripe for widespread rebellion. It opened in Sept. 1400 and by the end of 1401 had spread through most of north Wales; in 1402 it extended to central Wales and in 1403 to the south. Neither savage parliamentary proscription nor annual royal expeditions, 1400–3, did much to check the rebels' success, nor did the defeat of G.D.'s ally, Hotspur, at SHREWSBURY in 1403. In 1404, at the height of his power, G.D. proclaimed himself PRINCE OF WALES and summoned a parliament. Already in contact with Robert III of Scotland and Irish princes, he now allied with France and also, hoping to obtain from him an independent Welsh archbishopric and universities, with Benedict XIII of Avignon. In 1405, by the 'tri-partite indenture', he agreed to share the English realm with Northumberland and Mortimer. But French aid was insufficient, and in 1405–6 the tide turned against the rebels. Having in 1408–9 lost his last strongholds, G.D. became a hunted outlaw. After 1412 all is silence, and his ultimate fate is uncertain. Despite his failure, and the incalculable material harm done by his revolt, his effect on Welsh patriotism was, and remained, electrifying.   GW

Goa, Daman and Diu. The mainland Indian territories of G. and Daman became Portuguese in 1510 and 1531 respectively, the island of Diu in 1534. They were occupied by INDIA in Dec. 1961 and made a Union Territory.   IHE

Gold Coast was discovered by the Portuguese in 1471 and subsequently occupied and fought over by them, the Dutch (from 1600), Swedes (1645–57), Danes (from 1657), Brandenburgers (1681–1721) and English (from 1631). The AFRICAN COMPANY established a firm foothold in Cape Coast (captured from the Dutch in 1664); its successor, the Royal African Company, in 1694 joined a negro coalition which defeated the Dutch and their African allies. The first Christian missionary was sent out in 1752 by the Society for the Propagation of the Gospel; in 1760 the first African priest was ordained.

The Company was abolished in 1821 and the British government took over the G.C. forts, but from 1828 to 1842 left the management to a committee of merchants. Between 1807 and 1901 the warlike ASHANTI tribes of the interior frequently raided the coast and were in turn attacked and finally overthrown by the British. The Danes in 1850 and the Dutch in 1872 sold their remaining forts to Britain, which in 1874 organized the colony, moved the capital from Cape Coast to Accra in 1876 and in 1901 established the Northern Territories protectorate. From 1920 the trusteeship territory of TOGOLAND was administered by the G.C. government. In 1957 the G.C. attained its independence as a member state of the Commonwealth under the name of GHANA.   SHS

Gold Penny. Although gold pennies were minted by Offa, Edward the Elder, Aethelred II and Edward the Confessor, gold coins were rarely produced in England until the middle of the 14th century. Gold pennies and halfpennies (pennies and obols of musc), frequently referred to in the 13th century, were small gold coins mostly from Byzantium, not used as legal tender. In the second half of the 13th century the fine gold coins of Italy, the florin of Florence, first issued in 1252, and the sequin of Venice were widely imitated. In 1257 King Henry III minted an imitation of the florin, the g.p., alternatively called the bezant, after the Byzantine gold coin widely current in Western Europe. The g.p. was originally worth 20d., and its value was increased to 2s. in 1265. As few had need of such a valuable coin, the g.p. was withdrawn from circulation about 1270, and no more gold coins were struck in England until the FLORIN of Edward III.   RFW

Goldsmiths formed a GILD in London in the 12th century, obtaining a charter as the G.' Company in 1394. As dealers in foreign money and bullion the merchant g. became distinct from the working craftsmen, and in London the private banks first derived from the g.' shops. During the CIVIL

WARS the g. acted as guardians of coin and valuables, emerging as government bankers under the COMMONWEALTH. Their notes or deposit certificates came to serve as currency, and their running cash system was the forerunner of the current account. The Stop of the EXCHEQUER (1672) caused them temporarily to suspend payments, and they naturally showed initial hostility to the BANK OF ENGLAND.   IHE

Gold Standard, a monetary unit in which the currency unit is a fixed weight of gold or is kept at the value of gold, upon which there are no trading restrictions. In early times the currency of Britain was based on silver, later it was a mixed currency of gold and silver, and in the 18th century silver became subsidiary coin to the GUINEA. In 1816 provision was made for coinage of gold at the price of £3 17s. 10½d. per oz. and silver became legal tender for amounts up to 40 SHILLINGS only. Britain became the first country to adopt the g.s. when cash transactions (suspended in 1797 as a result of the FRENCH REVOLUTIONARY WAR) were resumed in 1821.

In the 1870s the g.s. was adopted by France, Germany and the U.S., and from the 1890s it became the almost universal currency system. It was disrupted by WORLD WAR I and although Britain remained on the g.s. (the £ being pegged at $4.76) export of bullion was difficult and the sovereign disappeared. In 1919 the g.s. was suspended, export being prohibited. In 1922 the £ became more or less stabilized at $4.40 on a free market. Already in 1919 the Cunliffe Report had recommended lifting suspension and the return to gold at the old parity was taken by Churchill, as Chancellor of the Exchequer, in 1925. Since regarded as a cause of deflation and a grave mistake, the return (to a g. bullion s. in which gold coin did not circulate) was strongly backed by the TREASURY and the BANK OF ENGLAND, Keynes and Lloyd George being among the few dissenters. The old parity possibly over-

valued sterling, but the real trouble was that Britain's ability to sell abroad had declined. The City did not win back from New York and Paris the dominant place it held in the pre-war heyday of the g.s., international conditions for the working of which no longer prevailed. The g.s. was finally abandoned by the newly. formed National government, 21 Sept. 1931, during the world financial crisis, and the U.S. followed in 1933.   MLH

Good Parliament, sat April to July 1376, longer than any previous session, its proceedings exceptionally well recorded, notably in the *Anonimalle Chronicle* of St Mary's York. The commons condemned the inept conduct of military operations against France, protested against burdensome taxation and waste of the proceeds, and chose Sir Peter de la Mare to put their case to parliament as a whole— the origin of the office of SPEAKER. In a conference with a committee of the lords, the commons asserted that certain councillors and officers were enriching themselves at the expense of the state, and demanded the punishment of the culprits. Lord Latimer and others were tried in parliament— an important step towards the procedure of IMPEACHMENT. Further demands, that Edward III's councillors and his rapacious mistress, Alice Perrers, should be removed, were acceded to, and new councillors were nominated and sworn in by parliament—apparently another innovation. The G.P.'s acts were annulled by a great council later in the year: the new councillors were dismissed; Alice Perrers returned; De la Mare was imprisoned; and in 1377 a more amenable parliament granted the first regular POLL TAX.   RFW

Goodwin's Case (1604). The Court of CHANCERY cancelled the return to Parliament of Sir Francis Goodwin, an outlaw, as one of the members for Buckinghamshire. The Commons successfully reasserted its sole jurisdiction over disputed election returns which had only that year been conferred on Chancery by a proclamation of James I.   IHE

Gordon Riots (2–9 June 1780) resulted from Savile's Roman Catholic Relief Act (1778). The eccentric Lord George Gordon headed a Protestant Association to secure its repeal and escorted by his London supporters presented a petition to Parliament (2 June 1780). In the evening the mob began to take control. Houses, chapels, breweries, distilleries were sacked and prisons opened while the orgy lasted. The magistrates evaded their duty, but order was eventually restored by regular troops and the militia under MARTIAL LAW. This dangerous outbreak destroyed the reliance of politicians on the nuisance value of the London mob.   IHE

Gorham Judgement (1850). The high-church bishop of Exeter, H. Phillpotts, refused to institute G. C. Gorham to a crown living (1847) on grounds of heresy. G.'s appeal was dismissed by the Court of Arches but allowed (March 1850) by the judicial committee of the PRIVY COUNCIL. The doctrinal question, baptismal regeneration, was unimportant except as illustrating the clash of opinion in the CHURCH OF ENGLAND between high and low church. The G.J., however, raised in acute form the constitutional issue of the right of a predominantly secular body to pronounce on matters of religious belief. Together with the reaction to anti-papal feeling aroused by the 'papal aggression' (ECCLESIASTICAL TITLES ACT), the G.J. resulted in further desertions of Anglicans to Rome (OXFORD MOVEMENT), in particular that of the later cardinal H. Manning (1851).   MLH

Gowrie Conspiracy (1600), one of the most mysterious events in Scottish history. James VI claimed that he was decoyed to G. House, near Perth, by the Master of Ruthven and made a prisoner (5 Aug.). James raised an alarm, and his attendants slew Ruthven and his brother, the earl of G., in a struggle. G.'s father was the author of the RUTHVEN RAID, and James owed

G. £80,000. It was held by many that the king designed the affair to get rid of the Ruthvens and his debt.   IHE

Grand Alliance, (1) (12 May 1689), was a militant league consequent upon the French invasion of the Palatinate (1688), between the Netherlands and the Empire joined by England (Sept.), Spain, Brandenburg, Saxony, Hanover, Bavaria and Savoy. It aimed to annul the French gains confirmed under the truce of Regensburg (1684), whereby she retained Strasburg, Luxemburg, Oudenarde, etc. A secret clause supported the imperial claims to the Spanish dominions on the death of Charles II. The war of the League of AUGSBURG (1688–97) is also known as the war of the G.A.

(2) (17 Sept. 1701), was formed between England, the Netherlands and the Empire against France to prevent the union of the thrones of France and Spain. Detailed territorial arrangements were largely left to further negotiation, but England and the Netherlands insisted that France was not to secure any trading rights in the Indies. It formed the basis of the European coalition against France in the SPANISH SUCCESSION WAR and was joined by Prussia (1702), Portugal and Savoy (1703).   IHE

Grand Assize, or assize of Windsor, probably. instituted by Henry II at Windsor in April 1179, provided an alternative to the judicial TRIAL BY BATTLE as the means of determining right to property. A tenant whose right was challenged might henceforth refuse the duel and claim the 'royal benefit' of the new procedure, by which four knights elected a jury of 12 knights, who in turn declared which litigant had the better right. The procedure soon proved popular, but it was subject to long delays, when, for instance, objections to the jury were lodged or ESSOINS were submitted.
                    RFW

Grand Remonstrance (22 Nov. 1641). Apprehensive of the growing strength of the supporters of EPISCOPACY and of those opposed to further

attacks on the royal PREROGATIVE, their opponents in the Commons drew up this document, which was carried only by 11 votes. It was printed and circulated as an appeal to the nation and contained a long statement of the king's errors, a list of reforms achieved by the LONG PARLIAMENT and of grievances awaiting redress. The king's ministers were to be approved by Parliament, which was to reform the church, aided by a synod of divines. Essentially a party manifesto, the threat to the Anglican church confirmed the politically moderate episcopalians in their support of the king.
IHE

Grattan's Parliament was the popular name given to the Irish Parliament of 1782–1800. It reflected recognition of Henry Grattan's efforts in the IRISH VOLUNTEER movement and in Parliament which resulted in the repeal of POYNINGS' LAW and the DECLARATORY ACT of 1719. The appellate jurisdiction of the Irish House of Lords was restored as well as the legislative independence of Parliament. The freedom of the constitution was largely illusory, however, as the British executive continued its effort to maintain control through influence and corruption until the Act of UNION (1800).
IHE

Graupius, Mons, battle of (A.D. 84), fought, probably near Forfar, between the Romans under Agricola, governor of Britain 78–85, and the warriors of CALEDONIA under Calgacus. Agricola aimed at the conquest of the whole island, and this battle broke the power of the Highland tribes for two or three generations. The ROMAN CONQUEST, however, never extended to the Highlands.
CFS

Gravelines, battle of. (1) (13 July 1558). England was involved in the Habsburg–Valois struggle, largely in the Spanish interest, and their land victory at G., east of Calais, was materially assisted by the guns of an English squadron.

(2) (29 July/8 Aug. 1588), the final defeat of the ARMADA. Having been scattered by fireships the previous night, the Spaniards were engaged by the English off G., lost four large ships after eight hours' action and suffered heavy damage and casualties. A northwest wind blew them towards the shoals of the Flemish coast, but a shift of wind to the south-west enabled them to escape into the North Sea.
IHE

Great Contract (1610–11), an attempt by Salisbury, the Treasurer, to come to an agreement with the Commons on the financial needs of the country. The crown was to commute its irksome practice of PURVEYANCE, right of wardship, etc., for a fixed sum of £200,000 per annum. Impositions were to be governed by statute. Before the details were settled fresh disputes arose over inadequate enforcement of the PENAL LAWS against Roman Catholics, NON-RESIDENCE of clergy, and the conduct of the Court of HIGH COMMISSION. James I resented Parliamentary interference in church matters and increased his financial demands. Attacks on his Scottish favourites and court extravagance led him to dissolve Parliament (Feb. 1611) and the G.C. was never concluded.
IHE

Great Officers of State, a term sometimes used in the middle ages to describe the king's principal ministers— the CHANCELLOR, the TREASURER and the keeper of the PRIVY SEAL—but normally used by historians of the g.o. of the Norman royal household, i.e. the STEWARD, the CONSTABLE, the MARSHAL, the CHAMBERLAIN and the BUTLER. Some of them had their equivalents in the Anglo-Saxon royal household, and all originally performed domestic duties in person: the steward was responsible for the service of meals, and the marshal for the care of the king's horses. In time, due partly to French influence, the offices became honorific and mainly ornamental dignities held by great lords and hereditary in their families, while the work was done by deputies and lower household officers. The g.o. now have mainly ceremonial duties, and some of them, e.g. the lord high steward and the lord high constable, are specially appointed to serve on a single day, that of the sovereign's CORONATION.   RFW

Great Rebellion, see CIVIL WARS.

Great Seal, the sovereign's chief SEAL, used to authenticate all important and many lesser documents: the first genuine surviving impression is of Edward the Confessor's seal. It is always circular and double-sided: one face shows the sovereign 'in majesty', crowned and enthroned, the other the sovereign mounted—in the Norman period this was known as the Norman side; the sovereign's style is given around the border of both faces. Though the size of the matrices has gradually increased, this basic design has been constant, except for the COMMONWEALTH period. The seal is normally kept by the CHANCELLOR, though a keeper could be appointed or the seal put in COMMISSION. In the early period the chancellor and the seal travelled with the sovereign— Richard I's seal was lost in a shipwreck. From the 13th century, as the CHANCERY settled at Westminster, the sovereign's verbal authority for the use of the seal was replaced by written warrant under the PRIVY SEAL (certified by a SIGN MANUAL from 1851). Apart from the chancery seal, there was another, smaller, G.s. for the EXCHEQUER, generally impressed on green wax. Occasionally this was used as the G.s. when the sovereign and his seal were abroad: later special g.s. 'of absence' were made.   PMB

Great Trek (1835–48), the exodus of some 20% of Dutch-speaking South Africans from CAPE Colony leading to the creation of Boer republics across the Orange and Vaal rivers and to the British annexation of NATAL. The primary causes were land hunger, discontent with governmental control and fear of the growth of equality between white settlers and natives; grievances about slave emancipation and Britain's vacillating frontier policy were subsidiary factors. Trekking began at the end of 1835, gathered strength throughout the later 1830s and fell

away during the 1840s. It led to conflict with the Griquas, Basuto, Matabele and Zulus and enormously complicated the frontier problems of the Cape government. The trekkers first moved into Transorangia but towards the end of 1837 the main body moved into Natal eventually routing the Zulus (DINGAAN'S DAY, 1838). When in 1843 the British government annexed NATAL, primarily to safeguard strategic imperial interests, many of the trekkers returned to the High Veld moving northward into the TRANSVAAL as did most of the new comers from Cape Colony. The G.T. substantially ended when the Cape high commissioner, Sir Harry Smith, annexed the ORANGE River Sovereignty in 1848, after overcoming Boer resistance at Boomplaats.
                                                              IHE

Green Cloth, Board of, the successor of the WARDROBE and CHAMBER as the financial office of the royal household. Presided over by the Lord STEWARD OF THE HOUSEHOLD with the Cofferer as its chief financial officer, the Board dealt with estimates and daily expenditure and, in conjunction with the court of the Verge (MARSHALSEA), the good government of the household. Its powers were much curtailed by an Act of 1782.   PMB

Grenada was discovered by Columbus in 1498 and named Concepción. It was from 1650 in *de facto* French possession after the failure of a British settlement in 1609. It was captured by the British in 1762, formally ceded in 1763 and attached to the WINDWARD ISLANDS, retaken by the French in 1779 and finally restored to Britain in 1783. Half of the Grenadines are administered by G., half by ST VINCENT. In 1967 G. became fully self-governing for internal affairs in free association with Great Britain and is one of the WEST INDIES Associated States.   SHS; IHE

Grenadines, see GRENADA.

Griqualand West, an area astride the Missionaries' Road north of CAPE Colony, assumed importance when diamonds were discovered near the junction of the Vaal and Harts rivers in 1868. It rapidly attracted a cosmopolitan population and was claimed by the Griqua chief Nicholas Waterboer, by the TRANSVAAL and the ORANGE FREE STATE. The Transvaal accepted the arbitration of Lieut.-Governor Keate of Natal, who awarded the diamond fields to Waterboer (17 Oct. 1871). The British high commissioner, Sir Henry Barkly, then annexed G.W. to Cape Colony, thus alienating the Boer republics and destroying prospects of confederation in South Africa. The Free State did not recognize the award but in 1876 accepted £90,000 for yielding its claims. G.W. was administered as a separate crown colony in 1873 but re-incorporated with Cape Colony in 1880.   IHE

Groat, or gross penny, the first multiple of the PENNY to be minted in England, worth 4*d.*, was issued in 1279, probably in imitation of the French *gros* and the *groot* of the Low Countries. The innovation proved to have been premature, and the minting was suspended until Edward III produced g.s for his continental dominions about 1339, and commenced the regular coining of silver g.s (4*d.*) and half-g.s (2*d.*) in England in 1351.
                                          RFW

Guadeloupe, from 1635 a French possession, was occupied by the British in 1759–63, 1794, 1810–14, 1815–16.

Guelph (German *Welf*), German dynasty of Swabian origin, after the extinction of the male line (1055) continued through the marriage of the heiress with the Italian house of Este, and was from 1138 the most powerful family in Lower Saxony. In 1714 the elector George Lewis of HANOVER became king of Great Britain, where the G. dynasty reigned until the death of Queen Victoria in 1901, when it was succeeded by the house of COBURG. SHS

Guienne (Guyenne), see GASCONY.

Guinea, originally G. POUND or sovereign (20*s.*) replacing the UNITE in 1663, was first minted from gold from the G. coast of West Africa. Its value rose to 30*s.* in 1694, but was fixed at 21*s.* in 1717. Last coined in 1813, its place was taken as the standard gold coin by the new sovereign (20*s.*) minted from 1817 until 1925. The g. is still used as money of account. IHE

Guinegate, battle of, see SPURS.

Gujarat, see BOMBAY.

Gunpowder Plot (1604–5) was conceived by Robert Catesby to destroy king, Lords and Commons, thus enabling the CATHOLICS to rise with possibility of success. Rookwood, Digby and Tresham were to lead the rising, and Guy Fawkes, an experienced soldier, stored barrels of powder in a vault under the House of Lords. Tresham informed his Catholic relative Lord Monteagle, who revealed the plot to Cecil. Fawkes was seized (5 Nov. 1605) and the rising collapsed. The conspirators were executed (1606) and the penal laws were rigorously enforced (BYE PLOT).
                                          IHE

Gurkhas, the ruling race of Nepal, which they conquered in 1768–9. Since 1816 the G. have been firm friends of the British and given valuable military aid during the mutiny and the two world wars. The Brigade of G. still forms part of the British army (nine surviving V.C.s in 1961).
                                          SHS

Guyana. The name under which BRITISH GUIANA became independent in 1966. It became a republic within the COMMONWEALTH on 23 Feb. 1970.
                                          IHE

Gwalior was first invaded by the Moslems in 1022, but incorporated in the Mogul empire only in 1558. The MARATHAS took it *c.* 1530, and their governor, Ranoji Sindhia, founded the reigning dynasty. Warren Hastings in 1782 recognized its independence, but a contested succession in 1843 reduced G. to protectorate status. During the mutiny (1857) the government remained faithful to the British. On 16 June 1948 G. was absorbed in

MADHYA BHARAT with (until 1956) the maharaja as rajpramukh of the state.

SHS

Gwynedd, i.e. land of the *Venedotae*, covered a great part of north Wales, including Anglesey and the mainland north and west of the Dovey and Clwyd. Rhodri Mawr (844–78) succeeded in uniting to G. a large part of south Wales, and his unifying efforts were followed by those of his descendants, Hywel Dda and Maredudd, rulers of DEHEUBARTH, and, more particularly, by Gruffydd ap Llywelyn (1039–63). Having almost succumbed in the reigns of William I and II to rapid Norman penetration from Chester, G. was rescued by Gruffydd ap Cynan (*c.* 1094–1137). He was the first of a dynasty which, by its own remarkable political insight and by exploiting geographical advantage and the continental and other entanglements of king and baron, made G. the spearhead of Welsh independence. Owain Gwynedd (1137–70), Llywelyn ab Iorwerth (1194–1240) and Llywelyn ap Gruffydd (1247–82), all patrons of literature and religion, had gifts as soldiers, and especially as statesmen, of a high order. They were resolute in their opposition to Norman encroachment, resourceful in their plans for strengthening the institutions and extending the territories of G. and solicitous of unity with lesser Welsh powers. Their state-building ambitions culminated in the treaty of MONTGOMERY, only to be extinguished by the EDWARDIAN CONQUEST and the statute of RHUDDLAN. GW

Habeas Corpus, Writs of, a group of procedural writs, developed from the early 13th century, to ensure the defendant's presence in court after attachment had failed, the attendance of jurors etc. Out of this expanding group one, the writ *habeas corpus capti in prisona* (have the body of the man imprisoned), sent to the SHERIFF, keeper of prison, etc., to produce the person named in court within a few days, gained special importance. First it was used by KING'S BENCH against

the COMMON PLEAS, releasing prisoners committed by inferior and rival jurisdiction, and secondly by the COMMON LAW courts against those of EQUITY. This latter use was seized upon in the Stewart period as a guarantee of the subject's right of free trial against improper use of the PREROGATIVE, an interpretation which led to the H.C. Act (1679) designed to prevent evasions of the writ and make its issue obligatory. This classic safeguard of personal liberty applied only to criminal charges, but was extended to other charges by the H.C. Act of 1816. An Irish H.C. Act was passed in 1782. PMB; IHE

Hadrian's Wall (*Vallum Hadriani*), built between 122 and 127 after personal inspection of the site by the emperor Hadrian (117–38), ran from Burgh Marsh on Solway to Wallsend on the Tyne. In the mid-2nd century an extension to Bowness on Solway made its length *c.* 73 miles. It was built of stone and cement except for a turf section on the west, was some 16 feet high with a parapet walk and was strengthened with mile-castles *c.* 1 Roman mile apart and two turrets between mile-castles. On the south were 17 forts, varying from 2½ to 5 acres in extent, and on the north a ditch *c.* 10 feet deep and 30 feet wide. Behind the Wall were a flat-bottomed ditch 30 feet wide and 7 feet deep with a bank on each side, and a military road, the Stanegate. Either of these in conjunction with isolated forts may represent the original frontier, but the ditch was soon disused. North of the Wall were a number of outlying forts. H.W. marked the permanent limit of the ROMAN CONQUEST. It was overrun and severely damaged in barbarian attacks of the late 2nd century, the late 3rd century and in 367, but was recovered and repaired in each case. There is, however, no evidence of rebuilding after the successful barbarian attacks of *c.* 383, when it ceased to be the effective frontier of ROMAN BRITAIN. CFS

Haldane reforms. As secretary of state for war (1905–12) R. B. (Lord)

Haldane was responsible for organizational reforms which produced a regular army and a reserve prepared for the first stages of WORLD WAR I. The H.r. included the extension and consolidation of the general staff, established by the previous administration, into the Imperial General Staff, and the formation of an expeditionary force of 6 infantry and 1 cavalry divisions (to be mobilized within 15 days) and a territorial force (14 infantry divisions and 14 cavalry brigades) recruited at county level. In addition, the volunteer corps at public schools were reorganized into officers' training corps.   MLH

Hales's Case (1686). A collusive action was brought against Sir Edward Hales, a Roman CATHOLIC, by his servant Godden, for holding a command in the army contrary to the TEST ACT. Convicted at Rochester assizes, he appealed to King's Bench, pleading the royal dispensation, and won his case. James II made him Lieutenant of the Tower and Master of the Ordnance by flagrant misuse of the DISPENSING POWER.   IHE

Halfpenny. Round silver halfpennies or obols (from *obolus*, a small Greek coin) were first coined in England in the 9th century by King Alfred and by Danish rulers such as Cnut of York (883–94), and continued to be minted for most of the 10th century. After the reign of King Edgar († 975) and up to the 13th century, halfpennies were usually made by cutting silver pennies in half. There is some evidence for the minting of round halfpennies by Henry I and by Henry III, but no examples have been found. Henry II and Edward, son of Henry III, produced round obols for Aquitaine. Edward, when king, started the regular issue of round, silver halfpennies or *mailles* in England in 1280. The h. minted by Charles II from 1672 was the first English copper coin; made of bronze from 1860 it was withdrawn in 1969.   RFW

Halidon Hill, battle of (19 July 1333), a heavy defeat of the Scots under the regent Archibald Douglas, who tried to relieve BERWICK which Edward III was besieging. The English here first employed the tactics (three divisions of dismounted men-at-arms, each with wings of archers) which they later effectively used in the HUNDRED YEARS' WAR. Berwick surrendered, and Edward Balliol, who, with the DISINHERITED, had fought on the English side, did homage to Edward III for the kingdom of Scotland and promised the cession of all south-east Scotland to England. However, although the young David II of Scots fled overseas, Edward III was unable to subdue Scotland.   RFW

Hall's Case (1581), an assertion of the privileges of the Commons. One Smalley, servant of Arthur Hall, M.P. for Grantham, was arrested during session (1576) and released by warrant of the mace. The Commons, finding he had himself arrested to avoid payment of a debt, consigned him to the Tower. The disgruntled Hall wrote pamphlets attacking the powers and privileges claimed by the Commons and was fined, imprisoned and expelled from the House for libel.   IHE

Ham (Old English: enclosure or farm), is a common element in English place names, possibly indicating something smaller than a TUN.   CFS

Hampden's Case, see SHIPMONEY.

Hampton Court Conference (1604) was called by James I after receiving the MILLENARY PETITION. Discussions took place between the king, the bishops and four Puritan clergy in the presence of the council. Contrary to the tendentious reports emanating from the Anglican bishops, James was inclined to meet the moderate requests of the PURITANS, but the intransigence of the bishops wrecked the conference. Therefore only a few small concessions were made and a new translation of the Bible, the AUTHORIZED VERSION, was decided upon. As a result some 300 Puritan clergy (the number is disputed) were ejected and the political significance of Puritanism was enhanced.   IHE

Hanaper, a wicker, leather or wooden box to keep documents in, the modern hamper. The container gave its name to the clerk of the H., who collected fees for documents passing the GREAT SEAL. Until 1324 he was answerable to the WARDROBE: thereafter he made his account with the EXCHEQUER. Like many offices, the clerkship came to be discharged by deputy. At its abolition in 1852 the last clerk, in office for 60 years, was given compensation. The h. was generally large enough for several documents; single documents were kept in smaller containers known as skippets.   PMB

Hanover. After the HANOVERIAN SUCCESSION (1714) the kings of England continued to rule their north German Electorate, thereby complicating the foreign policy and to some extent domestic administration of both countries. Although ruled as an independent state, George I and George II's preference for H. and frequent visits there handicapped their British ministers (e.g. during the South Sea Bubble crisis of 1720 and the Jacobite rebellion of 1745). The stock complaint of the opposition was that excessive attention was paid to Hanoverian interests. In fact, H. suffered greatly because of the English connexion during the SEVEN YEARS' and the NAPOLEONIC WARS, but fully shared in the literary and intellectual life of 18th-century England (foundation of Göttingen university 1736). In 1837 the connexion was severed: as long as there were any male GUELPHS, a woman was debarred from the throne of H., which passed to Victoria's uncle, the duke of Cumberland.   IHE

Hanoverian Succession to the kingdoms of England and Ireland was fixed upon the GUELPH dynasty of HANOVER by the Act of SETTLEMENT (1701) and accepted in Scotland by the Act of UNION (1707). To maintain the Protestant succession the claims of Charles I's descendants were set aside in favour of those of James I's daughter Elizabeth. Her grandson maintained contact with the English Whigs, who shared a common interest

in maintaining the SPANISH SUCCESSION WAR against France as well as supporting the H.S. The Tory peace of UTRECHT increased Hanoverian reliance on the Whigs, and although there were pro-Hanover Tories the party was divided, the leader Bolingbroke making a last-minute attempt to secure the succession for the Old Pretender. The Whig leaders, by prompt action, ensured George I's rights and the irreconcilables became JACOBITES.
                                                            IHE

Hansard, the *Official Report* of parliamentary debates. The name derives from T.C.H. who, from 1807, printed a series of unofficial reports established by W. Cobbett in 1804. From 1812 to 1890 these reports were published by the H. family (from 1855 with government subsidies) and then by various contractors; they appeared monthly and did not contain a full or accurate record. In 1909 the Commons appointed official reporters (the Lords in 1917); 'H.' contained thereafter 'substantially verbatim' reports, answers to oral and written questions, and division lists. It is issued in daily parts, weekly cumulations and revised volumes. In recognition of longstanding customary use the word 'H.' was placed on the title-page (Nov. 1943).   MLH

Hanse, at first an organization of German merchants trading in northern Europe. As middlemen they became an integral part of the medieval trading system acquiring a monopoly of the Baltic trade and dominating the North Sea routes. By the mid-14th century the H. had become a loose league of nearly 100 towns headed by Lübeck, but after 1380 its power began to decline as a result of Scandinavian, English and Dutch rivalry. Established in Hull, Lynn, Boston, Ipswich, Great Yarmouth and especially the London STEELYARD from the mid-12th century, the trading privileges of the H. merchants or Easterlings were increasingly resented by Parliament, and in 1463 Edward IV cancelled them, but granted even more favourable terms in 1474 as a reward for helping him recover the throne. Rivalry with the MERCHANTS ADVENTURERS caused abrogation of their privileges from 1552–3 and substantially in 1555–7. They returned to the Steelyard in 1560 with restricted privileges and were reduced to equality with other foreign traders in 1579. The formation of the EASTLAND COMPANY (1579) lessened dependence on the H. for naval stores, and they were expelled in 1598 in retaliation for the banishment of the Merchants Adventurers from Germany (1597). The concessions granted (1611) by Hamburg to the latter led to the return of the H. to London on similar terms. The last diet of the H. met in 1669.

IHE

Harfleur, on the mouth of the Seine, was the first objective of Henry V in his invasion of France in 1415. Because of the strong defences of the town and a serious outbreak of dysentery in the army, the siege lasted longer than Henry had expected (19 Aug.–22 Sept.). Many of the inhabitants were expelled, and English immigration was encouraged in order to turn H. into another CALAIS. Despite their defeat at AGINCOURT the French made strenuous efforts to regain H. in 1416–7, but their blockade by land and sea was raised after the earl of Huntingdon's naval victory over the Genoese allies of the French in July 1417. Lost in 1435, retaken in 1440, H. finally fell to the French in 1449.

RFW

Harroway, an ancient trackway following the high ground from Salisbury Plain to the English Channel via the North Downs. The medieval Pilgrim's Way to Canterbury followed part of its eastern section.   CFS

Harrying of the North. In the autumn of 1069 King Swein of Denmark invaded England, joined forces in Yorkshire with the English led by Edgar the Atheling and Earl Waltheof, and temporarily broke the Norman hold on the north. William I systematically devastated the country west and north of York, primarily to isolate his enemies concentrated in the city. When the Danes retired and made peace, William continued his 'harrying' through the winter, as far north as the river Tees. In the spring of 1070 north-west MERCIA was similarly devastated to crush lingering native resistance. William's main object in laying waste the northern shires was to eliminate the possibility of further revolts by a general destruction of life, stock, crops and dwellings. On the evidence of DOMESDAY BOOK large areas of Yorkshire and other northern counties were still lying waste in 1086.

RFW

Haryana. A State of India created 1 Nov. 1966 from Hindi-speaking parts of the PUNJAB with its capital at CHANDIGARH.   IHE

Hastenbeck, battle of (26 July 1757), near Hamelin on the river Weser. Both the Anglo-Hanoverian army (36,000 men) under William Augustus duke of Cumberland and the French (74,000 men) under the Duc d'Estrées believed themselves beaten, but Cumberland's precipitate retreat left the French on the battlefield, and the capitulation of ZEVEN confirmed their victory. Four successive defeats within four months (Kolin, H., Grossjägerndorf, Moys) at the hands of the Austrians, French and Russians marked the nadir of the Anglo-Prussian fortunes during the SEVEN YEARS' WAR.   SHS

Hastings, battle of (14 Oct. 1066). After the landing of William, duke of Normandy, in England on 28 Sept., King Harold led into Sussex an army of some 7,000 men, of which the HOUSECARLES of the king and his brothers formed the core. Many of the remainder were poorly armed peasants, and the speed of Harold's advance had not permitted him to make good the losses of STAMFORDBRIDGE. William's army, widely recruited on the continent but predominantly Norman, was inferior in numbers but superior in quality and discipline. The site of the encounter, that of the present town of Battle, some 8 miles from H., has at times been called SENLAC, but was called H. in DOMESDAY BOOK. The ANGLO-SAXON CHRONICLE describes the place as 'at the grey apple tree'. Despite William's skilful use of archers and his well-trained cavalry, Harold's men, all fighting on foot, maintained a resolute defence from morning until sunset, and the English position was not finally carried until Harold and his brothers Gyrth and Leofwine had been killed. Although nightfall prevented a pursuit, the victory proved decisive in effecting the NORMAN CONQUEST. Battle Abbey was founded on the site by William; its high altar where Harold fell.   RFW

Hawley-Shakell case (1378). Robert H. and John S., two squires imprisoned in the Tower after a dispute over a prisoner's ransom, escaped and took SANCTUARY in Westminster abbey. The constable of the Tower broke into the abbey during mass and H. was killed on the altar steps. The scandal seriously embarrassed John of Gaunt, who was—quite wrongly—held responsible, and who ill-advisedly attempted some defence of an act of sacrilege as notorious in its day as the murder of Thomas Becket at Canterbury.   RFW

Haxey's case (1397). In January the commons criticized the heavy expenditure of Richard II's household but were forced to apologize by the king, who obtained from the lords a resolution that incitement of the commons to reform the household amounted to treason. The commons attempted no defence of freedom of debate nor of Thomas Haxey, proctor of the abbot of Selby and author of the relevant clause in a commons' bill of complaint. H. was condemned to death as a traitor, but saved by his clerical status and later pardoned. The ease with which he had crushed parliamentary criticism encouraged Richard to proceed against the Lords APPELLANT.
RFW

Hay-Pauncefote Treaty (18 Nov. 1901), superseded the CLAYTON-BULWER TREATY (1850) by surrendering British claims to share control of any canal through Panama. John Hay, U.S. secretary of state, opened negotiations with the British ambassador, Sir Julian (Lord) Pauncefote (Dec. 1898). Substantial agreement was reached (11 Jan. 1899) but the Alaskan boundary dispute, then the senate's demand for canal fortification rights, delayed final settlement until 1901. Britain yielded to American requirements but Pauncefote secured neutralization and equality of tolls as embodied in the SUEZ CANAL convention of 1888.   IHE

Heads of the Proposals (1647) were produced by Ireton, approved by the council of the army and submitted to Charles I (July). The main provisions were franchise reform, equal electoral districts, biennial parliaments which were to control the army and navy for ten years and nominate the executive, a COUNCIL OF STATE to control foreign affairs for seven years, EPISCOPACY to be shorn of its coercive powers, toleration for all except papists, the COVENANT to be dropped and lenient treatment for DELINQUENTS. The king, intriguing with the Scots, failed to accept these favourable terms. His flight to Carisbrooke (11 Nov.) and the subsequent ENGAGEMENT ended the matter.   IHE

Health and Social Security, Department of. The 19th and 20th centuries, after centuries of piecemeal development and neglect, have produced a spate of legislation and activity in the fields of public health, sanitation, the poor law etc. A General Board of H. was appointed in 1848, to be superseded first, in 1858, by a Privy Council committee, then, in 1871, by the Local Government Board: the Board also replaced the Poor Law Board which in 1867 had superseded the commissioners appointed under the 1834 POOR LAW. The new Board covered the whole field of local government, public health and hygiene, gradually extending its powers. These, together with those of the commissioners appointed under the National Insurance Act 1911, were transferred to the Ministry of H. in 1919, much of whose work lay in controlling and co-ordinating locally provided services. The National Health Service Act 1948 greatly increased its work in the administration and co-ordination of the new regional authorities which assumed some former local government work: some duties were therefore transferred to the Ministry of HOUSING AND LOCAL GOVERNMENT, others to the Ministry of PENSIONS AND NATIONAL INSURANCE. On 1 Nov. 1968 insurance and health functions were again combined when the Ministry of H. and the Ministry of SOCIAL SECURITY were united in the D. of H. and S.S. under a SECRETARY OF STATE.   PMB ; MR

Hearth-penny, one penny paid by all free householders to the MINSTER church on the Thursday before Easter, in Old English and medieval times. CFS

Hearth Tax. Though a customary h.t. (Latin *furnagium*, Norman–French *fumage*, smoke-penny) was paid in some places before and after the Norman conquest (as well as PETER'S PENCE), a national h.t. was not imposed until 1662. At the rate of 2s. a hearth, with exemption for tradesmen and the poor, it was levied by local officers who, in 1664, were replaced by others specially appointed. Unpopular, though for the crown a welcome regular revenue, the h.t. was dropped in 1689 and replaced by the WINDOW TAX, but levied in Scotland in 1690.   PMB

Heathenism in ROMAN BRITAIN. Roman policy allowed the continuation of all local cults except DRUIDISM. The Celtic deities in some cases became associated with official Roman deities. The latter were formally venerated by the army and in tribal capitals; and formal observance included emperor-worship. In the 3rd century eastern religions gained ground among Romans, and, as earlier, individual soldiers continued to worship the deities of their homelands—African, Germanic, Eastern,

Central European, etc.; but none of this appears to have influenced native beliefs. There is no evidence of religious persecution until the spread of Christianity led to the establishment of the BRITISH CHURCH.   CFS

Heathenism, Old English. The surviving evidence for this is comparatively slight. The gods worshipped appear to have been those common to the Teutonic world, with Woden, Thunor, Tiw and, possibly, Frig the most popular. It is not known whether obscure deities peculiar to England, such as the goddesses Eostre (EASTER) and Erce, Mother Earth, were worshipped. Details of religious practice are not known, but there is no evidence of human sacrifice. Place-name evidence has given a large number of sites of worship, the great majority of which lie in the south midlands and the south-east. Eradication of heathen practices was slow and took long after the CONVERSION. But there is no evidence of a fanatical adherence to h. by the English—unlike continental Europe—and no missionary is known to have suffered martyrdom. In addition to these recognized religious practices, there existed a dark underworld of belief linked with the monstrous and the occult. Its origin is unknown, and it caused much trouble to churchmen, who associated it with the devil and his works. Many of its ideas survive in attenuated form as superstitions. CFS

Hedgeley Moor (near Wooler, Northumb.), battle of (25 April, 1464), checked the LANCASTRIAN revolt against Edward IV, led in the north by Henry Beaufort, duke of Somerset, and in Wales by Jasper Tudor, earl of Pembroke. Lord Montagu's victory over Somerset enabled him to negotiate a fifteen-years' truce with the Scots which excluded Lancastrian rebels from refuge in Scotland.   RFW

Heligoland was in 1807 taken from the Danes and used as a smuggling centre for breaking Napoleon's CONTINENTAL SYSTEM. The island was

formally ceded to Great Britain by the treaty of PARIS (1814). On 1 July 1890 H. (together with the Caprivi-Zipfel in S.W. Africa) was exchanged for the German protectorates of ZANZIBAR, UGANDA and Witu in EAST AFRICA. Nationalistic indignation at the surrender of the 'keys of Africa' for a 'trouser button' led to the foundation of the Pan-German League (1891), but H. was soon transformed into a strong submarine base and naval fortress for the protection of the Kiel canal. The fortifications were (ostensibly) dismantled under the treaty of VERSAILLES (1919), but rebuilt in 1935; they were blown up in 1947.
SHS

Heptarchy, term used by some historians for the seven Old English kingdoms of EAST ANGLIA, ESSEX, KENT, MERCIA, NORTHUMBRIA, SUSSEX and WESSEX. The expression 'the period of the h.' refers to the time when these existed at the same time with kings of their own, i.e. mid-6th to early 9th centuries. It is not a satisfactory term but has gained wide currency. CFS

Heralds, see COLLEGE OF ARMS.

Heriot (Anglo-Saxon *heregeatu*, military apparel), a death duty of early origin. Both before and after the Norman conquest VILLEINS' kin paid h.s, usually the best beast, to the lord of the manor: in time such payments almost automatically gave the heir entry to the deceased's tenement. Freemen also owed h.s, of armour and horses, to their lords or to the king, and tariffs of h.s appear in the later Anglo-Saxon laws. Here also the idea of payment giving right of entry developed, to survive the Norman conquest and mingle with the feudal RELIEF. PMB

Herrings, battle of the (12 Feb. 1429). An English provision train, carrying salt fish to the forces besieging ORLÉANS, was attacked at Rouvray by the French and Scots under the Count of Clermont and Sir John Stewart. The attack was skilfully beaten off by Sir John Fastolf and the English escort, and the convoy reached its destination safely. RFW

Hexham, battle of (15 May 1464), the final destruction of the duke of Somerset's army, after his defeat at HEDGELEY MOOR, by the Yorkist commander Lord Montagu. Somerset was captured and beheaded, and some twenty other Lancastrian nobles were eventually executed, the worst slaughter of notable prisoners so far perpetrated in the wars of the ROSES. RFW

Hidage, see CARUCAGE.

Hide, in Old English times the amount of land considered necessary to support a peasant and his household. Its acreage varied, being about 120 acres of arable land in the eastern counties, 40 acres in parts of WESSEX. It was subdivided into four virgates or eight bovates; to it were attached rights in woodland, pasture, etc. It was never used in KENT (SULUNG), and in the northern DANELAW it was replaced by the PLOUGHLAND. From the early 10th century or earlier the h. became also a unit of taxation assessment in Wessex, ESSEX, English MERCIA and the south midlands. Each SHIRE was assessed at a round number of h.s, which were divided among the constituent hundreds and, frequently in groups of five, among the vills within the HUNDRED. These 'GELD' h.s had no basis in agrarian fact. CFS

High Commission, a Tudor PREROGATIVE court. After the break with Rome, new institutions and courts had to be provided for the English church. H.C., the clerical STAR CHAMBER, began with the issue of temporary commissions, gradually becoming an established court. Its powers, over heresy, recusancy and other ecclesiastical offences, divorce etc., were comprehensively defined in 1611. By then PURITANS and common lawyers had condemned it, though it survived until 1641. As its records are lost, little is known of its detailed work: certainly most cases were initiated by individuals, not the crown, and as in Star chamber and CHANCERY, defendants were examined on oath, a procedure unknown at COMMON LAW.

PMB

High Commissioner, the representative of one self-governing member of the British Commonwealth in the country of another, having many of the functions of, and ranking equal with, an AMBASSADOR to a foreign court.

PMB

Himachal Pradesh, a centrally administered Indian territory, was on 15 Apr. 1948 constituted of 30 former PUNJAB hill states.   SHS

Hingston Down, battle of, near Callington, Cornwall (838). The West Saxons under king Egbert defeated a combined force of Britons from Cornwall and Danes. Cornwall, hitherto under an uneasy subordination to WESSEX, became part of that kingdom.

CFS

Historia Regum Britanniae, a 'chronicle' published by Geoffrey of Monmouth in 1136, purporting to give the history of the Britons from Brutus (allegedly 1000 B.C.) to Cadwaladr († 664). Derived from many sources, highly imaginative, and attractively written, it largely inspired ARTHURIAN literature in Europe and strongly influenced British antiquaries.

GW

Historical Manuscripts Commission. The 19th-century interest in manuscript sources, reflected in the founding of the PUBLIC RECORD OFFICE, led to the appointment of the first commission in 1869, empowered to list and abstract important historical documents in private hands. Periodically renewed, the commissions have produced many catalogues, that of the Cecil papers at Hatfield House among the more important. Its work continues, aided by the National Register of Archives (1945), which lists and registers smaller private collections.

PMB

Hoare-Laval plan for the settlement of the Italo-Abyssinian war was devised (7–8 Dec. 1935) by Sir Samuel Hoare (later Lord Templewood), British foreign secretary, and Pierre Laval, premier of France. Hoare's object was to evade the application of sanctions (as provided by the LEAGUE OF NATIONS) which might provoke reprisals. France would not risk war with Italy on any account; Britain was afraid to take unilateral action. The terms, which included ceding about two-thirds of Abyssinia to Italy, were accepted by Baldwin's cabinet for submittal to the League and the two parties, but a sharp public outcry in Britain against thus seeming to reward aggression led to Baldwin disowning the plan and to Hoare's resignation (18 Dec.). In the event Mussolini obtained his full reward. 'Collective security,' the *raison d'être* of the League, was abandoned.   MLH

Hold, a Scandinavian term used in the 10th and 11th centuries in NORTHUMBRIA to denote a noble superior in status to a THEGN.   CFS

Homage, the personal submission of a tenant to his lord, whereby the tenant was bound to serve his lord and the lord to warrant his tenant: thus all feudal tenants had to do h. and, after 1259, kings of England performed h. to kings of France for GASCONY and GUIENNE. The term was also applied to the body of suitors who formed the court baron in franchises and manors.

PMB

Home Office. Both Principal Secretaries of State dealt with domestic affairs until 1782, when the Southern Secretary became the SECRETARY OF STATE for Home Affairs with his own department, now the H.O. To his original duty of advising the sovereign on domestic matters and the use of the PREROGATIVE have been added those of the SIGNET OFFICE, administering the prison, police and other public services, the registration of ALIENS, care of children, etc., although some have been withdrawn, e.g. to the SCOTTISH OFFICE. Relations with ULSTER, the ISLE OF MAN and the CHANNEL ISLANDS are also conducted through the H.O.   PMB

Home Rule is the term used for the movement, lasting from 1870 to 1914, to obtain internal autonomy for Ireland under the British crown; it did not imply total repeal of the UNION as advocated earlier by O'Connell or the YOUNG IRELAND group. In 1870 the Home Government Association was formed (renamed H.R. Association in Nov. 1873). Aided by the BALLOT ACT, 59 Irish M.P.s so pledged were returned to Westminster in 1874 with the moderate Isaac Butt at their head. A policy of obstruction of government business was taken up by Charles Stewart Parnell, who quickly became dominant in this Irish Nationalist Party. In 1885 Gladstone became convinced of the necessity for h.r. and in the election of that year 86 Parnellites were returned. The Irish held the balance and the first h.r. bill was introduced (1886) which envisaged a one-chamber Irish parliament and the withdrawal of Irish M.P.s from Westminster. The bill was defeated on second reading by the dissident LIBERAL UNIONISTS. With the subsequent Conservative victory, h.r. was shelved until 1892 when the Liberals under Gladstone were again returned and the second h.r. bill (which differed from the first in that Irish members were to be retained at Westminster to vote only on Irish or imperial matters) passed the Commons but was killed by the Lords. Meanwhile the unity of the Irish Nationalist Party had been broken by Parnell's fall as a result of the O'Shea divorce case (1890)—a split which was not healed until 1900.

During the Conservative regime (1895–1905) h.r. went out of practical politics though a policy of social reform (e.g. an important LAND ACT) was pursued—'killing h.r. by kindness'. Both general elections of 1910 gave the Irish Nationalists once more a balance of power in the Commons; their leader, John Redmond, promised support for the Liberal government's Parliament bill curbing the House of Lords in return for h.r. The third h.r. bill (1912), similar to that of 1893, satisfied the Nationalist Party but was strongly opposed by two powerful rising political forces in Ireland—the Ulster UNIONISTS and the republican SINN FEIN party of the south. The situation, verging on civil war, became such that the H.R. Act, which finally received royal assent (Sept. 1914), was accompanied by a suspending act and never came into force. (See IRELAND, PARTITION OF.)   MLH

Homildon Hill, battle of (Sept. 1402), the severe defeat of a Scottish army under the earls of Douglas and Fife, which had raided Northumberland and Co. Durham and was intercepted on its homeward march by the earl of Northumberland and his son Henry Percy 'Hotspur'. The Scottish leaders were among the many notable prisoners, and Henry IV's demand for the surrender to him of Douglas was a contributory cause of the rebellion of the Percies in 1403 (SHREWSBURY).

RFW

Hong Kong island was ceded by China in Jan. 1841 (confirmed by the treaty of Nanking, 29 Aug. 1842) and received its colonial charter on 5 Apr. 1843. The peninsula of Kowloon was ceded in Oct. 1860 and further mainland tracts were added on 9 June 1898. From 25 Dec. 1941 to 30 Aug. 1945 H. was occupied by the Japanese.

SHS

Honor, a term of FEUDALISM meaning a number of knight's FEES administered as a unit from one centre, the *caput honoris*, normally a castle. The leading under-tenants on a h., the honorial barons, composed the honorial court. In early days h. described the holdings of important men, but in the 13th century could be applied to a modest under-tenancy. H.s in royal hands maintained their identity until the 16th century.   CFS

Hospitallers, the military order of the knights or brethren of the hospital of St John at Jerusalem. A hospital for Christian pilgrims to Jerusalem, dedicated to St John the Almsgiver, had been founded about 1070: after the first CRUSADE a military order devoted to giving protection and hospitality to pilgrims was established by Raymond of Le Puy. As organized by *c.* 1113 the H., like the TEMPLARS, included knights, sergeants and chaplains; the rule of St Augustine was adopted, and the dedication of the hospital was altered to St John the Baptist. The knights were distinguished by a white cross on a black ground. The whole order, divided into eight Langues (France, Auvergne, Provence, Aragon, Castile, Italy, Germany and England: its principal recruiting grounds), was ruled by a grand master, and its various provinces by grand commanders or priors. Individual houses in the English province were called either preceptories or commanderies. The head house of the order in England, the priory of Clerkenwell, London, and the earliest provincial foundations, e.g. Ossington (Notts), Mount St John (Yorks), Clanfield (Oxon), date from the 1140s. The commanderies, small manor houses, gave hospitality to pilgrims, travellers and the poor, but were mainly concerned with the farming of estates and recruitment for service in the Holy Land; they normally only housed the commander, one or two other members and secular servants. In 1338 there were 116 H. in England; 34 knights, 48 sergeants and 34 chaplains. After the suppression of the Templars, the H. received perhaps half of the order's English properties, and eventually possessed some 65 houses in England. The prior of the English province was summoned to Parliament until the dissolution of the order in England in 1540, when all its possessions passed to the crown. Only one knight remained to represent the English Langue in the great defence of Malta, 1565.   RFW

Housecarle, a specialized fighting man, introduced into England by king Cnut soon after 1016. H.s remained as a standing force until 1051. The h.s formed a disciplined and loyal brotherhood round the person of the king, probably some 3,000 strong. Their primary duty was military, but they were used for any task involving danger and responsibility. The status of a h. was that of a THEGN. The force

was financed by the levy of a GELD, and certain individuals received lands. After 1051 the majority received estates, on which they settled, but were available for garrison duties and war. The greatest of the king's subjects also had their forces of h.s. They disappeared as a class after the NORMAN CONQUEST, but the name long survived as a surname.   CFS

Household, Royal, see CURIA REGIS.

Housing and Local Government, Ministry of. The first government agency for local government affairs was the Board of L.G. established in 1871, most of whose powers were transferred to the Ministry of HEALTH in 1919. In 1943 a Ministry of Town and Country Planning was set up, to be vested in 1951 with most of the former Board's duties and the increasingly close relations between central and local government, being known first as the Ministry of L.G. and Planning, then of H. and L.G. Its work covers the whole field of local and central government relations except for education, the appointment of district auditors, administration of the Town and Country Planning Acts, government housing policy etc. In Oct. 1969 the Minister of H. and L.G. became a subordinate of the Secretary of State for LOCAL GOVERNMENT AND REGIONAL PLANNING.   PMB; MR

Hudson's Bay Company was created by royal charter in 1670 given to Prince Rupert and 17 other promoters for all the lands draining into Hudson Bay (which Henry Hudson had explored in 1610). British sovereignty was recognized by France in 1713. After 1763 a rival, the North-West Company, was formed to exploit the territories not covered by the charter. After years of cut-throat competition, the two companies amalgamated in 1821 and jointly exploited the NORTH-WEST TERRITORIES. In 1869 the H.B.C. surrendered its territorial rights for £300,000 to the government of CANADA.   SHS

Hue and Cry, a primitive police system of early and natural development: neighbours were bound to join the hue, crying aloud, and pursue a suspected criminal resisting arrest, or view a wounded person, carrying arms specified in the Assize of ARMS, the statute of WINCHESTER etc. Their obligation extended as far as the bounds of their manor etc., and they were punished both for non-attendance and for calling out the h. and c. without reason. In theory the accused ought to have been delivered to the SHERIFF for trial, but much summary justice took place. Though the h. and c. has disappeared, the public's obligation remains to assist the modern POLICE FORCE in arresting suspects.   PMB

Huguenots, the name (of uncertain origin) applied to the French Calvinists. At the outset of the French wars of religion (1562) Elizabeth I helped them with men and money, hoping to recover Calais. English and H. co-operated in Channel privateering, and help was sent to La Rochelle, their stronghold. After the massacre of St Bartholomew (1572) many sought refuge in England, and fresh immigrants came after the revocation of the edict of Nantes (1685). They settled chiefly in London, Norwich, Canterbury, Bristol and Southampton. Some went to Ireland, and emigration to the American colonies was encouraged. They contributed much to the development of the silk, linen and glass industries as well as the manufacture of satin, velvet and brocade. Their influence was also notable in banking, education, music and horticulture.
                                                                                                        IHE

Humble Petition and Advice (25 May 1657), an amendment of the INSTRUMENT OF GOVERNMENT put forward by Parliament, anxious for security and more constitutional rule than that typified by the MAJOR-GENERALS. Cromwell rejected the offer of kingship, but agreed to nominate his successor and a second chamber (consisting of not more than 70 and not less than 40 life peers). The composition of the COUNCIL OF STATE was altered and its powers diminished. Revenue was fixed, and Parliament's consent was needed for extra revenue. Religious toleration was to continue, and the Protector was not to exclude duly elected members from Parliament (a method widely used by Cromwell to prevent opposition).   IHE

Hundred, the subdivision of the SHIRE, except in Danish areas, where the equivalent unit was the WAPENTAKE. H.s are first definitely mentioned in the 10th century, but those in Wessex are probably older. Their numbers varied considerably, i.e. in the 11th century Staffordshire had 5, Berkshire 22. Their boundaries were far less stable than those of the shires, and new ones were created during the middle ages. In theory the h. consisted of 100 geld HIDES. The h. court (MOOT) met under the king's REEVE every four weeks, and was concerned with private pleas, criminal and lesser ecclesiastical matters and the apportioning of taxation. In most of England apart from East Anglia (LEET), Kent (LATHE) and Sussex (RAPE) there was no known unit of local government between h. and vill, but in the Danish shires of Derby, Leicester, Lincoln and Nottingham the wapentakes were divided into small units known, confusingly, as hundreds. H.s continued as units of local government until the late 19th century.   CFS

Hundred Rolls, a heterogeneous group of 13th-century records, the most important being the returns and abstracts of an INQUEST commissioned in Oct. 1274 by Edward I. The inquest, like chapters of the EYRE, covered various topics, notably abuses by local officials, usurped liberties and coin-clipping. Commissioners, often local men, put the questions to jurors of each HUNDRED, receiving also private complaints. The returns, colloquially called RAGMAN ROLLS, provided material both for the QUO WARRANTO proceedings 1278 and for early Edwardian legislation against corruption and liberties; incidentally they give a detailed picture of 13th-century local government. A similar inquiry was made in France at a slightly earlier date.   PMB

Hundred Years' War, the series of wars, punctuated by periods of peace or truce, fought between England and France from 1337 to 1453, arising from long-standing disputes about the English king's tenure of the duchy of AQUITAINE. By the treaty of PARIS, 1259, the kings of England held the duchy as vassals of the kings of France, but neither a series of short wars nor repeated attempts at a negotiated settlement (e.g. MONTREUIL, PERIGUEUX, AGEN) had defined or stabilized the territorial limits of the duchy or the respective rights of the kings therein. The French kings had on a number of occasions, e.g. after the affair of ST SARDOS, declared the duchy confiscated, but they had never proceeded to its complete military conquest. The English kings for their part had not gone so far as to sever their vassalage. The H.Y.W. might not have broken out when it did but for the alliance of France and Scotland. Edward III's attempt to subdue Scotland—notably through the agency of the DISINHERITED—had failed partly because of French assistance to his opponents; and in 1336 a French invasion appeared imminent. This situation would not have arisen if persistent papal attempts had succeeded in diverting the military energies of both kingdoms to a new crusade. There can be little doubt that a war with France, in France, was more to the taste of Edward III and the English nobility, and offered greater prospects of material profit and military glory, than war with either the Scots or the infidel. Moreover, Edward also had a pretext for war in his claim to the French throne. After the death of Charles IV of France in 1328, the claims of Philip of Valois, his cousin and nearest male heir, had been preferred to those of Edward, son of Charles' sister, Isabel. Edward, a boy of fifteen whose kingdom was ruled by his mother and Roger Mortimer (DEPOSITION of Edward II), had been unable to press his claim at the time and in 1329 had done homage for Aquitaine to Philip VI. By 1336 Edward was preparing for war. In 1337 renewed disputes in Aquitaine led to yet another French confiscation of the duchy, answered this time by the king of England laying claim to the throne of France and attempting to make good his claim by force. The claim in itself was strong—exclusion of females and their descendants being supported only by recent precedents— and there is evidence that Edward III took it seriously. But, failing the crown, Edward's principal objective was to obtain Aquitaine in full sovereignty.

Aided by family connexions and the application of economic pressure, Edward III concluded a series of alliances with the princes of the Low Countries, and in 1337 gained the support of the emperor Lewis IV. The allies, however, proved more impressive in appearance than in performance. Edward's first expensive but fruitless campaign near Cambrai in 1339 was offset by the acquisition of a further ally, Jacob van Artevelde and the burghers of the Flemish cloth cities. In 1340 Edward formally assumed the title of king of France and renewed his efforts on the kingdom's northern borders. The naval victory of SLUYS was followed, however, by the complete failure of the campaign against Tournai, and the truce of Espléchin temporarily halted hostilities. Edward's allies fell away and his debts mounted, but the disputed succession to the duchy of Brittany enabled him to open a new front, and by 1343 he had occupied most of the duchy on behalf of John de Montfort. French attacks on GASCONY had been checked, but the situation on its borders was critical in 1346 when Edward launched his next main campaign. His landing in Normandy, possibly by design, possibly because the weather ruled out the longer passage to Gascony, took the French by surprise, and his destructive progress from St Vaast-la-Hogue eastwards through Caen met little opposition. From Normandy Edward struck northwards to effect a junction with the Flemings, who still maintained the English alliance despite the murder of van Artevelde in 1345. Their military effort petered out before Edward appeared, but the king won the astonishing victory of CRÉCY and besieged CALAIS, which fell in the following year. Elsewhere, too, things went well for the English in 1346: in Brittany, in Gascony and on the Scottish border (NEVILLE'S CROSS). The following decade, however, did not fulfil its promise. The loss of the Flemish alliance was partly compensated by the adhesion to Edward of Charles the Bad, king of Navarre; the naval victory off WINCHELSEA maintained English command of the Channel; but no major effort was made in France in these years of financial crisis and the heavy onslaught of the BLACK DEATH. By 1355 Gascony was again hard pressed. The Black Prince's great raid across southern France from Bordeaux almost to the Mediterranean in 1355 inflicted vast material damage and re-established the security and loyalty of Gascony, and in 1356 the prince launched a second *chevauchée*, which ended in his crushing victory at POITIERS and the capture of Philip VI's successor, King John. Added to the loss of their king, the French faced grave internal problems—the ravages of the FREE COMPANIES, the rising of the Jacquerie and the seizure of control by the estates-general. Edward III seemed in reach of the greater prize of the crown of France, but the failure of his winter campaign in 1359–60 disposed him to accept the lesser, a sovereign and greatly enlarged duchy of Aquitaine, by the treaty of BRÉTIGNY.

In the nine years of peace, the succession war in Brittany was brought to a moderately successful conclusion (AURAY, 1364), but intervention in Iberian affairs, initially successful (NÁJERA, 1367), eventually produced the Franco-Castilian alliance which outweighed the English combination with Portugal (CASTILE, Way of PORTUGAL). Internal troubles in a heavily-taxed Gascony and French interference contrary to the terms of Brétigny led to a fresh 'confiscation' of the duchy and the renewal of the war in 1369. The last years of the Black

Prince (†1376) and Edward III (†1377) saw a succession of English disasters: the naval defeat of LA ROCHELLE (1372), the speedy loss of most of Aquitaine, the utter failure of English raids and the conspicuous success of the Franco-Castilian fleet in the Channel and against the southern coast of England. The reign of Richard II brought no better fortune: an occasional success, such as the action off MARGATE, did not halt the steady decline of English power in France, and it was a virtually beaten England which at last secured a truce in 1388. A long extension of the truce followed Richard II's marriage to Isabel, daughter of Charles VI of France, in 1396, but peace negotiations broke down over the English determination not to give up CALAIS. The DEPOSITION of Richard II in 1399 renewed French hostility but, despite French aid to the Welsh in the GLYN DŴR REBELLION and sporadic clashes in the Channel and on the borders of Gascony, the general Anglo-French war was not resumed.

The situation was radically changed by the incapacity of Charles VI of France and the emergence of the BURGUNDIAN and ARMAGNAC factions. Wooed by both groups, England sent military help to each in turn, to the Burgundians in 1411 and to the Armagnacs in 1412. Neither alliance brought firm territorial concessions, but the military success of the expeditions revealed that the English now had their best opportunity since the 1350s. This opportunity was seized by Henry V, who succeeded to the throne in 1413. Henry renewed the claim to the French throne 'inherited' by the house of Lancaster, negotiated with both French factions, seeking greater territorial concessions than those made at Brétigny as an acceptable alternative to the crown, and meanwhile made his military preparations. These were complete when, in July 1415, the French finally rejected his terms. Henry landed in France in August, besieged and took HARFLEUR, and won the great victory of AGINCOURT. The intervention of the emperor Sigismund in 1416 secured only a short truce. Unable as yet to win over the Burgundians, Henry embarked on a major effort in 1417, beginning the systematic conquest of NORMANDY, ROUEN itself falling early in 1419. The murder of Duke John of Burgundy by the Armagnacs drove his successor into a firm English alliance, soon followed by a truce with Charles VI, and, in 1420, by the treaty of TROYES. Despite the setback of BAUGÉ, the Anglo-Burgundians slowly but steadily reduced northern France until the premature death of Henry V (31 Aug. 1422) struck a severe blow for their adversaries. Henry's brother John, duke of Bedford, regent of France during the minority of the infant Henry VI, faced the accumulating difficulties of a chronic shortage of money and men, the disturbing conduct of his brother Humphrey, duke of Gloucester and regent of England, and the growing coolness of the Burgundians. Nevertheless, the tide of English military success still flowed strongly: the victories of CRAVANT (1423) and VERNEUIL (1424) enabled Bedford to secure his hold on the north and to proceed to the conquest of Maine and Anjou. By 1428 the English seemed to be firmly established on the Loire and had begun the siege of ORLÉANS. The tide turned when the dramatic appearance of Joan of Arc in 1429 was followed in swift succession by the relief of Orléans, a series of French victories, notably PATAY, and the coronation of the dauphin as Charles VII, at Reims. The coronation of Henry VI as king of France at Paris in 1430 was not an effective answer, while the capture of Joan of Arc and her trial and death at Rouen in 1431 did not halt the French recovery. Worst of all for the English, in 1435 the congress of ARRAS failed to produce a comprehensive peace settlement but ended in the reconciliation of the Burgundians with Charles VII. Bedford died in the same year and no successor of comparable ability appeared. Nevertheless, it took another fifteen years to expel the English from northern France. Calais was success-

fully held in 1436, and Normandy at least was retained, though with increasing difficulty. By the 1440s English resources were barely equal to holding even the remnants of their conquests, and domestic dissensions had their counterpart in the rivalries of their commanders in France, especially the dukes of York and Somerset. All hope of winning France for Henry VI had gone by 1444, when William de la Pole, earl of Suffolk, negotiated a truce and the marriage of Henry to Margaret of Anjou. Henry promised to give up MAINE in 1445, and the truce was extended to 1450—an interval profitably employed by the French in military reorganization. Provocative action by English troops brought a resumption of the war before the truce had expired, and an irresistible French invasion of Normandy. Rouen fell in 1449, and after the final defeat of FORMIGNY in 1450 the whole duchy, with the exception of the CHANNEL ISLANDS, was once again lost, this time for good. In 1451 the French overran Gascony, and although it was partly recovered in 1452, the defeat of CASTILLON in 1453 brought the last English effort in France to an end, and of all their French possessions only Calais remained. Although the empty title of king of France was retained by all English and British sovereigns down to George III (1801; the French coat of arms was displayed in the device of *The Times* newspaper even until 1932), the struggle to make it a reality had really ended in 1453, and the brief French campaigns of Edward IV (PICQUIGNY) and the Tudors were mere postscripts.   RFW

Hunne's Case (1514–15). Richard H., merchant, was imprisoned by the bishop of London on a charge of heresy and was found hanged. The church held it was suicide. The coroner's jury returned a verdict of murder against the bishop's chancellor and gaolers. Public opinion declared that H. was arrested for non-payment of a MORTUARY and for threatening an action of PRAEMUNIRE. The affair revealed the intense anti-clerical feeling of the City. There seems no doubt that H. was murdered. IHE

Husting, a Norse word (*hūs-thing*), adopted for many open-air meetings, notably those connected with parliamentary elections. Earlier h.s often had some legal business, preserved and extended in the City of London court of h. Founded before the NORMAN CONQUEST, exercising many COUNTY COURT powers, its business grew as City independence developed. Presided over by the mayor and sheriffs, it was a court of record, enrolling wills and deeds; though most of its powers have passed to later City courts, the h. still survives. Courts on the London model were established elsewhere, e.g. at Boston and Winchester. PMB

Hyderabad, a Hindu province of the Mogul empire (1687), from 1713 to 1956 under a Moslem dynasty, whose first ruler or nizam-ul-mulk made himself independent in 1724. After his death (1748) his successors played off the French against the English, sometimes in alliance sometimes at war with the sultans of MYSORE and the MARATHAS. By the treaty of 1766 with the EAST INDIA COMPANY (frequently broken by both parties) the nizam ceded the Northern Sarkars in return for an annual tribute. Eventually Lord Wellesley brought the nizam over to the English, to whom the treaty of 12 Oct. 1800 assigned the exclusive control of his foreign relations. In 1853 Berar was assigned to the Company. During the mutiny, H. gave valuable support to the British, and its position as the premier princely state was secure until Aug. 1948 when, after the nizam's refusal to join the Indian Union, H. was invaded by Indian troops and forcibly incorporated. In 1956 H. was partitioned between ANDHRA PRADESH and Mysore and ceased to exist. SHS

Iceni, a non-Belgic (BELGAE) tribe in the area of East Anglia, ruled during the earlier part of the 1st century A.D. by kings who issued coins. Their king submited to the Romans in 43, holding his kingdom thereafter as a client king. An attempt to disarm the tribe in 47-48 caused fierce resistance, which was defeated. On the death of the king in 61 Roman tax collectors seized his wealth, and during the course of this operation Queen Boudicca and her daughters were maltreated. The consequent revolt of the I. and neighbouring tribes almost overthrew the ROMAN CONQUEST, but was mercilessly suppressed. They became a CIVITAS with their capital at Venta Icenorum (Caistor by Norwich). CFS

Icknield Way, an ancient trackway following the line of high ground from the Wash to Salisbury Plain, crossing the Thames near Goring. It was used intensively from the BRONZE AGE; parts in East Anglia later became a ROMAN ROAD; in the period of the TEUTONIC CONQUEST it was one of the routes by which north WESSEX was settled; and it underlies sections of modern road. The meaning of the name is not known. See KING'S PEACE. CFS

Ilbert Bill (1883), named after Sir Courtenay Ilbert, legal member of the council of the governor-general of India, had the object of abolishing 'every judicial disqualification based merely upon race distinctions'. In particular, Europeans would no longer have had the guarantee of a British judge in case of trial. The European community protested vigorously in a Defence Association, and the bill was consequently modified. Strong racial feeling was aroused, and this formed the background for the organization of the Indian National Conference, 1883, the precursor of the INDIAN NATIONAL CONGRESS.

MLH

Impeachment, criminal trial in Parliament at the Commons' instigation. Several factors produced this procedure: the earl of Lancaster was condemned in Parliament in 1322 on the king's charge alone, and in 1330 Mortimer was condemned on the notoriety of his activities. Both convictions were later reversed because of increasing insistence on due legal process: by 1341 the king's word and notoriety, the clamour of the people, produced trials but not immediate convictions. The GOOD PARLIAMENT 1376 tried two officers on the i. and accusation by clamour of the Commons, acting for the people, giving i. its final form. In England i. was last used in 1805, but is still available in the U.S.A.   PMB

Imperial Conferences. Conferences on matters of common concern to Britain and other empire countries began when leaders were assembled for the jubilee of 1887. Colonial conferences of heads of self-governing colonies were held in 1897, 1902 and 1907, in which year they were put on a regular basis and renamed I.C. They met in 1911, 1917–8 (as an I. War C.), 1921, 1923, 1926, 1930 and 1937 and did much to ensure the smooth transition of self-governing colonies into independent dominions. Matters dealt with at these I.C. included IMPERIAL PREFERENCE, defence, nationality, communications and foreign policy; discussions on dominion status in 1926 and 1930 resulted in the statute of WESTMINSTER. Since 1944 the I.C.s have been succeeded by Commonwealth Prime Ministers' meetings. At the same time consultation has developed on many levels; finance and foreign ministers meet regularly, while conferences or standing councils have been established on many technical subjects (e.g. shipping, air transport, standards, agriculture and forestry, education and broadcasting).   MLH

Imperial Defence, Committee of, was evolved (1902–4) from a committee of the cabinet. Named C.I.D. (1903) and given a secretariat (1904), its chairman was the prime minister; there was no fixed membership. Until 1914 the C.I.D. was concerned mainly with problems of co-ordination between admiralty and war office; as a purely advisory body it did not become a centre of strategic planning. In WORLD WAR I the C.I.D. was virtually superseded in turn by the war council (1914–5), the Dardanelles committee (1915), the war committee (1915–6) and the war cabinet (1916–9). Re-established in 1919 as a body advisory to the cabinet, the most important of its many sub-committees became that of the chiefs of staff (1924). The appointment (1936–40) of a minister for the co-ordination of defence (as deputy chairman of the C.I.D.) was ineffective since he carried no executive powers. In WORLD WAR II the C.I.D. was again superseded. Under the war cabinet the most important policy-making bodies were the chiefs of staff committee and the defence committee (operations) of the cabinet, both of which were chaired by the prime minister as minister of defence. In 1946 the C.I.D. was not revived: the defence organization was reformed to include a defence committee of the cabinet and a separate minister of DEFENCE to whom the chiefs of staff committee became responsible.   MLH

Imperial Preference (officially known as Commonwealth P. since 1958) is the system of tariff concessions granted to each other by members of the COMMONWEALTH, Burma and the Irish and South African Republics. First steps towards I.P. were taken by Canada (1897), New Zealand and South Africa (1903) and Australia (1907), but Joseph Chamberlain's Tariff Reform Movement failed to wean Britain from FREE TRADE. The principle was accepted at the IMPERIAL CONFERENCE of 1917 and embodied to a limited extent in a slight move towards protection (1919–21). But there was little scope for concessions while Britain did not tax foodstuffs and raw materials. The situation was changed by the sharply protective reaction of the National government to the world slump and economic crisis of 1931. With the tariff authorized by the Import Duties Act 1932 Britain could bargain at the Ottawa economic conference (July–Aug. 1932). The series of bilateral agreements there negotiated were considerably limited by a mutual determination to protect home producers, but I.P. emerged in its most developed form. Britain agreed to keep the exemptions written into the 1932 Act and to raise tariffs on foreign foodstuffs and raw materials. The effect of I.P. on empire trade in the 1930s is difficult to assess; there was a swing in trade towards Britain and an increase in intra-empire trade at the expense of that with other areas, but in both cases other factors were also involved. Some modification in I.P. was effected by bilateral agreements with foreign governments (in particular the Anglo-U.S. agreement, 1938). After world war II I.P. agreements were extended but their effect was reduced by multilateral agreements under GATT, erosion of margins by rising prices and changes both in the commodity pattern and its direction.

MLH

Impositions, see BATE'S CASE, ELEVEN YEARS' TYRANNY.

Impressment, an ancient and arbitrary method of forcing men into military service. It took its name from the imprest money (French *prêter*) which was advanced on enlistment. It was still used for the army under 18th-century statutes applying to paupers, criminals, vagabonds, etc., but ceased after 1815. The merchant seaman was always the hardest hit by the press-gang, as the Royal Navy relied on this method until the 1830s when improvements in pay and conditions of service led to suitable volunteer enlistment.

IHE

Imprest, see PREST.

Impropriations. At the DISSOLUTION OF THE MONASTERIES their appropriated TITHES and PATRONAGE rights passed to the crown and were largely granted to lay rectors or impropriators. Tithe thus too often became a rent tribute to absentee laymen. As the impropriators, like their monastic predecessors, paid only a small fraction of the tithe to incumbents, the church found it increasingly difficult to provide adequate stipends for the clergy before QUEEN ANNE'S BOUNTY. Attempts to remedy the situation in the 16th and 17th centuries, notably by Laud, were frustrated by the gentry and partly explain the support of the National COVENANT by the Scottish nobility. A self-constituted corporation known as the Feoffees for I. from *c.* 1620 purchased i. and largely used the proceeds for the upkeep of Puritan ministers and LECTURERS until its suppression in 1633.

IHE

Inclosures, as intakes of moorland and waste were an ancient practice, but i. of common pastures and open fields aroused frequent complaints after 1500, especially in the midlands and north, where open-field farming was still prevalent. The main motive of inclosers was to secure more efficient and specialized use of land at times when population and prices were rising. I. were more often effected by agreement, but trouble arose when landlords disregarded commoners' rights. The i. of the sheepmasters undoubtedly caused grievances in the reign of Henry VIII, and agrarian unrest contributed towards the PILGRIMAGE OF GRACE (1536) and more especially to KETT'S REBELLION (1549). Government concern with the problem is shown by the various inquiries, statutes and proclamations, particularly with regard to the conversion of arable to pasture and the possibility of depopulation. I. continued in the 17th century, gathering momentum after 1700, and the process of inclosing by private bills promoted by landowners, begun in the 17th century, became the normal procedure in the 18th. The reign of George III covers the peak period of i. of common arable, pasture and waste; it is generally recognized that they contributed to the improved technical efficiency of farming during the AGRICULTURAL REVOLUTION. The work was completed under the General Inclosure Acts of 1801, 1836 and 1845. The social effects of i. have been exaggerated, but they did increase the amount of land in the hands of the wealthy, tend to drive out the small man and deprive the labourer of his customary and valuable rights of access to the land, especially over the waste; and the promoters of i. had most of the advantages on their side.

IHE

Income Tax was first levied in 1799 by Pitt as an extraordinary means of paying for the French Revolutionary war, the rate being 2s. in the £. Abolished in 1802, it was reimposed on resumption of war (1803) by Addington at 1s. and remained until 1816. In 1842 Peel introduced an i.t. of 7d. for a 3-year period and continued it in association with tariff reductions. Gladstone was prepared (1853) to abolish i.t. by 1860 but the CRIMEAN WAR (during which the rate rose to 1s. 4d.) upset his calculations and after 1860 it was renewed in association with his FREE TRADE policy. During the mid-Victorian period the i.t. was always regarded as temporary and the rate was continuously low. Hope of its abolition, raised by both Gladstone and Disraeli in the 1874 election (when the rate was 4d.) was not realized, and in the 1890s it became the major source of revenue although the rate remained low until 1914. In the first world war the rate rose to 6s. and in the second to 10s.

Classification of income by schedule was started in 1803, i.e. exemption and a graduated tax on low incomes and other allowances were present in Pitt's scheme. During the 19th century allowances practically disappeared but were revived with other innovations in the Liberal budgets prior to 1914: earned income relief in 1907, 'super-tax' on high incomes in 1909, child and other family allowances from 1909. The deduction of income at source by the 'Pay As You Earn' scheme was established in 1944. Consolidated I.T. Acts were passed in 1918 and 1952.   MLH

Indemnity and Oblivion, Act of (1660), was passed by the CONVEN-TION PARLIAMENT to implement the amnesty promised in the Declaration of BREDA. It pardoned all those concerned in the CIVIL WAR except some 50 named individuals. Of these, 13 regicides, together with Vane, were executed. Charles and his advisers withstood the demands of the more revengeful Cavaliers, and the Commons, which contained a strong Presbyterian element, naturally resisted the more vindictive policy of the Lords.   IHE

Indenture or chirograph, a type of document designed to prevent forgery. The text was copied twice or more on to a single skin of parchment, each text divided from the other by a word, e.g. *indentura*, *cyrograffum*, or a phrase, e.g. from the Vulgate. The texts were then separated by a cut, generally zigzag, through the dividing words; authenticity was tested by rejoining the parts. In Anglo-Saxon times i.s were commonly used for wills, and after the Norman conquest increasingly for public and private contracts, title deeds etc. Though the test of authenticity has lapsed, the form remains, e.g. in LEASES and articles of apprenticeship.

PMB

Independent Labour Party was formed (Jan. 1893) at a Bradford conference of labour and socialist organizations chaired by Keir Hardie with the object of co-ordinating the efforts of local labour unions in gaining parliamentary representation independent of liberal support. Under I.L.P. persuasion the Labour Representation Committee was formed (1900), an I.L.P. man, Ramsay MacDonald, being secretary. This committee became the LABOUR PARTY (1906) and the I.L.P. played a dominant part in its affairs until the first world war. Subsequently, however, I.L.P. influence in the Labour Party declined: the pacifism of some of its members was unpopular, while the decision of the Labour Party to adopt a more Socialist programme and to start local organizations (1918) stole much I.L.P. thunder. During the 1920s the I.L.P., advocating a more radical socialism, adopted an increasingly unhappy stance in the left of the Labour Party. Finally in the 1931 election Labour endorsement of I.L.P. candidates was withdrawn and the following year the I.L.P. disaffiliated itself from the Labour Party. In the Commons there were 46 I.L.P. members in 1923, 37 in 1929, 5 in 1931, 4 (all representing Glasgow constituencies) in 1935 and 3 in 1945. After the death of the leader of the I.L.P., James Maxton, in 1946 its remaining M.P.s joined the Labour Party (1947). The I.L.P. continues but has not won a parliamentary seat since 1959.   MLH

Independents. The BROWNISTS and BARROWISTS of Elizabeth I's reign were the first I., but the CIVIL WAR inevitably led to a multiplication of separatist sects which were collectively known as I. CONGREGATIONALISTS and BAPTISTS formed the two main groups. Each congregation was autonomous, and they rejected PRESBYTERIANISM and EPISCOPACY alike. They attracted eccentrics as well as those desiring liberty of thought and belief, and included ANABAPTISTS, Antinomians, Seekers, Divorcers, FIFTH MONARCHY MEN, Arians and other NONCONFORMISTS. They were particularly strong in the Parliamentary army. Toleration was essential to them, and Cromwell, although he restricted their political activities and proselytizing, ensured this until the RESTORATION.   IHE

India. In the 16th–17th centuries when I. came into permanent contact with the Europeans, the subcontinent was outwardly united under the Great Moguls of Delhi, the descendants of Babur, a Mogul chief, who in 1526 had made himself master of northern I. It reached its greatest extension under Aurangzeb (1658–1707), who incorporated most of the south. The way from the establishment of scattered trading posts by the Portuguese, Dutch, English and French to the foundation of a dominion by the British was paved by the inherent weakness of the Mogul

empire. Its very size undermined the authority of the central government and encouraged the defection of outlying provinces and the virtual independence of hundreds of petty feudal lords; the intolerance of the ruling Moslems permanently alienated the Hindus and other religionists; the invasions of Persians and Afghans and the rivalry between the French and the English in the 18th century accelerated the disintegration. The ousting of the French rivals and the gradual subjugation of the whole of I. by the EAST INDIA COMPANY from the middle of the 18th century was due to the inner dissensions among the Indian rulers, the naval superiority and brilliant generalship, administrative skill and financial power of the English.

From the governor-generalship of the marquess of Hastings (1813–23) it became the tacit and, later, open goal of the British administration to prepare I. for self-government and independence. The main stages on this road were the transfer of the administration from the Company to the British crown (1858), the revival of the imperial title (1876) with its emphasis on the unity of the country, the establishment of a national parliament (1919), the introduction of parliamentary government (1935), culminating in the India Independence Act (11 June 1947) and the proclamation of independence (15 Aug. 1947) of the two dominions of I. and PAKISTAN. On 26 Jan. 1950 I. proclaimed itself a republic within the COMMONWEALTH.

Parallel with this political development went the unification of I. in the spheres of education and law, both of which found their first champion in Lord Macaulay as member of the governor-general's council (1833–38) and led to the creation of an Indian civil and judiciary service (1861), the construction of nation-wide systems of roads (1839 ff.) and railways (1852 ff.) and the political awakening through the organizations of the INDIAN NATIONAL CONGRESS (1885) and the MOSLEM LEAGUE (1906). See

ANDHRA PRADESH; ASSAM; ANDAMAN
AND NICOBAR ISLANDS; BARODA;
BHUTAN; BIHAR; CENTRAL PROVINCES;
DADRA AND NAGAR HAVELI; GOA,
DAMAN AND DIU; HARYANA; HIMA-
CHAL PRADESH; JAMMU AND KASHMIR;
KERALA; LACCADIVE, MINICOY AND
AMINDIVI ISLANDS; MADHYA BHARAT;
MADRAS; MANIPUR; MYSORE; NAGA-
LAND; ORISSA; PONDICHERRY; PUNJAB;
RAJASTHAN; SIKKIM; TRAVANCORE;
TRIPURA; UTTAR PRADESH.   SHS; IHE

India Act. (1) 1784, introduced by
Pitt, was to correct the REGULATING
ACT of 1773 by restricting the
authority of the court of directors of
the EAST INDIA COMPANY; while
maintaining the dual control by
crown and company, the act vested
supreme power in the governmental
'board of control', whose president
represented India in parliament.

(2) 1813, curtailed the company's
monopoly in the India trade.

(3) 1833, terminated the company's
monopoly of trade with India and
China, confined the company to the
role of crown agent for administration
and patronage, admitted Indians to
the civil service and changed the title
of the governor-general of Bengal to
that of India.

(4) 1853, the last CHARTER ACT,
limited the company's patronage by
introducing appointment by competition.

(5) 1858, abolished company rule
and transferred the administration to
the crown; the president of the
board of control was made secretary
of state for India, the governor-
general became viceroy.

(6) 1919, based on the MONTAGU–
CHELMSFORD REPORT (1918).

(7) 1935, prepared by Sir Samuel
Hoare (1880–1959), reorganized the
Indian empire on a federal basis, with
responsible parliamentary government
at the centre (with a bicameral legislature, foreign affairs and defence
reserved to the viceroy) and in the
11 autonomous provinces (ASSAM,
BENGAL, BIHAR, BOMBAY, CENTRAL
PROVINCES, MADRAS, NORTH-WEST
FRONTIER PROVINCE, ORISSA, PUNJAB,

SIND, United Provinces) with safeguards for the protection of minori-
ties. BURMA was separated from
India. The act came into force on
1 Apr. 1937, but the federation was
never brought into being as the
necessary number of princes did not
agree upon the requisite instrument
of accession. The act was superseded by the Indian Independence
Act, 1947.   SHS

India Councils Act. (1) 1892,
authorized the nomination of Indians
to the legislative councils of the central
and provincial governments; (2) 1909,
part of the MORLEY-MINTO REFORMS.
                                    SHS

Indian Mutiny (1857–9), although
mainly a revolt of Indian troops
(sepoys) of the EAST INDIA CO's Bengal
army, had as its underlying cause a
conservative fear of British intentions,
particularly directed against the innovations of governor-general Dalhousie
(1848–56). Annexations (SIND, GWA-
LIOR, 1843; PUNJAB, 1849; OUDH,
1856) and use of the doctrine of 'lapse'
(Nagpur, 1853; Jhansi, 1854) bred insecurity among ruling families and
landowners, while measures such as
land reforms, encouragement of Christian missions, suppression of suttee
and infanticide, promotion of western
education and the introduction of
modern communications threatened
cherished traditions.

A greater proportion of high-caste
sepoys in Bengal than in the armies
of the other two presidencies made for
lax discipline, and grievance was
created by infringements of caste; in
particular, the use of an animal-greased
paper cartridge, which had to be torn
by mouth, precipitated the outbreak.
The Bengal army had, in 1857, about
151,000 sepoys of whom about one-
quarter took part in the m. British
strength was only 23,000, owing to
withdrawals to Persia and the CRIMEA;
about 13,000 of these were in the
Punjab area and therefore not immediately available. The m. started at
Meerut (10 May 1857) when sepoys
massacred Europeans and marched to
DELHI where they proclaimed a Mogul

emperor. By mid-June it had spread to the valley of the Ganges, Jumna and Gogra, and had been joined by the rani of Jhansi and Nana Sahib of Poona; Cawnpore surrendered on 26 June. But the m. was contained in this area and the Punjab was held firm by Sir John Lawrence. Delhi, strategic key and rallying-point of revolt, was captured after heavy fighting (20 Sept.) and the Lucknow residency was relieved (17 Nov.) by the new C.-in-C., Sir Colin Campbell (Lord Clyde), who next defeated Tantia Topi, Nana Sahib's lieutenant, near Cawnpore (6 Dec.). 1858 saw Campbell's pacification of Oudh (capture of Lucknow, 1 March) and the campaign of Sir Hugh Rose (Lord Strathnairn) in central India against Tantia Topi and the rani of Jhansi (capture of Gwalior, 20 June). Thereafter only 'mopping up' operations were necessary. The I.M. was followed by the INDIA ACT (1858). MLH

Indian National Congress was founded in 1885 by Allan Octavian Hume (1829–1912), a retired civil servant in Bengal, as an instrument of social reform. The viceroy, Lord Dufferin, however, encouraged it to become a political force as a kind of official opposition. From 1900 the Maratha, Bal Gangadhar Tilak, gave the party an anti-Moslem and anti-British tendency, so that in 1909 the majority of the Moslems seceded to the MOSLEM LEAGUE. Under the leadership of Mahatma Gandhi (1869–1948) and Pandit Nehru (b. 1889) the I.N.C. in 1947 achieved its aim of complete independence for India though it had to assent to the Moslem League's insistence on a separate state of PAKISTAN. SHS

India Office. When in 1858 the EAST INDIA COMPANY's powers were resumed by the crown there was little break with the past. The president of the board of control became secretary of state, and the council was mostly drawn from the old board. The I.O. succeeded the Company in the day-to-day administration of India through the viceroy, provincial governors and a specially recruited civil service containing, after 1917, an increasing proportion of Indians. As Indian self-government developed, the office's work diminished, and it was abolished when India and Pakistan achieved independence in 1947. Its library, a magnificent collection of books and MSS in ancient and modern Indian tongues, Persian, Chinese, Malay etc. was, however, not dispersed and is now in the custody of the FOREIGN AND COMMONWEALTH OFFICE. PMB; MR

Indirect Rule, the system introduced in NIGERIA by Sir Frederick Lugard from 1900, by which British residents acted as advisers to African rulers, councils and courts, whose customs and traditions were supported as far as compatible with British standards of humanity and justice. I.r. has gradually been superseded by parliamentary institutions. SHS

Indonesia. The scattered Portuguese settlements (from 1512) were from 1595 conquered by the Dutch and British EAST INDIA COMPANIES. In Sumatra the British held Atjeh (1601–23), Bantam (1603–19, 1628–84), Indrapura (1630–64), Batang, Benkoolen and Silebar (1685–1824); in Celebes, Macassar (1601–70). Finally, the Dutch ousted the British, but during the NAPOLEONIC WARS Sumatra, Borneo, Celebes, Bali and Java were conquered from the Batavian Republic (1810–12). Stamford Raffles was the governor of Java (1811–16) and Benkoolen (1818–23). Between 1816 and 1824 Britain handed all her Indonesian possessions over or back to the Netherlands. SHS

Indore, see MADHYA BHARAT.

Indulgence, see DECLARATION OF I.

Industrial Revolution, a term covering the many changes and influences which transformed Great Britain into an industrial state. Used by Arnold Toynbee in 1882 and by French observers as early as the 1820s, it has been frequently assailed on a variety of counts, e.g.: that it is misleading as the process had no precise beginning and no end, that it covers too long a period, that the rate of change varied from industry to industry, etc. It is customary to date the I.R. as falling somewhere between 1740 and 1850 and more often between 1760 and 1830, and if the limitations of the phrase are accepted a comparison between the Britain of 1750 and that of 1850 is its justification. The transition to the factory system, dependent on power-driven machinery, is its central feature and was most marked in the COTTON INDUSTRY earlier than in the still dominant WOOLLEN INDUSTRY. The I.R. owed much to the inventors, engineers and those who applied science to manufacture, but equally important were the great organizers. As commercial capitalists, manufacturers, managers and merchants, many of whom were NONCONFORMISTS, they concentrated the processes of industry, which became mainly centred in the Midlands, the North, Clydeside and South Wales, and used their imagination to develop new products and to exploit the opportunities of expanding markets. Good examples of this are to be found in the textile, pottery and iron industries. The development of mining, particularly of coal, road improvements effected by the TURNPIKES, the building of CANALS, the growth of coastal shipping and the later rise of the railways were as necessary to the I.R. as was the increased food production made possible by the AGRICULTURAL REVOLUTION. The I.R. enabled the rapidly rising population to be fed and clothed, but the uncontrolled growth of towns and factories created major social problems which governments were slow to appreciate. The industrial workers suffered much avoidable misery. Their conditions, especially during the post-war depression after 1815, led to demands for political REFORM, which though long delayed were essential to meet the needs of the changed society created by the I.R. IHE

Infangenetheof and Utfangenetheof, qualifications of private jurisdictions originating from before the NORMAN CONQUEST; i. was by far the more common. The essential in each was that a thief be taken with stolen goods on him: i. allowed the lord to do justice if the thief be taken within his estate, and u. wheresoever the thief be found. These powers lost their importance in the 12th century, for early Angevin kings insisted that royal officers should watch proceedings, and the privileges became valueless. PMB

Injunctions (ecclesiastical), orders requiring the observance of church law and customs, have a special significance during the period of the English REFORMATION. Royal Injunctions of 1536 made the 10 ARTICLES binding on the clergy and ordered a bible in Latin and English to be placed in every parish church. Those of 1538 were directed against popish and superstitious practices, ordered the bible in church to be in English and provided for the keeping of parish registers, those of 1547 emphasized the duties of the clergy. Elizabeth's Injunctions of 1559 caused the VESTIARIAN CONTROVERSY. Injunctions were usually preceded by visitations and articles of inquiry; they declined in importance after 1571 when Convocation began to replace them by canons. IHE

Inkerman, battle of (5 Nov. 1854), developed from a Russian sortie from Sebastopol in the CRIMEAN WAR. Although the British lines were weakly held at critical points, the attack was withstood, and after heavy fighting the Russians withdrew with the loss of about 12,000 men; British losses being about 2,500 and French losses about 1,000. MLH

Inland Revenue, Commissioners of. In 1848 the STAMP OFFICE and board of excise, divided since 1833, were re-united and a board, the C. of I.R., formally appointed in 1849. Of the many types of tax, e.g. stamp, window, death duties etc., income tax, established in 1842, came to dominate the c.' work, and by 1902 such revenue equalled that from excise, again detached in 1909. The c.' work, directed 'from Somerset House and carried out by the many local inspectors of taxes, was radically rearranged by the introduction of Pay-as-you-Earn in 1944. PMB

Inns of Court appear as centres of legal education, comparable with the colleges of Oxford and Cambridge, in the 14th century: the four great Inns, Gray's, Middle and Inner Temples and Lincoln's, were founded in the late 14th and early 15th centuries. Readers, from whom serjeants were chosen, taught the students; barristers stood next in rank, then the students; the whole was governed by the benchers. With modifications this system still persists. The Inns of Chancery, e.g. Furnival's, were subordinate to the great Inns, originally providing accommodation for CHANCERY clerks, then students, and later accommodation and training for ATTORNEYS and SOLICITORS excluded from the I. of C. PMB

Inquest, the means, in times of poor communication, of obtaining for the central government sworn and accurate information from a JURY of local residents on specific local questions put to them. I.s were increasingly used in England as governmental power grew. Their various uses can be seen in the history of the judicial jury, as well as in reports on the age of heirs, the extent and tenure of a deceased person's lands, the demarcation of boundaries and the possible effects of a royal grant of privileges etc. Their use has declined with the abolition of feudal tenures, the growth of local government and courts, better means of communication etc., and with the use of statutory investigations under, for example, the Town and Country Planning Acts. (CORONERS.) PMB

Instrument of Government (16 Dec. 1653), the constitution establishing the PROTECTORATE, was drawn up by the council of officers. Legislative authority was vested in the Lord Protector (Cromwell) and a House of Commons of 460 members, chosen by reformed constituencies. Parliaments were to be triennial. Executive power rested with the Protector and COUNCIL OF STATE, and they could issue ordinances when Parliament was not in session. Laws were to be in accordance with the I. of G. which provided for revenue, but Parliament was to grant extraordinary expenses. There was to be toleration except for papists and prelatists. The HUMBLE PETITION AND ADVICE amended the I. of G. in 1657. IHE

Intercursus Magnus (1496). Henry VII broke off trade with the Netherlands in 1493 owing to the support given to the pretender Perkin Warbeck. Resulting economic depression in the Netherlands and the failure of Warbeck's expedition of 1495 led to the I.M., which established substantial freedom of trade between the two countries, with mutual freedom of fishing in each other's waters. Both sides agreed to suppress piracy and not to assist each other's rebels. The I.M. was renewed in 1507. IHE

Intercursus Malus (1506). The Archduke Philip of Burgundy on his way to claim the throne of Spain was forced by weather to take shelter in Weymouth. Henry VII used the opportunity to secure a new commercial treaty, subsequently called the I.M., more favourable to England than the INTERCURSUS MAGNUS. Among other gains, English cloth was to be sold freely throughout the Netherlands in return for vague promises of reciprocal privileges in England. Philip never ratified this treaty. IHE

Interdict, a decree depriving persons or communities of the services and comforts of the church, was mostly used to bring pressure upon offenders against the canon law. In 1206 Pope Innocent III quashed the election to the see of Canterbury of the rival nominees of King John and the monks of Christ Church, whereupon the latter elected Stephen Langton, the papal candidate. The king refused to admit Langton to England, exiled the monks and seized the revenues of the see. Innocent eventually imposed an i. on England on 23 March 1208. After the failure of negotiations and the publication of his excommunication in Nov. 1209 John resorted to large-scale exactions from the church in England. In 1213 the increasing danger of his position, the threat of deposition by the pope and the imminence of a French invasion brought John to terms. He agreed to accept Langton, to recall the exiles and to compensate the church for its losses, and on 15 May formally surrendered England and Ireland to the pope and received them back as papal fiefs, paying an annual tribute of 1,000 marks to Rome. Langton, on 20 July 1213, absolved the king: the i. was not finally lifted until 1214, when agreement had been reached on John's compensation of the church.   RFW

Interregnum, usually denotes the period of the COMMONWEALTH and PROTECTORATE between the execution of Charles I (30 Jan. 1649) and the RESTORATION (8 May 1660). There was another i. between the flight of James II (22 Dec. 1688) and the accession of William and Mary (23 Feb. 1689). This lasted in Scotland until 20 Apr. 1689.   IHE

Intolerable Acts (Apr. 1774), the name given to a group of coercive acts directed against MASSACHUSETTS consequent upon the BOSTON TEA PARTY and consisting of the BOSTON PORT, TRANSPORTATION, MASSACHUSETTS GOVERNMENT and QUARTERING ACTS. The QUEBEC Act was also regarded as a retaliatory measure by the Americans. They aroused further resistance and resulted in the 1st Colonial Congress at Philadelphia (Sept.).   IHE

Intrinsic Service, service which, contrary to FORENSIC SERVICE, is defined in a contract, written or unwritten, between grantor and grantee, e.g. the payment of rent, the performance of knight service, etc.   PMB

Investiture, the delivery, generally symbolic, of a man's due by grant, election etc.; in modern times a ceremony of honour, in the 11th-12th century a cause of the I. CONTEST in England as elsewhere.   PMB

Investiture Contest, arose from the ecclesiastical reform movement, which had among its principal objectives the abolition of lay investiture of prelates and freedom of election. Before 1100 it had been customary for the Norman kings of England to receive the HOMAGE of newly elected prelates, and then to invest them with the ring and pastoral staff. From the king's point of view, royal control of election and payment of homage was necessitated by the dual position of the bishops and many abbots as spiritual leaders and as feudal tenants-in-chief owing military service. In 1100 Archbishop Anselm of Canterbury refused to do homage to Henry I and was backed by Pope Pascal II, who in 1105 excommunicated those English bishops who had accepted investiture from the king. A compromise negotiated at Bec in 1106 was published in England in 1107: Henry I renounced investiture with the spiritualities—by ring and staff—but retained his right to homage as a condition of investiture with the temporalities of a see or abbey. In practice, homage preceded the consecration of a new prelate, and the king continued to exercise a decisive influence in ecclesiastical elections.   RFW

Iona, a small island off the west coast of Scotland, about 1 mile out to sea from the Ross of Mull. It formed part of the kingdom of DALRIADA. St Columba, abbot 563–97, established a monastery there which became the main Christian centre of the north; and from it missions were sent that converted the northern PICTS and many of the English to Christianity. The community was of the SCOTTISH CHURCH, and its influence declined with the increase in strength of the Roman church and the adoption of Roman practices, which were adopted at I. in the early 8th century. In 794

I. was ravaged by Norsemen, but the monastery was soon rebuilt. Its exposed position left it open to further raids, and in 878 the relics of St Columba were removed to Ireland. The monastery was rebuilt in the mid-11th century, but declined; and in 1203 a Benedictine abbey was built there, surviving until the 16th century. CFS

The I. Community, founded 1938 by George Macleod, prepares ministers and laymen of the Church of Scotland for missionary work in industrial areas. The Community has rebuilt the abbey. MLH

Ionian Islands (Corfu, Paxos, Leukas, Ithaca, Kephallenia, Zakynthos, Kythera) were in 1797 captured by the French from Venice, which had acquired them from 1386 onwards. The I.I. were taken by the Russians in 1799, formed into a Russo-Turkish protectorate (1800), restored to France by the treaty of Tilsit (1807) and occupied by a British expedition in 1809/14. The treaty of PARIS (1815) established the I.I. as a British protectorate, but the desire of the inhabitants for union with Greece made the British government cede the I.I. to Greece in 1864. SHS

Iraq, formerly Mesopotamia, was in 637 conquered from Persia by the Arabs, who founded Bagdad as the capital in 763, fell under Mongol rule in 1258, was fought over by Persia and Turkey in the 16th century and eventually became a Turkish province in 1627. The MESOPOTAMIAN CAMPAIGN (1914–18) freed the country, which became a British MANDATED TERRITORY (2 March 1921). The amir Feisal, younger brother of King Abdullah of TRANSJORDAN, expelled by the French from Syria which had elected him king (1920), was installed as king of I. on 23 Aug. 1921 (†1933). The district of Mosul, contended for by Turkey and I., was in 1925 adjudged to I. by the LEAGUE OF NATIONS; on 25 Nov. 1933 the League fixed the frontier with Syria. The treaty of Bagdad (30 June 1930), concluded for 25 years, pro-

vided for the termination of the mandate and I.'s admission to the League of Nations; this took place on 4 Oct. 1932. During the second world war a rebellion fomented by and aided by the Germans was suppressed by General Wavell (Apr.–May 1941), but from that time British–Iraq relations lost their former intimacy. I. was a founding member of the Arab League and the UNITED NATIONS (1945), but repudiated a 20-year treaty of alliance with Britain (initialled on 15 Jan. 1948) and took part in the Arab war against Israel (1948–9). The expectations raised by the Bagdad pact of 1955 and the federation with JORDAN (14 Feb. 1958) were nullified by the nationalist revolution of 14 July 1958, which turned I. into a republic, terminated the federation with Jordan, took I. out of the Bagdad pact (CENTO), enforced the evacuation of the British air base at Habbaniyah (31 May 1959) and led I. into close, though often disturbed, relationship with the neutralist United Arab Republic and the communist Soviet bloc. SHS

Ireland, Conquest of. In 1166 Rory O'Conor, the high-king of I., drove out Dermot McMurrough, king of Leinster. Dermot sought the assistance of Henry II of England, who was already interested in the possibility of a c. of I. (see LAUDABILITER). With Henry's approval, Dermot obtained the support of a number of barons, notably Richard de Clare, earl of Pembroke ('Strongbow'), and a group of MARCHER LORDS. A Norman–Welsh invasion force took Wexford in 1169 and restored Dermot; Strongbow himself followed in Aug. 1170 and took Waterford and Dublin. On Dermot's death in 1171, Strongbow, who had married his daughter, succeeded him in Leinster. Henry II viewed the earl's success with some hostility but eventually confirmed him in possession of Leinster—less the chief ports and castles—as a fief held of the king of England. Henry II landed at Waterford on 17 Oct. 1171 and received the homage of the Irish kings of the south and centre; the submission of the church in I. was followed by papal recognition of Henry's lordship. Military conquest proceeded with Hugh de Lacy's acquisition of Meath, John de Courcy's conquest of eastern Ulster from 1177 and some progress in Munster, while Rory O'Conor retained Connaught and was recognized as supreme over all surviving native rulers. Henry II made his son John lord of I. in 1177, but John's two Irish expeditions in 1185 and 1210 did little to advance the frontiers of English rule. Nevertheless, by the early 13th century the English controlled all I. south and east of the Bann and the Shannon, had introduced feudal tenure, English laws and administration, and had secured their possessions with a network of castles. In the middle 1230s the De Burghs conquered Connaught, but the whole country was never brought securely under English rule. Under Edward I about three-quarters of the island were contained by the English shires and liberties, but there remained a number of centres of Irish resistance which were never reduced— notably western Ulster in the north, and Desmond and Thomond in the south.

The king's chief representative in I., the justiciar, headed an Irish counterpart of English administration, with his council, judges, chancery and exchequer at Dublin, while Irish parliaments were summoned from 1264. By the end of the 13th century English rule in I. had reached its peak: it was recognized that an extensive 'land of war' was in practice outside the king's control, and that the 'land of peace' of the eastern and southern shires was bounded by a marchland where the English hold was none too firm. For the subsequent history see KILKENNY; DUNDALK; PALE.   RFW

Ireland, Partition of (1920–2), resulted from Ulster's refusal to countenance HOME RULE from Dublin and the insistence of the other three provinces upon greater independence. The prospect, 1912–14, of the achievement of home rule provoked the raising of the Ulster Volunteers by Carson

and (Sir) James Craig (Lord Craigavon, prime minister of Northern Ireland, 1921–40), the signing of the Ulster covenant (28 Sept. 1912) and the establishment of a provisional government; the CURRAGH 'MUTINY' was a reaction to these events. In the south, the Irish Volunteers were recruited as a challenge to Ulster, while SINN FEIN (and the Irish Republican Brotherhood, a secret society of Fenians) were preparing for a republic. An explosive situation was temporarily masked by the outbreak of the first world war.

The method by which the EASTER RISING was suppressed and the proposal to enforce conscription (1918) ensured victory in the 1918 general election for Sinn Fein over the home rule Nationalists. Those Sinn Fein M.P.s not in prison constituted themselves a Dáil Éireann (national assembly), 21 Jan. 1919, and declared an Irish republic. Unity being impossible to attain, p. (already proposed as a temporary expedient during discussion on the 1914 Home Rule Act, and again by Lloyd George after the Easter Rising) featured prominently in the Government of Ireland Act 1920. This envisaged local self-government within the United Kingdom with separate parliaments for the six predominantly Protestant counties of Ulster and for the remaining 26 counties, and an all-Ireland council. The act was reluctantly accepted by Northern Ireland, but rejected in Southern Ireland by a majority demanding undivided independence. Then developed the 'Anglo-Irish war' (1920–July 1921)—ugly incidents, and out-of-hand reprisals, between the Irish Volunteers (renamed Irish Republican Army and ably led by Michael Collins) and the British army and Royal Irish Constabulary augmented by non-Irish recruits ('Black and Tans') and an auxiliary division. A truce was followed by a London conference (21 Oct.–6 Dec. 1921) resulting in hesitant Irish agreement to a treaty by which an 'IRISH FREE STATE' was offered dominion status, NORTHERN IRELAND to be given the option (which it quickly took, 1922) of withdrawing. The treaty was approved by the U.K. parliament, 16 Dec., and by the Dáil, 7 Jan. 1922, strong republican opposition led by de Valera being overcome after civil war (March 1922–May 1923). MLH

Irish Church. The origin of Christianity in Ireland is unknown, but it was widespread before the coming of St Patrick, who, taken as a slave from Britain in the 5th century, became the main figure in the development of the I.c. He visited Gaul and brought the I.c. up to date in doctrine and customs, but after his death earlier practices were revived, and the I.c. acquired many characteristics peculiar to itself. The prevailing organization was tribal, and each tribe had its own bishop or bishops and its own monastery. This tribal monastery was the centre of local religious life, bishops were members of it, and the abbot had disciplinary powers over them. The main differences from Roman practice lay in the calculation of the date of EASTER, the shape of the tonsure and the use of a pre-Vulgate version of the scriptures. Other peculiarities were an uncontrolled asceticism and a wanderlust that took Irish monks throughout the western world. Many of these practices, taken by the SCOTS to northern Britain, became characteristic of the SCOTTISH CHURCH there. CFS

Irish Free State, established as a dominion on 6 Dec. 1921 by the treaty partitioning IRELAND, was given its first constitution on 6 Dec. 1922 by the Dáil. This was revised by De Valera's FIANNA FÁIL government in 1937; the country's name was changed to Éire and a president became head of state. On 18 April 1949 Éire ceased to be a member of the British COMMONWEALTH. MLH

Irish Rebellion (1641), caused by the removal of Strafford's strong hand, the fear of Puritan domination and the bitter grievances resulting from the Protestant PLANTATIONS. On 23 Oct. the Irish made a savage assault on the English and Scots in Ulster, and several thousands were massacred. In December they were joined by the Roman Catholic nobility. The king's opponents in the English Parliament were now prepared to risk an open breach rather than entrust him with an army to suppress the Irish which might be used against them. The rebels appointed a supreme council to govern Ireland (May 1642), and the General Assembly of Confederate Catholics met at Kilkenny (Oct.). They offered troops to Charles I in return for redress of grievances, but a cessation of arms was arranged (15 Sep. 1643) which left them in control of most of Ireland except Cork and the coastline from Belfast to Dublin. (ADVENTURERS, GLAMORGAN TREATY.) IHE

Irish Rebellion (1798) was the hopeless effort of the Society of United Irishmen. Founded (1791) by T. Wolfe Tone and others in an attempt to unite Catholics and Protestants in enforcing reform of GRATTAN'S PARLIAMENT, the United Irishmen quickly turned to revolutionary means of gaining independence. In an atmosphere of agrarian disorder and increasing religious hostility the movement gained ground among the Presbyterians of the north and the Catholic peasants of the south—particularly after disappointment occasioned by the short-lived lieutenancy of the liberal and popular Lord Fitzwilliam (Jan.–March 1795). Appeals for French aid resulted in the sailing of a fleet from Brest with 15,000 troops under Hoche which reached Bantry Bay (22 Dec. 1796) but was dispersed by gales. A second large-scale expedition from Texel was abandoned after CAMPERDOWN (Oct. 1797). Meanwhile Lt.-Gen. (Lord) Lake disarmed Ulster (March–Oct. 1797) with savage assistance from local yeomanry. Leaders of the United Irishmen were arrested before a plot to secure Dublin could be realized (March 1798). But the now leaderless rebellion broke out sporadically (May–June) with something of the violence of a religious war.

The most serious insurrection occurred in Co. Wexford where Wexford town was captured by Catholic rebels (30 May); they were, however, heavily defeated by Lake at Vinegar Hill, Enniscorthy (21 June). In the north, Protestant rebels were finally crushed at Ballinahinch, Co. Down (13 June). When all was over, 1,100 French troops arrived at Killala Bay (Aug.) and surrendered at Ballinamuck, while a small French squadron with Tone aboard was captured at Lough Swilly, Co. Donegal (Oct.). The rebellion defeated, Pitt pushed UNION forward.

MLH

Irish Rebellion (1916), see EASTER RISING.

Irish Representative Peers, the 28 peers of Ireland elected by their fellows as life members of the British House of Lords in accordance with the Act of UNION of 1800. The remainder were eligible for election to the Commons. The four bishops lost their seats after the disestablishment of the Church of Ireland (1869). No further lay peers were elected after the creation of the Irish Free State in 1922; the last died in 1961. IHE

Irish Volunteers were a Protestant force formed in 1779 to protect Ireland from invasion when Great Britain was at war with the American colonies, France and Spain. The movement grew rapidly, and some 80,000 men were under arms by 1782. Their existence was used by 'GRATTAN'S PARLIAMENT' to secure concessions from the British government. Substantial freedom of trade was achieved in 1779 and legislative independence in 1782 when the Volunteer leaders supported the abolition of the PENAL LAWS against the Catholics. The movement subsided after 1785 and was abolished by the Arms Act of 1793.

IHE

Iron Age, the period characterized by iron implements and weapons, that followed the BRONZE AGE. It began c. 6th century B.C. in the lowland zone of Britain, but considerably later in the uplands, where bronze-age techniques long continued. The first main impulse came with the 5th-century invasions from mainland Europe, when CELTS of the Hallstatt culture invaded across the Channel and the North Sea. In the east and midland areas there was considerable continuity with bronze-age cultures; in the south intrusive influence was dominant, although social and agricultural organization appears to have been little changed. In the 3rd century a series of invasions by Celts of the more advanced La Tène culture led to the establishment of a wealthy military aristocracy in the areas of Lincolnshire and Yorkshire: articles of adornment and weapons were of high technical and artistic standards, the two-wheeled fighting chariot was introduced and burial took the form of inhumation, with very elaborate grave-goods under individual round barrows. Other and smaller La Tène groups settled in East Anglia and southern England, but in the latter the construction of hill forts by the inhabitants limited their success. In the south-west, however, La Tène invaders coming by sea overran the area and thence expanded towards Wales and the midlands. They constructed hill forts in considerable numbers; and built lake-villages at Meare and Glastonbury (Somerset). The latter especially shows a high technical standard in wood, iron and bronze work, pottery, and luxury goods, the wealth of the community being in part due to its good trading position. The use of the sling as a major weapon of war from the late 2nd century led to the development of hill forts with multiple ramparts, a marked feature in the present landscape of southern England. The coming of the BELGAE in the 2nd century B.C. introduced further technical advances, although these had not penetrated beyond the lowland area at the time of the ROMAN CONQUEST. CFS

Ironsides. In 1643 Cromwell raised a force of cavalry in the EASTERN ASSOCIATION, drawn largely from yeomen and freeholders, and INDEPEN-

DENTS. Distinguished for zeal and discipline, they showed their mettle at Gainsborough and Winceby Fights. Their prowess at MARSTON MOOR (1644) caused Rupert to nickname Cromwell 'Old Ironsides', which was afterwards applied to his men. IHE

Irvingites, see CATHOLIC APOSTOLIC CHURCH.

Israel, see PALESTINE.

Italian bankers, providing credit facilities, played an important part in the royal finances in the late 13th and the first half of the 14th centuries. Henry II had occasionally borrowed from Flemish sources; Richard I raised money from Lombard firms for the third CRUSADE; King John, while borrowing from both sources, depended mainly on what he could wring out of his kingdom. Henry III, unable to risk a repetition of John's extortions and ill-provided with taxes to supplement normal revenue, borrowed heavily from Tuscan firms to finance the 'SICILIAN BUSINESS'. Edward I enjoyed substantial new revenues, especially from the customs, which were frequently assigned to bankers in repayment of loans. Edward systematically raised loans from well-organized international firms whose resources far surpassed those, for example, of the JEWS in England, who had been exploited to the limit by the late 13th century. In return for their loans, firms received substantial 'gifts' from the crown—amounting to interest of 26% in the early 14th century—, obtained the assistance of the crown in collecting private debts and were accorded special advantages in their business as financiers, merchants and wool exporters. Considerable risk however attended their relations with the English kings. The Riccardi of Lucca, to whom Edward I owed £392,000 between 1272 and 1294, collapsed in 1294. The Frescobaldi of Florence, the crown's principal creditors between 1299 and 1311, were expelled by the Lords ORDAINERS. Their place was taken from 1312 on-

wards by the Bardi and Peruzzi of Florence, who rendered valuable service to Edward III in the opening years of the HUNDRED YEARS' WAR. By 1346, however, Edward's heavy borrowings had overstrained the still modest resources of the crown and brought about the bankruptcy of both houses. Thereafter, Edward and his successors had to rely on native merchants, but the difficulties in raising money eventually played their part in bringing about the financial collapse of the LANCASTRIAN dynasty. Although no distinct class of 'Lombards'— money-lenders and pawn-brokers— was established in England, Italian merchants and bankers continued to be active in the country, establishing trade connexions with the continent and contributing to the expansion of ports, especially Southampton, and to the development of native industries, particularly the cloth industry of the south-west. RFW

Itinerarium Cambriae, an account published by Giraldus Cambrensis in 1191 of his journey through Wales with Archbishop Baldwin in 1188. Together with his *Descriptio* (1194) it forms a primary source for early medieval Welsh society. GW

Jacobites were the supporters of the Stewart cause after the GLORIOUS REVOLUTION of 1688. Roman Catholics and NON-JURORS were natural J., but the cause was strongest in the Scottish Highlands, especially after GLENCOE (1692). In Ireland they were leaderless, and many went to serve in France, the main centre of Jacobitism until the death of Louis XIV (1714). Their intrigues increased after the death of Queen Mary (1695), and there was a plot to murder William III in 1696. James II died in 1701, and many politicians kept contact with his son James, the Old Pretender, but his Roman Catholicism and dependence on France weakened his cause in England. In 1708 he made an unsuccessful attempt to land in Scotland, and on Anne's death (1714) the Jacobite Tory leaders failed to

proclaim him James III. The FIF-
TEEN REBELLION followed, but the
TRIPLE ALLIANCE between England,
France and Holland (1717) prevented
further serious Jacobite threats until
1744. In 1719 Spain promoted a
Jacobite invasion, but Ormonde failed
to land in England and the Scottish
force was defeated at Glenshiel.
ATTERBURY'S PLOT (1722) revealed the
persistence of Jacobite intrigue but
Walpole's vigilance prevented further
attempts for many years. War with
France (1744) provided opportunity
for the last and most serious Jacobite
rising, when Charles Edward, the
Young Pretender, led the FORTY-FIVE
REBELLION on his father's behalf.
Lack of English support showed the
success of Walpole's economic policy
in creating political stability and the
hopelessness of the Jacobite cause.

                                                IHE

Jamaica was discovered by Columbus on 3 May 1494 and named Santi-
ago; but the Indian name ('well
wooded and watered') has survived.
From 1596 J. was frequently raided
by English expeditions, but occupied
only on 11 May 1655 by Admiral Sir
William Penn and General Robert
Venables who had failed to fulfil
Cromwell's order to take Hispaniola.
The conquest was recognized by
Spain in 1670. J. became the greatest
slave market in the Americas and the
chief producer of sugar, which was
introduced in 1672. A destructive
raid by the French in 1694 caused
great misery. The rebellion of the
Maroons, runaway slaves, in the 1790s
ended with their shipment to NOVA
SCOTIA (1796). The industrial production of beet-sugar (from 1802)
and the liberation of the slaves (after
1834) caused economic distress which
eventually exploded in a great insurrection of freed slaves in 1865.
Representative government was abrogated (1866) and only partly restored
in 1884. The constitutions of 1944
and 1953 eventually set up complete
self-government. In 1958 J. joined
the federation of the West Indies but
in 1961 opted out of it. On 6 Aug.

1962 J. became an independent member of the Commonwealth.
  The TURKS AND CAICOS ISLANDS,
the CAYMAN ISLANDS and the Morant
and Pedro Cays (occupied in 1862–3)
were Jamaican dependencies until 1962.

                                                SHS

Jameson Raid (1895–6), a foolhardy
conspiracy to overthrow President
Kruger's regime in the TRANSVAAL
where the Uitlanders bore the burdens
of taxation while being denied the
rights of citizenship. Cecil Rhodes,
prime minister of Cape Colony and
director of the British South Africa
Company, utilized Uitlander grievances in planning a rising in Johannesburg which was to be supported by a
force of company police and volunteers from Bechuanaland under Dr
L. S. Jameson. The high commissioner of Cape Colony, Sir Hercules
Robinson, was to be called in as mediator. The colonial secretary, Joseph
Chamberlain, was almost certainly
involved. The Johannesburg reformers, lacking unity and resolution,
postponed the rising (fixed for 28 Dec.
1895), but Jameson, ignoring instructions, left Pitsani (29 Dec.) with 470
men, hoping to force the issue and was
ignominiously taken at Doornkop
(2 Jan. 1896). The raiders were given
over to the British authorities for trial,
Rhodes resigned his premiership,
Afrikaner nationalism was consolidated while English JINGOISM was
further stimulated by the KRUGER
TELEGRAM.   IHE

Jammu and Kashmir, the northernmost Indian state, fell under Moslem
rule c. 1340, was incorporated in
Akbar's empire in 1586, conquered
by the Afghans in 1796 and annexed
by Ranjit Singh to the SIKH kingdom
in 1819. He handed over J. in 1820
to a chieftain, Golab Singh, who took
the title of maharaja and in 1846, by
the treaty of Amritsar, received K.
from the British on recognition of
British supremacy. On 27 Oct. 1947
the ruling Hindu maharaja acceded
to India, but the Moslem majority of
the population (80%) resented the
military occupation by India and

called in Pakistani troops, who set up
the state of 'Azad K.' in the half under
their control. In 1952 the hereditary
rule of the maharaja was abolished in
the Indian portion. The K. dispute
has been poisoning Indian–Pakistani
relations. The Tashkent Declaration
(Jan. 1966) confirmed the 1949
ceasefire line.   SHS; IHE

Jenkins' Ear, War of (1739–48), resulted from the abuse of the strictly
limited trading rights with Spanish
America obtained by Great Britain at
the peace of UTRECHT. Under cover
of the SOUTH SEA COMPANY's annual
ship and the ASIENTO a large-scale
illicit trade developed. Spain retaliated by seizing British shipping
and exercising the right of search, to
the detriment of honest traders. In
1738 Captain Jenkins told the Commons that his ship had been pillaged
and his ear severed by the Spaniards
in 1731. Walpole was forced to yield
to the general clamour for war, backed
by the trading interests, his opponents
and his own colleagues (19 Oct. 1739).
Essentially a maritime war, its main
incidents were Vernon's capture of
Porto Bello (1739), his disastrous raid
on Cartagena (1741), an unsuccessful
expedition to CUBA (1742) and Anson's
voyage round the world (1740–4)
capturing Spanish treasure *en route*.
Spain and Britain supported opposite
sides in the AUSTRIAN SUCCESSION WAR
(1740–8), and the Anglo-Spanish war
became part of a wider struggle. At
the treaty of AACHEN (1748) no mention was made of the Spanish right of
search.   IHE

Jesuits, members of the Society of
Jesus, a religious order founded in
1534 and approved by the pope in
1540, to propagate the Roman Catholic faith and combat heresy. They
arrived in England in 1580. Their
promotion of political conspiracies
and support of assassination plots increased the severity of the PENAL LAWS
and strengthened Protestant convictions that all Roman Catholics were
traitors. Their impractical scheme to
restore Mary Queen of Scots was
frustrated by the RUTHVEN RAID.

They soon became involved in conflict with the secular priests who resented their internationalism and
attempts to control them. In 1598
the J. secured the appointment of an
archpriest to supervise the Roman
Catholic priesthood in England and
Scotland, and in 1598 and 1602 the
seculars sought to obtain their recall.
In 1603 a Jesuit betrayed the BYE
PLOT, and their English Provincial
was executed after the GUNPOWDER
PLOT (1605). Although banished in
1585, 1604, 1606 and 1610, they remained, but suffered heavily as
victims during the POPISH PLOT. The
Order was suppressed by Pope Clement
XIV in 1773 but was reconstituted
in 1814. Former J. settled at Stony-
hurst (1794) but were not officially
recognized until 1829 through fear
of antagonizing the seculars.   IHE

Jews came to England after the Norman conquest, settling first in London which, with its Great Synagogue,
remained their centre, then in other
towns. Except for occasional outbursts of anti-Semitism, e.g. in 1190
and in the coin-clipping inquiries
1278–9, J. lived at peace beside Christians. They had many trades, notably
the financing of land transactions; in
this they had no monopoly, for
Cahorcin and LOMBARD BANKERS
found much business in 13th-century
England. In 1194 the king sought to
control their financial activities: copies
of STARRS were to be deposited at
chests set up in various towns in
charge of a Jew and a Christian, and
the starrs were to be enrolled. Soon
afterwards the Exchequer of the J.
was established, where TALLAGES put
upon them were collected. J. were
the king's personal chattels; this gave
them special protection and, in the
justices of the J. sitting at their Exchequer, a court for recovering debts.
In other cases they were subject to
COMMON LAW, where the word of a
Jew equalled that of two Christians.
Their special status had disadvantages, for they were increasingly
heavily tallaged; moreover, their debts
fell to the king on death. This, rather

than anti-Semitism, indebtedness etc., seems to have caused their expulsion. Edward I had constant financial difficulties: he expelled J. from Gascony in 1289, reaping handsome profits from their forfeitures. Seizure of the chests of starrs and expulsion from England followed in 1290. Certain J. re-settled in England in Charles I's reign, and moves, with the aid of continental communities, were made for general resettlement. Cromwell and his council took up the cause. A stormy conference in 1655 was abortive, but in 1656 a test case established J.' right to hold property. Thus they returned, following their religion, surviving the Restoration and taking an increasing part in mercantile life. Like NONCONFORMISTS and Roman Catholics, they sought full emancipation, achieving it, after ROTHCHILD'S CASE, in the Jewish Relief Act 1858.

PMB

Jingoism, a term now used to denote bellicose chauvinism, was first applied to those who favoured intervention on Turkey's behalf in the Russo-Turkish war of 1877-8. It originated from a music-hall song by G. W. Hunt (*refrain:* 'We don't want to fight, but by jingo if we do,—We've got the ships, we've got the men, and got the money too').

MLH

Johore, member state of the Federation of MALAYA, leased SINGAPORE to the EAST INDIA COMPANY in 1819-24, entered into treaty relations with Great Britain on 11 Dec. 1885 and, as one of the UNFEDERATED MALAY STATES, accepted a British 'general adviser' on 12 May 1914.

SHS

Jordan, formerly TRANSJORDAN, conquered in the war with Israel (1948-50) part of PALESTINE west of the river Jordan, including the old city of Jerusalem. After Abdullah's assassination (20 July 1951) the connexion with Great Britain weakened; the British officers were dismissed in 1956 and the 20-year treaty of 15 March 1948 was terminated on 13 March 1957.

SHS

Judicature, Supreme Court of. The English legal system was in confusion by the 19th century, with overlapping jurisdictions in COMMON LAW and EQUITY and cumbersome procedures, pilloried by Dickens. Small reforms were first attempted, e.g. KING'S BENCH became a first-instance court alone, and the EXCHEQUER equity jurisdiction was transferred to CHANCERY. By Lord Selborne's Judicature Act 1873, the Common Law and Equity jurisdictions of King's Bench, COMMON PLEAS, Chancery and Exchequer were united as divisions of the Supreme Court, together with the special jurisdictions of Admiralty, Probate and Divorce. The work of re-organization was crowned by the Appellate Jurisdiction Act 1876, creating Lords of Appeal, and by the amalgamation in the King's Bench division of the Common law jurisdictions of the Common Pleas, Exchequer and King's Bench divisions. These reforms, bringing order to the civil jurisdiction, also completed the fusion of law and equity in England and Wales.

PMB

Junius Letters (1769-72), a series of vitriolic personal attacks on public men and their policies first appearing in the press under the signature Junius 21 Jan. 1769. (His letters without this signature date from 1767.) Among those singled out were the Duke of Grafton, Sir William Blackstone, Lord Mansfield, the Duke of Bedford and Lord North. He attacked the shams and corruptions of political life and made full play of exposing private scandals. The attacks on Grafton helped to bring about the downfall of his ministry (1770). Their authorship is in dispute, but recent opinion favours either Philip Francis or Lord Shelburne.

IHE

Junto, from the Spanish *junta* (council), was used in the 17th century in much the same way as cabinet or CABAL. It was particularly applied to the Whig leaders of the reigns of William III and Anne, who were in office as a compact group between 1696 and 1697 and from 1708 to

1710. The lords of the Whig J., Somers, Wharton, Sunderland, Orford and Halifax, supported the wars of the League of AUGSBURG (after 1694) and of the SPANISH SUCCESSION and the trading and financial interests.

IHE

Jurats or jurates (Med. Latin *jurati*, 'sworn men'), sometimes used in medieval England as an alternative to 'jurors', but more frequently with a specialized meaning, varying in the different dominions of the crown.

(1) In England, in the late 12th and 13th centuries, j. were members of the new BOROUGH councils of 12 or 24, perhaps copied from the continental *communes*, elected by urban communities and bound by oath to maintain the liberties of their boroughs. By the mid-14th century many English boroughs were acquiring second, larger councils, 'common councils', and the j. came to be called aldermen, although in some 13th-century boroughs aldermen had been distinct officers. In some towns, however, the name j. survived as an equivalent of aldermen, notably in the CINQUE PORTS, Southampton and Portsmouth.

(2) In the CHANNEL ISLANDS the j. were magistrates rather than councillors. They may have originated in the 12 CORONERS appointed by king John to keep the PLEAS OF THE CROWN, or they may have existed earlier under a different name. In the 14th century each of the principal islands had a body of j. (12 in Jersey and in Guernsey, 7 in Alderney, 6 in Sark), elected for life by the king's ministers and the local magnates. The j. heard suits in the king's courts, presided over by the bailiff or prévôt, gave judgements, fixed fines and AMERCEMENTS, and were the principal guardians and interpreters of the customary law. When deliberative and legislative assemblies, the States, emerged in Jersey and Guernsey, the j. formed their nuclei.

(3) In Bordeaux in the early 13th century a body of 50 j. elected the mayor, held office for a year, chose their own successors, and together with the mayor chose the councillors.

Mayor and j. possessed a wide civil and criminal jurisdiction and a large measure of autonomy, as did other municipal authorities in the English part of AQUITAINE. The j. of Bordeaux were reduced to 24 in 1241 and to 12 in 1375, while a high property qualification secured a monopoly of office for the wealthiest citizens. J. performed similar functions in other cities in Aquitaine, e.g. Bayonne, Dax, La Rochelle, and were found elsewhere under different names, e.g. *échevins*, consuls.

RFW

Jury, a number of persons summoned by a royal officer to give true answers to specific questions. Its origin seems to lie in the practice of 9th-century Frankish kings in seeking unbiased local information from reputable local persons, a practice harnessed by the Norman kings to the English administrative and legal systems.

The j. in criminal cases was known in the DANELAW, but its continuous history begins with the Assize of CLARENDON 1166: jurors from each HUNDRED etc. were to appear before EYRE justices, presenting crimes in their areas and suggested criminals. To these presenting jurors other questions, chapters of the eyre, were put: gradually they were called Grand Juries, to be abolished in England for most cases in 1933.

Juries to try criminal charges, petty juries, began with the abolition of ORDEALS in 1215. New tests of guilt were needed, juries were seized upon, and experiments in their use, composition and source followed. For convenience they came to be drawn from grand jurors, thus losing much of their local origin, becoming judges of facts presented to them: in 1275 jury trial for serious charges was made compulsory. In later centuries juries have gained independence from external pressure, after BUSHELL'S CASE 1670, and from the consequences of bad verdicts, but lost any pretence to local ties.

Juries for civil cases appear first in the Grand Assize, then in the POSSESSORY ASSIZES. The modern optional civil jury derives from the action, regarded as partly criminal, of trespass, for which juries, modelled either on the assizes or petty juries, were adopted.   PMB

Justice, Lord Chief. As each branch of the sovereign's court took on a life of its own, a senior judge emerged: in COMMON PLEAS and KING'S BENCH, after the sovereign's withdrawal, a chief justice; in the EXCHEQUER, a chief baron; in CHANCERY, the Lord Chancellor or Master of the ROLLS; in the Tudor prerogative courts, Masters etc. Though orders of precedence were established, the office of L.C.J., senior judge of all courts under the Chancellor, was not created until the 1873 Judicature Act, which set up the modern High Court.   PMB

Justices, Mirror of, a fantastic legal treatise written *c.* 1290, probably by Andrew Horn, later chamberlain of London. It is a commentary, occasionally shrewd more often nonsensical, on contemporary English law compared with the golden age of king Alfred. Unknown in the middle ages, revived and revered by 17th-century historians, it has been condemned by those of the last 150 years.   PMB

Justices of the Peace. Local lords and gentry as conservators of the peace were first given judicial powers in 1361 when their duties were combined with those of the justices of labourers. As J.P.s they acted through courts of QUARTER SESSIONS and were commissioned under the crown from CHANCERY. Summary jurisdiction (PETTY SESSIONS) developed in the 16th century and appellate jurisdiction is based on acts of 1848. The governmental work of wage-fixing was soon given to the J.P.s, and their administrative duties enormously increased from Tudor times onward. Essentially unpaid, the gentry welcomed the powers they wielded, but with the downfall of paternal and conciliar government after the RESTORATION they tended to act in the interests of property. They remained the mainstay of county government and law enforcement until the Local Government Acts of 1888 and 1894 left them with few administrative powers other than in connexion with the licensing laws and visiting prisons and mental hospitals.   IHE

Justiciar (Latin *justiciarius*, a justice), the viceroy of the Norman and Plantagenet kings, although the title j. was never regularly employed. As William I and his successors established a strong, centralized monarchical government in England but retained an over-riding loyalty to Normandy, the English government required a head to act while the king was overseas. Bishop Odo of Bayeux, William I's half-brother, probably exercised some of the powers later entrusted to j. while his brother was in Normandy: Ranulf Flambard was the 'chief agent of the king's will' in William Rufus' reign, and in Henry I's time the j. position was firmly established. He stood below the king but above the departments of government while the king was in England; while the king was abroad he governed in his name. Henry I's j., bishop Roger of Salisbury, kept office into Stephen's reign; his dismissal and humiliation in 1139 show clearly the political pre-eminence and power of the office. Most j.s were men trained in the royal service and dependent on royal patronage. They were all administrators, but several displayed special skills, reflecting their masters' special interests; thus Ranulf Flambard was an astute financier, Ranulf de Glanvill, one of Henry II's j.s, was a learned judge, and the j.s of Richard I and John were principally administrators. John's last j., Hubert de Burgh, retained office under Henry III, achieving political eminence in the last years of the minority and the early years of the majority of the young king. Hubert was disgraced in 1232 and, although a successor was appointed, the justiciarship lapsed in 1234. It was revived by the baronial reformers in 1258 but, when the j., Hugh Despenser, was killed with Simon de Montfort at EVESHAM in 1265, the office finally lapsed.

As a step towards central control of justice and to provide skilled judges in all parts of the country, local j.s were appointed in many counties, probably during William Rufus' reign, certainly during Henry I's and Stephen's. Local men of some standing and proven loyalty, their business was to keep the crown PLEAS and hear, with or without the SHERIFF, cases referred to them by the king. Local j.s were still appointed in the earlier years of Henry II's reign, but they were replaced by the new system of busy central courts and judicial eyres.

PMB

Jutes, are mentioned by Bede (†735) as one of the Teutonic groups that invaded Britain (TEUTONIC CONQUEST). He located their continental homeland as north of that of the ANGLES, i.e. in Jutland; and attributed to them the conquest of KENT and of the Isle of Wight and the mainland opposite. West SAXON tradition and archaeology support these latter settlements, which were probably offshoots from Kent. The settlement in Kent was more complicated than Bede suggests: a more primitive minority of invaders probably came direct from northern parts, but all evidence points to the lower Rhine area as that from which the majority came. Literary evidence suggests that the J. originally entered Kent as FOEDERATI, and it is probable that such a body included elements from various Teutonic areas.   CFS

Jutland, battle of (31 May 1916), the only major fleet action in WORLD WAR I. The German Adm. von Scheer and the British Adm. Jellicoe were both seeking an action, which began when Adm. Beatty with 6 battle cruisers encountered the German advance force of 5 battle cruisers on the afternoon of 31 May. Beatty, losing 2 ships, turned north leading the Germans towards the Grand Fleet. Indecisive action followed but the Germans effected escape in the gloom, although there were some confused night actions with British light forces. The British losses included 3 battle cruisers, 3 cruisers and 8 destroyers; the Germans lost 1 battleship, 1 battle cruiser, 4 cruisers and 5 destroyers. Although a tactical German victory, the battle of J. was a strategic British success as the Germans never again challenged the British navy.   IHE

Kashmir, see JAMMU AND KASHMIR.

Kedah, member state of the Federation of MALAYA, ceded PENANG (1786) and Province Wellesley (1800) to the EAST INDIA COMPANY, was released from Siamese suzerainty on 10 Mar. 1909 and became one of the UN-FEDERATED MALAY STATES.   SHS

Keeling Islands, see COCOS ISLANDS.

Kelantan, see UNFEDERATED MALAY STATES.

Kenilworth, Dictum of (31 Oct. 1266), the most important step towards re-establishing peace after the BARONS' WARS. The efforts of the more moderate royalists to secure the submission of the DISINHERITED on acceptable terms were powerfully backed by the papal legate Ottobuono. The D., as finally agreed upon, stated the king's full resumption of his powers, annulled the acts of Simon de Montfort and all acts to which Henry III had given unwilling consent since 1258. More important, it gave the rebels the opportunity of redeeming their confiscated property, by paying the king a certain multiple of its annual value determined in proportion to the seriousness of their offences. In Sept. 1267 special justices were appointed to apply the terms of the D., accepted by the rebels with special modifications in some cases.   RFW

Kenilworth, Siege of. On 31 July 1265 Simon de Montfort the younger was surprised at night outside K. castle by Henry III's son, Edward. Although most of his men were captured, Simon escaped into the castle, where he held out after the battle of EVESHAM. Henry III began to besiege K. in December, but its close investment did not begin until June 1266. By then Simon and many others had moved to the Isles of AXHOLME and ELY. The garrison continued to hold out after the publication of the DICTUM OF K., but accepted it when they eventually surrendered on 14 Dec. 1266.   RFW

Kent. According to tradition, Hengest and his followers were invited to settle, in 449, as FOEDERATI, in the modern county of K., and they subsequently conquered the area (JUTES). This may be true, for K. shows some slight continuity between Romano-British and Teutonic civilizations there, and the Teutonic *Cantware*, 'dwellers in Kent', is derived from the Romano-British name *Cantiaci*. It also differed from other Teutonic kingdoms in agrarian, administrative and social organization, and in these and in cultural activity it shows Frankish influence. Its most important king was Ethelbert (died 616), who was converted to Christianity by the ROMAN MISSION, and who was recognized as overlord of the southern English (BRETWALDA). In 686 Caedwalla, king of WESSEX, invaded K. but failed to maintain his conquest. The names of the kings of K. are known, and it appears that the original dynasty died out soon after the mid-8th century. From this time until 825 K. generally recognized the overlordship of MERCIA. In that year the men of K. submitted to Ethelwulf, son of Egbert king of Wessex, and K. became a SHIRE of Wessex.   CFS

Kenya. The Portuguese who had taken Mombasa in 1508 were expelled by the Arabs in 1728, and in the 1830s the whole coast came under the rule of ZANZIBAR. From 1885 the German East Africa Association acquired Witu; in 1887 Mombasa and in 1889 the whole coast were leased from the sultan of Zanzibar by the British EAST AFRICA COMPANY, which controlled the 'British East Africa Protectorate' after Germany had relinquished her claims to Witu by the HELIGOLAND treaty of 1 July 1890. The country was placed under the crown in 1895, transferred from the foreign to the colonial office in 1905 and constituted the 'colony and protectorate of K.' on 23 July 1920; the protectorate included the coastal strip which the sultan of Zanzibar ceded to Kenya on 8 Oct. 1963. The frontier with Ethiopia was delimitated in 1908; Jubaland was ceded to Italy in 1924 and now forms part of Somalia. Indians immigrated from 1896 as workmen on railways. The uninhabited highlands, which had been depopulated by Masai raids, were opened to white settlers in 1900; the Masai received compensation in steppe land. From 1918 when the first elections were held, constitutional progress was interrupted only by the measures necessary to suppress the atrocities of the Mau Mau cult. Kenya became independent on 12 Dec. 1963 and a republic within the COMMONWEALTH on 12 Dec. 1964.   SHS; IHE

Kerala, historic name of the most highly literate and industrialized Indian state, which was created in 1956 as a Malayalam-speaking unit out of TRAVANCORE–Cochin and parts of MADRAS.   SHS

Kett's Rebellion (1549), began as a local riot early in July at Wymondham, but gathered strength under the leadership of Robert Kett, and for six weeks (12 July–26 Aug.) some 16,000 insurgents encamped on Mousehold Heath dominating Norwich. Offers of a pardon were rejected, and the government forces under Warwick entered Norwich (24 Aug.). Kett moved to Dussindale where his supporters were routed by Warwick (27 Aug.). Retribution followed, and Kett and his brother were executed (Dec.). K.R. was an attempt to gain governmental support against agrarian grievances, largely caused by inclosures and encroachments on the commons. It was not actuated by religious motives but showed Protestant sympathies.   IHE

Keys, House of (*keise*, Old Nordic 'the chosen') the representative assembly of the Isle of MAN, elected (from 1866) by the four municipalities and six sheadings.   SHS

Khaki election (Oct. 1900) was so called because it was regarded as an attempt by the Conservative government to benefit from recent victories in the SOUTH AFRICAN WAR. Salisbury had been persuaded to dissolve parliament by Joseph Chamberlain, whose personality and policy as colonial secretary became the main issue. The government were returned with a slightly increased majority.   MLH

Kilkenny, statutes of (1366). Although the Scottish invaders had been driven out of Ireland after the battle of DUNDALK, English control markedly declined. Many of the old Norman families died out and were not effectively replaced. After the extinction of the De Burghs or Burkes of Ulster the earldom of Ulster broke up and was largely reconquered by the Irish. The Burkes of Connaught, on the other hand, became almost indistinguishable from Irish chiefs. Many English heirs to Irish lordships did not take up their inheritances in person, and despite continual legislation the English government failed to compel them to do so. Parts of Leinster, Leix and Carlow were lost, and the MacMurroughs revived a native kingdom of Leinster. A few lords of English descent—notably the Fitzgeralds and the Butlers—increased their power, but English government and institutions, law and customs and the English language were all steadily losing ground. When Edward III's son Lionel, duke of Clarence, went to Ireland as lieutenant in 1361, it was soon apparent that a major reconquest could not be undertaken. Instead, the 35 statutes of the parliament held by Lionel at K. in Feb. 1366 amounted to a recognition that the conquest of Ireland had failed, and attempted to ensure that the third of the country, the PALE, where English rule was still effective, remained English in character. Intermarriage and fosterage with the Irish were forbidden to the English, and they were bound to the exclusive use of English law, customs, dress and language. Although the statutes were frequently re-enacted and were not finally re-pealed until 1613, their enforcement proved impossible. The merging of the races, the 'degeneracy' of many powerful lords of English descent and the recovery of the Irish had progressed too far to permit a rigid partition of Ireland.   RFW

Killiecrankie, battle of (27 July 1689). The restoration of PRESBYTERIANISM ensured the success of the GLORIOUS REVOLUTION of 1688 in Scotland, but the Highland supporters of James II rose under Viscount Dundee. They were met by William III's troops under General Mackay at K. near Blair Atholl, Perthshire. The Highlanders won the battle, but Dundee was killed. After an attack on Dunkeld the Highlanders began to disperse and were finally routed (June 1690).   IHE

Kilmainham Treaty, the name given to an informal bargain between Gladstone and the Irish leader, Parnell, Joseph Chamberlain being an intermediary. Parnell and two other Irish M.P.s were released on 2 May 1882 from K. gaol, where they had been since Oct. 1881. Parnell was to use his influence to discourage violence in Ireland; Gladstone to introduce a bill by which Irish tenants would have arrears of rent paid and thus be able to take advantage of the LAND ACT of 1881. In spite of the PHOENIX PARK MURDERS and consequent new Coercion Act, Parnell and Gladstone stood by their agreement; the latter passed an Arrears Act, which, however, gave tenants little benefit.   MLH

King's Bench, Court of. In origin the king's personal court which, after the establishment of COMMON PLEAS, came to be known as the court *coram rege*, 'in the king's presence', and later as K. (Queen's) B., reviewing cases from Common Pleas and hearing cases of particular interest to the king and the law. Its early history was sporadic: Henry II and John regularly held courts as they travelled about their realms; in their absence, as in Richard I's reign, it lapsed. In Henry III's minority the council held the court. Later, Henry III sat occasionally with the judges, but in Edward I's reign the sovereign withdrew, special judges were appointed and the court was finally established, though maintaining close connexions with the king and council for some decades. Sometimes settled at Westminster, the court was regularly sent through the country in the later 14th century, in an attempt to replace the general EYRE: at this period too it began its conflict with the Common Pleas for particular types of cases, offering different procedures, in the growing complexities of COMMON LAW. Conflict lasted until the 19th century. The court first lost its reviewing powers, then it became a division of the High Court, finally as the Queen's Bench Division uniting all the common-law jurisdictions in 1881. See also APPEAL; CROWN OFFICE; CURIA REGIS; ENROLMENT; HABEAS CORPUS; JUDICATURE, SUPREME COURT OF; NEWGATE PRISON; QUARTER SESSIONS; REMEMBRANCER; TRAILBASTON.   PMB

King's Bench Prison, established in Southwark at least by the 14th century to hold prisoners for the court of KING'S BENCH, the prison was increasingly used for debtors who, in return for payments, might be allowed to live semi-free in the 'Rules' adjoining the prison proper. The prison was rebuilt in 1754, renamed Queen's Prison in 1842 and abolished, with the end of imprisonment for debt, in 1869. PMB

King's Evil, was the name given to scrofula ('surgical' tuberculosis) supposedly cured by the king's touch. This custom of touching existed in France before it was introduced into England by Edward the Confessor. Ceremonial proceedings were instituted by Henry VII and the sufferers were presented with gold coins. The practice was very popular after the RESTORATION, and Charles II distributed special touch pieces or medallions. William III scorned the custom, and it was last practised in this country by Queen Anne.   IHE

King's Friends, the name given early in the reign of George III to those politicians who, for varying reasons, supported the crown or the administration. In 1766 such a group met to further the view that the king should appoint his servants freely and not be dominated by the party leaders. Many of them were ambitious for office and became permanent PLACEMEN, others were less self-seeking and supported the crown for more honourable reasons. They were mainly TORIES, and when used by their Whig opponents K.F. was a derogatory term. Their importance as a political unit as well as their undue subservience to the crown has been exaggerated.   IHE

King's Peace, a concept developed in Old English times and reflecting the changing position of the king. In the earlier Old English period kings were little more than war leaders; but time and Christian influence, symbolized by the rite of anointing, produced the idea of a king responsible to God for the well-being of his kingdom. The k.p. supplemented the general peace (FRITH) and the MUND that each free man possessed, but even at the end of the O.E. period it was not universal. During the 11th century it covered widows, strangers, churches, attendance at moots and military service. The laws of Edward the Confessor, compiled after the NORMAN CONQUEST, state that it also lay over the three great feasts, the four main highways (ERMINE STREET, FOSS WAY, ICKNIELD WAY, WATLING STREET) and navigable rivers. Breach of the k.p. was punished by a special WITE enforced by royal officials. After the Norman conquest it became general.   CFS

Kingston-on-Thames, treaty of (12 Sept. 1217), between Prince Louis of France, the baronial nominee to the English throne, and the supporters of the young Henry III ended the civil war of 1215–17. Louis agreed to cease aiding the baronial party and to secure the restoration of the Channel Isles to England. A general amnesty was proclaimed, and both royalists and rebels were to recover their lost possessions. Louis retired to France, speeded by a grant of 10,000 marks. RFW

Kirkby's Quest (1284-5), one of Edward I's large-scale inquiries, conducted by the treasurer, John Kirkby, and a staff of Exchequer officials. The first object was the investigation of debts owed to the Exchequer in the various shires, but it was specially notable for its recording of the details of knight's fees held in chief of the crown, probably to facilitate the collection of the scutage of 1285. The original returns have mostly disappeared but have been largely reconstructed. RFW

Knight, derived from Old English CNIHT, the mainstay of English medieval society. At the beginning of the feudal period a k. was required, in return for his FEE, to join the feudal army for 40 days, perform castle-guard, castle-work and escort duty: as an heir under age he was his lord's ward, if of age he paid relief, subscribing also to feudal AIDS. The various classes of k. existing soon after the Norman conquest, household, enfeoffed, VAVASSORS, had by the mid-12th century became a single group, some of whose duties, e.g. castle-work, could be commuted to rent, and whose army service might be discharged by payment of SCUTAGE with, on occasion, a fine for non-attendance. As medieval warfare changed, so did the k.'s military duty. The feudal host was not designed for long campaigns: in the 12th and 13th centuries fees were grouped to produce a quota of their service; mercenaries were employed; k.s, acting as officers to the increasing numbers of infantry, were first paid for service over 40 days in Edward I's Scots wars, and in Edward III's French wars all k.s were paid full time. The last feudal army was summoned in 1385, but by then the new conception of a paid k. dedicated to the glory of war was established and commemorated in the founding of the order of the GARTER in 1341. However, the non-combatants were not idle. As men of standing in their

shires, they became SHERIFFS, tax-collectors and commissioners of ARRAY; harnessed to the developing legal system as provers of ESSOINS, members of the Grand Assize, amateur judges, CORONERS and J.P.s: experience of all these tasks they brought to Parliament as k.s of the SHIRE. The successors of the medieval k.s are to be found not only in the ORDERS OF CHIVALRY and the armed forces but also in Parliament, commissions of the Peace and the many aspects of local government. PMB

Kotsetla, a free peasant in Old English times (CEORL). Such men formed the lowest class of the free peasantry, holding some 5 acres of land and being liable to a considerable number of services on their lord's estate. Economically their position resembled that of the later bordar.
CFS

Kruger Telegram (3 Jan. 1896), a congratulatory message sent by the German emperor, William II, to President Kruger of the TRANSVAAL following the defeat of the JAMESON RAID. William II also ordered troops to embark for Delagoa Bay (Portuguese East Africa) and to entrain for Pretoria: the Portuguese, however, refused transit. The telegram provoked violent reaction in Britain and seriously embittered Anglo-German relations. In so far as it encouraged Kruger to seek foreign support the K.t. was a factor in events leading to the SOUTH AFRICAN WAR (1899-1902). MLH

Kuwait, see PERSIAN GULF.

Labour, Ministry of, see EMPLOYMENT AND PRODUCTIVITY.

Labourers, Statute of (1351). After the BLACK DEATH the reduced labour force was in great demand, wages rose and VILLEINS escaped more frequently: the ancient pattern of rural society was disrupted. Reinforcing a 1349 ordinance, the statute attempted to hold wages at their pre-plague levels: men could demand no more, their lords had first claim on their

services, contracts were rigorously enforced. Penalties for infringement,
imposed by local justices, were severe,
but this first labour legislation failed
because of the labourers' resistance
and continuing labour shortage. The
resentment generated, however,
helped eventually to produce the
PEASANTS' REVOLT.   PMB

Labour Party, dates from a meeting of
TRADE UNIONS and socialist bodies,
27–28 Feb. 1900, pursuant to a resolution of the T.U.C. annual conference
of 1899. A Labour Representation
Committee was formed to sponsor
Parliamentary candidates, the chief
supporters being the INDEPENDENT
L.P., the FABIAN SOCIETY and the
newer unions of the unskilled. At the
1900 election two candidates were returned. Continuance was ensured by
a great increase in union affiliation
after the TAFF VALE DECISION and by
a secret agreement with the LIBERAL
PARTY under which, at the 1906 election, they opposed only 18 out of 50
L.R.C. candidates, of whom 29 were
returned. Thereupon the L.R.C. took
the title L.P. During the period 1906–
14 dependence upon the Liberals provoked discontent and finances were
hampered by the OSBORNE JUDGMENT,
but membership increased and included the Miners' Federation with
their 'Lib.–Lab.' M.P.s. The first
world war threw a strain on the L.P.
for several of the leaders were anti-war
while others joined the coalition
government. A socialist constitution
was drawn up in 1918, a policy statement adopted and the party machine
re-organized. Strength in the Commons increased from 57 (1918) to 142
in 1922. In 1923, 191 seats were won
and the first Labour government under
MacDonald was formed, dependent
upon Liberal support (Jan.–Nov.
1924). MacDonald formed his second
minority government when Labour
gained 287 seats in 1929; during the
financial crisis of Aug. 1931 the cabinet
split over cuts in unemployment benefits and MacDonald formed a National
government, all but a small minority of
the L.P. going into opposition. Under

Clement (later earl) Attlee's leadership
the L.P. joined Churchill's coalition
government, May 1940. The 1945
election gave Labour 393 seats, an
overall majority of 146 and Attlee
formed an administration. In 1950
strength in the Commons shrank to
315, a majority of 6, and the L.P. was
defeated in 1951 with a minority of 17.
Gaitskell, leader from 1955, died in
1963 and was succeeded by Wilson,
who brought the L.P. to office in 1964
with a majority of 4, increased in 1966
to 96.   MLH

Labuan, on BORNEO, was ceded to
Great Britain by the sultan of BRUNEI
in 1846, incorporated with NORTH
BORNEO in 1889, attached to SINGA-
PORE in 1907, made a separate settle-
ment in 1912 and re-united with
North Borneo in 1946.   SHS

**Laccadive, Minicoy and Amindivi
Islands,** off the coast of Kerali, form
a Union Territory of INDIA with their
administrative centre at Kozhikode
(Calicut). See MADRAS.   IHE

Lagos, battle of (18 Aug. 1759), a
British naval victory during the
SEVEN YEARS' WAR. The French fleet
escaped from Toulon to join the
Channel fleet at Brest preparatory to
the invasion of England. Pursued by
Boscawen from Gibraltar they were
scattered, 1 ship being taken in battle,
5 escaping to Cadiz and 4 run ashore
and destroyed at L. on the coast of
Portugal.   IHE

La Hougue, battle of (29 May 1692),
the decisive naval battle in the war of
the GRAND ALLIANCE. The French
set out to engage the Anglo-Dutch
forces preparatory to the invasion of
England, but encountered a fleet of
twice their strength and were defeated. The allies made subsequent
attacks at La Hougue and Cherbourg,
destroying 15 ships of the line, and
the French were reduced to privateering and commerce raiding for the
rest of the war.   IHE

Laing's Nek, battle of (28 Jan. 1881).
Failing to regain their independence
from the Gladstone government, the

TRANSVAAL Boers proclaimed the restoration of the republic (DINGAAN'S DAY 1880) and besieged the small British garrisons at Pretoria, Potchefstroom and Lydenburg. Sir George Colley, setting out with some 1,000 men from Natal to their aid, was repulsed by Joubert at the pass of L.N. near the Transvaal border. Colley's second attempt resulted in his rout at MAJUBA HILL.   IHE

Lambeth, treaty of (4 May 1212), between King John and Renaud de Dammartin, count of Boulogne, who pledged themselves not to conclude a separate peace with France. Dammartin, who received fiefs in England and a generous annuity, was the vital link in the chain of alliances against Philip II of France: helping to bring other princes of the Low Countries, notably the count of Flanders, to John's side. John's plan to recover the ANGEVIN EMPIRE ended at BOUVINES.   RFW

Lambeth Conferences of the bishops of the Anglican communion. The first assembled at Lambeth Palace, London, on 24 Sept. 1867 at the instigation of the Church in Canada. It met in response to an urgent desire for a unity which had been shaken by the COLENSO affair and controversies emanating from Darwin's theory (1859) and the *Essays and Reviews* by Frederick Temple and others (1860). In his invitation to the 242 bishops (of whom 76 accepted—none from the province of York) Archbishop Longley of Canterbury stated: 'such a meeting would not be competent to make declarations or lay down definitions on points of doctrine. But united worship and common counsels would greatly tend to maintain practically the unity of the faith.' This principle has remained true of the succeeding L.c. held at intervals of about ten years. Resolutions arising from the discussions have no binding force but are significant as expressions of the common opinion of the Anglican hierarchy. The tenth L.c. in 1968 was attended by 468 bishops.
                                        MLH

Lambeth Palace, the London residence of the archbishop of Canterbury, situated in the diocese of Rochester (since 1905, in Southwark). The first L.P. was built in the 12th century. CFS

Lancaster, Duchy of, began as an institution with Henry III's desire to set up his son Edmund as a territorial magnate in England, after his failure to establish him in a kingship on the continent. This object Henry successfully contrived in 1265 and the following years by using the spoils of the BARONS' WAR. In 1267 Edmund was created earl of L., first of a line of earls and dukes who played a notable part in English history in the 14th century, being greatly helped in this by the extensive lands and jurisdiction of their inheritance. The last of these dukes, Henry of Bolingbroke, became Henry IV in 1399; he did not let the inheritance be merged in the crown lands, but under the name D. of L. it thenceforward kept its separate identity and administration.

The D. was at its greatest extent and power in the 15th and 16th centuries: it then shared the fate of the crown lands and was shorn of large portions to provide, through the sales, ready money for the early Stewarts. In the 18th century the D. was fairly moribund, but since then it has improved in value and efficiency as a landed estate, its surplus revenue going directly to the sovereign's privy purse. Thus the D., though classed as a public office or department of state, is in no way under Treasury control. Nevertheless, by a further anomaly, it provides in its chancellor a minister of the crown (as often as not in the cabinet) who is free from departmental burdens and therefore can be assigned to special tasks. As the chief officer of the D. the chancellor was usually closely connected with the royal household in the 15th century, and in the 16th century became almost one of the chief officers of state. Thus when the cabinet and ministerial system developed the chancellor of the D. found his natural place in it.

The chancellor presides over the D. council. Although the council is now only advisory and comprises some non-official members, for centuries it was composed of the principal officers and, like other councils of the sort, it was at once advisory, executive and judicial. Known in its judicial capacity as the Court of D. Chamber, it administered an EQUITY jurisdiction with procedure similar to that of the High Court of CHANCERY, but limited to matters arising on D. lands and LIBERTIES. This was extensive enough, and in the 16th and 17th centuries the court was at its busiest; it declined with the contraction of the D. itself.

The D.'s interests at one time lay in every county in England and in several in Wales, but Lancashire requires a special mention. This county palatine is part of the D., and in it the dukes of L. had royal powers on the model of Chester. These descended to the D.; administration of justice in the county was therefore largely the D. concern; an attenuated jurisdiction still survives.

R. Somerville, *History of the D. of L.* (1953.)   RS

Lancastrians. (1) The kings of the house of Lancaster, i.e. Henry IV (1399–1413), his son Henry V (1413–22) and his grandson Henry VI (1422–71) who, however, after his DEPOSITION by Edward IV, of the house of York, in 1461, only briefly regained the throne during the 'READEPTION' of 1470–1. Henry's son Edward, Prince of Wales, the last of the legitimate line of Lancaster, was killed at the battle of TEWKESBURY in 1471.

(2) The Lancastrian party in the wars of the ROSES, i.e. the supporters of Henry VI and his son Edward, and later of Henry Tudor, earl of Richmond, who gained the throne as Henry VII in 1485, against the YORKISTS.

(3) Sometimes applied to the followers of Thomas, earl of Lancaster (†1322), under Edward II, and of John of Gaunt, duke of Lancaster (†1399), under Edward III and

Richard II. (See LORDS ORDAINERS; DEPOSITION OF RICHARD II.)   RFW

Land Acts, Irish. During the 19th century the agrarian problem in Ireland, characterized by divided holdings, absentee landlords, lack of tenant right, evictions, reprisals and coercion, grew more acute. Attempts to pass legislation protecting the tenants foundered chiefly on a general ignorance of Irish conditions. The first effective measure was Gladstone's Land Act of 1870, which provided for compensations for eviction as well as for improvements by tenants, and recognized the tenant right system of Ulster and similar customs elsewhere. But there was no compensation for eviction due to failure to pay rent, and no security of tenure. Increased evictions owing to tenants being unable to pay rent at a time of bad harvests and agricultural depression led to the formation of the LAND LEAGUE in 1879 and renewed terrorism, including the 'BOYCOTT'. A Coercion Act was followed by Gladstone's second Land Act of 1881, which gave tenants the 'three F's'— Fixity of Tenure, Fair Rents and Free Sale of the interest in their holdings. Land courts were established for adjudication.

In 1885, a solution of the land problem was found. The Ashbourne Act advanced £5m. to facilitate tenant purchase of land—the landlord being paid in Consols an average of 17½ times the rent. The amount was raised by £5m. in 1888 and by £33m. in 1891 (with amended terms of repayment); but by 1902 only 74,000 tenant-owners had been created. Finally, the movement towards universal peasant-proprietorship was speeded by George Wyndham's Land Act of 1903, which offered a bonus to landlords to sell entire estates, landlords being paid in cash, tenants paying interest at 3¼% over 68 years. The system worked satisfactorily until 1932 when De Valera's Irish Free State government withheld these 'annuities' (amounting to about £3m. a year). The British government imposed a tariff on imports from Ireland, and in 1938 the Irish government paid £10m. in settlement of all claims.

MLH

Landavensis, Liber, a MS. mostly in Latin and partly in Welsh, compiled at Llandaff probably in the third quarter of the 12th century, contains chiefly lives of saints associated with Llandaff and grants made to them. Acute controversy exists concerning its authenticity and purpose.   GW

Land League, Irish, was formed in Oct. 1879 by Michael Davitt, a socialist Fenian, its ultimate object being the overthrow of 'landlordism'; Parnell was president. 'Proclaimed' in 1881, it was renewed as the National League (1882), and, being responsible for the 'plan of campaign' (1886), was again 'proclaimed'. The L.L.'s importance is that it coupled solution of the land problem to the achievement of HOME RULE. The L.L.'s activities were investigated by the PARNELL COMMISSION.   MLH

Land Registry. Though Acts of 1535 and 1563 attempted to enforce registration of certain deeds, they were evaded: registries for local deeds were established in Yorkshire from 1704 onwards and in Middlesex in 1708, but the extension of registration to other parts of the country was slow. The L.R. was founded under an Act of 1867, with power to issue, for convenience, registered titles acceptable in a court without ancillary proof, on evidence normally acceptable to CHANCERY; but comparatively few titles were so registered, and in 1897 compulsory registration was introduced, in such areas as the Privy Council should ordain. Modern registration at the central and district registries is governed by an Act of 1925. (See also ENROLMENT.)   PMB

Land Revenue, Auditors of. In 1554 the Auditors of the Exchequer took over the work of the Court of AUGMENTATIONS and were known as A. of L. R., auditing the accounts of receivers, SHERIFFS, ESCHEATORS etc., and later of land and other taxes, also enrolling grants and leases of crown lands. The ancient revenues of the crown fluctuated and then steadily declined. An Act of 1799 allowed the offices to lapse on the death of the then holders: the last office was finally abolished in 1832 and the auditors' functions divided between the Audit Commissioners and the office of Land Revenue Enrolments and Records.

PMB

Lands Commissioners, see TITHE REDEMPTION COMMISSION.

Land Tax, the oldest surviving direct tax, deriving from the monthly assessments of the INTERREGNUM; it continued after the RESTORATION, being replaced by a tax on real estate and personal property in 1692. Difficulties of assessment made it a L.T. only fixed on 1692 valuations and varying from 1s. to 4s. in the £. It did much to finance the 18th-century wars but was unpopular with the gentry. Walpole kept it as low as possible and hoped to abolish it through his EXCISE BILL (1733). In 1798 Pitt fixed it at 4s. and promoted a scheme for its redemption, and many landowners took the opportunity provided. New taxes on unearned increment of land values were introduced by Lloyd George (1909) but discontinued in 1920.   IHE

Langport, battle of, near Bridgwater (10 July 1645), enabled the Parliamentarians to continue their subjugation of Somersetshire.   IHE

Langside, battle of (13 May 1568). After the marriage between Mary Queen of Scots and the earl of Bothwell the nobles rose under the earl of Moray. Mary was defeated and confined in Lochleven Castle and induced to abdicate. She escaped and was joined by her Catholic supporters but routed by Regent Moray at L. near Glasgow. She fled to Cumberland (17 May) and was subsequently removed to Bolton Castle.   IHE

La Rochelle, naval battle off (June 1372), one of the worst English defeats in the HUNDRED YEARS' WAR. A fleet of armed merchantmen carrying reinforcements to AQUITAINE was intercepted by Castilian galleys and virtually destroyed, the commander, the earl of Pembroke, and many other leaders being captured. The victory demonstrated the superiority of well-handled galleys over the sailing ships of the period, given favourable conditions. It was a direct consequence of the failure of English policies in the Iberian peninsula, which had produced the Franco-Castilian alliance, and was the prelude to England's temporary loss of control of the Channel.   RFW

La Rochelle Expeditions (1627–8). Charles I's attempts to mediate between Louis XIII of France and the HUGUENOTS, personal issues and maritime disputes resulted in a drift to war. In 1627 Buckingham led an unsuccessful expedition to seize the island of Rhé, off La Rochelle, as a base from which to help the Huguenots and attack enemy shipping. In May 1628 Denbigh failed to relieve La Rochelle and Buckingham was murdered at Portsmouth before the third unsuccessful expedition sailed (Aug.). La Rochelle capitulated (Oct.) and peace was made with France in 1629.   IHE

Lastage, a duty, possibly of Anglo-Saxon origin, on goods exported from the country, assessed on the last or load, e.g. 10 sacks of wool made a last. Though collected for many centuries, l. was overshadowed from the later 13th century onwards by national customs.   PMB

Lathe, the primitive unit of local government and taxation in KENT, where there were six (cf. PROVINCIA). It later became an intermediate unit between SHIRE and HUNDRED, and although it lost many of its functions to the latter, it long remained the main assessment area for taxation in this county (GELD).   CFS

Latin. At the Norman conquest the language common to educated Englishmen and Normans was L., which became the language of government,

courts and diplomacy. A vast proportion of English governmental and private documents down to the Tudor period are in L., witnessing the conservatism of government and law against the VERNACULAR, and the vested interests of professional clerks, scriveners etc. Parliament abolished the use of L. for governmental records in 1651: it was revived at the RESTORATION, to be finally abolished in 1733, lingering only rarely, e.g. in names of judicial processes.   PMB

Latitudinarians, a name applied from the mid-17th century to those favouring latitude of thought, belief and practice in religion. They were given preferment by George I and George II and their Whig ministers to weaken the High Church party (BANGORIAN CONTROVERSY). Their attacks on the Creeds, confirmation and episcopacy, their indifference and opportunism encouraged laxity in all forms but favoured ideas of toleration and in many ways reduced the church to a department of government. Latitudinarianism was checked by the rise of the EVANGELICALS and further weakened by the OXFORD MOVEMENT. It became the theological liberalism of the 19th century.   IHE

Laudabiliter, a papal bull probably granted by the English Pope Adrian IV to Henry II in 1155 but not acted upon until 1171–2. Neither the original bull nor Pope Alexander III's confirmation (1172) have survived, and the text was preserved only by Giraldus Cambrensis. Long questioned, the authenticity of L. is now generally accepted. Henry was encouraged to proceed with his plan for the conquest of IRELAND, on condition that he preserved the rights of the Irish church and secured the payment of PETER'S PENCE from Ireland. The papacy's principal interest was to secure reform of the Irish church by forging closer connexions with England and Rome.   RFW

Laudians refers to the supporters in the Anglican church of the ideas and policies of William Laud (bishop of

London 1628, archbishop of Canterbury 1633–45). As ARMINIANS they strove to introduce discipline and uniformity of worship according to the Prayer Book, emphasizing the Catholicism of the church and the use of vestments and ceremonial. To the Puritan they seemed bent on eliminating the Protestant character of the church. They supported the suppression of Puritan preaching and pamphleteering and used the law and prerogative courts to secure enforcement. They supported the royal supremacy, and the attempt to Anglicize the Scottish Church (1633–8) led to the BISHOPS' WARS and their own eclipse.   IHE

Lawman, see MOOT.

Law Terms. The names, Michaelmas, Hilary, Easter and Trinity, derive from the first day of business in each term fixed, in the medieval manner, by religious festivals, e.g. Michaelmas term began on the octave, seven days, after Michaelmas (29 Sept.). The length of the term was variously determined: Michaelmas term ended at Advent, for the church forbade the necessary oaths from Advent to the octave of Epiphany; Hilary term was closed by a similar ban from Septuagesima to 14 days after Easter, and Easter term by a ban on the successive religious festivals from Ascension to Corpus Christi. The Trinity term, however, was brought to an end by fear of sickness in the summer in towns, by the harvest and by annual accounts. The old terms were abolished in 1873: sitings, retaining the old names, are now fixed by rule of the Supreme Court of JUDICATURE.   PMB

League of Nations (1920–46), an association of independent states for the maintenance of peace and security, was suggested by the American President Woodrow Wilson in 1916. Its statute, largely the work of Lord Phillimore (1845–1929), was incorporated in the peace treaties of 1919–20; the L. of N. became operative on 16 Jan. 1920, with its seat at Geneva.

The United Kingdom and all members of the British Empire and Commonwealth were among the original members, and Sir Eric Drummond (16th earl of Perth, 1876–1952) was its first secretary-general (1919–32). Owing to the refusal of the U.S.A. to join the L. of N., the belated admission of Germany (1926) and the Soviet Union (1934), numerous withdrawals (Brazil 1928, Japan and Germany 1933, Italy 1937, etc.) and the expulsion of the Soviet Union (1940) the L. of N. was at no time fully representative of the comity of nations. Its failure to stop the invasion of China by Japan (1931) and of Ethiopia by Italy (1935) and to take any decisive steps towards disarmament showed its impotence in fulfilling its main objective, the preservation of peace, even before Hitler started the second world war. On the other hand, the functional agencies and organizations created by the L. of N. did much useful work: the International Labour Organization, the International Court of Justice, the supervision of the MANDATED TERRITORIES, assistance to refugees, technical and cultural co-operation, etc. In April 1946 the L. of N. dissolved itself and transferred its functions and assets to the UNITED NATIONS.   SHS

Leake, treaty of (9 Aug. 1318), an agreement between Thomas, earl of Lancaster, and representatives of the MIDDLE PARTY, provided for the reconciliation of Lancaster and his followers with King Edward II, the maintenance of the ORDINANCES of 1311 and in particular the formation of a standing council, on which Lancaster was to be represented by a knight banneret of his choice. The king was not to exercise his powers without the consent of those members of the standing council who were in attendance. The treaty heralded a marked decline in the influence of Lancaster and a corresponding increase in that of the Middle Party.   RFW

Lease, a transaction giving the lessee the lessor's rights etc. in property for a period, without permanent alienation. In the early middle ages l.s were used both for agricultural lands and dwelling-houses and, by exacting capital before completion, as equivalents to mortgages: terms varied, for a fixed period of years or for the life of the lessee. L.s for lives were developed in the age of much building, the term depending on the life of the longest lived of persons named, often royalty: such l.s gave long-term security for capital expenditure without diminution of the lessor's estate.   PMB

Lecturers. Since the reign of Elizabeth I the bishops tried to restrain Puritan preachers, and Laud instituted a vigorous campaign against them. He especially attacked the use of IMPROPRIATIONS by which individuals and corporations maintained unbeneficed clergy to lecture after service had been read. A royal instruction was issued to the bishops in 1630 and from 1633 to 1637 the l. were suppressed.   IHE

Leet, a group of villages forming a subdivision of a HUNDRED in EAST ANGLIA. It was a unit of local government and was concerned with the collection of tax. In size l.s seem similar to the small hundreds of the DANELAW, but their origin is unknown. They were assessed for GELD payments in terms of pence instead of HIDES.
                                    CFS

Leeward Islands, consisting of ANTIGUA, ST KITTS, MONTSERRAT, the VIRGIN ISLANDS and DOMINICA, were separated from BARBADOS in 1681 and had its first federal legislature in 1705–11. The five presidencies were again federated in 1871, lost Dominica to the WINDWARD ISLANDS in 1940, joined (without the Virgin Islands) the West Indies federation in 1958 and were federated with the Windward Islands in 1960.   SHS

Le Goulet, treaty of (22 May 1200). After the death of Richard I in 1199 the succession to the various dominions of the ANGEVIN EMPIRE was disputed between his brother John, accepted in England, Normandy and Aquitaine, and his nephew Arthur, accepted in Brittany, Maine, Anjou and Touraine. Philip II of France originally supported Arthur, but by the treaty of Le G., on the Seine near Vernon, he accepted John as Richard's heir to all his French possessions and received his homage. John agreed to pay a feudal relief of 20,000 marks, and ceded important border districts of Normandy. Arthur was to rule in Brittany as John's vassal.   RFW

Lend-Lease agreement was a means by which the United States lent or leased arms and supplies to Britain and other countries during WORLD WAR II. Various conditions were attached but repayment in cash was not envisaged. The L.-L. Act passed Congress, 11 March 1941, when British Commonwealth reserves were almost exhausted. Between that date and the end of L.-L. (25 Aug. 1945) the U.K. received from the U.S. an estimated £5,049m. worth of materials while L.-L. to the U.S. amounted to an estimated £1,201. The loan agreement of Dec. 1945 provided for a credit of $650m. to cover goods 'in the pipeline' when L.-L. ended, installations, etc.   MLH

Leinster, see O'NEILL'S REVOLT; PLANTATION OF IRELAND.

Lesotho, kingdom of, established 4 Oct. 1966, the former BASUTOLAND. A state of emergency was proclaimed on 30 Jan. 1970.   IHE

Letters patent, see PATENT ROLLS, WRIT.

Levant Company. In 1581 London merchants, having obtained privileges from the sultan, established the joint-stock Turkey Company to develop the Levant trade. In 1583 the Venice Company was formed on a joint-stock basis to trade with Venice in sweet wines, oils and currants. They amalgamated as the L.C. in 1592. It became a regulated company in the

17th century, developing the Mediterranean trade with cloth as a staple export, but suffered setbacks from the DUTCH WARS, and from competition from the French, the EAST INDIA COMPANY and interlopers. It still traded in the 18th century, surrendering its charter only in 1825.   IHE

Levellers, the name given to the more extreme democrats of the CIVIL WAR and COMMONWEALTH period. Led by John Lilburne and others, they advocated republicanism, manhood suffrage, toleration, abolition of the House of Lords, etc. They dominated the ranks of the army (1647–9), were prominent among the AGITATORS and largely responsible for the AGREEMENT OF THE PEOPLE. Their distrust of Cromwell led to a mutiny (15 Nov. 1647) and, after trying to revive the council of the army, a more serious outbreak in May 1649. They were antagonistic towards the Commonwealth, which they considered little better than the monarchy, but after the suppression of Lilburne's activities in 1653 their influence declined.   IHE

Lewes, battle of (14 May 1264). As Simon de Montfort and Gilbert de Clare, earl of Gloucester, moved out of London, Henry III's army, which had taken Tonbridge castle and unsuccessfully tried to secure the CINQUE PORTS, fell back on L. Halting at Fletching, 9 miles to the north, the MONTFORTIANS offered peace, provided Henry III would maintain the PROVISIONS OF OXFORD with such modifications as might be negotiated. Henry replied with a formal defiance of the rebels, and on the night of 13 May the Montfortians moved to the down north-west of L. The royal army attacked on the morrow and was utterly defeated, despite the success of Edward, the king's son, against the Londoners opposed to him. Henry III, his brother Richard, Edward and the majority of the royalist nobles were eventually captured, and had to agree to the Mise of L. (See also FORMA REGIMINIS.)   RFW

Lewes, Mise of (15 May 1264), an agreement concluded between the MONTFORTIANS and royalists the day after the battle of L. Peace was proclaimed; royalist-held CASTLES were to be surrendered; Montfortians taken prisoner at NORTHAMPTON and many MARCHER LORDS and northerners on the king's side captured at L. were to be released. Tentative proposals for French arbitration were made in the hope of bringing all royalists into a general peace settlement.   RFW

Lexington, battle of (19 Apr. 1775). After the 1st Colonial Congress (1774) local American committees organized militia and began to store munitions. Governor Gage of Boston sent 700 troops to destroy military stores at Concord. On their way back they were met by some 50 militia men near L. A shot was fired and in the resulting skirmish eight Americans were killed. After this so-called battle the British were attacked all the way to Boston, losing many more men than their adversaries. This event precipitated the revolution.   IHE

Libel of English Policy, an anonymous English political poem, written 1436–8, at a critical point in the HUNDRED YEARS' WAR. The alliance of France and Burgundy by the treaty of ARRAS (1435) placed most of the continental shores of the narrow seas in hostile hands, but the royal navy built up by Henry V had been largely sold or scrapped after his death. Philip, Duke of Burgundy, banned the entry of English merchants and goods into the Low Countries, with severe effects on the English export trade in cloth and wool, and in 1436 unsuccessfully besieged CALAIS, the seat of the STAPLE. The L. (i.e. *libellus*, 'little book'), probably written by a protégé of Humphrey, Duke of Gloucester, captain of Calais and an inveterate enemy of Burgundy, strongly advocated a revival of sea power, which, with the safe keeping of Calais, would enable England to command the narrow seas, to control foreign sea-borne trade with the

Low Countries, and to suppress piracy;

Cheryshe marchandyse, kepe thamyralte,
That we bee maysteres of the narowe see.

Very well informed of the details of European maritime commerce, the writer argued that English blockade, and especially the cutting off of supplies of wool to the Low Countries, would force Burgundy to make peace. By implication the L. did not favour the determined prosecution of the land war in France: resources would be better employed in restoring English authority in Ireland, which could be valuable to England economically and strategically.

Of foreigners in general, and Flemings in particular, the L. expressed a lively hatred, while foreign merchants, especially Italians, whose English trade was booming during the Burgundian embargo, aroused its envy and resentment. It alleged that the Italians' dexterous use of credit and exchange facilities enabled them to make undue profits in the English export trade; their imports were mainly unnecessary luxuries, and their bribes influenced government policy; their activities should therefore be severely restricted. In fact, Italian imports and enterprise played an important part in the development of the cloth industry, and English merchants benefited by their use of international financial machinery set up by the Italians.

The L. failed to change the policy of the English council, which concentrated its limited resources on retaining Normandy. Calais was neglected, the navy was not revived and the keeping of the seas was left to private enterprise. English trade, however, and particularly the import of wool for the Flemish cloth industry, proved indispensable to the Low Countries, and in 1439 Duke Philip had to raise the ban, which was already being widely evaded. Well known in its own day, though not acted upon, the L. continued to command the interest of naval historians and advocates of sea power—e.g. Richard Hakluyt, who

printed it in his *Principall Navigations,* John Selden and Samuel Pepys, who possessed a MS.—largely because its essential message did not lose its relevance:

Kepe than the see, that is the wall of
*   Englond,*
And than is Englond kepte by Goddes
*   hond.*
The Libelle of Englyshe Polycye,

ed. Sir George Warner (1926)   RFW

Liberal Party. The term L. was first applied, after the French Revolutionary wars, to the more advanced groups of WHIGS and came into creditable use after the REFORM ACT (1832). Gladstone headed the first administration (1868–74) generally called L., imposing a semblance of unity upon Whig aristocrats, Peelite CONSERVATIVES and RADICALS; important legislation included CHURCH OF IRELAND disestablishment, EDUCATION and Irish LAND ACTS, the BALLOT ACT and a Supreme Court of JUDICATURE Act. In his second ministry (1880–5), formed after the MIDLOTHIAN CAMPAIGN, Gladstone had to contend with discontent from the under-represented Radicals under Joseph Chamberlain and Irish obstruction as well as Conservative FOURTH PARTY opposition. The record in foreign affairs (first SOUTH AFRICAN WAR; EGYPT) was dismal; at home, the most important measure was the third Reform Act (1884). Gladstone's third ministry ended when 93 Liberals voted down his HOME RULE bill. Complete split of the L.P. was shown at the subsequent election when 78 L.Unionists were returned. These dissidents, led by Chamberlain and Hartington, allied with the Conservatives; they included the remnants of the Whigs. The loss of Chamberlain and the radical unionists cost the L.P. the working-class vote. Reluctance to adopt working-class candidates and policies led to the formation of a separate LABOUR PARTY.

After the 1886 debacle the L.P. was out of office until 1905—except for the period 1892–5 when Gladstone again

attempted Home Rule, retired and
was succeeded by Rosebery. Disagreements on the second SOUTH
AFRICAN WAR seemed to presage a
further split but the L.P. united
against Chamberlain's tariff proposals
and triumphed in the 1906 election,
gaining 377 seats. The last L. governments under Campbell-Bannerman
(1905–8) and Asquith (1908–15) were
responsible for the PARLIAMENT ACT
of 1911 and social legislation including
old-age pensions and health insurance.
But the period also saw Britain's
involvement in Europe (ENTENTE
CORDIALE) and entry into WORLD WAR I.
The replacement, in 1916, of Asquith
(who had headed a coalition government since 1915) by Lloyd George
caused a further split in the L.P.; this
was confirmed by the COUPON ELEC-
TION (1918). L. decline continued in
the election of 1922, in which the
Labour Party ousted the L.P. as
official opposition. The minority
Labour governments of 1923 and 1929
held office with L.P. support; in 1929
the L.P., once more united (1927) and
with a good programme, could muster
only 60 M.P.s. A final disastrous
split came in Oct. 1931 when the L.
National Party was formed shortly
before the election of that month;
under Sir John (Lord) Simon it was
pledged to full support of Mac-
Donald's national government and
gained 33 M.P.s as against the L.P.'s
35. The latter, under Sir H. (Lord)
Samuel, not being able to stomach
permanent protection, withdrew from
the national government in 1932.

The L.P.'s membership in the
Commons varied from 12 in 1945 to,
9 in 1950, 6 in 1951, 1955 and 1959,
9 in 1964 and 12 in 1966. In 1964 it
mustered over 3m. votes (11.2%).
The L. National Party (now National L.
Party) has remained in close agreement
with the Conservative Party.   MLH

Liberal Unionists, see CONSERVA-
TIVE PARTY; LIBERAL PARTY.

Liberties, areas with freedom, generally by royal grant, from royal officials
and jurisdictions, in part or in whole,
embracing a wide range from manorial
lords entitled to hold certain pleas to
the quasi-royal holders of palatinates.
Creation of l., begun before the Norman conquest and briefly expanded
thereafter, arose partly to honour the
recipient, partly from necessity, e.g.
the PALATINATE of Durham to guard the
Scots border. The Welsh MARCHER
LORDS claimed their l. not of the crown
but by right of conquest as heirs of the
Welsh princes, to which the crown at
first acquiesced. L., particularly the
greater, displeased stronger kings as
breeding grounds of disaffection as
well as inconveniences to government
and justice. In the 12th and early 13th
centuries some judicial encroachments
were made: in Edward I's time the
greater l.' power was attacked by the
QUO WARRANTO proceedings and the
attempt to curb the Marchers, but was
not broken. At this period, however,
new l. were created, both in the royal
principalities of Wales and in the increase of burghal independence.
These and many lesser, often usurped,
l. long survived. The greater l., such
as the right of SANCTUARY, sources of
disruption in the 15th century, were
diminished by the Tudors after 1534;
the boroughs were attacked for
political reasons in Charles II's reign
and reformed in the 19th century; the
lesser l. fell into decay or had their
privileges steadily whittled away; the
palatinates and principalities were
firmly attached to the crown, that of
LANCASTER alone preserving its independent existence.   PMB

Licence, a permission, generally in
return for a payment, for a transaction
otherwise forbidden by custom or
statute. Royal l.s have three principal
but inter-acting purposes: first and
earliest to control, e.g. to alienate in
perpetuity, later to import; second to
register, e.g. marriage licences; third,
and of increasing importance, to raise
revenue, e.g. road fund licences. PMB

Licensing Act (1662), following upon
the Act of UNIFORMITY, established
a press censorship in the interests of
ecclesiastical conformity. PRINTING
was restricted to London, York,
Oxford and Cambridge, and the

number of master printers was limited. Books licensed by the appropriate civil or ecclesiastical censor were to be registered by the Stationers' Company. Initially for two years, the act was not renewed after 1695 and was in abeyance 1679–85, but publications, especially political writings, were subject to a severe law of libel.   IHE

Life peerage, comprises: (i) the lords of appeal, eminent lawyers who have taken over the judicial functions of the house of lords as the ultimate court of appeal (under the Appellate Jurisdiction Act, 1876); (ii) peers and, for the first time in parliamentary history, peeresses created under the L.P.s Act, 1958.   SHS

Limerick, treaty of (3 Oct. 1691), ended the Williamite war in Ireland. The supporters of James II were allowed to quit the country or take an oath of ALLEGIANCE to William and Mary and receive complete amnesty. Roman Catholics were to retain such privileges 'consistent with the laws of Ireland' that they had held under Charles II. The treaty was to be confirmed by the Irish Parliament, but its spirit was broken by the subsequent introduction of a new PENAL CODE for Catholics.   IHE

Lincoln, battles of, (1) (2 Feb. 1141). While besieging L. castle, which had been seized by Ranulf, earl of Chester, late in 1140, King Stephen gave battle to a relieving army led by the earls of Gloucester and Chester and other supporters of the empress Maud. The royalists were defeated; Stephen himself was captured and taken to Bristol. This was for Stephen the most critical phase of the ANARCHY, but by the time he was released in exchange for the earl of Gloucester, captured in Sept. 1141 in the 'rout of WINCHESTER', the royalists had largely re-established their position.

(2) (20 May 1217). While Prince Louis of France besieged DOVER, his baronial allies operated in the Midlands, undertaking the siege of L. castle. The royalist army under William Marshal, earl of Pembroke, on 20 May reinforced the garrison and broke into the city. In a street battle the French and baronial army was completely defeated, some 300 knights being captured. The victory, which caused Louis to give up the siege of Dover and induced many barons to change sides, was a most important step towards the peace treaty of KINGSTON-ON-THAMES.   RFW

Lincoln, Parliament of (1316), see ORDAINERS.

Lincolnshire Rebellion (Mar. 1470), followed a small-scale disturbance in L., which made Edward IV imprison the Lancastrian Lord Welles (already involved in the risings of 1469), and was led by Lord Welles' son, Sir Robert. Ostensibly caused by royal exactions in the shire, it was probably a mainly Lancastrian movement, although the earl of Warwick and his faction within the Yorkist party may have been secretly in league with the rebels. After defeating the rebels at LOSE-COAT FIELD, Edward IV denounced Warwick for complicity in the rising. Failing to muster support in England, the earl fled to France and openly allied himself with Henry VI's exiled queen, Margaret of Anjou, bringing about the READEPTION of Henry VI.   RFW

Lindisfarne, a small island off the coast of NORTHUMBRIA. In about 634 Aidan (†651), the leader of the Scottish mission to Northumbria, established a monastery there. From here Northumbria and other English kingdoms were converted to Christianity. The situation of the island and the outlook of the SCOTTISH CHURCH gave the community there a harshly ascetic existence. The most famous member of the community was St Cuthbert (died 687). In 793 L. was sacked by VIKING raiders, and in 875 fear of Danish attacks led the monks to flee with the coffined body of St Cuthbert. After more than a century of wandering the community was re-established at Durham. The body of St Cuthbert was accompanied by the most famous of Old English manuscripts, the L. Gospels.　　CFS

Lindsey, a kingdom of the ANGLES, occupying Lincolnshire north of the river Witham, came into being early in the 6th century. The first element of the name is British, but nothing more is suggested of the relations between invaders and natives. Its history is very obscure, for although the names of its kings are known, it was under the control of either MERCIA or NORTHUMBRIA until the later 7th century, when it passed to permanent Mercian control. Its last recorded king occurs at the end of the 8th century, and at the end of the 9th century it was settled by a Danish army (DANES) that divided it into three RIDINGS. It was converted to Christianity by Paulinus early in the 7th century, and the bishopric established there disappeared at the time of the 9th-century Danish invasion.　　CFS

Linen Industry existed in medieval England and was widespread as a home industry in Tudor times. Attempts were made to encourage production in the 17th century, and HUGUENOT immigrants developed the manufacture of fine linen in Charles II's reign, but by the mid-18th century production only partially met home demands. Cotton-spinning machines were first adapted to a linen thread in Scotland in the 1790s and power-driven mills were established in England and Scotland from the 1830s. In Ireland the l.i. was first encouraged by Strafford from 1635 and was further stimulated at the end of the century by Huguenot immigration and by free admittance to England in compensation for the restrictions on Irish woollens. After the mid-19th century the l.i. became mainly concentrated in Northern Ireland with a substantial export trade.　　IHE

Livery and Maintenance. L. (Lat. *liberatio*) had the general meaning of 'pay' in the middle ages. As the pay received by a lord's retainers frequently included cloth or robes, the term came to be applied particularly to the distinctive, uniform clothing in the colours supplied by a lord to his household servants, military retainers etc., often together with his badge. M., unlawfully supporting by words or actions the law suit of another person, became closely associated with l. in the late-medieval 'BASTARD FEUDALISM'. It was part of a lord's feudal responsibilities to support his own tenants and servants in court, but from the mid-13th century lords were extending their support and protection to others. With the development of the system of retaining by indenture and the growth of lords' 'affinities' in the 14th and 15th centuries, such protection became part of the benefits of 'good lordship' which a wide circle of retainers and other adherents might expect, and it frequently amounted to m. Judges, jurors, witnesses, counsel or opposing parties might be bribed, intimidated or kidnapped, or court sessions might be prevented or broken up by violence, and liveried retainers played a prominent part both as the recipients and the agents of m. Legislation attempted to deal with the concomitant evils of retaining, notably m. and disorder involving liveried retainers. The statute of l. and m. of 1390 was directed particularly against the keeping of short-term retainers, as opposed to retainers for life (who formed the essential cadres of lords' retinues in the national army), and it defined and restricted the social ranks who might retain or be retained, and give or receive l. The statute and its 15th-century successors proving ineffective, m., as part of the problem of the 'overmighty subject', remained to be tackled by the Tudors. The so-called Star Chamber Act of 1487 provided for the stricter enforcement of earlier legislation and the surer punishment of powerful offenders, and in 1504 the Act against Unlawful Retainers forbade the retaining of, or the giving of liveries and badges to, any but *bona fide* household servants and officers, and gave parliamentary sanction to judicial action by the council against offenders. With the king's licence, subjects might still enlist retainers to serve the king in war, and lords' retinues still had a place in the national army under Henry VIII. The abuses of the system of retaining lingered on, declining gradually and only disappearing with the achievement of a monopoly of armed force by the state.   RFW

Local Government, see COUNTY; HEALTH; HOUSING AND LOCAL GOVERNMENT; HUNDRED; JUSTICES OF THE PEACE; LATHE; MUNICIPAL CORPORATIONS; PARISH; POOR LAW; SHIRE.

Local Government and Regional Planning, Secretary of State for, was appointed in Oct. 1969 to superintend the Ministries of HOUSING AND LOCAL GOVERNMENT and TRANSPORT. In addition, he was made responsible for local government reform.   MR

Lollard Rising (1414). Sir John Oldcastle, Lord Cobham (b. 1387), a personal friend of Henry V when Prince of Wales, was suspected of heresy by 1410. He appears to have been in contact with John Hus and his followers in Bohemia, and may have been the recognized secular leader of the English LOLLARDS. Oldcastle retained Henry's favour until 1413, when his appearance before an ecclesiastical court left no doubt of his heretical opinions. Refusing to submit, he was excommunicated and imprisoned in the Tower but contrived to escape and was hidden by sympathizers in London. Oldcastle then organized a daring plot: London Lollards were to join provincial contingents outside the city, while Henry V and his brothers were to be captured on Twelfth Night 1414 at Eltham Palace by a band of Lollards disguised as mummers. The plans leaked out, however. Henry left Eltham hastily, the London rising was nipped in the bud, and although some parties of armed Lollards from the provinces reached a rendezvous in St Giles' Fields on the night of 9–10 Jan., they were met by Henry himself and speedily routed. There followed the hanging and burning of Lollard leaders captured in the fight, and a widespread hunt for rebels and their sympathizers. The principal provincial centres of the rising were Bristol, the Chilterns, Essex and the Midland towns, while urban craftsmen were prominent among the rebels. Oldcastle himself remained at large until 1417, when he was captured near Welshpool, and subsequently hanged and burned.   RFW

Lollards or Lollers, the name given to the followers of John Wyclif by about 1380, apparently derives from the Middle Dutch *lollaerd*, a mumbler. Wyclif, who had originally won distinction in the University of Oxford as a philosopher of the realist school, had turned his attention to theology by 1372, when he entered the royal service. Anti-clerical feeling in England was running high, and in his initial attacks on the worldliness of the clergy and in his assertions of the superiority of the secular over the ecclesiastical power Wyclif was sure of a sympathetic audience among the lay magnates and gained the favour and protection of John of Gaunt. As Wyclif turned increasingly to attacks upon orthodox doctrine, his radical views attracted the unfavourable attention of the papacy and the English hierarchy. Specially objectionable were his view that sinful priests could have no authority, his rejection of the doctrine of transubstantiation, his forbidding doctrine of predestination —of being 'foreknown' to God for salvation or damnation—and his demonstration that papal powers lacked scriptural justification. Although certain of Wyclif's tenets were condemned by the papacy in 1377 and by an English synod in 1382, and he was suspended from teaching at Oxford, he was never formally tried as a heretic—probably owing to John of Gaunt's protection—and died unmolested as rector of Lutterworth (Leics.) in 1384.

Wyclif had gained a strong academic following in Oxford, but after vigorous action against his chief disciples by Archbishop Courtenay in 1382 the university ceased to be the centre of the Lollard movement. Oxford followers of Wyclif, notably Nicholas Hereford and John Aston, were, however, responsible for spreading Lollardy outside the university, and winning converts who in turn evangelized new areas. Groups of L. were established in the towns of the midlands and south—at Leicester, Coventry, Northampton and Bristol, for instance—and in rural areas of the west midlands. Recruits came mainly from urban tradesmen and craftsmen and the poorer clergy, but comparatively few gentry joined the sect despite the prevalence of anti-clericalism. With the accession of the LANCASTRIAN dynasty there came sterner measures against heresy, notably the statute DE HERETICO COMBURENDO in 1401. The LOLLARD RISING of 1414 was a failure, but it demonstrated that Lollardy had spread widely and had gained some degree of organization. Though there were sporadic outbreaks of violence later in the 15th century, Lollardy disappeared as a significant political movement after 1414. There is ample evidence, however, of its survival as a dissenting religious movement and of its continued spread. Fifteenth-century Lollardy was a somewhat diluted version of Wyclif's difficult doctrines: it was characterized particularly by rejection of transubstantiation, equation of the papacy with Anti-Christ, rejection of some or all of the sacraments, anti-clericalism, 'Puritanism' and Bible reading. Radical doctrines amounting to social revolution were probably confined to a fringe of extremists.

Wyclif had insisted on the importance of the scriptures, which should be made available for all men to read. The first complete English BIBLE was produced before Wyclif's death, possibly by Nicholas Hereford, and a second and much improved version which appeared c. 1396 is attributed to John Purvey, Wyclif's secretary. Despite the vigilance of the authorities, Lollard Bibles and tracts continued in circulation in manuscript, and the latter were eagerly printed by 16th-century Protestant propagandists. Evidence shows that Lollardy continued to survive in the early 16th century, especially in the towns, and that it was still spreading to new areas—East Anglia, Yorkshire, even Scotland—nourished by preachers and occasionally protected by the gentry. Though always a minority movement, Lollardy popularized beliefs and practices—especially reading the Bible in English—which provided a direct link with the REFORMATION, and 16th-century Protestants came to claim Lollard teachers and martyrs as their own. Since the teachings of Wyclif were more radical than those of the Henrician reformers, Lollardy may be regarded rather as the forerunner of English Nonconformity. RFW

Lombards, see ITALIAN BANKERS.

London Company founded the first permanent English settlement in America. James I issued a patent (Apr. 1606) establishing a Royal Council for Virginia to superintend the colonization of the American coastline between latitudes 34° and 45° N. Two companies were formed from London and Plymouth groups. The L.C.'s concession lay between 34° and 41° N., and their first expedition entered Chesapeake Bay (May 1607) with 120 emigrants and founded Jamestown. The L.C. was newly chartered (23 May 1609) with more financial backing as the VIRGINIA COMPANY. IHE

London convention, see PRETORIA CONVENTION; SOUTH AFRICAN WARS; TRANSVAAL.

Londonderry, siege of (17 Apr.–30 July 1689). James II, having landed at Kinsale with French support, was joined by the Irish under Tyrconnel, moved on Ulster and besieged L. The siege lasted 105 days, but the boom laid across the river Foyle was broken by ships sent by Colonel Kirke, and the starving remnants of the garrison were relieved. This was followed by a victory for the Ulstermen at Newtown Butler (2 Aug.). IHE

Long Parliament (1 March–22 Dec. 1406), held in three sessions, covering 158 days. Two succession acts were passed, the second of which secured the right of daughters of an elder son to succeed to the throne before a younger son. Although Parliament repeatedly complained of the king's inability to crush the GLYN DŴR REBELLION and to protect English shipping against pirates and the French, the measures proposed were ineffective, and its financial aid to the crown was grudging and inadequate. Henry IV, seriously ill in 1406, had to accept the appointment of a continual council of 17, which was both to advise him and to regulate his appointment of officials until the next parliament met.   RFW

Long Parliament (3 Nov. 1640–16 Mar. 1660) was summoned after Charles I's defeat in the second BISHOPS' WAR. It secured the execution of Strafford (May 1641) and Laud (Jan. 1645), passed a bill against dissolution without its consent and a TRIENNIAL ACT. Its permanent achievements were the abolition of the courts of STAR CHAMBER and HIGH COMMISSION and the COUNCILS OF THE NORTH and Wales; and the condemnation of MONOPOLIES, SHIP-MONEY and the levying of TUNNAGE AND POUNDAGE without consent. It was divided over the abolition of EPISCOPACY, but passed the GRAND REMONSTRANCE (1641) and the MILITIA BILL (1642). After the rejection of its NINETEEN PROPOSITIONS and the beginning of war, Parliament, shorn of its royalist members, entered into the SOLEMN LEAGUE AND COVENANT (1643), established the COMMITTEE OF BOTH KINGDOMS and the WESTMINSTER ASSEMBLY. Mainly Presbyterian, its power was weakened by the failure of the UXBRIDGE NEGOTIATIONS and the formation of the NEW MODEL ARMY controlled by the INDEPENDENTS, who were further strengthened by fresh elections after NASEBY to fill vacant royalist seats. The army's seizure of the king from Parliament (1647), and the latter's negotiations with him in 1648, in spite of the VOTE OF NO ADDRESSES, led to PRIDE'S PURGE. The RUMP, after the king's execution (1649), established the COMMONWEALTH, but was dismissed by Cromwell (20 Apr. 1653). The rift between Richard Cromwell and the army led to the restoration of the Rump (7 May 1659), but it was expelled by Lambert (13 Oct.). Restored again (26 Dec.), Monck reinstated the excluded members, and it dissolved itself (16 Mar. 1660) after arranging for a CONVENTION PARLIAMENT.   IHE

Long Parliament (1661–79), see CAVALIER PARLIAMENT.

Lord Lieutenant (properly 'H.M.'s lieutenant of and in the county of . . .'), the sovereign's personal representative in a COUNTY. The Tudors made various experiments in decentralization, one the establishment of regional COUNCILS; another, more flexible, firmly tied to the central government and less expensive, in the appointment of L.s, whose main task was to control the county militia. Lord Russell's appointment in the west country 1539–40, after the PILGRIMAGE OF GRACE, was followed by other temporary appointments. In 1551 the system was made permanent and used with skill by Elizabeth I: her L.s, appointed over one or more counties, working with the aid of the JUSTICES OF THE PEACE and gentry to maintain order, were generally experienced Privy councillors, to be appointed or dismissed at will. From being an important agent of central government the L.L., often simultaneously the CUSTOS ROTULORUM, has now become a figure of local dignity.   PMB

Lords, House of, see PARLIAMENT.

Lose-coat Field, battle of (12 March 1470), near Empingham, Rutland; so called because the rebels, routed by Edward IV, threw off their coats in order to run away more quickly. Their leader, Sir Robert Welles, was, however, captured and beheaded, and the

LINCOLNSHIRE REBELLION was crushed.   RFW

Lostwithiel, surrender at (2 Sep. 1644). After CROPREDY BRIDGE Charles I followed Essex into Cornwall and surrounded his troops at L. The cavalry escaped to Plymouth, but the infantry surrendered. This defeat emphasized the need for reorganization of Parliament's armies which was effected by the NEW MODEL ARMY.
                                     IHE

Louviers, treaty of (15 Jan. 1196). After his release from captivity Richard I opened a campaign in Normandy in 1194 to win back recent losses to Philip II of France. By the t. of L. Richard recovered most of eastern Normandy, but not the Norman Vexin, and the war was renewed in 1198.   RFW

Lower Canada, see QUEBEC.

Luddite Riots (March 1811–Jan. 1813) were caused by acute distress owing to unemployment and reduction of wages in the textile industry at a time of wartime economic depression, the increase of food prices, the impossibility of lawful COMBINATION and obsolescent regulations concerning the fixing of wages and apprenticeship. Trouble started in Nottinghamshire, where disciplined bands (under a mythical 'King Ludd' or 'General Ludd') destroyed knitting-frames, cheap products from which had swamped the market. In Jan. 1812 outbreaks spread with the smashing of new machinery—cotton power-looms in Lancashire and Cheshire, woollen shearing-machines in the West Riding. With military aid the government followed a policy of severe repression, breaking of stocking-frames being made a capital offence. Further sporadic outbreaks occurred in 1816 and later.   MLH

Ludford (or **Ludlow**), **Rout of** (12–13 Oct. 1459). Although the forces of Richard, duke of York, and the earl of Salisbury succeeded in uniting after the latter's victory at BLORE HEATH, there was no general muster of YORK-

IST supporters, and, after advancing to Worcester, York had to fall back to Ludlow, followed by a superior LANCASTRIAN army. On 12 Oct. the two armies were divided by the R. Teme at Ludford, but overnight the Yorkists' morale collapsed, and their men deserted or fled. York himself was compelled to take refuge in Ireland.
                                     RFW

Lunacy, Master in. From the middle ages onwards the landed lunatic enjoyed the benevolent guardianship of the king and the law over the administration of his estates and the maintenance of himself and his family. Extents of his lands were made and returned into CHANCERY, which, through MASTERS of the Court, came to regulate the administration of such lands, etc. This work is now carried out by the Master, in the Court of Protection, and his staff.   PMB

Madhya Bharat was created a 'B-state' on 15 June 1948 through the merger of 25 princely MARATHA states, including GWALIOR and Indore (a British protectorate since 1818). On 1 Nov. 1956 it was merged in Madhya Pradesh.   SHS

Madhya Pradesh, see CENTRAL PROVINCES.

Mad Parliament, see OXFORD PARLIAMENT.

Madras was in 1639 leased by the ruler of Chandragiri to the EAST INDIA COMPANY, who built Fort St George, which soon superseded Masulipatam (1611) as the chief factory on the Coromandel coast and in 1653 became the seat of M. presidency. In 1746 the French stormed M. but had to relinquish it in 1749 under the peace of AACHEN (1748). The failure of the French to take M. in 1758–9 cost them their dominion in the Carnatic. The MYSORE wars (1766–99) and the corrupted government of the nawab of the Carnatic allowed the Company to bring under their control the whole area from the Northern Sarkars to Cape Comorin. The CHARTER ACT of 1793 subjected M. to the authority of the governor-general of BENGAL, but legislative and administrative independence was restored in 1861. In 1956 the Telugu-speaking northern districts were transferred to KERALA and Mysore, and the Malayalam-speaking Laccadive Islands were separated from M. as a centrally administered territory, while some districts of TRAVAN-CORE-Cochin were assigned to M., now a Tamil-speaking state called Tamil Nadu.   SHS

Maerdref, see COMMOTE; VILLEIN.

Mafeking, siege of (14 Oct. 1899–17 May 1900). At the outset of the SOUTH AFRICAN WAR the Boers invested Kimberley and M. on the western borders of the Orange Free State and Transvaal respectively. M. was held for seven months, by 1,300 men under the resourceful Colonel Baden-Powell. Kimberley was relieved in Feb. 1900 but M. only on 17 May. The siege of M. had been spotlighted by the press and news of the relief led to riotous celebrations in London and elsewhere (18–19 May), hence the word 'mafficking'. The military importance of the siege seems to have been exaggerated.   IHE

Magna Carta, the 'great charter' of liberties granted by King John, is dated 15 June 1215, though its final form was probably settled several days later. Literally a 'great charter', M.C. is a long document, drawn up in the most solemn form, embodying the concessions made by the king to the English church and all free men of the realm.

Although King John was in many ways an able ruler, his reign was a series of disasters. Far from accepting defeat, John devoted much of his energies and resources to the recovery of his lost possessions, making unprecedented financial and military demands upon an English baronage that had comparatively small interest in NORMANDY, lost to the French in 1204. John's difficulties were aggravated by the loss of Norman revenues and by the increasing cost of government and military operations in a period of rising prices. To secure greater revenues from England John exploited his rights as feudal overlord and, in addition to frequent feudal taxes, imposed the new taxes on MOVABLES. Substantial exactions from individuals to have justice or the king's favour swelled the already considerable profits of the king's courts. Despite growing opposition, John persisted in his efforts to recover the ANGEVIN EMPIRE until the decisive defeat of BOUVINES (1214) confirmed the verdict of 1204. By this time John had alienated a large part of the BARONAGE —about half of them eventually went into rebellion—and there had already been a series of incipient revolts. Royal exactions, John's extensions of royal powers and the stern efficiency of John's servants played their part, but John's bad personal relations with his barons were of particular importance. Of his many defects of character perhaps the most damaging were his incredible suspicion, even of his best servants, the capriciousness of his favour and the pitiless tenacity with which he pursued the objects of his hatred. Despite John's own indifference to religion and his long quarrel with the church which had culminated in the INTERDICT, his firmest ally after 1213 was the papacy; but, a few close adherents excepted, the king could command little support from the English church.

Before John's departure for his last French campaign baronial opposition was being organized by Archbishop Stephen Langton into a constitutional movement for the preservation of liberties formerly granted, especially by Henry I's CHARTER OF LIBERTIES. When, after the total collapse of his continental plans in 1214, John renewed his financial demands, the extremists of the baronial party resorted to force. Rejecting the suggestion of papal arbitration, in the spring of 1215 they mustered at Stamford, sent their formal defiance to the king and began operations against royal castles in the Midlands. In mid-May the rebels were able to enter

London, and at the end of the month Langton secured a truce which enabled negotiations to be resumed. While still proposing papal arbitration without success, John made the preliminary concession that he would not proceed against any baron except by due process of the law. Further efforts by moderates led by Langton finally brought John and his opponents together at RUNNYMEDE on 15 June and produced agreement on the terms incorporated in M.C.

Modern editors have divided the main body of M.C. into some 60 articles, opening with John's confirmation of the liberties of the English church. Many articles met the particular grievances of the baronial class arising from John's exploitation of their feudal obligations. For example, article 12 provided that no SCUTAGE or AIDS (except three) should be taken by the king without the counsel of his barons, and article 14 laid down the procedure by which the king might obtain such counsel. Article 2 fixed the amount of RELIEF to be paid by tenants-in-chief, while others aimed at restricting the king's abuse of his rights of WARDSHIP, marriage and ESCHEAT. Articles 15 and 60 provided that the concessions made by the king to his tenants-in-chief should also be made by the tenants-in-chief to their tenants. The feudal articles were distinctly conservative, their framers being concerned to define what the feudal law provided and to obtain John's acceptance of their definitions.

No attempt was made by the barons to destroy or even greatly to modify the machinery of royal government and of royal administration of justice. A number of articles sought to ensure, however, that it should be worked efficiently and fairly, and that the king himself should not act outside the law. Articles 17 and 18 provided that while COMMON PLEAS should be heard in one fixed place, the POSSESSORY ASSIZES of NOVEL DISSEISIN, MORT D'ANCESTOR and DARREIN PRESENTMENT should be taken locally and frequently. Articles 20–22 provided that AMERCEMENTS should be reasonable and proportion-

ate to the gravity of the offences. The most famous articles of all, 39, *No freeman shall be arrested or imprisoned or deprived of his freehold or outlawed or banished or in any way ruined, nor will we take or order action against him except by the lawful judgment of his equals and according to the law of the land*, and 40, *To no one will we sell, to no one will we refuse or delay right or justice* were more than statements of high principles, they were specific renunciations by John of his former unlawful actions. Several articles were designed to check the oppression of royal officers, notably the SHERIFFS: article 24, for example, forbade all royal officers to hold PLEAS OF THE CROWN—where they might be both accusers and judges. Three articles reducing the area of the royal FORESTS and regulating the administration of the forest law were later to be expanded into the separate charter of the FOREST. Though the baronial class derived most benefit from M.C., many of its concessions also favoured free tenants in general, while townsmen and merchants at least received a general confirmation of municipal liberties and freedom of movement for trading.

A group of articles sought to effect a reconciliation between John and his opponents: the king undertook to redress the grievances of individuals against whom he had proceeded without lawful judgment, and to do justice to Llywelyn and the Welsh and to Alexander II of Scots. It remained to ensure that John should honour his undertakings, and it was not enough that he should promise to dismiss his foreign mercenaries and their hated captains. An unprecedented provision, article 61, distinguished by the heading *concerning the security of peace*, authorized the barons to appoint a committee of 25 who, if John did not carry out his promises, should hear complaints and, if necessary, compel the king to observe the charter by seizing his castles and lands.

The reconciliation effected in June 1215 was short-lived. Not only were the barons understandably distrustful of John's intentions, but the more radical of them were not satisfied with the settlement. For his part, John was clearly not prepared to accept M.C. as permanently binding, and here he was backed by the papacy, whom he had further obliged by undertaking to go on crusade. By the time that Innocent III's condemnation of M.C. reached England in the autumn of 1215, however, the BARONS' WAR was already under way. Shorn of the provisions more obnoxious to the crown, M.C. was reissued by the regent, William Marshal, shortly after John's death in 1216, this time with papal approval, and helped to bring the civil war to an end in 1217, when it was again issued with modifications. Further revisions were made in 1225 by Henry III, and it was this version that came to be accounted first in the exclusive body of English statutes. In the 13th and 14th centuries M.C. remained of the greatest importance as a fundamental definition of the restrictions upon royal power accepted by the king, and the CONFIRMATION and extension of the charter were among the foremost objectives of constitutional movements. By the 15th century many of its provisions were obsolete, and by the end of the 16th century it was possible for Shakespeare to write a *King John* without even alluding to M.C. The constitutional upheavals in the 17th century brought M.C. a new, if unhistorical, celebrity. While its fame has justly survived, not the least service of modern historians to M.C. has been to restore its importance in its original setting.   RFW

Maharashtra, see BOMBAY.

Maine, (south of Normandy) conquered by the English in the 1420s, was ceded to France in 1445–8 after the military failures of the early 1440s during the HUNDRED YEARS' WAR. The English council, led by William de la Pole, earl of Suffolk, attempted to come to terms with the French, but in 1444 only gained a two years' truce and the betrothal of the young Henry VI to Margaret of Anjou, niece of Charles VII of France. Before

the couple were married, in 1445, Suffolk was induced to promise the surrender of the fortresses still held by the English in M.—a promise later confirmed by Henry VI in return for a further truce, but not generally disclosed in England. Suffolk delayed the surrender on various pretexts, but its completion in 1448 and the revelation of his undertaking swelled the rising tide of his unpopularity and contributed to his eventual disgrace and death in 1450.   RFW

Maine (U.S.A.) was part of the COUNCIL FOR NEW ENGLAND's territories confirmed to Sir Ferdinando Gorges in 1635 by royal proprietary grant. Thinly populated largely by woodcutters and fishermen, it was seized by MASSACHUSETTS in 1652. Early in Charles II's reign there was a short-lived attempt to set up a royal administration and in 1678 Massachusetts forestalled the king's attempts to obtain possession by buying out the Gorges' rights for £1,250. It formed part of the Dominion of NEW ENGLAND (1686–9) and was incorporated with Massachusetts from 1691 to 1820.   IHE

Main Plot (1603), a project of Lord Cobham's to overthrow James I in favour of his English-born cousin Arabella Stewart. Raleigh was aware of it, and there was some negotiation with Spanish agents. Cobham and Raleigh among others were condemned but reprieved. They were tried with the instigators of Watson's plot as though the two schemes were one. Hence the names M.P. and BYE PLOT.   IHE

Mainprise. In the middle ages persons accused of criminal acts were, with certain exceptions made more stringent by the statute of WESTMINSTER I, 1275, not kept in prison but released if mainpernors (Latin *manucaptores*) could be found to pledge their appearance in court: if the accused did not appear the mainpernors were amerced. The modern bail system, applicable to lesser criminal charges, wherein the pledge enters

H

into a recognizance which forfeits if the accused defaults, is a development of m. PMB

Maintenance, see LIVERY AND M.

Major-Generals. After PENRUD-DOCK'S RISING (Mar. 1655) Cromwell divided England and Wales into 10, later 11, areas under the control of M.G. placed in charge of the re-organized MILITIA. They collected the decimation tax on royalists for its upkeep, held the JUSTICES OF THE PEACE to their duties, exercised wide powers of police in the interests of public order and strengthened central government at the expense of the local gentry. They were withdrawn at the end of 1656. IHE

Majuba Hill, battle of (27 Feb. 1881), the culminating incident of the first SOUTH AFRICAN WAR. Major-general Sir George Colley on 26 Feb. 1881 occupied M.h. commanding the pass of Laing's Nek. His dispositions were bad, and at dawn the Boers under Joubert attacked and routed Colley's small force of 550, which sustained 280 casualties; Colley was killed. The psychological effect was far-reaching. General Sir Ian Hamilton of GAL-LIPOLI fame, who was wounded in the action, described it as 'a sort of BUN-KER HILL in Afrikander history'. MLH

Malacca was founded by Malays from SINGAPORE in 1253, occupied by the Portuguese in 1511, taken by the Dutch in 1641, captured by the British in 1795, returned to the Dutch in 1814 and ceded by them to the EAST INDIA COMPANY in 1825 in exchange for the settlement of Bencoolen in Sumatra. Administered as part of the STRAITS SETTLEMENTS, M. was joined to the Union (Federation) of MALAYA in 1946. SHS

Malawi. The name under which NYASALAND became independent in 1964. M. became a republic within the COMMONWEALTH on 6 July 1966 and is a one-party state. IHE

Malaya, Federation of, was con-stituted as the Union of M. on 1 Apr. 1946 and as the F. of M. on 1 Feb. 1948 by treaty between Great Britain and the nine rulers of the FEDERATED and UNFEDERATED MALAY STATES, to which the settlements of PENANG and MALACCA were joined. The F. of M. became a sovereign member state of the COMMONWEALTH on 31 Aug. 1957. Its constitution provides for a head of state (Yang di-Pertuan Agong) elected from among the rulers for a five-year period, and two houses of federal parliament. The federal capital is Kuala Lumpur (in Selangor). SHS

Malaysia, federation of, was in 1963 created an independent Common-wealth country by the merger of MALAYA, SINGAPORE, NORTH BORNEO (renamed Sabah) and SARAWAK. Singapore gained separate indepen-dence in 1965. SHS; IHE

Maldive Islands, a sultanate origin-ally tributary to the kings of CEYLON, became a British protectorate in 1887 and was granted complete indepen-dence in internal affairs in 1960. The M.I. left the COMMONWEALTH in 1965. SHS; IHE

Maldon, battle of (in Essex, Aug. 991). Englishmen under Byrhtnoth, EALDORMAN of ESSEX, were defeated by Danish raiders. Byrhtnoth was killed; a group of his THEGNS fought to the death long after hope of victory was gone. The battle was commemorated in the greatest of all late Old English poems. CFS

Maletolt (Norman-French 'bad toll'), unpopular levies in general, and in particular the new customs duties on wool, wool fells, etc., imposed 1294–7 and abolished by the CON-FIRMATION OF THE CHARTERS. PMB

Malignants and DELINQUENTS, the names given to Charles I's advisers and supporters by his opponents, especially after the second CIVIL WAR. IHE

Malplaquet, the most sanguinary battle of the SPANISH SUCCESSION WAR (11 Sept. 1709), was forced upon Marlborough and Prince Eugene by the French marshal Villars, who wanted to raise the siege of Mons. The frightful losses of the allies (24,000 out of less than 100,000 combatants) made it impossible to exploit their hard-won victory, but Mons surrendered on 20 Oct.   SHS

Malta, consisting of the islands of M., Gozo, Comino and Filfla, was held successively by Phoenicians, Greeks, Carthaginians, Romans (218 B.C.), Vandals, Ostrogoths, Byzantines, Arabs (870), Normans (1090) and their successors as kings of Sicily. Charles V gave it to the knights of St John in 1530 after their expulsion from Rhodes. The grand master, Jean de la Valette, in 1566 founded the capital, Valletta. Bonaparte on his way to Egypt annexed M. in 1797, but a popular rebellion against the French aided the British blockade, and M. surrendered in 1800. Its restoration to the order of St John as a Russian protectorate, stipulated by the treaty of AMIENS (1802), never took place, and the treaty of PARIS (1814) finally confirmed M. as a British possession. In recognition of the heroism of the Maltese during the second world war against almost uninterrupted German and Italian air-raids, M. was awarded the George Cross (17 Apr. 1942). The constitution of 1887 was repealed in 1903, the constitution of 1921 granting self-government was suspended in 1930 and abolished in 1936 because of the disturbing effects of Italian fascist propaganda. Self-government with ministerial responsibility was granted on 5 Sept. 1947. An attempt to integrate M. with the United Kingdom (approved by referendum in M. and by Parliament in London in 1956) proved abortive. In 1961 a new constitution was introduced and the island became the 'State of M.' This achieved full independence within the COMMONWEALTH on 21 Sept. 1964.   SHS; IHE

Man, Isle of, was occupied by Edwin of Northumbria (c. 625) and settled by VIKING raiders (c. 800), whose jarls ruled as dependants of the Norwegian kings of Dublin and, from

c. 1150, of Norway. It was acquired by Alexander III king of Scots by the treaty of Perth (2 July 1266), but came under English suzerainty in 1290 and finally in 1333. The lordship passed from the Montague earls of Salisbury (1333–93) to William Le Scrope earl of Wiltshire (1393–9), Henry Percy earl of Northumberland (1399–1405), the house of Stanley (1405–1736) and the Murray dukes of Atholl (1736–65) whom the English crown bought out by the Revesting Act (10 May 1765). The I. of M. was brought wholly under the crown in 1827, but does not form part of the United Kingdom. It is administered, under a governor, by the Court of TYNWALD.   SHS

Manchester School originated in meetings of the Manchester chamber of commerce (founded 1820). Its members were RADICALS and strong supporters of FREE TRADE, practical business men rather than economic theorists; they were generally advocates of a *laissez-faire* which included individualism, antagonism to empire, non-intervention in foreign affairs and the least possible state interference in commerce and industry. Led by Cobden and Bright, they formed the Anti-CORN LAW League.   MLH

Mandated territories, the former German colonies and parts of the Turkish empire which the Paris peace conference of 1919, at the suggestion of Jan Smuts, placed under the tutelage of the allied powers so as to avoid the charge of outright annexation (art. 22 of the LEAGUE OF NATIONS covenant). The 'A' m.t. were to attain full independence; the 'B' m.t. were to be administered as colonies; the 'C' m.t. were to be treated as integral territory of the mandatory power. Great Britain accepted Iraq and PALESTINE under category A, TANGANYIKA and parts of the CAMEROONS and TOGOLAND under category B and (together with Australia and New Zealand) NAURU under category C; as 'C' m.t. the German part of NEW GUINEA and other Pacific Islands was accepted by Australia, Western SAMOA by New

Zealand, and SOUTH WEST AFRICA by the Union of South Africa.

Iraq attained its independence in 1932, Jordan in 1946, Israel in 1948. Under the UNITED NATIONS charter the 'B' and 'C' m.t. were transformed into TRUST TERRITORIES; only the Union of South Africa refused to place South West Africa under trusteeship.

SHS

Manipur was conquered by BURMA in 1813 but regained its independence under British protection after the first Anglo-Burmese war in 1826. The murder of the chief commissioner, J. W. Quinton, and his staff by the ruler of M. in 1891 led to an administrative reorganization under a political agent. M. acceded to India on 15 Aug. 1947 and was taken over by the Indian government as a centrally administered territory on 15 Oct. 1949.

SHS

Manitoba, known as the Red River Settlement until 1870, formed part of the NORTH-WEST TERRITORIES. Its capital, Winnipeg (founded in 1783), was the most important trading centre of the North-West Company and the gateway to the west. The Red River rebellion (1869–70), a protest against the surrender of the HUDSON'S BAY COMPANY's rights to the Canadian government, was quickly suppressed, and M. entered CANADA as a province on 15 July 1870. Its boundary with ONTARIO was settled in 1884. SHS

Manor (Fr. *manoir*, Med. Lat. *manerium*), a term originally meaning 'a dwelling place', introduced into England after the NORMAN CONQUEST to describe both the m. house and the lands attached to it. In its simplest form a m. consisted of one village, having one lord. The lord had his m. house, and part of the estate was reserved for his maintenance—the DE-MESNE—and was worked for him by his unfree tenants, VILLEINS. Free tenants paid money rents or rents in kind for their lands and might owe relatively light labour services. However m.s varied almost infinitely in size and organization. They might

consist of only a part of a village, or of several villages, or of a number of scattered settlements. Some were compact, others made up of lands in different villages, perhaps in different counties. There might be demesne, and no villeins, or villeins and no demesne; villeins might not owe labour services but rents; even the m. house might be missing. Methods of land use differed from one area to another, and the m. was associated with the open-field system of agriculture only in certain parts of England. In brief, it is difficult to define a 'typical' m. Lords who possessed a number of m.s. would entrust the supervision of a particular m. or group of m.s to a steward. The work of a manorial estate would be directed by a bailiff, while the labour force would be under the orders of the REEVE, often himself a villein. A lord possessed a limited jurisdiction over his free tenants in the COURT BARON and wide powers over the unfree in the Customary Court, which dealt, *inter alia*, with breaches of the regulations of husbandry, tenurial matters and minor misdemeanours. Many lords possessed the privilege of holding half-yearly COURTS LEET which were regarded as royal courts, with jurisdiction delegated to the lord.

In addition to local variations the manorial system underwent many changes—in methods of land-use, in the ways lords exploited their demesnes, in the substitution of rents for labour services, and in the general decay of villeinage. Although these changes began in the early 14th century, their pattern, and the speed with which they came about, differed greatly from one part of the country to another. The last lingering survivals of the manorial system were abolished in 1926. RFW

Mansfield's judgment (1772), pronounced by the lord chief justice, earl of M. (1705–93), in the case of a fugitive negro slave, James Somersett; it stated that SLAVERY is not 'allowed or approved by the law of England'.

SHS

Manumission. VILLEINS could obtain freedom by purchase, through a third party since in theory they had no private funds, or by grant for services rendered. The solemn act of m. was done publicly, often in the COUNTY COURT, for it might be challenged: the lord quit-claimed his villein and gave him arms, the marks of a freeman. The act could be confirmed by charter or letters patent, e.g. as by the Black Prince in North Wales.   PMB

Maori, the Polynesian inhabitants of NEW ZEALAND, immigrated during the 10th–14th centuries from 'Hawaiki' (Society Islands?). A 'king movement' in the 1850s to 1870s tried in vain to unify the tribal organization. The MAORI WARS, on the whole, accelerated the integration of the M. in the political and economic life of New Zealand. In 1909 the first M. minister was appointed in a New Zealand cabinet. The M. population has risen from under 40,000 in 1890 to over 214,000 in 1968.   SHS

Maori wars broke out over the enforced sales of land in contravention of the treaty of WAITANGI. They lasted intermittently from 1845 to 1848 and from 1860 to 1872. The majority of the Maori remained friendly or neutral; the beaten tribes lost most of their lands. During the final stages of the war, a Native Land Court was set up (1865), a Maori school system was inaugurated (1867) and the Maori were granted four elected members in the NEW ZEALAND House of Representatives (1867).   SHS

Marathas, a warlike people in the Deccan, achieved national unity in their fight against the Mogul empire under the military and administrative genius, Shivagi (†1680). They were the paramount power in India from 1714 to 1761, including the later Rajputana, Central Provinces, Bombay, Orissa, Gwalior, Baroda, etc. The federated principalities were ruled by a Peshwa (prime minister), the dignity becoming hereditary in the family of Balaji Viswanath (†1720). The crushing defeat at the hands of the Afghans in the battle of Panipat (14 Jan. 1761) broke the power of the M. Internal dissensions among the Peshwa dynasty (1772–6) led to interference bv the British, whose first treaty with the M. (1739) had made possible the pacification of the coast between Bombay and Goa. The M. wars (1779–81, 1803–4, 1817–8) resulted in the complete subjugation of the M. empire and the abolition of the Peshwaship. The INDIAN NATIONAL CONGRESS was particularly strong and radical in the M. territories.   SHS

Marcher Lords. The first of them were powerful vassals placed by William I at Hereford, Shrewsbury and Chester. From these and other strongpoints Norman adventurers penetrated into all parts of Wales down to 1135. Checked by a national rising, 1094–8, and thrown back during the ANARCHY of 1135–54, they established a balance of power between themselves and the Welsh princes during Henry II's reign, by which a large part of south and east Wales remained in their hands. They enjoyed the regalian rights of the MARCHES and were prominent in baronial opposition to the crown as well as a check on the Welsh. Though Edward I after his Welsh conquests of 1282–3 had to increase their number, he also tried to limit their power. But under his weaker successors, and fortified by their participation in wars with France, they played a dominant role in English politics, especially during the wars of the ROSES. Greatly reduced in numbers and prestige, they were finally deprived of their peculiar privileges by the Act of UNION. GW

Marches of Wales are those areas in south and east Wales conquered by MARCHER LORDS between c. 1067 and 1283 which were removed from Welsh rule but not absorbed into the English realm until 1536. The M. were made up of individual lordships, won by conquest, whose boundaries were usually those of the previous Welsh COMMOTES. Taken over with the territory of the commote were its regalian, military, fiscal, administrative and judicial rights, which gave the marcher lordships their virtually independent character. Most lordships were divided into the low-lying ENGLISHRY, into which castles, boroughs, manors, feudal tenures, Anglo-Norman law and Latin-style monasteries were introduced, and the upland Welshry, where WELSH LAWS and customs prevailed and the inhabitants paid a communal rent and acknowledged only a shadowy overlordship. The economic difficulties of the 14th century, the civil wars of the 15th, and early Tudor policy brought all but four of the lordships into royal possession by 1521. Subjected to increasing control by means of the COUNCIL OF THE MARCHES, they were finally abolished in 1536 by the Act of UNION.   GW

Margate, naval battle off (24 March 1387), was won over a Franco-Spanish fleet by the earls of Arundel and Nottingham; nearly 100 ships were captured. The victory ended the threat of an invasion which Charles VII of France had been preparing since the spring of 1386. Arundel's subsequent successes in the Channel increased the popularity of the party led by the duke of Gloucester, Arundel's close associate, and opposed to Richard II and his friends.   RFW

Marian Exiles were the many protestant clergy and laymen who fled to the continent (1553–4) before the MARIAN REACTION began. The majority gathered in Frankfurt, Zurich and Geneva, where they produced the Geneva BIBLE. They returned in strength in 1559 to play a prominent part in the ELIZABETHAN SETTLEMENT.   IHE

Marian Reaction (1553–8). Queen Mary's chief purpose was to restore papal authority in England, and in 1553 the Act of UNIFORMITY was repealed and married clergy were ejected. In 1554 all anti-papal legislation since 1528 was repealed, the heresy and treason laws re-enacted, and a solemn reconciliation with Rome effected. Mary found it impossible to restore confiscated church lands in view of the solid opposition of the nobility and gentry. In 1555 the burning of Protestants was begun and some 300 perished, including Archbishop Cranmer. This persecution, together with the Spanish marriage, strengthened nationalist and anti-papal sentiment and defeated Mary's purposes.   IHE

Mark, a Danish monetary unit current in much of the DANELAW, was not an actual coin, but represented 128 silver pennies, i.e. 10s. 8d. It later became current as money of account over the whole country, its value rising to two-thirds of a POUND, i.e. 13s. 4d.   CFS

Marlborough, statute of (18 Nov. 1267), for the 'amelioration of the realm' after the BARONS' WAR, fostered by prince Edward, was the precursor of the outburst of legislation in his reign. Re-iterating the 1225 MAGNA CARTA and adopting many of the MONTFORTIANS' innovations, including some of the PROVISIONS OF WESTMINSTER, the statute introduced new legal procedures to safeguard feudal rights, curbed the reviewing powers of local courts and regulated replevin and DISTRESS.   PMB

Marprelate Tracts (1587–9), scurrilous, ribald and anonymous attacks on the bishops, were secretly printed and first distributed in London in 1587, commanding wide attention. They threatened to set up 'a young Martin' in every parish able to 'mar a prelate'. Disowned by moderate Puritans, they led to a severe CONVENTICLE ACT against the BROWNISTS and an act against seditious writings (1593). John Penry, the presumed chief author, was executed. The expulsion of French and Dutch typefounders, suspect of Calvinism, retarded English typefounding by about 150 years.   IHE

Marque, Letters of, licences granted at least from the 14th century to allow private ships to engage lawfully in naval warfare; similar licences were issued to take reprisals against foreign shipping for unredressed piracy. Since 1870 British subjects have been debarred from receiving l. of m.   PMB

Marquis (Medieval Latin *marchio*; Old French *markis*), originally a European title for the commander of a frontier area (march). Writers in England at times used it informally in that sense, e.g. in styling Brian fitz Count, during the ANARCHY, *marchio* of Wallingford. In the late 14th century it became a style of NOBILITY, the variant spelling marquess (now exclusively used) developing later. The spelling of the female style, marchioness, has remained closer to the Latin original.   CFS

Marriage Act, Hardwicke's (1753), was passed to prevent the clandestine marriage of minors and other abuses, especially of the kind associated with the Fleet district. Valid marriages must be held in the established church after the publication of banns or by special licence. Minors must obtain consent of parents or guardians. The act excepted the royal family, Jews and Quakers and did not apply to Scotland or the Channel Islands. An amendment of 1836 permitted marriage before a registrar or with religious rites other than Anglican.   IHE

Marshal was, with the CONSTABLE, a senior member of the royal household, responsible for regulating the household and its travelling arrangements, for keeping tallies, receipts etc. at the EXCHEQUER and, in wartime, keeping records of services performed and maintaining discipline. As the personal importance of the m. grew, two deputies were appointed, the m. of the Exchequer and the m. of the Household. In Henry I's reign the office belonged to the Marshal family, and in the 13th century passed to the Bigod earls of Norfolk: it has remained with the Norfolk earldom, and, later, dukedom, despite successive creations. The earl marshal's duties, apart from his presidency of the COLLEGE OF HERALDS, are now principally ceremonial.   PMB

Marshall Plan (1948–51) was a scheme, originated by the U.S. secretary of state, George C. Marshall, in a speech at Harvard University (5 June 1947), for assistance by the U.S.A. to European countries economically exhausted by the SECOND WORLD WAR. The European Recovery Programme, as it was formally known, came into existence 1 July 1948; 18 countries of Western Europe received large loans and grants apportioned by the Organization for European Economic Co-operation, the biggest share going to the U.K. Recovery of production being speedier than envisaged and the Korean War having cleared the European dollar deficit, the Plan ended 31 Dec. 1951 instead of six months later as previously envisaged, the U.K. having suspended receipt of aid 31 Dec. 1950. The M.P. was succeeded by the Mutual Security Programme.   MLH

Marshal Rebellion (1233–4) of a section of the English baronage against Henry III was led by Richard Marshal, earl of Pembroke, who allied with Llywelyn the Great and the Welsh. The rising was principally directed against the king's advisers, led by the Poitevins, Peter des Roches, bishop of Winchester, and Peter de Rivaux. Among its causes were hatred of foreigners and arbitrary government, and resentment at exclusion from the king's counsels. The civil war which broke out in Aug. 1233 was fought mainly in the Welsh Marches and in Ireland. In Wales the Marshal and his allies had much the better of the fighting, but in Ireland the royalists were victorious, and the Marshal himself was mortally wounded and captured on the Curragh of Kildare on 1 Apr. 1234. The peace settlement was largely the work of the English bishops, led by Edmund of Abingdon, archbishop of Canterbury. Henry III was reconciled with the Marshal family; the Poitevins and their English associates were replaced by Richard's brother, Gilbert, and other leading rebels.   RFW

Marshalsea, the transport office of the royal household, headed by the MARSHAL of the household, and the title of a court presided over by him and the STEWARD OF THE HOUSEHOLD. The court, set up to discipline offenders in the household, came also to hear cases of crime committed within its bounds or 'verges', as it travelled about the country, a source of irritation in the later 13th century. It thrived throughout the middle ages and beyond, entertaining some civil cases, to be reconstituted in the changed circumstances of James I's reign in 1612 as the Court of the Verge, hearing cases arising within royal residences and 12 miles radius thereof, limited in civil cases to damages of £5. Renamed Palace Court in 1630, it existed until 1849: the position of the sovereign's household is, however, still recognized by the appointment of a special coroner. PMB

Marshalsea Prison. Prisoners of the MARSHALSEA of the household were kept in Southwark from the 13th century; special buildings were provided in the 14th century which, from 1430 onwards, received admiralty prisoners and those committed for debt. To these the Tudors added political prisoners, but from 1601 onwards the M.P. was chiefly used for debtors, together with some admiralty prisoners. Removed to newer buildings in 1799, which in 1824 confined Dickens' father, the M. was abolished in 1842. PMB

Marston Moor, battle of (2 July 1644), a decisive battle in the CIVIL WAR. Rupert, after relieving York, followed the Parliamentarians and their Scottish allies westwards to M.M. The Roundhead armies unexpectedly attacked in the evening. Cromwell and Leslie routed Rupert on their left, and although Fairfax was defeated on the right, the advent of Cromwell's cavalry which turned on the royalist centre completed the victory. The royalists lost 3,000–4,000 men, and the king's power in the North was shattered. IHE

Martello Towers, were built along the south and east coasts of England during the NAPOLEONIC WARS against the threat of French invasion. These relatively low round towers, about 45 ft. in diameter with a gun platform at the top and usually protected by a moat, proved ineffective against vertical fire. The M.T. were modelled upon a tower at Cap Mortella, Corsica, which offered strong resistance to a British attack in 1794. IHE

Martial Law, not a code of law but the suspension by proclamation of the normal legal processes, usually in times of grave civil disturbance, the maintenance of law and order being delegated to military forces. England was partially under m.l. in 1715 and 1745, when local commanders were empowered to deal with JACOBITES, and in 1780 during the GORDON RIOTS. Full m.l. was imposed in Ireland 1798–1801, 1831 and later, and in various colonies in the 19th and 20th centuries. PMB

Martinique, from 1635 a French possession, was occupied by the British in 1762–3 and 1794–1815. SHS

Martin's Case (1587), an assertion by the House of Commons of the privilege of members of freedom from arrest during session and for 'a reasonable time' before and after. Martin's arrest 20 days before the reassembling of a prorogued Parliament was held by the Commons to be within the limit of privilege. The House would not commit itself to 'a time certain'. IHE

Marxist parties have never been significant in British politics. Although the First International (International Working Men's Association) was founded by Karl Marx in London (1864), it had more effect in Europe than in Britain. The first British M.p., the Social Democratic Federation, was organized by H. M. Hyndman in 1881 but soon lost influence to the FABIANS and the INDEPENDENT LABOUR PARTY. The Socialist Labour Party (1903) and the British Socialist Party (1911) were offshoots of the Federation; the B.S.P. was the largest element in the foundation, under Third International (Comintern) influence, of the Communist Party of Great Britain (1920). The C.P.G.B. had

2 members in the Commons in 1922–3 and again 1945–50, but did not win a seat in any other election; in 1961 it mustered 162,112 votes.   MLH

Maryland, a proprietary colony on the northern part of Chesapeake Bay granted to the first Lord Baltimore in 1632. A settlement was established at St Mary's in 1634. The proprietors and many of the early settlers were Roman Catholics, but there was toleration and efforts were made to avoid antagonizing the Protestants. M. repudiated the COMMONWEALTH but the 2nd Lord Baltimore's tact secured the restoration of his proprietorship, which was again in abeyance from 1689 to 1715. The Anglican church was officially established in 1692 and the Catholic element decreased. By the early 18th century negro slaves constituted one-third of the population and tobacco was the main export. M. made no effective contribution during the Anglo-French struggle in North America and from 1774 supported colonial resistance to British policies.
                                                                              IHE

Massachusetts was established as a Puritan colony by the M. BAY COMPANY (1629) and was soon conspicuous for its intolerance and defiance of the home authorities. Its exiles established themselves in RHODE ISLAND (1636–8). In 1643 it joined the NEW ENGLAND Confederation, but eventually accepted the English republic's authority. It unlawfully absorbed NEW HAMPSHIRE (1641–79) and MAINE in 1652. Its high-handedness led to the cancellation of the M.B.C.'s charter (1684) by Charles II, and it was swept into the Dominion of New England under Sir Edmund Andros (1686–9). The new charter (1691), incorporating PLYMOUTH, Maine, ACADIA (conquered 1690) and NEW BRUNSWICK, established a council and assembly, the latter being elected by property owners instead of church members. The governor was a crown nominee, and there was soon constant friction with the assembly which tried to assume executive powers. M. con-

stantly evaded the NAVIGATION ACTS, but provided substantial contingents during the Anglo-French struggle (1744–63). Shortly after the treaty of PARIS (1763) it shared the lead in disaffection with VIRGINIA. From 1765 M. played a major part in the resistance which led to the AMERICAN REVOLUTION as is evidenced by the BOSTON MASSACRE (1770), the BOSTON TEA PARTY (1773), LEXINGTON and BUNKER HILL (1775).   IHE

Massachusetts Bay Company. In 1628 a group of English Puritans obtained a grant from the COUNCIL FOR NEW ENGLAND and made their first settlement at Salem under John Endicott. They obtained a charter (Mar. 1629) for the M.B.C. which significantly made no provision for the government to be fixed in England, and in 1630 the shareholders migrated as a body under John Winthrop. By 1631 the colony was on a firm basis but run by an intolerant oligarchy. The governor and officials were appointed by the shareholders, but in 1631 approved church membership became the qualification for electoral rights. Laud attempted to suppress the M.B.C.'s charter in 1635, but it was not revoked until 1684.   IHE

Massachusetts Government Act (1774), one of the INTOLERABLE ACTS remodelling the M. charter to strengthen British control. The upper house of the legislature was no longer to be elected but nominated by the crown. Judges were to be appointed by the governor, and town meetings were limited to one session per year.
                                                                              IHE

Master, a title widely used in the middle ages and beyond. In the classical usage, teacher, it described the medieval university graduate licensed, after a period, to teach: it is still so used by the ancient universities, though in more modern foundations it implies a second degree by examination. A second usage, of proficient, master, craftsman, has gradually been extended from a select band, through the many masters of apprentices and official m.-generals etc., to the modern courtesy title. The title M. in Chancery probably combined these two elements. As the CHANCERY grew in business and size senior clerks, known from 1330 as m.s, presided over juniors. Their experience and proficiency in drafting documents was used to settle specialized problems as chancery became an EQUITY court, and their clerical work was gradually abandoned for the law. Specialized evidence, production of deeds etc., which slowed trials, was regularly referred to them, and they returned certificates to the court. The Chancery M.s were abolished in 1855, but M.s of the Supreme Court of JUDICATURE, performing similar functions in all divisions, are now appointed.   PMB

Matapan, battle of Cape (28–29 Mar. 1941), in World War II a successful night action by the British Mediterranean fleet under Admiral Cunningham against strong Italian forces seeking to intercept British troop convoys from Egypt to Greece. The Italians, west of Crete and heading south-east, were sought out by the British fleet (28 Mar.) and turned for home with one battleship damaged by torpedo-bombers. In the ensuing actions three powerful cruisers and two destroyers were sunk for the loss of one British aircraft. This victory considerably helped the subsequent evacuation of British troops from Greece (24–29 Apr.).   IHE

Mauritius, known to 10th-century Arab and 15th-century Malay sailors, discovered by the Portuguese c. 1510, was named (after Prince Maurice) and settled by the Dutch in 1598. They abandoned M. in 1710, and were succeeded in 1715 by the French, who renamed it Isle de France. The British occupied the island in 1810 and obtained its formal cession in 1814. It served as a naval base in the fight against Portuguese slave traders. The emancipation of the slaves (1834) led to the introduction of indentured labourers from India and China, whose descendants now form two-

thirds of the population. French is still the second official language. Rodrigues, the Chagos and other small islands are dependencies of M.   SHS

Mayflower, the 180-ton vessel in which the PILGRIM FATHERS sailed to NEW ENGLAND, left Southampton (5 Aug. 1620) with the smaller *Speedwell*, which, however, became unseaworthy beyond Land's End and put back to Plymouth. The M. finally sailed (6 Sept.) and made land at Cape Cod. The leading emigrants drew up the M. Compact (11 Nov.) to provide for future government and settled at New Plymouth.   IHE

Meal Tub Plot (1679). During the POPISH PLOT scare one Thomas Dangerfield claimed to have discovered a Presbyterian or Whig plot to prevent the duke of York's succession. The alleged evidence was concealed under the meal tub of his associate, Mrs Cellier. When this was found to be false, he accused leading Roman Catholics of promoting the conspiracy as cover for a real popish plot.   IHE

Medina del Campo, treaty of (Mar. 1489), was made between England and Spain who wished to prevent France absorbing Brittany; Spain hoped to regain Cerdagne and Roussillon, and England ostensibly Normandy and Aquitaine. Neither signatory was to make a separate peace until his territorial claims had been met. This was obviously to Spain's advantage, but Henry VII was primarily interested in the freedom of trade established between the two countries and in securing recognition of his dynasty by alliance with the rising power of Spain. The treaty provided for a marriage between Henry's infant son Arthur and the Spanish princess Catherine. (ÉTAPLES.)   IHE

Medway, battle of the (A.D. 43), fought between the Roman invaders under Aulus Plautius and the British of the south-east under Caratacus. The military superiority of the Romans won after two days of fighting. The battle was decisive for the early stages of the ROMAN CONQUEST.   CFS

Mercantilism, a term first popularized when Adam Smith attacked the commercial or 'mercantile system' of Great Britain in *The Wealth of Nations* (1776) and used to cover a wide range of ideas and policies varying from age to age not peculiar to Britain. Smith held that labour not trade was the real source of wealth and sought to demolish m. in favour of free trade and *laissez-faire.* His ideas steadily gained ground, m. was abandoned and free trade fully established by 1860. M. in Britain was accepted national policy between the mid-16th and mid-18th centuries. Involved with concepts of state power and security, its central feature was the idea of a favourable balance of trade, and in Elizabeth I's reign it was argued that this would involve an influx of coin or treasure. These ideas led to over-insistence on the importance of the precious metals (condemned by Smith), and to legislation designed to reduce imports and increase national self-sufficiency, which found their fullest expression in the NAVIGATION ACTS. Colonies were monopolized as sources of raw materials and markets for manufactured goods primarily in the interests of the mother country. Thus England excluded the Scots from her colonial trade until the Act of UNION (1707), and Irish trade was remorselessly subordinated to English interests. The protective system thus built up lasted until the 19th century when m. was abandoned.   IHE

Mercenaries, soldiers serving for pay rather than as a national or feudal duty, were seldom absent from medieval armies. As the inadequacy and inefficiency of the feudal host became more marked the English kings came to rely increasingly upon m. King John, for example, employed m. from Flanders, Brabant and elsewhere both for his continental campaigns and in England, where they speedily earned an evil reputation: the 1215 version of MAGNA CARTA provided for their expulsion from the realm. The word 'soldier' itself derives from Latin *solidarius,* one paid with *solidi,*

shillings—a shilling was the daily wage of a man-at-arms in the mid-13th century. During the 13th–16th centuries Scottish m., the GALLOGLASSES, played an important part in the history of Ireland. By the reign of Edward III the whole national army—including the troops raised by commission of ARRAY—had become a paid force. During the HUNDRED YEARS' WAR foreign soldiers were frequently taken into English pay while English soldiers, lacking employment by the king, took service as m. with other paymasters or formed part of the notorious FREE COMPANIES. The military resources of late-15th- and 16th-century English rulers were not always adequate or sufficiently reliable to enable them to retain their thrones without calling in foreign m.; Henry VIII also used German m. against the Scots. Although hated and feared, m. were indispensable until a large, permanent and efficient royal army could be created.   RFW

Merchants Adventurers, formed local gilds in the 14th century primarily to develop the export of cloth to Europe and in 1407 a regulated company of M.A. was formed in London which became a national organization, although the other ports frequently had to contest London's attempts to monopolize the trade. Its European headquarters were fixed at Bruges, but political difficulties caused removals to Antwerp (1446) and to Calais (1493). They returned to Antwerp after the INTERCURSUS MAGNUS (1496) and became the successful rivals of the HANSE, securing the temporary annulment of the latter's English privileges in 1552 and 1555. In 1567 difficulties in the Netherlands sent them to Hamburg, but opposition from the Hanse drove them to Emden (1579), then Stade (1587), and in 1611 they returned to Hamburg on favourable terms. They regained a Dutch mart at Middelburg in the 1580s, moving to Delft (1621), Rotterdam (1635) and Dordrecht (1655–1751). After Napoleon's conquests the company was dissolved in 1808.   IHE

Merchet, generally an incident of VILLEIN tenure. Since the villein, his kin and his chattels belonged to the lord, compensation, merchet, must be paid if his daughter was married outside the manor, his son schooled or his beast sold. In Scotland each freewoman paid m. on marriage; in Wales a similar payment, *amobyr*, was made.

PMB

Mercia (derived from *Mierce*, 'boundary folk'), a kingdom of the ANGLES, originally in the frontier area between the British and the earlier Teutonic settlers. From its nucleus in the area of Lichfield and Tamworth the kingdom expanded to fill the area between the Humber and Thames and between Wales and East Anglia, the land of the MIDDLE ANGLES and LINDSEY being incorporated. Its first known king was the heathen Penda (632–54), who claimed descent from the famous 4th-century Offa of Angeln; and the prestige of this descent probably facilitated acceptance by other Anglian settlers in the midlands of the M. royal house. Penda invaded NORTHUMBRIA three times, twice killing its king and being finally killed himself. M. was converted to Christianity soon after his death. During much of the later 7th and 8th centuries M. kings were supreme in England south of the Humber (BRETWALDA). WESSEX lost land on the lower Severn and north of the Thames, and although the former was regained by Wessex, M. gained Berkshire; ESSEX lost London and MIDDLESEX, which became part of M. Mercian supremacy reached its height under king Offa (757–96): he was recognized as overlord in southern England and, possibly, in Northumbria; he corresponded as an equal with Charlemagne and the pope; he established an archbishopric at Lichfield (abolished 803); he introduced a new type of coinage, the PENNY; and he had a dyke built to mark the Mercian-Welsh boundary (OFFA'S DYKE). The power of M. declined rapidly under his successors: lordship over Wessex and Northumbria was lost, and although there was a series of successful Mercian attacks against the North Welsh (816–22), the victory of king Egbert of Wessex at the battle of ELLENDUNE (825) reduced M. power to that kingdom alone. In 829 Egbert conquered M., but it regained its independence in 830, retaining land in Berkshire until the mid-9th century. In 855 there occurred the first raid by the DANES into M., and from 867 Danish activity was frequent. In 874 Burgred of M. abandoned his kingdom and the Danes appointed a king's THEGN as client ruler. In 877 they divided the kingdom, the eastern part being settled by the Danes, the western part, later known as English M. and consisting of the counties of southern Buckinghamshire, Cheshire, Gloucestershire, Herefordshire, Oxfordshire, Shropshire, Staffordshire Warwickshire and Worcestershire, soon coming, although by unknown steps, under the control of king Alfred's son-in-law. M. had no genuine kings of its own after 874, but in 924, 955 and 957 the Mercians independently accepted the west Saxon ruler as king. Under king Cnut (1017–37) Leofric was made earl of M. The earldom came to an end with the murder of his grandson Edwin in 1070.

CFS

Merciless Parliament (1388). The defeat of Richard II's supporters at RADCOTE BRIDGE in Dec. 1387 and the adhesion of London to the Lords APPELLANT left Richard at the mercy of his opponents. Threatened with deposition, the king was compelled to stand aside while the M.P., which met on 3 Feb. 1388, dealt with his friends. Following the condemnation of their principal opponents, whom they appealed of treason, the Appellants secured the impeachment, condemnation and execution of four knights of the king's chamber. Lesser enemies were exiled to Ireland. It is very doubtful if the offences of the victims amounted to treason, and the manner in which the Appellants dealt with their opponents furnished the precedent which Richard II was to follow in 1397. The support which the

Appellants enjoyed both in Parliament and outside was a measure of dissatisfaction with the ministers' conduct of affairs. But the Appellants themselves did little better, and when Richard declared himself of age in May 1389 they had to acquiesce in the king's assumption of full responsibility for government.   RFW

Merton, statute of (Jan. 1236), a series of provisions issued after a meeting of the great council at M. Priory, defining and clarifying the law. Certain new writs were designed, and legal processes in Ireland were brought into line with English practice. The council is best remembered for the decision not to change the law concerning children born before the marriage of their parents. By canon law such children were legitimized by their parents' marriage, but by English law they remained illegitimate.
                                                              RFW

Mesne Tenure. If the king granted land to A for knight service, for example, and A granted it to B for rent etc., A was the mesne, 'intermediate', tenant between B and the king, but if A did not perform knight service and the land was taken into the king's hand, B not A suffered damage. His remedy was the common action of *mesne*, regulated by the Statute of WESTMINSTER II, 1285, to compel A to perform the service. Sub-infeudation, attacked by Edward I, and other long chains of tenure made the position of the actual tenant of land difficult, for in law suits all tenants between him and the king were interested parties who had to be informed, if they could be traced.
                                                              PMB

Mesolithic (Gk. *mesos*, middle; *lithos*, stone), is the general name given to the cultures of the period 8th–4th millennium B.C. that grew out of the PALAEOLITHIC when climatic change forced a modification in the way of human life. Native developments were affected by those from without, especially by the Maglemosian culture;

but during this period, probably *c.* 6000, Britain became an island, with increased potentiality for the development of its own cultural variations. The standard of civilization may have been lower than in late Palaeolithic times. Hunting—on a lesser scale— and food-gathering remained the methods of subsistence; and shell and other fish were consumed in increasing quantities. Bone implements were manufactured, but the typical artefacts were microliths, small flint flakes mounted in wood for use. Dugout canoes were made, the dog was apparently domesticated, and tree-felling techniques were employed. But no great developments took place during this period, and its later stages were marked by a change to a wetter, Atlantic, type of climate. This raised the water-level and encouraged the spread of thick deciduous forests, both affecting the river valleys, the favoured dwelling areas. Mesolithic cultures continued in parts of the island for some time after the introduction of NEOLITHIC cultures by newcomers from the mainland. The term did not come into general archaeological use until well into the 20th century.   CFS

Mesopotamian campaign, an important operation of WORLD WAR I. With the limited object of safeguarding oil installations and ensuring allegiance of the shaiks of Kuwait and Mohammerah, a small force from India was landed at Abadan, 6 Nov. 1914. It quickly took Basra and Qurna, at the junction of the Tigris and Euphrates. Reinforced, an advance up Tigris was made to Amara (3 June 1915) and Kut al Amara (28 Sept.). The cabinet, feeling the political need of a victory over the Turks to compensate for the Dardanelles, then authorized an attack on Bagdad; this failed at the battle of Ctesiphon (21 Nov.), and the commander, Maj.-Gen. C. Townshend, retired on Kut where he was besieged. Attempts at relief failing, Kut fell 29 Apr. 1916, about 10,000 prisoners being taken by the Turks. Responsi-

bility then passed from the C.-in-C.,
India to the war office and Lt.-Gen.
Sir S. Maude was appointed to command a force of 120,000 fighting
troops. Maude retook Kut (24 Feb.
1917) and entered Bagdad (11 March).
Further reinforced, he captured Ra-
madi (on the Euphrates) in Sept. and
Tigrit (on the Tigris) in Nov. Maude
died (18 Nov.) and was succeeded by
Lt.-Gen. W. R. Marshall. The
Russian collapse of 1917 demanded a
diversion for the protection of the
Baku oilfield; 'Dunsterforce' (under
Maj.-Gen. L. C. Dunsterville, the
original of Kipling's *Stalky*) got
through to Baku in Aug. 1918 but
could not hold the town. The final
assault on the Turks in Mesopotamia
was launched, 23 Oct. 1918, and they
surrendered at Sharqat, 30 Nov.
Total Anglo-Indian casualties in the
M. c. were 92,501 (15,814 killed in
battle, 12,807 dead from disease).

MLH

Methodists, English. The members
of Charles Wesley's 'Holy Club'
founded at Oxford in 1729 were soon
called M. and John Wesley became
their leader. These Anglican clergy
really began their evangelical movement in 1738, and their unfashionable
enthusiasm deprived them of the use
of church pulpits. Open air preaching, first among the Kingswood col-
liers near Bristol, steadily developed
into a national crusade noted for its
attention to the needs of the poor and
degraded. The ARMINIAN John Wesley parted company with the Calvinistic George Whitefield in 1741. With
the aid of lay pastors local societies
were organized, and the first Conference was held in 1744; it was legally
constituted by John Wesley in 1784.
At his death (1791) relations with the
Church of England were still unsettled, but the Conference decision
of 1795 against the need for episcopal
ordination marked the break. Various
secessions ensued over the years,
largely from organizational differences.
The Methodist New Connexion separated in 1797, the Independent M.
1805, the Primitive M. 1810, the Bible

Christians 1815, the Wesleyan M. Association 1835, the Wesleyan Reformers 1849, these latter two becoming the
United Methodist Free Church in
1857 and linking up with the New
Connexion and Bible Christians in
1907 as the United Methodist Church.
This body joined the original Wesleyan Methodist Church and Primitive
M. to form the Methodist Church of
Great Britain in 1932. IHE

Methodists, Welsh. The Welsh
church after 1660 suffered from lati-
tudinarian, absentee, non-Welsh
bishops, from pluralism, nepotism,
non-residence and, above all, poverty.
But constructive and reinvigorating
energies are observable in the huge
increase in the number of devotional
books published and circulated in
Welsh, in active support for the
S.P.C.K. and CIRCULATING SCHOOLS.
These prepared the way for the M.
who, c. 1735, began their revival independently of, though closely in touch
with, English counterparts, notably
Whitefield. Following the founding of
early societies the first association
(*sasiwn*) was held in 1742. The leaders
were Howell Harris (1714–73), supreme as itinerant and organizer,
Daniel Rowland (1713–90), outstanding as preacher, and William Williams
(1717–91), Wales's greatest hymnist,
and Thomas Charles (1755–1814),
'architect of his denomination'. Welsh
M. were Calvinist in theology and
PRESBYTERIAN in organization. Despite dissensions within and opposition without, they multiplied greatly
within the established church, until
in 1811, after being suspected of
treason during the wars, 1793–1815,
they reluctantly decided to form a
separate denomination. The revival
had profound effects: it made nonconformity dominant, though M.
themselves were the most numerous
sect only in the largely rural areas of
the north and west. It implanted the
Calvinist ethos of personal morality,
restraint and seriousness, with its
accompanying perils of cramped self-
righteousness, hypocrisy and gloom.
At first inhibitive of cultural and

political activities, it later gave them invaluable support.   GW

Methuen Treaty (1703), a commercial treaty between England and Portugal named after its negotiator John M. (†1706) and consequent upon other treaties bringing Portugal into the GRAND ALLIANCE of 1701. It lasted until 1836, and its importance was not diminished until the time of Pitt's commercial treaty with France in 1786. English woollens were re-admitted into Portugal. In return, Portuguese wines were imported into England at two-thirds of the duties payable on French wines, and the adverse balance was paid in gold. It also opened the Brazilian market to English trade until the reign of George III, when it was confined to Portuguese companies.   IHE

Middle Angles occupied the area between MERCIA, EAST ANGLIA and LINDSEY, extending south towards the Thames. The settlement had begun before the end of the 5th century, the settlers were comparatively numerous and their culture included a SAXON element. They probably formed a loose alliance of kindred groups, for there is no record of any ruling dynasty. Before the mid-6th century they had come under Mercian control, but there is no evidence that this was the result of conquest. They were converted to Christianity in 653.
                                                          CFS

Middle Party (1316–21), a moderate group of barons and bishops, between the extreme ORDAINERS led by the earl of Lancaster and Edward II's favourites. After the execution of Piers Gaveston on BLACKLOW HILL a group of Ordainers led by Aymer de Valence, earl of Pembroke, had moved away from Lancaster, and it was around Pembroke that the M.P. was formed in 1316. It included the bishops of Ely and Norwich, the earls of Norfolk and Hereford, a group of MARCHER LORDS, and some of Edward II's new favourites. The party aimed to maintain and execute the ORDINANCES of 1311, but with the co-operation of the king.

Lancaster was pushed out of his dominant position in 1318, adherents of the party secured offices of state and household, and the party remained in control for some three years, despite continued failure in the war with the Scots. The rise of the Despensers eventually caused the break-up of the M.P.: the marcher element rejoined Lancaster, while Pembroke and others moved closer to the king, so that by the middle of 1321 the party had practically ceased to exist.   RFW

Middlesex probably represents what was originally an independent kingdom of the Middle SAXONS. But there is no record of any royal line, and by the beginning of the 7th century it formed part of the kingdom of ESSEX. It was later taken by MERCIA. Its boundaries seem to have included the modern counties of M. and Hertford; and it is possible that SURREY, whose name means 'Southern district', was originally settled by the Middle Saxons, although any connexion was early lost. It was in the 10th century that M. became a SHIRE. It lost its separate identity in 1965.   CFS

Middlesex Election. In 1768 John Wilkes, an outlaw, was elected M.P. for Middlesex and was expelled the House on government initiative as ineligible. Thrice re-elected and expelled, although his outlawry had been reversed, he was again returned in the election of 1774 and allowed to sit. In 1782 the Commons' resolutions of 1769 against him were erased from their records. By arousing popular agitation he established the right of electors to return the member of their choice. (GENERAL WARRANTS.)   IHE

Midlothian campaign (24 Nov.–7 Dec. 1879), an election tour of southern Scotland made by Gladstone as Liberal candidate for Midlothian. His speeches, castigating the foreign policy and financial waste of 'Beaconsfieldism', were warmly received and widely reported. Gladstone won the seat from Lord Dalkeith and (the Liberals being returned with a majority of 157) reassumed the party leadership and premiership. A precedent had been set for statesmen to appeal thus directly to the mass of voters.   MLH

Military Law, a code devised for army discipline, which in wartime may include some civilian offences. The modern laws derive from slowly developing articles of war, proclaimed for successive campaigns until 1689, when a standing army was first recognized. In 1879 the articles were attached to the MUTINY ACT but later separated and continuously enforced by the Army Act 1881. Under m.l. courts range from the summary jurisdiction of commanding officers to general courts martial. The court is formed of officers, with the aid of a judge advocate, and decision reached by simple majority. The rules of evidence, procedure etc. are akin to criminal law, and the accused may be assisted by an officer or by counsel. A courts martial appeal court was instituted in 1951. (MARTIAL LAW.) PMB

Militia, this national levy, a development of the ancient FYRD, controlled by the SHERIFFS, came to be organized by the LORDS-LIEUTENANT under the Tudors. Called m. in the 17th century, it was a defensive force supplied by county quotas for local service mainly by IMPRESSMENT. King and Parliament struggled for its control (MILITIA BILL), but it was placed under royal command by the M. Act (1661) and reorganized by Acts of 1662 and 1663. The obligation to provide men and arms was placed on the property owners, and individuals called to serve could provide substitutes. They became liable for service anywhere in the kingdom. It was never effectively trained and Pitt's M. Act (1757) made service compulsory, county quotas being determined by ballot. Substitutes were permissible, and it was embodied during the SEVEN YEARS' WAR and subsequent FRENCH WARS. An act of 1852 substantially made it a volunteer force, and it was taken out of the hands of the lords-lieutenant in 1882. It ceased to exist after the Territorial and Reserve Forces Act (1907) although the name was applied to the Special Reserve (1921), and revived by the Military Training Act (1939).   IHE

Militia Bill (1642). After Charles I's attempt to seize the FIVE MEMBERS, Parliament passed the M.B. to assume control of the MILITIA and of the appointment of governors of fortresses. The king refused his consent, and Parliament took the unprecedented step of passing the Militia Ordinance (5 May), thereby assuming sovereign powers. The king replied by proclamation (27 May) forbidding the militia to obey the ordinance.   IHE

Millenary Petition (1603), an appeal to James I after his entry into England, reputedly from some 1,000 Puritan clergy, requesting certain moderate changes in liturgy and worship. They urged the discontinuance of the sign of the cross in baptism and the ring in marriage; optional use of cap and surplice, shortening of the service and more scope for preaching, simplification of music and stricter sabbath observance. They also asked for the prevention of pluralities and NON-RESIDENCE, that bishops should not hold livings *in commendam*, and more careful use of excommunication. As a result, James called the HAMPTON COURT CONFERENCE.   IHE

Minden, battle of (1 Aug. 1759), on the river Weser, in which Ferdinand duke of Brunswick, commander of the Anglo-Hanoverian army, defeated the French and subsequently liberated Hanover. A complete rout of the French was prevented by the incompetence of the British cavalry commander, Lord George Sackville, who was court-martialled and dismissed.
                                              SHS

Mines Acts resulted from the same growing awareness of need for some government regulation as prompted the FACTORY ACTS. The first M.A. (1842) prohibited employment underground of women and girls and of boys under 10 years of age (increased to 12 in 1860). Acts, mainly concerning safety and inspection, were passed in 1850,

1855, 1860, 1862, 1872 and 1887. The foundation of the Royal School of Mines (1851) to train inspectors enabled the 1872 act to enforce the holding by managers of certificates of competency. The 1908 M.A. limited the underground shift to 8 hours per day—the first time that the state directly limited the hours of work of adult men; this was reduced to 7 hours in 1920 but increased to 8 again after the GENERAL STRIKE (1926). A further innovation was that of a minimum wage (on an area basis) under the Coal M.A., 1912.

The post-war condition of the coal mining industry led to government support and regulation: the Coal M.A., 1930, set up a central council and executive boards to fix output quotas and minimum prices; a reorganization commission, to promote colliery amalgamation, proved ineffective. Coal royalties were nationalized in 1938. The industry came under full government control in 1942 and under public ownership in 1946.　MLH

Ministerial Responsibility is both individual and collective. Individual ministers are responsible for the actions of their departments; the cabinet and ministry are collectively responsible to Parliament. Fortunately for the development of M.R. the clause in the Act of SETTLEMENT (1701) which would have excluded ministers from the Commons was modified (1705–7). M.R. developed gradually during the 18th century with the growth of cabinet solidarity under the more effective prime ministers, and more rapidly after the 1770s. By the time of the American Revolution ministries were generally regarded as collectively responsible for their policies, but ministers still occasionally voted with the opposition: as late as 1792 Pitt obtained the dismissal of Lord Chancellor Thurlow to secure ministerial unanimity. With the decline of political PATRONAGE and the passing of the REFORM ACT of 1832 M.R. to Parliament was emphasized, but it was not until after 1841 that collective resignation became the normal procedure consequent upon an important defeat in the Commons. M.R. also implies that the cabinet offers unanimous advice to the crown.　IHE

Minorca, one of the Balearic Islands with the strategically important harbour of Port Mahon, was captured from Spain by a British expedition in 1708 and ceded to Britain by the treaty of UTRECHT (1713). During the SEVEN YEARS' WAR M. surrendered to the French (1756); Admiral John Byng was court-martialled and shot for having failed to relieve it. The treaty of PARIS (1763) restored M. to Great Britain, but in 1782 the combined Spanish and French fleets took it, and the treaty of VERSAILLES (1783) gave it back to Spain. Reoccupied by the British in 1798, M. was finally ceded to Spain by the peace of AMIENS (1802).　SHS

Minster (Old English *mynster*, Latin *monasterium*), a monastery, until the 8th century or even later also a church served by a group of priests. Because of this usage, some cathedral and older PARISH churches are still known as m. churches. In some cases, however, they may represent former monastic foundations.　CFS

Mint, Royal. There were many local m.s working in Anglo-Saxon times: after the Norman conquest the numbers were gradually reduced, until in 1242 only the London and Canterbury m.s and exchanges remained. Local m.s were revived for subsequent recoinages, but after the coin-clipping trials of 1278–9 the monopoly of these two was almost permanently established (minting being done at London) under the charge of a warden or master. At first the London minters worked in the City, but from at least 1299 until it moved to Tower Hill in 1811, the m. was within the Tower of London. Occasionally temporary branches were established, e.g. at Rhuddlan, or permanent in the countries of the Commonwealth. On 17 Dec. 1968 a new m. was opened at Llantrisant, near Cardiff, to produce the new British decimal coinage. As well as British coinage, the M. has worked for foreign countries, from Spanish coins in the reign of Mary I to modern Costa Rican coinage.

The district of Southwark called the M. dates from a m. established there in 1545 and closed because of fraud in 1551; in the 18th century it was the haunt of thieves and coiners. PMB; MR

Mise, a word of varied medieval usage, describing miscellaneous expenses, the issue in an action on the writ of right and the payment made to each new earl of Chester by his tenants in Cheshire to maintain their special privileges. In the sense of an agreement it was used both for the final settlement of accounts and for the conclusion of disputes, as in the M. of AMIENS and of LEWES.   PMB

Missionary Societies. The Church of England Society for the Promoting of Christian Knowledge (1698) and the Society for the Propagation of the Gospel (1701) were founded to further the cause of Christianity in the colonies, but the main missionary effort began at the end of the 18th century consequent upon the religious revival, which owed much to the METHODISTS. The Baptist M.S. was founded in 1792, the London M.S. in 1795 (mainly CONGREGATIONALIST), the Church M.S. in 1799 by the CLAPHAM SECT opponents of the SLAVE TRADE, and the Wesleyan M.S. in 1813. These M.S. among others carried out pioneer work in many parts of the world. The inter-denominational British and Foreign Bible Society (1804) assisted by providing bibles in native languages.   IHE

Model Parliament (Nov. 1295), the most representative so far summoned —hence its 19th-century title. To it were summoned 7 earls and 41 barons, the archbishops and bishops, 70 abbots and heads of religious houses, the heads of all cathedral chapters, archdeacons, 1 proctor for the clergy of each chapter, 2 proctors for the clergy of each diocese, 2 knights from each shire and 2 representatives from each city and borough. Its summons was occasioned by Edward I's pressing need for financial aid because of the coincidence of crises in Wales, Scotland and in Edward's continental dominions. All elements present in parliament granted taxation, including the clergy (prior to the bull CLERICIS LAICOS of 1296). The parliament did not, however, provide a model upon which subsequent parliaments were consistently based. The number of lay peers summoned was to vary considerably; in the 14th century the representation of religious houses was to be considerably decreased, and the lower clergy were to drop out of Parliament; and the number of boroughs represented was far from constant. Parliament was not yet divided into Lords and Commons, and until the reign of Edward III parliaments were summoned in which the Commons were not represented at all.   RFW

Modus Tenendi Parliamentum, a treatise on 'the manner of holding Parliament' surviving in two versions, English and Irish, of the late 14th and early 15th centuries. The author is unknown, but may have been William Ayreminne, Keeper of the Rolls of Chancery and a clerk of parliament. Historians are not agreed as to the date of composition, but the majority, consider the English version to be the earlier, written about 1316–24, and the Irish version to have been written near the end of the 14th century. In form the M. purports to be a description of Parliament at the time of the Norman conquest, but in fact it describes Parliament, partly as it was in the early 14th century, and partly as its author thought it ought to be. Its historical value is therefore limited, though it would gain in importance if its background and the connection of its author with the constitutional reform movement under Edward II could be established more certainly.   RFW

Monasticism in Anglo-Saxon England falls into two distinct periods, before and after king Alfred (871–99), for the Danish wars of that reign brought a temporary end to organized monastic life in England. Monastic foundation began with the CONVERSION. Houses founded by the SCOTTISH CHURCH had at first the organization typical of that church, but they gradually adopted the essentials of the rule of St Benedict. This was first introduced into southern England by St Augustine (597) and into NORTHUMBRIA by Wilfred and Benedict Biscop in the 7th century. Monastic organization, as distinct from the rule, in this first period took various forms: the independent house, the most usual; the federation of equal monasteries, where the founder kept control; the monastery with dependent cells; the double monastery, under the control of an abbess and very popular in England; and the family monastery, which was frequently a device to avoid taxation. The federation and the double and family monasteries did not survive into post-Alfredian times. During this first period the founder of a monastery had considerable powers over his foundation, for it could be a source of profit due to pious benefaction; and bishops of the time strove constantly to keep abuses arising from this within bounds.

The second period is marked by the monastic revival of the 10th century, often known as the Tenth Century REFORMATION. In its earlier stages it was a native development, but it later drew much inspiration from reformed houses in Lorraine and the Low Countries. The layman who did most to develop it was Edgar, who became king of all England in 959; and the foremost churchmen were Dunstan, Ethelwold and Oswald. The rule generally adopted was that of the REGULARIS CONCORDIA. Territorially the foundation of houses was virtually limited to the south and south midlands. The movement lost much of its force in the early 11th century, and although houses did not disappear, the general standard in 1066 was lower than that on the continent.   CFS

Monasticon Anglicanum, published in 3 volumes 1655–73, was planned by Sir Henry Spelman and Roger Dodsworth. Dodsworth set about collecting materials and was joined by (Sir) William Dugdale, later Garter king of Arms, to whom the book is generally if unjustly attributed. The *M.* contains essential documents for the early history of almost every English religious house. Many were printed uncritically and have since been re-edited, but the book taught scholars the importance of CHARTERS and remains today a monumental and essential work. The Record Commission edition 1817–30 contains additional material: it is generally cited, but enjoys an unmerited reputation.

PMB

Monmouth's Rebellion (1685) was the last desperate attempt of the duke of Monmouth to assert himself against James II as champion of the Protestant cause (EXCLUSION BILLS, RYE HOUSE PLOT). Landing at Lyme Regis (11 June), he gathered a following of some 4,000 countryfolk and was proclaimed king at Taunton and Bridgwater. His attempts on Bristol and Bath failed, as did ARGYLL'S REBELLION, and his forces were totally routed at SEDGEMOOR (6 July). Monmouth was caught and executed (15 July); his followers were punished by the BLOODY ASSIZES.   IHE

Monopolies in trade had been granted to companies since the mid-14th century (STAPLE, MERCHANTS ADVENTURERS), but during Elizabeth I's reign a new form developed. The sole right to sell commodities was granted to reward individuals or raise money for the crown. Parliament challenged them especially in 1597, 1598 and 1601. James I granted numerous m., partly in order to regulate trade, but mainly to profit the crown; they were often granted corruptly to courtiers and financiers for articles in common use. In 1621 Michell and Mompesson, notorious monopolists, suffered IMPEACHMENT. The statute of monopolies (1624) forbade their issue except to cities, boroughs, trading companies and individual inventors. Charles I created new monopolies (1632–5) which were revoked in 1639, and the LONG PARLIAMENT finally abolished them.

IHE

Mons, battle of (23 Aug. 1914), the first large-scale British engagement in WORLD WAR I. The small British Expeditionary Force under Sir John French, positioned along the Mons–Condé canal west of Mons, a Belgian town 34 miles S.W. of Brussels, held six divisions of the German 1st Army (von Kluck), but the withdrawal of the French 5th Army (Lanrezac) on French's right (after heavy fighting around Charleroi and French reverses in the Ardennes) necessitated the retreat of the B.E.F. also.

MLH

Montagu–Chelmsford Report, presented to Parliament in July 1918 by the secretary of state for India (Edwin S. Montagu) and the viceroy (Lord Chelmsford), implemented a cabinet declaration, Aug. 1917, on 'the progressive realization of responsible government in India'. Modified recommendations were embodied in the Government of INDIA ACT 1919. 'Dyarchy' was introduced in eight provinces: certain subjects of administration were transferred to ministers responsible to legislatures which were 70% elected on a property or special qualification and on a communal basis. At the centre there was a bicameral legislature (an assembly with 106 elected and 40 nominated members; a council of state with 61 members and an unofficial majority); the executive council was enlarged and now had 3 Indian members; an advisory chamber of princes was formed. Reserve powers were vested in viceroy and governors. The constitution, to be reviewed after 10 years, was inaugurated 21 Feb. 1921.

MLH

Montfortians, the followers of Simon de Montfort, earl of Leicester, in the period 1258–65. The reform movement which produced the PROVISIONS OF OXFORD in 1258 originally enjoyed the support of the great majority of the English baronage, whereas Henry III had little support outside the circle of his kinsmen. The machinery of government set up by the Provisions worked for some 18 months, but baronial unity was short-lived. There were signs of a breach between the earls of Leicester and Gloucester as early as Mar. 1259; Henry III's son, the Lord Edward, though in alliance with de Montfort in 1259, was building up a party of his own; and there was a decided royalist reaction setting in. Henry III gradually strengthened his position, was released by the papacy from his oath to observe the Provisions (May 1261), dismissed the more determined reformers and had virtually recovered full control in 1262. De Montfort, who had gone abroad at the end of 1261, returned in Apr. 1263 and was soon joined by a party of younger barons, with a strong MARCHER element. Especially important was the alliance of the new earl of Gloucester, Gilbert de Clare. The M.'s struggle for the observance of the Provisions met with some initial success, but by the end of 1263 the royalists were again recovering, and in particular the Lord Edward was building up his support at the expense of de Montfort. When civil war broke out early in 1264, after the publication of the Mise of AMIENS, de Montfort's leading supporters were the earls of Gloucester and Derby; a number of bishops and a strong minority of the barons favoured his cause, and of increasing importance was a strong party of knights and gentry and of townsmen, notably of London and the CINQUE PORTS. While the M. were strongest in the south and east, the king was supported by a majority of the barons of the north and of the Marchers whom de Montfort failed to reconcile after his victory at LEWES. The strength of the Lord Edward's personal following, the continued hostility of the Marchers and defections from his own party—particularly that of the earl of Gloucester—contributed to de Montfort's final defeat at EVESHAM in 1265. It was not until 1267, however, that the war was brought to an end by the submission of the 'DISINHERITED' M.　　　RFW

Montgomery, treaty of (25 Sept. 1267), between Henry III and Llywelyn ap Gruffydd, ruler of GWYNEDD, following a period of intermittent warfare from 1256. Its most significant provision was the recognition of Llywelyn's right to the title of PRINCE OF WALES, which carried with it feudal suzerainty over almost all other Welsh chieftains. This was an overlordship having no historical precedent in Wales which brought Llywelyn legally as near to independence as he could hope to attain. Important territorial concessions in northeast and mid-Wales were also made to him. In return he agreed to pay 25,000 marks by annual instalments. The treaty lasted until 1277.　　　GW

Montreuil, process of (1305–6), the deliberations of an arbitration commission to consider disputes between Edward I of England and Philip IV of France. No decision acceptable to both parties was reached, although meetings were not finally abandoned until 1311, after Edward's death. RFW

Montserrat, one of the LEEWARD ISLANDS, was discovered by Columbus in 1493 and named after the 'serrated mountain' near Barcelona. M. was colonized from ST KITTS by Sir Thomas Warner in 1632, captured by the French in 1644 and again in 1782, but restored to Britain in 1668 and 1783 respectively. A form of ministerial government was introduced on 1 Jan. 1960.　　　SHS; IHE

Moot (Old English *gemot*, a meeting or assembly). In the Old English period such gatherings dealt with legal and administrative affairs both lay and, in the more important, ecclesiastical. They occur wherever organized communities are found, the main being SHIRE and HUNDRED m.s; BURH and PORT m.s (borough courts), and hall m.s (manorial courts). The smaller the community, the less the competence of its m., and little is known of those below the shire and hundred,

which formed the main units of local government. Those attending were those who owed suit of court. In judicial matters these, under the presidency of the appropriate royal official, acted as the judges, the function of the president being to declare the law. In most cases action had to be initiated by the injured party or his kin. The procedure was that of compurgation, followed, if necessary, by the ORDEAL. In the DANELAW bodies of 12 lawmen, i.e. men with specialized legal knowledge, took a leading part in directing the activities of a local court (JURY). Administration covered the reception of royal commands, apportionment of GELD payments, calling out of the FYRD, view of FRANKPLEDGE, witnessing of wills and land transfers, etc. The greatest of these m.s was that for the whole kingdom (WITAN). The word has survived in the expression 'a moot point'.　　　CFS

Morley–Minto Reforms were Indian constitutional changes proposed by the secretary of state, John (viscount) Morley, and the viceroy, 4th earl of Minto. Mainly embodied in the INDIAN COUNCILS ACT 1909, they resulted in a greater measure of representative but not of responsible government. Membership and powers of both the imperial legislative council and provincial legislatures were increased, the latter with a non-official majority mostly indirectly elected by sectional interests (Moslems gaining the right to racial representation). Morley and Minto set store by giving office to Indians; in 1907 two were placed on the Indian council in London, and in 1909 Satyendra (later Lord) Sinha was appointed to the viceroy's executive council.　　　MLH

Mort d'Ancestor, Assize of. Devised by Henry II to make feudal lords admit their under-tenants' heirs to their ancestors' tenements, it derived from the Assize of NORTHAMPTON 1176, c. 4, and had to be brought by a near relation, e.g. brother, son or nephew, of the deceased. The jurors were asked: if O. father (or other relation) of G. was seised in his demesne as of fee of land etc. on the day when he died, if he died within the assize and whether G. is his next heir. The restriction to close relations was eased in the 13th century by other actions, aiel, besaiel etc. which, although not POSSESSORY ASSIZES, allowed remoter relationships to be pleaded. All these actions aided the development of the hereditary principle.   PMB

Mortimer's Cross, battle of (2 Feb. 1461). The LANCASTRIANS came near to complete victory after the death of Richard, duke of York, at WAKEFIELD, and would certainly have gained possession of London after the second battle of ST ALBANS but for the defeat of their western army, under the earls of Pembroke and Wiltshire, at M. (Herefordshire) by Edward, earl of March, eldest son of Richard of York. Among the Lancastrians captured in the battle and afterwards executed at Hereford was Owen Tudor, grandfather of the future Henry VII. After joining Warwick on 22 Feb. Edward pushed on to London, where he was crowned as Edward IV on 4 Mar. 1461.   RFW

Mortmain. Ecclesiastical tenants holding lands in FRANKALMOIN were, in law, self-perpetuating bodies not subject to ESCHEATS, RELIEFS etc.: the dead hand, *mort main*, of the church had fallen on the lands. In the 13th century the consequent loss of revenue to lay feudal lords led to attempts to control m., culminating in the Statute of M. 1279, which laid down that the king's licence must be obtained for future transactions. The problem was not peculiar to England, e.g. in France an ordinance of 1275 foreshadowed the English statute.   PMB

Mortuaries, developed from SOUL SCOT, becoming the gift of the second best beast of the deceased to the incumbent of the parish church, later the offering of the first or second best possession, although local custom varied. When m. became fees they were more open to abuse, and they frequently aroused anti-clerical feeling as in HUNNE'S CASE. The Parliament

of 1529 limited m. to moderate amounts. They were still collected in some parishes in the 18th century.
                                                IHE

Moslem League, founded in 1906 as a rival political organization of the INDIAN NATIONAL CONGRESS which had become almost wholly Hindu. From 1940 the M.L. advocated the creation of a separate PAKISTAN, which was achieved in 1947 under the leadership of Mohammed Ali Jinnah (1876–1948) and Liaqat Ali Khan (1895–1951). After their deaths the M.L. became tainted by graft and corruption and was swept from power in 1954.
                                                SHS

Mosquito Coast ('Mosquitia'), the territory of the Moskito Indians along the coast of Nicaragua and Honduras, received a British resident in 1844 and was placed under British protection in 1847. At the insistence of the U.S.A. the protectorate was ceded to Honduras and Nicaragua (1859–60), but the Moskitos enjoyed a measure of British protection until 1905.

The offshore islands of St Andrew and Old Providence were granted to the earl of Warwick and John Pym in 1630, frequently changed hands but after 1671 passed under Spanish (now Colombian) rule.   SHS

Mount Badon, see BADONICUS.

Movables, Taxes on. Such taxes, assessed on variable proportions of all or a section of the chattels of laymen and clergy, began with the tenth of 1188, the SALADIN TITHE, followed by other similar impositions of fifteenths, thirteenths, twentieths etc. and became a regular, non-feudal source of revenue. Assessment was sometimes based on individuals' sworn declarations, otherwise on the verdicts of jurors under the direction of commissioners appointed to assess and collect the revenue. In the 13th century, particularly under Edward I, such taxes came to be negotiated between the king, his barons and later Parliament, and the convocations, playing an important part in early parliamentary history. The tax was soon standardized to a tenth from towns and ancient DEMESNE, elsewhere a fifteenth; in 1334 it became virtually a tax on holdings. The assessments remained unaltered until it was last levied in 1623, by which time its value had declined from c. £100,000 in the 14th century to little more than £20,000.   PMB

Mund. In Old English times every free man had his m. or peace that lay over his dwelling. It increased with rank, and payment due for housebreaking, fighting in a man's hall, etc., depended on the m. of the owner of the property. In late Old English times a man who commended himself to a lord came under the lord's m. The king's m. was the most valuable.
                                                      CFS

Munich agreement (29 Sept. 1938) was instigated by Neville Chamberlain in an effort to avert war by sacrificing Czechoslovakia to Nazi Germany. The question at issue was the timing of Hitler's occupation of the Sudeten German areas of Czechoslovakia adjacent to Germany and Austria.

In the preceding weeks Chamberlain had worked hard to soften the will of France to honour her treaty commitments and had brought maximum pressure to bear on Czechoslovakia to make wounding concessions. At the same time Hitler had increased his demands: first, autonomy for the Sudeten areas; next, self-determination (conceded after Chamberlain's first visit to Hitler, at Berchtesgaden, 15 Sept.); and finally, occupation by 1 Oct. (presented in the Godesberg memorandum on Chamberlain's second visit, 22–23 Sept.). The M.a., which was signed by Hitler, Chamberlain, Daladier and Mussolini, allowed occupation over 10 days. Czechoslovakia was not represented and was given no option but to accept. She lost her heavily fortified frontier and key industrial areas. Joint guarantees of her new frontiers proved worthless, for border areas in the south and east were occupied by Poland and Hungary, and in March 1939 Hitler took

over the remainder of the country. The M.a. allowed Britain to enter WORLD WAR II better prepared both physically and morally. To the apologists this is its justification.   MLH

Municipal Corporations. The M.C. Act (1835) marks the beginning of local government reform. A uniform system of councils, directly elected by the ratepayers, was imposed on 178 old borough corporations; mayors and aldermen were indirectly elected. The election of JUSTICES OF THE PEACE was abolished and the POLICE was placed under watch committees. The m.c. took over the powers of improvement commissioners, and during the next 40 years other bodies controlling local services were eliminated. Many new functions (including in particular those effecting public health) were imposed on the m.c. by a large number of amending statutes, both compulsory and adoptive. These were consolidated in the M.C. Act of 1882, which also added 25 boroughs to the 62 incorporated since 1835. By the Local Government Act (1888) larger municipalities were made county boroughs with functions analogous to those of the COUNTY. Further important consolidation took place under the Local Government Act (1933); an amending act (1958) provided that small m.c. might become rural boroughs within rural districts.   MLH

Municipium, a town in Roman times that had special rights of self-government and whose inhabitants had a status approaching that of Roman citizens. The only one in ROMAN BRITAIN was Verulamium (St Albans), the capital of the CATUVELLAUNI. Later any special privileges appear to have been lost, and it became legally indistinguishable from any chief town of a CIVITAS.   CFS

Munitions, Ministry of, a short-lived department set up in 1915 after the scandal over the supply of munitions to the Western front. It was abolished in 1921, and its powers were divided between the WAR OFFICE and the AIR MINISTRY: the TREASURY was entrusted with the dispersal of surpluses etc., a process lasting until 1927. Similar functions were discharged by the Ministry of SUPPLY in the second world war.   PMB

Munster, see IRELAND, CONQUEST OF; DESMOND REVOLT; PLANTATION OF IRELAND.

Murage, a tax destined for the provision and maintenance of the walls of medieval boroughs, levied from the burgesses by royal licence.   PMB

Murder Fine, a modification of the Anglo-Saxon WERGILD, introduced by William I as punishment for killing a Norman. If the HUNDRED could neither produce the murderer nor successfully present ENGLISHRY, it had to pay the fine, originally 40 marks to the king and 6 marks to the victim's family, but later decreased. The Norman and English races soon mixed and the fine became a levy of £5 on a HUNDRED in which an unsolved murder occurred: it was eventually abolished in 1340.   PMB

Murmansk–Archangel expedition (1918–19), resulted from the Russian revolutionary government's withdrawal from WORLD WAR I (15 Dec. 1917) and was primarily intended to re-establish the eastern front and to prevent the extensive stocks of military equipment at M. and A. (the property of the western allies) from falling into German or Bolshevik hands. In April 1918 a small force of British marines landed at M. and in June and July allied troops (mainly British) occupied the area and A. (3 Aug.); further troops arrived (30 Sept.) under General Ironside, who subsequently took over the command. At the same time an allied force under Japanese control had landed at Vladivostok. The expedition developed into support of the anti-Bolshevik Russian forces, but the futility of intervention became increasingly apparent and withdrawal was decided upon (Mar. 1919). Additional troops were sent in May to assist in the evacuation and, after a limited summer offensive, withdrawal from A. (27 Sept.) and

finally from M. (12 Oct.) was effected. Little was achieved and the Russian civil war was prolonged.   IHE

Muscat and Oman, fought over between Arabs, Portuguese and Turks in the 17th–18th centuries, was seized by the founder of the present dynasty, Sayyid Sultan, at the end of the 18th century. He also conquered some places on the Persian coast of the PERSIAN GULF which in 1958 were ceded to PAKISTAN. The theocratic rule of the imam was confined to the interior. In 1800 Sayyid accepted a British political agent. Subsequent treaties for the suppression of the slave-trade strengthened the ties with Britain, culminating in the treaty of friendship of 1951. From 1828 to 1861, the sultan was also ruler of ZANZIBAR, Pemba and the coast of KENYA. The Kuria Muria islands were ceded to Britain in 1854 and retroceded to the sultan in 1967. SHS

Muscovy Company. In 1553 an influential London company supported Sebastian Cabot's project to search for a north-east passage to Asia. The first voyage (1553–4) under Willoughby and Chancellor resulted in the opening of trade (largely in naval stores) with Russia. The joint-stock company incorporated in 1555 was given a monopoly of this trade, becoming known as the M. or Russia Company. Search for the passage soon ceased, but company voyages for this purpose continued until 1608; the passage was first traversed by the Swedish ship *Vega* in 1879. Between 1562 and 1579 Anthony Jenkinson on behalf of the M.C. opened up an overland trade with Persia which was revived again in the late 1730s until 1746. English merchants were excluded from Russia in 1646, largely owing to Dutch influence, but the trade was reopened after the Restoration when the M.C. was reorganized as a regulated company. It continued to exist until after the Russian revolution of 1917.   IHE

Mutiny Act. The first such act was passed in 1689 to deal with a mutiny among disaffected troops at Ipswich and was valid for six months only. It was re-enacted annually, with some exceptions, and provided for the punishment of mutiny and desertion by court-martial within the kingdom in time of peace, thus legalizing the existence of a standing army. The Act of 1718 provided for the establishment of courts-martial in any of the crown's dominions and authorized the crown to draw up articles of war. The MILITIA was brought under its provisions in 1757, and in 1803 it was extended to troops outside the dominions. In 1879 the M.A. was replaced by the Army Discipline and Regulation Act, and since 1881 by Army (Annual) Acts, which from 1917 applied to the R.A.F., becoming Army and Air Force (Annual) Acts.

IHE

Mynydd Carn, battle of (1081), fought at an unidentified site not far from St David's between Gruffydd ap Cynan of GWYNEDD and Rhys ap Tewdwr of DEHEUBARTH on the one side, and rival Welsh princes on the other. It ended in complete victory for the former and went far towards establishing their dynasties as the rulers of Gwynedd and Deheubarth.

GW

Mysore, an old Hindu kingdom, from the 14th to the 17th centuries part of the Vijayanagar empire, became a powerful state under the Moslem adventurer Hyder (1761–82). The so-called first Anglo–M. war (1765–9), in which the nizam of HYDERABAD and the MARATHAS changed sides several times, ended in a draw. During the second Anglo–M. war (1780–4) Hyder, allied with the French (Hyderabad and the Marathas again found on both sides), invaded the Carnatic, took ARCOT and, despite the English victory of Porto Novo (1781), died unvanquished (7 Dec. 1782). His son, Tipu, continued the war and concluded peace (Mangalore, Mar. 1784) on the basis of the *status ante*. Lord Cornwallis provoked the third Anglo–M. war (1789–92), but Tipu opened it by attacking the English

protectorate of TRAVANCORE. The peace of SERINGAPATAM (Mar. 1792) deprived Tipu of half his dominions, which were allotted to Hyderabad, the Marathas and the Company. Tipu took advantage of the REVOLUTIONARY WARS to ally himself ('citoyen Tipu') with France, but the fourth Anglo-M. war (1799) was of short duration and ended with the complete defeat of Tipu, who was killed in the gallant defence of his capital, Seringapatam (4 May). M., again reduced in favour of Hyderabad and the Company, was brought under a Hindu dynasty whose misgovernment caused the English to take M. under direct administration from 1831 to 1881. In 1956 a Kannada-speaking state called M. was created by amalgamating the previous states of M. and COORG with some districts of BOMBAY, Hyderabad and MADRAS.

SHS

Myton, battle of (20 Sept. 1319). While Edward II was trying to retake BERWICK, a Scottish force under Sir James Douglas carried out a diversionary raid into Yorkshire. At M. in Swaledale Douglas routed an army hastily raised by William Melton, archbishop of York, which included a large number of priests and monks: hence the Scots called the fight 'the chapter of M.' Douglas' raid achieved its main purpose in causing the English to abandon the siege of Berwick.

RFW

Nabobs, a nickname given to those servants of the EAST INDIA COMPANY who, having made their fortunes, returned to England to buy estates and seats in Parliament, where they had a vested interest in preventing reform of Indian government.

IHE

Nagaland. A state of INDIA, constituted Sept. 1962, from the Naga Hills and Tuensang districts. Christians (mostly Baptists) outnumber Hindus.

IHE

Nagpur, see CENTRAL PROVINCES.

Nájera, battle of (3 Apr. 1367). An Anglo-Gascon army under the Black Prince came in 1367 to the assistance of Peter the Cruel of Castile against his half-brother Henry of Trastamara, who had dethroned him with the aid of French mercenaries. After some initial reverses, the prince, together with Navarese and loyalist Castilian forces, advanced upon Burgos, and at N., near the Castilian-Navarrese border, completely defeated the Franco-Castilian army of Henry of Trastamara and Bertrand Duguesclin in a battle which demonstrated afresh the effectiveness of English tactics and the generalship of the prince. Although Peter was temporarily restored, English intervention in Castile was a failure in the long run. Peter's failure to pay the Black Prince's expenses led to the withdrawal of the English army, and important prisoners taken at N. were ransomed by the English and eventually assisted Henry to regain the throne in 1369. Thereafter England faced a firm Franco-Castilian alliance when the HUNDRED YEARS' WAR was resumed, and lost the command of the seas to the combined fleets of her enemies.   RFW

Nanking, treaty of (29 Aug. 1842), ended the first Chinese war (1839–42, the 'opium war'). HONG KONG was ceded to Britain and 4 more ports (Amoy, Foochow, Ningpo, Shanghai) were licensed for trade, consuls being recognized in each; whereas previously British merchants had been confined to Canton and had no diplomatic representation. British nationals acquired an extra-territorial legal status which was to cause much friction. Similar treaties were negotiated by the U.S.A. and France (1844). Shanghai quickly rivalled Canton as a commercial port, Chinese diplomatic exclusiveness was weakened and western influence considerably increased.   MLH

Napoleonic wars, see FRENCH REVOLUTIONARY AND N.W.

Naseby, battle of (14 June 1645), the decisive battle in the CIVIL WAR.

Charles I left Oxford and stormed Leicester. Fairfax and Cromwell hurried after him and the armies met at N. near Market Harborough. The NEW MODEL outnumbered the royalists by two to one. As at EDGEHILL, Rupert galloped far in pursuit of the Parliamentary left wing, but Cromwell routed the opposite wing and turned on the centre. The royalist army was destroyed, and captured correspondence revealed the king's intrigues for foreign aid.   IHE

Natal (Portuguese 'Christmas'). Vasco da Gama landed on Christmas day 1497 near the site where English traders settled in 1823 and in 1835 founded Durban. These were on good terms with the Zulu chiefs Chaka (1818–28) and Dingaan (1828–40). In 1837 the Boer Trek reached N.; the massacre of Piet Retief and his companions by Dingaan (6 Feb. 1838) was avenged by Andries Pretorius in the battle of Blood River (16 Dec. 1838) and the supplanting of Dingaan by his brother Panda who became a Boer vassal (1840). The republic was annexed to CAPE colony on 12 May 1843, whereupon most Boers emigrated to the TRANSVAAL. N. was made a separate colony on 15 July 1856, given responsible government in 1893 and enlarged by ZULULAND and Tongaland in 1897. From 1860 Indians immigrated in large numbers, first as workers on sugar plantations. In the discussions preceding the formation of the UNION OF SOUTH AFRICA, N. favoured a federal constitution. In 1960 it was the only province to reject the republican constitution.   SHS

National Assistance Board, the government agency for relieving individual distress. It was set up as the Unemployment Assistance Board in 1934 during the slump to aid the able-bodied unemployed, administering the means test. Allied schemes were subsequently assigned to it, e.g. supplementing the Old Age Pension from 1940 onwards, when it was known as the Assistance Board: the whole non-contributory Old Age Pension scheme was transferred to it in 1947 and, with modern terms of reference, it was renamed the N.A.B. in 1948. In Aug. 1966 the N.A.B. became the Supplementary Benefits Commission of the Ministry of SOCIAL SECURITY.   PMB; MR

National Coal Board. The working of coal, known from the 13th century at least, was greatly and haphazardly extended to serve the INDUSTRIAL REVOLUTION. Apart from improving conditions of work (MINES ACTS), government interfered little until 1920, when the mines department of the Board of TRADE was established. Though given powers over the production and sale of coal in 1930, the department could not prevent great distress in the mining areas during the inter-war depression or rationalize the industry. The first step towards nationalization was taken in 1938, and coal commissioners appointed to buy mines: full nationalization came only with the 1946 Act, under which the N.C.B. was appointed to plan and administer every aspect of the industry.   PMB

National Debt, originated in its permanent form from a scheme to finance war with France in 1692 when £1m. was borrowed and secured on the national revenue. In 1694 a further loan of £1·2m. was obtained from the newly formed BANK OF ENGLAND, which has managed the debt since 1750. Mainly due to wars the N.D. increased rapidly reaching £20m. in 1697, £243m. in 1784 and £798m. in 1903. The SOUTH SEA COMPANY's conversion schemes (1711–20) were followed by more successful conversions in the 18th and 19th centuries, especially that of Goschen in 1888 and more recently in 1932. Attempts at systematic capital redemption were started by Walpole's SINKING FUND (1717), by the younger Pitt (1786) and by Northcote (1875). In 1968 the debt stood at £34,194m.   IHE

National Debt Office, the secretariat of the National Debt Com-

missioners first appointed in 1786 to administer the SINKING FUND established by the younger Pitt to reduce the NATIONAL DEBT. Other smaller funds have since been entrusted to the commissioners, e.g. under the National Annuities Act 1808, as well as administration of the Trustee Savings Banks, established from 1799 onwards.   PMB

National Incomes Commission, see PRICES AND INCOMES.

National Insurance, see PENSIONS AND N.I.

Nationalist Party, see HOME RULE; IRELAND, PARTITION OF.

National Register of Archives, see HISTORICAL MANUSCRIPTS COMMISSION.

N.A.T.O. The North Atlantic Treaty Organization established in 1949 for collective defence between Great Britain, Belgium, France, Italy, Luxembourg, Netherlands, Denmark, Ireland, Norway, Portugal, Canada and the U.S.A. Greece and Turkey joined in 1952 and the Federal Republic of Germany in 1955.   IHE

Nauru, a Pacific island, discovered in 1789, was annexed by Germany in 1888 and surrendered to the Australian forces in 1914. It was made a MANDATE (1920) and TRUSTEESHIP territory (1947) common to Great Britain, Australia and New Zealand, which agreed that AUSTRALIA was to appoint the administrator. N. was occupied by the Japanese from 26 Aug. 1942 to 13 Sept. 1945. It became an independent republic on 1 Feb. 1968 maintaining special relationship with the COMMONWEALTH.   SHS; IHE

Navarino, battle of (20 Oct. 1827). By the Treaty of London (6 July) Great Britain, France, and Russia agreed to interfere in the Greek War of Independence to secure an armistice. A British squadron under Vice-Admiral Codrington joined by French and Russian ships was sent to the Morea to enforce terms and entered

N. Bay. The Egyptian leader Ibrahim Pasha opened fire on a boat carrying a flag of truce and in the ensuing battle the Turko-Egyptian fleet was virtually destroyed. When Wellington became Prime Minister in Jan. 1828 he adopted a pro-Turkish policy and N. was lamented as an 'untoward event'. IHE

Navigation Acts were first designed to develop English shipping (1382, 1485, 1540), but the ordinances of James I and Charles I were primarily to regulate the colonial trade in the interests of revenue. The Commonwealth ordinance of 1650 forbade foreign ships to trade in the colonies. That of 1651 restricted all colonial trade to English and colonial ships manned by 75% English crews, and only English ships or those of the exporting country could import European goods to England. Directed against the Dutch carrying trade, they were the basis of the act of 1660, which also provided that specified colonial goods could only be shipped to England or her plantations. This policy of MERCANTILISM was furthered by acts of 1663 (Staple Act), 1672 and 1696. The colonies gained greatly by monopolies in the English market, but the acts were frequently violated and difficult to enforce. They were modified in 1822 and 1825 to permit foreign countries to trade with the colonies under certain conditions and were repealed in 1849. IHE

Nechtansmere, battle of, near Forfar in Angus, Scotland (20 May 685). King Ecgfrith of NORTHUMBRIA suffered a crushing defeat at the hands of the PICTS under King Bruide, and Ecgfrith was killed. The battle marked the end of Northumbrian expansion north of the Firth of Forth, although it was not until the early 11th century that the Scots acquired territory to the south (CARHAM). CFS

Neck verse, see BENEFIT OF CLERGY.

Negri Sembilan, see FEDERATED MALAY STATES.

Neolithic (Gk. *neos*, new; *lithos*, stone), is the general name given to the cultures of the period beginning in the latter part of the 4th millennium B.C. that succeeded the MESOLITHIC. It saw the major advances of domestication of animals, cultivation of crops and making of pottery. These had originated in the Near East *c.* 7000 B.C., and were brought to Britain by invaders or immigrants from western Europe. The type-site that has given its name to their culture is Windmill Hill, near AVEBURY, Wiltshire; characteristic features of the culture are an efficient, sparsely decorated, handmade pottery, and long barrows constructed for communal burial. Other immigrants reached the west coast of Britain, their main known characteristic being the construction of the so-called megalithic tombs, which are scattered over the countryside as far east as Berkshire (Wayland's Smithy). Native Mesolithic cultures were gradually affected: the best studied are the Peterborough and Rinyo-Clacton cultures, which show a combination of new ideas together with surviving techniques of hunting and fishing. These native Neolithic cultures were generally of a lower standard than those from outside, but they appear responsible for certain religious sanctuaries whose construction implies a high degree of tribal organization, and which are unique to Britain: examples are Arminghall (Norfolk), Woodhenge (Wilts) and the first works at STONEHENGE. These may imply a change in religious belief from fertility cults towards a form of sun-worship. The better flint and stone implements of this age were products of specialized manufacture, Langdale (Westmorland) and Grimes Graves (Norfolk) being two main centres; implements of bone and wood were also used. BRONZE-AGE cultures began to enter the country soon after the beginning of the 2nd millennium, but Neolithic continued in many areas until *c.* 1400, and in the north until considerably later. The term originated in the later 19th century. CFS

Nepal. The kingdom was conquered by the GURKHAS in 1768 and became a neighbour of British India on the cession of Gorakhpur by Oudh in 1801. The only armed conflict (1814–16) was settled by the treaty of Sagauli (28 Nov. 1815), by which N. withdrew from SIKKIM and several frontier districts and gave permission, in return for an annual subsidy, to recruit Gurkha regiments. The N. government, from 1846 to 1951 under the hereditary premiership of the Rana family, has remained loyal to the alliance with India and Great Britain as confirmed by the treaties of 1923 and 1950.   SHS

Neville's Cross, battle of (17 Oct. 1346). Although Edward III was still in France, besieging CALAIS, in the autumn of 1346, he had left the forces of the northern shires behind in England to guard against a probable Scottish invasion. David II, the ally of France, duly invaded England, but was disastrously defeated and captured at N.C., just outside Durham. The Black Rood of Scotland, evidently restored after the treaty of NORTHAMPTON in 1328, fell into English hands for the second time. David remained in captivity until 1356, when he was ransomed for 100,000 marks, but his absence did not weaken Scottish resistance to Edward III.   RFW

New Amsterdam. Consequent upon the discovery of the Hudson River (1609) and the trading activities of the New Netherland Company (1614–23) and the Dutch West India Company (1621), New Netherland was established as a Dutch colony (1622) and Fort Amsterdam became its governmental centre. New Sweden (founded 1638) was annexed in 1655, and there was a steady influx from the surrounding English colonies. N.A. became a centre for illicit trade with the English settlements, and in 1664 Charles II granted it to the duke of York as a proprietary colony. It was occupied with little resistance and renamed NEW YORK, although temporarily re-occupied by the Dutch

(1673–4) during the third DUTCH WAR.
                                                      IHE

New Britain Archipelago, see NEW GUINEA.

New Brunswick, part of the French colony ACADIA and, from 1713, of NOVA SCOTIA, was constituted a separate colony in 1784 after the large influx of loyalists from the lost American colonies. The frontier with MAINE was finally settled in 1842.

N.B. received responsible government in 1848 and joined the Dominion of CANADA in 1867 as a province.
                                                      SHS

Newbury, first battle of (20 Sep. 1643). The London militia under Essex, returning from the relief of Gloucester, were confronted at N. by the ROYALISTS, who withdrew after severe losses, and Essex continued his march to London.

Second battle of (27 Oct. 1644), an attempt of Parliamentary forces under Manchester to cut off Charles I's return from Cornwall, checked the king's advance to London, but he secured his retreat to Oxford.   IHE

Newcastle, Propositions of (14 July 1646), peace proposals delivered from Parliament and the Scots to Charles I at N. after his surrender (5 May), made up of 19 clauses and similar to the negotiations of UXBRIDGE. Charles was to accept the COVENANT, abolish episcopacy, agree to the punishment of his supporters and allow Parliament to control the army and foreign relations for 20 years. He would not desert the Anglican church and played for time. The Scots tired of waiting, made a settlement with Parliament over monies due to them, handed over the king and left England (Feb. 1647).
                                                      IHE

New England, the territory of the PLYMOUTH COMPANY, was so named by Captain John Smith in 1614 and was taken over by the COUNCIL FOR NEW ENGLAND (1620–35). It was largely settled by PURITANS who rejected the

ARMINIANISM of the Anglican Church. The first colony was established at PLYMOUTH (1620), followed by MASSACHUSETTS (1628–9), CONNECTICUT (1633–6), RHODE ISLAND (1636–9) and NEW HAVEN (1638–9). N.E. also included the colonies of NEW HAMPSHIRE (1629) and MAINE (1635). Massachusetts, Plymouth, Connecticut and New Haven formed the N.E. Confederation (1643–84) to maintain uniformity of external relations etc., probably in view of the English CIVIL WAR. To enforce royal authority and maintain the NAVIGATION ACTS James II combined them all, together with NEW YORK and NEW JERSEY, into one short-lived Dominion of N.E. (1686–9). Separatist and democratic in outlook, they resented the restraints of English MERCANTILISM and took the most prominent part in the events leading to the AMERICAN REVOLUTION.

IHE

New Forest, an ancient woodland forming part of the forest of Andred which covered much of Hampshire and Sussex, but traditionally first preserved for the king's hunting by William I who is alleged to have destroyed many villages within its bounds, and who imposed the severe Norman forest laws.

On 2 Aug. 1100 William II (Rufus) was killed by an arrow shot by Walter Tirel while hunting in the N.F. near Brockenhurst. The king's death may have been deliberately planned by adherents of his younger brother, Henry.

RFW

Newfoundland, possibly visited by Bristol sailors from 1481 (or 1491), was made publicly known by John Cabot in 1497. Its codfish soon attracted fishermen of various nations. N. was formally annexed by Sir Humphrey Gilbert in 1583, and the drying of codfish led to permanent settlement. By the peace of UTRECHT (1713) France acknowledged British sovereignty, but French fishing rights were finally bought out as late as 1904. The colony was granted a legislature in 1832 and a constitution in 1855 and raised to Dominion status in 1917.

Financial collapse led in 1934 to the suspension of the constitution and government by commission. A referendum in 1948 voted for confederation with CANADA, of which N. became the tenth province on 31 Mar. 1949.

SHS

Newgate Prison. The new gatehouse of the City of London was used as a prison for both City and, from the 13th century onwards, some KING's BENCH prisoners. Rebuilt in 1672 and 1770, the prison was equipped to administer the *peine forte et dure* allowed by the law, and executions were transferred there from Tyburn after 1783. Adopted as a government prison in 1877, N.P. stood empty for some years before its demolition in 1902: the Central Criminal Court (Old Bailey), opened in 1905, now covers its site.

PMB

New Guinea, discovered by the Portuguese in 1526, was later claimed by the Dutch, who effectively occupied the western half in 1828. Eastern N.G. was in 1883 annexed by QUEENSLAND in order to prevent its occupation by Germany but, owing to the objections raised by the colonial office, only the southern portion was on 6 Nov. 1884 declared the protectorate of British N.G. (in 1906 renamed PAPUA). North-eastern N.G. and the New Britain archipelago became German protectorates in 1884 and were renamed Kaiser-Wilhelms-Land and Bismarck Archipelago. Australian forces in Sept. 1914 conquered the German colony, which subsequently became an Australian MANDATE (9 May 1921) and TRUST TERRITORY (13 Dec. 1946) and in 1945/6 was administratively combined with Papua.

SHS

New Hampshire, one of the 13 American colonies. From 1622 the COUNCIL FOR NEW ENGLAND made grants in the area, and small fishing and trading settlements developed. The name was first applied (1629) to John Mason's concession, confirmed in 1635 shortly before his death, and in 1641 N.H. was absorbed by MASSA-

CHUSETTS whose dissidents had spread into the area. Charles II reversed this high-handed action by re-establishing N.H. as a royal colony (1679). It became part of James II's Dominion of NEW ENGLAND (1686) but was restored as a separate colony in 1691. It was the first colony to establish an independent government in 1776. IHE

New Haven was established as a Bible commonwealth to the west of the Connecticut estuary in 1638 by a group of wealthy Puritans who had arrived in Boston in 1637. In 1639 government was established on a narrow basis of church membership. N.H. was taken over by CONNECTICUT in 1662 in spite of its protests. IHE

New Hebrides (Nouvelles-Hébrides), discovered in 1606 and surveyed by Cook in 1774, were occupied by France in 1886 and subsequently (1887, 1906) created an Anglo-French condominium; it was in 1922 placed under the jurisdiction of the WESTERN PACIFIC HIGH COMMISSION. SHS

New Jersey was originally part of the Dutch settlement of NEW AMSTERDAM in America taken over for the duke of York in 1664. He transferred the land between Hudson and Delaware to Lord Berkeley and Sir George Carteret. Renamed N.J., East Jersey was taken over by Carteret and West Jersey by Berkeley. During the Dutch re-occupation (1673–4) Berkeley sold his rights to two Quakers, who were bought out in 1682 by William Penn and his associates for £3,400. It became part of the Dominion of NEW ENGLAND (1688), was restored to its proprietors 1689 and became a crown colony in 1702. IHE

New Model Army was established by Parliamentary ordinance (15 Feb. 1645). The armies of Essex, Waller and Manchester were reorganized as a single force of 22,000 men under Sir Thomas Fairfax, but the troopers of the EASTERN ASSOCIATION were its main strength. Planned to consist of 6,600 horse, 1,000 dragoons and 14,400 foot, the cavalry was much increased and a more powerful artillery established. Better pay arrangements improved discipline, but many soldiers were still pressed men. The majority were INDEPENDENTS. Cromwell was soon appointed lieutenant-general. IHE

New Monarchy. This term was first used by J. R. Green in the 1870s and has since been widely bestowed on the Tudor monarchy with special emphasis on Henry VII's contribution. It suffers from the same misconceptions as the view that the N.M. was the political manifestation of the Renaissance. It was supposed to reveal new tendencies towards centralization, absolutism and constitutional changes of a fundamental character. The modern view is that the Tudor monarchy (rather than N.M.) developed with the aid of existing machinery, no significant changes coming before the 1530s. The essential significance of 1485 was that then an extremely able ruler ended the struggle between York and Lancaster and created a stable and effective dynasty and a strong central government. IHE

New South Wales was sighted and named (after its supposed resemblance to Glamorganshire) by Cook in 1770, and served as a penal settlement from 1788 to 1853. The first party of 736 convicts, sent out in 1787 under Capt. Arthur Phillip, was settled at Botany Bay and (26 Jan. 1788) founded Sydney. The worst elements were later transferred to NORFOLK ISLAND and Tasmania. Transportation ceased in 1840 and was eventually abolished in 1853 (except to Western Australia). By fostering the exploration of the interior (from 1813), introducing sheep grazing on a colossal scale (merinos were first introduced from the Cape by John Macarthur in 1797), granting land to the convicts after the expiry of their sentences and encouraging the immigration of free settlers (after 1815), the governors Lachlan Macquarie (1809–19) and Sir Thomas Brisbane (1821–5) transformed the penal settlement into a real colony. A nominated council was set up in 1823, followed by the establishment of representative (1843) and responsible (1856) government. The colony originally comprised the whole of Australia except WESTERN AUSTRALIA; successively TASMANIA (1825), SOUTH AUSTRALIA (1836), VICTORIA (1851), QUEENSLAND (1859), the NORTHERN TERRITORY (1863) and CANBERRA (1909) were carved out of its territory. N.S.W. joined the Commonwealth of AUSTRALIA on its creation, 1 Jan. 1901.   SHS

Newspapers, see PRINTING.

New York, formerly NEW AMSTERDAM, was occupied by the English in Aug. 1664 and granted as a proprietary colony to the duke of York. NEW JERSEY was given to other proprietors at the outset and DELAWARE was ceded to William Penn in 1682. By the duke's laws freedom of conscience and worship and trial by jury were granted. N.Y. was included in the Dominion of NEW ENGLAND in 1688. A cosmopolitan population of Dutch, Germans, Huguenots and New Englanders favoured the growth of faction, and from 1689 to 1691 the colony was controlled by the popular party under Jacob Leisler. Royal government was re-established in 1691 with an assembly which developed on British Parliamentary lines. In the 18th century N.Y. constantly violated the NAVIGATION ACTS, resisted the STAMP ACT (1765) and the Tea Act (1773). The assembly was suspended (1767–9) and the patriot party usurped its powers in 1775 and joined the AMERICAN REVOLUTION. In 1776 Washington's troops were driven out by British forces, and it remained the British headquarters for the rest of the war.   IHE

New Zealand (Maori: Aotearoa), discovered by Tasman in Dec. 1642, first charted by James Cook and explored by Joseph Banks in 1769–70, was intermittently settled by whalers from NEW SOUTH WALES, the Church Missionary Society (from 1814) and other missionary bodies and the N.Z. Association (1837; renamed N.Z. Company, 1839; dissolved 1851). On 6 Feb. 1840 British sovereignty, under the governor of New South Wales, was established by the Treaty of WAITANGI. N.Z. was made a separate colony in May 1841 and granted provincial (1846) and colonial (1852) self-government. Ministerial responsibility was introduced in 1856. The capital was moved from Auckland to Wellington in 1865. The gold rushes (1852, 1857–70) increased the population and altered its composition (influx of Irish, Jews, Chinese); state-aided immigration on a large scale began in 1870. The frozen-meat and dairy industries became the backbone of the N.Z. economy after 1880. The provinces (six in 1852, nine in 1874) were abolished in 1876. N.Z. was the first country to grant votes to women (1893) and to develop the modern welfare state.

N.Z. refused to join the Commonwealth of AUSTRALIA in 1900 and was ranked as a Dominion in 1907, receiving its first governor-general on 11 May 1917; the 1931 Statute of WESTMINSTER was ratified as late as 23 Nov. 1947. The upper house (legislative council) was abolished with effect from 1 Jan. 1951.

N.Z. troops took part in the Boer war and the two world wars (ANZAC). In 1919 N.Z. joined the League of Nations, in 1945 the United Nations, in 1952 the ANZUS pact and in 1954 SEATO.

In 1887 N.Z. annexed the Kermadec Islands, in 1901 the Cook Islands (since 1888 a British protectorate), in 1923 the Ross Dependency and in 1949 the Tokelau Islands (in 1926 transferred from the GILBERT AND ELLICE ISLANDS to Western Samoa). WESTERN SAMOA (conquered from Germany by N.Z. forces in Aug. 1914) became a N.Z. MANDATE in 1919, a TRUST TERRITORY in 1946 and independent on 1 Jan. 1962. NAURU was a joint N.Z.–United Kingdom–Australia trust territory, administered by Australia.   SHS

Nigeria was from 1472 visited by Portuguese, Dutch, French and English traders in pepper, ivory, palm oil and slaves. After the ASIENTO (1713) British influence became paramount along the coast. Despite British efforts from 1808 to stamp out the slave-trade, Portuguese, Spaniards, Brazilians and U.S. Americans continued it until the 1840s. The great increase of legitimate trade caused the British government to appoint in 1849 the governor of FERNANDO Pó consul for the coast between the capes St Paul and St John and to commission Heinrich Barth to explore in 1850–5 the interior where the river Niger had first been sighted by Mungo Park in 1796. Methodist, Anglican and Presbyterian missionaries took up work from 1841.

The first armed intervention took place in Dec. 1851: a British squadron expelled a pretender to the throne of Lagos and reinstated King Akitoye, who on 1 Jan. 1852 placed his kingdom under British protection. The misrule of Akitoye's successor led to the annexation of Lagos (6 Aug. 1861). In 1862 Lagos was proclaimed a colony, but it was placed under the governors of SIERRA LEONE (1866–74) and the GOLD COAST (1874–86). It was actually run by the local businessmen, who in 1854 established courts of equity which enjoyed much respect and assisted the expansion of trade. In 1879 (Sir) George Goldie (1846–1925) brought about the amalgamation of the traders in the United Africa Company, which, in 1882 reorganized as the National African Company, in 1884 bought out a rival French company and on 10 July 1886 was chartered as the Royal Niger Company. The company concluded a series of treaties with African rulers which resulted in the proclamation (5 June 1885) of a protectorate over the 'Niger districts', which in 1893 was renamed Niger Coast Protectorate. The company set up the machinery of government and gradually extended its territory. The frontier with German CAMEROONS was fixed between 1885 and 1893; but French advances

in the north and east constituted grave difficulties: Yorubaland (1888), Borgu (1894), Nupe, Ilorin and Benin (1897) were secured against stiff French opposition before the frontier was settled in 1898.

In 1899 the company gave up its charter for a compensation, and on 1 Jan. 1900 government assumed direct control. The Niger Coast Protectorate was renamed Southern N. and on 1 May 1906 amalgamated with Lagos as the Colony and Protectorate of Southern N. The submission of the slave-raiding Aro in 1902 brought the last important tribe under control; Egbaland, subdued in 1895 but left independent, was incorporated in 1914. Northern N. was placed under Sir Frederick Lugard (1848–1945) as high commissioner (1900–1906); he had fought slave traders in NYASALAND, opened up UGANDA, served the N. company from 1894 and was to become governor of HONG KONG (1907–12), governor of both Southern and Northern N. (1912–14), the first governor-general of N. (1914–19) and a peer (1928). Between 1902 and 1906 Lugard dealt with the slave-raiding emirs of Kontagora, Yola, Bornu, Kano, Sokoto, Keffi and other regions and pacified the country by his system of INDIRECT RULE. The slavery proclamation of 1901 abolished legal slavery, prohibited the slave-trade and declared free all children born after 1 Apr. 1901. The main causes of the need for slaves—lack of free labour, minted currency and mechanical transport—were abolished through the building of railways and roads (from 1896).

On 1 Jan. 1914 Northern and Southern N. were amalgamated as the Colony and Protectorate of N. Nominated advisory and legislative councils, both including African members, were set up. They were in 1923 superseded by a partly elected council which, in turn, in 1947 gave way to a central legislative council for N. and CAMEROONS (administered by N. from 1924), regional houses of assembly and a council of chiefs for the Northern region, all with unofficial African majorities. A council of ministers responsible to the house of representatives was created in 1951; a new constitution with greater regional autonomy came into force on 1 Oct. 1954 when the name of the country was changed to Federation of N. The Federation achieved independence on 1 Oct. 1960 becoming a republic within the COMMONWEALTH on 1 Oct. 1963. In Jan. 1966 the constitution was overthrown by a military *coup d'état*, and in May 1967 the eastern states attempted secession as the Republic of Biafra. Bitter civil war followed until Jan. 1970.   SHS; IHE

Nile, battle of the (1 Aug. 1798), destroyed French naval power in the Mediterranean and ruined Napoleon's eastern ambitions. Napoleon left Toulon (19 May), took MALTA (12 June), landed at Alexandria (1 July) and won the battle of the Pyramids (21 July). Nelson with 13 ships of the line had preceded the French at Alexandria (28 June), continued his search to Syracuse, returned and sighted their fleet (13 ships of the line, 4 frigates) at anchor in Aboukir Bay. Although at dusk and on the verge of shoal water, he attacked from both landward and seaward sides. Only 2 French ships of the line and 2 frigates escaped and their Admiral de Brueys was killed. Nelson was made Baron Nelson of the Nile.   IHE

Nineteen Propositions (1 June 1642) were delivered by Parliament to Charles I at York, stating its political demands. Parliament was to appoint his council, officers of state, governors of fortresses and judges. It was to supervise the education and marriage of his children, control the militia and determine the form of church settlement. The anti-Catholic laws were to be strictly enforced, the DELINQUENTS abandoned to Parliament and the appointment of new peers was to be approved by both Houses. Charles rejected them as depriving him of all executive power, but they provided Parliament with a programme for the ensuing war.   IHE

Nisi Prius. As the JURY system developed and the king's courts settled at Westminster, the trouble and cost of bringing jurors there to give verdicts grew, as MAGNA CARTA recognized. The n.p. system, wherein pleadings were heard at Westminster and verdicts, other than POSSESSORY ASSIZES, were given in the county unless an EYRE should first appear, *nisi prius justiciarii veniant*, was developed after the Statute of WESTMINSTER II, 1285. Specially commissioned justices, necessarily judges, were appointed, and in process of time other special commissions were given to them, resulting in the modern system of judges on circuit.   PMB

Nithing, a man without honour. To be publically pronounced n. by a formal assembly was, in the late Old English period, the most serious reflection that could be cast on a man's character; it put him outside the social pale in any part of the Scandinavian world including England. The concept was introduced into England by king Cnut (1017–35). Its last formal use was by king William II in 1088 as a threat against those defaulting in service with the FYRD.   CFS

Nobility, titles of. In Old English and Anglo-Norman times title generally indicated service and responsibility rather than personal dignity, but from the early 12th century the title of EARL began to be given for personal reasons. The term BARON, originally applied to any important tenant-in-chief, likewise came to indicate personal worth rather than the extent of a man's lands. The increased stress on personal dignity during the 14th and 15th centuries differentiated the n. by introducing DUKE and MARQUIS above earl, VISCOUNT between earl and baron.   CFS

Noble. Gold n.s, half-n.s and quarter-n.s, worth 6s. 8d., 3s. 4d. and 1s. 8d. respectively, were issued by Edward III in 1344 to replace the FLORIN. The name n. apparently referred to the metal, gold. The design of the obverse of the n. and half-n., showing the king armed and standing in a ship, has often been thought to refer to Edward's naval victory of SLUYS (1340) and English command of the seas, but it is uncertain whether any such reference was intended. In 1464 the n. was revalued at 8s. 4d., and in 1465 replaced by the ROYAL, or rose n., and the ANGEL.   RFW

Nominated Parliament, see BARE-BONE'S PARLIAMENT.

Nonconformists, a term usually applied to those Protestants, called dissenters in the 17th century, who do not conform to the usages of the CHURCH OF ENGLAND. Their early history is that of the separatists, PURITANS and INDEPENDENTS, among whom the CONGREGATIONALISTS and BAPTISTS were the most important. With Roman CATHOLICS they were subject to the PENAL LAWS, but gained a temporary ascendancy after the CIVIL WAR until the RESTORATION, when the Act of UNIFORMITY (1662) added PRESBYTERIANISM to their ranks, although many of the latter became UNITARIANS in the 18th century. They were largely responsible for the colonization of NEW ENGLAND, and as late as 1681 PENNSYLVANIA was founded as a refuge for QUAKERS. Persecuted under the CLARENDON CODE and TEST ACTS, they gained freedom of worship by the TOLERATION ACT (1689), but various disabilities remained until the late 19th century. The METHODISTS were the last main group to become N. (1784–95). As champions of civil and religious liberty, N. were historically associated with the Whigs and the Liberal party and also contributed to the founding of the Labour party. N. now co-operate in the Free Church Federal Council (formed 1940).   IHE

Non-jurors, a term applied to some 400 High Church clergy, including Archbishop Sancroft and five other bishops, who on grounds of NON-RESISTANCE refused oaths of ALLEGIANCE to William and Mary. They were deprived in 1690 despite William

III's attempts at conciliation and were augmented by those who refused allegiance to George I in 1714 (BANGORIAN CONTROVERSY). Supported by Anglican JACOBITES, they maintained their own episcopal succession until 1805. Their secession enabled the government to replace them by Low Churchmen and LATITUDINARIANS. Most of the Scottish Episcopal Church were n.-j., but it was disestablished in 1689, and their opposition ceased after the Young Pretender's death (1788).   IHE

Non-residence of beneficed clergy was a major abuse in the medieval church and continued in England in varying degrees until the reign of Queen Victoria. Much of it resulted from pluralism, which was widely practised by the higher clergy, who often held livings 'in commendam' (i.e. to which no incumbent was appointed). 'That n.-r. be not permitted' was one of the requests in the MILLENARY PETITION (1603), and residence was required by canons of 1604. It was prevalent in the 18th and early 19th centuries (more than half the clergy were non-resident in 1810), some bishops rarely visited their sees and pluralist bishops held livings long distances apart. The Ecclesiastical Commission's report and the appointment of a permanent commission (1836) led to its discontinuance.   IHE

Non-resistance began as an Anglican doctrine of passive obedience even if royal commands were unlawful or against the divine will. This doctrine was taught in the *Homily on Wilful Disobedience* (1569) directed against Roman CATHOLICS and was developed as a natural corollary to the theory of the DIVINE RIGHT of kings to condemn resistance to Charles I. It assumed a new importance after the Restoration, when Anglican clergy and Tories went to extreme lengths to proclaim it against Whigs and Dissenters. In 1675 a n.-r. bill was unsuccessfully introduced to debar from Parliament those who advocated change in church or state. The policies of James II turned many moderate Anglican advocates of n.-r. against him, including the SEVEN BISHOPS. Even at the GLORIOUS REVOLUTION Archbishop Sancroft tried to preserve n.-r. by suggesting the appointment of a regent. Thereafter its devotees became NON-JURORS.

IHE

Nootka Sound dispute (1789–90). Captain Cook's discovery of King George's (Nootka) Sound, Vancouver Island (1778), led to a settlement by British fur traders (King George's Sound Company). These were ejected by a Spanish expedition in 1789. Spain claimed a prescriptive right by prior discovery of the whole west coast of North America up to 60° N.; Pitt asserted British ownership on the grounds of effective occupation. Parliament voted £1m. for war and Spain prepared to fight, but failing to get satisfactory support from revolutionary France, yielded to Pitt's claims (28 Oct. 1790).

IHE

Norfolk Island, discovered by Cook in 1774, was used as a settlement for dangerous convicts from NEW SOUTH WALES (1790–1805) and as a general penal colony (1826–56). Free settlers from PITCAIRN occupied N.I. in 1856. Administered by New South Wales (1856–96) and TASMANIA (1896–1913), it became a territory of the Commonwealth of AUSTRALIA in 1913.

SHS

Norham, arbitration of (1291). Edward I's arbitration on the claims of John Balliol, Robert Bruce and others to the throne of Scotland opened on 10 May 1291. Edward's claims to the overlordship and the custody of Scotland during the interregnum were acknowledged in June, and it was agreed that the successful candidate for the throne should do homage to Edward and grant him the rights 'incidental to homage'. The actual arbitration was submitted to 80 assessors (40 chosen by Balliol and 40 by Bruce) and 24 of Edward's council, who met at Berwick and eventually chose Balliol as king. Balliol was

duly crowned at SCONE on 30 Nov. and did homage to Edward on 26 Dec. 1292.

RFW

Norham, treaty of (1212). After some years of hostility between King William the Lion of Scotland and King John, the latter brought an army to the Scottish border in Aug. 1212. Without recourse to battle, however, John got his opponent to accept the treaty concluded at N. The precise terms are uncertain, but John was promised the payment of £10,000, and it is likely that William acknowledged John as overlord of Scotland. Scottish claims to the northern counties of England were not abandoned, however, until 1237.

RFW

Norman Conquest. On the death of Edward the Confessor (5 Jan. 1066) Harold Godwinson succeeded to the throne with the approval of the WITAN and Edward's dying consent, and was crowned the next day. The claims of Duke William of Normandy were disregarded, although Edward had probably promised the kingdom to William in 1051 or 1052, and Harold in 1064 had taken an oath to help William. William, whose claim was backed by pope Alexander II, recruited an army in France, Flanders and the Norman duchies in southern Italy, and assembled an invasion fleet. During the summer of 1066 Harold was harassed by the raids of his brother Tostig on the south and east coasts which were a prelude to the invasion of northern England by Tostig's ally, the king of Norway, in early September. The English defeat at FULFORD (20 Sept.) was speedily wiped out by Harold's victory at STAMFORDBRIDGE (25 Sept.).

As the English fleet guarding the Channel had been withdrawn to the Thames early in September, William's crossing (27–28 Sept.) was unopposed. After disembarking at Pevensey, the Norman army moved eastwards and won the decisive battle of HASTINGS, in which Harold was killed (14 Oct.). William then moved to Canterbury, and on to London, which was held for Edgar the Atheling, the native claimant to the throne. Unable to cross the Thames, William marched westwards, devastating the country as he went, forded the river at Wallingford and advanced north-eastwards as far as Berkhamsted. There Edgar, Edwin, Morcar and other English leaders submitted, and William was able to occupy London. On 25 Dec. he was crowned king in Westminster abbey.

However, resistance increased during William's absence from England (Mar.–Dec. 1067), and on his return the king had to deal with a series of local risings, notably in the south-west. In the summer of 1068 Edgar fled to Scotland, and Edwin and Morcar raised the north. The year 1069 was critical. William regained his grip on the north after the destruction of his garrison at Durham, only to lose it again in the autumn to a Danish invading army. Other risings in the south-west and in the west midlands demanded the king's attention before he could return to the final HARRYING OF THE NORTH in the winter of 1069–70. By Easter 1070 the last resistance along the Welsh border had been crushed, and thereafter William's position was not seriously threatened by local exploits like those in the Isle of ELY. By the summer of 1071 the most important English leaders had finally submitted. William's invasion of Scotland in 1072 and the resulting treaty of ABERNETHY removed the danger of rebels obtaining assistance from King Malcolm III, and the N.C. was complete.

The conquest brought fundamental changes. The Normans turned the face of England from Scandinavia to France: within 100 years the ANGEVIN EMPIRE stretched from the Tweed to the Pyrenees, from the Atlantic to the Massif Central; Norman kinsmen governed S. Italy and Sicily and played leading parts in the CRUSADES. FEUDALISM, as later medieval England knew it, was a Norman import; strongly centralised government, in which the king's chief instruments were his household and court (CURIA REGIS), took over useful Anglo-Saxon institutions—a royal secretariat

(CHANCERY), the treasury, a system of national taxation (GELD)—and adapted and developed them. In local government the main units of the SHIRE and HUNDRED were retained, although overlaid by a new pattern of feudal institutions. The bishop-administrators were trained in the Norman schools in an alien tradition, their cathedrals were designed by Norman architects. Much of the social order of the old English state, some of its culture and institutions were swept away. LATIN became the language of government, Norman-French the language of the upper classes, and not for more than three centuries did English recover its position as a literary and official language (VERNACULAR). The achievements of the Anglo-Saxon state are not to be despised, but the Normans revitalized it and gave it a new drive and direction.   RFW

Normandy, conquest of. (1) by Henry I, see TINCHEBRAI and BRÉMULE.

(2) by Henry V. After AGINCOURT Henry V renewed his invasion of France in the summer of 1417 with the naval victory off HARFLEUR. While the French were distracted by the feud of ARMAGNACS and Burgundians, Henry systematically reduced N., first securing a firm hold on the coast and the central part of the duchy, capturing Caen, Bayeux and Lisieux, and then pushing south to the borders of MAINE. This phase was rounded off by the capture of Falaise early in 1418, after a long siege. From central N. Henry's forces advanced in 1418 eastwards to the Seine, while south-western N. was overrun by Warwick and Huntingdon, and the duke of Gloucester reduced the Côtentin, being held up six months by the resistance of Cherbourg. The English then concentrated on ROUEN, which fell eventually on 19 Jan. 1419. The capture of Gisors and CHÂTEAU GAILLARD cleared the approaches to Rouen, while the fall of Pontoise in July 1419 brought Henry within striking distance of Paris. The murder of John the Fearless at Montereau in

Sept. brought the Burgundian faction into open alliance with the English and prepared the way to the treaty of TROYES and the Anglo-Burgundian control of all northern France. N. remained the stronghold of English military power in France, and particular efforts were made to make Henry's rule acceptable in the duchy.   RFW

Normandy, loss of. (1) under King John (1201–4). Before Philip II's final assault on the duchy, its defences had been weakened by the cessions of border territories by the treaties of LOUVIERS and LE GOULET. Having divorced his first wife, in 1200 John married Isabella of Angoulême, previously betrothed to Hugh de Lusignan. The latter raised a rebellion in Poitou, and when John seized their lands the rebels appealed to Philip, John's feudal overlord, who summoned him before his court. When John failed to appear, Philip's court sentenced him to the loss of all his French possessions, and the king proceeded to execute the sentence by military force in the spring of 1202. John won some initial success, in particular when he relieved Mirabeau (1 Aug.), capturing his nephew Arthur of Brittany and many of the Poitevin rebels. Arthur was probably murdered by John the following spring. From then on John's position rapidly deteriorated. The Bretons allied with Philip and eventually attacked N. from the west; to the south MAINE was lost; and Philip himself reduced the fortresses of eastern N. with surprising speed, helped by the treachery of John's castellans. John left N. for England in Dec. 1203, and in 1204 Philip met with only pockets of stout resistance. CHÂTEAU GAILLARD fell on 8 Mar., central and western N. put up virtually no resistance and Rouen and the surviving castles surrendered on 24 June. Of the whole duchy only the CHANNEL ISLANDS remained to John.
(2) under Henry VI, see FORMIGNY.   RFW

Norsemen or **Northmen,** see VIKINGS.

North, Council of the, see COUNCIL OF THE NORTH.

Northampton, assize of (probably Jan. 1176), a reissue and revision of the assize of CLARENDON of 1166. Forgery and arson were added to the list of offences to be dealt with by juries of presentment and the king's justices. More severe punishment—by mutilation and exile—was decreed for convicted criminals. The dangerous rebellion of 1173 prompted some precautionary measures: the justices were to take oaths of fealty to the king from all men, to inquire into the custody of castles, to ensure the complete destruction of ruined castles and the demolition of others which ought to be destroyed. Increased powers given to the justices were probably a consequence of the Inquest of SHERIFFS. The assize of MORT D'ANCESTOR originated in the assize of N.   RFW

Northampton, battle of (10 July 1460). In June 1460 the YORKIST earls of Warwick, Salisbury and March returned to England from Calais, and quickly mustered strong support despite their ignominious failure of the previous year at the Rout of LUDFORD. Henry VI and the duke of Buckingham assembled the LANCASTRIAN forces at N., but before their muster was complete they were attacked by Warwick who, assisted by treachery, stormed the entrenched camp of his opponents and gained an easy victory. Buckingham and almost all the Lancastrian nobles present were killed and Henry VI himself was captured.   RFW

Northampton, siege of (6–7 Apr. 1264). Civil war having broken out after the publication of the Mise of AMIENS, Henry III assembled his army at Oxford in Mar. 1264, while the MONTFORTIANS mustered at N. and London. Advancing from Oxford, the royalists stormed the town of N. on 6 Apr., and compelled the castle to surrender the following day. Simon de Montfort the younger was among the many important prisoners taken.

Simon the elder had set out from London to assist his son, but was too late, and had to retire to the capital.

RFW

Northampton, treaty of (28 Aug. 1290), Edward I's ratification of the treaty of BIRGHAM.

Northampton, treaty of (4 May 1328), the English ratification of the treaty concluded at Edinburgh on 17 Mar. 1328, between Robert Bruce and Queen Isabella and Roger Mortimer, the real rulers of England after the DEPOSITION of Edward II. In return for the payment of £20,000 the English recognized Robert as king of Scots and acknowledged the independence of Scotland. The Anglo-Scottish border was fixed as it had been in 1286. The treaty made no reference to the restoration of the Stone of SCONE to Scotland. RFW

North Borneo was in 1878 ceded by the sultan of Sulu to a British syndicate which in 1881 was chartered as the British N.B. Company. The company placed it under British protection in 1888. The frontiers with Dutch Borneo were delimited in 1891. From 20 Jan. 1942 to 10 Sept. 1945 N.B. was under Japanese occupation. It became a crown colony on 15 July 1946 and was joined to MALAYSIA in 1963 as the State of Sabah. SHS

North Carolina, the scene of Ralegh's early colonial ventures (1584–91), south of the present VIRGINIA, was granted to Sir Robert Heath (1629) but first planted by a group of eight influential proprietors who obtained their patent from Charles II (1663). Virginians had moved into the area in the 1650s, and the new syndicate established their settlement at Albemarle. Populated mostly by emigrants from the existing colonies, Scotch, Scotch-Irish, Huguenots and Germans, it was soon noted for its disorderliness and proved a disappointment to its founders. It became a crown colony (1729), supported the AMERICAN REVOLUTION (1775) and was the scene of bitter fighting (1780–1). IHE

North-East Passage, see MUSCOVY COMPANY.

Northern Ireland, an integral part of the United Kingdom, was established after the partition of IRELAND (1920–2). It consists of 6 of the 9 Ulster counties: Armagh, Antrim, Down, Fermanagh, Londonderry and Tyrone. N.I. has an executive government and bi-cameral parliament of its own, but sends 12 members to the U.K. parliament. MLH

Northern Rebellion (1569) was led by the earls of Northumberland and Westmorland with hopes of Spanish help from Alva in the Netherlands. Norfolk, who was originally involved, submitted to the government, but the northern earls rose when summoned to London (Nov.). They demanded a return to Catholicism, restoration of ancient liberties and customs and the removal of the queen's evil counsellors. Aiming at releasing Mary Queen of Scots from Tutbury, they retired and dispersed when Sussex gathered his forces against them (Dec.). The leaders fled to Scotland. Another rising under Dacre (Jan. 1570) was destroyed by Hunsdon. Retribution was severe; some 800 rebels were hanged. IHE

Northern Rhodesia was occupied from the mid-18th century by the Barotse, Bemba and some 50 other Bantu tribes. The Bemba were among the worst raiders and traders of slaves, selling them as far as ZANZIBAR and Arabia; they were brought under control as late as 1896. Under the influence of French Protestant missionaries Lewanika, the ruler of the warlike and well-organized Barotse, from 1870 repeatedly applied for British protection before this was granted on 27 June 1890. N.R. and NYASALAND were administered by one commissioner until 1895, when north-western and north-eastern Rhodesia were separated. The north-west, Barotseland proper, was placed under the high commissioner of South Africa in 1899; the north-east was put under the commissioner for Nyasaland in 1900. After further concessions made by Lewanika (who died in 1916) in 1898, 1900 and 1909, the north-east was gradually absorbed by the north-western administration. The two provinces were amalgamated on 4 May 1911 as N.R. under a resident commissioner with effect from 17 Aug. On 1 Apr. 1924 the crown took over from the British South Africa Company, which had administered N.R. since 1889, and instituted a governor with excecutive and legislative councils (the latter with an unofficial majority since 1945); but the Barotseland protectorate remained under the rule of its paramount chief. N.R. joined the Federation of RHODESIA AND NYASALAND in 1953 which was dissolved in 1963. N.R. became the independent Republic of ZAMBIA on 24 Oct. 1964. The economy of N.R. is based on copper, which was discovered along the Katanga border in 1902 but exploited only from 1928.   SHS; IHE

Northern Territory of Australia, originally part of NEW SOUTH WALES, was on 6 July 1863 annexed to SOUTH AUSTRALIA and on 7 Dec. 1907 transferred to the Commonwealth (effective 1 Jan. 1911). It has a legislative council (1948) and a non-voting member in the house of representatives, and administers the uninhabited Ashmore and Cartier islands.
SHS

Northstead, Manor of, see CHILTERN HUNDREDS.

Northumbria, a kingdom formed by the union of BERNICIA and DEIRA, was ruled, apart from the reign of the Deiran Edwin (616–32), by the Bernician royal line. Territorially it included all England north of the Humber, S.W. Scotland and E. Scotland to the Firth of Forth. Further expansion towards the north was checked by the victory of the PICTS at the battle of NECHTANSMERE (685). During much of the 7th century N. was the strongest English kingdom and its kings, Edwin (616–32), Oswald (633–41) and Oswiu (king 642–70, overlord

654–7), exercised lordship over the kings of southern England (BRETWALDA). But invasions of the kingdom from MERCIA in 632 and 641 resulted each time in the death of the N. king and the ravaging of his kingdom; and fighting between the two kingdoms from 670 to 678 resulted in the final gain by Mercia of the kingdom of LINDSEY. The hilly terrain that composed most of N. made royal control difficult, and although the main royal line continued until the beginning of the 9th century, the hundred years from 704 saw a number of pretenders to the throne. The troubles culminated during the years 758–808 in a series of revolts, and this was followed by a generation of political isolation broken only in 829 with the nominal submission of the Northumbrians to the king of WESSEX. In 844 the king of N. was killed by the DANES, and in 867 both claimants to the throne were killed at York in battle against the Danes. The tributary king set up by the Danes was expelled in 872, and in 876 the kingdom of N. came to an end. A Danish kingdom was established round YORK, and obscure English kings and nobles continued to rule in the wilder northern parts. N., less lands north of the Tweed lost to Scotland, was an earldom in the 11th century, but the later earldom of Northumberland covered only that county. N. was converted to Christianity by a ROMAN MISSION in 625 (CONVERSION OF ENGLAND), largely relapsed into HEATHENISM during the Mercian invasion of 631–2 and was after 634 reconverted by the SCOTTISH CHURCH. Differences between Scottish and Roman practices were settled by the synod of WHITBY (663). During the later 7th and 8th centuries N. became the leading western European centre of learning, and the reputation of its scholars continued long after its political decline.   CFS

North-West Frontier Province, the mountainous country west of the river Indus, gained importance when the Russian advance in Central Asia threatened Afghanistan and the approaches to India. The Russian occupation of Bukhara, Turkestan, Samarkand, Khiva and Merv (1866–84) was countered by the British advance all along the Afghan frontier, beginning with the occupation of Quetta (1877) and ending with the delimitation of the boundary by Sir Mortimer Durand (1893). The districts were combined in the N.W.F.P., carved out of the PUNJAB, under a chief commissioner (1901), later (1932) a governor; the old N.W. Province being renamed United Provinces. Serious risings of the Waziris, Afridis and other hill tribes, however, continued to drain Indian resources and manpower. In 1947 the N.W.F.P. became part of PAKISTAN.   SHS

North-West Passage. After 1498 the realization that John Cabot's New Found Land was not the coast of Asia led to the search for a N.W.P. The most important early English attempts were those of Sebastian Cabot to Hudson's Bay (1509), Frobisher and the CATHAY COMPANY (1576–8), Davis (1585–7), Waymouth (1602), Knight (1606) and Hudson (1607–8). Hudson made another voyage on behalf of the Dutch (1609), and for an English syndicate (1610–11) which as the N.W.P. Company promoted further voyages (1612–19) when Baffin and Bylot reached 78° N. in Baffin Bay (1616). Voyages were made in 1631 by James and Foxe, and the search was resumed by the HUDSON'S BAY COMPANY from 1742. Cook reached Bering Strait from the Pacific side (1778), and his work was continued by Vancouver (1792–5). The passage was first traversed by the Norwegian Amundsen in 1903–5. IHE

Northwest Territories, since 1867 the name of Rupert's Land and the Northwest Territory. Out of it were carved the provinces of BRITISH COLUMBIA, ALBERTA, SASKATCHEWAN and MANITOBA and the YUKON TERRITORY. Since 1952 the N.T. has been governed by a commissioner assisted by a council.   SHS

Norwegians. Attacks on England by N. VIKINGS were less important than those of the DANES. The majority of raids before 835 were probably made by N., but there is no mention of them in the happenings of the later 9th century. In 991 and 994 the exiled Norwegian leader Olaf Tryggvason, presumably with N. among his followers, ravaged in England. On the second occasion he was associated with Swein, the Danish king; and between 1009 and 1012 a Norwegian force under Olaf the Stout (later St Olaf) aided the Danes in their continuous ravaging of the land. Between 1012 and 1014 this force took service under the English king, Ethelred. In 1015 the Danish army under Cnut that attacked England included a Norwegian force. However, in two enterprises against England N. took the leading role. In the early 10th century a force of N. from Ireland, in association with Danes from Ireland and native Irish, occupied N.W. England and established the Norse kingdom of YORK. In 1066 Harold Hardrada, king of Norway, led an expedition to England to enforce his claim to the English crown. He defeated an English force at the battle of FULFORD, but was defeated and killed by the English under king Harold II at the battle of STAMFORDBRIDGE.   CFS

Notary, a clerk, descended from the *tabelliones* of the Roman empire, licensed to prepare documents in due form for civil and canon law requirements. On the continent there were two classes, imperial notaries (later licensed by national authorities) and papal. In England, where COMMON LAW flourished, there were originally few n.s, licensed by bishops under papal authority. The growth of the civil law court of admiralty and the advance of international trade led to an increase. In modern times the office is usually held by a SOLICITOR. At first n.s did not use seals to authenticate documents, but put on them distinctive marks, generally elaborately decorated crosses: a SEAL is, however, now generally employed.   PMB

Nottingham, Richard II's consultation of the judges at (Aug. 1387). In 1386 the opponents of Richard II and his favourites, led by the duke of Gloucester and the earl of Arundel, secured the appointment in Parliament of a commission of government —or continual council—of which they were to be members, and which was to have full powers until Nov. 1387. Richard, already nearly 20 years old, bitterly resented the appointment and in Feb. 1387 went on a prolonged tour of the Midlands, seeking to raise support and to undo the work of the parliament of 1386. On two occasions in Aug., first at Shrewsbury and later at N., Richard put a series of questions to his judges, of which the most important were whether the commission of government was detrimental to the royal prerogative, and how those responsible for its appointment should be dealt with. The judges, who afterwards pleaded that they acted under coercion, produced a formal written answer on 25 Aug. at N., declaring that the commission infringed the prerogative and that those responsible should be dealt with as traitors. The judges' reply was kept secret at first, but had leaked out by mid-Nov., when it alarmed Gloucester and Arundel and their party, the Lords AP-PELLANT, into preparing drastic action against the king's friends.   RFW

Nova Scotia, part of the French colony ACADIA, was ceded to Great Britain by the treaty of UTRECHT (1713). In 1749 the capital was moved from Annapolis (until 1710 called Port Royal) to the newly founded Halifax. The influx of American loyalists from the lost colonies led in 1784 to the constitution of NEW BRUNSWICK as a separate colony. In 1820 Cape Breton Island was incorporated in N.S. An elected legislative assembly had been granted as early as 1758, and responsible government was introduced in 1848. N.S. became a province of the Dominion of CANADA in 1867.   SHS

Novel Disseisin, Assize of, the first POSSESSORY ASSIZE, introduced in 1166.

The jurors were asked: if A. disseised B. of his free tenement unjustly and without judgement within the assize. Originally the action was limited to disseisins within a short period, fixed by ordinance. The limiting date was infrequently changed, and in Henry VIII's time it was still 1242, fixed in 1272. Designed to protect rightful SEISIN, the assize gave equal protection to wrongful seisin: later it was frequently adopted as a fictitious action to establish doubtful titles.
                                  PMB

Nyasaland was opened up by Livingstone (1858–63) and the Scottish Presbyterian missionaries (from 1875), but was dominated by Arab slave-traders who were finally suppressed only in 1895. The 'British Central Africa protectorate' was proclaimed on 15 May 1891 after Portuguese and German claims had been repudiated in 1890. The boundaries with Moçambique and NORTHERN RHODESIA were settled in June 1891. The common administration with north-eastern Rhodesia was abolished in 1895, and control was transferred from the foreign to the colonial office in 1904. A protectorate constitution of the renamed N. was introduced in 1907. Africans and Indians were nominated to the governor's legislative council from 1949 and, after the accession of N. to the Federation of RHODESIA AND N. in 1953, the nominated members were replaced by elected members in 1955. Fully responsible government was introduced in 1961. In 1963 N. opted out of the Federation and, as MALAWI, became an independent member of the COMMONWEALTH on 6 July 1964.
                              SHS ; IHE

Oath Helpers supported by oath the defendant's oath denying the accusation (WAGER OF LAW). Originally o.h. came from the accused's kinsfolk; but it was later laid down that they should be men of the same class as the accused but unrelated, and for refuting serious accusations should include at least one man of high rank. The oath of such would be more valuable, for the value of a man's oath varied according to his WERGILD.   CFS

Occasional Conformity Act (1711). To hold office many NONCONFORMISTS took communion in the Church of England once, evading the CORPORATION and TEST ACTS. The Tories introduced bills to prevent this (1702,3,4) but these were opposed by the Whigs and rejected in the Lords. The Whigs discreditably passed the O.C.A. in order to secure the support of the Nottingham group of Tories against the government's peace preliminaries with France. It was not strictly enforced and was repealed in 1719.   IHE

Offa's Dyke, traditionally the boundary between England and Wales, was an earthwork running along the border, though not continuously, from near Prestatyn in the north to the Wye near Monmouth in the south. It was probably constructed by Offa of MERCIA *c.* 784–96 and intended as a boundary rather than for defence. In general, despite Welsh retreats—as in western Herefordshire—and similar fluctuations, it remained the frontier between England and Wales until after the Norman conquest.   GW

Old Bailey, see NEWGATE PRISON.

Oléron, Laws of, international maritime laws promulgated in 1160 on the island of O. off La Rochelle by Eleanor queen of England and duchess of Aquitaine. The laws, akin to classical and early mediterranean codes, seem to have been adopted for England by Richard I. Thereafter they were augmented and interpreted as need arose and the ADMIRAL's jurisdiction developed.   PMB

Oman, see MUSCAT.

Omdurman, battle of (2 Sept. 1898), destroyed the Mahdist rule in the SUDAN. The reconquest of the Sudan, planned by Kitchener and Cromer, was approved by the British government in March 1896 when French and

Belgian expansion into the upper Nile regions and finally the Italian debacle at Adowa (1 March) at the hands of the Abyssinians (in collusion with the French and Mahdists) threatened the British position in EGYPT, ADEN and UGANDA. By the end of Sept. 1897 the northern Sudan as far as Merowe had been conquered by Kitchener's Egyptian troops. Reinforced by a British brigade, Kitchener, pushing along the railway which he was constructing simultaneously, gained a decisive victory at Atbara (8 April 1898). With now about 26,000 men, of whom one-third were British, Kitchener then advanced upon O., the Mahdi's capital, and within a few hours wiped out the main Mahdist army for the loss of 48 killed. The extrusion of the French from FASHODA and the final defeat of the Mahdists by Sir Reginald Wingate (24 Nov.) completed the campaign.   SHS

O'Neill's Revolt, (1) (1559–67), arose from a disputed succession to the earldom of Tyrone. Shane O'N. was accepted by the clan. The English government supported the rival claimant but failed to dislodge Shane, who by a compromise became captain of Tyrone in 1562. By war and terrorism he gained control of Ulster (1563–7), aiming at full independence, but was eventually overthrown by the efforts of the lord deputy and Shane's enemies, the O'Donnells.

(2) (1594–1603), a rising of the northern Irish dominated by Hugh O'N., earl of Tyrone, against English control. His great victory at Yellow Ford (Aug. 1598) encouraged rebellion in Munster, Connaught and Leinster, and the English position became precarious. It was largely suppressed in 1600 by Charles Blount, Lord Mountjoy, but a Spanish force landed at Kinsale, Co. Cork (23 Sept. 1601). The Spaniards and Tyrone's Irish army were decisively defeated (24 Dec.) and Tyrone eventually surrendered (Mar. 1603).   IHE

Ontario was in 1791, under the name of Upper Canada, separated from

QUEBEC and theoretically comprised an area stretching some 500 miles to the west, but was actually confined to the region of the great lakes. Its capital York (Toronto) was founded in 1794. The wish of the U.S.A. to absorb Upper Canada was partly responsible for the war of 1812; the victory of QUEENSTON HEIGHTS saved the colony. The inefficiency of the government and the dominance of small privileged sections caused the emergence of political groups demanding reform. Although they obtained in 1828 the majority in the assembly under the leadership of William Lyon Mackenzie (1795–1861), their efforts availed nothing. The plans for responsible ministerial government urged in 1829 by the conservative William Baldwin (1775–1844) and his son Robert (1804–58) were also turned down by the governor, but its main features were afterwards embodied in the DURHAM REPORT (1839). Mackenzie's rebellion in Dec. 1837 was suppressed even more quickly than that of Lower Canada. In 1840 Upper and Lower Canada were re-united, but again separated on the establishment of the Dominion in 1867, which O. joined as a province. About 1850 O. became more populous than Quebec and the capital, originally Montrèal and from 1849 alternating between Quebec and Toronto, was in 1858 fixed at Ottawa.   SHS

Ora, a Danish monetary unit, not an actual coin, representing 16 silver pennies. It was current in much of the DANELAW.   CFS

Orange Free State (Oranje Vrystaat). The territory between the rivers O. and Vaal was occupied by some 15,000 Boers from the CAPE during the GREAT TREK in 1836–7 and organized as a republic in 1842. From 1848, when the 'O. River sovereignty' was claimed by Great Britain, British settlers and businessmen followed, but the Bloemfontein convention of 1854 recognized the independence of the republic, which enjoyed stability and tolerance unknown in other Boer states. Its

economy was deeply influenced by the discovery in 1867 of diamonds on the O. river, with Kimberley as the centre. The dispute over the mine fields led to the establishment of a separate colony of GRIQUALAND WEST (1873), which despite the well-founded claims of the O.F.S. was annexed to the Cape in 1880.

Until the JAMESON RAID O.F.S. acted as a mediator between the Cape and TRANSVAAL, sharing a common president from 1860 to 1863, but in 1896 concluded an alliance with the latter which was maintained during the SOUTH AFRICAN WAR. Known as the O. River Colony from 1902, it joined the UNION OF SOUTH AFRICA under its old name in 1910.   SHS

Ordainers, Lords, the executive committee of the baronial opposition to Edward II. Early in 1310 the earls presented their grievances, notably Edward's wastefulness and the loss of Scotland. Faced by a show of force, the king was compelled to appoint, on 16 Mar., a committee with powers until Michaelmas 1311, to reform the realm and the royal household—the L.O. Twenty-one O., not all unsympathetic to Edward, were chosen by indirect election: the archbishop of Canterbury and 6 bishops, 8 earls, among whom Thomas of Lancaster was the most extreme opponent of the king, and 5 barons. The committee duly produced the ORDINANCES of 1311 but Edward evaded their provisions as soon as he could. The outbreak of fighting in 1312 led to the capture of Edward's favourite, Piers Gaveston, his execution on BLACKLOW HILL and the consequent split among his opponents. Peace was patched up, but by late 1313 it seemed that the reform movement had failed. In 1314, however, the disastrous BANNOCKBURN campaign so weakened the king's position that Lancaster was able to demand the execution of the ordinances. They continued to be enforced through the period of Lancaster's dominance and subsequently under the rule of the MIDDLE PARTY. The rise of Edward's favourites, the Despensers, led to the break-up of the Middle Party and the final defeat of Lancaster and the more extreme O. at BOROUGHBRIDGE in 1322.   RFW

Ordeal, a method of determining guilt or innocence in criminal cases by appeal to God's judgment. In Anglo-Saxon times o. followed if the accused was unable to get OATH-HELPERS or if oath failed. At the Norman conquest the alternative of TRIAL BY BATTLE was introduced. In England there were three main o.s: for the freeman, by hot iron (carrying a heated iron 9 ft in church during mass, with no scars after three days under bandages); for the unfree, by cold water (lowering bound into cold water, sinking proving guilt); for the clergy, the cursed morsel (a feather etc. in food, choking proving guilt): all were supervised by the church. In 1215 all clergy were forbidden to assist in o.s, and in England the 1219 EYRE justices were advised on new procedures to replace them. Their abolition marked a turning-point in English criminal law and the development of the JURY.   PMB

Orders in Council are issued by the sovereign on the advice of the PRIVY COUNCIL. Their scope has steadily decreased with the gradual transference of sovereignty from the crown to PARLIAMENT, and it is now agreed that, though o.c. may be issued by virtue of the royal PREROGATIVE, they should not substantially alter the law. Instances of o.c. where prerogative exists are those made for the armed forces and crown colonies. The majority of o.c. are now, however, issued under statutory authority (e.g. defence regulations in the second world war). They therefore form an alternative to the statutory instrument as a means of delegating legislation. A famous series of o.c. were issued in connexion with Napoleon's CONTINENTAL SYSTEM.
                                              MLH

Orders of Chivalry. The earlier CRUSADES saw the foundation of religious orders of knights—the HOSPITALLERS, TEMPLARS and others—who combined a monastic life with active military service in the cause of Christendom. In the later middle ages there were formed secular orders or brotherhoods of knights, whose institutions and ideals owed much to the chivalric literature of the time. These orders, far less international than their religious predecessors, were exclusive societies of distinguished soldiers, usually headed by their sovereign, sworn to military brotherhood, with a more or less elaborate hierarchy of officers. They included chaplains, the orders had their patron saints, and their own chapels and halls where their special festivals were solemnly and magnificently celebrated. Of the nine British orders of knighthood (knights bachelor and BANNERETS were never orders) only that of the GARTER dates from the middle ages. The premier Scottish and Irish orders of the Thistle and of St Patrick date from 1687 and 1788 respectively, while George IV and the romantic revival were responsible for the reorganization of the order of the BATH and the foundation of the order of St Michael and St George (1818). The latter has been associated since its foundation with colonial and imperial service, as were the 'imperial' orders of the Star of India (1861), the Indian Empire (1877, the year of Queen Victoria's assumption of the title of Empress of India) and of the British Empire (1917–18). The Royal Victorian Order (1896), awarded for special service to the sovereign or the royal family, had continental precedents. The Irish and Indian orders, which had the lord lieutenant and the viceroy as their grand masters, must be regarded as moribund. The introduction in the newer orders of ranks below that of knight—companions and members—has made possible the public recognition of a wider range of merit than military service, while an order like that of the British Empire, with its many grades, embraces very many fields of public service or celebrity. Not all modern orders have knighthood as their highest rank, but the Distinguished Service Order

(1886), for example, is none the less
an order of chivalry.   RFW

Ordinance, see STATUTE.

Ordinances (1311), the work of the
Lords ORDAINERS, appointed in Mar.
1311, the main body of which was
worked out by Aug. and assented to
by Edward II early in Oct. A further
group of o. made in 1311–12—when
the term of the Ordainers had expired
—was not accepted by the king. In
the first place the O. required the renewed exile of Piers Gaveston and
penalized others of Edward's favourites. Further, baronial control of
policy was secured by establishing
control of the administration: the
chief ministers, the officers in charge
of overseas possessions and some local
officers were to be appointed by the
baronage in parliament. Parliaments
were to be held twice or at least once
a year. A committee of ministers was
in turn responsible for the appointment of sheriffs. The king himself
was not to leave the realm without
baronial consent; his lavish grants
were revoked, and future grants were
to be agreed to in parliament until his
debts were paid. All revenue was to
be paid direct to the Exchequer. The
king's ITALIAN BANKERS, the Frescobaldi, whose loans had assured him a
degree of financial independence, and
who had been in receipt of the customs,
were arrested, and their goods seized.
The o.—41 in all—covered a wide
field, e.g. Exchequer accounting, the
jurisdiction of courts, amendments of
law and procedure. A committee of
five was to report to Parliament on
breaches of the o., but no effective
machinery was devised to ensure that
the o. were obeyed. They were finally
revoked by the statute of YORK, 1322.
                                     RFW

Ordnance, Board of. With the developing use of gunpowder, a master
of the king's O. was appointed with,
from Tudor times at least, an establishment at the Tower of London.
The master (later master-general) and
others formed the B. of O. which,
from Charles II's reign, was charged

with the supply of arms and munitions
to the services and the maintenance of
barracks and fortifications: the master-
general became the commander-in-
chief of artillery and engineers. The
B. of O. existed until 1855, when it
was merged with the WAR OFFICE.
                                     PMB

Ordovices, a primitive tribe occupying north-central Wales. They
offered considerable resistance to the
ROMAN CONQUEST but were defeated
in A.D. 51. Events elsewhere postponed Roman penetration of the area
until the mid-70s, and the conquest
was brutally completed by Agricola
in 78. They never became a CIVITAS,
probably remaining under military
government.   CFS

Oregon boundary treaty (Washington, 15 June 1846) divided the original
'Oregon territory' (i.e. present-day
British Columbia south of 54° 40′ N.
lat. and the present states of Washington, Oregon and Idaho) along the 49th
parallel, which in 1818 had been
agreed upon as the Canadian–U.S.A.
frontier from the Lake of the Woods
to the Rocky Mountains. The treaty
of 1846 continued this frontier to the
Pacific coast, assigning BRITISH COL-
UMBIA and Vancouver Island to Great
Britain, the rest to the U.S.A.   SHS

Orissa, Indian state, was absorbed by
the Mogul empire in 1592, ceded to
the MARATHAS in 1751 and conquered
by the British in 1803. As the 'district
of Cuttack' it was placed under BEN-
GAL administration (1804), split up
into three districts and a number of
tributary states (1822), combined with
BIHAR (1912) and eventually constituted a separate province enlarged
by some districts from the CENTRAL
PROVINCES and MADRAS. The 25 O.
states surrendered their authority to
the Indian government on 14 Dec.
1947; 23 of them were merged in O.,
2 in Bihar.   SHS

Orléans, siege of (1428–9). O., commanding an important passage of the
Loire and one of the principal fortresses of that part of France which
acknowledged the Dauphin Charles,

was invested by the English under the earl of Salisbury in Oct. 1428. Salisbury was killed early in the siege and was succeeded by the earl of Suffolk. Although the English were not strong enough either to storm or to enclose the city completely with their works, the defenders, disheartened by the 'battle of the HERRINGS', might have surrendered but for the appearance of Joan of Arc and a relieving army, which entered the city on 29 Apr. 1429. Inspired by Joan, the French captured some of the principal forts of the besiegers and within a few days forced Suffolk to abandon the siege.   RFW

Osborne judgment (21 Dec. 1909) allowed an injunction to restrain the Amalgamated Society of Railway Servants from spending its funds on political objects: the law lords decided that such activity was *ultra vires* as not mentioned in the defining clause of the Trade Union (Amendment) Act, 1876. Thus TRADE UNIONS were barred from contributing to the support of Labour M.P.s and the LABOUR PARTY was struck a financial blow. The O.j. conduced to the serious strikes of 1911–12. It also precipitated the payment of M.P.s (£400 p.a. from 1912). The decision was reversed by the Trade Union Act (1913).   MLH

Otterburn, battle of (15 Aug. 1388). A Scottish army under the earl of Douglas raided Northumberland and defeated Henry Percy, 'Hotspur', in a skirmish near Newcastle. Percy assembled superior forces and attempted a night attack on the Scots' camp at O. Although Douglas was killed, the Scots won a striking victory and Hotspur himself was captured. The battle became the subject of two famous ballads, the Scottish *Otterburn* and the English *Chevy Chase.*   RFW

Oudenarde, battle of (11 July 1708), one of the decisive battles in the SPANISH SUCCESSION WAR. The French, having resumed the offensive in the Netherlands after RAMILLIES, were admitted into Ghent and Bruges by the inhabitants. They next besieged O., but were utterly routed in

a surprise attack by numerically inferior forces under Marlborough and Eugene. The allies were again masters of the Netherlands and the capture of Lille followed (Dec.).   IHE

Outlawry, the final legal sanction against the absentee accused of a criminal charge, equivalent to conviction. The accused was summoned at four consecutive shire courts: if he failed to appear he was outlawed, with such words as 'let him bear the wolf's head'; he forfeited his goods to the crown, his lands to the crown for a year, then to his lord; he could be captured, in some areas killed on sight, and only the king could reverse the decision. In Anglo-Saxon times o. was widely used; after the Norman conquest the development of lesser criminal penalties brought gradual decline. In civil cases, however, a coercive, procedural o. in such matters as debt was used from the 13th century onwards.   PMB

Oxford Movement, a religious movement so-called because its leaders were members of Oxford University, was an attempt to reassert the authority of the CHURCH OF ENGLAND against a decline of standards, the spread of 'liberal' theology and dangers thought to be latent in such state action as CATHOLIC EMANCIPATION. The O.M. dates from an Assize sermon on *National Apostasy,* preached 14 July 1833 by John Keble, attacking a bill for the suppression of 10 Irish bishoprics. Keble, R. Hurrell Froude and John Henry Newman (all Fellows of Oriel College) thereupon wrote a series of *Tracts for the Times.* Edward Pusey was a valuable adherent in 1834. The Tractarians, or Puseyites as they later became known, strongly asserted the historical continuity of the Church of England as a divine institution and the foundation on catholic faith of its doctrines and ceremonies. This was backed by scholarly editions of the works of the Fathers and the Caroline divines. Opposition was soon expressed (by the University authorities, many of the bishops, EVANGELICALS and broad churchmen) to an insistence on clerical authority and doctrine which could be regarded as Romish. The O.M. grew, but within it emerged a party who gradually tended towards Rome. Newman's *Tract 90* on the Thirty-Nine Articles (1841), a defence of an extreme position, was widely attacked. In Oct. 1845 he was received into the Roman church, many supporters following him. A further secession occurred in 1850, following the GORHAM JUDGEMENT. Pusey and Keble remained firm. Despite widespread hostility their views gained ground in the next 20 years and had permanent influence. The lasting gain for the Church of England lay in the movement's emphasis on the importance of the ministry, of worship and ceremonial, and of religious community life.   MLH

Oxford Parliament (1258). Faced with the financial demands and the prospect of excommunication by Alexander IV if he failed to meet his obligations incurred in the SICILIAN BUSINESS, Henry III was forced in the London parliament of Apr. 1258 to give way to the barons, now on the verge of revolt. The barons promised financial aid on condition that the pope moderated his terms and Henry accepted reforms to be agreed upon by a committee of 24, half chosen by himself and half by the barons. The 24 met in the parliament which assembled at Oxford on 11 June and there produced the PROVISIONS OF OXFORD as the first stage of reform. The O.p. used to be called, erroneously, the 'Mad Parliament': one contemporary chronicle apparently referred to it as *illud insane parlamentum*, but the word *insane* has been shown to be a later substitution, possibly for *insigne*, 'famous'.   RFW

Oyer and Terminer. The general EYRE was slow, expensive and increasingly unpopular. From the 13th century onwards special justices, not necessarily judges but frequently SERJEANTS, were commissioned to 'hear and determine' some or all PLEAS OF THE CROWN which would have come before an eyre in the county. Like other special commissions, o. and t. was gradually merged into the commission of the modern judge on circuit.   PMB

Pahang, see FEDERATED MALAY STATES.

Pakeha, Maori name of the white New Zealanders.

Pakistan. The word was coined by Moslem students at Cambridge in 1933 and variously interpreted as 'land of the pure' (in Persian and Urdu) or as a combination of the initials of Punjab, Afghanistan (or Afghania, i.e. North-West Frontier Province), Kashmir, Iran (or Islam), Sind and the last syllable of Baluchistan; to describe the territorial aims of the MOSLEM LEAGUE, which from about 1940 agitated for the creation of P. comprising the Moslem-inhabited parts of India. This was achieved against the strenuous opposition of the INDIAN NATIONAL CONGRESS when on 15 Aug. 1947 India was partitioned and the dominion of P. was inaugurated, accompanied by the mass emigration of populations (over 10 millions) and the indiscriminate slaughter of over a million Hindus, Sikhs and Moslems. P., since 23 Mar. 1956 called the Islamic republic of P., comprises the former provinces of BALUCHISTAN, SIND, NORTH-WEST FRONTIER PROVINCE and parts of BENGAL, PUNJAB and KASHMIR. The provinces were abolished in 1955 in favour of a unified state. A new constitution was introduced on 1 Mar. 1962. Martial law was proclaimed on 25 March 1969, but unrestricted political activity was allowed from 1 Jan. 1970, and a constitution-making National Assembly planned for Oct.   SHS; IHE

Palaeolithic (Gk. *palaios*, ancient; *lithos*, stone), the name given to the first phase of human pre-history, lasting for over half a million years to about the 8th millennium B.C. The major developments of the period included tools, fire and speech. It coincided with the Ice Age of four very cold phases interspersed with milder interglacials. The ice reached the Thames valley area and fundamentally altered the surface features of the land, which was still joined to mainland Europe.

The main relics—and which have given the age its name—are stone implements. These were made by striking flakes from a core and using either the core or flakes as tools etc.; and various stone industries have been identified, showing a gradual development to more effective implements. Varieties of these 'core' and 'flake' industries known in Britain in early and middle Palaeolithic times are respectively: Abbevillian and Acheulian; Clactonian and Levalloisian. The physical types identified with these are Swanscombe man and Neanderthal man, although the latter has not been identified in Britain. They were probably organized in small kindred-groups, surviving by hunting and food gathering. The earliest known cave dwelling, Kent's Cavern in Torquay, was occupied by people with a mixed Acheulo-Levalloisian industry during the last glacial phase. In late Palaeolithic times earlier industries were gradually superseded by 'blade' industries, so-called from the characteristic parallel-sided flakes. The people of these new cultures were *homo sapiens* in type, appear to have practised a fertility religion, were skilful in bone-carving and were accomplished artists, although examples of cave artistry are not found in Britain. The varieties of 'blade' industry reaching Britain included the Aurignacian and Magdalenian, although the latter, the height of Palaeolithic achievement, was poorly represented. The warmer climate caused by the recession of the ice resulted in changes in fauna and flora; the former herds of wild animals disappeared and forests developed. Palaeolithic hunting techniques became increasingly difficult to apply, and a British development of the earlier Aurignacian 'blade' industry, the Creswellian (first discovered at Creswell, Derbyshire), shows the development of microliths and a way of life characteristic of the MESO-LITHIC.   CFS

Palatinate or County Palatine, an area—in England usually a county-earldom—whose lord, although a subject and a feudal tenant-in-chief of the king, possessed quasi-regal jurisdiction. Four p.s appear to have been created after the NORMAN CONQUEST, mainly for military reasons: Cheshire and Shropshire on the Welsh border, Durham in the north, and Kent, the nearest county to the continent; however, Shropshire and Kent were soon suppressed after the rebellion of their earls. The institution was older than the name—derived from Latin *palatinus*, associated with the imperial palace and therefore specially privileged—which only came into use in England in the mid-14th century, probably borrowed from Germany. The p. earldom of Chester was acquired by the crown in 1237 but retained its peculiar institutions and its separate character: Cheshire was not represented in PARLIAMENT until 1541. In the later middle ages it was closely associated with the Principality of WALES and held by the sovereign's eldest son. An Irish p., Co. Tipperary, was created in 1328, and the largest English p., LANCASTER, in 1351; like Cheshire, Lancaster retained much of its character of a kingdom within a kingdom. Durham was unique in that its lords were ecclesiastics, the bishops of Durham, who did not finally lose their palatine jurisdiction until 1836. The term p. is also occasionally applied to the territories of the Welsh MARCHER LORDS, most appropriately to those with a county organization, *viz.* Pembroke and Glamorgan.   RFW

Pale, the English. As early as the reign of Edward I Ireland was in practice divided into the 'land of war', the areas still ruled by the Irish, the 'land of peace', where English rule was secure, and the marches in between, ruled by English lords but frequently disturbed by war. By the time of the statutes of KILKENNY (1366) the 'English' area, where royal government was still effective, was considered to consist of Louth, Meath, Trim, Dublin, Kildare, Kilkenny, Wexford, Waterford and Tipperary. These areas, where English settlement was thickest and English rule most strongly entrenched, came to be called the Pale. Its frontiers, however, continued to shrink, partly because of the further encroachments of the Irish chiefs, partly because of the rise of the great earls who dominated Munster and parts of Leinster and ruled with little reference to the royal government in Dublin. Thus Waterford fell under the influence of the earl of Desmond, Kilkenny and Tipperary under that of the earl of Ormond, and Kildare under that of the earl of Kildare. In 1465 the parliament which met at Trim and Drogheda defined the Pale as consisting of four counties only—Louth, Meath, Dublin and Kildare. An act of Poynings' parliament in 1495 provided for the enclosure of the Pale by a great ditch, and shows that the area thus defined was considerably smaller than that of the four modern counties. The Pale continued to shrink until Henry VIII and his successors embarked on what amounted to a reconquest of Ireland. See also CALAIS.

RFW

Palestine, a Turkish province from 1516, was conquered by imperial forces under Allenby in 1917/18 and granted by the League of Nations to Great Britain as one of the MANDATED TERRITORIES (1920; in force 1923). On 25 May 1923 (Trans-)JORDAN was separated from P. proper, where the British administration implemented the BALFOUR DECLARATION of 2 Nov. 1917. Under the mandate about 400,000 Jewish immigrants were admitted, but this did not satisfy the Zionists who wanted a Jewish national state, whereas it alienated the Arabs who foresaw their relegation to an impotent minority while the neighbouring Arab countries were gaining their independence. The constructive work of the mandatory administration was continuously hampered by murderous riots between Arabs and Jews but directed increasingly also against the British. Various plans for a reorganization of P. on a tripartite or bipartite basis were rejected by Arabs or Jews or both. On 31 Aug. 1947 the security council of the United Nations recommended the political bisection of the country while maintaining its economic unity, and the neutralization of Jerusalem. When this project was turned down the British government decided to terminate the mandate and to withdraw the administrators and troops on 14 May 1948. On the same day the Jews proclaimed the independent state of Israel.

SHS

Pannage, a customary manorial rent paid by VILLEINS for the privilege of pasturing their pigs in woodland: the rates were often 1d. for a yearling pig, $\frac{1}{2}d$. for a younger.

PMB

Papal provisions, see PROVISIONS, PAPAL.

Papua, the south-eastern part of NEW GUINEA, was declared the protectorate of British New Guinea on 6 Nov. 1884, the administrative costs being borne by QUEENSLAND, NEW SOUTH WALES and VICTORIA until the Commonwealth of AUSTRALIA took over the territory in 1901 (effective 1 Sept. 1906), changing its name to P. In 1945–6 P. and New Guinea were placed under a single administration. A House of Assembly was introduced in 1964 and under the P. and New Guinea Act of 1968 the Administrative Council is to become an Executive Council.

SHS; IHE

Parage, a form of tenure found in English lands in France, possibly spread by Henry II from Anjou to Normandy and elsewhere. In p. the eldest brother held the fief as sole lord, and his brothers held of him without doing HOMAGE to him: fiefs, therefore, were not split by subinfeudation. Primogeniture was early accepted in England where true p. is not found.

PMB

Paris, Declaration of (16 Apr. 1856), issued by Great Britain, France,

Russia, Austria, Prussia, Sardinia and Turkey to regularize the usages of naval warfare. It abolished PRIVATEERING, defined the nature of contraband and blockade, laid down the principle of 'free ships, free goods' (other than contraband of war) and required a blockade to be 'effective' in order to be binding on neutrals.   SHS

Paris, Parlement of, was the French king's court both of first instance and appeal, which emerged from his curia in the late 12th and early 13th centuries to administer justice and, in consequence, to extend French domains and jurisdictions. The p. followed Roman or customary law according to the area from which a case came, periods in each session being allocated to areas of the country. English kings were concerned with the p. from 1259, when Henry III did homage for AQUITAINE, to 1340, when Edward III renounced his homage, with a brief revival in 1360–9. Generally represented by PROCTORS, their chief concerns were breaches etc. of treaties between England and France, and appeals from Gascon courts which the English seneschal of GASCONY ought to have heard but the French kings entertained.   PMB

Paris, first peace of (30 May 1814), was concluded, after Napoleon's abdication, by the allies with king Louis XVIII of France. France was allowed to keep the frontiers of 1792, even with certain rectifications in her favour; the colonies annexed by Britain during the FRENCH REVOLUTIONARY AND NAPOLEONIC WARS were restored, with the exception of TOBAGO, ST LUCIA, MAURITIUS, MALTA and the IONIAN ISLANDS. Of the conquered Dutch colonies, Britain retained the CAPE, CEYLON and BRITISH GUIANA; and Denmark ceded HELIGOLAND. France also recognized the freedom of shipping on the rivers Rhine and Scheldt and promised to abandon the slave-trade within five years. Unsolved questions were to be treated at the congress of VIENNA.   SHS

Paris, second peace of (20 Nov. 1815), was concluded after Napoleon's final defeat at WATERLOO and the second restoration of Louis XVIII. On the whole, it confirmed the first peace of P. and the decisions of the VIENNA CONGRESS, since both Alexander I of Russia and the duke of Wellington regarded France as a potential future ally against their respective present allies. Therefore France had only to cede certain frontier districts to Prussia (Saarland), Bavaria (Landau), Switzerland (Fort Joux), Savoy (Haute-Savoie) and the Netherlands (Bouillon, Philippeville, Mariembourg), restore some of the pilfered art-treasures, pay an indemnity of 700m. francs and accept for five years an allied occupation which, however, was terminated in 1818.   SHS

Paris, peace of (30 Mar. 1856), terminated the CRIMEAN WAR. Russia relinquished the protectorate over the Danube principalities and the Orthodox Christians in the Turkish empire, ceded southern Bessarabia to Moldavia and the mouth of the Danube to Turkey, acknowledged the freedom of navigation on the Danube under international control and the neutralization of the Black Sea where she was not to keep warships or build fortifications. On 15 Apr. Britain, France and Austria guaranteed the integrity and independence of Turkey. However, when Russia in Oct. 1870 repudiated the Black Sea clause, France was prostrate, Austria powerless, and Britain eventually yielded at the London conference (17 Jan.–13 Mar. 1871) in return for a solemn declaration of the great powers that international treaties must not be annulled or altered unilaterally.   SHS

Paris, treaties of, (1) (1259), sometimes called the treaty of Abbeville. Only a series of truces had been negotiated between France and England since Philip II had declared King John's French possessions forfeited; and the king of England maintained his claim to NORMANDY and other lost dominions, and the king of France his claim to GASCONY. Henry III, encouraged by the papacy since peace between England and France would facilitate the 'SICILIAN BUSINESS', opened negotiations with Louis IX in 1257, and agreement had been reached by 28 May 1258. Negotiations continued after the OXFORD PARLIAMENT of 1258; both parties had ratified the peace by Nov. 1259, and it was formally published in Paris on 4 Dec. Henry III gave up his claims to Normandy, Maine, Anjou and Poitou, but was confirmed in possession of Gascony—as a vassal of the king of France. Compromise was reached concerning other areas of the duchy of AQUITAINE. In the dioceses of Limoges, Périgueux and Cahors Louis ceded his domains to Henry; Saintonge was to revert to Henry after the death of Alphonse, count of Poitou; Quercy and the Agenais would either revert to Henry after the death of the count and his wife, or Henry would receive compensation. The treaty recognized the French conquest of most of the ANGEVIN EMPIRE and secured peace for 35 years, but it left a host of thorny problems and, by substituting English vassalage for the English king's practical independence in Gascony, ultimately contributed to the outbreak of the HUNDRED YEARS' WAR.

RFW

(2) (1286), one of the series of treaties by which England and France sought to agree upon the application of the t. of P. of 1259. Edward I did homage to Philip IV of France on 5 June 1286 for the lands which were his by the treaty of 1259. During Edward's stay in Paris an agreement was reached under which Edward received Saintonge, while Philip retained Quercy and paid Edward compensation. The treaty was formally published in August.   RFW

(3) (1303). After his defeat by the Flemings at Courtrai in 1302 Philip IV of France was disposed to come to terms with Edward I. After Edward had sworn fealty for GASCONY on 20 May 1303, Philip's daughter Isabella was betrothed to Edward's son, Edward of Caernarvon. Edward then renewed his homage for Gascony and recovered his French lands, most

of which had been in Philip's hands from 1294.   RFW

(4) (10 Feb. 1763), between Great Britain, France, Spain and Portugal ended the SEVEN YEARS' WAR, being followed by the peace of Hubertusburg (15 Feb.) between Austria and Prussia. Prussia retained Silesia, Great Britain received MINORCA, CANADA, NOVA SCOTIA, Cape Breton Island, Senegal, GRENADA, ST VINCENT, DOMINICA and TOBAGO from France, and FLORIDA and concessions in Honduras from Spain. France recovered Belleisle, Goree, Guadeloupe, Mariegalante, Martinique, ST LUCIA and her trading posts in India, ceded Louisiana to Spain and again agreed to demolish the fortifications of DUNKIRK. France retained fishing rights off NEWFOUNDLAND and in the Gulf of St Lawrence with St Pierre and Miquelon. These rights remained a source of friction until the ENTENTE CORDIALE (1904). Great Britain restored Havana and Manila to Spain. British gains were considerable, due to maritime supremacy, but they were considered inadequate by much of public opinion.   IHE

Parish, civil, originated when Tudor POOR LAW and highway legislation made the p. a unit of local government under JUSTICES OF THE PEACE. Since the 16th century the boundaries of c.p. and ecclesiastical p. have diverged. During the 18th and 19th centuries government in the open or closed vestries of the c.p. proved increasingly inadequate and they lost significance to other bodies created by acts of parliament, first local (e.g. TURNPIKE trusts, improvement commissions) then general (poor law unions, sanitary districts, MUNICIPAL and COUNTY councils). Civil functions of the vestry in rural c.p. were taken away in 1894 when p. councils or p. meetings were substituted. Urban c.p. remained rating authorities until 1927, losing their last civil functions to boroughs or district councils in 1933.

MLH

Parish, ecclesiastical, the area served by a church with a resident priest or, in earlier times, a group of priests. The earliest reference to an e.p. is of the 7th century, and the creation of parishes still continues. Parochial development after the CONVERSION OF ENGLAND depended on the willingness of the upper classes to build and endow churches (PATRONAGE). The earliest type of parish church was the old or ordinary MINSTER or *matrix ecclesia* that served a wide area and was usually a royal or episcopal foundation. These areas were later divided into smaller parishes, each served by a lesser church with graveyard and usually founded by lay nobles. The possession of a graveyard, a source of income for the priest and a place of SANCTUARY for the parishioners in time of trouble, was generally regarded as the criterion of an established church; and any loss of revenue to the *matrix ecclesia* was usually made good by an annual payment from the parish. The building of a field church (a church without a graveyard) was often the first step in the parochial development of a new area, but in early post-conversion times a stone cross might suffice temporarily for service of prayer. Parishes are the basic territorial units in ecclesiastical organization, and are grouped to form rural deaneries. The incumbent of a parish church in the middle ages received his income from three main sources. These were: (1) a grant of land, later known as the parson's GLEBE; (2) offerings and payments for services rendered, the main being SOUL-SCOT, PLOUGH ALMS, Easter offerings and fees for non-sacramental services; (3) a compulsory payment, usually in kind, from the parishioners; this first took the form of food-rent, known later as CHURCH SCOT, but was superseded by TITHE.

CFS

Parisi, a British tribe occupying the area of east Yorkshire. Conquered by the Romans in *c.* A.D. 70 they probably became a CIVITAS with their capital at Petuaria (Brough on Humber). Their name indicates that they were a branch of the Parisii of northern France. They probably first settled in Britain in the 3rd century B.C.　CFS

Parliament. (Fr. *parlement*, Med. Lat. *parliamentum*). The term, with its general meaning of 'a talk', was applied in mid-13th-century England to a wide variety of meetings for discussion. From the 1240s it was increasingly used to describe important assemblies of the king and his nobles which might discuss military, financial, judicial and domestic affairs or foreign policy. A p. was essentially a meeting when the king took counsel not only with the inner circle of royal councillors, but also with a large number of magnates, lay and clerical. P. under Henry III has been described as an occasion rather than an institution—an occasion when many kinds of important business might be transacted, rather than a body of men with certain tasks. The period of baronial reform (1258–65) temporarily emphasized its political and legislative functions (PROVISIONS OF OXFORD). The MONTFORTIAN p.s introduced a wider representative element: in 1264 four knights of each shire and in 1265 two knights of each shire and two burgesses from each of certain boroughs were summoned to attend; and this experiment was followed up by Edward I.

Although the reigns of Edward I (1272–1307) and Edward II (1307–27) were of critical importance in the development of p., scholars differ as regards the relative importance of its functions—as an enlarged council, as a high court of justice or as a representative assembly. Certainly the competence of p. in the late 13th and early 14th centuries was very wide, its meetings were short periods of intense activity, and p., usually summoned more than once a year by Edward I, had apparently gained a permanent place in the constitution. Judicial business loomed increasingly large after 1265. Petitions poured in for the consideration of king and council in p. as the highest court in the realm, necessitating the development of machinery for dealing with them, but

p. did not become primarily a court of justice, a *parlement*. The representative elements were not an essential part of p. under Edward I (MODEL PARLIAMENT) but they were present most often when taxation was being discussed. Knights and burgesses came to p. with full powers as representatives of their shires and boroughs, and their assent to royal taxation was binding on the communities whom they represented. While not yet a legislative body under Edward I, its meetings were convenient occasions for the announcement of legislation. Under Edward II p. was becoming an institution where constitutional and political issues might be discussed and decided. The ORDINANCES of 1311 confirmed the practice of calling p. at least once a year, and made its meetings occasions when the baronage might give its assent to the appointment of the king's ministers. The statute of YORK of 1322 clearly envisaged p. as the proper body for dealing with constitutional issues. Notable too under Edward II are the increasingly active part played by the baronage in the general work of p., and the growing frequency with which shire and borough representatives were summoned: after 1325 the 'commons' were regularly present. Kings might still summon magnates and councillors alone (meetings eventually distinguished as 'Great Councils') and Edward III occasionally called representative assemblies of merchants, but by the middle of the 14th century p. had come to mean an assembly to which the king summoned both magnates and commons, even though the commons might not remain for the entire session.

P., an established part of the constitution in the later middle ages, still normally depended for its existence on the king, who summoned, prorogued and dismissed it when he wished. Quasi-parliaments, however, summoned in the king's name, played an important part in the DEPOSITION of Edward II and Richard II. Edward III summoned on the average one

p. a year as did the LANCASTRIAN kings; but under the YORKISTS the number of p.s fell sharply. The king might summon whom he wished, though by the 15th century the lords were claiming hereditary right to be summoned. Legislation in p. depended on the king's assent, and his presence was felt to be essential.

The spiritual lords comprised the archbishops and bishops of the provinces of Canterbury and York, including the four Welsh bishops (21 in all), and a varying number of abbots (70 in 1295, 27 from 1364). In the 15th century the attendance of the spiritual lords was poor. From the reign of Edward II onwards the lay lords claimed the right to attend, but 14th-century kings summoned widely varying numbers (90 in 1321, 30 in 1334) on no clear principle, even including BANNERETS. From 1387 the kings created new baronies by letters patent, and the list of lords to be summoned tended to become stereotyped: an hereditary peerage possessing an exclusive right to be summoned was evolved. Individual officials, notably the royal judges, might be summoned by individual writ. In the late-14th and 15th centuries usually about 40 lay lords attended, about half the number customarily summoned.

Heads of cathedral chapters, archdeacons and three proctors for the clergy of each diocese were indirectly summoned to p. by Edward I. Although royal orders that the lower clergy should attend were discontinued in 1341, some lower clergy continued to appear until much later. At all events, full clerical representation had become less important with the development of clerical taxation through their own convocations.

Thirty-seven English shires (all save Cheshire and Co. Durham) were regularly represented by two knights each. In spite of intermittent royal demands that the shire members should be knights, many were not, though they tended to be men of some wealth and standing, with experience in local government. Sheriffs were forbidden to return themselves as members in 1372, but attempts to exclude lawyers ultimately failed (UN-LEARNED PARLIAMENT), and they were prominent in 15th-century p.s. Many 15th-century knights of the shire were retainers or dependants of lords, often their professional servants, and by 1450 there had been a notable increase in shire members who were in some way connected with the royal service. The knights were elected in the county court by, in theory, the 'common assent' of the electors, defined by the statute of 1429 as freeholders of lands worth at least 40s. a year, and resident in the shire. In practice, the considerable pressure which local magnates brought to bear often determined the choice of the electors. The number of boroughs represented by two burgesses apiece varied considerably (86 under Edward I, 70 under Edward II, over 80 in the later years of Edward III); the highest figure, 101, was reached in 1478. Few new boroughs appeared in the list from the mid-14th century, but there was greater regularity in the summonses received by boroughs. Electoral procedure varied from borough to borough, but the choice of burgesses tended to be exercised by small oligarchies. Payment of members by boroughs during sessions of p. was usual from the early years of Edward III. The social status of 14th-century parliamentary burgesses ranged from knights and wealthy merchants down to quite humble townsmen. A statute of 1413, imposing a residence qualification for borough members, was widely ignored. While there is evidence that some boroughs regarded representation in p. as a burden rather than a privilege, there was clearly a growing appreciation of the importance of membership of p.

Sessions were usually short, a week or ten days, though there were some marked exceptions such as the 15th-century LONG PARLIAMENT. When summoned to the capital, p. assembled in the palace of Westminster. Formal sessions of the whole of p. were held, usually in the painted chamber, but for deliberation p. split up into groups. In the second half of the 14th century the knights and burgesses usually deliberated together, either in the painted chamber, or in the chapter house of Westminster Abbey, while in the 15th century they met in the refectory of the abbey. The knights and burgesses were called collectively 'the commons' in the 14th century, and they acquired a clerk of their own (probably by 1363) and a common spokesman in the SPEAKER, who first appears in the GOOD PARLIAMENT of 1376. Nevertheless they still tended to be regarded as two separate bodies into the 15th century, with the knights as the superior order: the Speaker was almost invariably chosen from among the knights. The lords spiritual and temporal sometimes met separately in the 14th century, but more often met together, usually in the white chamber. In 1440 the term 'lower house' was used in an institutional sense, and in 1454 the terms 'higher house' and 'commons house' were similarly employed. The 'higher house' does not seem to have been called 'house of lords' until the 16th century. Although the term 'houses of Parliament' was not used in the middle ages, while P. might be described as the 'estates of the realm', the development of P. in the middle ages determined that there should be two 'houses' and not three or more 'estates' as in continental representative assemblies.

The principal functions of the medieval p. were giving counsel to the king, granting taxation, doing justice and passing legislation. Deliberation upon general and particular problems of foreign and domestic policy, and giving advice to the king, remained an important part of the work of p., in which the commons came to share under Edward III. Generally speaking, medieval kings experienced a more pressing need of p.'s financial aid than of its counsel. By the reign of Edward III it had become the established practice that grants of taxes on MOVABLES should be made in p., with the assent of the representative knights and burgesses. By 1362 p. had also gained control of the imposition of taxes on wool and merchandise. For the grant of taxation the assent of the commons was essential: it was conceded in 1407 that they alone might initiate money grants, and 15th-century subsidy bills took the form of grants by the commons to the king, with the assent of the lords. Although it might on occasion be conceded that p. should be informed how money granted had been spent, p. had no control of spending nor did it succeed in making supply dependent on the redress of grievances. However, the needy Lancastrian kings had to hear complaints and make concessions to secure the grant of taxation. The sounder finances and stronger government of the Yorkists, with the infrequency of summons, severely restricted p.'s opportunities in the later 15th century.

The strictly judicial work of p. decreased in the later middle ages, although the lords gained the right to try peers accused of treason and felony (a right retained until 1948), and although the lords became judges and the commons accusers in the new procedure of IMPEACHMENT, introduced by 1376. Early in the 14th century machinery was developed for dealing with petitions. Originally all petitions coming to p. may have passed from the receivers (chancery clerks) to the auditors or triers (lords and royal justices), who might deal with them themselves, pass them to the courts or refer them to the council or to the king and lords. Private petitions seeking a legal remedy were generally the concern of the courts or the council; a large class of petitions, however, became the particular concern of p.—the 'common petitions', best defined as petitions on matters of general or public interest. These might originate from individual members of the commons, from the commons collectively, from individuals or groups outside p.; others might be the outcome of deliberations between

lords and commons, or be proposed by the lords and adopted by the commons. From the late 14th century onwards an increasing number of groups and individuals were including the commons among their addressees and seeking their mediation. The importance of the common petitions is that they could result in the making of a STATUTE, that they provided a way by which the commons could share in, and initiate legislation. It is unlikely that the procedure of three readings had been developed by the early 15th century, as was once thought—but the common petitions did pass, either singly or in groups, to the lords for their assent, and finally to the king for his assent, which might be withheld. At a late stage a petition might be edited, on legal advice, to become a 'BILL'—having the form of the ultimate statute; but it appears that by the early 15th century some petitions were professionally prepared as bills before submission. Legislation could, of course, originate with the king or the lords, or could take place outside p. in the form of an ordinance. But by the mid-14th century it was felt that an ordinance lacked the permanent character of a statute, and by the second half of the 15th century it was held that a statute must necessarily receive the assent of the commons. Although they controlled the grant of taxation, although they had come to play a part in legislation and were far from being dominated by the lords, the commons still possessed only a limited authority in the 15th century, while p. as a whole still played a less important role in government than the council.

Although p. was summoned infrequently by the Tudors, their use of statute law as the essential basis of state authority inevitably strengthened the powers of p. This was especially due to the work of the Reformation p. in ecclesiastical concerns and p.'s part in the Elizabethan settlement, as well as in social and economic legislation (e.g. statute of APPRENTICES, 1563). P. became the supreme authority under royal management but it was not a mere instrument, although nearly all legislation was of governmental or conciliar origin. In the commons FREE SPEECH was claimed and PRIVILEGE asserted, aided by the keeping of Commons' Journals from 1547. The committee system began to develop and the UNION of England–Wales increased the size of the commons as did the creation of new boroughs. Elections were more keenly contested although influence was used. The Reformation p. ended the clerical majority in the lords by removing 30 abbots, and crown control of the bishops was consolidated (CONGÉ D'ÉLIRE), whilst a statute of 1593 limited membership of the upper house to peers of the realm. The gentry became dominant in the commons, largely composed of landowners and merchants, and from the 1560s the growth of militant protestantism led to criticisms and attacks on royal PREROGATIVE.

The inability of the first two Stewarts to compromise with an increasingly assertive commons, which refused to face up to the financial problems of the crown and whose Puritan members challenged Charles I's support of the Arminians in the Church of England, caused both sides to strain the constitution. Growth of friction is illustrated by the APOLOGY OF THE COMMONS (1604), the ADDLED P. (1614), the PROTESTATION (1621), the revival of the IMPEACHMENT of ministers (from 1621), the PETITION OF RIGHT (1628), attacks on foreign policy etc. The majority of the lords supported the crown. The ELEVEN YEARS' TYRANNY and the summoning of the SHORT PARLIAMENT (1640) marked the failure of conciliar government and the proceedings of the LONG PARLIAMENT led to the CIVIL WARS, the establishment of the COMMONWEALTH and the apparent triumph of the RUMP P., until it was dismissed by Cromwell in 1653. The failure of BAREBONE'S P. and subsequent frictions between p. and the protector emphasized the weakness of the republic which was ended by the RESTORATION and return to government by king, lords and commons. The bishops returned to the lords in 1661.

The prerogative was much weakened and the initiation of the CLARENDON CODE by p., and not the crown, reveals the extent of the change. The CAVALIER P. eventually showed dissatisfaction and resisted Charles II's claims to the SUSPENDING POWER but PATRONAGE was increasingly used to manage p. In this period WHIGS and TORIES began to emerge as political groups but Charles II's seeming triumph over p. after 1681 (EXCLUSION BILLS) was ended by James II's arbitrary use of prerogative, resulting in the GLORIOUS REVOLUTION (1688). The DECLARATION OF RIGHTS (1689) ensured the ascendancy of p., as did the TRIENNIAL ACT (1694) and Act of SETTLEMENT (1701). Control of the army was secured by the MUTINY ACT and by the appropriation of supplies for fixed purposes, voted annually. Thus p. has met annually since 1689. The right of the lords to amend money bills was denied by the commons (1671, 1678) and their right of rejection was dropped until the Paper Duties Repeal Bill (1860). Their rejection of this bill led to the commons including all financial proposals in one annual finance bill or budget which was not challenged until 1909.

The electoral system of the Restoration with its large majority of borough members substantially remained until 1832, other than with the additions made by the UNION of Scotland–England (1707) and the UNION of England–Ireland (1800), and SCOTTISH and IRISH REPRESENTATIVE PEERS joined the lords (see also PEERAGE BILL). In 1707 of 558 members 432 sat for boroughs, 122 for counties and 4 for universities. The life of a p. was increased by the SEPTENNIAL ACT (1716) which remained in force until the PARLIAMENT ACT (1911) limited it to five years. The claim of the lords to original civil jurisdiction was abandoned after the case of SKINNER v. EAST INDIA COMPANY (1666–70). With the emergence of the cabinet (from the reign of Charles II) the

PRIVY COUNCIL declined, and when George I and his successors substantially ceased to attend (from 1717), the appearance of a PRIME MINISTER was a natural consequence, further enhancing the powers of p., and MINISTERIAL RESPONSIBILITY gradually developed. Attempts to limit crown influence by excluding PLACEMEN (PLACE ACTS) were frequent in the 18th century but the attempted exclusion of the executive from p. did not take place. Agitation for the reform of p. grew from the time of the MIDDLESEX ELECTION (1768), encouraged by the spread of democratic ideas, and royal patronage was again attacked by DUNNING'S RESOLUTION (1780), CREWE'S ACT (1782) and Burke's Civil Establishment Act (1782).

During the ministry of Pitt the younger the executive increased its authority at the crown's expense owing to the personal incapacity of the king and to administrative reforms which reduced royal PATRONAGE. Yet until 1832 the crown could hold and win an election and thus provide support for a ministry of its choice with a majority in both houses.

During the regency and the reign of George IV middle-class 'public opinion' became vociferous on definite political issues—more time of both houses was taken up in discussion of public petitions; reports of parliamentary proceedings (HANSARD) were being widely disseminated. The demand for electoral reform was satisfied by the first REFORM ACT (1832) which fundamentally altered the balance of power between crown, lords and commons. The crown's choice of PRIME MINISTER was henceforth confined to those with the widest support in the commons (witness Peel's defeat (1835) and the BEDCHAMBER CRISIS). The lords, by passing the bill when threatened with the creation of sufficient peers to ensure a majority, tacitly admitted that the will of the lower house must prevail. Practically the peers' hold over the commons by patronage was destroyed: in 1816 about 250 members were returned by peers' nomination or influence, but after 1842 peers'

influence remained strong in only about 60 constituencies.

The commons, on the other hand, won an increased ascendancy over the lords by the vindication of the representative principle and entered upon a period of notable independence, released from control of crown and peers and not yet bound by modern party ties to the cabinet.

The introduction by the 1832 REFORM ACT of electoral registration led to the formation of associations to ensure voting support for particular candidates. The second REFORM ACT (1867), which almost doubled the electorate, made organization essential. Thus, with the foundation of central bodies to which local associations could be affiliated, the machinery of the modern political parties evolved. Many more seats were contested (284 in 1859, 542 in 1880) and candidates generally accepted party labels. With the civil service to provide administrative continuity the system of alternating government by party became accepted. After the third REFORM ACT (1884) there was a general tightening up of party organization together with an elaboration of policy programmes put directly to the electorate by the leaders (a tendency noticeable in the MIDLOTHIAN CAMPAIGN). Influence was further reduced by forbidding practices leading to corruption (e.g. BALLOT ACT, 1872).

The development of the party system restricted the liberty of action of members of the commons as did the streamlining of procedure to cope with increased legislation. Upon the ancient 'practice' of the house, whose purpose was to preserve the rights of members in debate, was superimposed a growing body of standing orders intended to help the government get through its business, hindered not only by sheer bulk but by Irish obstruction. So was instituted, e.g., the closure (1882) and its refinement, the 'guillotine'. Acceptance of these standing orders was assisted by the neutrality of the Speaker, established on the election of Shaw-Lefevre (1839). Another means of dealing with growing pressure of work was the institution of standing committees (1882); these were increased from 2 to 4 (1907), to 6 (1919) and to an unlimited number (1947). Questioning of ministers as a means of curbing the power of the executive was recognized by 1832, and the number of questions per session rose from 200 in 1850 to 4,000–5,000 by the 1890s and to over 13,000 by the 1950s. In 1967 a Parliamentary Commissioner for the Administration (acting only at the instance of M.P.s) was appointed to investigate complaints of personal injustice of maladministration by the central government.

The increased influence of the executive over p. was also shown in the rapid growth from the mid-19th century of delegated legislation. This power given to ministers and other bodies to formulate regulations in accordance with the general terms of statutes limited the supremacy of p. itself, but recent procedure has endeavoured to reduce abuse to a minimum; a large proportion of general statutory instruments are laid before the house and subjected to scrutiny by a select committee appointed in 1946.

Membership of the house of commons stood at 558 until 100 were added by UNION with Ireland (1801); membership thereafter has been 670 (1885), 707 (1918), 615 (on establishment of the Irish Free State, 1922), 640 (1945), 625 (1950) and 630 (1955). Payment of members was reintroduced in 1912 (the result of the advent of the LABOUR PARTY and of the OSBORNE JUDGMENT); salaries were raised from £400 to £600 (1937), to £1,000 (1946) and to £3,250 (1964). Pensions (minimum £600 for 10 years service) were instituted in 1965. Qualification for membership remained from 1710 to 1858 at £600 a year for county and £300 a year for borough members. Disqualifications have included English and Scottish peers, clergy of the English (1801), Welsh (1914) and Roman Catholic churches (1829), Roman Catholics until CATHOLIC EMANCIPATION, Jews (until ROTHS-

CHILD'S CASE), atheists (BRADLAUGH'S CASE) and women (until 1918). Until its destruction by fire in 1834 St Stephen's chapel was the meeting-place of the house; temporary occupation of the house of lords was followed by a move into the new chamber in 1852. After its destruction by bombing (1941) the commons again took over the lords' chamber until 1950.

Estimates of the residual power of the crown differ. Discounting personal influence, variable and largely inestimable, the crown's chief constitutional duty has become the appointment of a head of government. Almost always there is no real choice, any element of doubt (e.g. 1923, 1956) being dispelled by advice.

The first Reform Act relegated the lords to the minor position. In 1839 Wellington refused the premiership because its holder ought to be in the commons; the last peer appointed, other than Home in 1963, was Salisbury in 1895. The lords' power to veto legislation, however, caused a number of collisions with the commons, whilst domination of the lords by the CONSERVATIVE PARTY made LIBERAL legislation particularly vulnerable. Notable clashes occurred over repeal of the paper duties in 1860 (rejecting a money bill), disestablishment of the Irish church (1869), the third Reform Act (1884) and the HOME RULE bill of 1893. During the first 2 years of the Liberal administration of 1906 important education and licensing bills were rejected and other bills mutilated. The struggle came to a head with the rejection of the Finance Act (1909), the social provisions of which were regarded by the lords, with some justification, as tantamount to the revival of 'tacking'. The sequel was the PARLIAMENT ACT (1911). Its preamble envisaged imminent lords' reform, a hope unfulfilled largely because change of composition must affect function, on which parties have little common ground. Abortive reform projects have included those of Rosebery (1888), Lansdowne (1911) and the Bryce committee (1917–18); conferences between the party leaders failed in 1910, 1948 and 1968. In 1968 the government introduced, but withdrew (1969), a Parliament Bill which would have effected exclusion of peers by succession, loss of voting rights by non-attendance and reduction of the lords' delaying power.

Since the 18th century the judicial functions of the lords have been almost entirely appellate, its original jurisdiction being limited to IMPEACHMENT (last used against Dundas (Melville) in 1805) and peerage claims. Trial by peers for treason or felony—last used when de Clifford was acquitted of manslaughter in 1935 and abolished by the Criminal Jurisdiction Act of 1948—was a privilege of peerage rather than of the house. As a court of review, appeal lay from the KING'S BENCH and from the Exchequer Chamber by writ of error, from CHANCERY and from the Scottish and Irish courts. But after the first years of the 19th century it was not common for lay peers to sit on appeal cases; the convention that they should not take part was firmly established in 1844. An attempt to create life peers with legal qualifications was foiled by the Wensleydale peerage case (1856). Congestion of business (particularly of appeals from Scotland) resulted in heavy arrears, though some of the earlier reforms of the legal system (e.g. institution of the divorce court, 1858) alleviated the position. The Judicature Act (1873) aimed to abolish the lords' judicial powers but this decision was reversed by the Appellate Jurisdiction Act (1876) which appointed lords of APPEAL in ordinary and finally established the lords as a court of appeal. In 1907 jurisdiction was extended to criminal cases certified of exceptional legal importance by the ATTORNEY-GENERAL; and to courts martial (1951). An appellate committee, formed temporarily (1948) to hear cases and report, has survived.

Membership of the house of lords was greatly increased during George III's reign, notably by Pitt who (1783–1801) was responsible for advising 141 creations. By 1836 there were 352 peers. The Union with Ireland (1800) added 28 IRISH REPRESENTATIVE PEERS elected for life and 4 bishops. Lords of appeal in ordinary were given the right to sit for life in 1887; they now number 9. LIFE PEERAGES were instituted in 1958. The creation of bishoprics since that of Manchester (1847) has not affected the number of spiritual peers, reduced by Irish (1869) and WELSH DISESTABLISHMENT (1914); there are now 26 (2 archbishops, the bishops of London, Durham and Winchester and 21 others by seniority of appointment). About 1,050 peers are entitled to sit, but some 200 usually claim leave of absence (provided for in 1958); normally 80–120 attend. The Peerage Act (1963) allowed peers to disclaim their peerages for life and admitted peeresses in their own right (previously barred—Lady Rhondda's case, 1919) and all Scottish peers. In 1957 peers were entitled to claim expenses (since 1969 £6 10s. for each daily attendance). The house met in the White chamber until 1801 and then in the White or Lesser hall; from 1834 it occupied the Painted chamber until its present chamber was completed in 1847; the bombing of the house of commons entailed a move to the king's robing room (1941–50).

RFW; IHE; MLH

Parliament Act. (1) (1911). Opposition of the lords to legislative proposals of the Liberal government culminated in the rejection (30 Nov. 1909) of Lloyd George's controversial budget. After two general elections (Jan. and Dec. 1910) the P. bill was forced through the lords (Aug. 1911) on pain of creating sufficient peers to overcome resistance. A money bill, as defined in the Act and certified by the SPEAKER, may receive royal assent one month after being sent to the lords notwithstanding that the lords has not consented. A PUBLIC BILL, other than a money bill or one to extend the duration of p., not passed by the lords (with agreed amendment) in three successive sessions might also receive royal assent provided that two years had elapsed since the second reading in the commons. The maximum duration of p. was reduced from 7 years (SEPTENNIAL ACT) to 5 years.

(2) (1949). In 1947 the Labour government feared that the lords might reject the nationalization of iron and steel, a bill for which could not be passed under the 1911 P.A. before the p. ended. The P.A. (1949) reduced the delaying power of the lords as regards a public bill other than a money bill to one year, provided that it had not been passed by the lords in two successive sessions; the act was made applicable to any bill introduced during its passage.   MLH

Parnell Commission. On 18 Apr. 1887 *The Times* published, in a series of articles on 'Parnellism and crime', a facsimile letter ostensibly written by the Irish Parliamentary leader, Charles Stewart Parnell, in extenuation of the PHOENIX PARK MURDERS. On advice, Parnell did not sue for libel and was denied a committee of inquiry. However, after an action by another Irish M.P. (O'Donnell *v.* Walter) in which further letters allegedly written by Parnell were produced, a special commission of three judges was appointed to report on the responsibility of Parnell and other Irish M.P.s for violence in Ireland; it sat from 17 Sept. 1888 to 2 Nov. 1889 and reported 13 Feb. 1890. The letters were shown to be forgeries of an Irish journalist, Richard Pigott, who confessed and fled to Madrid where he committed suicide, 1 Mar. 1889. Parnell was cleared, but other Irish leaders were charged with incitement to intimidation and extenuation of agrarian crime. *The Times* had to pay costs of £250,000.   MLH

Partition Treaties were made between England, the Netherlands and France to settle the succession problem which would arise on the death of Charles II of Spain. The first secret P.T. (11 Oct. 1698) allotted Spain, the southern Netherlands and the Indies to the Electoral Prince of Bavaria; Milan and Luxemburg

to the Archduke Charles of Austria; Naples, Sicily etc., to the Dauphin. The death of the Electoral Prince (Jan. 1699) led to the second P.T. (25 Mar. 1700). The Archduke Charles was to have Spain, the Indies, the Netherlands and Sardinia, and the Dauphin the other Italian territories of Spain, ultimately exchanging Milan for Lorraine. The Emperor did not accept this arrangement. Charles II died (1 Nov. 1700), leaving all his dominions to the Dauphin's second son, Philip of Anjou. Louis XIV of France disregarded the P.T. and supported his grandson against the GRAND ALLIANCE in the SPANISH SUCCESSION WAR.   IHE

Passchendaele, see YPRES.

Paston Letters. Probably the most famous collection of English private correspondence, these letters of the Paston family of Paston, Norfolk, contain much, often of great charm, about the way of life and private affairs of a middle-class family in the years 1422–1509, as well as information and comment on current affairs: as a source for 15th-century social history they are invaluable. Most of the P.L. are now in the British Museum.   PMB

Patagonia, Welsh colony in. Inspired by patriots who wished to see emigrants from WALES preserve their own traditions and not become assimilated into English-speaking communities in North America, the colony was founded by a party of 153 Welsh immigrants who reached the Chubut river on 28 July 1865. The enterprise was badly planned and the immigrants inexperienced and ill-prepared for the immense difficulties they faced: an inhospitable terrain and climate; Indians; bandits; and the suspicions of the Argentinian authorities. Nevertheless, they survived, prospered, increased in number and extended the colony up to the Andes, where the boundary with Chile was delineated in 1902. The settlers can reasonably claim to have founded the first genuinely democratic community in South America.

The Welsh language and culture are still preserved in their midst, and their links with Wales were reinforced during the centenary celebrations of 1965.   GW

Patay, battle of (18 June 1429). Joan of Arc and her commanders followed up the relief of ORLÉANS by destroying the remnants of the besieging army and capturing the garrisons at Jargeau, Meung and Beaugency, with their leader, the earl of Suffolk. An English force arrived too late, was taken by surprise and routed at P., the most important French success in a campaign which culminated in the coronation of Charles VII at Reims on 17 July and the reconquest of the Loire valley, Champagne and much of the Île de France.   RFW

Patent Rolls, CHANCERY enrolments of royal letters patent under the GREAT SEAL, i.e. open letters of more than passing importance with pendant seals. The first roll dates from 1201–2 and the series continues still. Early P.R. cover most government business, but the development of new departments narrowed their scope to patents of nobility, crown appointments etc. The rolls are now compiled by the Clerk of the CROWN IN CHANCERY. Some letters patent under the Exchequer seal were enrolled on the memoranda rolls, but patents of invention ceased to be enrolled in 1853 and are now registered in the Patent Office.   PMB

Patronage, ecclesiastical, the right of a person to nominate the priest of a church, originally the one who built and endowed it (PARISH, ECCLESIASTICAL). A church so established was regarded as the property of the patron, who could bequeath it to his heirs. From the 8th century the position of the priest was safeguarded by the rule that no clerk could take possession of a church until instituted by a bishop. By the end of the Old English period rights of p. were limited to the nominating of the priest, subject to negative control by the bishop and the disposal of part of the TITHE. The importance

of p. in O.E. and medieval times was very great, for it encouraged the founding and protection of parish churches by giving the upper classes a vested interest in them (ADVOWSON). After the DISSOLUTION much monastic p. reverted to lay ownership (IMPROPRIATIONS) and in the 17th century BAREBONE'S PARLIAMENT attempted to abolish p. After the RESTORATION its increasing use by the crown for political purposes, especially in the higher appointments, led to the ERASTIANISM of the 18th century, while its use by the gentry safeguarded tory church interests and prevented undue subjection of the clergy to both bishops and state. During the 19th century p. came to be used with an increasing sense of responsibility to the needs of the church. In 1930 parochial church councils were allowed to object to transfers of p. and in 1931 to make representations to the patron other than the crown, also, in some cases, to refuse to agree to an appointment. In 1933 they were enabled to purchase advowsons except when the crown or bishop is the patron. Diocesan boards of p. were set up in 1932 and advowsons may not be sold after 2 vacancies have occurred since 14 July 1924. The crown still appoints bishops and deans and possesses very extensive benefice p. Church commissions to consider crown patronage were set up in 1935, 1952, and 1961.   CFS; IHE

Patronage, political, was increasingly used by the crown after the RESTORATION to secure support in Parliament, especially in the Commons. In the 18th century the crown came to depend on ministers who could manage Parliament by this distribution of offices and appointments, as the natural aims of the ambitious or the professional politicians were to secure them personally or for their relatives and friends. Ministerial and civil service posts, appointments in the army and navy, colonial offices, church preferment and sinecures opened a wide field. That the increase of crown influence through p.p.

alarmed the Commons is shown by the many attempts to exclude PLACE-MEN as well as by DUNNING'S RESOLU-TION. The CIVIL LIST Act (1782) did not succeed in preventing p.p., which was more effectively checked by the administrative reforms of the younger Pitt after 1784; but civil service patronage did not end until Gladstone made entry dependent on competitive examination (1870). Such patronage as remains is controlled by the prime minister as first lord of the Treasury, acting on behalf of the sovereign.

IHE

Paty's Case, see AYLESBURY ELECTION.

Pavage. A levy for the repair and maintenance of roadways, dating at least from the 12th century and most common in towns. With increasing urbanization, the duty of road repair fell on the parish as well as borough authorities, and thence to their successors, the urban, rural district and county councils and, for trunk roads, the Ministry of TRANSPORT. PMB

Paymaster-General. In 1835 the powers exercised by many officers in disbursing public money were brought together and vested in the P.-G.; further consolidation took place in 1848. All funds voted by Parliament are paid into his account and administered by his officers. Modern P.G.s, relatively free from departmental duties, are frequently allotted special duties outside the framework of existing departments. PMB

Peace, Commissions of, naming local laymen to assist in maintaining law and order, were first issued in the 12th century: nearly two centuries of experiment in their form followed. Commissions in every county were first issued in the baronial experiment of 1263. In 1285 enforcement of the police regulations in the statute of WINCHESTER were added to other duties, which included development of the local MILITIA. Power to try cases was first granted in 1329, then withdrawn and again granted: powers under the statute of LABOURERS (1351) were added. Finally, in 1361 statutory authority for the inclusion of judicial powers was provided, giving the commission something approximating to that of modern JUSTICES OF THE PEACE. PMB

Peasants' Revolt, the name given to the widespread risings, urban as well as rural, of 1381, motivated by a great variety of social and economic grievances. The immediate cause was the imposition of the third and most burdensome POLL TAX. The most determined opposition and the most radical demands were encountered in Kent and Essex, where the peasantry had already achieved comparative freedom and prosperity. Open resistance to the collection of the tax was first encountered in Essex, where violence was chiefly directed against royal officials and judges. In Kent the rebels captured Rochester castle on 6 June, established contact with the rebels in Essex and on 7 June chose Wat Tyler as their leader. The priest John Ball joined the rebels when they released him from prison in Canterbury. On 11 June the Kentish rebels marched on London and encamped on BLACK-HEATH, while the Essex rebels moved up to Mile End. After the breakdown of their meeting with Richard II on 13 June, the rebels moved into the southern suburbs of London and were admitted over London bridge by sympathizers within the city. Many lawyers, clergy and foreigners were slaughtered, and John of Gaunt's great house, the Savoy, was destroyed, but on the whole the leaders kept control of their followers. Richard II, who had taken refuge in the Tower, met the Essex rebels at Mile End on the 14th. While Richard was promising the abolition of villeinage and the revocation of the labour laws, the rebels in the city obtained possession of the Tower: among the refugees dragged out to execution on Tower Hill were Archbishop Sudbury of Canterbury and the Treasurer, Sir Robert Hales. On the 15th, at Smithfield, Richard received the demands of the Kentish men, including the radical proposals of John Ball. In a sudden scuffle Wat Tyler was killed by William Walworth, the mayor, and an ugly situation was saved by Richard himself, who led the rebels off. The peasants then in London dispersed, many still relying on Richard's promises and the charters he had issued, and the loyalist faction gained control of the city.

In the provinces the most serious outbreak occurred in the eastern counties, with isolated risings as far afield as York and Winchester. The risings took many forms: in St Albans and Bury St Edmunds the townsmen rose against their overlords, the abbots; in Cambridge violence was mostly directed against the University; in Norfolk the rebel leader, Geoffrey Litster, was joined by some of the gentry. Vigorous military action by the bishop of Norwich crushed the East Anglian revolt by the end of June. By 23 June Richard II was already withdrawing his promises, and on 2 July the fight at BILLERICAY brought serious armed opposition to an end. Judicial inquiries and action followed, but the government contented itself with the execution of the surviving leaders. Much investigation remains to be carried out into the causes, character and scope of the risings. RFW

Peep of Day Boys were Protestants in Ulster who, from about 1785, banded together to search the houses of Catholics for arms; their counterpart were the Catholic Defenders. After the battle of the Diamond (21 Sept. 1795) most of the P. of D.B. joined the newly formed Orange society whilst the Defenders were largely merged with the United Irishmen. MLH

Peerage Bill (1719) was to ensure a permanent Whig majority in the Lords. Excluding princes of the blood, it restricted the creation of new peerages to 6 and established 25 hereditary Scottish Lords of Parliament instead of 16. It passed the Lords but was rejected in the Commons where its constitutional and political dangers were ably exposed by Walpole. IHE

Peine forte et dure, see WESTMINSTER, FIRST STATUTE OF.

Penal Code (Ireland). After the Reformation of the Irish church (1560) office holders were subject to the oath of SUPREMACY and RECUSANTS were fined, but there was never much active persecution. The P.C. proper was enacted by the Irish Parliament between 1695 and 1727 in violation of the treaty of LIMERICK. Apart from enforcing existing PENAL LAWS, Catholics were excluded from Parliament (1692), disarmed, forbidden to keep schools or take degrees, excluded from the Bar (1698), etc. Catholic bishops were banished (1697). Restrictions were also placed on Irish trade by the English Parliament. Savage legislation after 1703 completed the exclusion of Catholics from the professions, restricted their holding of land, encouraged their heirs to turn Protestant and deprived them of the franchise (1727). These statutes were annulled between 1778 and 1829, the strictly penal measures being abolished by 1782. IHE

Penal Laws refer historically to the statutes penalizing the RECUSANTS. After Elizabeth I's excommunication (1570) and increasing threats from Catholic conspiracies severe anti-Catholic laws were passed between 1571 and 1593. Fines, imprisonment, banishment and, in exteme cases, death were accompanied by a wide range of private and public disabilities. These laws were confirmed in 1604 and made more comprehensive in 1606 and 1610. Never completely or constantly enforced, they were mitigated by the Stewart use of the DISPENSING POWER even after the TEST ACTS and, except for the continuance of public disabilities until 1829, were largely inoperative by the 18th century. Many Protestant sectaries were driven abroad by a severe act of 1593, but they escaped most discriminatory legislation until the introduction of the CLARENDON CODE. IHE

Penang (Prince of Wales Island) was in 1786 ceded by the sultan of KEDAH to the EAST INDIA COMPANY which in 1800 also bought Province Wellesley. P., together with MALACCA, was incorporated in 1826 in the Incorporated (from 1867: STRAITS) SETTLEMENTS and in 1946 joined to the Union (Federation) of MALAYA. SHS

Peninsular War (1808–14) was the most important contribution on land which Britain made to victory in the FRENCH REVOLUTIONARY AND NAPOLEONIC WARS. Napoleon's attempt to control the Iberian peninsula secured for Britain a strategic foothold in Europe which was well sustained and exploited. Sir Arthur Wellesley with 12,000 men landed at Mondego Bay (1–8 Aug. 1808) and advanced on Lisbon. Junot's attack on his positions at VIMEIRO failed, but Burrard and Dalrymple, both Wellesley's superiors, negotiated the convention of Cintra (30 Aug.) which allowed the French to evacuate Portugal. The recall of all 3 generals left Sir John Moore in command. His advance into Spain (Oct.) diverted Napoleon from completely shattering Spanish opposition, but he had to retreat on CORUÑA (Feb. 1809).

Wellesley, back in command at Lisbon, assumed the offensive. By a surprise crossing of the Douro he captured Oporto (May 1809), forcing Soult to retreat into Galicia. He next advanced up the Tagus against Victor. The failure of Spanish co-operation, however, brought about the hard battle of TALAVERA (July); although victorious, heavy losses and lack of supplies dictated a retreat on Portugal. A series of Spanish defeats, the most disastrous being Ocaña (Nov.), laid Andalusia open to the French. In the spring of 1810 Masséna attacked Portugal and Wellesley (now Lord Wellington), after a victory at Busaco (27 Sept.), retreated on his prepared triple defence lines round Torres Vedras. After a winter of discomfort Masséna retired (March 1811) and

K

Wellington followed, aiming to capture the Spanish frontier fortresses, Almeida, Badajoz and Ciudad Rodrigo. Almeida fell after a close fight at Fuentes de Oñoro (5 May), but, in spite of ALBUERA (16 May), Marmont (Masséna's successor) and Soult saved the other two and Wellington again retired. Withdrawal of French troops for Russia and widespread dispersal of armies in Spain allowed Wellington to make a mid-winter attack on Ciudad Rodrigo, which fell 19 Jan. 1812, and to storm Badajoz with heavy loss (6 April). Although a brilliant victory over Marmont at SALAMANCA (22 July) was followed by occupation of Valladolid and Madrid (12 Aug.) and investment of Burgos, Wellington's advance drew Soult from Andalusia and he was once more forced back to Portugal for the winter. The French were now in grave difficulties; the supply problem was immense, and momentary concentration of forces against the British laid the occupied provinces open to guerilla attack; only the north-east was held.

Heavily reinforced, Wellington's campaign of 1813 opened in May. One part of his force moved against Salamanca while the other under his second-in-command, Graham, marched through the Tras-os-Montes. By a series of outflanking movements Burgos was quickly reached. Over the Ebro, the French were crushingly defeated at VITORIA (21 June) and fell back on the Pyrenean passes. Soult's counter-attacks were defeated (July) and the fortresses of San Sebastian and Pamplona fell (Sept.–Oct.). Wellington crossed the Bidassoa and Nivelle and was again unsuccessfully attacked by Soult on the Nive (Dec.). Leaving a strong force blockading Bayonne, he followed Soult towards the Garonne and defeated him at TOULOUSE (10 April 1814). Two days later news of Napoleon's abdication was received and hostilities were quickly suspended (17 April). MLH

Pennsylvania, a proprietary colony founded (1681) by William Penn as a refuge for English QUAKERS who were suffering under the CLARENDON CODE. Part of the Delaware country previously settled by Swedes and Dutch was surrendered by the duke of York. There was complete religious toleration and all Christians were enfranchised subject to a property qualification. The assembly confirmed Penn's scheme of government (1682) and a treaty of amity was made with the Indians (1683). There was a steady influx of Quakers from England, Wales and Ireland, Mennonites and Lutherans from Germany, and early in the 18th century Presbyterians from Ulster (Scotch-Irish). DELAWARE became a separate colony (1702) but shared a common governor until 1776, when the Penn proprietorship terminated. By the time of Penn's death (1718) Philadelphia, the capital, was the next largest city to Boston, and P. was exceeded in population only by VIRGINIA and MASSACHUSETTS. Clashes with the French on the western boundary ceased with the capture of Fort Duquesne (1758). There was resistance in Philadelphia to the STAMP ACT (1765), and the Presbyterian counties were largely responsible for P.'s support of the AMERICAN REVOLUTION. The 1st and 2nd Continental Congresses were held in Philadelphia, and it was Richard Penn, one of the proprietors, who unsuccessfully took the Olive Branch Petition to England (1775).   IHE

Penny, a coin whose name is probably derived from that of Penda king of MERCIA (killed 654) under whose authority such coins first circulated. These early pennies were silver coins with varying designs; but during the reign of Offa of Mercia (759–96) an improved type of coin superseded all earlier types in England south of the Humber. It was reckoned that 240 of these new pennies (Latin *denarii*) could be struck from 1 POUND (Latin *libra*) of silver, and that a SHILLING (Latin *solidus*) should be reckoned as worth 12 of them (hence £ s. d.). They had the king's name and, later, portrait on one side, the name of the moneyer and, later, the MINT on the

other. Until the later 13th century they were the only coins in circulation, pounds, MARKS and shillings being money of account. They were cut into two or four parts to give HALFPENNIES or FARTHINGS. The p. became a copper coin in 1797. Struck in bronze from 1860, it is still colloquially called a *copper*.   CFS

Penruddock's Rising (Mar. 1655). After the dissolution of the first PROTECTORATE Parliament (Jan. 1655) discontent with army rule revealed itself in republican and royalist conspiracies which met with little success. At Salisbury 200 ROYALISTS under Col. Penruddock seized the judges but were easily crushed. The leaders were executed and others were transported to BARBADOS. A major-general was put in charge of the West, and by June the whole country was under military rule, the expense being met by a 10% tax on royalist incomes.   IHE

Pensionary Parliament, see CAVALIER PARLIAMENT.

Pensions and National Insurance, Ministry of. The Ministry of Pensions, established in 1916 to administer war pensions and provide medical care for the disabled (transferred to the Ministry of HEALTH in 1953), was amalgamated in 1953 with the Ministry of National Insurance, set up in 1944 under the social services legislation. The function of the amalgamated M. of P. and N.I. was to administer, and sometimes to adjudicate on, cash allowances under war and national insurance pensions, industrial accident benefit and family welfare schemes. In Aug. 1966 the M. of P. and N.I. was merged in the Ministry of SOCIAL SECURITY.
PMB; MR

Perak, see FEDERATED MALAY STATES.

Perlis, member state of the Federation of MALAYA, became a British protectorate on 23 Mar. 1907 and was released from Siamese suzerainty on 10 Mar. 1909 as one of the UNFEDERATED MALAY STATES.   SHS

Persian Gulf was in 1505 entered by the Portuguese, who in 1507 sacked MUSCAT and established a customs office at Bahrain. English traders in 1583 first sailed from Basra through the P.G. to India. The EAST INDIA COMPANY, in alliance with Persia, ousted the Portuguese, Dutch and French from the P.G. in the 17th century and used Kuwait as a station on its mail services Aleppo–Bagdad–India. Treaties for the suppression of the slave-trade were concluded with the shaiks of the Pirate Coast (1820) and Bahrain (1847), and led to the establishment of British protectorates: Pirate Coast, 1892 (renamed Trucial States, 1903); Kuwait, 1899 (independent, 19 June 1961); Qatar, 1916. Formerly famous for its pearl fishing, the P.G. is now one of the world's largest producers of oil (discovered 1932; exploited from 1946).

SHS

Peterborough Culture, see NEOLITHIC AGE.

'Peterloo massacre' (16 Aug. 1819) is the name ironically (after WATERLOO) given to the bloody dispersal of a parliamentary reform meeting in Manchester. Economic distress following the Napoleonic wars was particularly felt by the handloom weavers of Lancashire who supported popular RADICAL agitation timed to reach a height when Henry ('Orator') Hunt addressed some 60,000 people on St Peter's Field. The magistrates, to whom this unarmed meeting 'bore the appearance of insurrection', commanded local yeomanry to lead the way for Hunt's arrest and then called on the 15th Hussars. In the mêlée 11 persons were killed and at least 400 injured. For more effective control of such agitation the SIX ACTS were passed.

D. Read, *Peterloo* (Manchester, 1958).   MLH

Peter's Pence, a payment to the papacy. Although king Offa in the 8th century and king Ethelwulf in the 9th made monetary gifts to the pope, the true beginning of P.P. should probably be placed in the reign of Alfred (871–99). It was a HEARTH TAX and became standardized at £200 a year for the country. It was abolished in 1534 by act of Parliament.   CFS

Petitioners. The strength of the supporters of the EXCLUSION BILLS caused Charles II to prorogue a newly elected Parliament (Oct. 1679). Shaftesbury and the COUNTRY PARTY by means of petitions from the constituencies sought to coerce Charles to call a meeting of Parliament. The supporters of the court abhorred this interference with the royal PREROGATIVE. Hence the use of 'P.' and 'Abhorrers' as party labels, which were soon superseded by the abusive names of WHIGS and TORIES.   IHE

Petition of Right (1628). Charles I's third Parliament met after the disastrous expedition to Rhé. The release of those imprisoned for non-payment of the FORCED LOAN (1627) resulted in 27 of them being returned to Parliament, and they attacked arbitrary taxation and imprisonment as breaches of the fundamental laws. After conference with the Lords they produced the P. of R. It forbade the levying of gifts, loans and benevolences without consent of Parliament, also arbitrary imprisonment, compulsory BILLETING and the issue of commissions of martial law. The Lords supported the Commons, and Charles, needing subsidies, eventually gave his assent as to a private bill (7 June). In 1629 the Commons tried to assert that the levying of TUNNAGE AND POUNDAGE was contrary to the P. of R. and the king dissolved Parliament.   IHE

Petty assize, see POSSESSORY ASSIZES.

Petty Bag Office. The three clerks of the P.B., officers of CHANCERY, drafted writs of summons to Parliament, CONGÉS D'ÉLIRE, patents of offices and some legal proceedings, administered oaths to solicitors and officers of chancery and, until 1835, enrolled specifications for patents of invention. From 1835 until the abolition of the office in 1889 they assumed the work of the CURSITORS. The clerks' functions are now mostly discharged by the CROWN OFFICES.   PMB

Petty Sessions. Local criminal charges requiring a jury are heard before JUSTICES OF THE PEACE at QUARTER SESSIONS. P.s. of two or more justices, sitting as required, were devised to deal summarily with minor charges: from Tudor times their jurisdiction has been enlarged by innumerable statutory offences. In London and some other large cities lay justices have, under Acts of 1839–82, been replaced by stipendiary professional magistrates, sitting daily. Juvenile courts, under the Children's Act 1908, are an offshoot of the p.s.
PMB

Philiphaugh, battle of (13 Sept. 1645), a disastrous defeat of the Scottish royalists near Selkirk, after which their leader Montrose fled abroad.
IHE

Philippines were conquered from the Spaniards by the British in 1762, but restored by the peace of PARIS (1763).

Phoenix Park Murders (6 May 1882). Lord Frederick Cavendish, newly appointed Irish chief secretary, and Thomas Henry Burke, the undersecretary, were stabbed to death in Phoenix Park, Dublin. English opinion suffered a severe shock, and a new Irish Coercion Act was passed. The assassins, members of a secret society identified as 'the Invincibles', were eventually arrested, two turning queen's evidence; five were hanged, three sent to life penal servitude. Parnell's lack of complicity was established by the PARNELL COMMISSION.
MLH

Picquigny, treaty of (29 Aug. 1475). No peace-treaty had brought the HUNDRED YEARS' WAR to a formal end. In 1475 Edward IV, his domestic troubles behind him, renewed the attack on France in alliance with Charles the Bold of Burgundy. Edward's army landed at Calais on 4 July, but made little progress and received no effective aid from Charles. Negotiations were opened between Edward and Louis XI of France, and the terms of a treaty were ratified at a meeting of the two kings on a bridge over the Somme at P. near Amiens. In return for giving up his invasion and abandoning his ally, Edward secured payment of a substantial lump sum and an annual pension which helped to free him from financial dependence on Parliament in the last years of his reign.
RFW

Picts. The Latin *Picti* means painted (i.e. tattooed) men, but possibly the word was used as an equivalent of the Celtic word *Priteni* (BRITAIN) rather than as a simple description of the colouring of the warriors. The term embraced a number of racial and cultural groups, of which a substantial pre-Celtic population and a strong Celtic group from the southern part of Britain were the most important. The first known use of the name occurred at the end of the 3rd century (CALEDONIA), and thereafter P. were frequently mentioned with SCOTS and SAXONS as raiders of ROMAN BRITAIN. By the 7th century a distinct Pictish kingdom and language were recognized, and it is possible that the kingdom had been in existence since the 3rd century. This Pictish kingdom covered Scotland north of the Clyde–Forth line less Argyll (DALRIADA), but including the Orkneys and, possibly, the Shetlands. The conversion of the P. to Christianity was begun in the 5th century by the BRITISH CHURCH and was completed in the 6th century by the SCOTTISH CHURCH. The main territorial threat to the kingdom came from NORTHUMBRIA, but after the battle of NECHTANSMERE (685) the southern boundary of the Pictish kingdom was re-established on its previous line. In 756 the king of Northumbria allied with the king of the P. to force the surrender of the Britons of STRATHCLYDE. The reign of this king, Angus (731–61), who exercised power also in Dalriada and Strathclyde, saw the kingdom in an unusually powerful position. Generally, however, the kingdom does not appear to have been strong due to divergent racial groups, geography and the practice of matrilineal succession to the throne; and its superiority in the north was due to the weakness of Strathclyde and Dalriada and the decline of Northumbria after the mid-8th century. It was this system of matrilineal succession that in the mid-9th century gave Kenneth mac Alpin, king of Dalriada, a claim to the throne of the Pictish kingdom, and he apparently made it good by conquest. Thereafter the Pictish kingdom lost its separate political identity.

In the 4th century A.D. camouflaged scouting vessels of the *classis Britannica* were known colloquially as *picti*.
                                                    CFS

Piepowder Courts, held at fairs and markets in the middle ages, principally to deal with the commercial transactions of itinerant merchants. Their name seems to derive from the French *pieds poudrés*, describing the dusty feet of the travelling dealers.   PMB

Pilgrimage of Grace (1536–7), a northern rising largely due to political discontent among the gentry, agrarian unrest caused by INCLOSURES and rising rents, and the religious changes culminating in the DISSOLUTION OF THE MONASTERIES. A rising in Lincolnshire (Oct. 1536) was easily suppressed, but in Yorkshire under the leadership of Robert Aske the 'pilgrims' with the five wounds of Christ on their banner, took York and assembled a force of 30,000 men at Doncaster (24 Oct.). Eventually the duke of Norfolk secured a truce and promised to present their demands, including a reformed Parliament and the punishment of Cromwell. A full pardon was offered, and Aske persuaded his supporters to disperse (6 Dec.). Further outbreaks (Jan. 1537) gave Henry VIII the excuse to break the promises given, and over 220 rebels were executed. As a result the COUNCIL OF THE NORTH was reconstituted in 1537.   IHE

Pilgrim Fathers, the name (first used 1799) given to the 102 emigrants who sailed to NEW ENGLAND in 1620. In 1608 a Puritan congregation left Scrooby (Notts.) and settled at Leiden, but eventually decided to look for a new home across the Atlantic. Obtaining a patent from the LONDON COMPANY to settle in its northernmost territory (1620) and supported by London financiers, they finally left Plymouth in the MAYFLOWER. They established themselves, however, at New PLYMOUTH (Nov. 1620) in the COUNCIL FOR NEW ENGLAND's territory, from whom they obtained a grant in 1621. Only 35 of the *Mayflower* passengers were Puritans, and the P.F. are more important in American folklore than history.   IHE

Piltdown, near Lewes, Sussex, was the scene of a major archaeological hoax. In 1908 a humanoid skull was found there, and by 1912 Charles Dawson, a local lawyer, and his friends had located a jawbone and an upper canine tooth, together with flints and animal bones, from ostensibly the same gravel. All were, on the strength of the finder's report, identified as belonging to the lower (i.e. early) PALAEOLITHIC, but scholarly opinion was divided as to whether the jawbone and canine tooth were human or simian. The former was more favoured and so-called P. man received the scientific name of *Eoanthropus dawsoni*. As more remains of early man came to light P. man seemed increasingly unique, but not until the 1950s did improved scientific techniques disclose a deliberate hoax in that the various remains were either recent but deliberately stained and rubbed or old but imported. The widespread reconstructions of the skull of P. man hastily vanished from museum cases.   CFS

Pinkie, battle of (10 Sept. 1547). Protector Somerset, anxious to weaken the French in Scotland and achieve union by the marriage of Edward VI and Mary, crossed the border (4 Sept.) supported by an English fleet. At P., east of Edinburgh, the Scots were routed with heavy losses. Garrisons were left but the victory was not followed up. The Scots turned to the French for support, and by the treaty of

Boulogne (1550) the English evacuated Scotland.   IHE

Pipe Rolls, EXCHEQUER documents, the oldest and longest series of public records which begins in 1131 and is almost unbroken from 1156 to 1831. The P.R. contain, county by county, the yearly accounts of SHERIFFS, and later other officers, with the Exchequer, of income from the farm of the county and other sources, judicial, feudal etc., offset against the sheriff's expenditure on the king's behalf. Thus the P.R., though important and particularly so in the 12th and 13th centuries, are not national balance sheets. As other departments and other forms of revenue developed, the P.R. decline in importance. Duplicates, chancellors' rolls, were kept for the CHANCELLOR.   PMB

Pirate Coast, see PERSIAN GULF.

Pitcairn was sighted by and named after a midshipman P. in 1767, but remained uninhabited until 1790, when the mutinous sailors of HMS *Bounty* and their Tahitian women occupied the island, where they remained unknown until 1808. P. was formally annexed in 1830. In 1856 the majority of the inhabitants emigrated to the ex-convict settlement of NORFOLK ISLAND. P. was placed under the jurisdiction of the WESTERN PACIFIC HIGH COMMISSIONER in 1898 and transferred to the Governor of FIJI in 1962.   SHS; IHE

Place Acts were intended to weaken crown and governmental influence in the House of Commons by excluding PLACEMEN. Place Bills were introduced in 1675 and repeatedly from the 1690s until the 1740s and thereafter less frequently but few passed both Houses. Excise officers were excluded from the Commons by an act of 1699 and customs officers in 1701. The Act of SETTLEMENT (1701) contained a general place clause, but it was repealed (1705) before it became operative. The Succession to the Crown Act (1707) excluded specified office holders and holders of 'new' offices created after 1705. Others could seek

re-election, but the vagueness of the act led to the majority being re-elected. (The requirement of re-election for ministers was abolished in 1926.) The act of 1716 excluded pensioners for a period of years and the act of 1742 most lesser civil servants. In 1780 the Commons passed DUNNING'S RESOLUTION excluding certain officers of the Household; Clerk's Act (1782) excluded government contractors, and CREWE'S ACT disfranchised revenue officers.   IHE

Placemen were those members of the House of Commons holding places of profit under the crown. They included ministers, civil servants, household and court officials, sinecurists, legal officers, pensioners, contractors, and officers of the army and navy. Distribution of crown PATRONAGE by the Treasury, rapidly increasing after 1660, helped the government of the day to secure support in the Commons. From the reign of William III constant attempts were made to limit this influence by means of PLACE ACTS, but this end was eventually achieved by administrative reforms (1782–1870) which abolished places.   IHE

Plague, The Great (1665–6), the last outbreak of the bubonic plague which had occurred at intervals since the BLACK DEATH (1348). There were serious outbreaks in London in 1603, 1625 and 1647, which was again its chief centre. It raged from Apr. 1665, reached its peak in Sept. and largely died out by the autumn of 1666. Total deaths in London are estimated at 100,000 (the bills of mortality give less than 70,000). The court, Parliament, many people and some of the clergy left town, but not the Lord Mayor. The stoppage of trade was serious.   IHE

Plaid Cymru ('Party of Wales'). Founded in 1925 as Plaid Genedlaethol Cymru ('Welsh Nationalist Party'), it adopted the aim of dominion status for WALES in 1930 and fought its first election. In the 1930s its fortunes were impaired by the association of nationalism with fascism and nazi-ism, though the imprisonment of its three leaders following their symbolic act of destruction against a bombing-school in 1936 won much sympathy. Between 1945 and 1966 the party put up a number of candidates at all general elections with little success. Its president, Gwynfor Evans, won a parliamentary by-election at Carmarthenshire in May 1966 and it has since made considerable inroads into the Labour vote in Wales. It stands for home rule to be achieved by constitutional means, is radical in its economic policy and internationalist in its approach to world affairs. A dual appeal emphasizing preservation of the language and opposition to English 'economic neglect' has not proved easily reconcilable.   GW

Plantagenet, the name by which, since the middle of the 17th century, English historians have regularly referred to the ANGEVIN (Henry II to Richard II), LANCASTRIAN and YORKIST (Henry IV to Richard III) kings. The name originated with Geoffrey, count of Anjou, father of Henry II of England, who was nicknamed P., probably because of his habit of wearing a sprig of broom, *plante genêt*, in his cap. Other explanations include Geoffrey's fondness for hunting among broom, or his having planted broom to protect game. The name was never used by Henry II or his successors or applied to them by contemporaries, until about 1448, when Richard, duke of York, father of Edward IV, adopted it as a surname.   RFW

Plantation of Ireland began in 1556 when Offaly and Leix were planted by English settlers and renamed King's and Queen's Counties. This method of subjugating the Irish continued until the RESTORATION. The first Protestant p.s by west-country undertakers or ADVENTURERS failed (Leinster, Munster 1568–70; Ards 1572–3; Antrim 1573–5). The p. of Munster by Raleigh and his associates (1586) was destroyed by O'NEILL'S REVOLT (1598). Others followed under James I and Charles I, but the extensive p. of Ulster (1608–11) by English

and Scottish undertakers (BARONETCY), and Wentworth's proposed p. of Connaught largely provoked the IRISH REBELLION (1641). This led to fresh land grants to the Adventurers of 1642 and wholesale confiscations under Cromwell.   IHE

Plassey, battle of (23 June 1757), north-west of Calcutta, was won by Robert Clive over the vastly superior forces of Suraj-ud-daulah, nawab of Bengal, and some French auxiliaries. However, the nawab's generals, previously bribed by Clive, abandoned their master during the battle. One of them, Mir Jafar, was proclaimed subahdar of Bengal, and his son murdered the captured Suraj-ud-daulah a few days later. The victory, made possible largely by the navy's command of the sea and river communications, established British supremacy in BENGAL.   SHS

Pleas of the Crown. Justice produces profits, from AMERCEMENTS, forfeitures etc.; kings may become more powerful if their courts and punishments are employed, and certain kings saw that good law and good government go hand in hand: as a result, certain cases, broadly the more serious criminal charges, were reserved to the king and his courts, to be known as the P. of the C. The king's control of them and the courts provided to hear them were the foundations of the English legal system criminal and civil, for primarily criminal courts came also to hear civil cases. Their origin is unknown; but matters covered by the KING'S PEACE, MUND and WITE tended to form a coherent group of offences. The first list of crown pleas, from Cnut's reign, is brief, including ambush, housebreaking etc.; as monarchy grew the list lengthened, to include homicide, treason, arson, any breach of the peace and then innumerable statutory offences. The right to hear crown pleas could be granted away, in small sections to franchises, in entirety to a palatinate; elsewhere they were enshrined in the chapters of the EYRE, in the work of the various courts which succeeded it and in the jurisdiction of KING'S BENCH.   PMB

Pleas of the Sword, the equivalent in Normandy of the English PLEAS OF THE CROWN, i.e. cases reserved for hearing before the duke or his representatives. Though first listed in 1091, such pleas were reserved considerably earlier: as in England, they were enlarged by the legal innovations of Henry II. The sword was the symbol of ducal authority in Normandy, as the crown for royal authority in England.   PMB

Plimsoll line, a mark indicating the maximum load line of a merchant vessel in saltwater, named after Samuel Plimsoll (1824–98), M.P. for Derby, who began in 1870 his campaign against the overloading and overinsuring of ill-found ships. When Disraeli's government abandoned the shipping bill (1875), Plimsoll's sensational protest in the commons was supported by public opinion and immediate legislation resulted, but the Merchant Shipping (Plimsoll) Act, 1876, left the fixing of the load line to the shipowners. The Act of 1890 secured its enforcement by the Board of Trade and these regulations were applied to foreign ships using British ports in 1906. The London load-line convention (5 July 1930), signed by 40 states, was embodied in the Merchant Shipping Act of 1932.   IHE

Plots, see ATTERBURY, BABINGTON, BYE, CAMBRIDGE, CATO STREET, DESPARD, GOWRIE, GUNPOWDER, MAIN, MEAL TUB, POPISH, RIDOLFI, RYE HOUSE, THROCKMORTON.

Plough Alms, a payment made in Old English and medieval times to the PARISH priest of 1*d.* for each plough-team in the parish, paid 14 days after Easter.   CFS

Ploughland, a unit of land holding and taxation assessment in the northern DANELAW, where it replaced the earlier HIDE. Like the SULUNG, it represented the area that could be kept in cultivation by an eight-ox plough-team in the year, but in practice it resembled the hide in acreage. To it were attached rights in woodland, pasture etc. It was subdivided into eight oxgangs. From the 10th century the p. became also the unit of taxation assessment in this area. Each SHIRE was assessed at a round number of p.s, which were subdivided among the constituent WAPENTAKES and, frequently in groups of 6 or 12, among the vills within the wapentake. These 'GELD' p.s had no basis in agrarian fact. The Latin equivalent of p. is *carucata terrae,* and in modern historical usage 'carucate' frequently appears as a synonym for p.   CFS

Plymouth Brethren are a Christian sect formed of communities the most influential of which was founded at P. by J. N. Darby in 1830. Calvinist, fundamentalist and millenarian in outlook, they have no church organization. The most important of several schisms was that in 1849 between the 'open' or 'neutral' b. led by G. Müller and the 'exclusive' b. who followed Darby.   MLH

Plymouth Colony (1620–91) was established by the PILGRIM FATHERS and noted for its toleration and purity of administration under the governorship (1621–57) of William Bradford. The seven years communal working insisted upon by the London financiers was terminated in 1623, but the fur-trade was reserved to them. In 1627 the settlers bought out the entire interest in the colony for £1,800. P.C. joined the NEW ENGLAND Confederation (1643), was made part of James II's Dominion of New England and was finally incorporated with MASSACHUSETTS by William III (1691).   IHE

Plymouth Company (1606–20) shared the commercial and colonial concessions in VIRGINIA with the LONDON COMPANY operating between latitudes 38° and 45° N. After an unsuccessful attempt to plant a colony on the mouth of the Kennebec (1607–8) it confined itself to its trading and fishing monopolies and was reconstituted as the COUNCIL FOR NEW ENGLAND in 1620.　　IHE

Pocket Borough, see ROTTEN BOROUGH.

Poitevins. Many P., subjects of the kings of England as dukes of AQUITAINE and counts of POITOU, entered the royal service in England in the late-12th and 13th centuries. Historians of the 13th century apply the name specifically to a group of councillors and ministers chosen by Henry III after the justiciar, Hubert de Burgh, had lost his confidence. Their leaders, Peter des Roches, bishop of Winchester, and his nephew, Peter des Rivaux, were P., but the majority of the group were English. The P. were Henry III's principal agents from 1232 until 1234 when the success of the MARSHAL REBELLION and their growing unpopularity—to which English hatred of foreigners in general contributed—compelled their dismissal.　　RFW

Poitiers, battle of (19 Sept. 1356). With an Anglo-Gascon army of about 7,000 men the Black Prince carried out a large-scale raid into the heart of France in the summer of 1356, starting from Bergerac on the Dordogne and penetrating as far as Aubigny south-east of Orléans. He then turned westwards to Tours, possibly with the idea of concerting operations with the duke of Lancaster north of the Loire. However, when King John of France brought superior forces over the Loire the prince started a hasty retreat to his base in Gascony. Encumbered by their plunder, the prince's men were outmarched by the French, and the tracks of the armies crossed twice before the prince finally took up his position in an area called Maupertuis, some 7 miles south-east of P. The exact site and some details of the battle are still in dispute, but it is clear that, while the ground favoured the English combination of archers and dismounted men-at-arms, the prince did not fight a purely defensive action, and that it was only after a very hard fight that the French, who numbered 15,000–16,000 men, were defeated and King John captured. The prince then completed his withdrawal to Bordeaux, and King John was sent to England. Possession of him was a most valuable bargaining counter for Edward III and made possible the favourable treaty of BRÉTIGNY in 1360.　　RFW

Poitou, county of, part of the ANGEVIN EMPIRE, brought to Henry II of England by his wife Eleanor of AQUITAINE in 1152 and conferred by him in 1172 on his second son, later Richard I, who in 1196 enfeoffed his nephew, later the emperor Otto IV, with the county. Noted for their turbulence and unstable allegiance, the nobles of P. were frequently in rebellion, notably against Henry II in 1173 and against John in 1200. Having declared all John's French possessions forfeited, Philip II of France invested John's nephew Arthur with P. Arthur, however, was captured by John at Mirabeau in 1202 and subsequently murdered. Despite the loss of NORMANDY and other territories John maintained a foothold in P., notably at La Rochelle, and in 1206 recovered most of the county, which in 1214 was the base of one prong of John's final, and unsuccessful, counter-attack on Philip II (see BOUVINES). John and Henry III continued to hold parts of P. until 1224 when Louis VIII of France took La Rochelle and conquered the whole county. English attempts to reconquer P. failed in 1226, 1230 and 1242 (see SAINTES), and Henry III surrendered his claim to P. by the treaty of PARIS, 1259. During the HUNDRED YEARS' WAR P. was ceded to Edward III by the treaty of BRÉTIGNY, 1360, but was quickly recovered by the French after the resumption of the war in 1369. LA ROCHELLE, again the main English base, fell shortly after the English naval defeat off the port in 1372.　　RFW

Police Forces. By the latter part of the 18th century the traditional method of preserving the king's peace, by the use of unpaid constables acting under JUSTICES OF THE PEACE, was proving inadequate, even though supplemented in the larger towns by salaried watchmen and in London by the BOW STREET RUNNERS. Legislation was delayed by fear that the creation of effective p.f. would be a threat to personal liberty. In 1829, however, Peel's Metropolitan P. Act established a single p.f. in the London area (except the City whose separate p.f. dates from 1839) and placed it under direct control of the Home Secretary. The MUNICIPAL CORPORATIONS ACT (1835) required boroughs to appoint p.f. under control of watch committees and in 1839 justices were empowered to maintain p.f. in the counties; in 1856 county p.f. were made compulsory. This network of local p.f. preserved the common-law rights of the constable and his control by the magistrates. Voluntary and compulsory amalgamation of small p.f. was instituted by acts of 1840, 1856, 1888, 1946 (by which date p.f. were maintained—with the exception of the City of London—by counties and county boroughs only) and 1964. HOME OFFICE inspection and financial aid was established in 1856; grants-in-aid to efficient p.f. were raised from ¼ to ½ charge for pay and clothing in 1874 and to ½ net expenditure in 1919 (since 1950 variable by statutory instrument). Power to make regulations for administration of p.f. was granted to the Home Secretary in 1839; by the 1919 P. Act these are made by statutory instrument. MLH

Political Parties, see COMMON WEALTH PARTY, CONSERVATIVE PARTY, COOPERATIVE MOVEMENT, FOURTH PARTY, INDEPENDENT LABOUR PARTY, LABOUR PARTY, LIBERAL PARTY, MARXIST PARTIES, PLAID CYMRU.

Poll Tax, a personal tax (*poll*, head) assessed on either a fixed or sliding scale and collected locally by special officers. Though first levied in 1222 for the Holy Land, it became a regular tax only in the later 14th century. Always unpopular, the tax of 1380–81 was a major contributory cause of the PEASANTS' REVOLT. The last P.T. was

imposed in 1698. Apart from financial matters, the collectors' returns are useful sources for population figures, though not entirely reliable because of the extent of tax evasion.   PMB

Pondicherry, on the Coromandel Coast, was acquired by the French East India Company in 1673 and soon became the centre of their Indian possessions. P. was in Dutch hands 1693–9, and occupied by the British (after an abortive siege, 1748) 1761–5 (WANDIWASH), 1778–85, 1793–1814). It was transferred to India by treaty on 1 Nov. 1954 and (with Karikal, Mahé and Yanaon) became a Union Territory in 1962.   SHS; IHE

Pontage, a toll for the upkeep and repair of bridges, generally those near towns, levied by royal licence from regular and casual users.   PMB

Pontefract, in May 1321, the scene of a meeting of the northern lords with Thomas, earl of Lancaster, and the conclusion of a defensive alliance between them, possibly against the Scots, possibly against Edward II's favourites, the Despensers. In the spring of 1322 Lancaster mustered his forces at P., and he was beheaded there on 22 Mar. after his defeat at BOROUGHBRIDGE. The earl, though thoroughly undeserving, became a popular saint and P. the resort of pilgrims.   RFW

Pontefract, in 1399–1400 the prison of Richard II, removed there from Leeds (Kent) after his DEPOSITION. Before the end of 1399 rumours of Richard's death or escape were circulating, and the rising of his supporters in Jan. 1400 seems to have convinced Henry IV that Richard was too dangerous a prisoner. The council considered the desirability of Richard's death early in February, and he was soon officially announced to have died on 14 Feb. The manner of his death is unknown. Shakespeare's version, derived ultimately from a French chronicle, is improbable: no marks of violence were discovered when Richard's remains were examined in 1871. He may have been deliberately starved and ill-treated, or the ordinary rigours of a medieval prison in winter were sufficient to secure the desired end.   RFW

Poor Law. In medieval England relief of the poor was a charitable obligation upon the churches, monasteries, gilds and other benefactors. In Tudor times main responsibility was placed on the PARISH; but when parish poor funds relying on private benevolence became inadequate, a compulsory rate was introduced (1572), and in 1576 materials were to be provided to set the poor to work. These provisions, together with relief of the helpless poor and an apprenticeship scheme for pauper children, were embodied in an act of 1598. Parish overseers were to be appointed by the J.P.s, and those unwilling to work were treated as VAGABONDS. This formed the basis of the P.L. Act of 1601, which was steadily less effectively administered, and the growth of vagrancy provoked the Act of SETTLEMENT of 1662. In 1691 controlling powers were given to the vestries and J.P.s, and in 1723 overseers were empowered to establish workhouses, contract for employment of the inmates and deny relief to those refusing to enter. GILBERT'S ACT (1782) once more allowed outdoor relief, which was indiscriminately applied after the spread of the SPEENHAMLAND SYSTEM. The resultant rate burden and demoralization of the poor led to the P.L. Amendment Act (1834), which aroused great resentment by largely seeking to abolish outdoor relief except to the aged and infirm. It never fully achieved this end. Some 600 unions under elected boards of guardians replaced the 15,000-odd parish units and were centrally controlled by three P.L. commissioners until the establishment of the P.L. Board, 1847 (often under a cabinet minister). The latter's work was taken over by the Local Government Board (1871); the Local Government Act (1929) abolished the boards of guardians in favour of the county and county borough councils with their public assistance committees. A consolidating act was passed in 1930. The introduction of old-age pensions (1908), unemployment and national health insurance (1911), followed by the comprehensive National Insurance Act (1946) and National Assistance Act (1948) completed the replacement of the P.L. by schemes of social security under the Ministry of HEALTH.   IHE

Popish Plot (1678) was a fictitious Jesuit conspiracy to murder Charles II, fire the City and enthrone the Roman Catholic duke of York with the aid of French and Irish troops. Its scoundrelly authors were Titus Oates and Israel Tonge. Their allegations were strengthened when the duke's secretary was found to be in treasonable correspondence with France. Before the panic abated in 1681 some 35 victims were judicially murdered, including the Roman Catholic Primate of Ireland. It led to the exclusion of Roman Catholics from Parliament by the TEST ACT of 1678, the scare of the MEAL TUB PLOT and the fall of Danby. The Whigs made use of the occasion to introduce EXCLUSION BILLS to debar the duke of York from the succession. After James II's accession Oates was convicted of perjury.   IHE

Port, a market town in the Old English period, whether on the coast or inland. See BOROUGH.   CFS

Porteous Riots (8 Sept. 1736). Robertson, one of two smugglers awaiting death in Edinburgh for robbing a customs' officer, escaped with the aid of his fellow prisoner Wilson. At the latter's execution Lieutenant Porteous, fearing an attempt at rescue, ordered the town guard to fire on the crowd. Porteous was condemned to death but temporarily reprieved, whereupon some citizens stormed the prison and hanged him in the Grassmarket. The city was fined £2,000 and the Lord Provost was dismissed. Scottish opposition prevented severer measures.   IHE

Portugal, The Way of, an alternative
to 'the way of FLANDERS' as a plan for
indirect attack upon France, involving
an attack upon France's ally Castile in
conjunction with Portugal. John of
Gaunt, duke of Lancaster, favoured
the scheme especially since Portugal
might prove the way to achieving his
own ambitions in CASTILE. Lancaster's
brother Edmund, earl of Cambridge,
led a small army to Portugal in 1381,
but after his lamentable failure in
Extremadura in 1382 the Portuguese
made peace with Castile. The accession of João I in Portugal in 1384 and
the outbreak of a war against Castile
renewed English interest in the
Peninsula. Some English troops
assisted João at ALJUBARROTA in 1385,
and in 1386 Lancaster invaded Galicia.
In Feb. 1387 João married Lancaster's
daughter Philippa. Their concerted
invasion of León in the spring of 1387
failed completely, however: Lancaster
departed to Gascony and in July 1388
came to terms with Castile. Nevertheless, partly due to the influence of
Queen Philippa, Portugal maintained
the friendship with England formed in
the 1380s.   RFW

Port Way, a ROMAN ROAD forming the
Silchester–Old Sarum part of the
main western road London–Staines–
Silchester – Old Sarum – Badbury
Rings–Dorchester–Axminster–Honi-
ton–Exeter. The Staines–Silchester
section is known as the Devil's Highway; part of the Old Sarum–Badbury
Rings section as Ackling Dyke. The
name P.W. is used for many other
stretches of Roman and non-Roman
road and means the way to the PORT.
                                          CFS

Possessory (or Petty) **Assizes.** Designed by Henry II to counter the
ANARCHY of Stephen's reign and extend
good justice through his courts, NOVEL
DISSEISIN attacked self-help, MORT
D'ANCESTOR encroached on feudal
courts and DARREIN PRESENTMENT on
church courts. P.a., deciding SEISIN
not right, had to be heard in the
king's courts and were made attractive.
They were quick, originally a year or
less was allowed to bring an action and

few or no ESSOINS were allowed; they
were simple, replacing the cumbersome procedure of the writ of RIGHT
with the JURY of 12 free and lawful
local men, whose answer to set questions settled the action; they were
cheap, for they could be heard before justices of ASSIZE in the county
of the alleged offence, not at Westminster or in the king's travelling
court, as MAGNA CARTA emphasized,
DARREIN PRESENTMENT alone being
reserved to central courts or general
EYRES. Undoubtedly the p.a. were
successful and popular, for innumerable cases survive on the rolls of late-
12th- and early-13th-century courts.
Thereafter they gradually changed;
pleading was allowed and p.a., designed as preliminaries to the writ
of right, became final actions. UTRUM,
not a p.a. in origin, was adapted as a
form of *novel disseisin* and a final
action.   PMB

Post-nati. James I tried to secure the
union of England and Scotland
(1604–6), but the Commons refused
to agree to the naturalization of his
Scottish subjects or to free trade,
except on a basis of a common parliament and law for both countries, and
the plan was abandoned. By a collusive action (Calvin's Case 1606–7)
the judges decided all those born in
Scotland after James's accession (*Post-
nati*) were natural born subjects of the
king of England.   IHE

Post Office. In the middle ages a
system of messengers developed,
carrying government documents, riding the main roads and changing
horses at the posts maintained by
postmasters. Its extension to private
correspondence was slow: a master of
the posts was appointed in 1512, possibilities of additional revenue were
realized, private letters accepted and
wider services, re-organized in 1660,
established. Posts were first 'farmed'
by the COMMONWEALTH, and while
producing guaranteed revenue, the
practice led to high rates payable on
delivery, based on time in transit, and
to inefficient service. Though 'farming' ended in 1711, inefficiency and

expense remained while England became industrialized and in need of
good, cheap communications. At
last Rowland Hill's reforms of 1840
brought the basic 1d. post and better
service. Since then the P.O.'s work
has increased in volume and scope,
with the foundation of the Savings
Bank in 1859, acquisition of telegraph
services 1868, monopoly of telephone
services acquired from 1880 onwards,
control over radio and television
stations and establishment of National
Giro. It also acts as agent for other
departments, e.g. in issuing licences,
paying pensions etc. On 1 Oct. 1969
the P.O. ceased to be a department of
state and became a public corporation.
A Minister of Posts and Telecom-
munications took over the licensing
and certain other functions of the
Postmaster General, but he has no
responsibility for the commercial
operations of the P.O.; these are the
concern of the P.O. Board.   PMB; MR

Potsdam Conference (17 July–2
Aug. 1945) of allied delegations,
headed by Churchill (later Attlee),
Stalin and Truman, took place in a
deteriorating political atmosphere;
the need for military cohesion was
lapsing whilst the U.S.S.R. was
disregarding the YALTA agreement on
free elections in Poland and other
east European countries. The P.c.
established a council of foreign
ministers (to include also China and
France) to draw up treaties with
Germany's allies in WORLD WAR II
and ultimately with Germany herself;
and further detailed political and
economic principles for the government of Germany and for the payment
of reparations. Recognition of Soviet
power in eastern Europe was conceded:
northern East Prussia was transferred
to the U.S.S.R.; the Oder–W. Neisse
line as Poland's western frontier was
endorsed 'pending final determination
of territorial questions at the peace
conference'.
Differing interpretations of the P.
agreement marked the start of the
'cold war'. The U.S.S.R. regarded
the territorial changes as final and

flouted the cardinal decision that
Germany should be treated as a
single economic unit; this led to the
fusion of the British and U.S. zones
(1947) and eventually to the establishment of the Federal Republic of
Germany (Sept. 1949) and the communist German Democratic Republic
(Oct. 1949).   MLH

Pound, originally the weight of silver
making 240 silver pennies. The P.
sovereign (20s.) was a large gold coin
first minted by Henry VII in 1489,
named from the design embodying
the enthroned monarch. The sovereign became a 30s. piece under
Edward VI and Mary. Elizabeth I
minted gold sovereigns (30s.) and
pounds (20s.). James I substituted
the UNITE (20s.). in 1604. See also
TREASURY NOTES.   IHE

Poundage, see TUNNAGE.

Power, Ministry of. A ministry of
Fuel and P. was set up in 1942 to take
over functions in relation to the fuel
and power industries formerly exercised by the Board of TRADE. After
World War II, new responsibilities
were added of advising and inter-
preting government policy to the
boards operating the nationalized coal,
electricity and gas industries. In 1957
the title was changed to M. of P. and
functions relating to iron and steel
were added; and subsequently responsibilities for inspecting and licensing nuclear installations, for controlling the construction and operation of
pipe-lines, for licensing prospecting
for and exploiting petroleum and
natural gas in the United Kingdom
and within territorial waters. Since
Oct. 1969 the title of Minister of P.
has been held in conjunction with that
of M. of TECHNOLOGY.   MR

Powys, the ancient kingdom of
central WALES, extended at its greatest
from near Mold in the north to the
Wye near Glasbury in the south, and
from the English border to the Dovey
estuary. The kingdom maintained its
unity under a dynasty founded early
in the 5th century by Cadell until 854.
Thereafter, despite temporary sub-

ordinations to GWYNEDD, it retained its separate identity, and early in the 12th century, under the descendants of Bleddyn ap Cynfyn, attained a short-lived supremacy in Wales. Shorn of its provinces between Wye and Severn and hemmed in by Gwynedd on the north, P. was further weakened from 1197 onwards by fission into P. Fadog (north) and P. Wenwynwyn (south). Its rulers throughout the 13th century oscillated between uneasy alliance with England and uneasier vassalage to Gwynedd. After the Edwardian conquest of 1282–3 southern P. was held directly of the crown as a kind of Welsh MARCHER LORDSHIP.   GW

Poynings' Law (1494), a measure promoted by the Irish Lord Deputy Sir Edward Poynings (1459–1521) restricting the powers of the Irish Parliament. Its object was to reinforce English sovereignty and destroy YORK-IST influence, but its implications changed after 1534. The Irish Parliament was not to meet without the king's consent and until its legislative programme had been approved by the king in council. By another act of the 1494–5 Parliament, laws made in England were to apply to Ireland. These acts were virtually repealed in 1782.   IHE

Praemunire, Statute of. The first s. of p. was granted in Parliament 1353 and was one of many measures, beginning with the Constitutions of CLARENDON 1166, followed by writs of prohibition and CIRCUMSPECTE AGATIS, regulating the bounds of church and lay jurisdictions. Opposition to papal provisions had produced the Statute of PROVISORS in 1351, but bishops and patrons adhering to it could be cited before a church court for ignoring a provision, with appeal to Rome. Under COMMON LAW patronage disputes belonged to lay courts, and such appeals had been discouraged throughout the earlier 14th century. The s. of p. forbade them entirely, leaving spiritual appeals unchecked, but supplementing the 1351 statute; although it was not until the 2nd s. of p. (1365) that appeals to

the papal court were specifically prohibited. The 3rd s. of p., sometimes called the Great S. of P. (1393), laid it down that no suits of PATRON-AGE were to go to Rome, and no bulls concerning excommunication or provisions were to enter England. In the event these statutes were of little immediate effect as kings had no desire to enforce them. Their importance came at the REFORMATION.   PMB

Pragmatic Sanction was a decree, first promulgated by the Emperor Charles VI in 1713, that all his territories should pass to his daughter Maria Theresa if there was no male heir. To secure its acceptance became his main objective. It was eventually guaranteed by all the important European states except Bavaria, in return for territorial, dynastic and commercial concessions by the Emperor. By the suspension of the Ostend East India Company (1731) he obtained Great Britain's support. After his death Prussia's invasion of Silesia (Dec. 1740) led to the AUSTRIAN SUCCESSION WAR. France repudiated the P.S., which she had guaranteed as late as 1738. Great Britain and the Netherlands supported Austria.   IHE

Precipe Writs. Many WRITS begin with the word *precipe*: that referred to in MAGNA CARTA, *precipe quod reddat* an early writ of ENTRY, required the addressee to surrender the claimant's land or answer in the king's court, thus removing pleas from a lord's court. The old theory, that the barons objected to the writ because their courts lost business, conflicts with the evidence. Plaintiffs chose the writ because of the tardiness or partiality of lords' courts; such courts were not competent to try cases between the tenants of different lords, and many men held of two or more lords. Cases could be removed to the lord's court if it were successfully claimed in the king's court. The rule that a man need not answer for his free tenement except in the king's court was current in Henry I's reign. The object of the clause appears to have been to save the lords claiming their courts. After the Charter the use of the writ was modified, and plaintiffs found other means of bringing cases to the king's courts.   PMB

Prerogative, historically came to imply the recognized rights and privileges as well as the undefined powers of the monarchy, of which the Tudors made full and judicious use in administration, war, diplomacy etc. The extent of the p. became a matter of dispute in the early 17th century, and the use made of it by James I and Charles I led to ceaseless attacks from Parliament and the common lawyers, and to statutory curtailments, especially by the LONG PARLIAMENT. The CIVIL WAR forced the king to accept limitation of the p. by statute, and it was further restricted by the BILL OF RIGHTS (1689). The right to choose ministers, other than in exceptional circumstances, disappeared after 1832, and the right to interfere in policy was finally whittled away during the reign of Queen Victoria. The residue of discretionary powers is exercised by the government in the sovereign's name. (PROCLAMATIONS; ORDERS IN COUNCIL.)   IHE

Prerogative Courts exercised the judicial PREROGATIVE of the crown through the PRIVY COUNCIL and were widely used by the Tudors to maintain law and order and give cheap and swift justice. They often dealt with matters for which there were no administrative precedents, such as the control of PRINTING. The p.c. included the courts of STAR CHAMBER, REQUESTS and HIGH COMMISSION as well as those of the COUNCILS OF WALES, THE NORTH and THE WEST. They administered the COMMON LAW of the land mingled with EQUITY and were naturally unpopular with the Common lawyers, but not with the public at large until unwisely used by the early Stewarts.   IHE

Presbyterianism, the system of church government by presbyters or elders, was introduced into the CHURCH OF SCOTLAND after the

REFORMATION although EPISCOPACY was not finally overthrown until 1690. P. was established by the Scots in Ulster in 1642 and it was aided by crown grants from 1670 until 1870. In England attempts to set up P. (from the 1570s) and to convert the Church of England from within were checked by the HIGH COMMISSION and the archbishops. It was stimulated by the activities of the LAUDIANS and ARMINIANS, and its temporary triumph was marked by the SOLEMN LEAGUE AND COVENANT with the Scots (1643). The WESTMINSTER ASSEMBLY (1643–9) revealed the strength of P. among the beneficed clergy of the Anglican church but the ascendancy of the INDEPENDENTS and the army largely prevented its official establishment. The Presbyterians naturally welcomed the RESTORATION but failed to secure comprehension at the SAVOY CONFERENCE (1661) and were badly hit by the Act of UNIFORMITY (1662). There were over 200 Presbyterian congregations in George I's reign but they dwindled away during the 18th century when many became UNITARIANS. The Presbyterian Church of England, revived in 1876, has never gained a large following. The Presbyterian Church of Wales (Calvinistic Methodists) was established during the METHODIST revival.   IHE

Press-gang, see IMPRESSMENT.

Prest or imprest, a loan. Medievally loans from the sovereign were often made to private individuals, to the army away from home, to messengers and to officers for day-to-day expenditure; all these had eventually to account, and this useful system of advancing cash before accounting has survived to the present time. Loans to the crown, voluntary or FORCED, though given the semblance of consent, have likewise survived in the modern government stock, savings schemes, post-war credits etc.   PMB

Prestonpans, battle of (21 Sept. 1745). Having proclaimed his father, James, king at Perth, the Young PRE-

TENDER entered Edinburgh (16 Sept.). He then marched out to meet the English forces under Cope advancing from Dunbar, and completedly routed them within a few minutes. Cope and his cavalry escaped to Berwick, and the Highlanders with greatly enhanced morale advanced on Carlisle. IHE

Pretender, the Old and the Young, see JACOBITES.

Pretoria Convention (3 Aug. 1881) ended the first SOUTH AFRICAN WAR. British troops were withdrawn, and the independence of TRANSVAAL was recognized subject to the 'suzerainty of Her Majesty' and to certain 'reservations and limitations', the more important of which concerned external relations and the position of the natives. The Transvaal was made responsible for debts incurred before and during the British occupation.

The terms were modified in the London convention of 27 Feb. 1884, which did not mention suzerainty; Transvaal became the South African Republic and its frontiers were precisely delimited. MLH

Prices and Incomes, National Board for. A National Incomes Commission was established in Nov. 1962 to provide impartial and authoritative advice on matters relating to incomes. It was superseded in 1965 by the N.B. for P. and I., which had its terms of reference extended to take account also of prices. At the end of 1969 plans were announced for the merger of the N.B. for P. and I. and the Monopolies Commission, which was set up in 1948 and had its powers extended in 1965 to enable it to investigate mergers where the assets would be more than £5 million or where a single firm would cover one-third of the market. The new body was to be known as the Commission on Industry and Manpower. MR

Pride's Purge (6 Dec. 1648). Parliament, having made the treaty of Newport with Charles I, ignored the REMONSTRANCE OF THE ARMY and removed him from Carisbrooke to Hurst (1 Dec.). Consequently Colonel Pride, with his soldiers, arrested 45 M.P.s and debarred 78 more from entry. Of the 78 left about 20 more refused to sit. P.P. transferred power to the hitherto Independent minority now nicknamed the RUMP. IHE

Prime Minister, the head of the government, chairman of the cabinet, leader of the majority party in the House of Commons and first lord of the TREASURY. In the latter capacity he is free from departmental duties which fall on the CHANCELLOR OF THE EXCHEQUER. In the 18th century the control of POLITICAL PATRONAGE and the resulting management of Parliament by the first lord of the Treasury made him the most important member of the cabinet. After the HANOVERIAN SUCCESSION when the king ceased to attend cabinet meetings regularly, the way was open for the personal ascendancy of an outstanding parliamentarian who could control the cabinet and manage PARLIAMENT. Walpole is generally recognized as the first P.M. (1721–42), and the position was notably consolidated by the younger Pitt (1783–1801, 1804–6). The P.M. is the main link between crown and cabinet, he secures the appointment and dismissal of ministers, advises on the dissolution of Parliament and controls the remaining patronage in church and state. Nowadays the P.M. is customarily a member of the Commons, as are most of the members of the cabinet, which consists of some 20 of the most important ministers (mainly heads of major departments). The origins of the cabinet go back to the reign of Charles II (1660–85), but it did not emerge in its modern form until the development of cabinet solidarity and MINISTERIAL RESPONSIBILITY which inevitably increased the P.M.'s influence at the expense of both crown and Parliament. IHE

Primrose League was founded (1883) by members of the FOURTH PARTY in support of the CONSERVATIVE PARTY; the p. was wrongly thought to be Disraeli's favourite flower (it was the late Prince Consort's). The objects of the P.L., which was formed on masonic lines with archaic titles regarded as attractive to the working classes, were stated to be 'the maintenance of religion, of the estates of the realm and of the imperial ascendancy'. Its success (over 1m. members in 1891; over 2m. in 1910) was in part due to the HOME RULE issue. Since then the P.L.'s membership and influence have largely declined.

MLH

Prince Edward Island was discovered by Jacques Cartier in 1534 and claimed by France in 1603. It was occupied by the British in 1758 and, after its cession by France in 1763, annexed to NOVA SCOTIA, but in 1769 constituted a separate colony. It was granted responsible government in 1851 and on 1 July 1873 entered the Canadian Confederation as a province.   SHS

Prince of Wales. Llywelyn ap Gruffydd of GWYNEDD (1247–82) was the first to assume the title and had it recognized by the treaty of MONTGOMERY. In 1301 Edward I revived the title for his eldest son, Edward, to whom he entrusted the PRINCIPALITY. Edward III created the Black Prince p. of W. in 1343, and his grandson, Richard, in 1376. Owain GLYN DŴR in the course of his rebellion assumed the title, but since the 15th century it has been normally conferred by the sovereign on his eldest son and heir. The present p. is the twenty-first.   GW

Princes in the Tower. About midMay 1483 the boy king Edward V was lodged in the Tower of London. There he was joined on 16 June by his younger brother, Richard, duke of York. Ten days later, after Edward's DEPOSITION, the princes' uncle, Richard, duke of Gloucester, was proclaimed king. There is no evidence that the boys ever left the Tower, and the date and manner of their death remain unsolved mysteries. The familiar stories of their murder on Richard III's orders, written 30 years later by Sir Thomas More and Poly-

dore Vergil, are no longer generally accepted, but no fully convincing explanation of their disappearance has yet been substituted.

By the time of Richard's coronation (6 July 1483) the princes were no longer being seen in the precincts of the Tower. Rumours that they had been murdered by their uncle soon arose and had spread overseas by the beginning of 1484. In 1674 two skeletons, thought to be those of the princes, were found during demolition work adjoining the White Tower. Four years later those bones that had not been lost in the meantime were transferred to Westminster Abbey. In 1933 the remains were examined by experts, who concluded that the bones were those of two children, one aged between 12 and 13, and the other about 10: Edward V was born in 1470 and his brother in 1473. If the bones are really those of the princes, then they probably died between July and Sept. 1483.

The surprising facts that the princes' sisters remained at liberty, that Richard's relations with their mother were good, and that, after BOSWORTH, Henry VII did not specifically accuse Richard of murdering his nephews, have led some historians to argue that they were still alive in 1485 and that Henry VII had them murdered as possible rivals. But there is no conclusive evidence that the boys were alive in 1484 or 1485.

According to More, Sir James Tyrell confessed in 1502 that he had been Richard's agent in the murder. Other possible agents have been suggested, notably Henry Stafford, duke of Buckingham, who may have murdered the princes without Richard's knowledge in order to further his own king-making designs. Nevertheless, Richard III remains the most likely instigator of the murder, though the case against him stands not proven.   REW

Principality (of Wales), strictly speaking, did not come into existence until Edward of Caernarvon was created PRINCE OF WALES in 1301;

but the term is usually applied to those lands in Wales retained in the direct possession of the crown from the statute of RHUDDLAN in 1284 to the Act of UNION in 1536, as opposed to the MARCHES. The term is now often loosely applied to the whole of WALES. GW

Printing. The technique of printing from movable types was invented by Johannes Gutenberg in Mainz *c.* 1440, and brought to England in 1476 by William Caxton (died 1491) who, by trade a mercer, had learnt and practised the craft in Cologne and Bruges. He established a printing house in the precincts of Westminster abbey and produced nearly 100 books, usually popular or literary titles, several in his own translations. On his death his business passed to his workman, Wynkyn de Worde, who later moved to Fleet Street in the City of London. In Scotland the first printing press was established in Edinburgh in 1508 by Walter Chepman and Andrew Myllar.

The chief craftsmen in the trade were foreigners trained abroad until the 1530s, when legislation forbidding the employment of aliens began to be passed. As only members of a City company could engage in trade in London, the early printers and booksellers probably infiltrated the STATIONERS' COMPANY, which until the early 18th century remained the central organization of the printing and publishing trade. In order to control a potentially dangerous weapon of political and religious propaganda, the government placed the control of the trade in the hands of the Stationers, which gave the Company so complete a monopoly that during the 16th and for much of the 17th centuries there was no printing outside London except for small businesses at the two university towns. The number of presses and employees in any one house was rigorously restricted, and no printing could be undertaken without official approval.

The control of printing included the suppression of news publications, particularly of home news. For this reason, and also for technical reasons, the periodical press, usually in book format, was slow to develop. After 1640, when home news could be published, regularity of publication was achieved and newsbooks and soon news-sheets were issued on settled days of the week. Although these periodicals were suppressed after 1655, two official newspapers continued in existence until by 1695 the restrictions were so laxly observed that newspapers were freely founded. The first daily newspaper was the *Daily Courant*, which appeared from 11 March 1702. Periodicals other than newspapers, such as magazines and literary and technical journals, began to appear after 1690, and the *Gentleman's Journal*, the first miscellany, appeared monthly after Jan. 1692.

Jobbing, which covers all printed matter apart from books and periodicals, including forms, handbills, tickets and trade cards, expanded greatly during the 18th century, and work was of high quality.

The first English typefounder of consequence was William Caslon (1692–1766), whose distinctive old-face, derived—as all English types had been—from continental originals, was cut between 1720 and 1726. The first significant departure from the standard basic design was made by John Baskerville of Birmingham (1706–75), a writing-master turned printer, who transformed the old-face design on principles he had learned from calligraphy. Hitherto, few English printers, with the exception of Dr John Fell, vice-chancellor and bishop of Oxford, who controlled the press at that university, had attempted to raise the standard of printing. Though Baskerville's chief reputation was on the continent, there was beginning in the 1780s a period of 'fine' printing, initiated by John Bell (1745–1831), William Bulmer (1757–1830) and Thomas Bensley (1785–1833).

Booksellers increasingly stocked not only the books they published themselves but also those of other publishers and booksellers. The emergence of such firms as Rivington & Co, founded 1711 by Charles Rivington, and Longmans, Green and Co., founded 1724 by Thomas Longman, marks the emergence of the modern publisher and the separation of the bookselling trade from that of PUBLISHING.

The INDUSTRIAL REVOLUTION stimulated the production of printed matter (for example, of technical journals), increased the markets, initiated publicity printing and improved techniques. The demand for cheap books, including cheap Bibles, arose among the working classes, and the system of publishing in numbers was generally practised. Lending libraries, the first of which in London was founded in 1730, expanded. The increase in periodical publishing was even more startling, and besides technical and commercial journals, periodicals for juveniles became numerous. Many new type designs in a variety of sizes were required, and during the first part of the 19th century the highly skilled British typefounders enjoyed a pre-eminence that later passed to Germany.

In all countries the methods of printing had scarcely changed since the 15th century until in 1800 Lord Stanhope designed an all-metal hand press. The real advance was on 29 Nov. 1814 when *The Times* newspaper was printed on a steam-powered press invented by Friedrich König and Andreas Bauer, which quadrupled the speed of printing and thus enabled periodical printers for the first time to seek mass circulations. Successive improvements in printing speed were made in the office of *The Times*, which also in 1857 pioneered stereotyping for newspapers; stereotyping for book printing had been invented by the Scotsman, William Ged, in 1727. Stereotype plates taken from moulds of *papier mâché*, which could be curved round a printing cylinder, permitted the development of rotary printing, and the first British reel-fed rotary perfecting press, designed and built by *The Times* in 1866, used a continuous reel of paper instead of sheets, and printed both sides in one run. Composing was fully mechanized by American inventions, the Linotype, which casts a whole line of text as a slug of metal, and the Monotype, which casts single units. Most British newspapers are now set on the Linotype and most British books on the Monotype.

The industrialization of printing and the loss of skilled craftsmanship during the 19th century caused a reaction led by William Morris, who in 1891 founded in London the Kelmscott Press, which was deliberately restricted to work that could be done by hand. The influence and methods of Morris had an important effect on standards not only in Britain but also in Europe and in the U.S.A.

The London master printers began to organize themselves in the late 18th century, when their membership of the Stationers' Company ceased to be effective; in 1900 they formed the Federation of Master Printers. Organization among the men followed—for example, the London Union of Compositors was founded in 1824—and printing unions today are banded together in the Printing and Kindred Trades Federation.

In the course of the 19th century copper-plate and wood-block illustrations were gradually replaced by other processes, mainly due to the application of photography. Process-engraving, half-tone, lithography, rotary photogravure and offset are the chief methods used for printing black-and-white as well as coloured illustrations in books, magazines and newspapers. The main developments of the 20th century have been in the application of electronics to printing equipment of all kinds. Because the British national daily newspapers have a circulation unparalleled in other countries, their managements have been eager to develop any invention that promises economy and increased speed.   BWF

Prisage. The sovereign's right to purchase, not necessarily at commercial prices, part of goods shipped into the country, e.g. prise of wine was 1 cask from before the mast, 1 from aft. Ancient prises were extended by Edward I, and goods collected by special officers at ports were used to defray war expenses: this extension was opposed and restricted by baronial opposition in the later years of his reign. Ancient prises were long lived: a payment in lieu of prise of wine persisted until 1809.   PMB

Prison Commissioners. Though medieval imprisonment was usually a means of producing the accused in court, increasingly it was adopted for punishment and restraint of criminals and of debtors. Maintained by sheriffs or local authorities, prisons were ancient, open to bribery and ill-kept until the work of the reformers John Howard (1726–90), Elizabeth Fry (1780–1845) and their fellows. They, together with the increasing prison population as TRANSPORTATION, suspended in 1846, dwindled and the move to house prisoners singly in cells, brought new prison building, e.g. Millbank 1816, Pentonville 1840. At the same period work to maintain prisoners' health was introduced and the need to reform as well as restrain recognized. P.C. were first appointed in 1877 to administer prisons, their inmates and staff, and experiment in penal reform, under the guidance of the Home Secretary to whom the powers of the P.C. were transferred on 1 Apr. 1963.   PMB; MR

Private Bill is promoted from outside Parliament by means of petition from the interest concerned, either private persons, groups or corporations; the expenses are borne by the promoters. P.b.s used to be much more common, and until 1675 could be presented by M.P.s. Many general Acts now give Ministers powers to issue orders which obviate the need for P.b.s. They can be introduced in either House and on passing the second reading, if opposed, go before a committee which hears the case on both sides. If it accepts the preamble the final form of the bill follows the same procedure as a PUBLIC

BILL. Parliament essentially exercises a judicial function.   IHE

Privateering was conducted under letters of MARQUE licensing private ships to attack their country's enemies in return for shares of the booty. English, Dutch and French privateers were active in Tudor times. In 1568 Huguenots from La Rochelle joined the English, as did the Dutch Sea Beggars in 1569. The Hawkinses of Plymouth and their like were active privateers, and from 1570 they spread to the Caribbean until the peace of 1604. In the next two centuries DUNKIRK was a noted centre, and in the 18th century Spain and France made much use of p. in the face of British sea supremacy, and it was widespread during the FRENCH REVOLUTIONARY WARS. The maritime powers agreed to its abolition by the declaration of PARIS 1856, but it was not finally recognized as obsolete until the Hague Convention (1907).   IHE

Privilege, Parliamentary, includes especially Parliament's right to regulate its own proceedings, to punish for breach of p. or contempt, free speech, freedom from civil arrest and in the case of the Commons the right to regulate membership. See APOLOGY OF THE COMMONS, ASHBY, AYLESBURY ELECTION, BILL OF RIGHTS, CROMWELL, DIGGES, FERRERS, GENERAL WARRANTS, GOODWIN, HALL, HAXEY, MARTIN, MIDDLESEX ELECTION, PROTESTATION, RUSSELL, SHIRLEY, SHIRLEY v. FAGG, SPEAKER, WILKES.   IHE

Privy Council. In the centuries following the NORMAN CONQUEST the barons and great officers of state formed the king's council: in practice, however, much everyday business must have been done by such councillors as were about the court, and the king's personal staff. As the council developed into Parliament, so the informal council gained importance and was known, from the late 14th century, as the Privy ('private') Council. In Richard II's youth and in Henry VI's reign it had an important political role: under the Yorkists and the

Tudors its judicial and administrative functions were emphasized, e.g. in STAR CHAMBER. In the 17th century administration, notably of colonies and trade, was an important part of its business but, with the growth of political parties and the cabinet system, its political influence waned. It retained, however, administrative functions in authorizing ORDERS IN COUNCIL, and in the 19th century laid the foundations of, for example, the ministry of EDUCATION. In 1833 its first Judicial Committee was appointed, to hear appeals from civil law courts and the colonies. In recent years its members, of considerable political, administrative or judicial experience and bound by the special councillor's oath, have been employed in inquiries into such matters as national security.   PMB

Privy Purse Office, the last in the long succession of offices, beginning with the CHAMBER, established to administer the sovereign's domestic finances. The office of the keeper of the P.P., charged with administering the CIVIL LIST, assumed its modern form in the early 19th century.   PMB

Privy (or Secret) **Seal.** A royal P.s. is first mentioned in John's reign, but the earliest surviving impression comes from that of Edward I. The seal is single-sided, smaller than the GREAT SEAL, bears the coat-of-arms with a brief legend and is normally impressed on red wax, the impression being applied and not pendant. The seal gave its name to a type of document originally less formal than letters close or patent, generally written in French, then English. These documents were particularly important in the late 13th century as the CHANCERY went out of court, were temporarily overshadowed by the SIGNET letters, and with the 15th- and 16th-century dominance of the council, with which the P.s. came to be associated, assumed a new importance. P.s.s on the royal model were soon adopted by magnates.

The first special keeper of the P.s. was, in the reigns of Edward I and Edward II, the controller of the WARD-

ROBE, but from 1311 onwards a keeper was appointed. The title was retained until Thomas Cromwell held the seal as Lord P.S., a style lapsing in Elizabeth I's reign in favour of keeper, but subsequently revived. Though at times the Signet overshadowed the P.s., the keeper had, by the late 14th century, become a high officer of state called, on occasion, to hear cases with the CHANCELLOR: later the keeper was regularly appointed Master of the Court of REQUESTS. His staff, originally household clerks, were known as the P.S. Office, and received Signet warrants for drafting and issuing warrants to the Great seal. Though the office was abolished in 1884, the Lord P.S. has remained important and a cabinet officer able, because of few regular duties, to attend to special governmental tasks.   PMB

Probate, Admiralty and Divorce Division, the division of the supreme court which united courts other than those of COMMON LAW and EQUITY. Until the 19th century probate of WILLS was primarily administered in diocesans' and metropolitans' courts, then in 1857 a lay probate court was created; divorce was at first a church matter later usurped by Parliament; admiralty courts administered maritime law. The three jurisdictions, though linked for convenience under the JUDICATURE Act 1873, have remained specialized and distinct. PMB

Proclamations, similar to medieval ordinances, were widely used by the Tudors to supplement STATUTES and fill in legislative and administrative gaps. Issued under royal PREROGATIVE, they dealt with a wide range of subjects (e.g. trade, industry, INCLOSURES, PRINTING, ANABAPTISTS, RECUSANTS, etc.). An essential part of good government when Parliament met infrequently, p. were approved, subject to conditions, by the Statute of P. (1539). The repeal under Edward VI (1547) did not affect their legality, and their use was enforced by STAR CHAMBER. The Commons petitioned against their abuse in 1610, and the judges decided that no new offence could be created by p. nor could they change the Common law. The abolition of Star Chamber greatly curtailed their use which is now restricted to such pronouncements as the proroguing, dissolution and summoning of Parliament or as authorized under the RIOT ACT (1714) and the Emergency Powers Act (1920). IHE

Proctor, the representative of his principal in canon and civil law courts: though akin to the attorney-in-law, his powers to commit his principal were limited by the terms of his letters of proxy. Royal agents sent on the frequent missions to the parlement of PARIS in the 13th and 14th centuries, those maintained in the papal curia and those negotiating treaties and truces had, of necessity, to be appointed proctors. PMB

Procurator-General. As in COMMON LAW proceedings ATTORNEYS and later Attorneys-General acted for the crown, so in civil and ecclesiastical cases proctors or procurators, then a P.-G., were appointed but, because of the predominance of Common law, the P.-G. never achieved the political importance of the ATTORNEY-GENERAL. In modern times the work of the P.-G., joined to the office of TREASURY SOLICITOR in 1876, has chiefly been to act as Queen's Proctor in matrimonial cases when ordered by the court or on suspicion of collusion, and in time of war to conduct all prize proceedings in the United Kingdom, also advising overseas courts thereon. PMB

Prohibition, Writs of, issued out of one court to bar the jurisdiction of another: both plaintiffs and judges who heard the suit were endangered if the writ was ignored. In the 12th and 13th centuries the writ was used to bar the church courts, particularly in cases of goods not concerned with testamentary or matrimonial suits. Later the writs, with other devices, were used by Coke and his followers to defend COMMON LAW from EQUITY, e.g. to take cases from CHANCERY or mercantile matters from the ADMIRAL'S court. PMB

Propagation Act for the propagation of the Gospel in Wales (1650), delegated authority to 71 commissioners, authorizing them to establish a Puritan ministry and appoint schoolmasters. It is notable as the first state provision for schools, of which more than 60 were founded, and as an early experiment in autonomy for WALES.
GW

Protectorate (16 Dec. 1653–25 May 1659) established by the INSTRUMENT OF GOVERNMENT. Protector Cromwell ruled with a COUNCIL OF STATE but failed to work with Parliament—his first lasted only five months (1654–5). PENRUDDOCK'S RISING was followed by the arbitrary rule of the MAJOR-GENERALS (1655–6), and about 100 potential opponents were excluded from the Parliament of 1656. After the HUMBLE PETITION AND ADVICE (1657) the re-admission of the excluded M.P.s renewed dissension and Cromwell finally dissolved Parliament (4 Feb. 1658). A union with Scotland and Ireland was effected and peace made with the Dutch (1654). There was interference with private life and amusement but substantial religious toleration, except for 'papists' and 'prelatists', and the JEWS were re-admitted. The maintenance of the army and navy and an aggressive foreign policy produced financial difficulties. The expedition to Hispaniola and the capture of JAMAICA (1655) led to war with Spain and a French alliance (1657), the defeat of the Spaniards at the battle of the DUNES and the occupation of DUNKIRK (1658). A British fleet defeated the BARBARY CORSAIRS at Algiers and Tunis. Oliver died (3 Sept. 1658) and his son Richard, failing to secure the support of the army, abdicated (25 May 1659).
IHE

Protestation (18 Dec. 1621). The Commons, disagreeing with James I's policy of securing Spanish support to recover the Palatinate for his son-in-law, drafted a petition on foreign policy and were sharply rebuffed. A protest against his interference with their freedom of speech and jurisdiction followed, and James replied that their privileges were not of right but of grace. The Commons entered their P. that their liberties, privileges, jurisdictions and freedoms of discussion were of right. After the dissolution the king tore out the page from their journals.   IHE

Protestation of the Lords and Commons (May 1642) was made shortly before the Civil War, that princes err in assuming that they can do what they will with their kingdoms 'as if their kingdoms were for them, and not they for their kingdoms'.   IHE

Provincia. The Roman empire consisted of a number of provinces each responsible for its internal administration, defence, etc. Britain originally formed one p.; at the end of the 2nd century it was divided into two (Britannia Inferior and Superior); at the beginning of the 4th century, into four (Britannia Prima and Secunda, Maxima and Flavia Caesariensis); late in the 4th century land reconquered, probably in Wales, became a fifth province, Valentia.

There is no continuity with the p. or *regio*, the term used by early writers for the sub-division of a Teutonic kingdom. The word had originally the sense of a tribe or folk rather than a district. It formed the earliest known unit for local government and taxation, and presumably goes back to the early days of the Teutonic settlement. In most of England it was replaced by the SHIRE and HUNDRED or WAPENTAKE. But the LATHES of KENT and the RAPES of SUSSEX are relics of this older organization; and it is possible that some of the later hundreds elsewhere have their origin in former *provinciae*.
                                          CFS

Provisions, Papal. During the 13th century the popes increasingly exercised their supreme power in making appointments to vacant benefices in England, overriding the rights of PATRONAGE of English laymen and ecclesiastical bodies. Considerable opposition, and in 1231 armed resistance,

was encountered by papal nominees, especially from lay patrons. Although p.p. came to be confined to benefices in the gift of ecclesiastics, opposition continued in the 14th century, notably on the grounds that papal nominees were often foreigners and absentees and that the revenues of their livings were consequently being sent overseas. On the other hand the popes frequently provided deserving clergy who lacked other patrons, and in nominating cardinals and members of their households to English benefices were, not unreasonably, requiring England to share in the maintenance of the central organization of the church. Here the interests of the papacy and the crown clashed, since the kings were accustomed to inducing ecclesiastical patrons to provide livings for members of the royal household and administration. Although the parliaments of Edward III and Richard II produced the antipapal statutes of PROVISORS and of PRAEMUNIRE, these were only strictly enforced when the king desired to bring pressure to bear on the pope. A workable compromise was in fact reached: in 1398 Richard II and Boniface IX agreed to share p. to English bishoprics, while a third of the major offices of cathedral and collegiate churches were reserved for papal nominees; and in the 15th century p.p. frequently secured livings for the king's nominees.   RFW

Provisions of Oxford (1258) for the future government of England made by the committee of 24 at the OXFORD PARLIAMENT in June 1258. Henry III, if unwillingly, assented and took an oath to observe them. A long list of grievances, the petition of the barons, was brought forward in the parliament; the p., however, did not give immediate redress, but rather established a limited monarchy and set up machinery with which the desired reforms could be undertaken. The most revolutionary measure was the appointment of a council of 15, indirectly elected by the 24, as the permanent advisers of the king; in practice they were the real rulers of England. The council, which was in being by 6 July, included the archbishop of Canterbury, the bishop of Worcester, Simon de Montfort, Richard de Clare and four other earls. Instead of limiting the king's powers by insisting on the observance of MAGNA CARTA, the barons now themselves exercised the king's powers through the new council. Contact with the barons was to be maintained at regular parliaments, three every year, at which the council would consult with a committee of 12 representing the baronage. Another committee of 24, whose membership overlapped with that of the council and the Twelve, was to arrange for the financial aid which the king so desperately needed. A justiciar was appointed for the first time since 1234, and together with the chancellor and the treasurer was made responsible to the council. Other p. regulated the appointment and conduct of local officials. Little change was made in the administrative machinery, but it was placed under the control of the council. Immediate inquiries in every shire into the misconduct of officials foreshadowed the intense judicial activity which was to follow, and wider schemes of reform and redress which became the work of the council of 15 when the Oxford Parliament broke up at the end of June. The term 'p. of O.' was extended by contemporaries to the later measures of the reforming barons now generally known as the PROVISIONS OF WESTMINSTER.   RFW

Provisions of Westminster (1259), the reforming legislation, less revolutionary than the PROVISIONS OF OXFORD, issued in the parliament which assembled at W. at Michaelmas. The legislative p., defining or modifying the common law, were the product of the deliberations of the council of fifteen with the committee of twelve and the royal judges. On many points the p. met the grievances expressed in the petition of the barons in 1258. They included the obligations of feudal lords and tenants in respect of

suit of court, WARDSHIP and DISTRESS; modifications in the law of ENGLISHRY; and the MORTMAIN legislation of Edward I was anticipated. The jurisdiction of feudal courts was further limited, appeals against false judgement being reserved to the royal courts. Following the legislative p., issued on 13 Oct., came a series of administrative enactments. The king was provided with councillors in constant attendance, a finance committee was set up to supervise the revenues and to choose sheriffs, and machinery was devised for the judicial investigation of complaints in the shires. The legislative p., often regarded at the time as part of the P. of Oxford, were reissued in 1263 and, after the defeat of the baronial reform movement, incorporated, with some changes, in the statute of MARLBOROUGH, 1267.   RFW

Provisors, Statute of (1351). To quieten the current popular dislike of papal PROVISIONS, the s. of p. confirmed powers already used by the crown to exclude, and if necessary imprison, persons provided to benefices. Though it had some success in halting papal provisions, the crown acquired greater patronage at the expense of private patrons, for it could present to a vacant church if a patron was unwilling so to do in the face of a provision. Waived by the crown to suit its convenience, the s. of p. was reinforced by another, sterner, measure in 1390.   PMB

Public Bill, the draft of a proposed law affecting the public generally (BILL). Most controversial p.b.s originate in the commons. Initiated by a cabinet memorandum, a government bill is drafted by the office of the parliamentary counsel (not available to private members). The bill is lost if agreement between lords and commons is not eventually reached. P.b.s involving public expenditure have to be authorized by a committee of the whole house.   IHE

Public Building and Works, Ministry of. Medievally king's works were improvised by sheriffs and castellans, etc., later reinforced by surveyors at

each royal residence. By the 16th
century general surveyance lay with a
central office, which in 1660, was
created the Board of Works. It gradually acquired power over public buildings, e.g. Westminster Bridge, and in
1782 all public buildings were put in
its charge. Briefly after 1832 it was
merged with the Commissioners of
Woods and Forests, but later separated, acquiring new powers, e.g. over
ancient monuments, but losing others,
notably to the Metropolitan Board of
Works, the forerunner of the London
County Council. Created a ministry
in 1940, it exercised town and country
planning powers until 1943. Its
responsibilities include the upkeep of
public buildings and ancient monuments, arrangements for public ceremonies, organization of exhibitions,
etc. In July 1962 the title was changed
from M. of Works to M. of P.B. and
W. In Oct. 1962 the M. took over
responsibility for construction for
service needs from the ADMIRALTY,
WAR OFFICE and AIR MINISTRY.

PMB; MR

Public Record Office, was established under the direction of the
Master of the ROLLS by an 1838 Act
as a central repository for legal and
governmental records. The present
building, which stands on part of the
Rolls estate, formerly the Liberty of
the Rolls and site of the DOMUS CON-
VERSORUM, was begun in 1851. There
the documents accumulated over centuries were gradually brought together
from the Tower, the Westminster
Chapter House etc. to be sorted,
listed and made available. The founding of the office marked a turning-
point in English historical studies. As
these developed, increasing anxiety
was felt about documents accumulating in modern government offices. In
1952 a committee was appointed to
examine the problem, and as a result
a 1958 Act was passed, regulating the
transfer of recent documents and
transferring the office's direction to
the Lord Chancellor.

The collections, unparalleled in
Europe, broadly cover the centuries
between DOMESDAY BOOK and the last
few years. They contain not only
documents written in government departments, courts etc. but also confiscated deeds and such groups as the
records of the Duchy and Palatinate
of LANCASTER. Most public records
are open for inspection after 30 years,
but this may be varied by the Lord
Chancellor at the request of the
department concerned. A later development in the keeping of historical
materials has been the establishment
of many local authority record offices,
performing tasks analogous to the
P.R.O. in their respective areas, as
well as the care for some public
records, e.g. of QUARTER SESSIONS.

PMB; MR

Public Schools had their origin in the
endowed grammar schools of medieval
and Tudor times. Winchester (founded 1382) and Eton (1440) held an
exceptional position; some other
schools were recognized as 'great' or
'p.' in the 18th century when, ceasing
to cater for local needs, they accepted
fee-paying boarders—change of status
owing much to the headmaster's
personality. The educational needs of
the Victorian middle classes were
satisfied by the foundation of many
new p.s., a potent influence in development being the example of Thomas
Arnold at Rugby (1828–42). Constitutions of 7 foremost p.s. (Eton,
Winchester, Westminster (1560),
Charterhouse (1611), Harrow (1571),
Rugby (1567) and Shrewsbury (1552))
were reformed by the P.S. Act (1868).
There are now about 220 p.s. in the
United Kingdom and 50 in the
COMMONWEALTH if the official definition (1942)—membership of the Head-
masters' Conference (founded 1869) or
of the Governing Bodies Association—
be accepted; this figure includes
state-aided schools.   MLH

Publishing. In the early days of
PRINTING the functions of publisher,
printer and bookseller were hardly
separated. The printer usually performed all three: he initiated and
financed the work, printed it and sold
it to the public. In 1553 the licensing

of printing was introduced in England and the STATIONERS' COMPANY (chartered in 1557) was charged with its control. This had two important consequences: first, all books published (with special exceptions) had to be entered in the register at Stationers' Hall, a system which later became important in establishing the claim of the publisher to COPYRIGHT; and second, in course of time the Company won for its members virtual control of printing and bookselling.

The LICENSING system was continued by various Acts of Parliament during the 17th century, but gradually became increasingly ignored or abused. During the civil war passions were again inflamed; it became impossible to prevent clandestine printing at home or the importation of pirated copies from abroad, and the Company could not control its own members. Finally the booksellers appealed to Parliament, which passed the epoch-making Copyright Act of 1709. This for the first time gave the author a copyright in his work, as well as the publisher—for 21 years from 1710 for books already published, and 14 years from publication (extensible to 28) for new works. This Act incidentally, in establishing a limited statutory copyright, killed the claim to perpetual copyright at common law on which publishers had relied with varying success hitherto. But it has been succeeded and extended by other Acts, of which the latest is the Copyright Act, 1956. The term of protection is now the life of the author and 50 years thereafter.

The Act of 1709 provided some security for author and publisher, the two parties chiefly at risk in publication, and hastened the process of specialization in the trade. Publishers increasingly threw off their printing and bookselling ties and concentrated on what we now know as publishing. For a time risk-sharing was common, several firms contributing to the costs and sharing proportionately in the profits. Some outstanding figures of the late 17th and the 18th centuries, with the dates of their careers, are:

Jacob Tonson (1678–1720), publisher for Dryden, Addison and Steele; Bernard Lintot (c. 1700–28), Pope; Robert Dodsley (1735–59), Pope, Johnson, Gray and Sterne; John Newbery (1744–67), who published many of Goldsmith's works and was a pioneer of books for children. In 1768 the first John Murray started the career of a firm, still a household word today, which with Macmillan (started in 1843) and Longmans (1724) formed a publishing triumvirate of dominating influence through the 19th century.

Publishers have reacted to, or even anticipated, the changes of demand and fashion in reading occasioned by the political and social developments since the industrial revolution. The growth of the franchise, the coming of railway travel, compulsory education and general literacy, the spread of public libraries and the demand for invented stories have all found authors and publishers quick to respond with relevant reading matter. The most important advance of the 20th century has been the rise of the cheap paperbound book pioneered by Sir Allen Lane, who founded Penguin Books in 1935. Publishing firms are now numbered in hundreds, and besides the giants who take all writing for their province, there are many smaller firms specializing in all conceivable spheres of knowledge.   BWF

Punjab, the land of the 'five rivers' (Jhelum, Chenab, Ravi, Beas, Sutlej) flowing into the Indus, centre of the earliest Indian civilization (3000 B.C.), gateway to India of all north-western invaders from Alexander the Great (327–25 B.C.), and home of the SIKH religion. From the 16th to the 18th centuries the P. was mostly under Afghan rule. The Sikh governor, Ranjit Singh (1780–1839), revolted and created a powerful kingdom. The rapid decline of the Sikh power after his death paved the way for the English, who after the SIKH WARS annexed the P. (30 Mar. 1849). The efficiency and benevolence of British administration made the Sikhs remain stead-

307 PURVEYANCE

fastly loyal during the mutiny. The chief commissionership set up in 1853 was transformed to a lieutenant-governorship (including Delhi) in 1859. In 1901 the NORTH-WEST FRONTIER PROVINCE and in 1911 DELHI were separated from the P., which in 1937 became an autonomous province. On the partition of India in 1947 the eastern P. (⅓ of the area with ½ of the population) went to India, the western portion to PAKISTAN. On 1 Nov. 1956 the Patiala and East Punjab States Union was integrated with P. state, the hills states were merged in HIMACHAL PRADESH. The irrigation and colonization schemes undertaken from 1875 created one of the greatest economic assets of India before 1947.
SHS

Puritans, the more extreme Protestants of the 16th and 17th centuries within and without the Church of England and including Presbyterians and Independents. Characterized by a high sense of duty and morality, they reacted against certain forms of art and amusement and emphasized individualism in religion. They became prominent under Elizabeth I, and the BROWNISTS and BAPTISTS were the earliest organized separatists. The first disputes in the church were over ritual (VESTIARIAN CONTROVERSY) and then over EPISCOPACY. Their strength was shown by the MILLENARY PETITION (1603) but their demands were rejected by the HAMPTON COURT CONFERENCE (1604). Elizabethan persecution had driven Puritan exiles to Holland but the reigns of James I and Charles I witnessed the great migration to NEW ENGLAND. With the growth of ARMINIANISM under Charles I the LAUDIANS drove them into violent opposition, and they became a major political force in the struggle between crown and Parliament. The LONG PARLIAMENT and CIVIL WARS led to the triumph of PRESBYTERIANISM, especially after the SOLEMN LEAGUE AND COVENANT (1643), but it was of short duration. The Parliamentary army championed the INDEPENDENTS and toleration for all protestants other than

Anglicans, and after 1649 they took control. After the RESTORATION the Act of UNIFORMITY (1662) deprived Puritan clergy of their livings, those who conformed came to be known as the Low Church party, the remainder Dissenters or NONCONFORMISTS. IHE

Purpresture, an illegal incroachment on royal land, roads, rivers etc., by buildings etc. In the middle ages p.s were listed and valued at the general EYRE: in theory, all an incroacher's lands were forfeit, but generally he subsequently paid a rent for his p. The rent was collected by the SHERIFF and appeared in his account on the PIPE ROLL together with small ESCHEATS.
PMB

Purveyance, the compulsory, though paid-for, acquisition by government of food, land, etc. Goods for the king's itinerant court in the middle ages were normally either purchased from tradesmen in the places where the king stayed or compulsorily purchased (purveyed) from producers by local officers, warned in advance of the king's arrival. Such compulsory purchases, particularly if local surpluses were small, caused hardship and grievance, especially as the requisitioning of carts to transport what was purveyed was an essential part of the practice. In war-time the whole country became the field for p., and local officers were supplemented by itinerant purveyors employed to buy foodstuffs for which ready payment was rarely forthcoming; in addition, merchants were forbidden to export and compelled to sell to the crown. The system was inevitable, but it produced constant grievance which occasionally came to a head, e.g. complaints against p. contributed to the CONFIRMATION OF THE CHARTERS (1295) and figured in the ORDINANCES of 1311; subsequently it was regulated by many statutes, but was still a major source of grievance in the early Stewart period and reckoned to be worth many thousands of pounds yearly to the monarch. It has persisted to the present day, although its scope has decreased with the growth of commerce. Horses were purveyed in the First World War, houses and property compulsorily requisitioned in the Second, and in the purchase of land for roads and other improvements some vestiges of p. still remain. PMB

Putney Debates (Oct.–Nov. 1647), meetings of the council of the NEW MODEL ARMY held in Putney church when the generals, two officers and two AGITATORS from each regiment discussed the AGREEMENT OF THE PEOPLE. Cromwell and Ireton withstood the more radical demands of the LEVELLERS, but the debates revealed fundamental differences of social and political attitudes between the officers and the lower ranks. Ireton opposed universal suffrage and republicanism. Cromwell held that they were not practical politics, and the Agitators were sent back to their regiments (8 Nov.). IHE

Quadruple Alliance. (1) (2 Aug. 1718), between Great Britain, the Netherlands, France and the Emperor, was an extension of the TRIPLE ALLIANCE (1717); later joined by Savoy. It sought to maintain the peace of UTRECHT and prevent war arising between Spain and the Empire over their conflicting claims, especially in Italy. The Emperor was to cede Sardinia to Savoy in exchange for Sicily; Don Carlos of Spain was to secure the reversion of Parma and Tuscany. Spain was to be coerced if these terms were refused, and after the battle of CAPE PASSARO a short war with Spain ensued. Spain and France attempted to invade each other's territories, and Spain supported attempted Jacobite invasions of England and Scotland. In 1720 Spain accepted the terms of the Q.A.

(2) (20 Nov. 1815), between Great Britain, Austria, Russia and Prussia to guarantee the peace of PARIS of the same date. It provided for periodical meetings of the powers which resulted in the European congresses of 1818, 1820, 1821 and 1822.

(3) (22 Apr. 1834), was negotiated by Palmerston between Great Britain,

France, Spain and Portugal to expel the pretenders Don Carlos from Spain and Dom Miguel from Portugal. IHE

Quakers, the usual name for the Society of Friends founded by George Fox (1624–91), a shoemaker. His active preaching began in 1647 and his missionary journeys at home and abroad continued until his death. Their interruption of church services and emphasis on personal inspiration brought persecution from the Presbyterian COMMONWEALTH, but Cromwell gave them protection. They built up an organized society between 1656 and 1668 and were strong enough to survive victimization under the Quaker Act (1662) and CLARENDON CODE. Emigration to MASSACHUSETTS established them in America, and it increased after the foundation of PENNSYLVANIA (1681) which was of Quaker origin. The TOLERATION ACT (1689) recognized their objection to oathtaking by allowing them to make a declaration instead. At first characterized by rigid puritanism, they gained respect for their sincerity and subsequently for their prominence in humanitarian and philanthropic enterprises. IHE

Quare impedit, see DARREIN PRESENTMENT.

Quartering Act (1774), one of the INTOLERABLE ACTS, forced Boston to accommodate royal troops in the town barracks. IHE

Quarter Sessions. After the failure of general EYRES various expedients in criminal jurisdiction were tried. Finally, from 1368 onwards, JUSTICES OF THE PEACE were permanently empowered to hear criminal charges. Sitting four times a year in Q.S., they dealt with cases presented by grand juries (JURY): their jurisdiction has subsequently been enlarged by innumerable statutory offences, but from the 18th century capital charges have been heard at ASSIZES, and most grand juries were abolished in 1933. Q.S. also review PETTY SESSIONS'

309 QUEEN

cases: q.s. decisions were first reviewed by KING'S BENCH, later by the court of CRIMINAL APPEAL. PMB

Quatre-Bras, battle of (16 June 1815), in which Wellington's British and Hanoverian troops checked Marshal Ney, while on the same day Napoleon defeated Blücher's Prussians at Ligny. Contrary to Napoleon's expectations, Wellington and Blücher decided to combine their forces: Wellington retreated northward to the hills covering Brussels, where Blücher joined him two days later in the last phase of the battle of WATERLOO. SHS

Quebec (French 'Québec'; Indian 'closed place'), founded as a trading post by Samuel de Champlain in 1608, became the capital of the French colony of New France (1627) and seat of a bishopric under François de Laval (1658 titular, 1674 established) and has remained the metropolis of the province of Q., with the exception of the years 1844–58, when the capital was moved to (Ville Marie de) Montréal (founded in 1642). Despite the temporary occupation by English adventurers under David Kirke (1629–1632), the colony of Q. was the complete oversea counterpart of the France of the Ancien Régime, ruled by priest and seigneur in an authoritarian, feudal and paternalistic way, and administered (from 1665) by the dual system of an *intendant de justice, police et finance* and a governor; the law being, since 1637, the *coutume de Paris*. The first British attempt to conquer Q. in 1690 failed; but during the SEVEN YEARS' WAR Pitt's amphibious strategy and Wolfe's generalship overthrew the French regime by the capture of Louisbourg (28 July 1758), the battle on the Plains of Abraham (1759) and the surrender of Montreal (8 Sept. 1760). When Q. was ceded to Britain in 1763 the French inhabitants numbered about 60,000.

The Q. Act of 1774 won over the ruling classes by perpetuating Roman Catholic religion and seigneurial rule in the new British colony—and thus indirectly inflamed the revolutionary sentiments in the 13 colonies. Q.

never thought of joining the rebels, and an attack on the capital was decisively repelled (31 Dec. 1775). With the influx into Upper Canada of white and Red Indian loyalists, Quakers, Mennonites, Methodists—mainly of Scots and Ulster extraction—the government deemed it prudent to divide the colony into Upper and Lower Canada (1791). Q. city remained the common capital, and the governor of Lower Canada was superior to the lieutenant-governor of the other provinces.

The effect of the French Revolution, which found no echo in Q., was indirect in that the *seigneur* was superseded by the *avocat* in public importance and popularity. Grievances over the spoliation of public lands and the monopolizing of administrative and judicial posts by the English led to the rebellion of 1837–8. Their leader was Louis Joseph Papineau, speaker of the assembly 1815–36, who from 1831 had agitated for complete control of the administration by an elected council. The cause of the 'Patriots', who received support from bands of U.S. adventurers, speedily collapsed, mainly because the clergy opposed Papineau's secularist doctrines. The much-needed reforms were indicated in the DURHAM REPORT of 1839. In 1840 Upper and Lower Canada were re-united and in 1846 renamed Canada West and Canada East, and responsible government was introduced in 1848. On the establishment of the Dominion of CANADA (1867), Q. joined the confederation under its old name as the province of Q. SHS

Queen Anne's Bounty, the fund established (1704) for the relief of poorer Anglican clergy by Queen Anne's gift of the revenue from first fruits (ANNATES) and tenths. Grants were somewhat haphazardly made to livings not exceeding £10 per annum; those over £35 did not qualify until 1788. Loans for the building and repair of parsonages began in 1777. The fund was augmented by Parliamentary grants (1809–20) and private gifts. Q.A.B. became responsible for the collection and distribution of church tithes (1925) and was merged with the Ecclesiastical Commission to form the CHURCH COMMISSIONERS for England (1948).   IHE

Queen's Gold. From at least the mid-12th century the queen consort was entitled to 1 gold MARK, i.e. £6, for every 100 silver marks levied as fines in the king's courts. The practice gradually lapsed: hopes of a 17th-century revival led William Prynne to dedicate his monumental history, *Aurum Regine* (1668), to Catherine of Braganza, Charles II's queen.   PMB

Queensland, with Brisbane as its capital, was established in 1824 as a penal settlement and in 1842 opened to free settlers. After the discovery of goldfields in 1858, the colony was separated from NEW SOUTH WALES and given responsible government in 1859. From 1860 the sugar planters imported some 50,000 Polynesians (Kanakas) before this virtual slave-trade was stopped in 1890 and the Kanakas were repatriated. Q. joined the Commonwealth of AUSTRALIA on its creation, 1 Jan. 1901. The upper house (legislative council) was abolished in 1922.   SHS

Queenston Heights, battle of (14 Oct. 1812). Canadian militia and British regulars defeated the American invaders and thereby saved Upper Canada from annexation by the U.S.A.—one of the main, though not admitted, aims of Jefferson's war. SHS

Quia Emptores, Statute. Taking its name from the first words of its preamble ('since purchasers'), the statute, granted in Parliament in 1290, aimed at preserving lords' feudal incidents when their tenants sold lands held of them. While permitting free sale, it forbade subinfeudation, i.e. performance of service to the MESNE tenant. Though successful in its aim, the statute aided the break-up of feudal holdings by increasing the number of men holding direct of the king.   PMB

Quiberon Bay, battle of (20 Nov. 1759). After Boscawen's victory at LAGOS the main French fleet of 21 ships of the line at Brest escaped to sea. Pursued by Hawke's somewhat larger English fleet, they fled to Q.B. Despite the weather and the dangers of reefs and shoals Hawke engaged the enemy and inflicted heavy losses. The 14 surviving French ships escaped as a divided force and the invasion plan collapsed.   IHE

Quiberon Expeditions (1795) were intended to support royalist insurgents in La Vendée and Brittany during the FRENCH REVOLUTIONARY WAR. 3,600 emigrés and released French prisoners, escorted by a British squadron, landed at Q. (27 June) and were joined by a large number of royalists (*Chouans*). Divided leadership, timidity and treachery ensured defeat by Hoche (19 July) who captured some 6,000, including 1,000 emigrés of whom 690 were shot; about 1,800 were re-embarked. In Sept. 5,000 British troops escorted the Comte d'Artois to the island of Yeu, near Q. Ludicrously unplanned and ill-equipped this expedition also proved a fiasco and was withdrawn (Dec.).

                                          MLH

Quit Claim, a general release and disclaimer of all rights, interests and potential legal actions from the grantor to the grantee of property etc., either incorporated in the conveyance or given in a separate document. The q.c. belongs to the age of imprecise legal titles, the counterpart of warranty, which compelled the grantor to guarantee in court a conditional title derived from him.   PMB

Quo minus, see EXCHEQUER OF PLEAS.

Quo Warranto. FRANCHISES perturbed the crown in the 13th century: inquiries about them were made from 1254 onwards, but the real attack began with those of 1274–5. The old writ q.w., to show 'by what WARRANT', was adapted to compel known franchise holders to prove their titles.

From the 1278 eyre onwards many pleas ensued, resented because of the four years delay for the Welsh war and because royal grant, not long user or imprecise grant, was at first the acceptable defence: the statute q.w., 1290, allowed long user, if subsequently confirmed, to be pleaded. Certain resumptions, fines for confirmations and increased technical skill in drafting conveyances resulted from these pleas. In the 17th century the action was used to revoke company or borough charters. (See also HUNDRED ROLLS.)   PMB

Radcote Bridge, battle of (20 Dec. 1387), destroyed Richard II's only hope of organizing military resistance against the Lords APPELLANT. Robert de Vere, earl of Oxford, tried to bring some 4,000 men from Cheshire to the king at London. Finding his direct road blocked, De Vere marched by way of Stow-on-the-Wold and Burford, and was attempting to cross the upper Thames at R.B. when he was suddenly attacked and routed by Henry Bolingbroke, earl of Derby, and Thomas, duke of Gloucester. De Vere himself escaped and eventually fled overseas.   RFW

Radicals, an indefinite term used in the 19th and early 20th centuries of persons in favour of wide social, particularly parliamentary, reform. 'Radical reform', an expression probably first used about 1780, and of which Radical is a shortened form, was demanded by leaders of the opposition to George III's parliamentary control. Besides the FRANCHISE, the R. later advocated reform of the ecclesiastical laws, the CIVIL LIST, the House of Lords, local government, taxation and education. Never an organized party, they became identified with the more extreme section of the LIBERAL PARTY. By 1914 a large number of their aims were realized or in sight and, after the Liberal split of 1916, many of them drifted into the emergent LABOUR PARTY.   MLH

Ragman Rolls, the colloquial name, on account of ragged appearance (caused by the many pendant seals), for the returns to the inquest of 1274–5, otherwise HUNDRED ROLLS. The name is also given to the roll of professions of HOMAGE and FEALTY made by the Scottish clergy and nobility to Edward I at Berwick in Sept. 1297.
                                                                  PMB

Railways developed rapidly in the second quarter of the 19th century, when a demand by commerce and industry for speedier, cheaper transport than CANALS and TURNPIKES could provide coincided with the technical progress necessary for the production of the steam locomotive and wrought-iron rail, and with the availability of large amounts of private capital for exploitation. The first authorized r., starting with the Wandsworth–Croydon line 1805, were for drawing goods by horse waggon and were similar to the colliery r. and canal feeders of the 18th century. The Stockton–Darlington Railway, 1825, was permitted to carry passengers but did not use steam locomotives along its whole length. The first line built for passengers and goods and using only steam locomotives (Stephenson's *Rocket*) was the Liverpool–Manchester, 1830. Its immediate success heralded the beginning of the railway age. The next 20 years saw the building of the main trunk lines; by 31 Dec. 1849, 6,031 miles were open for traffic. Companies were promoted to serve local ends; the r. thus grew up piecemeal and in sometimes inviable competition. The ill-effects were alleviated by amalgamation, tending to be cumulative, which produced such companies as the Midland Railway (1844) and the North Eastern (1854). An Act of 1846 established a uniform gauge (4 ft 8½ in.) for the future.

In 1870 there were some 15,500 miles of line. At this point amalgamation was discouraged by the government which had long feared the dangers of monopoly. Much legislation, such as Gladstone's Act (1844) and Cardwell's Act (1854), was prompted by this motive. Acts of 1888, 1893 and 1894 provided for maximum rates for freight, which proved most unsatisfactory; labour troubles culminated in the national railway strike of 1911. A Railway Commission, first appointed 1873, was in 1888 reconstituted with wider powers of supervision.

By the first world war Britain had a railway network of some 23,000 miles, operated largely by 11 companies. As a result of experience gained in 1914–18 when the r. were operated by the government, the Railways Act, 1921, grouped the companies into 4 territorial units. A wide variety of statutory obligations were consolidated in 1928. However, the 4 companies did not achieve the anticipated 'standard revenues'; economy and efficiency anticipated from the amalgamations did not materialize, whilst statutory restrictions and traditional methods made the r. uncompetitive with road transport. At the beginning of the second world war the r. were again taken over by the government.

The r. were nationalized by the Transport Act, 1947, which set up a Railway Executive to administer 6 railway regions under the British Transport Commission. In the 1950s modernization was financed by government loans. But loss of traffic to road transport continued. The 1960s saw administration reorganization (1963) and elimination of many branch lines: route mileage, 17,481 in 1962, was 13,721 in 1966, and employees were reduced from 441,000 to 336,000.   MLH

Rajasthan, an Indian state formed in 1949 out of the 19 princely states and 3 chiefships of the former Rajputana Agency, and reorganized in 1956 by the addition of AJMER and parts of BOMBAY and MADRAS. The Rajputs were a brave and chivalrous people, and the defeat of their powerful confederacy at Khanua (1527) made possible the foundation of Babur's Mogul empire; Akbar's dominion was mainly based on his success in conciliating the Rajputs. In the 18th century the Rajputana was torn by the rivalries of the leading feudatories (Bikaner, Udaipur, Jaipur, Jodhpur) and ravaged by the MARATHAS, Pathans and Pindaris, so that the princes willingly submitted to British protection and paramountcy (1817–23) and remained quiet during the mutiny.   SHS

Ramillies, battle of (23 May 1706). After BLENHEIM the major campaigns in the SPANISH SUCCESSION WAR took place in the Netherlands. At R. near Namur Marlborough gained another great victory over the French, inflicting heavy losses. Brussels and Antwerp were taken and by the end of the year the French were only left with Mons, Charleroi, Namur and Luxemburg.   IHE

Ransom, King Richard I's. On his way home from the Third Crusade, Richard I was captured near Vienna by Duke Leopold of Austria in Dec. 1192 and subsequently handed over to the Emperor Henry VI, whose chief opponents in Germany were allies of Richard. Philip II of France had already been attacking NORMANDY in Richard's absence, and now attempted to have Richard kept a prisoner. Richard's brother John made preparations to seize the English throne with Philip's assistance. Their plans were thwarted by the loyalty Richard commanded and the prompt action of his mother, Queen Eleanor, and his justiciars in England. In the spring of 1193 the emperor fixed Richard's r. at 150,000 marks: an AID was levied in England, heavy taxes on revenues and goods were imposed, the wool crop of the Cistercian and Gilbertine houses was seized, and the total was swelled by fines laid upon the supporters of John; Richard's continental dominions also made their contribution. Enough of the r. was paid to secure Richard's release on 4 Feb. 1194 and his return to England on 13 March—which was soon followed by a reconciliation with John. The whole of the r. was never paid, part being remitted by the emperor in 1195, and although Richard had been compelled to agree to hold his kingdom henceforth as a fief of the empire, Henry VI released him from his promise in 1197.

RFW

Rape, apparently the primitive unit of local government and taxation in SUSSEX, although it is not mentioned by name in O.E. times (PROVINCIA). It later became an intermediate unit between SHIRE and HUNDRED, although the latter took over most of its functions. In the Norman period each r. became a CASTLERY.

CFS

Ravenspur (1) (4 July 1399). While Richard II was on his second Irish expedition, the exiled Henry Bolingbroke sailed from France and, after touching the coast of Sussex, eventually landed at R. in Holderness, a port which coastal erosion has entirely destroyed. From R. Henry made for Pontefract, joined the northern lords, who had probably been prepared for his arrival, and began the brief campaign which ended with the DEPOSITION of Richard II and the invader's coronation as Henry IV.

(2) (14 March 1471). After being driven from England by the earl of Warwick in Sept. 1470, Edward IV landed at R. with a force of German mercenaries, after eluding the Lancastrian fleet and making an unsuccessful attempt to land in Norfolk. Edward's skilfully conducted march southwards culminated in his entry into London and the capture of Henry VI, whose READEPTION thus came to an end.

RFW

Readeption of Henry VI (Oct. 1470–11 April 1471). Edward IV having been driven overseas on 29 Sept. 1470, Henry VI was released by the earl of Warwick on 3 Oct. and was recrowned as king on the 13th. Henry dated documents during his brief restoration 'in the 49th year of our reign, and the first of our readeption of the royal power'. After Edward IV's landing at RAVENSPUR and his advance to London, Henry VI again became a prisoner on 11 April 1471 and remained in the Tower until he died, presumably murdered, on 21 May.

RFW

L

Rebecca Riots, said to have got their name and inspiration from Genesis xxiv, 60, were clandestine disturbances by bands of tenant-farmers dressed as women, confined mainly to the three south-western counties of WALES during June 1839 and, more specially, 1842–3. Directed chiefly against turnpike gates, they were a symptom of mass-hysteria and brought emotional relief to a peasantry rendered desperate by the strain on an antiquated economy of over-population, inequitable land-tenure, high rents, rates and tithes, and agricultural depression. A class-ridden and corrupt magistracy had to invoke military aid to suppress the riots, which were followed by a government commission of inquiry and a turnpike bill.

David Williams, *The Rebecca Riots* (1955).

GW

Receiver-General, a senior financial officer, collecting revenues through subordinate receivers and preparing accounts. Rs.-G. were once appointed for many departments and sources of revenue, e.g. court of WARDS, inland revenue, but the title is now used only in the Duchy of LANCASTER.

PMB

Recognizance, a deed recognizing a debt made before a court of RECORD, giving the creditor power to levy his debt with the aid of the crown within a stated term, without recourse to a legal action of debt. In mercantile law the r. was called a statute and special arrangements were made to enrol such documents at local registries. See also MAINPRISE.

PMB

Reconstruction, Ministry of. With the hope of avoiding the disruption of industry so disastrous after the NAPOLEONIC WARS, committees of r. were appointed in 1916 and 1917 to plan the re-organization and development of industry and employment: later in 1917 these were superseded by a M. of R., wound up in 1919. A minister of R. was again appointed in Nov. 1944; his post was abolished in May 1945.

PMB

Record, Court of, a court whose evidence in a case is accepted, without

additional proof, by another jurisdiction. The king's own court was the
first such court, and the record was
embodied in its judges' memories,
written matter only slowly being accepted. C.s of r. have since become
more numerous, partly with the granting of such privileges to boroughs etc.,
partly with the proliferation of royal
courts for judicial convenience. PMB

Record Commissions. In 1800
Charles Abbott proposed and led a
Select Committee of inquiry into the
preservation, arrangement etc. of the
public records. To remedy the par-
lous and disorganized state of such
records up and down the country a
series of R.C. was issued 1800–36.
The commissioners achieved no centralization, but some listing was done
and a series of important volumes
printed, somewhat unevenly edited.
In the 1830s the commissioners' financial and printing policy was much
criticized and a pamphlet war raged.
On William IV's death the last commission lapsed, to be replaced in 1838
by the PUBLIC RECORD OFFICE. PMB

Recorder, in origin an officer appointed by cities etc., to keep legal
records of their courts of QUARTER
SESSION who, in course of time, came
to be the city's chief legal officer and
sole judge at quarter sessions. Modern
r.s., appointed by the crown, are required to be barristers of 5 years
standing. PMB

Recovery, Action of Common, a
collusive legal fiction, known in the
13th century and widely used later to
bar entails, remainders, DOWER etc.
A. sought land against B., the tenant,
by writ of ENTRY; B. called upon C.,
the court's Common Vouchee, to warrant the title allegedly derived from
him; C. failed to appear in court;
judgment on C.'s default was given to
A., who thus 'recovered' the land,
without the question of the title or its
encumbrances being raised. PMB

**Rectitudines Singularum Person-
arum,** a treatise on estate management probably composed by a REEVE

in the earlier part of the 11th century.
It gives an account of the rural classes
and the services they owed, and is of
great importance to historians. CFS

Recusants, those refusing to attend
Church of England services. The first
fines for recusancy were imposed
under the Acts of UNIFORMITY of 1552
and 1559 at the rate of 1s. per Sunday
but increased to £20 per month in
1581. An act of 1587 authorized
seizure of two-thirds of a defaulter's
property. Under Elizabeth I fines
were imposed on Protestant and
Catholic r. alike. Catholics especially
were subjected to a mass of PENAL
LAWS but they were only intermittently
enforced. IHE

**Red River Rebellion; Red River
Settlement,** see MANITOBA.

Reeve (Anglo-Saxon *gerefa*, Latin
prepositus), the local representative
and officer of his lord. Medieval r.s
ranged from the SHERIFF to the
humble manorial r., generally a VIL-
LEIN, elected by his fellows to organize
the daily affairs of the MANOR. This
latter office was unpopular, and attempts to escape it were regularly
made. PMB

Reform Acts. (1) In the second half
of the 18th century House of Commons reform was advocated by M.P.s,
including Chatham, John Wilkes and
the younger Pitt, and by political
societies formed for this purpose.
The REVOLUTIONARY and NAPOLEONIC
WARS proved a setback, but the issue
was reiterated in the 1820s under the
leadership of Lord John Russell. In
1830 a Whig administration pledged
to reform was returned under Earl
Grey; after an unprecedented Parliamentary struggle which, in a period of
industrial depression, led to serious
civil disorder, the 'Great Reform Bill'
(introduced 1 March 1831) was passed
on 4 June 1832. The Act disenfran-
chised 56 'ROTTEN' BOROUGHS and deprived 30 others of 1 member each;
of the 143 seats thus released, 65 were
allotted to counties whilst 22 large
boroughs previously unrepresented
received 2 members and 21 boroughs

one member each; 8 seats went to
Scottish and 5 to Irish boroughs. In
the counties the franchise was extended from the 40s. freeholders to
include £10 copyholders and long-
leaseholders, and £50 short-lease-
holders and tenants; in boroughs a
uniform £10 household franchise was
established. The effect of the 1832
Act (and of analogous Acts passed for
Scotland and Ireland) was to give the
vote to the middle classes, increasing
the electorate from about 478,000 to
814,000.

(2) The second Reform Act, 1867,
largely the work of Disraeli, extended
the franchise further to include, in the
counties, leaseholders and copyholders
of property valued at £5 p.a. and occu-
piers of property rated at £12; in the
boroughs, all householders and also
rentpayers of £10 p.a. 45 boroughs
with less than 10,000 inhabitants lost
1 member each; thereby the counties
gained 25, the University of London 1
and the boroughs the remainder
(Liverpool, Manchester, Birmingham
and Leeds now having 3). The Act,
and similar Acts for Scotland and Ireland, increased the electorate from
1,359,000 to 2,456,000, the new voters
coming mainly from the urban working classes.

(3) The agricultural labourers,
many of them illiterate, were not enfranchised until the third Reform Act,
1884, introduced by Gladstone at the
instance of the RADICALS led by Joseph
Chamberlain; the extension of household suffrage to the counties added
over 2½m. to the electoral registers.
A separate Act followed (1885) fundamentally altering the distribution of
seats; except in 23 large boroughs
which kept 2 seats, the country was
divided into single-member constituencies, boroughs of less than
10,000 inhabitants being merged into
the counties.

(4) The Representation of the
People Act, 1918, sometimes referred
to as the fourth Reform Act, conceded
adult male suffrage and realized to a
great extent the aims of the SUFFRA-
GETTE MOVEMENT by giving the vote to
women over 30 who (or whose hus-

bands) were local government electors; about 2m. men and 6m. women
were enfranchised. The electoral map
was revised in an attempt to provide,
with some exceptions, single-member
constituencies of about 70,000 electors.
The 1918 Act also regularized the
university and business votes. Universal adult suffrage was finally
achieved by the Representation of the
People (Equal Franchise) Act, 1928.

The Representation of the People
Act, 1948, abolished the university
and business votes and the last 12
double-member constituencies. A
similarly entitled Act, 1969, lowered
voting age to 18 years.

See also BALLOT ACT.   MLH

Reformation,   Edwardian.   On
Henry VIII's death (1547) the nation
(although theoretically still catholic)
was doctrinally divided but the influx
of continental refugees increased the
spread of Zwinglian and Calvinist
teaching. The Protestants gained
ascendancy in the council, the heresy
laws and 6 ARTICLES were repealed,
and Cranmer issued a Book of Homilies
accompanied by INJUNCTIONS which
conflicted with the King's Book of
1543. The BOOK OF COMMON PRAYER
(1549), although an ineffective compromise, marked a stage in the doctrinal reformation and the second
book of 1552 was definitely Protestant.
Both were accompanied by Acts of
UNIFORMITY and Cranmer's 42 AR-
TICLES followed (1553). The marriage
of clergy was permitted in 1549, the
removal of altars was ordered (1550)
and further spoliation of church property was effected by the CHANTRIES
Act (1547), the confiscation of 'super-
fluous' church plate (1552–3) and the
annexation of lands belonging to the
bishops. The rapidity of these
changes facilitated the MARIAN RE-
ACTION.   IHE

Reformation, Henrician, was political rather than doctrinal in origin,
and effected by government and parliament rather than clergy and people.
The determining factors were the endeavour of the council (under Thomas
Cromwell) to strengthen the power of

the crown at the expense of the church, the anti-clericalism of the R. PARLIA-MENT (1529–36) and the inability of pope Clement VII (who was the virtual prisoner of the emperor Charles V) to annul Henry's marriage with Catherine of Aragon. By 1534 the state's victory over the church was complete. The DISSOLUTION OF THE MONASTERIES (1536–40) and the attack on the CHANTRIES (1545) created vested interests in these changes, while opposition was shown by the PILGRIMAGE OF GRACE. The Church of England position was defined by the 10 ARTICLES (1536) enforced by royal INJUNCTIONS which also author-ized an English BIBLE. The Bishops' Book (1537) was an essentially ortho-dox book of faith and the more radical injunctions of 1538 were fol-lowed by the conservative 6 Articles (1539). After Cromwell's execution (July 1540) the king maintained a policy of moderate conservatism and in 1543 the right of reading the Bible was reserved for the propertied classes and the King's Book provided an orthodox definition of doctrine. Henry also became supreme head of the church of Ireland and the Irish abbeys were dissolved (1536–7).   IHE

Reformation, Scottish. Protestant-ism gained ground in Scotland in the 1540s and was strengthened by a visit from Knox (1555–6) and the advent of MARIAN EXILES. In 1557 nationalism and protestantism combined against the French Catholic regent Mary of Guise when the Protestant Lords of the Congregation signed the COVEN-ANT. In 1558 they petitioned for reform of the church, and the return of the militant Calvinist John Knox (1559) led to the outlawry of the preachers, the destruction of church and monastic property by mob vio-lence, and open hostilities with the French. In 1560 the Estates adopted a Calvinistic confession of faith and abolished papal jurisdiction. English help was gained by the treaty of BERWICK and the French left Scotland in accordance with the treaty of EDIN-BURGH (1560). The arrival of the

Catholic Queen Mary (1561) made the r. precarious but her disastrous mar-riages led to her overthrow in 1567. Although a General Assembly of the Reformed Church had met since 1561, a nominal episcopate was re-stored in 1572 but superseded by a full PRESBYTERIAN system in 1592. Most of the ecclesiastical estates were appropriated by laymen but in 1561 revenues were set aside for the minis-ters of the reformed church. Existing clergy retained their incomes.   IHE

Reformation, Tenth-century, a term applied, in its strictest sense, to the monastic revival in England; but as this revival affected the whole church the term is frequently taken in a looser and wider sense. In addition to the revival of monastic life and the founding of new monasteries (MONAS-TICISM) it resulted in great advances in learning and in the development of vernacular literature. Further, every bishopric at some time between 975 and 1066 had a professed monk as its bishop. The parish clergy, however, do not seem to have been influenced to any great extent.   CFS

Reformation Parliament (Nov. 1529–Apr. 1536), effected an eccle-siastical revolution substituting the royal supremacy for papal power in England. Its legislation was largely the work of Henry VIII's minister, Thomas Cromwell. In 1529 it passed acts attacking abuses of MORTUARY and probate fees, SANCTUARY, pluralities and NON-RESIDENCE of clergy and in 1531 ratified the king's pardon to the clergy for their illegal recognition of Wolsey's legatine authority (PRAE-MUNIRE). In 1532 it presented the SUPPLICATION AGAINST THE ORDI-NARIES and passed the first Act of ANNATES. This was followed by the Act in RESTRAINT OF APPEALS (1533) and in 1534 by a second Act of Annates, acts prohibiting licences and dispensations from Rome and pay-ment of moneys to the papacy, a Heresy Act, Treasons Act, an Act for the Submission of the Clergy, SUC-CESSION ACTS and the Act of SU-PREMACY. In 1536 it authorized the

DISSOLUTION OF THE smaller MONAS-
TERIES and incorporated WALES with
England. IHE

Regency Act. In modern times
provision for the youth or incapacity
of the sovereign has been made by
statute. Precautionary R.A.s to deal
with particular situations were passed
in 1751 (death of Frederick Prince of
Wales), 1765 (possible recurrence of
George III's first illness), 1830
(accession of William IV), 1840
(marriage of Victoria) and 1910
(accession of George V). In 1788–9
George III recovered before a R.A.
could be passed; on his final illness
the R.A. (1811) appointed the Prince
of Wales regent subject to specified
limitations. The R.A. (1937), slightly
amended in 1953, is designed as a
permanent measure to deal systematically with several possibilities. MLH

Registrar-General. Before 1836 the
clergy of all denominations kept
registers of baptisms, marriages and
deaths, but reforms of the period required more exact information, and a
General Register Office under the
R.-G., with local offices throughout
the country, was established. Apart
from such regular duties, the R.-G.
is responsible for organizing and
assimilating CENSUS returns. Plans
have been announced for the merger
of the General Register Office and the
Government Social Survey in a single
Office of Population, Censuses and
Surveys. PMB; MR

Regium Donum (1), the annual
grant paid towards the upkeep of
Presbyterian ministers in Ulster.
From 1670 Charles II made a crown
grant of £600 per annum for this
purpose which was discontinued by
James II but restored by William III
in 1691 at £1,200. Again withdrawn
in 1710, it was renewed in 1718 at
£2,000. Substantially increased after
1802, it was abolished in 1871 when
£770,000 was given to the Presbyterian church from the revenues of
the Church of Ireland after its
disestablishment and partial disen-
dowment in 1869.

(2), an English R.D. of £1,000 per
annum to the widows of dissenting
ministers was introduced as a con-
ciliatory measure by Walpole in 1723
and later extended to Presbyterian,
Baptist and Congregationalist ministers. This grant was abolished in 1851
largely as a result of nonconformist
agitation against it. IHE

Regnal Year. Before Henry II the
method of computation is uncertain,
though the practice was introduced
from the continent in the 8th century.
Henry II, Richard I, John and Henry
III dated their reigns from the day of
their coronation, despite John's coronation on Ascension day, a movable
feast. Edward I was abroad when his
father died and did not return to
England for 2 years: his reign dated
from 4 days after Henry III's death.
Thereafter r.y.s dated from the day
of the predecessor's death. The Exchequer r.y. ran from Michaelmas
day (29 Sept.) to Michaelmas. The
first exchequer r.y. of a reign ended at
the first Michaelmas day after the
king's accession. The numbering of
Acts of Parliament by r.y. was abolished in 1962. See also CALENDAR;
EASTER; EASTER TABLES. PMB

Regnenses or Regni, a group of
British tribes in the area of Sussex
and S. Surrey that was part of, or
normally controlled by, the kingdom
of the ATREBATES. They had, however, a king of their own immediately
before the ROMAN CONQUEST, but
were under heavy pressure from the
CATUVELLAUNI. The speedy submission of their king to the Romans
gained him Roman citizenship and the
style *Rex et Legatus Augusti in
Britannia*. Although the style died
with him it was perpetuated in the
name Regnum (Lat. kingdom) of the
territory he had controlled. They
became a CIVITAS with their capital at
Noviomagus (Chichester). CFS

Regularis Concordia, drawn up at a
synod at Winchester between 965 and
975 in an attempt to bring uniformity
into monastic practice in England.
It is essentially an elaboration of the

Benedictine rule as extended by St Benedict of Aniane in the early 9th century, but it borrowed points of practice from various continental houses and laid unusual stress on prayers for the royal family. It remained the basic rule of English MONASTICISM until the NORMAN CONQUEST. CFS

Regulating Act (1773), the first CHARTER ACT, introduced by Lord North, aimed at giving the crown direct control over the EAST INDIA COMPANY which had become financially and administratively incapable of discharging its responsibilities. The R.A. vested the administration of BENGAL in a governor-general and council appointed by the crown, and gave them control of the other presidencies. The obstruction of the governor-general by the council led to the passing of the first INDIA ACT (1784). SHS

Relief, a feudal incident, the sum paid by the heir to his lord to succeed to his predecessor's land: the development of r. owed something to the acceptance of primogeniture in feudal tenures, something to the Anglo-Saxon HERIOT. In the 12th century the idea of a reasonable r. arose, e.g. 100s. for a knight's fee, perhaps copied from the VAVASSOR's r. with suitable figures for larger or smaller units. Lords, however, determined r.s and kings, notably John, demanded large sums from greater tenants. After MAGNA CARTA had laid down a tariff, r.s ceased to be a political issue, though they were collected, energetically by the Tudors, until the abolition of feudal tenures in 1661. PMB

Remembrancer. By the late 13th century two Exchequer clerks were called R., one the Lord Treasurer's, the other the King's. At first each seems to have duplicated the other's work, but by the COWICK Ordinances 1323 the Lord Treasurer's R. was made responsible for collecting fixed revenues and debts established by the King's R., thus becoming closely associated with the Pipe Office. The R. declined in importance with the crown's ancient revenues: the office was abolished in 1833 and the remaining duties re-assigned.

By the Cowick Ordinances the King's R. was particularly assigned to casual crown revenues and documents, e.g. inquisitions relating thereto, preliminary audit and proceedings against defaulters. To these duties were added, in Elizabeth I's reign, that of registrar of the EXCHEQUER OF PLEAS equity court, and in 1833 the AUGMENTATIONS OFFICE and some of the Lord Treasurer's R.'s duties. The office was transferred to the Supreme Court in 1877: it is now discharged by the senior Master of the Queen's Bench division, who registers revenue cases. PMB

Remonstrance of the Army (18 Nov. 1648) was adopted by the council of officers and presented to Parliament demanding, among other matters, that Charles I be brought to trial. IHE

Remonstrants. Defeat at DUNBAR (1650) increased dissensions among the Scots. The stricter Covenanters, attributing the disaster to ungodliness in high places, presented a remonstrance to the Committee of Estates (30 Oct.), refusing to acknowledge Charles II until he had proven the sincerity of his devotion to the COVENANT. This was condemned by a resolution of the Estates. The supporters of the remonstrance were known as Remonstrants or Protesters. Their opponents were called RESOLUTIONERS. IHE

Rental, a common type of document, the modern rent-roll, in early periods often scarcely distinguishable from a survey. R.s provide information about distribution of estates, tenants, current land values etc., as well as some genealogical matter. PMB

Replevin, see DISTRESS.

Requests, Court of, more correctly Court of Poor Men's Causes, an EQUITY court, primarily for civil cases, formed from the king's council to give formal hearing to complaints to the sovereign and confirmed by statute 1487. The court settled at Westminster c. 1516, though even thereafter one of its masters often travelled with the sovereign. It became a popular institution dispensing cheap and speedy justice. Between 1536 and 1540 its members ceased to be privy councillors and from the end of the century its jurisdiction was challenged by the common-law courts. It ceased to sit at the outbreak of the CIVIL WAR (1642) but was not abolished by statute.

The City of London Court of Conscience, the EAST INDIA COMPANY's Courts of R. and the Councils of Wales and the North had similar jurisdictions, and the archbishops' and bishops' Courts of Audience performed like functions in ecclesiastical cases.   PMB; IHE

Resolutioners were those Scottish Presbyterians led by Argyll, who, after DUNBAR, wished to unite with the Scottish royalists against Cromwell. They effected this alliance and supported the relaxation of the Act of CLASSES opposed by the REMONSTRANTS.   IHE

Restoration (1660) was made possible when Monck secured the final dissolution of the LONG PARLIAMENT and its consent to the election of a CONVENTION PARLIAMENT. It met in April, accepted the Declaration of BREDA and recalled Charles II (May). It began the R. settlement by passing an Act of INDEMNITY AND OBLIVION, providing for the king's revenue, and effecting a land settlement which however failed to meet the claims of those royalists who had sold their properties to meet the demands of the decimation tax. The religious settlement was left to the CAVALIER PARLIAMENT which restored the Anglican Church and enacted the CLARENDON CODE against those who rejected the Book of Common Prayer of 1662. The MILITIA was reconstituted (1661–3) but Parliament would not make provision for a standing army. DIVINE

RIGHT reappeared shorn of its absolutist powers and the PREROGATIVE remained limited by the enactments of the Long Parliament passed between 1640 and 1642. Arbitrary taxation and the prerogative courts were not revived and the triumph of EPISCOPACY involved the downfall of PRESBYTERIANISM. Henceforward the propertied classes exercised increasing power through Parliament and their control of local administration.   IHE

Restraint of Appeals, Act in (Mar. 1533), prevented appeals to Rome in testamentary and matrimonial cases, thus making possible Henry VIII's divorce. The preamble asserted the supremacy of the royal jurisdiction in spiritual and temporal affairs and effectively destroyed papal authority in England. Archbishop Cranmer opened court at Dunstable and pronounced Catharine's marriage void (23 May) and Anne's (contracted secretly in Jan.) valid.   IHE

Rhode Island grew from a combination of settlements formed by religious and political exiles from MASSACHUSETTS. Roger Williams and his followers established themselves at Providence (1636), Anne Hutchinson and her adherents settled at Portsmouth, renamed R.I. (1638), Samuel Gorton at Shawomet (Warwick) in 1638, and William Coddington founded Newport (1639). Williams obtained a charter from the Parliamentary commissioners for plantations (1644) and the 4 settlements (combined as Providence Plantation in 1647. R.I. was not allowed to join the NEW ENGLAND Confederation (1643) but obtained a royal charter in 1663 which was revoked in 1686. It became part of the Dominion of New England (1687) but regained its charter in 1691. Until the AMERICAN REVOLUTION it was a centre for illicit trade (especially in rum) as witness the GASPEE AFFAIR (1772).   IHE

Rhodesia. After the break-up of the R. AND NYASALAND FEDERATION, NORTHERN R. became the Republic of ZAMBIA in 1964 and SOUTHERN R.

came to be known as R. as a self-governing colony. Disagreement with Great Britain over the implementation of majority rule led to Prime Minister I. D. Smith's unilateral declaration of R.'s independence on 11 Nov. 1965. Britain imposed economic sanctions which were backed by the United Nations in 1966. (Portugal and South Africa did not observe the trade embargo.) Abortive talks were held between British Prime Minister Wilson and Mr Smith in 1966 and 1968 and a new constitution based on racial segregation and white supremacy was approved by the electorate or R. in June 1969. On 2 Mar. 1970 the break with the British crown and COMMONWEALTH was completed by Mr Smith's declaration of a republic.

IHE

Rhodesia and Nyasaland, Federation of. Association of Southern and Northern Rhodesia was mooted from about 1910. A definite proposal of amalgamation made by the British South Africa Company in 1915 was rejected by Southern Rhodesia. Various suggestions about amalgamation, federation and co-operation led to the establishment in 1945 of a consultative Central African Council which extended and created a number of common services for the Rhodesias and Nyasaland. After a conference of delegates at Victoria Falls in 1949 had unanimously decided in favour of federation on the Australian model, details were worked out in a series of conferences (1951–3) and approved by referendum in SOUTHERN RHODESIA and by the legislatures of NORTHERN RHODESIA, NYASALAND and the United Kingdom. The F. was proclaimed on 1 Aug. and came into being on 3 Sept. 1953. Its constitution maintains the status of the 3 territories, above all the retention of responsibility by the British Parliament for the protectorates. Until 1962 the majority of the white electorate adhered to the programme of 'partnership', proclaimed by Sir Godfrey Huggins (later Lord Malvern) in 1948 against the South African policy of APART-HEID. The majority of the Africans, politically represented by the African National Congress (founded 1944), opposed federation from the beginning. By 1963 white and black racialism led to the dissolution of the federation on 13 Dec. 1963. SHS

Rhuddlan, Statute of, was proclaimed on 3 March 1284 to provide for the government of the PRINCIPALITY. GWYNEDD west of the Conway was divided into the shires of Anglesey, Caernarvon and Merioneth, though existing CANTREFS and COMMOTES and their officials were retained. The existing counties of Cardigan and Carmarthen were enlarged and made into SHIRES, and SHERIFFS and CORONERS were introduced. A chancery and exchequer, under the justice and chamberlain of North Wales respectively, were established at Caernarvon, with similar arrangements for West Wales at Carmarthen. The new shire of Flint was placed under Chester. English criminal law and methods of apprehension were enforced, and a great sessions, COUNTY COURT and SHERIFF'S TOURN established. Only minor modifications were otherwise made to Welsh customary law. The statute remained in force until 1536. GW

Riding (from the Old Norse word for a third part that became anglicized as *thrithing*), a division found in the former kingdom of LINDSEY (N., W. and S. Ridings) and in Yorkshire (E., W. and N. Ridings). They were units of local government established by the DANES who settled those areas in the later 9th century. CFS

Ridolfi Plot (1571) was organized by Roberto R., a Florentine banker, aided by the bishop of Ross. Pius V, Philip II, Mary Queen of Scots and the duke of Norfolk were involved. There was to be a Catholic rising helped by Alva's troops from the Netherlands. Mary was to supplant Elizabeth I and marry Norfolk. This impractical scheme was discovered in September while R. was abroad.

Norfolk was executed (1572) and Mary was gravely discredited.　IHE

Right, Writ of, emerged in the mid-12th century. Sent either to the SHERIFF or, if both parties held of the same lord, to their lord, it ordered the recipient to give the plaintiff the land he claimed or to hear the case. When the parties joined issue, the defendant could chose whether the case was decided by TRIAL BY BATTLE or by the grand assize. Battle could be waged in any court, but the grand assize could only be taken in the king's court. To make the assize 4 knights were summoned to elect 12 to form the JURY; the jury was asked: whether A or B has greater right in the land etc.; their verdict was final, as was the result of judicial combat. The writ was valuable in establishing rightful tenants but it was slow: ESSOINS were allowed and, in a seigneurial court, a case could take 7 years to decide. In time it was replaced by the POSSESSORY ASSIZES.　PMB

Rinyo-Clacton Culture, see NEOLITHIC AGE.

Riot Act (1715) was promoted by the Whigs disturbed by the unpopularity of the Hanoverian king and Jacobite riotings. It was made a felony if an assembly of 12 or more persons refused to disperse when ordered by the lawful authority (subsequently held to include soldiers as well as magistrates). It removed local riots from the operation of the treason law (DAMMAREE).　IHE

Ripon, treaty of (26 Oct. 1640), concluded the second BISHOPS' WAR. The Scots were to receive £850 per day and remain in occupation of Northumberland and Durham pending a final agreement. Charles I was forced to summon the LONG PARLIAMENT which concluded the peace (10 Aug. 1641).　IHE

Robin Hood Legend. Five narrative poems of the adventures of R.H. survive in mid-15th-century MSS, while the stories in the *Lytell Geste of Robyn Hode*, printed before 1500, may derive from a late-14th-century MS. The background of the tales is that of late-14th-century and 15th-century England; the king, when he appears, being called either Edward or Henry. Rhymes of R.H. are mentioned in the 1377 version of *Piers Plowman*, and the outlaw had become a household word by the early 15th century, partly no doubt because of the popular appeal of the stories in an age of peasant discontent. The earliest stories, set in Sherwood Forest and in Barnsdale in southern Yorkshire, include Little John, Will Scarlet, Much the miller's son, and their enemy, the sheriff of Nottingham. Maid Marian and Friar Tuck seem to have been added later—although a certain outlaw was known by the *alias* of Friar Tuck in the reign of Henry V. Fifteenth-century historians thought that Robin had lived in the late 13th century, the time of the DISINHERITED. Later writers pushed his date back to the reign of Richard I or forward to that of Edward II. Various outlaws, named Robert or R.H., active in the northern forests in the 13th or early 14th century, have been identified as the original hero. One of them may well have supplied the name, but the adventures are probably drawn from the careers of several historical outlaws as well as from a common stock of legend, and have been added to ever since.　RFW

Rochdale Pioneers, the 'founders' of the COOPERATIVE MOVEMENT, on 21 Dec. 1844 opened their shop in Toad Lane, Rochdale, Lancs., £28 being found by 28 subscribers. By no means the first cooperative store, Rochdale's claim to priority lies in its success; this was primarily due to rules (soon to be copied widely) combining fixed interest on capital with 'dividends' on purchases.　MLH

Rochester, sieges of (1) (1088). The rebellion of Odo of Bayeux, restored as Earl of Kent in 1087, was the most serious of many outbreaks against William II. After being captured by the king Odo undertook to arrange the surrender of R. castle, but instead joined the garrison. William II finally forced R. to surrender, and Odo was exiled.

(2) (1215). King John's siege of R. was the first major operation of the BARONS' WARS. The barons had obtained possession of R. on 30 Sept., but their garrison had to surrender after a seven weeks' siege on 30 Nov. Thereafter John met with little resistance until the barons received aid from France in May 1216.

(3) (1264). After the MONTFORTIANS' defeat at NORTHAMPTON, Simon de Montfort from London and Gilbert, earl of Gloucester, from Tonbridge converged on the royalist garrison at R. They captured the city and the outer works of the castle on 18 April, but were then compelled to withdraw to London by the approach of the main royal army under Henry III and his son, Edward.   RFW

Rolls, Master of the. A keeper of the rolls of CHANCERY appears first in Henry III's reign: thereafter he gradually ceased to be an administrator, becoming instead the CHANCELLOR's chief legal assistant and senior chancery master. From the late 15th century the title M. of the R. was used and by the mid-16th century he ranked second among all judges. In the 19th century law reforms he became the chief judge of the chancery division. Throughout the Master has retained, though delegated, his custody of the chancery records. In 1838 all public records were put in his charge but in 1958 his powers were once more restricted to the chancery records.   PMB

Rolls Series, properly *Chronicles and Memorials of Great Britain and Ireland during the Middle Ages,* published between 1858 and 1899 under the direction of the Master of the ROLLS. 99 works were issued, ranging from Anglo-Saxon times to Henry VII's reign; the standard of editing varied, but each text is of importance in its respective period.   PMB

Roman Britain, a term covering in time the period from mid-1st century A.D. to the early 5th, and in territory Wales and England to the northern limits established by the ROMAN CONQUEST. Britain was an imperial PROVINCIA, ruled by a governor (*propraetor*) and a financial official (*procurator*), and normally defended by three legions, auxiliary troops and a fleet. The upland areas of Wales and northern England were under military government; elsewhere there was much local self-government (CIVITAS, COLONIA, MUNICIPIUM). Coinage and taxation were as in other parts of the empire; export trade was mainly in raw materials, import in luxuries. The adoption of Roman ideas, techniques etc. was encouraged from the earliest days. These had comparatively little effect in northern and western areas, but in the south and east an equal standard of life was not regained until modern times. Town life was fostered, but eventually the cost of public buildings proved overmuch for a comparatively poor province, and towns in general declined from the 3rd century. The majority of the population was rural, living in villages or VILLAS or on imperial estates. There were many religious cults (HEATHENISM) but with the introduction of Christianity the BRITISH CHURCH came into being. Communications were provided by a system of ROMAN ROADS. From the end of the 2nd century the province was on the defensive against external attack, although the lowland area continued to enjoy long periods of peace until the 5th century. Britain was affected by the decline of the empire as a whole, and other parts were affected by events in Britain. In 195 Albinus, governor of Britain, was proclaimed emperor and took all available troops to Gaul. This left HADRIAN'S WALL and the north open to barbarian attack, and they suffered badly. The northern defences were restored by order of the emperor Septimius Severus (193–211) who himself led major punitive expeditions (208–11) into CALEDONIA before dying at York.

The northern frontier was thereafter quiet for a century. In 286 Carausius set himself up as emperor of Britain. His successor, in an unsuccessful attempt to maintain his position, took troops from the northern defences, which were again badly damaged by barbarian attack. They were restored by the Caesar Constantius Chlorus (292–305) who also campaigned successfully in Caledonia and organized the defences of the SAXON SHORE. The general reforms of the emperor Diocletian (284–305) made Britain a diocese divided into 4 provinces, and military responsibility was divided between the Duke of the Britains (*Dux Britanniarum*) and the Count of the Saxon shore (*Comes Litoris Saxonici*): the former was in charge of defences in the north and west, the latter was responsible for southern defences against pirates. In 368 there was a major attack by PICTS, SCOTS, SAXONS and Franks which resulted in severe damage to the Wall and in widespread devastation throughout the province. The situation was temporarily restored by an army sent under Theodosius, but in 383 and 407 troops were again removed to Gaul. The first occasion resulted in the final loss of Hadrian's wall to the barbarians; the second led, in 410, to a request to Rome by the Civitates for military aid. But the emperor, himself threatened by barbarian attacks, instructed them to look to their own defence. Any small reinforcements and officials subsequently sent ceased to operate c. 428, and Britain entered on what is known as the SUB-ROMAN PERIOD.

CFS

Roman Conquest. Attacks on Britain were made by Julius Caesar in 55 and 54 B.C. due to assistance given to the Gallic by the British BELGAE and possibly because he aimed at conquest. On each occasion he landed on the open Kent coast and his exposed fleet suffered damage. On the second occasion he captured Wheathampstead (nr St Albans) after heavy fighting, but trouble outside Britain forced his withdrawal. During the next hundred years traders from the empire visited Britain, and its known wealth, the rising anti-Roman feelings of the Belgae, prestige and available troops resulted in invasion in A.D. 43. The defeat of Caratacus at the battle of the MEDWAY allowed the triumphant entry of the emperor Claudius into Colchester, capital of the CATUVELLAUNI; and self-interest, fear of the Catuvellauni or conquest secured the submission of many tribes. The Romans advanced fanwise in three columns from London, building ROMAN ROADS and establishing police posts; and by 47 controlled Britain behind the line of the FOSS WAY. A revolt by the ICENI was put down, but an advance into north Wales c. 48 was halted when troops had to intervene against the anti-Roman party among the BRIGANTES. In 51 the ORDOVICES and SILURES under Caratacus were heavily defeated. Caratacus, the leading figure in the British resistance, was captured soon after; but the Brigantes, Ordovices and Silures attacked Roman posts and tribes that had submitted. In 61 the Romans occupied the territory of the DEGEANGLI and stormed Anglesey, a centre of DRUIDISM. In that year the Iceni and others revolted under queen Boudicca, destroying London, Colchester, St Albans and the IX legion. Roman power was almost overthrown, but the revolt was crushed by the governor, Suetonius Paulinus. Vengeance and reorganization lasted until 71 when the second stage of the conquest began. Between 71 and 79 the Brigantes, Ordovices and Silures were conquered, and in 80 Roman forces under Agricola reached the Clyde–Forth line. Further penetration north-east led to a Roman victory at Mons GRAUPIUS, but the withdrawal of a legion from Britain prevented further advance. Roman forts in the Lowlands of Scotland were held for some years, but attacks by northern tribes led in 122 to the establishment of the frontier on the line of HADRIAN'S WALL. In 140–2 the frontier was extended to the ANTONINE WALL, enclosing the Lowlands. Unrest and attacks by the northern tribes in the 150s, 160s and 170s culminated in major destruction on the Antonine wall in the early 180s. It was rebuilt but evacuated soon after and the frontier was taken back to Hadrian's wall. There were no further attempts at conquest and Roman forces were thereafter concerned only with the defence of ROMAN BRITAIN.   CFS

Roman Mission. Pope Gregory I (590–604) planned, for religious and political reasons, the CONVERSION OF ENGLAND to Christianity. Unable to go himself, he sent a number of missionary monks under Augustine who landed at Thanet in 597. The first mission was reinforced with a second in 601 and members of these missions succeeded as archbishops of Canterbury until 652. It was in connexion with his plans to convert England that pope Gregory is reputed to have made his famous puns, when he saw certain Anglian youths in Rome: *non Angli sed Angeli* (not ANGLES but Angels); they come from DEIRA and must be rescued *de ira Dei* (from God's wrath); Ælle is their King and Alleluiahs will be sung in his land.   CFS

Roman Roads were first built under legionary control during the ROMAN CONQUEST. Radiating from London these ran S.E., S.W., N.W. and N. (WATLING STREET, PORT WAY, ERMINE STREET) with the FOSS WAY forming a lateral connexion. Eventually over 6,500 miles were built. Construction varied with local materials, but common characteristics were a width of *c.* 20 feet, a high camber, drainage ditches on both sides, kerb stones, and construction in straight lengths between intermediate points. The majority were surfaced with gravel etc.; a few, where stone was available, with stone slabs. Rivers were crossed by bridges or paved fords. In some cases the line of existing tracks (i.e. ICKNIELD WAY) was chosen, and many stretches of R.r. have continued in use to the present day. The standard of construction was not again attained until the 19th century. These roads connected the main military and civil centres; smaller settlements were connected by lighter roads or trackways.

I. D. Margary, *Roman Roads in Britain* (2 vols, 1957–9).   CFS

Rome, appeals to, see PRAEMUNIRE.

Rome, Saxon School at. A *schola* was a unit in the later Roman militia. The name was applied in the early middle ages to groups of foreigners resident in Rome who were militarily organized for the defence of the city; later the term was applied to the premises in which they lived. The S.S. consisted of Englishmen either permanently or temporarily resident in Rome. The area they occupied, described as the *vicus Saxonum*, lay between Nero's circus and the Tiber; and traces of their occupation survive in the street name of the Borgo (A.-S. BURH), and in the church name of Santo Spirito in Sassia (formerly Saxia). The Anglo-Saxon chronicle records that king Burgred of Mercia was buried in St Mary's church in the S.S. (874), and that pope Marinus (882–4) freed the S.S. from taxation at the request of king Alfred. The S.S. came to an end in 1204.   CFS

Root and Branch Petition (1641) was signed by some 15,000 Londoners asking for the abolition of EPISCOPACY and debated in the Commons (Feb.). A Root and Branch bill was introduced (27 May) to abolish bishops, deans and chapters and to give ecclesiastical jurisdiction to joint commissions of clergy and laity in every shire controlled by two central commissions. It did not get beyond a second reading and convinced episcopalians of the need to support the monarchy against the GRAND REMONSTRANCE.   IHE

Rose noble, see ROYAL.

Roses, Wars of the (1455–85), the civil wars in England which brought about the replacement of the house of Lancaster by the house of York, and eventually the replacement of the latter by the house of Tudor. The name, derived from the supposed use of roses as badges by the partisans of the rival houses, seems to have been a produot of tho romantio movomont, but its adoption was probably prepared by the Temple-garden scene in Shakespeare's *King Henry VI*, Pt. I, II, iv. While the white rose was a widely used badge of the YORKISTS, the LANCASTRIANS used other badges long associated with their house, such as the swan. The association of the red rose with Lancaster was fostered by the adoption of a red and white rose as a badge by the TUDORS, who represented both houses.

Henry VI (1422–61, 1470–1) was the grandson of the usurper Henry IV, who in 1399 had contrived the DEPOSITION of Richard II, and the great-grandson of John of Gaunt, duke of Lancaster, third son of Edward III. Richard II, only surviving son of the Black Prince, eldest son of Edward III, was himself childless. The best hereditary claim to succeed Richard II had been that of Edmund Mortimer, earl of March, great-grandson of Lionel, duke of Clarence, second son of Edward III. Edmund's claim descended through his sister Anne to her son, Richard, duke of York, who on his father's side moreover was the grandson of Edmund, duke of York, fifth son of Edward III. After the death in 1447 of Henry VI's last surviving uncle, Humphrey, duke of Gloucester, Richard was Henry's heir presumptive. After the birth of a son, Edward, to Henry VI in 1453, however, Richard's claim to be the true heir of Edward III and Richard II, excellent as it was, would not have been pressed but for the incapacity of Henry VI as a ruler and the failures of the Lancastrian government.

Succeeding Henry V in 1422, Henry VI was declared of age—at fifteen—in 1437. While the pious and gentle Henry would have made a good monk, he was not capable of ruling 15th-century England, and government was exercised in practice by those nobles who could gain Henry's confidence and hold the principal offices of state. In the 1440s the influence of Humphrey, duke of Gloucester, the former regent, rapidly declined, and the dominant position

wao hold by tho king'o kinomen, tho BEAUFORTS, by William de la Pole, duke of Suffolk, chief architect of Henry's marriage to Margaret of Anjou in 1445, and by Margaret herself, who gathered about her a group of nobles who were to form the hard core of the Lancastrian faction. The position of the dominant party was imperilled, however, by their conspicuous failures at home and abroad and by Henry VI's lapse into insanity, inherited from his Valois mother. The obvious choice as regent or 'protector' during Henry's insanity was Richard of York, long excluded from a part in government by the Beauforts and further alienated from them by their incompetence in the closing phases of the HUNDRED YEARS' WAR.

Suffolk's failure to conclude an honourable peace with France, the cession of MAINE and the loss of NORMANDY led to his impeachment, exile and murder in 1450. The Beauforts shared his unpopularity and added to their own by the inadequacy of their measures to hold Normandy, finally lost in 1450, or the remnants of AQUITAINE, finally lost in 1453. At the same time they were manifestly failing to suppress local disorder in England itself: both in 1450 and in 1453 the opinion was expressed in Parliament that securing domestic peace—not saving Lancastrian France—demanded the government's most urgent attention. In 1456 popular discontent boiled over in the rebellion of Jack Cade, and prominent among the rebels' complaints were the government's failure to maintain good order, to repress the corruption and oppression of its local officers, and to dispense impartial justice. The rebels also proposed to remedy a fundamental weakness of the Lancastrian dynasty, its failure to secure adequate revenues from its own demesnes, from regular sources and from Parliamentary taxation or to maintain the necessary credit to obtain loans. To the rebels, and many others, a preliminary condition for reform was the removal of the king's evil counsellors: Richard of York appeared as a possible leader of a new council—but not yet as an alternative sovereign. The civil war did not spring directly from popular protest against misgovernment nor from the many local conflicts between lords and their retainers struggling to control local government and administration of justice in their own interests. The crucial contest was at the centre and for the control of the central government. Here the queen, the Beauforts and their adherents were confronted from 1450 onwards by York, supported by a small group of nobles, most of them members or connexions of his mother's family, the prolific Nevilles, and led by the earls of Salisbury and Warwick. The growth of the Yorkist party was, however, slow. In Parliament, York as yet enjoyed rather more support among the commons than among the lords. Family feuds and local struggles—like that of the Nevilles and the Percies in the north—deeply influenced the alignment of lords and gentry, and self-interest often dictated a change of sides. The system of indentured retainers, one of the causes of 15th-century disorder in general, provided much of the military resources of both sides in a conflict in which ordinary folk, townsmen and countrymen alike, took little active part save when compelled.

York's appearances with an armed following in 1450 and in 1452 caused considerable alarm but no change of ministers, despite Henry VI's promises. Tension and disorder mounted, until in August 1453 Henry became insane and York, despite the queen's opposition, became protector and gained temporary control. York was still a reformer—though the short duration of his protectorate gave him little opportunity to prove himself—not a claimant to the throne: he recognized Edward, Henry's son born in Oct. 1453, as the heir apparent. Henry's recovery late in 1454 was soon followed by a restoration of York's opponents to office and military preparations by both parties,

though it was only with reluctance that there was a resort to war. Still protesting their loyalty to the king, York and the Nevilles defeated the royal army at ST ALBANS, capturing the king and killing Edmund, duke of Somerset, the head of the house of Beaufort. Yorkists once again filled the principal offices, York himself became protector a second time, 1455–6 (though Henry did not relapse into madness as was once believed) and, most important for the future, Warwick was appointed captain of CALAIS, where the Yorkist sympathies of the merchants secured his control of the large but restive garrison.

The influence of Queen Margaret again led to the dismissal of Yorkist ministers, but for three years, 1456–9, there was an uneasy peace. A formal reconciliation in 1458 did not prevent the leaders of both sides from mustering support until in 1459 they again resorted to open war. Warwick from Calais and Salisbury from the north—thanks to his victory at BLORE HEATH —were able to join York at Ludlow, but in the ensuing rout of LUDFORD the Yorkist army dispersed and its leaders were forced to seek safety overseas, Warwick in Calais and York in Ireland. The severity with which the Lancastrians dealt with local disorders increased Yorkist support, which had proved none too strong in 1459. The main Lancastrian effort, based on SANDWICH, was now made against Calais, but Warwick had far the better of a series of raids and counter-raids across the Straits. The military measures taken by the Lancastrians increased their unpopularity, and when Warwick again landed in England in June 1460, he met comparatively weak opposition. After entering London, Warwick brought the main Lancastrian army to battle at NORTHAMPTON. The Yorkist victory again removed a number of Lancastrian leaders, notably the heads of the Stafford and Talbot families, and gave the Yorkists possession of the king's person; after a siege the Tower of London was taken. On the high tide of victory Richard of York returned from Ireland to claim not the protectorship but the crown. However, his supporters were not yet prepared to dethrone Henry VI, and the duke had to accept (Oct. 1460) a compromise which designated him as Henry's successor and gave him the principality of Wales. But the Lancastrians still commanded powerful support, particularly in the north, and the duke's Yorkshire campaign ended in his defeat and death near WAKEFIELD. After securing promises of help from Scotland—at the price of the cession of BERWICK—Queen Margaret advanced on London, defeated Warwick at the second battle of ST ALBANS and rescued Henry VI (1461). A western Lancastrian army had, however, already been destroyed at MORTIMER'S CROSS by Richard of York's son Edward, earl of March. Warwick joined Edward with the remnants of his forces, and together they secured London, which had been fearfully negotiating terms of surrender to the queen. Edward was acclaimed by the people and formally installed at Westminster as King Edward IV after the DEPOSITION of Henry VI. Coronation followed after Edward had decisively defeated Margaret and the northern Lancastrians at TOWTON. For another three years, with French and Scottish aid, Margaret desperately attempted to secure a foothold in the north, taking, losing and regaining a group of castles, of which BAMBURGH served as her headquarters, only finally to lose them after the last Lancastrian field forces had been scattered in 1464 by the successive defeats of HEDGELEY MOOR and HEXHAM. Meanwhile the Lancastrian strongholds in Wales were reduced by William Herbert, earl of Pembroke, the last, Harlech, falling in 1468. Henry VI himself again fell into Yorkist hands in 1465.

After 1464 the greatest danger to the new dynasty came from within the ranks of the Yorkists themselves. No one had done more for the Yorkist cause in the critical years 1459–61 than Richard Neville, earl of Warwick. Edward IV's secret marriage to Elizabeth Woodville in 1464 displeased the earl, who had been planning a royal marriage alliance with France, and brought on the scene as rivals to the Nevilles a group of the queen's kinsmen, former Lancastrians. More serious was the sharp difference between Warwick and Edward over foreign policy. While Warwick continued to work for an alliance with Louis XI of France against Burgundy, Edward favoured, and in 1468 effected, an alliance with Burgundy. Encouraged by the generous promises of Louis, Warwick prepared to replace Edward by his brother George, duke of Clarence, whom inspired rumours declared to be the eldest legitimate son of Richard of York. In 1469, when Edward's attention had been drawn to the north by the rising of 'Robin of Redesdale', engineered by Warwick, and by a genuine Lancastrian rising, Warwick and Clarence crossed from Calais, entered London and with their northern confederates defeated Yorkist forces loyal to Edward near BANBURY. Edward himself was captured at Olney (Bucks), but the conspirators found that Edward's co-operation proved necessary for the suppression of disorder, and the increasing liberty he received enabled him to gather his friends. When the complicity of Warwick and Clarence in the LINCOLNSHIRE REBELLION of 1470 was revealed, they fled to France where, as early as 1467, Louis XI had considered the restoration of Henry VI by a combination of Queen Margaret and the die-hard Lancastrians with Warwick, backed by France. In 1470 he brought about the reconciliation of the queen and the earl, and Warwick invaded England and effected the short-lived READEPTION of Henry VI. Caught surprisingly unprepared and deserted by his chief northern supporter, Warwick's brother, John Neville, marquess of Montagu, Edward took refuge in the Burgundian Netherlands. He returned in the spring of 1471, landing at RAVENSPUR, and, aided by the hesitation of his opponents and the desertion of Clarence to his side, once more entered London and captured Henry VI. Edward then finished Warwick and Montagu at the battle of BARNET. The last large-scale Lancastrian effort ended in complete disaster at TEWKESBURY, where Henry VI's son Edward was killed. The capture of Margaret and the death of Henry himself made Edward's tenure of the throne secure. Many former opponents became reconciled to Edward's triumph, and after the destruction of the BEAUFORT family few die-hard Lancastrians were left—Jasper Tudor and his nephew Henry being notable exceptions.

The main phase of the W. of the R. ended in 1471, but they may justifiably be considered to have been renewed under Edward IV's brother, Richard III, who after crushing the duke of Buckingham's rebellion in 1483, was defeated and killed at BOSWORTH in 1485 by Henry Tudor, representing the house of Lancaster through his Beaufort mother. Perhaps the most satisfactory terminal date is 1497, when Henry VII captured the pretender Perkin Warbeck and became free from the attempts of surviving Yorkists and their candidates for the throne to reverse the decision of Bosworth.
                                                    RFW

Rothschild's Case. In 1847 Baron L. N. de Rothschild, a Jew, was elected M.P. for the City of London. The terms of the ABJURATION OATH, however, included the phrase 'on the true faith of a Christian', thus barring practising JEWS from Parliament. Disagreement between the political parties and between the two Houses over amending the oath was prolonged. R. had been elected fruitlessly 5 times before an Act of 1858 allowed him to take his seat by permitting the omission of the offending words in particular cases. By the Parliamentary Oaths Act, 1866, the phrase was dropped entirely.   MLH

Rotten Borough, a term originating from Chatham's description of borough representation as the 'rotten part of the constitution', is applied to those borough constituencies in the gift of patrons which, though seriously depopulated, continued to send M.P.s to the Commons until the REFORM ACT of 1832. Worst examples included Old Sarum, Gatton, Dunwich, Winchelsea, Rye and Bossinney. An almost synonymous expression is 'pocket borough', used generally of those borough seats at the disposal, or in the pocket, of patrons.   MLH

Rouen, the most important city and fortress of the duchy of NORMANDY, although the administrative centre in the 12th century was at Caen. R. put up a long resistance to Geoffrey of Anjou when he invaded the duchy in 1144, and was one of the last places to fall to him. Philip II of France besieged the city unsuccessfully in 1193, while Richard I was a prisoner in Germany, but it surrendered to him on 24 June 1204, after he had conquered almost all the duchy from King John.

R. endured a long siege by Henry V in the summer and autumn of 1418. Terrible hardship was suffered by refugees who were shut out by the city, which could not feed them, and not allowed through the English lines. After faint-hearted attempts at relief by the duke of Burgundy, R. finally surrendered on 19 Jan. 1419. R. was the scene of the burning of Joan of Arc (29 May 1431) and remained the centre of English military power in France until a rising of the inhabitants gave the city to Charles VII, the duke of Somerset surrendering the castle on 29 Oct. 1449.   RFW

Roundheads, a name applied to the PURITANS and parliamentarians during the CIVIL WARS and subsequently. Like the term 'Cavalier' it was originally derogatory. Both names appeared in 1641 during the scuffles at Westminster between the mobs of close-cropped apprentices (Roundheads) demonstrating against the bishops and the swaggering soldiers supporting the king (Cavaliers). See ROYALISTS.   IHE

Round Table Conferences (1930–2) between representatives of British

India, the Indian states and the British government were held in London to discuss Indian constitutional changes. At the first conference (Nov. 1930–Jan. 1931) the princes agreed in principle to an all-Indian federation, whilst the British government conceded responsible government in the provinces. At the second conference (Sept.–Dec. 1931) the INDIAN NATIONAL CONGRESS was represented by Gandhi, whose intransigence led to little progress on detail and to deadlock on the question of communal representation. After a third conference (Nov.–Dec. 1932) the British government issued its constitutional proposals (Mar. 1933) which formed the basis for the Government of INDIA ACT, 1935.

MLH

Rowlatt Acts (1919) embodied proposals of a committee on sedition in India chaired by Sir S. Rowlatt, an English high court judge. Government was empowered to allow judges to try political cases without juries and to allow provincial governments power of internment. Bitterly opposed by all shades of Indian opinion, their enactment nullified support for the MONTAGU–CHELMSFORD proposals and led to widespread disorder, a long-remembered incident being the AMRITSAR 'MASSACRE'. Undoubtedly the seriousness of the original emergency was misjudged, and the R.A. were never enforced. MLH

Royal assent, see BILL.

Royal (Ryal) or Rose Noble. Edward the Black Prince issued for Aquitaine in 1364 a gold coin called the r. or *pavillon*: the obverse showed the prince seated under a canopy. The first English r. was issued in 1465 by Edward IV, to replace the NOBLE, and was worth 10s. The obverse of the r. continued the famous type of the noble—the king standing in a ship—while the reverse introduced a rose in a sun with rays, giving the coin its other name, the rose noble. The minting of r.s appears to have ceased by 1470, but the coin was revived, with the same value and similar design, by Henry VII. RFW

Royal Historical Society is the premier national society for those, amateur or professional, concerned with the serious study of history. It was founded in 1868 and in 1872 received permission to use 'royal' in its style. Its headquarters are now (1970) at University College, London. It publishes (*Transactions, Guides and Handbooks*, Camden Series), holds monthly meetings during the winter and has a library. Membership as an Associate or a Fellow is by application. There are about 1,000 of these and over 600 subscribing libraries.

CFS

Royalists were the supporters of the king and the Anglican Church during the CIVIL WARS (1642–8). The GRAND REMONSTRANCE (1641) converted many Anglicans and moderates into royalists, and the majority of the largest landowners and peers as well as the Roman Catholic gentry supported the king. Some were motivated by personal loyalty to Charles or to the monarchical idea. They were strongest in the North and West. The nickname Cavalier was in use by 1641, originally as an uncomplimentary term. After their defeat the 'DELINQUENTS' suffered confiscation in spite of the Ordinance of Pardon and Oblivion (1652) and a decimation tax was imposed after PENRUDDOCK'S RISING (1655). The Cavaliers returned to power at the Restoration with the CAVALIER PARLIAMENT (1660).

IHE

Royal Marriage Act (1772), to prevent undesirable royal marriages. All descendants of George II under 25 years of age (except the issue of princesses marrying into foreign families) must obtain royal consent. Others might marry without crown approval provided 1 year's notice was given to the Privy Council and no Parliamentary objections were made. This did not affect the exclusion from the throne, as laid down in the BILL OF

RIGHTS (1689), of those marrying Roman Catholics. IHE

Royal Society, partly inspired by the ideas of Francis Bacon (1561–1626), grew out of gatherings of scientists, philosophers and others meeting at Gresham College, London, as early as 1645. Removing to Oxford during the CIVIL WAR they returned to London at the RESTORATION. In 1660 a group of 12, including Boyle, the father of chemistry, and Wren, the architect, founded a society which was incorporated as the R.S. in 1662. A symbol of the SCIENTIFIC REVOLUTION, the society developed at first as an experimental centre corresponding with continental scientists and arranging visits from them. Its *Philosophical Transactions* were first published in 1665. Fellowship of the R.S. has become the most coveted distinction among British scientists, and it is now an independent organization of eminent research workers fostering international co-operation in science. IHE

Rump, the remainder of the LONG PARLIAMENT, left after PRIDE'S PURGE (6 Dec. 1648), consisted of less than 60 M.P.s but later some were re-admitted and new ones elected; by 1652 its numbers did not exceed 125, and 50 was the average attendance. It abolished the House of Lords and the monarchy, established the COUNCIL OF STATE and declared England a COMMONWEALTH. Members frequently accepted bribes from ROYALISTS and were prone to nepotism. It faced up to external threats from the Irish, Scotch and Dutch, but failed to co-operate with the army and achieve internal reconstruction. It was dismissed by Cromwell when seeking to pass the 'Perpetuation Bill' (20 Apr. 1653). It resumed its sittings in 1659 and Monck secured the readmittance of the purged members in 1660 and it finally dissolved itself (16 Mar.). IHE

Runes, the Germanic and Scandinavian alphabet until it was superseded by the Latin alphabet that came with Christianity. It was devised for carving and in England consisted of 31 characters. Runic inscriptions were made until the 10th century and some runic poems are known. Three runic characters continued in use until the later middle ages. One of them, representing *th*, originally written as þ later as *y*, survived into modern times: hence such present-day efforts as 'Ye olde tea shoppe'. CFS

Runnymede (1215). MAGNA CARTA is dated 'in the meadow which is called Runnymede, between Windsor and Staines, on the 15th day of June, in the 17th year' of the reign of King John. The charter was apparently given the place and date of John's meeting with the barons when he sealed a draft agreement. The formal reconciliation of king and barons followed on the 19th, and it is unlikely that the final version of the charter was drawn up and sealed by John before 23 June. RFW

Rupert's Land, the name given in 1670 to the territories under the jurisdiction of the HUDSON'S BAY COMPANY of which Prince Rupert (1619–82) was the patron. SHS

Russell's Case (1576). The House of Commons asserted its right to settle questions of membership during the reign of Elizabeth I by precedents in individual cases. In 1576 the Commons confirmed the right of the eldest sons of peers to sit in their house. Lord John Russell, eldest son of the earl of Bedford, was allowed to sit as a burgess for the borough of Bridport following a similar precedent in the case of his father in 1550. IHE

Russia Company, see MUSCOVY COMPANY.

Ruthven Raid (1582). After 1579 the young James VI of Scotland was under the control of the earls of Lennox and Arran who planned to restore his mother Mary to the throne and re-establish Roman Catholicism. In Aug. 1582 the Protestant and pro-English earls of Mar, Gowrie and others abducted James to Gowrie's castle of Ruthven. Lennox fled to

France, but in June 1583 James escaped to St Andrews, the Ruthven faction was overthrown with the aid of the French and Arran returned to power. Gowrie was executed in 1584 but his associates escaped.   IHE

Rye House Plot (Apr. 1683). After the failure of the EXCLUSION BILLS Whig extremists and old Cromwellians planned to murder Charles II and the duke of York (on their return from Newmarket) near R.H., Hoddesdon, Herts., the home of Rumbold, a Cromwellian. The royal brothers left early and spoilt the plan. The plot, in which Monmouth was also involved, was betrayed (June) and the conspirators executed, including Lord Russell and Algernon Sidney who were not actively involved.   IHE

Ryknield Street, a ROMAN ROAD on the line Bourton on the Water–Alchester – Birmingham – Wall – Derby–Chesterfield–Templeborough (near Sheffield).   CFS

Ryswick, peace of (20 Sept. 1697), between England, the Netherlands, France and Spain ended the war of the GRAND ALLIANCE. The Emperor made peace subsequently (30 Oct.). By these treaties the Dutch restored PONDICHERRY to France, gained commercial concessions and the right to garrison certain barrier fortresses in the Spanish Netherlands. France restored all gains made since 1678 except Alsace and Strasbourg, recovered ACADIA and retained all the HUDSON'S BAY COMPANY's forts except Fort Albany. France recognized William III as king of England and Anne as his successor. French aggression had been checked but it was a truce rather than a peace.   IHE

Sabah, see NORTH BORNEO.

Sac and Soc. Used in grants of land these words conveyed to the grantee the right to hold a court for his tenants and receive its profits: such rights the king granted to his tenants and they, in turn, to their tenants. The two words are first found together in 956

but the idea of private jurisdiction may long antedate this. S. and S. grants were probably fairly common before the Norman conquest: thereafter they increased until the words were almost common form.   PMB

Sacheverell affair. In 1709 Dr Henry S. preached 2 sermons, subsequently printed, attacking the principles of the GLORIOUS REVOLUTION, the Dissenters, and the Whig ministry which ill-advisedly impeached him before the Lords (1710). Conviction was carried by 69 to 52 votes, but the light sentence of 3 years' suspension from preaching virtually gave the victory to S. and his high church supporters. Tremendous excitement was aroused in London and Dissenters' meeting houses were destroyed. (DAMMAREE.)   IHE

St Albans, battles of. (1) (22 May 1455), the first pitched battle of the wars of the ROSES. Henry VI's recovery of sanity late in 1454 terminated the first protectorship of Richard, duke of York, and he and his followers were excluded from any share in the government. The YORKISTS raised an army in the north and marched on London, though proclaiming their loyalty to the king himself. A LANCASTRIAN army under the dukes of Somerset and Buckingham advanced from London, and after futile parleys was attacked and routed in the streets of St A., leaving Henry VI in the power of York.

(2) (17 Feb. 1461). After the defeat and death of Richard, duke of York, at WAKEFIELD, the LANCASTRIAN army of Queen Margaret met little resistance on the way to London until it encountered the earl of Warwick defensively posted at St A. A surprise attack through the town led to a complete Lancastrian victory and the rescue of Henry VI. But for the success of York's son, Edward, in the west, the YORKIST cause might have been irretrievably lost.   RFW

Saintes, battle of (21 July 1242). The investiture of Alphonse, brother of Louis IX of France, as count of Poitou in 1241 caused widespread resentment among the nobles of south-western France. In 1242 Henry III of England sought to recover what he could of the lost Angevin dominions in alliance with the counts of La Marche and Toulouse. In fact Henry received little assistance from his allies, and his invasion of Saintonge was a fiasco. Left dangerously exposed when the French army forced the Charente at Taillebourg, Henry fought a skirmish at S. and beat a hasty retreat into Gascony. Despite a considerable outlay nothing had been achieved: thereafter Henry made no attempt to reconquer the ANGEVIN EMPIRE and finally cut his losses by the treaty of PARIS in 1259.

RFW

St Helena was discovered by the Portuguese in 1502, captured by the Dutch in 1600, secured by the EAST INDIA COMPANY in 1673 and surrendered to the crown in 1834. It was occasionally used for detaining prisoners (Napoleon, 1815–21; Boers, 1899–1902). Ascension Island (1922), TRISTAN DA CUNHA, Gough, Inaccessible and Nightingale Islands (1938) are dependencies of the colony.

SHS

St Kitts (St Christopher) was discovered by Columbus in 1493 and colonized by (Sir) Thomas Warner (†1649) in Jan. 1624 as the first English settlement in the WEST INDIES. In 1625 French settlers arrived but in 1629 the Spaniards virtually annihilated both the British and French colonies. The French soon recaptured the whole island which was divided between them and the British until the peace of UTRECHT in 1713 when France ceded her portion which the British had captured in 1702. It was taken by the French in 1782 but restored by the treaty of VERSAILLES in 1783. It joined the federation of the LEEWARD ISLANDS (1871) as a presidency together with its dependencies of Nevis (settled 1628) and Anguilla (settled 1650). In 1967 it became one of the West Indies Associated States. Anguilla attempted secession (1967–9).

SHS; IHE

St Lucia was discovered by Columbus on 13 Dec. 1502 and, after abortive attempts to establish a British colony (1605, 1638–41), remained in dispute between France and England throughout the 17th and 18th centuries. Britain eventually ceded it to France in the treaty of VERSAILLES (1783), but recaptured it in 1795 and, after a short Spanish interlude (1802), again in 1803 and finally obtained it by the peace of PARIS (1814). In 1838 it was attached to the WINDWARD ISLANDS. On 1 Mar. 1967 it became one of the WEST INDIES Associated States.

SHS; IHE

St Pierre and Miquelon shared the history of NEWFOUNDLAND until 1763 when the islands, important for their cod fishing, were ceded to France. SHS

Saints, battle of the (12 Apr. 1782). The French, allies of the United States in the American War of Independence, captured the LEEWARD ISLANDS and planned to attack Jamaica. Rodney decisively defeated the French off Les Saintes (now a dependency of GUADELOUPE), thus recovering British control in the West Indies. IHE

St Sardos, war of (1324–5), the most serious Anglo-French hostilities between 1303 and the opening of the HUNDRED YEARS' WAR in 1338. Edward II of England delayed doing homage for GASCONY, and before a date was fixed trouble broke out in the Agenais, where Edward's seneschal of Gascony destroyed a new fortified town which the French had started building at St S. When Edward postponed his homage further and did not carry out preliminary undertakings towards a judicial settlement of the dispute over St S., Charles IV declared Gascony confiscated. A French invasion of the duchy met with some success, but after papal intervention a truce was concluded in 1325. Edward's son, Edward, did homage for Gascony to Charles, who retained the Agenais as an indemnity. RFW

St Vincent, one of the WINDWARD ISLANDS, was discovered by Columbus on 22 Jan. 1498, granted to the earl of

Carlisle in 1627, but remained in the hands of the native Caribs until captured in 1762 and formally ceded by France in 1763. The French retook it in 1779 but restored it by the treaty of VERSAILLES (1783). On 1 June 1967 it became one of the WEST INDIES Associated States.   SHS; IHE

St Vincent or St Valentine's Day, battle of (14 Feb. 1797), a daring and timely British naval victory in the French Revolutionary wars when Great Britain had abandoned the Mediterranean and was threatened by the Dutch, French and Spanish fleets. Admiral Sir John Jervis with 15 sail of the line sighted 27 Spanish ships west of Cape St V. making for Cadiz. Jervis attacked the rear force of 18 ships, whose escape was prevented by Commodore Nelson breaking out of line without orders. In the mêlée 4 Spanish ships were taken, others mauled and the Spanish threat broken. Jervis was created Earl St Vincent and Nelson made a Knight of the Bath.   IHE

Saladin Tithe, a tax levied by Henry II in 1188 for the recovery of Jerusalem. The levy was of a tithe, one tenth, of each man's rents and MOVABLES, and produced very considerable returns.   PMB

Salamanca, battle of (22 July 1812), one of Wellington's decisive victories in the PENINSULAR WAR. Advancing from Badajoz but outmarched by Marmont, Wellington took up position south of S. Marmont overextended his line, giving opportunity for surprise attack. After some hours confused fighting (in the early stages of which Marmont was wounded) Clausel extricated the French with heavy loss (perhaps 14,000 to the British 5,000) and the road to Madrid lay open.   MLH

Salvation Army had its origin in the Christian Revival Association, founded (1865) in Whitechapel by William Booth (1829–1912). Known from 1867 as the (East London) Christian Mission, it was modelled on quasi-military lines as the S.A. in 1878,

Booth being first 'general'. The S.A. quickly became international, work starting in, e.g., Australia (1881), India and Canada (1882), South Africa and New Zealand (1883). Unconventional methods were used to reach the lowest classes, care for whose material condition was an essential part of its mission. When the S.A. procured evidence of the need for the Criminal Law Amendment bill (1885), it attracted national attention. This was magnified by Booth's *In Darkest England and the Way Out* (1890), formulating a scheme which greatly increased the S.A.'s social work. Booth nominated as successor his son, W. Bramwell Booth, who as chief of staff from 1880 was the real organizer of the S.A.; Bramwell was general until his dismissal in 1928 (†1929), when the post was made elective.   MLH

Samoa, first visited by Europeans in 1722, was through the greater part of the 19th century a flourishing entrepôt of American, British and German traders. The Americans concluded a commercial treaty in 1839, but from 1855 the Hamburg firm of Godeffroy exercised a virtual trade monopoly. On 14 July 1889 the U.S.A., Great Britain and Germany declared the islands neutral but on 7 Nov. 1899 Britain withdrew and Germany renounced her rights to the islands east of 171° W. long. in favour of U.S.A. The German colony was occupied by New Zealand forces on 29 Aug. 1914 and, under the name of Western S., became a NEW ZEALAND mandate on 7 May 1919. The advisory body of headmen, established in 1905, was gradually transformed into a legislative assembly (1947) and an executive council (1952), both under a council of state, consisting of the high commissioner and the two Fautua, representing the two ancient royal lines; and cabinet government was introduced in 1959. On 1 Jan. 1962, Western S. became independent, with the Fautua as joint heads of state. American S. is an 'unorganized and unincorporated American territory'.   SHS

Sanctuary was a right of the church, existing from Anglo-Saxon times, to provide refuge for fugitives generally in all churches and churchyards. After 40 days the coroner went to the s. and imposed the ABJURATION oath. Special sanctuaries granted by the crown such as the great LIBERTIES of Durham, Ripon and Beverley provided permanent refuge. In 1486 the judges decided s. gave no protection in cases of treason and for second offenders. Most of the remaining rights were drastically curtailed by acts of Henry VIII (1529–40) and 8 cities of refuge, on the biblical model, were appointed, Wells, Westminster, Northampton, Norwich, York, Derby, Manchester and Lancaster, giving some s. to debtors. S. for criminals was finally abolished in 1623 and for civil offenders by acts of 1697 and 1723.   IHE

Sand River convention (17 Jan. 1852) recognized the independence of the Boers beyond the river Vaal. The clause forbidding slavery was never observed by the Boers.   SHS

Sandwich, naval battle off (24 Aug. 1217). In the BARONS' WAR the royalists were rapidly gaining ground after their victory at LINCOLN, while Prince Louis badly needed reinforcements from France. A convoy of French troops crossing the Straits of Dover, commanded by Eustace the Monk— the terror of the Channel and the hero of a medieval French romance—was intercepted by an English fleet under Hubert de Burgh, based on S. Although the troopships escaped, the French supply ships were captured. Eustace himself was captured and beheaded forthwith. The failure of his reinforcements persuaded Louis to come to terms with the supporters of Henry III at KINGSTON-ON-THAMES.
                                 RFW

Sandwich, battles of (1459–60). After the rout of LUDFORD the earl of Warwick had found refuge in Calais. A Lancastrian force under the duke of Somerset crossed from S. to Guisnes, but effected nothing against Calais and was isolated by Warwick's control of the Straits. A second Lancastrian force under Lord Rivers was surprised at S. by a daring Yorkist raid from Calais on 7–8 Jan. 1460, which captured both its leaders and its shipping. During Warwick's absence in Ireland a further Lancastrian attempt on Calais was foiled, largely by bad weather. Finally, about 20 June, part of Warwick's troops landed at S. to defeat yet another Lancastrian force and to secure a bridgehead for the landing of Warwick's main army.
                                 RFW

Sangatte, see CALAIS, siege of.

Sankey commission (1919) was a statutory c. on the coal industry, appointed by Lloyd George to stave off a strike. Composed of miners' representatives, coal-owners, industrialists and socialist economists, it presented various minority reports; a bare majority (including the chairman, Sir J. S.) finally recommended nationalization. Lack of unanimity was taken as excuse for proposing an unacceptable compromise; the only results of the S.c. were the MINES ACT (1920) and a labour bitterness which led directly to the GENERAL STRIKE.   MLH

Saratoga, surrender at (17 Oct. 1777). In 1777 the British planned to shorten the war of the AMERICAN REVOLUTION by cutting off NEW ENGLAND from the other colonies. Burgoyne left Canada and reached the upper waters of the Hudson river to join forces with Howe from New York, but owing to confusion of plan Howe left by sea to attack Philadelphia instead. After several defeats Burgoyne, surrounded by some 17,000 opponents under Gates, surrendered his remaining 4,500 men at S. Although not an irretrievable military disaster it was a decisive point in the war as it encouraged France to join the Americans (6 Feb. 1778).   IHE

Sarawak. Uninterrupted human occupation of the country goes back to the middle palaeolithic age (c. 40,000 B.C.); Chinese and Indian trading stations existed from A.D. 600. When Portuguese sailors in 1521 first visited S., it was part of the Malay sultanate of BRUNEI. James Brooke (1803–68), invalided from the EAST INDIA COMPANY, in 1839–40 helped Rajah Muda Hassim, uncle of the sultan, to quell a revolt and was rewarded by being installed as rajah of S. (24 Sept. 1841). The U.S.A. in 1850 and Great Britain in 1864 recognized the independence of S. which James Brooke pacified and civilized by suppressing piracy and head-hunting; he set up (1855) two representative councils. His nephew and successor, Sir Charles Johnson Brooke (1829–1917), developed the country which in 1861, 1882, 1885, 1890 and 1905 was enlarged by cessions by the sultan of Brunei and the British North BORNEO Company and by voluntary submission of the natives. The country was placed under British protection in 1888. Economic prosperity and educational and medical services continued to flourish under the third rajah, Sir Charles Vyner Brook (1874–1963), who on 21 Sept, 1941 relinquished his absolute powers and granted a constitution. S. was occupied by the Japanese from 16 Dec. 1941 to 11 Sept. 1945 and under British military administration until 15 April 1946. The rajah ceded S. to the British crown on 1 July 1946, and the council authorized the cession by 19 to 16 votes, the majority including 7 British officials. A new constitution came into force on 1 April 1957, providing for executive and legislative councils. In 1963 S. joined MALAYSIA.   SHS

Sark, see CHANNEL ISLANDS.

Saskatchewan, named after the S. river (*Kis-is-ska-tche-wan*, 'fast flowing'), was carved out of the NORTHWEST TERRITORIES and constituted a province of CANADA on 1 Sept. 1905.
                                        SHS

Savoy Conference (Apr.–July 1661), between bishops and Presbyterian clergy, commissioned to review the BOOK OF COMMON PRAYER, marked the failure to attain comprehension or

toleration favoured by Charles II The Puritans drew up their 'exceptions' to the Prayer Book and the 'Savoy Liturgy', a Presbyterian service book. Most of the 'exceptions' as well as the liturgy were rejected by the bishops but minor modifications were included in the revised Book of Common Prayer (1662). Toleration was refused and the CAVALIER PARLIAMENT enacted the CLARENDON CODE.
                                        IHE

Saxons, one of the Teutonic groups that invaded Britain in the late 5th and early 6th centuries (TEUTONIC CONQUEST). By the 4th century they formed a strong and populous group between the rivers Elbe and Weser, and extending into Frisia. S. was the generic description in the Roman world for Teutonic pirates whose attacks, beginning in the 2nd century A.D., had led to the construction in ROMAN BRITAIN of the coast defences of the SAXON SHORE. During the conquest of Britain Saxon kingdoms were established in the southern part of the island, the main ones being ESSEX, MIDDLESEX, SUSSEX, WESSEX.
                                        CFS

Saxon Shore, the 400 miles of coastline from the Wash to the Solent, was fortified *c.* 300 to check the forays of SAXON and Frankish pirates, as part of the reorganization of the defences of ROMAN BRITAIN. Ten major forts were erected to guard the main harbours and estuaries; each had a garrison and a detachment of the fleet (*Classis Britannica*) based on it, and the whole was commanded by the Count of the S.S. (*Comes Litoris Saxonici*). In the later 4th century the scheme was extended by a line of coastal signal stations from the Wash to north Yorkshire.   CFS

Schellenberg, battle of (2 July 1704). France aimed at deciding the SPANISH SUCCESSION WAR by capturing Vienna (1703–4). Marlborough, realizing the danger, abandoned his campaign on the Moselle without informing the Dutch and marched his armies across Germany, being joined by Margrave

Louis of Baden. His victory over the French and Bavarian forces on the heights of the S. overlooking Donauwörth established him in Bavaria. IHE

Schism Act (1714) was promoted by Tories and Anglicans to weaken the political and social influence of the Dissenters and Whigs. The relevant clauses of the Act of UNIFORMITY (1662) were being disregarded, therefore Nonconformists were forbidden to teach or keep a school. The act also applied to Ireland. Anne's death brought the Whigs to power, making it ineffective. It was repealed in 1719. IHE

Science, Minister of, see EDUCATION AND SCIENCE.

Scientific and Industrial Research, Department of, see TECHNOLOGY.

Scientific Revolution is a term applied to the changes and developments in scientific ideas and methods in the 16th and more especially the 17th century. This revolution was essentially the product of Western Europe, particularly of England, France and Holland, and was aided by the widening horizons created by geographical discovery, commercial development and the increasing secularization of thought. Rational scientific method led to the discarding of magic and the world came to be regarded as a machine working by cause and eflect. In England the empiricism advocated by Bacon (1561–1626) was united with the mathematical logic of Descartes (1596–1650) and brought to fruition by the genius of Newton (1642–1727). Astronomy was the central field of scientific research, and Newton built on foundations laid by Galileo (1564–1642) and Kepler (1571–1630) to produce his laws of motion and theory of the universe. The progress of the S.R. was marked by the formation of the ROYAL SOCIETY (1660–2) and the Académie Royale (1666). There were important achievements in other fields which collectively made these developments in natural science the most revolutionary influence in European and world civilization. IHE

Scone, Stone of, or Stone of Destiny, was, according to an early-14th-century legend, the stone which had formed Jacob's pillow at Bethel and had been brought to Scotland by way of Egypt, Spain and Ireland (where it had been the inauguration stone of the high-kings at Tara). Another legend associates the stone with St Columba. Geologists have identified the stone as Old Red Sandstone and quite possibly Scottish in origin. After their defeat of the PICTS the SCOTS are said to have brought the stone to S., where a long line of medieval Scottish kings was certainly crowned, and where their councillors assembled on the Moot Hill.

The last Scottish king to be seated on the stone at his coronation was John Balliol in 1292. In the summer of 1296, after his apparent reduction of Scotland, Edward I carried off the stone to England together with the Scottish regalia. It was incorporated in a wooden chair about 1307 and has since regularly played its part in the coronation of English and British sovereigns. Although no provision for its restoration to Scotland was made in the treaty of NORTHAMPTON (1328), its return seems to have been intended by the English government. At Christmas 1950 the stone was carried back to Scotland by Scottish Nationalists, but it was subsequently restored to Westminster Abbey. RFW

Scot, see CHURCH SCOT; SOUL SCOT.

Scot and Lot, payments by burgesses for various kinds of borough (and national) taxation, roughly corresponding to modern rates; in course of time they came to be regarded as qualification for the burghal FRANCHISE, particularly important in parliamentary elections. PMB

Scots, Goidelic-speaking CELTS from Northern Ireland. They raided the western coastal regions of ROMAN BRITAIN from the 3rd to the 5th centuries. During the 4th century they were associated with PICTS, SAXONS,

Attacotti and Franks in major attacks on Britain. None of their settlements in Wales and the north-west maintained its independence, but in the 5th century they successfully established the kingdom of DALRIADA in Pictish territory. The term later became political rather than racial, and from the 11th century was applied to those living within the boundaries of the kingdom of Scotland. CFS

Scottish Church. The SCOTS in Ireland followed the practices current in the IRISH CHURCH, and these spread to DALRIADA when the Scots set up their kingdom there. From the monastery of IONA the northern PICTS were converted and missions sent on royal invitation to NORTHUMBRIA (634). That kingdom was speedily converted from the monastery at LINDISFARNE, and the sphere of activity of the S.c. soon extended to the southern midlands. The practices and methods of the Scottish churchmen in England came into conflict with those of Rome, and the decision of the synod of WHITBY (663) in favour of the latter led to the submission of the S.c. in England. During the 8th century the S.c. outside England conformed. The enthusiasm and saintliness that characterized the S.c. made it ideal for conversion work, but it lacked the stability and organization of the Roman church. However, its missionary zeal possibly influenced the united church in England in its great 8th-century missionary activity in Frisia and Germany. CFS

Scottish nationalism. A growing national consciousness produced the Scottish Home Rule Association in 1886. Home Rule bills came to a division in the House of Commons ten times, 1889–1913; latterly at least 80% of S. members voted in favour. Both S. Labour and Liberal parties backed self-government, but absence of practical political prospects led to formation of the Scottish National Party in 1927. One parliamentary candidate gained a by-election seat in

1945, but lost it at the immediately subsequent general election. In 1949 a 'covenant' to secure a S. Parliament was signed by 2m., a majority of the electorate. In the 1960s the S. party was revitalized; 23 candidates unsuccessfully contested the 1966 election, but one was returned at a by-election in 1967. MLH

Scottish Office. After the Act of Union 1707 Secretaries of State for Scotland were intermittently appointed 1709–45; thereafter Scots affairs were entrusted to one of the Secretaries of State, later the Home Secretary, aided 1745–1827 by the Lord Advocate and a Scot in the cabinet. In 1885 a Secretary for Scotland, created Secretary of State in 1926, was appointed. His work was to oversee Scots affairs in general and especially matters of strong Scots tradition. Replacing many separate boards, the S.O. has four main departments, agriculture, development, education, home and health, comparable with their English counterparts. PMB

Scottish Representative Peers, the 16 peers of Scotland elected by their fellows to sit in the British House of Lords, during the lifetime of a Parliament, in accordance with the Act of UNION of 1707. Non-representative peers were ineligible for seats in the Commons. The 1963 Peerage Act has enabled all Scottish Peers to sit in the lords. IHE

Scriveners, clerks, descended from the *notarii* of the Roman empire, employed in writing documents for private persons, much as the CURSITORS wrote WRITS. In England s. specialized in drafting the simpler types of documents, e.g. BONDS, and through this business themselves acted as usurers. At all times they were lowly men of little professional status. PMB

Scutage, a financial composition for KNIGHT service, though occasionally taken from some serjeants. The practice probably developed soon after the Norman conquest, though the term was not used until 1100. The method of levy before Henry II is uncertain: thereafter s. was assessed at a fixed sum for each knight's fee, i.e. for each shield, *scutum* (see CARTE BARONUM). A tenant-in-chief paying s. recouped himself from his tenants, and in the 13th century obtained the king's writ to do so. With the decline of feudal armies s. became more valuable to the crown than the military service it replaced, but owing to the division of knight's fees and other complications, s. became increasingly difficult to collect. After a 20 years' break Edward I revived it in 1277 for his Welsh and Scottish campaigns; it was levied last in 1327.   PMB; RFW

Seal, a means of authentication in illiterate times, becoming widespread with the development of government, law and commerce, now maintained by custom and statute. Single- or double-sided, seals can be applied directly to documents, frequently to close them, hung from them by strips of leather or parchment, strings of silk etc., or embossed on them. Beeswax, sometimes with added chalk, shellac and gutta percha were common materials, and plastic is now used. Applied seals are made by pressing the matrix into warm wax: wax for single-sided pendant seals is pressed into the matrix with the fingers, and for double-sided seals is enclosed between 2 matrices with a press. In CHANCERY the wax was prepared by the chaffwax and the seal affixed by the spigurnel.

Royal seals are always round: so generally are those of lay magnates and corporations. Seals of bishops and religious houses are pointed oval, a shape frequently chosen by other ecclesiastics and women. The legend, either the owner's name and style or, a text or pious phrase, runs clockwise outside the device, and seals are good illustrations of contemporary design and taste. Non-royal seals generally belonged to one person, but could be inherited or borrowed if the borrower had no seal or thought his own unknown: this latter practice was common with ecclesiastics' seals. Alternatively a second seal, e.g. that of a town, could be put on the document for additional guarantee. (COMMON SEAL; GREAT SEAL; PRIVY SEAL; SIGNET.)   PMB

SEATO, the South-East Asia Treaty Organization, implements the South-East Asia Collective Defence Treaty which was signed in Manila on 8 Sept. 1954 by Australia, France, New Zealand, Pakistan, the Philippines, Thailand, the United Kingdom and the United States. The undertaking of mutual aid against aggression and subversion also covers Cambodia, Laos and South Vietnam. On the same day the signatories issued the Pacific Charter, proclaiming the principles of equal rights and self-determination of peoples, economic, social and cultural co-operation, and the defence of sovereignty and territorial integrity.   SHS

Second World War, see WORLD WAR II.

Secretary of State, an office much dependent on the character and ability of its tenant. A king's secretary was established by the late 14th century, keeping the SIGNET and advising, often as a member of the council, on affairs both foreign and domestic. The appointment of a subordinate secretary to deal with French affairs from 1468 onwards shows the growing importance and business of the senior office which, with the appointment of able men such as the Cecils, grew to be one of the most important in the realm. From 1540 onwards two Principal Secretaries were appointed: no formal division of their work was made, but character and personal interests frequently produced an informal division. In 1660 one secretary was assigned to the Northern department, i.e. relations with Protestant countries, the other to the Southern department and Roman Catholic countries. These titles were retained, with varying allocations of duties, until 1782 when the Northern Secretary became responsible for foreign affairs and the Southern for home, colonial and Irish business, setting the modern pattern. From time to time additional S.s of S. have been appointed, e.g. 1709–45 for Scottish affairs, since revived. Modern Secretaries still retain their connexion with the sovereign, receiving signets on their appointment.   PMB

Sedgemoor, battle of (6 July 1685) brought about the collapse of MON-MOUTH'S REBELLION. With the royal forces closing in upon him, Monmouth withdrew from Bath to Bridgwater where he was soon confronted by the king's troops under Feversham and Churchill on the flat plain of S. Monmouth attempted a surprise attack at night but was discovered. His cavalry took flight and at daylight Monmouth, seeing his cause lost, abandoned his men to their inevitable destruction.   IHE

Seisin, a COMMON LAW term denoting possession not ownership, since possession was, in an age of unwritten titles, more easily proved than ownership. The conception of s. probably dates from before the Norman conquest, but the post-conquest lawyers developed it extensively, and Henry II's POSSESSORY ASSIZES, particularly NOVEL DISSEISIN, gave it new impetus. S. was at first concerned with land: e.g. a grant came into force only when the grantor gave the grantee livery of s., often by a symbol such as a turf; the s. thus given could only be upset by an earlier lawful s. Later the conception was applied to services, goods, chattels etc.   PMB

Selangor, see FEDERATED MALAY STATES.

Self-denying Ordinance (3 Apr. 1645). The indecisive second battle of NEWBURY (1644) led to this ordinance as the least offensive way of dismissing inefficient commanders, especially Manchester. All members of both Houses were to relinquish every civil and military command but nothing was said against their re-appointment. This latter clause was inserted after the Lords had earlier rejected the ordinance in its original form.   IHE

Senlac, as the name for the battle of HASTINGS was first used in the 12th century and was popular in the 19th century. It is an Old French form of Old English *Sandlacu,* the name of a stream near the English line. It survived for some centuries as Sandlake, but has now disappeared.   CFS

Separatists, see ANABAPTISTS, BAPTISTS, BARROWISTS, BROWNISTS, CONGREGATIONALISTS,   INDEPENDENTS, METHODISTS,   NONCOMFORMISTS, PURITANS, QUAKERS.

Septennial Act (1716) was promoted by the Whig ministry to prolong its tenure of office in view of the unsettled state of the country arising from the FIFTEEN REBELLION. The election due in 1718 in accordance with the TRIENNIAL ACT (1694) was to be held in 1722 and the maximum duration of a Parliament was to be 7 years. This was altered to 5 years by the Parliament Act (1911).   IHE

Seringapatam, the fortress-capital of the sultans of MYSORE, was the scene of two sieges. In March 1792 Lord Cornwallis, governor-general, invested the stronghold and forced the sultan, Tipu Sahib, by the first treaty of S. to give up half his territory, thus ending the third Mysore war.

In April–May 1799, during the fourth Mysore war, Gen. G. Harris besieged S. The assault, 4 May, was made by Maj.-Gen. D. Baird, Tipu being killed and the town sacked. British supremacy in southern India was established: Kanara, Coimbatore and S. were annexed to the presidency of MADRAS; the territory of the Nizam of HYDERABAD, who had supplied troops under Arthur Wellesley (later Duke of Wellington), was enlarged; by the second treaty of S. (1 Sept. 1799) the infant heir of the former Hindu raja was made ruler of Mysore, subject to the EAST INDIA COMPANY.   MLH

Serjeants-at-law. As COMMON LAW became increasingly complex, professionals were employed to conduct cases: ATTORNEYS-in-law represented their principals, and narrators, called

s. by the early 14th century, undertook oral proceedings. The s. became a gild, small in numbers but of great legal authority, with its own Inn: each s. also had an office in St Paul's cathedral. The gild, often called the order of the Coif from the s.' white caps fastening under the chin, was dissolved in 1877. PMB

Serjeanty, a name covering a wide range of tenures in return for service: while some serjeants did military service and paid fines or SCUTAGE, most undertook domestic services for their lord, some almost negligible, receiving land in lieu of wages. Among the king's serjeants were his DISPENSER, his tailor, the keeper of the FLEET PRISON and the man who boarded a hawk. Except at great feasts the greater serjeanties were of little importance. Later lawyers divided the tenures into Grand and Petty S.: both were abolished in 1922. PMB

Settlement, Act of (1701), was passed after the death of Anne's son, the duke of Gloucester. If William III and the Princess Anne left no heirs the throne was to pass to the Electress Sophia of Hanover or her Protestant descendants. It also continued the constitutional settlement begun by the BILL OF RIGHTS. Future sovereigns must be communicants of the Church of England and must not leave the kingdom or engage the country in war to defend their continental territory without consent of Parliament. Foreigners were debarred from office and Parliament. Other clauses excluded all office holders from the Commons (modified 1705–7), attempted to check the growth of the cabinet council (repealed 1707) and provided that judges were to hold office 'during good behaviour'. IHE

Settlement Acts. (1) (Ireland, 1652), was passed by the English Parliament classifying and punishing those who took part in the IRISH REBELLION (1641) according to their guilt. The mass of the poor were pardoned. Participants in the early stages of the revolt forfeited their lives and estates, all others lost two-thirds of their estates and those of dubious loyalty one-third, and by an act of 1653 they were forced to accept transportation to Clare and Connaught. The confiscated lands were divided among the ADVENTURERS and Cromwellians.

(2) (1662), was passed by the Cavalier Parliament to check vagrancy. It empowered parish overseers to remove any new-comers likely to become chargeable on the rates. It severely limited the mobility of the poor but was restricted in 1795 substantially to those applying for relief.

(3) (Ireland, 1662), was an attempt, based on a royal declaration of 1660, to lessen the hardships imposed on the Irish by the act of 1652. The ADVENTURERS of 1642 retained their lands and 'innocent' protestants were to regain theirs if they had not already accepted compensation in Clare or Connaught. 'Innocent' Catholics were to be restored but the definition was narrowly interpreted and many were excluded. Certain others were included by royal favour but English opinion prevented further adjustment. Moreover the settlers were too well entrenched. IHE

Settlement and Explanation, Act of (Ireland, 1665). There was not enough land available to meet conflicting claims arising from the Act of SETTLEMENT (1662). Accordingly ADVENTURERS and Cromwellians had to surrender one-third of their lands held in 1659 to compensate loyalists. All doubtful cases were decided in favour of Protestants who were left with about two-thirds of the total profitable land. IHE

Seven bishops, trial of (June 1688). After James II's DECLARATION OF INDULGENCE Archbishop Sancroft and 6 bishops petitioned the king against the order in council by which the bishops were to distribute it and have it read in all churches on two successive Sundays. They also challenged the legality of the DISPENSING POWER and were put on trial for seditious libel. The jury gave a verdict 'not guilty' which was applauded by the nation. IHE

Seven Years' War (1756–63) resulted from the commercial and imperial rivalry which led to the DIPLOMATIC REVOLUTION. After the French attack on Minorca Great Britain declared war (15 May), Prussia invaded Saxony (29 Aug.) and by 1757 was opposed by Austria, the Empire, France, Russia, Poland and Sweden. Prussia, though victorious in Saxony, had to evacuate Bohemia, and the English, defeated by the French at HASTENBECK (July), lost Hanover. The victory at Rossbach saved Prussia and was followed by the recovery of Silesia (Dec.). In 1758 the French were defeated at Crefeld (June), the Russians checked at Zorndorf (Aug.), but the Austrian victory at Hochkirch (Oct.) left Prussia in a perilous position. In 1759, after the defeat of the French at MINDEN (Aug.), the Austro-Russian victory at Kunersdorf (Aug.) made the Prussian case desperate, but she held on until 1762 when Russia and Sweden made peace and Britain abandoned her ally. General exhaustion ended the war in 1763.

The Anglo-French struggle was primarily fought at sea, in North America, the West Indies and India. The French capture of MINORCA was followed by successes in North America until 1758 when the British took Louisbourg and Fort DUQUESNE but failed at TICONDEROGA. British naval victories at LAGOS and QUIBERON BAY and the capture of QUEBEC made 1759 a decisive year. Montreal fell in 1760 and Spain's entry into the war in 1762 resulted in her loss of CUBA and the PHILIPPINES. In India the British capture of the French factory at Chandernagore and Clive's victory at PLASSEY (1757) limited the contest to southern India. The French took Fort St David and besieged MADRAS (1758) but their defeat at WANDEWASH (1760) was followed by the fall of PONDICHERRY (1761). The treaty of PARIS (1763) confirmed British success in the colonial struggle. IHE

Sewers, Commissions of. Until 1930 land drainage was partly the result of local necessity and enterprise, partly of crown interest. From an early period areas such as Romney Marsh were reclaimed by local residents, and in the 17th century the 4th earl of Bedford drew up the plans for new Fenland drainage. Crown interest was first shown by the appointment of temporary, later regular, commissioners de walliis et fossatis, of walls and ditches, to oversee repairs of river banks, dykes etc. Such commissions were legalized in 1427 and their powers etc. restated and amplified in 1532. Holding courts and hearing juries' presentments, the commissioners attempted to enforce local and personal responsibility for repairs, later levying rates. Their first aim was to maintain existing land drainage and navigable waterways, but from the 16th century new works were commissioned. Some commissions, e.g. in London, were vested in local authorities in the 19th century; the remainder were abolished in 1930 and replaced by local Drainage Boards. PMB

Seychelles, discovered by the Portuguese, were colonized and (1768) annexed by the French to break the Dutch monopoly of the spice trade. The islands (92 in number) were captured by the British in 1794 and formally ceded in 1814. First administered as a dependency of MAURITIUS, with its own executive and legislative councils since 1888, S. became a fully separate crown colony in 1903. A new constitution based on adult suffrage was introduced in 1967. SHS; IHE

Sherburn-in-Elmet, assembly at (1321). Thomas, earl of Lancaster, did not actively assist the MARCHER LORDS in their war against the Despensers early in 1321. But after his meeting with the northern lords at PONTEFRACT he summoned the northern prelates, together with many lay nobles of both north and south, to S. on 28 June. This meeting, which has sometimes been regarded as a 'counter-parliament', considered the conduct of the Despensers and their malign influence over Edward II, and a body of barons swore to achieve the destruction of the king's favourites. Although Lancaster does not seem to have secured the unanimity of northerners and Marchers, the barons were sufficiently united in the July parliament at Westminster to secure the exile of the Despensers. RFW

Sheriff (Anglo-Saxon *scirgerefa*, Latin *vicecomes*). In the early 11th century the term s. (shire reeve) superseded the older designation of REEVE as the administrator of the royal DEMESNE in a SHIRE and the deputy of the EALDORMAN in local government. With the replacement of ealdormen by EARLS in the 11th century the s. became the key figure of local administration, appointed by and responsible to the king. As the king's courts developed, much of their routine work fell to the s., e.g. he delivered writs; he accounted yearly at the EXCHEQUER for the ancient demesnes of the crown, often holding them at farm, as well as for the expanding extraordinary revenues of the crown; he controlled the county forces. Such power was open to abuse. After the 1170 inquest into s.s' malpractices many were dismissed, and at the end of the century new officers, CORONERS etc., were being introduced further to check s.s' powers, while counties made fine to elect the officer from among themselves. In the 13th century the s.'s business increased, e.g. with purveyance for the wars of Edward I, but with new courts, methods of keeping the peace and of administration, the office steadily declined, with a brief revival in the later 15th century in an attempt to curb the magnates' powers: modern s.s' powers are principally of minor judicial and ceremonial importance.

S.s were introduced into crown lands in Ireland and South Wales after their conquest, and in North Wales by the statute of RHUDDLAN 1284: there an inquiry similar to the 1170 inquest was made after Madog ap

Llywelyn's rebellion in 1295. Alexander I (1107–24) introduced s.s on the English model into Scotland, but the office rapidly became hereditary, unlike the short-term, now annual, English appointments: it so remained, with a brief lapse during Edward I's conquest, until 1748, when hereditary offices were progressively abolished. Since 1769 s.s-depute have been appointed for life, most of their duties being discharged by a deputy, the s.-substitute. Their courts have been restricted to criminal cases and, among civil actions, recovery of debts and some land cases; their duties also include preliminary investigation of some criminal charges. PMB; CFS

Sheriffmuir, battle of (13 Nov. 1715), marked the failure of Mar's rising in the FIFTEEN REBELLION. After raising the standard at Perth (6 Sept.), the earl of Mar advanced towards Dunblane. With 10,000 men he met Argyll's army of 3,300 men at S. and after an indecisive action began his retreat. No further effort was made. Mar abandoned his followers (4 Feb.) who were finally dispersed by Cadogan. IHE

Sheriffs, Inquest of (April 1170), an inquiry instituted by Henry II into the conduct of all his sheriffs and of other royal, baronial and ecclesiastical officers. A commission investigated among other things what moneys the sheriffs had received since 1166, what sums they had collected as an aid in 1168, whether they had given or taken bribes, and how they had discharged their custody of the royal demesne. The result of the inquest, of which some returns survive, was the dismissal of most of the sheriffs and their replacement by professional administrators trained in the king's service. Henry II was probably more concerned with ensuring that the crown got its dues than with relieving his subjects from the oppression of local officials. RFW

Sheriff's Tourn, a court held twice yearly by the SHERIFF in each royal HUNDRED, for the inspection of the TITHING and FRANKPLEDGE systems and to deal with certain criminal matters, reserving others for the justices in EYRE: in private hundreds owners held their own tourns. Similar functions were performed at COURTS LEET in manors with private jurisdiction.   PMB

Shilling, a silver coin worth 12 pennies first minted by Henry VII after 1504, bearing a portrait of the king and at first known as a testoon, from an Italian coin of that name. After 1816 they became of token value.   IHE

Ship-money. Piratical attacks on English shipping, the need to protect the North Sea fisheries, and to strengthen the navy against the Dutch and French, gave Charles I grounds for issuing writs of s. on maritime towns and counties (1634). Based on ancient precedents and previously used, the demand was extended in 1635 to inland shires and towns and writs were issued annually until 1640. In 1637 John Hampden refused to pay his due of 20s. and a test case resulted in the EXCHEQUER OF PLEAS —7 of 12 judges declared against him. This evasion of the PETITION OF RIGHT led to general loss of confidence in the courts of law. S. was made illegal by the LONG PARLIAMENT (5 July 1641).   IHE

Shipping, Ministry of, see TRANS-PORT.

Shire (O.E. *scir*, a part), the main unit of local government in Old English times. The great majority of s.s had come into being by the end of the 10th century, replacing the older PRO-VINCIAE, and their boundaries have remained virtually unchanged. WES-SEX proper was divided into s.s before the end of the 8th century; Western MERCIA in the 10th century, probably in the reign of Edward the Elder (899–925), each s. taking the name of a leading town in its area and no regard being paid to earlier divisions. The Danish area of Eastern MERCIA was probably shired at about the same time; the s.s of Derby, Leicester, Lincoln and Nottingham represent the territories dependent on four of the FIVE BOROUGHS; those of Bedford,

Cambridge, Huntingdon and North-ampton, the territories settled by Danish armies whose respective head-quarters were at those towns. ESSEX, KENT, MIDDLESEX and SUSSEX were former Teutonic kingdoms. Norfolk and Suffolk represent the old division of the kingdom of EAST ANGLIA into a north and south folk. Yorkshire probably represents the area of the Danish kingdom of YORK, and North-umberland the remnant of the former kingdom of NORTHUMBRIA that was not conquered by the Danes, i.e. the southern part of BERNICIA. Of the later s.s county Durham was the area administered by the bishop of Dur-ham; Westmorland the area where lived the people of the western moors; Cumberland the relic in England of the old kingdom of STRATHCLYDE (Cumbria); Lancashire the formerly unshired lands belonging to the HONOR of Lancaster; Rutland that part of Northampton assigned in dower to the queen of England. The s. in Wessex was originally controlled by an EALDORMAN, but after the 10th cen-tury the effective royal representative in any s. was its SHERIFF, although an EARL could if he desired take pre-cedence in any s. within his earldom. For taxation purposes the s. was assessed at a round number of HIDES or PLOUGHLANDS on which GELD was paid. The s. authorities were respon-sible for calling out the local militia (FYRD) when ordered by the king. The s. court (MOOT), presided over jointly by the local bishop and the sheriff or earl, dealt with administration and justice, both lay and ecclesiastical, within the s. S.s were divided into HUNDREDS or WAPENTAKES. Under Norman-French influence the name was transformed into COUNTY. The English system was introduced in Wales under the Act of UNION.   CFS

Shirley's Case (1604). Sir Thomas S., M.P. (1542–1612) had been im-prisoned for debt. By bills which received the royal assent Parliament asserted the privilege of its members to freedom from arrest during session, except for treason, felony or breach of the peace. Shirley was released to take his seat. IHE

Shirley v. Fagg, case of (1675). Dr Thomas S. appealed to the Lords against a Chancery decision in favour of Sir John F., M.P. The Commons claimed that F. was exempted by privilege during session from legal proceedings and that the Lords had no jurisdiction in equity cases. The resulting deadlock was ended only by prorogation of Parliament (Nov. 1675–Feb. 1677). S. abandoned his case and the Lords maintained their right of jurisdiction. IHE

Short Parliament (13 Apr.–5 May 1640) was summoned on Strafford's advice to obtain supplies for waging the second BISHOPS' WAR. Charles I offered to give up SHIP-MONEY in return for subsidies but the Commons insisted on redress of grievances in church and state as a first condition. Learning that they were about to petition against the Scottish war, the king dissolved Parliament. IHE

Shrewsbury, or Hateley Field, battle of (21 July 1403). The Percies, foremost supporters of Henry IV in the DEPOSITION of Richard II, but subsequently disillusioned kingmakers, rebelled in 1403, nominally in support of the claim to the throne of Edmund, earl of March, but possibly on their own account. Before the earl of Northumberland had assembled his full power in the north, his son, Henry 'Hotspur', marched south, raised Cheshire and descended with superior forces on Henry, Prince of Wales, at S. But whereas the Percies' ally, Owain GLYN DŴR, was too far away—at Carmarthen—to help, Henry IV hurried to his son's aid, reaching S. on 20 July, just ahead of Hotspur. The following day, three miles north of S.—the present Battlefield—a desperate battle was fought before Hotspur was killed and his army broken. Hotspur's uncle, Thomas, earl of Worcester, and other rebel leaders were captured and executed forthwith; Northumberland was forced to

submit; and Henry IV had survived the most serious crisis of his reign.
RFW

Shrewsbury, parliament of (Jan. 1398). After the destruction of Richard II's enemies in the session at Westminster in 1397, Parliament was adjourned to S., where it sat for four days. Oaths to maintain the acts of the preceding session were taken, and the acts of the MERCILESS PARLIAMENT were repealed. On 3 Jan. 1398 Henry Bolingbroke accused Thomas Mowbray, duke of Norfolk, of plotting against Richard II. A committee of 18 was set up to consider the accusation, which led eventually to the meeting of Bolingbroke and Mowbray in the lists at COVENTRY. Another committee, of similar membership, was to deal with outstanding petitions. While the view that Richard II was seeking to replace Parliament by this second committee is no longer widely held, the king did increase its powers in 1399, when it was used as the instrument of the perpetual exile of Bolingbroke and other acts of royal vengeance.
RFW

'Sicilian business'. In March 1250 Henry III took the cross, later promising to set out for the Holy Land by midsummer 1256. Intent on the destruction of the Hohenstaufen rulers of Sicily, Conrad IV (†1254) and Manfred, sons of the emperor Frederick II, Pope Innocent IV was seeking a powerful papal candidate for the kingdom. Henry III's brother, Richard, earl of Cornwall, declined, but in 1254 Henry accepted Sicily for his second son, Edmund, as a papal fief. In 1255 Pope Alexander IV permitted Henry to fulfil his crusading vow by overthrowing the enemies of the papacy in Sicily. Henry undertook to meet the expenses already incurred by the papacy; but the proceeds of clerical taxation, which Henry had been granted in 1252 (VALUATION OF NORWICH) for three years to finance his crusade, proved quite insufficient to finance the 'S.b.'. While Manfred consolidated his hold on Sicily and Henry's hopes faded, papal demands for money and men became more exorbitant and peremptory, and though not beyond the resources of England they exceeded what Henry was able to draw from his kingdom. Failing to obtain papal dispensation from his obligations, by the spring of 1258 Henry III was in imminent danger of excommunication and interdict. To obtain the financial aid of his barons, who had heartily disapproved of the whole adventure, and their intercession with the papacy, Henry was forced to surrender control of England to them (OXFORD, PARLIAMENT OF; PROVISIONS OF OXFORD). In Dec. 1258 the papal grant of Sicily was withdrawn; it was finally cancelled by Urban IV in 1263.   RFW

Sierra Leone (Portuguese: Lion Mountains) was sighted in 1447 by the Portuguese who in 1505 shipped the first consignment of Negro slaves from S.L. to America. Dutch, English and French slave-traders followed (Sir John Hawkins, 1562); the first permanent British factory was established at Bunce in 1672. In 1787 the London abolitionists set up at Granville a colony of ex-slaves from the West Indies and the southern American colonies, who had fought with the British and first been settled in NOVA SCOTIA. Granville was burnt down in 1789 by hostile tribes, and the S.L. Company (chartered in 1791) sent out colonists who in 1792 founded Freetown and in 1800 were strengthened by settlers from JAMAICA ('Maroons'). Between 1807 (Abolition of the Slave Trade Act) and 1870 about 70,000 slaves were rescued from slave-traders and set free by the S.L. courts. The 'Nova Scotians' and 'Maroons' formed a new African race, the Krios, with their own Krio language. The discovery of diamonds in 1930 strengthened the predominantly agricultural economy.

The Church Missionary Society in 1799 had 29 boys and 4 girls educated in London, in 1804 sent out the first missionaries (followed by Methodists in 1811) and in 1816 founded the first school in S.L. out of which grew

M

Fourah Bay College, since 1845 under African principals and since 1876 affiliated to Durham university. One of its tutors, Samuel Adjai Crowther, in 1864 became the first non-European Anglican bishop.

S.L. became a crown colony in 1808 and from 1860 expanded into the interior which in 1896 was declared a protectorate. S.L. was administered together with the GOLD COAST and Lagos until 1874 and the GAMBIA until 1888. S.L. received a constitution in 1925, and in 1951 internal self-government with a majority of elected members in the legislature. Independence and membership of the Commonwealth were achieved on 27 April 1961; in Oct. S.L. became the 100th member of the United Nations.

Army leaders overthrew parliamentary government in Apr. 1967, civilian rule was restored on 26 Apr. 1968, but a state of emergency was proclaimed 20 Nov.

C. Fyfe, *A History of S.L.* (1962).
                                                    SHS; IHE

Signa, a means of authenticating and guaranteeing documents in illiterate times, used on the continent from an early period and in England from at least the 8th century. The guarantors' names were written at the foot of the document and they added their *signa crucis*, autograph crosses. S., not seals, were used on documents in Normandy before the conquest of England: after the conquest a SEAL was also appended. The S. soon gave way before the CHARTER with WITNESSES and seal.
                                                    PMB

Signet, a single-sided SEAL, smaller than the PRIVY SEAL, first appearing in Edward II's reign. Early s.s had varied designs and several were in use together, e.g. the griffon of Edward III associated with the CHAMBER, the eagle of Henry V etc. associated with the Duchy of LANCASTER. From Richard II onwards most s.s bear the royal arms with a Garter or border of SS. S.s were kept successively by the king's secretary and the SECRETARIES OF STATE. Like the Privy seal the s. gave its name to the documents to which it was applied. Modern Secretaries of State are vested with office by receiving from the sovereign their s.s, three for all departments except the Home Office, which has four. PMB

Signet Office, the secretariat of the keepers of the SIGNET, later the Principal SECRETARIES OF STATE. Its work of preparing WARRANTS for the issue of PRIVY SEAL warrants was discharged by a small body of clerks; it was abolished in 1851, certain of its duties passing to the Home Office. PMB

Sign Manual. The earliest known royal signature is Edward III's, and from Richard II onwards the S.M. was increasingly used for WARRANTS: Henry VIII and some later sovereigns employed wooden stamps. The tendency for S.M. warrants to by-pass the SIGNET and PRIVY SEAL was checked in 1535, thus preserving clerks' fees. The modern procedure, requiring a S.M. on a Privy seal as warrant for the GREAT SEAL was instituted in 1851. PMB

Sikhs ('pupils'), a sect founded by Nanak (1469–1538) with the aim to unite Hindus and Moslems, but afterwards filled with implacable hatred of Islam, so that in 1947 the S. were expelled from West Punjab. The sect throve in the PUNJAB which its leaders ('guru') wrested from the Mogul empire only to fall under Afghan (1750) and finally British (1849) rule. The last *guru*, Gobind Singh (1675–1708), gave the S. a tight military organization which made them, together with the GURKHAS, the outstanding soldiers of the later Indian army. SHS

Sikh War. (1) (1845–6) was caused by the invasion of British India by the Khalsa army of the PUNJAB, which had assumed control after the death of Ranjit Singh (1839). The well-trained Sikhs were driven back across the Sutlej by Sir Hugh Gough after two pitched battles (Mudki, 18 Dec. 1845, and Firozshah, 21–2 Dec.). Again crossing the Sutlej, they were defeated by Sir Harry Smith at Aliwal (28 Jan. 1846) and finally by Gough at Sobraon (10 Feb.). Casualties on both sides were heavy. By the treaty of Lahore (March) the Sikhs lost cis-Sutlej territory and accepted military limitations; a British resident, Henry Lawrence, was to advise the infant Dulip Singh—9 months later Lawrence became head of a regency council; as part of an indemnity KASHMIR was handed over and subsequently sold to a Hindu.

(2) (1848–9). Lawrence's reforms provoked the hostility of S. chiefs who regarded the 1846 settlement as a mere respite. A local revolt at Multan soon assumed national proportions. After costly and inconclusive battles at Ramnagar (22 Nov. 1848) and Chillianwalla (13 Jan. 1849) Gough shattered the S. army at Gujarat (22 Feb.). The governor-general, Dalhousie, then annexed the Punjab on his own responsibility. MLH

Sikkim, an Indian protectorate under a dynasty established in the mid-17th century. The raja obtained from Nepal a tract separating NEPAL and BHUTAN (treaty of 10 Feb. 1817), ceded Darjeeling to the British in 1835 and put S. under British protection in 1890. India succeeded as the protecting power on 5 Dec. 1950. The political officer in S. also represents the Indian government in Bhutan. SHS

Silures, a large and powerful British tribe occupying the area between the ORDOVICES, the DEMETAE and the west bank of the Severn. They fiercely opposed the ROMAN CONQUEST and despite a defeat in A.D. 51 continued to resist until they were finally conquered in the mid-70s. They became a CIVITAS with their capital at Venta Silurum (Caerwent). CFS

Simony, the purchase of spiritual office or authority for money, named after Simon Magus who offered money in return for apostolic power (Acts VIII, 18–24). In the middle ages the blatant sale and purchase of spiritual office found few defenders although many practitioners; but the problem was complicated by the landed estates and other sources of profit that came under the control of churchmen. In such a case it could be argued that the overlord was entitled to some gain. The problem was never solved, and the standard pun of the middle ages was that the gate of heaven was opened by the key of Simon rather than of Peter.   CFS

Sind, the fertile lowlands of the Indus valley, was the centre of a great civilization of the 3rd and 2nd millennia B.C. In 732 it came under Moslem rule and was in 1590-1 incorporated in the Mogul empire on whose break-up it fell under Persian (1739) and Afghan (1757) sway. The conquest of S. by the SIKHS in the 1830s was opposed by the EAST INDIA COMPANY who had been in treaty relations with the amirs of S. since 1809. The country was placed under British protection in 1839 and, in flagrant violation of the treaties, annexed in Aug. 1843. The amirs were exiled and S. was placed under the BOMBAY presidency. It was separated in 1936 and made an autonomous province in 1937. On the division of India in 1947, S. joined PAKISTAN.   SHS

Singapore (Sanskrit 'Lion town') was founded by Malays from Sumatra c. 1160 and was an important trading centre in the 13th–14th centuries. The Javanese destroyed S. in 1377 and the place was desolate when Sir Stamford Raffles (1781–1826) leased it from the sultan of JOHORE in 1819 and quickly restored its former greatness. The EAST INDIA COMPANY acquired the whole island on 2 Aug. 1824 and in 1826 made it, together with PENANG and MALACCA, an Indian presidency, of which S. became the capital in 1832. S. was under Japanese occupation from 15 Feb. 1942 to 5 Sept. 1945. On 3 June 1959 it was created a state with full internal self-government under a Malayan head of state (Yang di-Pertuan Negara). In 1963 S. entered the federation of MALAYSIA, seceded 7 Aug. 1965 and became an inde-

pendent republic within the COMMONWEALTH on 15 Oct. 1965.

The COCOS ISLANDS in 1882, CHRISTMAS ISLAND in 1888 and LABUAN in 1906 were placed under the governor of the STRAITS SETTLEMENTS and incorporated in S. in 1903, 1900 and 1907 respectively; Labuan was transferred to North Borneo on 10 July 1946, the Cocos Islands to Australia on 23 Nov. 1955.   SHS; IHE

Sinking Fund, first established in 1717 to pay off the NATIONAL DEBT, achieved some success but was raided to increase the CIVIL LIST and reduce taxation. Pitt the younger established a S.F. in 1786, administered by independent commissioners. £1m. was to be set aside annually to buy up stock and re-invest the interest but after the outbreak of war in 1793 money was borrowed at high rates of interest to maintain the S.F., thus creating a loss. It was abandoned in 1828, thereafter casual surpluses were used for debt redemption. A new S.F. was established in 1875, and new schemes were introduced in 1923 and 1928, but funds were frequently diverted to meet extraordinary expenditure.   IHE

Sinn Fein ('We Ourselves'), an Irish political movement formed (1905) by Arthur Griffith to further self-determination. S.F. gained support from the Irish Nationalists' inability to achieve HOME RULE, became republican and supported the EASTER RISING (1916). Led by de Valera and being almost unanimously returned at the 1918 election, it set up a Dáil, declared a republic and organized government services whilst prosecuting the 'Anglo-Irish war' (1920–1). The S.F. as a political power was shattered by disagreement over the treaty of 1922 (IRELAND, PARTITION), de Valera eventually forming FIANNA FAIL (1927). S.F. lost its last 4 seats in the Dáil in 1961 but continues as a nationalist republican party seeking to end partition by force. In 1955 2 S.F. candidates for Northern Ireland constituencies won seats in the U.K.

House of Commons, but were disqualified as felons.   MLH

Six Acts were hurriedly passed (Dec. 1819) to curb radical agitation such as had resulted in PETERLOO: (1) prevented drilling and training in the use of arms; (2) for 27 months authorized seizure of arms in certain counties; (3) prevented imparling in cases of misdemeanour; (4) for 5 years limited meeting upon public grievances to not more than 50 persons living locally, arms, flags etc. being forbidden; (5) empowered seizure of copies of material judged blasphemous and seditious libel; (6) extended newspaper stamp duties to periodicals published more than once every 26 days and costing less than 6d.   MLH

Six Clerks, established by the late 16th century, they received and filed all CHANCERY judicial proceedings, each with 10 subordinates, the Sixty clerks. Since the Six acted very much as parties' solicitors, they regarded their documents almost as personal papers: the resulting confusion makes the tracing of suits difficult. The S.C. were abolished in 1842: their duties passed first to the Clerk of the Writs and Records then, in 1880, to the central office of the Supreme Court.   PMB

Skinner v. **East India Company** (1666–70). Thomas Skinner petitioned the king for redress for damage done to his property in India by the EAST INDIA COMPANY. The case was referred to the Lords who awarded damages. The Company then petitioned the Commons who denied the right of the Lords to exercise original jurisdiction. After sharp conflicts between the Houses the king persuaded them to drop the dispute and erase the records. The Lords ceased thenceforward to claim to be a court of first instance in civil cases.
                                                      IHE

Skippet, see HANAPER.

Slavery. A slave is one who has no rights, can possess nothing of his own and is entirely at the mercy of another. S. of this type occurred in Roman Britain and in Anglo-Saxon England. But from the time of the CONVERSION churchmen worked to ameliorate the conditions of slaves and encouraged emancipation as a form of good works: in various law-codes slaves, by a legal fiction, were given opportunities to purchase their freedom. But considerable numbers still existed in 1066. S. was not common in Normandy, and by the mid-12th century little remained in England. The VILLEIN of the middle ages, although unfree, was not a slave. S. was declared illegal in Britain by Lord MANSFIELD'S JUDGMENT (1772) and abolished in the British Empire by an Act of 1833.   CFS

Slave-trade. Bristol was in Anglo-Saxon times the centre of a prosperous s. between England and Ireland. S. entered a new phase with the colonization of the Americas and from the early 16th century negro slaves were shipped under Portuguese licences from the Guinea coast to the Spanish colonies. English participation in the s. began when John Hawkins broke in on this monopoly (1562–9). The English s. developed steadily in the 17th century with the demands for negro labour in the West Indies, Virginia, Maryland, the Carolinas etc. S. eventually became the monopoly of the African Company which obtained the ASIENTO in 1713, but in the 18th century Bristol and Liverpool merchants acquired most of the trade. QUAKERS opposed it from 1727 but it was not abolished until 1807 after some 35 years of humanitarian agitation. England secured its condemnation by the VIENNA CONGRESS (1815) but the Atlantic s. persisted in various forms until the 1870s.   IHE

Sluys, naval battle of (24 June 1340). In 1340 Edward III planned to invade France by way of Flanders, and the French fleet was concentrated in the Zwyn estuary to block the approaches to Bruges. The French and their Genoese allies were attacked at their moorings at S. by the English fleet commanded by Edward III in person. After a quasi-military engagement, in which Edward employed archers and men-at-arms, the French were decisively beaten and their fleet destroyed. However, Edward neither followed up this victory by a vigorous land campaign nor did he pay much attention to maintaining the command of the Narrow Seas. RFW

Smoke-penny, see HEARTH-TAX.

Socage, a free, non-servile, non-military tenure, encompassing many degrees of freedom from large reserved to nominal rents and services. Land held in s. could be alienated by its tenants: it was divisible among the heirs, though primogeniture was slowly adopted, the heir paying 1 year's rent for entry. Relatively uncommon in the middle ages, s. is now the only fee-simple freehold tenure in England, following the commutation to s. of feudal tenures in 1660 and SERJEANTY, COPYHOLD and other tenures in 1926. PMB

Social Security, Ministry of. In Aug. 1966 the M. of PENSIONS and NATIONAL INSURANCE and the NATIONAL ASSISTANCE BOARD (renamed the Supplementary Benefits Commission) were merged in the M. of S.S. On 1 Nov. 1968 this M. was in turn merged with the M. of Health to form the Department of HEALTH AND SOCIAL SECURITY. MR

Soke, an organization, peculiar to the DANELAW, where rights of private jurisdiction, SAC AND SOC, were exercised. Personal relationships seem to lie behind the s.: the freemen of the 9th-century Danish armies settling in England commended themselves to a lord and acknowledged his court. Thus there are two features peculiar to the s.: tenants were freemen, and the s. was not compact; sokemen could be scattered over many villages. In time the personal tie was replaced by a tie of land: it could not be taken out of a s., though the sokeman could still sell to whom he chose. Some s.s were in decline before the Norman conquest, others lasted until the 18th and 19th

centuries. The modern S. of Peterborough retains the name, though not the form, of the old Danelaw sokes. PMB

Solemn League and Covenant (25 Sept. 1643), an alliance between the English Parliamentarians and the Scots, which both parties considered important for their survival against Charles I. The signatories were pledged to establish PRESBYTERIANISM in England and Ireland 'according to the example of the best reformed churches'. Vane's addition of the phrase 'and according to the word of God' permitted later evasions by supporters of wider religious liberty. The Scots undertook to provide an army in return for a monthly payment of £30,000. IHE

Solicitor. In the early EQUITY courts COMMON LAW practitioners had no place: instead routine work for the parties was done, from the 15th century onwards, by agents, the s.s. Their professional status rose steadily until in the 19th century they dealt with common law and equity business, as well as the specialist and originally separate work of conveyancing and drafting pleadings: their professional and examining body, the Law Society, was formed in 1827. Later, s.s were allowed to represent clients in inferior courts. PMB

Solicitor-General. Crown solicitors are first mentioned in 1461 and a single S.-G. came to be appointed who, from 1530 onwards, regularly succeeded the retiring ATTORNEY-GENERAL. In Elizabeth I's reign the S.-G. was either elected to the Commons or summoned to the Lords to expound legal policy, a link between Parliament and the law strengthened when Attorneys-General were also regularly elected. Both officers, from the 16th century onwards, were assisted by king's counsel learned in the law, an appointment now regarded almost exclusively as a professional distinction. PMB

Solomon Islands, discovered by the Spaniards in 1568, rediscovered by

Carteret and Bougainville in 1767–8. The islands of Bougainville and Buka were annexed by Germany in 1884, occupied by the Australians in 1914 and added to the mandate of NEW GUINEA. The rest of the S.I. became a British protectorate in 1893 (enlarged 1898–9) and forms part of the WESTERN PACIFIC HIGH COMMISSION. The S.I. were occupied by the Japanese from 1942 to 1945.   SHS

Solway Moss, battle of (24 Nov. 1542). In 1540 Henry VIII unsuccessfully tried to persuade James V of Scotland to abandon his pro-Catholic and pro-French policy. Border fighting was renewed (1542) and the English under Norfolk invaded from Berwick. The Scots counter-attacked in the west and were ignominiously routed at S., many prisoners being taken. The news killed James V, the French party was temporarily overthrown, and the treaty of Greenwich (1543) provided for a marriage between the infant Mary Stewart and Prince Edward (later King Edward VI).   IHE

Somaliland was occupied by British forces after the departure of the Egyptians in 1884 and attached to India. In 1887 S. was declared a British protectorate but from 1910 to 1920 control was limited to the coastal towns while the interior was ruled by Mohammed bin Abdulla, the 'mad mullah', who from 1901 waged a 'holy war' against the British. From Aug. 1940 to March 1941 S. was under Italian occupation. On 1 July 1960 S. and the Italian trusteeship territory of Somalia merged in the independent Somali republic.   SHS

Somers Islands, see BERMUDA.

Somme, battle of (1 July–18 Nov. 1916), was the first large-scale mainly British offensive on the western front in WORLD WAR I. After failure of frontal attacks a battle of attrition developed; deteriorating conditions, particularly mud, terminated it. 55 British, 20 French and 95 German divisions were engaged. Casualties: British, 418,654; French, 194,451;

German, about 650,000. Haig's premature use of tanks (32 went into action, 15 Sept.) has been criticized but loss of surprise may be excused by importance of occasion, early discovery of mechanical faults and experience of infantry cooperation.   MLH

Soul Scot, in O.E. times an offering from the goods of the deceased made to the parish priest at the time of burial. It possibly originated in heathen times. Later the term was used loosely to cover all bequests made for religious purposes. It continued throughout the middle ages, in reduced form, as the corpse present or MORTUARY.   CFS

South African Republic, see TRANSVAAL.

South African (Boer) Wars. (1) (1880–1). The Transvaal Boers, disappointed when Gladstone took office (Apr. 1880) and failed to reverse Disraeli's annexation of 1877 or to grant self-government, rose under Kruger's leadership, beleaguering the small British garrisons and defeating relieving forces at LAING'S NEK and MAJUBA HILL. After these humiliations the British granted self-government to the TRANSVAAL by the PRETORIA CONVENTION (Aug. 1881) whilst preserving suzerainty and the right of veto on native legislation. By the convention of London (Feb. 1884) this veto was dropped, the revival of the title 'South African Republic' permitted, suzerainty omitted but still limited by prohibiting diplomatic relations and treaties with foreign powers other than the ORANGE FREE STATE.   IHE

(2) (1899–1902). After the defeat of the JAMESON RAID Afrikaner distrust of the British government was increased by the leniency shown to the raiders. The ORANGE FREE STATE concluded an offensive and defensive alliance with the TRANSVAAL (17 Mar. 1897) and Kruger intensified his warlike preparations, while the British colonial secretary, Joseph Chamberlain, complained of the Transvaal's violation of the London convention of 1884. The appointment of the Liberal imperialist, Sir Alfred Milner, as high commissioner at the Cape (5 May 1897) ensured that British paramountcy in South Africa would be upheld. Milner, convinced that British suzerainty was the solution of the South African problem, tried in vain to persuade Kruger to modify his policies. The failure of the Bloemfontein conference (31 May– 5 June 1899) hastened the drift to war which Milner had come to regard as inevitable. Last-minute negotiations broke down, when British reinforcements arrived at Durban (3 Oct.), Kruger sent an ultimatum demanding their withdrawal. This challenge the British government was unlikely to ignore and war began (12 Oct.). With initially superior forces the Boers besieged MAFEKING and Kimberley and advanced into Natal. After sharp contests at Talana Hill (20 Oct.) and Elandslaagte (21 Oct.) Joubert's forces drove Sir George White's troops into Ladysmith which they invested (1 Nov.). Across the Orange River the Boers occupied Colesberg where many Cape Afrikaners joined them. General Buller, the newly arrived British commander-in-chief, led his main army towards Ladysmith, sending forces under Methuen towards Kimberley and under Gatacre to Colesberg. During Black Week (9–15 Dec.) Gatacre was defeated at Stormberg (10th), Methuen disastrously by Cronje at Magersfontein (11th) and Buller himself by Botha at Colenso (15th). Buller suffered further defeats at Spion Kop (24 Jan. 1900) and Vaal Krantz (5 Feb.). Meanwhile the British effort was intensified by reinforcements, including contingents from Canada, Australia and New Zealand and a new commander-in-chief, Lord Roberts, assisted by Lord Kitchener. Sir John French relieved Kimberley (effected 15 Feb.) and trapped Cronje with 4,000 men at Paardeberg (27 Feb.); Buller at last relieved Ladysmith (28 Feb.). Roberts entered Bloemfontein (13

Mar.) and annexed the Orange Free State (24 May). He next occupied Johannesburg (31 May) and Pretoria (5 June) and by August large-scale fighting was over. Kruger sailed for Europe to seek foreign aid. The Transvaal was annexed (1 Sept.) and at the end of November Roberts left Kitchener to complete the conquest. Instead the war entered a new phase. Boer commandos under such resolute leaders as de Wet, de la Rey, Botha, Smuts, Hertzog and Steyn maintained a successful guerilla warfare. After abortive peace negotiations at Middelburg in March 1901 the conflict became increasingly embittered. The difficulties of rounding up the commandos, often operating in civilian clothing and sheltered by their compatriots, led to Kitchener's systematic destruction of farmsteads and the erection of lines of blockhouses and barbed wire. The dispossessed were interned in inefficiently organized concentration camps and the death rate at the outset was scandalously high (total deaths c. 4,000 women and 16,000 children). The last significant commando success was de Wet's raid on Tweefontein Camp (Dec. 1901) and by the spring of 1902 peace talks were initiated. Retention of independence by the republics was still the stumbling block but agreement was finally reached by the peace of VEREENIGING (31 May), at the cost of some 22,000 British lives (about 16,000 of whom died from wounds and sickness). In addition to concentration camp deaths, Boer losses in the field probably exceeded 5,000.   IHE

South Australia, with Adelaide as its capital, was established in 1836 as a colony of free settlers under a charter granted to the South Australian Association founded by Edward Gibbon Wakefield in 1834. To overcome the colony's economic difficulties, the charter was suspended and S.A. made a crown colony in 1841; its prosperity began with the governorship of Sir George Grey (1841–6) but remained shaky until the mid-1930s. Up to 1850 the immigrants included a large number of religious and political refugees from Prussia. Representative government was instituted in 1851 and responsible government in 1857. S.A. was the first British colony to separate church and state (1851). From 1863 to 1910 S.A. administered the NORTHERN TERRITORY. S.A. joined the Commonwealth of AUSTRALIA on its creation, 1 Jan. 1901.   SHS

South Carolina was colonized under the same proprietary grant as NORTH CAROLINA and the first permanent settlement was established on Charlestown harbour by English emigrants and recruits from the West Indies in 1670. They removed to the present Charleston in 1680. Huguenots, Swiss, Germans and Scots joined the colony and by 1690 North and S.C. were separated. A rebellion against the proprietors in 1719 led to the surrender of its charter. Prosperity was assured by the introduction of rice planting (about 1688) and by 1763 there were some 70,000 negroes to 30,000 whites. In 1775 the secessionist elements took over and with North Carolina it witnessed severe fighting in the campaigns of 1780-1.   IHE

Southern Rhodesia was occupied about 1840 by the Matabele whom the Boers had forced out of TRANSVAAL. They formed a powerful kingdom under Moselikatse (†1868) and Lobengula (1870-94) and oppressed the Mashona tribes in the east. In 1887 President Kruger obtained a fraudulent treaty from Lobengula which would have placed Matabeleland under the control of Transvaal. Thereupon John Smith Moffat, who had befriended Lobengula in 1859 when a missionary and was now a commissioner for BECHUANALAND, was at the instigation of Cecil Rhodes dispatched to Bulawayo, Lobengula's residence, and on 11 Feb. 1888 concluded a treaty which placed Matabeleland and Mashonaland under British protection. The Rudd concession of Sept. 1888 and the Lippert concession of Oct. 1891 gave Rhodes the exclusive rights over all metals and minerals in Lobengula's domain. The British South Africa Company, chartered on 29 Oct. 1889, occupied Mashonaland and founded Salisbury in 1890 and, after a war with the Matabele, captured Bulawayo (4 Nov. 1893) and brought Matabeleland under its control. Company government was established by order-in-council of 18 July 1894; the name Rhodesia was formally adopted in 1895. Risings of the Matabele and Mashona, who massacred a tenth of the whites, were suppressed (1896-7). The post of the company-nominated administrator was in 1896 changed to that of a resident commissioner appointed by the government, and the constitution of 20 Oct. 1898 transferred most of the power of the company to the crown and the white settlers who in 1907 obtained the majority in the legislative council. Churchill's suggestion that S.R. should join the Union of SOUTH AFRICA was rejected twice by S.R. (1907, 1922). On 12 Sept. 1923 S.R. was formally annexed to the crown and on 1 Oct. responsible government was established. The company's mineral rights were bought out in 1933, and S.R., although technically a 'self-governing colony' was treated almost as a full member of the Commonwealth. By a referendum in April 1953 a two-thirds majority endorsed the Federation of RHODESIA AND NYASALAND. This was dissolved in 1963 and S.R. came to be called RHODESIA.   SHS

South Sea Company was founded (1711) as a joint-stock company with the monopoly of British trade in Spanish America and to undertake a conversion of part of the NATIONAL DEBT to a lower rate of interest. It was granted the management of the ASIENTO and annual-ship concession obtained from Spain at the peace of UTRECHT (1713), but its hopes of large-scale trade with the Spanish colonies and of dominating the BANK OF ENGLAND and EAST INDIA COMPANY did not materialize. In 1720 Parliament accepted its offer to take over and convert the total national debt in return for a monopoly of trade to the South Seas. Feverish gambling in South Sea and other stocks followed, with an inevitable disastrous slump ruining many people (the 'South Sea Bubble'). Ministers were involved in charges of corruption and Walpole restored credit by transferring £18m. of South Sea stock to the Bank of England and East India Company. It ceased to trade with Spanish America after 1750 and continued, largely as a financial house, until 1856.   IHE

South-West Africa. The only usable port, Walvis Bay, was occupied by Britain in 1878 and administered (until 1922) by CAPE colony. In 1884 Germany annexed the no-man's land, fixing the frontier with Angola in 1886 and with the Cape in 1890. The Germans surrendered to South African troops under Botha on 9 July 1915. S.-W.A. was entrusted to the UNION OF SOUTH AFRICA as a MANDATE on 17 Dec. 1920. As the United Nations in 1945 rejected the incorporation in the Union, the Union refused a trusteeship agreement and in 1949 virtually transformed S.-W.A. into a province.   SHS

Sovereign, see GUINEA, POUND.

Sovereignty in Great Britain now resides with Parliament and there are no fundamental laws which it cannot alter. In medieval times it resided with the king although it came to be held that he was not above the law. The Henrician REFORMATION established the concept of national s. free from outside authority. The royal supremacy in church and state based on the s. of king in Parliament, rested on Parliamentary statute and laws administered by the courts. The DIVINE RIGHT theories and absolutist tendencies of the Stewarts made the problems of s. the chief cause of the constitutional conflicts of the 17th century. After the GLORIOUS REVOLUTION s. resided in the legislature, although this was not fully realized or claimed until the mid-18th century.   IHE

Spanish Main, the north-east coast of South America between the isthmus of Panama and the delta of the Orinoco, was thus named by the privateers in the 16th–17th centuries. The erroneous application of the term to the Caribbean sea is probably due to Longfellow (*Wreck of the Hesperus*, 1839).   SHS

Spanish Succession War (1702–13) began after Louis XIV of France repudiated the PARTITION TREATY and refused compromise proposals. Both English and Dutch wished to prevent the Spanish Netherlands and colonies falling into French hands and English participation was made certain when Louis XIV forbade British imports, secured the ASIENTO (1701) and recognized the Old Pretender as king of England. The GRAND ALLIANCE declared war (4 May 1702) and was joined by Prussia, Hanover and the Palatinate. Savoy changed over to the allies (1703). Portugal's cooperation was secured by the METHUEN TREATY (1703). France was supported by the Electors of Cologne and Bavaria and initially Savoy. The French plan of ending the war by taking Vienna was defeated at BLENHEIM (1704), and Marlborough's victories at RAMILLIES (1706), OUDENARDE (1708) and MALPLAQUET (1709) drove them out of the Netherlands. In Spain the Archduke Charles received English support. Barcelona (1705) and Madrid (1706) were taken but defeats at ALMANZA (1707) and Brihuega (1710) secured the throne for his rival Philip of Anjou. In Italy the French were at first successful but Eugene's victory at Turin (1706) led to their withdrawal (1707). Elsewhere England took GIBRALTAR (1704), MINORCA and Sardinia (1708) and ACADIA (1710). The Tories, now in office in England, began peace negotiations with France without consulting their allies (1711). England withdrew from the war (July 1712). All powers except Austria and the Empire consequently agreed to the peace of UTRECHT (11 Apr. 1713). France made the peace of Rastatt with the Emperor and the peace of Baden with the Empire in 1714.   IHE

Speaker, the name given to the presiding officers of both houses of Parliament. The lord CHANCELLOR is S. of the Lords but his powers are inferior to those of the S. of the Commons. The latter claims the 'ancient and undoubted' privileges of the Commons from the crown at the beginning of a parliament, is chairman of the House with a casting vote, has powers to censure, suspend and expel members, and certifies money bills. The office emerged in and after the GOOD PARLIAMENT (1376). The S. was at first a crown servant but since 1679 direct royal interference with his election ceased although George III used indirect influence in 1780. The S. ceased to hold ministerial office after 1742 and to take part in debate after 1839. He is elected by the Commons after consultation between government and opposition.

P. Laundy, *The Office of Speaker* (1964). IHE

Speenhamland System, name given to the method of poor relief adopted by the Berkshire justices at a meeting at S., Newbury (6 May 1795). Wages were to be supplemented from the rates according to a basic minimum-wage scale related to the price of bread and the size of the family. This action was due to the distress among the agricultural labourers caused by high prices and low wages. It systematized the practice of outdoor relief already permitted by GILBERT'S ACT (1782) and was endorsed by an act of 1796 which also abandoned the workhouse test. The S.s. was widely adopted in southern and eastern England and to a lesser extent in the north. It kept down wages, tended to demoralize the recipients and greatly increased the rate burden. The Poor Law Amendment Act (1834) was designed to discontinue outdoor relief, except to the aged and infirm, but circumstances prevented its complete abolition. IHE

Spigurnel, see SEAL.

Spurs, battle of the (16 Aug. 1513). In 1511 Henry VIII joined the Holy League of the Pope, Spain and Venice against France, largely over issues in which England was not directly concerned. This royal military adventure met with failure in 1512 but in 1513 Henry landed at Calais, was joined by the Emperor Maximilian, and they besieged Thérouanne. The French relieving force was routed at Guinegate, called the b. of the S. from the speed of the French retreat; but there were few casualties on either side. Thérouanne and Tournai were taken and the latter retained at the peace in 1514. IHE

Stainmore, battle of, near Edendale, Westmorland (954), was fought between Norsemen under Eric Bloodaxe king of YORK and men of English NORTHUMBRIA under their earl. Eric was killed and this battle brought to an end the Norse kingdom of York. CFS

Staller, a Norse loan-word that came into use in England after the Danish conquest (1016). Its meaning was 'place-man', and it seems to have been applied to any important official in the royal household. It was not used after 1066. CFS

Stamford Articles (July 1309). Having achieved the return of Piers Gaveston from exile, Edward II was prepared to make concessions to his barons. The Articles agreed to by the king at the S. parliament amounted, however, to little more than a confirmation of Edward I's ARTICULI SUPER CARTAS. Gaveston's increasing arrogance and Edward's continued favour aggravated baronial discontent and in 1310 led to the establishment of the Lords ORDAINERS. RFW

Stamfordbridge, battle of, on the crossing of the river Derwent, northeast of York (25 Sept. 1066), was fought between the English under king Harold II and the NORWEGIANS under king Harold Hardrada, supported by Tostig, formerly earl of NORTHUMBRIA. The Norwegians, recently victorious at the battle of FULFORD, suffered a crushing defeat, and Harold Hardrada and Tostig were killed. During the absence of the English king in the north, William of Normandy landed on the south coast (NORMAN CONQUEST).   CFS

Stamford Secession (1334). On several occasions in the middle ages groups of masters and scholars left Oxford as the result of town-and-gown fights or disorders within the university itself. In 1238 and 1263 there were 'secessions' to Northampton, and a group of Oxonian exiles seems to have maintained itself at Salisbury from 1238 until 1278 at least. The best-known secession occurred in 1334, when, after their defeat in a fight with the southerners, a group of northern masters and scholars migrated to S. and set up a rival 'university'. The royal authority was soon invoked by Oxford, and stern measures taken by Edward III in 1335 seem to have dispersed the S. scholars for good. It was not until 1827 that Oxford University ceased to demand an oath from its M.A.s not to lecture at S.   RFW

Stamp Act (1765) was carried by Grenville's ministry imposing stamp duties on legal documents, advertisements, newspapers etc. in the American colonies to provide revenue for colonial defence. It raised the question of Britain's right to tax the colonies and riots and resistance made it unenforceable. Representatives of 9 colonies met in the Stamp Act Congress to frame a protest. After its repeal by Rockingham's ministry the DECLARATORY ACT was passed (1766).
                                    IHE

Stamp Duties, at first imposed on paper etc. for legal documents, were later extended to other commodities. A short-lived duty, following continental models, was imposed in 1670, and a general tax in 1690, with stamps ranging in value from 40s. to 1d., the appropriately valued stamp to be fixed to each piece of paper or parchment used for legal business. The subsequent history of the duties is of innumerable variations in scale and scope, generally increasing in the 18th and declining in the 19th and 20th centuries. Scotland, at first exempted by the Act of Union, enjoyed lower rates until 1808, then uniform rates on most documents. The STAMP ACT of 1765 was a contributory cause of the AMERICAN REVOLUTION.   PMB

Stamp Office. Commissioners, known as the Board of STAMP DUTIES, later of Stamp Duties and Taxes, were charged with collecting revenues under the successive Stamp Acts. Though moneys were lodged with the Bank of England, their secretariat, the S.O., organized the whole system. In 1849 the Boards of Stamps and of Excise were amalgamated as the Board of INLAND REVENUE.   PMB

Standard, battle of the (22 Aug. 1138). During the period of the ANARCHY David I of Scots launched a number of invasions of England in order to regain lost territories in the north-west and to win Northumberland, which he claimed by hereditary right, and even Durham. During the invasion of 1138 the behaviour of the Scots was exceptionally brutal and gave the efforts of the English defenders something of the character of a 'holy war'. The defence was organized by Archbishop Thurstan of York, and the army which met the Scots on Cowton Moor, north of Northallerton, had as its rallying point a cart carrying the banners of St Peter of York, St John of Beverley and St Wilfrid of Ripon (probably inspired by the famous *carroccio* of Milan). The mast with its banners gave its name to the battle, and the word 'standard' (Old French *estandard* = banner) entered the English language. The Anglo-Norman army under William, count of Aumale, completely defeated David and the Scots. The victory did not finish the campaign however, and on 9 April 1139, by the treaty of Durham, Stephen secured peace with the Scots only at the price of granting the earldom of Northumberland to David's son, Henry.   RFW

Stanegate, see HADRIAN'S WALL.

Stane Street (O.E. *stan*, stone) two ROMAN ROADS, one running from London to Chichester, another from Braughing (Herts) to Colchester.

CFS

Stannaries, the tin mines of Cornwall and Devon appurtenant to the crown and after 1337 to the duchy of CORNWALL. Mining, known in early times, produced considerable revenues which, in the middle ages, was used to guarantee and repay loans from LOMBARD BANKERS or finance re-coinages. Under the lord warden, vice-warden and stewards stannary courts met, in prosperous times, every three weeks to administer stannary law. Though primarily concerned with trade regulation, other cases were heard for no tinner could be impleaded elsewhere save for life, limb or land. The coinage dues were abolished in 1838 and stannary jurisdiction in 1897, although the lord warden still heads the council of the duchy of Cornwall.

PMB

Staple, in the middle ages a town specially appointed to be an exclusive market for the principal products of England, especially wool. In 1294 Edward I directed that wool should be collected at certain towns and exported to Dordrecht for sale to foreign buyers, thus facilitating the collection of customs. The continental s. was moved to Malines in 1295, to Antwerp in 1296, to St. Omer 1314 and to Bruges after 1325. In 1326 the ordinance of Kenilworth appointed 14 home s.s—York, Newcastle, Lincoln, Norwich, London, Winchester, Exeter, Bristol, Shrewsbury, Cardiff, Carmarthen, Dublin, Cork and Drogheda. The system was abandoned in 1328 but revived by Edward III, to whom the wool trade was an important diplomatic bargaining counter and a security for foreign loans. The continental s. moved with the needs of Edward's diplomacy: to Antwerp in 1337, to Bruges in 1340 and to Middelburg in 1348. The ordinance (1353) and statute (1354) of s.s reappointed most of the home s.s of 1326 except Cardiff and Shrewsbury, adding Canterbury, Chichester and Waterford; English merchants were specifically excluded from the export trade in wool, which was to be carried on by foreign merchants from the English s.s. In 1363, however, a continental s. was established at CALAIS, in English hands since 1347 and made a s. for tin, lead and cloth in 1348. The home s.s were retained as sources of supply for Calais, and the export and sale of wool were concentrated in the hands of 26 merchants, the Company of Merchants of the Staple—a number increased by the mid-15th century to 38. Opposition from other merchants, diplomatic needs and the dubious security of Calais prompted several changes, but from 1392 onwards the continental s. was fixed at Calais. The security of Calais involved heavy royal expenditure on fortification and the maintenance of a large garrison in the 15th century. While the merchants of the s. profited from their monopoly, they paid for the privilege by contributing large loans to the hard-pressed Lancastrian kings and by becoming increasingly responsible for the keeping of Calais. In 1466 Edward IV made them entirely responsible for the financial administration of the port. In general the English wool trade seems to have declined markedly when concentrated in Calais, but the decline is partly attributable to the increase of English cloth manufacture, itself stimulated by the export duties imposed on wool. The s. system was not watertight: apart from the activities of smugglers, individual merchants outside the staplers might obtain royal licences to export, northern merchants were allowed to export direct to the Low Countries, and Italian exporters were not obliged to deal through the s. The importance of the s. continued to diminish with the increase of the English cloth trade and the rise of the MERCHANTS ADVENTURERS. After the loss of Calais in 1558 the overseas s. was transferred to Middelburg and later to Bruges, where it remained until the prohibition of the export of English wool by a proclamation of 1617 effected its abolition. The merchants of the s. turned to the home wool trade, and under the Commonwealth became officially the 'Merchants of the S. of England'.   RFW

Star Chamber, Court of. From an early period subjects' petitions were heard by the king and his council. Edward IV so confined the council's political activities that it dealt almost solely with such matters, particularly criminal petitions and public order: it sat frequently in the S.C. in Westminster palace. The council in its judicial aspect over criminal matters thus became the C. of S.C. Its business was considerable, for it was quicker than the COMMON LAW courts, and was enlarged by statutory offences created by the Tudors. Attacked by the Common lawyers and unjustly described as harsh, it was abolished by the LONG PARLIAMENT in 1640. The COUNCILS OF Wales and THE NORTH had similar jurisdictions.   PMB

Starr. Derived from the Hebrew *sh'tarr* or *shetar*, a contract, the name was applied to all agreements between JEWS and Christians and, occasionally, to other Jewish documents before the Jews' expulsion in 1290. Starrs were written in 2 languages, Latin or Norman-French, with an acknowledgement at the foot in Hebrew: many survive, recording the Jews' diverse activities.   PMB

State Paper Office, developed from informal reference collections of papers made by the personal clerks of successive SECRETARIES OF STATE. It became a formal office with the appointment in 1613 of keepers to register and care for papers deposited with them. From this time until 1782, when the work of the Secretaries was re-arranged, the office accumulated large numbers of reports, despatches, memoranda, minutes, letters etc. of vital importance to historians. In 1852 the collections were transferred to the Master of the ROLLS' charge and are now in the PUBLIC RECORD OFFICE. Though important they are not complete, not only because of the passage of time but also because of the habit of retiring Secretaries of keeping considerable numbers as their private papers. Notable collections, of the Cecils, father and son, are at Hatfield House and in the Lansdowne MSS in the BRITISH MUSEUM.   PMB

Stationers' Company, organized in 1403 and chartered in 1557, comprised the London printers, booksellers and publishers. It was given monopolistic control over PRINTING and PUBLISHING and under the Tudors and Stewarts almost acted as a government instrument, supported by STAR CHAMBER, for the censorship of religious and seditious writings, a position confirmed until 1695 by the Licensing Act of 1662. Their registration system was made part of the COPYRIGHT Act of 1842 but compulsory 'entering' of publications at Stationers' Hall ended in 1923. It became the S. and Newspaper Makers' Company in 1933.   IHE

Statute (Latin *statutum*), a fixed, written declaration reforming old or establishing new rights, procedures, laws, departments etc., at first much concerned with legal affairs, now, by gradual extension, affecting many aspects of everyday life. Early s.s had divers forms, codes of laws, CHARTERS, ASSIZES, instructions to justices etc.; their authority derived first from the king's will, to which the council's, then Parliament's agreement was later added; producing from the later 14th century onwards the distinction between ordinances, made by the king and the council, and s.s, made by Parliament. Parliament's increasing power in legislation is marked by the change from mere presentation for assent, even though drafted at its request, to the use of BILLS, begun in the 15th century, thrice read, a Tudor innovation. In the courts s.s were regarded as new law, compared with the old, unwritten COMMON LAW. Their interpretation, first undertaken by king, council and Parliament, had by the mid-14th century passed to the judges, by then withdrawn from the council.   PMB

Steelyard, the London factory of the HANSE. Occupying quarters between Upper Thames Street and the river from 1320, with additional premises granted by Edward IV (*c.* 1475), the German merchants enjoyed full self-government under their own strict regulations. The S. was attacked by the London mob in 1493 and during the expulsion of the Hanse in 1598–1611 it was used as a naval storehouse. The buildings were destroyed in the FIRE OF LONDON 1666, but subsequently rebuilt and eventually sold in 1853 and demolished in 1863 for the construction of Cannon Street station. IHE

Steinkirk, battle of (3 Aug. 1692). On land the war of the GRAND ALLIANCE went against the allies. When the French, after taking Namur, threatened Brussels, William III attempted a surprise attack at S. but was forced to retreat, the English contingent suffering heavy losses. He abandoned the idea of invading France and was again defeated at Landen or Neerwinden (29 July 1693). IHE

Steward, Lord High. Stewards, king's dishbearers, Latin *dapifer* or *senescallus*, came to England with the Norman ducal household. Of several dapiferships noted in DOMESDAY two, the Courci (later associated with Normandy) and the Bigod became hereditary: Henry II created a third for the earls of Leicester. In John's reign the Bigods renounced their claim to the earls of Leicester, and Simon de Montfort acquired the united office with the earldom. At his death it passed to the earls and dukes of Lancaster and thence, on Henry IV's accession, to the crown. Henry's second son, Thomas duke of Clarence, was created S. for life: since his death in 1421 L.H.S.s have been appointed for special occasions only, e.g. coronations, trials of peers etc. PMB

Steward of the Household, Lord. Though hereditary stewardship-became honorary, working stewards were still required for the royal household. In the 11th and 12th centuries several were appointed; only one, occasionally two, were appointed in the 13th century and from the early 14th century a single S. of the H. has been appointed. At first concerned with the service and, jointly with the MARSHAL, the discipline of the household, stewards acquired political influence as intimate advisers, then reverted to the sovereign's personal service, organizing the affairs and establishment of the household. PMB

Stewarts (Stuarts), the family reigning in Scotland 1371–1714 and in England 1603–1714. Walter Fitz-Alan, a younger son of the lord of Oswestry, became high steward of Scotland in the reign of David I (1124–53) and Walter, the 6th steward, married Margery, daughter of Robert I (Bruce). Their son became king as Robert II in 1371. Then followed Robert III (1390–1406), James I (1406–37), James II (1437–60) and James III (1460–88). James IV (1488–1513) married Margaret, daughter of Henry VII of England. The direct male line ended with James V (1513–42) when the crown passed to his infant daughter, Mary Queen of Scots, whom the Scottish REFORMATION forced to abdicate in 1567 in favour of her one-year old son, James VI of Scotland, who succeeded his great-aunt Elizabeth I in 1603 as James I of England. His son Charles I (1625–49) was executed after the CIVIL WARS. Charles, prince of Wales, was proclaimed king of Great Britain by the Scottish Estates but fled abroad after Cromwell's victories at DUNBAR (1650) and WORCESTER (1651) until the RESTORATION of 1660. In 1685 his Roman Catholic brother, the duke of York, inherited as James II but was driven into exile by the GLORIOUS REVOLUTION of 1688. Mary, the Protestant elder daughter of his first marriage, became joint ruler with her husband, the prince of Orange, William III. Mary died childless in 1694 and her sister Anne succeeded on William III's death in 1702. In 1714 the Stewart monarchy ended with the HANOVERIAN SUCCESSION. James II's

son, James (III), the Old Pretender (1688–1766), was considered the lawful king by the JACOBITES, as were his sons, Charles Edward, the Young Pretender (1720–88), and Henry (IX) who died in 1807 as cardinal of the Roman church and pensioner of George III.
IHE

Stirling bridge, battle of (11 Sept. 1297), the most important victory of William Wallace. Although Scotland had apparently been conquered by Edward I in 1296 and had been formally delivered to Edward by John Balliol, widespread revolts broke out in 1297. The rebels in the south-west were compelled to submit at Irvine (July), but William Wallace and Andrew of Moray gained control of most of central and north-east Scotland. Edward's guardian of Scotland, John de Warenne, earl of Surrey, underestimated the seriousness of the rebellion: when he did move at last, he was soundly defeated by Wallace at S.B. The English hold on Scotland was almost completely broken, and Edward's task of conquest had to be repeated from scratch.
RFW

Stoke, battle of (16 June 1487), the last battle of the wars of the ROSES. In 1486 the Yorkist leaders, Lord Lovell and the earl of Lincoln, arrived in Ireland with Lambert Simnel. Masquerading as the earl of Warwick he was crowned in Dublin as Edward VI (May 1487). Landing in Furness with Irish supporters and German mercenaries they met Henry VII's army at S. near Newark and suffered complete defeat. Simnel was made a royal scullion, Lincoln was killed and Lovell disappeared.
IHE

Stone Age, see PALAEOLITHIC, MESOLITHIC, NEOLITHIC.

Stonehenge, the best-known of the stone-circle monuments although enclosing considerably less space than AVEBURY. Situated in Wiltshire some 8 miles north of Salisbury, the first definite reference to it under this name was in the 12th century A.D. It was reconstructed and altered several times. The first simple erection (Stonehenge I) was in the late NEO-

LITHIC; reconstructed under the BEAKER CULTURE (Stonehenge II), it assumed its known form under the WESSEX CULTURE (Stonehenge III). Its known use ceased c. 1400 B.C., and legends developed that attributed its origin and use to DRUIDS, Romans and even Danes. From the early 17th century it attracted antiquarians and visitors, but no systematic excavation was attempted until 1901. In 1918 it was presented to the nation, and extensive research has taken place in the 1920s and since 1950.
CFS

Stonor Papers, the deeds, accounts and letters of the S. family of S. near Henley, Oxfordshire, 1290–1483. They show the public and private lives of the S.s and their contemporaries both as country gentlemen, with considerable estates, and as merchants of the staple. Sir William S. was attainted in 1483 and his papers, together with his lands, seized by the crown. Though the lands were restored by Henry VII, the papers remained in crown hands and are now in the PUBLIC RECORD OFFICE.
PMB

Straits Settlements, consisting of MALACCA, PENANG, SINGAPORE and (from 1907) LABUAN, was in 1826 organized as an Indian presidency under the name of Incorporated Settlements and in 1832 included in BENGAL (with transfer of the seat of administration from Penang to Singapore). The S.S. became a crown colony in 1867 and was dissolved in 1946.
SHS

Strathclyde, a British kingdom occupying for most of its existence the shires of Ayr, Dumbarton, Lanark, Renfrew and Stirling. Its capital was originally at Carlisle, later at the hill fort of Dumbarton. It was one of the native kingdoms that appeared after the withdrawal of the Roman military forces, and the only one outside Wales and Cornwall that survived beyond the 7th century. Its inhabitants were known to the English as the S. Welsh. Originally it had included territory in north-western England, and this area retained the old name of Cumbria (cf.

Cambria) by which the whole kingdom had once been known. It played a subordinate part in northern affairs and was generally under pressure from NORTHUMBRIA, the PICTS and, later, the VIKINGS. In the early 10th century a temporary military resurgence extended its boundaries to the south of Solway. Although it retained its gains it was during the 10th century twice ravaged by the king of England whose overlordship was three times recognized by the king of S. In 937 he was with other northern rulers defeated at the battle of BRUNANBURH. In 945 S. was ravaged by king Edmund of England who handed it over to the king of the SCOTS. Within a few years it regained a precarious independence, but in 1018 Malcolm II, king of Scots, made Duncan his grandson and heir king of S. On Duncan's succession to the throne of Scotland in 1034 S. lost its separate political identity. Part of its territory in northern England later became an English SHIRE, Cumberland.   CFS

Style and Title, royal, a guide to the descent and aspirations of the crown, as well as changing political circumstances. Among the various titles since the Norman conquest, some were hereditary: duke of NORMANDY, used 1066–1259; duke of AQUITAINE, acquired on Henry II's marriage with duchess Eleanor, 1154–1340; count of POITOU, similarly acquired, 1154–1259; count of Anjou, acquired by the marriage of the empress Maud and count Geoffrey, 1154–1259; elector of HANOVER, 1714–1837. Of the political titles, king of France, adopted by Edward III in 1340, was used until 1801; lord of Ireland, granted to John before his accession by the pope and changed to king of Ireland by Henry VIII, was used from 1199 until the Act of UNION 1801, which also replaced the style king of England and Scotland with the style of Great Britain. The frequent modern changes have been adopted to suit imperial changes: Empress of India, devised in 1876, was dropped when India became independent in 1947; Head

of the COMMONWEALTH was added in 1949, to accommodate new republics. The longest style was that jointly employed by Philip and Mary I, combining English and Spanish titles.

PMB

Sub-Roman Period, the period between the end of ROMAN BRITAIN and the TEUTONIC CONQUEST. It can be taken as beginning c. 430 by which date Roman troops and officials had certainly withdrawn, although the makeshift governmental system by the civitates (CIVITAS) continued until 446, when they made a last vain appeal to Rome. After this time political and military power in the land was exercised by the less civilized and slightly romanized rulers from the west; Vortigern, whose power extended from south Wales to Kent, is the best known. They gave a generation of strong rule, but it was marked by a decline in material standards, the abandonment of towns and VILLAS, and the cutting off of Britain from the rest of the Roman world. On the other hand there was a revival of Celtic art, great activity by the BRITISH CHURCH, and a large-scale invasion of Brittany. In the west this phase lasted into the 6th century: in the east the Teutonic invaders had established themselves before the end of the 5th century despite strong opposition with which the name of Arthur (ARTHURIAN LEGEND) is associated.   CFS

Subsidy, a medieval term loosely used to cover a financial grant to the crown over and above customary revenue. It was used more specifically in 3 cases, all of which required parliamentary sanction: (1) A tax on MOVABLES first imposed under Edward I. This was later known as the Fifteenth and Tenth; its results were recorded in the s. rolls. (2) A tax on lands and goods first successfully levied in 1514. It is usually known as the Tudor s. and continued until the civil war; its results were recorded in the s. books. The standard grant on any one occasion was one s. and two fifteenths and tenths. (3) S. on wool, including wool-fells and leather, was first levied by Edward III to help meet the expenses of the HUNDRED YEARS' WAR. This export tax of 40s. per sack on wool was additional to the ancient custom of ½ mark per sack first imposed in 1266. It eventually became part of the general customs system.   CFS

Succession Acts. The act of 1534 fixed the succession on the issue of Henry VIII and Anne Boleyn, bastardized Mary, created new treasons for any criticism of the new marriage and imposed oaths to maintain these provisions. It was cancelled by the act of 1536 asserting the rights of any issue of the marriage with Jane Seymour and creating new treasons and new oaths. Henry could also settle the succession by will or letters patent. This provision was retained in the act of 1544 which vested the crown in Edward, Mary and Elizabeth in that order. Henry's will of 1546 put the heirs of his younger sister Mary, duchess of Suffolk, next in line after the heirs of his children.   IHE

Sudan (Arabic, '(country of) the blacks') was conquered in 1821–2 by Mohammed Ali, khedive of Egypt, and administered as his and his successors' personal estate, with, from 1830, Khartoum as the capital. From 1869 British administrators were employed, among them Charles Gordon (governor of Equatoria 1874–6, governor-general of the S. 1877–9) who established orderly government and fought the slave-traders. Otherwise the Egyptian record was one of misgovernment and inefficiency. This led in 1881 to the revolt of the Mahdi, Mohammed Ahmed, who quickly made himself the ruler of the S. An Egyptian expedition commanded by Col. William Hicks was wiped out near El Obeid (5 Nov. 1883) and the last bastion, Khartoum, fell on 25 Jan. 1885, owing to the pusillanimity of the British Liberal government who, although since July 1882 in control of EGYPT, wished to abandon the S. and sacrificed their emissary, Gordon, and his men. The reconquest of the S. took 13 years and was achieved by Kitchener (battle of OMDURMAN, 2

Sept. 1898) and Wingate (defeat and death of the Khalifa, the Mahdi's successor, 24 Nov. 1898); only Darfur remained independent until 1916. A French attempt to seize the S. was prevented by Kitchener who in Sept. 1898 stopped the French advance at FASHODA; the boundaries were fixed on 21 March 1899.

An Anglo-Egyptian condominium was agreed upon (19 Jan. 1899), which made the S. autonomous under a governor-general appointed by the khedive on the recommendation of the British government. The condominium was re-affirmed in the Anglo-Egyptian treaty of 26 Aug. 1936. An elected legislative assembly was created in 1948. On 12 Feb. 1953 the co-domini agreed on the complete Sudanization of the administration, police and army; this was completed by Dec. 1954. The first all-Sudanese cabinet took office on 9 Jan. 1954, and the S. became a sovereign independent republic on 1 Jan. 1956.   SHS

Suez Canal, a 101-mile shipping lane across the isthmus of S. connecting the Mediterranean and Red Sea, was constructed by the French engineer Ferdinand Vicomte de Lesseps (1805–94), who followed up projects drafted by scientists accompanying Napoleon I to EGYPT. Lesseps's plan was approved by Said Pasha in 1854 and financed by Napoleon III and the *Compagnie Universelle du Canal maritime de Suez*, which was founded in 1858 and obtained a 99-year concession for running the canal (1869–1968). The British government, parliament and press strongly opposed the S.C., and not a single one of the 400,000 shares was taken up by British investors. Construction began in 1859 and the canal was opened to traffic on 17 Nov. 1869. In 1875 Disraeli bought the 176,602 shares of the bankrupt Khedive Ismail for £4m. (the money being advanced by Rothschild, anticipating parliamentary approval) and thus secured British government control of this vital link with India. The convention of Constantinople (29 Oct. 1888), signed by all European maritime nations, declared the S.C. 'open to vessels of all nations' and 'free from blockade.' The 1936 treaty between Britain and Egypt created the S.C. zone where British troops, withdrawn from Egypt proper, were concentrated; but on 19 Oct. 1954 Britain recognized the S.C. as an integral part of Egypt and the canal zone was finally evacuated on 13 June 1956. On 26 July 1956 President Nasser nationalized the S.C. British attempts to secure the interests of the canal users were thwarted by the American secretary of state, John Foster Dulles, who was also the leading opponent of the Anglo-French military operation aimed at re-establishing international control of the S.C. (Nov. 1956). In 1958 the S.C. company recognized the nationalization in return for £28m. payable 1959–64, and changed its name to Suez Financial Company.   SHS

Suffragette Movement. The term s. was coined about 1906 to denote a militant supporter of female parliamentary suffrage. Women's right to vote, advocated in William Thompson's *Appeal* (1825) and first subjected to legislative denial in the 1832 REFORM ACT, was championed in Parliament from the late 1860s by J. S. Mill and Jacob Bright amongst others. Many local suffrage societies (the first permanent one being formed by Lydia Becker in Manchester, 1867) were affiliated in 1893 to the National Union of Women's Suffrage Societies under the presidency of Mrs Fawcett. Its methods—private member's bills and petitions—educated opinion but neither political party would support legislation. Members of the Women's Social and Political Union (organized by Mrs Emmeline Pankhurst in 1903) therefore attempted to coerce the Liberal government of 1905. Mildly lawless advertisement was later accompanied by arson; hunger strikes by female prisoners were met by forced feeding (the 'Cat and Mouse' Act (1913) enabling temporary release of physically weak strikers). Such militant tactics, which irritated supporters and confirmed opponents, were halted by the First World War. In 1918 the vote was given to women over 30 who (or whose husbands) were local government electors; finally all adult women were enfranchised in 1928.   MLH

Sulung, a PLOUGHLAND (O.E. *suhl,* a plough), being the area that could be kept in cultivation by a ploughteam of 8 oxen in the year. It was larger than the HIDE, consisting of possibly 200 acres of arable land with appurtenant rights in woodland, pasture etc. It was subdivided into 4 yokes. The s. was unique to KENT and was later adopted as the unit of taxation assessment there.   CFS

Sunday Schools (1) in England substantially date from 1780 when the printer, Robert Raikes (1735–1811) opened his school in Gloucester. Poor children were taught reading, the catechism etc. and were afterwards taken to church. The idea spread rapidly and a society for establishing S.s. was founded in 1785, supported by most denominations. Teachers, at first paid, were soon replaced by enthusiastic volunteers who carried out valuable pioneer work in elementary education on a religious basis. S.s. developed in Ireland from the 1780s and similar work was begun in Scotland by the evangelist James Haldane in the late 1790s.   IHE

(2) in Wales were first organized by the Methodist, Thomas Charles, *c.* 1789. They soon displaced CIRCULATING SCHOOLS and became the most potent medium of popular education. By 1846 their pupils numbered 296,000 and as late as 1905, 222,000. They have had a character of their own, being intended for adults no less than children. Before state schools were founded, and afterwards, they exercised an enormously beneficial interest in extending literacy, fostering the discussion of abstract ideas and raising the level of general as well as religious education.   GW

Supplementary Benefits Commission, see SOCIAL SECURITY.

Supplication against the Ordinaries (18 Mar. 1532), presented by the Commons to Henry VIII, was based on a petition of 1529 revised by Thomas Cromwell and set in motion by the crown. It attacked clerical jurisdiction and particular abuses but stressed the objections to independent legislation by the church. The king referred it to Convocation which prepared a not unsatisfactory reply, but Henry insisted on their acceptance of his proposals. No canons were to be enacted without royal licence and existing canon law was to be reviewed by a committee nominated by the crown. Thus the king used the S. to become the master of Convocation, which was effected by the submission of the clergy (15 May).   IHE

Supply, Ministry of. Following the precedent of the Ministry of MUNITIONS, the M. of S. was created in 1939 to provide all war material except aircraft and ships. Since the second world war it has had a variety of additional tasks, including the supply and development of aircraft, development of atomic energy and control of the iron and steel industry. De-nationalization and the establishment of independent bodies soon detached various of these functions, and in 1959 the M. was dissolved: some of its functions were transferred to the Ministry of AVIATION, others to the service departments.   PMB

Supremacy, Acts of. The act of 1534 declared that the king 'justly and rightly is and ought to be supreme head of the Church of England', with power to make ecclesiastical visitations, reform and correct heresies and abuses. This did not merely set aside papal authority but marked the establishment of the royal supremacy over the national church. On Elizabeth I's accession a second breach with Rome was effected and by the A. of S. (1559) the queen was styled supreme governor 'as well in all spiritual or ecclesiastical things or causes as temporal'.

The change of title from head to governor inevitably led to the lessening of the crown's personal control in favour of the crown in parliament.   IHE

Surinam (Netherlands Guiana) was discovered by Alonzo de Ojeda in 1499, visited by Dutch traders from 1551 and settled by English colonists in 1630. Charles II assigned the colony to Lord Willoughby and Lawrence Hyde in 1663; it changed hands several times but was returned to the Netherlands by the peace of Breda (31 July 1667) in exchange for New Amsterdam (NEW YORK). It was again conquered by the British in 1799, restored to the Batavian Republic by the peace of AMIENS (1802), reconquered in 1804 and finally handed back to the Netherlands in 1816.   SHS

Surrey, probably a primitive PROVINCIA which, until it was finally incorporated in WESSEX in 825, was at various times under the control of that kingdom, KENT or MERCIA. After 825 it became a SHIRE of Wessex. See also MIDDLESEX.   CFS

Suspending Power, the use of the royal PREROGATIVE to suspend entirely the operation of a law. Instances of its use in matters of trade and taxation occur from the 11th century but it was not often used. The constitutional conflicts of the 17th century greatly affected the prerogative and Charles II had to cancel his DECLARATION OF INDULGENCE (1672), Parliament having declared this use of the s.p. illegal. The use of the s.p. by James II caused the SEVEN BISHOPS to petition against it. The use of the s.p. without consent of Parliament was made illegal by the BILL OF RIGHTS (1689).   IHE

Sussex, the kingdom of the South SAXONS, occupied the area of approximately the modern county of S. less Hastings and its surroundings. Although Teutonic settlers came early and in considerable numbers, it was primitive and backward. Nothing is known of its kings between Ælle (BRETWALDA) who conquered the area in the last quarter of the 5th century and Æthelwalh who was baptized about 675. It was the last kingdom to be converted to Christianity. The scanty evidence that survives indicates that S. at any one time had more than one king. In 685 it was conquered by Cædwalla, king of WESSEX, but lost to Wessex after his death; in 722 and 725 it was invaded by Ine, king of Wessex; in the later 8th century it was controlled by Offa, king of MERCIA. In 825 the men of S. submitted to Egbert, king of Wessex; and S., including the area around Hastings, became a SHIRE of Wessex.   CFS

Sutton Hoo, a village near Woodbridge, Suffolk, overlooking the estuary of the river Deben, where in 1939 an undisturbed ship-burial was excavated (now in the British Museum). No body was found but it commemorates an EAST ANGLIAN king of the earlier 7th century. It is one of the richest of such burials found anywhere in Europe, and its discovery revolutionized ideas of the wealth and cultural contacts of 7th-century English kingdoms.   CFS

Swan River Settlement, see WESTERN AUSTRALIA.

Swans, Feast of the (22 May 1306). On Whit Sunday Edward I knighted his eldest son, Edward of Carnarvon, who in turn created 300 knights in a magnificent ceremony. At the feast which followed, swans were carried in, and the king swore 'before God and the swans' to avenge Robert Bruce's murder of the Red Comyn—and his usurpation of the throne of Scotland. In the following summer Edward I set out on what was to be his last Scottish campaign.   RFW

Swaziland was occupied by the Swazi about 1820, kept its independence between Boers and Britons who however in 1890 agreed to place it under the administration of the SOUTH AFRICAN REPUBLIC. From 1902 S. was in charge of a British commissioner and in 1906 together with BASUTOLAND and BECHUANALAND was placed under a High Commissioner for the 3 terri-

tories. It became an independent Kingdom within the COMMONWEALTH on 6 Sept. 1968.   SHS; IHE

Tables, the name given to a group of four representative committees which practically assumed control of Scotland in 1637 to resist Charles I's innovations. They drew up the National COVENANT and prepared for war.   IHE

Taff Vale judgement (1901). The T.V. Railway successfully sued for damages the Amalgamated Society of Railway Servants which supported a strike. The award (£23,000) was reversed on appeal but upheld in the Lords where it was found that a TRADE UNION was sufficiently a legal entity to make it liable for tortious acts. Until this decision it was widely assumed that the 1871 Trade Union Act had granted immunity. The unions sought political redress, in particular by supporting the embryo LABOUR PARTY, and this was obtained by the Trade Disputes Act (1906).
                                                        MLH

Talavera, battle of (27–8 July 1809). Wellesley (Wellington), advancing up the Tagus with 20,000 men and attempting to cooperate with 35,000 Spaniards under the incompetent Cuesta, was faced 70 miles S.W. of Madrid by 40,000 French under Victor and King Joseph. Victor's attacks were almost wholly upon the British lines and after very heavy fighting (Wellesley called it a 'murderous battle') the French withdrew. British casualties were 5,365 compared with French losses of 7,268, but Wellesley had lost over a quarter of his force. This and a hopeless supply situation prevented pursual of the victory in the PENINSULAR WAR.
                                                        MLH

Tallage, a tax raised in two fields: manorial t. was paid by VILLEINS at the lord's will, as an obligation of the unfree; royal t. fell on ancient DEMESNE, notably towns and boroughs, forfeited and escheated lands. The name was first used in 1173–4, though similar taxes, complementary to feudal dues, had been levied earlier. Based on special assessments, t.s were often connected with campaigns. They were abolished by the 1340 Parliament, by which time new methods of taxation, such as AIDS and SUBSIDIES, had been developed. PMB

Tally, a medieval accounting device: a peg of wood was notched with cuts of varying sizes for each denomination of money, then slit down the centre. The creditor received the stock, hence the Stock Exchange etc., the debtor retained the foil: the parts were reunited and retained by the debtor when the debt was discharged or otherwise acknowledged. The burning of old Exchequer tallies, struck until 1826, led to the destruction by fire of the old palace of Westminster in 1834. PMB

Tamworth Manifesto (1834), Peel's address to his constituents at T. prior to the election of Jan. 1835. Intended for a wider audience, the T.M. was a ministerial appeal in the cause of orderly government by a prime minister (newly appointed and without parliamentary support) contending with novel circumstances arising from the REFORM ACT. Peel accepted this act as 'final and irrevocable' and pledged review of grievances 'without infringing on established rights'. Although the principles of the T.M. became identified with the growing CONSERVATIVE PARTY (led by Peel in the succeeding years but organized by others), it had nothing in common with the modern party programme. MLH

Tanganyika in 1890 became the colony of 'German East Africa' after agreements with Britain and the sultan of ZANZIBAR. The German forces resisted throughout the first world war and capitulated only on 14 Nov. 1918. In May 1919 the territory became a British MANDATE (transformed into a TRUSTEESHIP in 1946); Ruanda-Urundi was allotted to Belgium and the Kionga triangle to Portugal. Slavery, which was maintained by the Ger-

mans, was abolished in 1922. A legislative council was set up in 1926, responsible government was introduced in 1959, and T. became fully self-governing on 1 May, independent on 9 Dec. 1961 and a republic on 9 Dec. 1962. On 26 Apr. 1964 T. combined with Zanzibar to form the United Republic of T. and Zanzibar, renamed TANZANIA (29 Oct.).

SHS; IHE

Tangier, the capital of the Roman and later Byzantine province of Tingitania, was conquered by the Arabs (682) and Portuguese (1476) and was in Spanish hands 1580–1656. As part of the dower of Charles II's Portuguese queen, Catherine of Braganza, it became English in 1661 and proved a valuable base for the English trade in the Mediterranean and for operations against the BARBARY CORSAIRS. Charles, however, in 1683–4 evacuated it allegedly as too expensive, in fact to oblige Louis XIV. After the division of Morocco between France and Spain (27 Nov. 1912), T. was constituted a demilitarized international zone guaranteed by France, Spain and Great Britain. It was annexed by Spain in 1941 but re-established in 1945. On 29 Oct. 1956 the international status was abolished and T. was incorporated with Morocco. SHS

Tariff Reform Movement, see FREE TRADE, IMPERIAL PREFERENCE.

Tanzania. The name adopted (29 Oct. 1964) by the United Republic of TANGANYIKA and ZANZIBAR. It is a one-party state and the 'interim constitution' of 1964 provides for a separate executive and legislature for Zanzibar. IHE

Tasmania was discovered by Abel Tasman in 1642 and named Van Diemen's Land after the governor o the Dutch East Indies; it was renamed T. in 1853. It was visited by Cook in 1777 but its insularity was ascertained only in 1798. The island was used by NEW SOUTH WALES as a convict settlement from 1803 to 1853; the first juvenile reformatory was established in 1835. It became a separate colony in 1825 and was granted representative government in 1851 and responsible government in 1856. The last native (of originally perhaps 2,000) died in 1869. T. joined the Commonwealth of AUSTRALIA on its creation, 1 Jan. 1901. SHS

Taxation, see AID; CENSUS; DANE-GELD; CUSTOMS AND EXCISE; HEARTH TAX; INCOME TAX; INLAND REVENUE; MAJOR-GENERALS; MOVABLES; POLL TAX; SCOT AND LOT; SCUTAGE; STAMP DUTIES; SUBSIDY; TALLAGE; TAXA-TION OF NICHOLAS IV; TOLL; VALOR ECCLESIASTICUS; WINDOW TAX.

Taxation of Nicholas IV. In 1291 pope Nicholas IV granted Edward I six years' tenths from the clergy for a crusade (never undertaken). In 1292–3 papal collectors made a new survey of every benefice in England to assess the tenth: the surveys were copied into two volumes, one for each province, known as the *Taxatio.* Until super-seded by the VALOR ECCLESIASTICUS, most ecclesiastical taxation was assessed by these books. PMB

Technology, Ministry of. A Com-mittee of the PRIVY COUNCIL for Scientific and Industrial Research set up in 1915 became the Department of Scientific and Industrial Research under the Lord President of the Council in Dec. 1916. Under the Department several research boards were established to study specific fields of scientific and industrial research. When the M. of T. was established in Oct. 1964 it took over the industrial research work of the Department and its boards, fundamental scientific research becoming the responsibility of the Science Research Council. In Feb. 1967 the M. of T. took over those functions of the M. of Aviation which were not related to civil avia-tion. In Oct. 1969 the M. of T. took over responsibilities for regional eco-nomic development from the Depart-ment of ECONOMIC AFFAIRS and the industrial functions of the Board of TRADE; at the same time the Minister of T. became also Minister of Power. The M. of T. is also responsible for the Atomic Energy Authority and the National Research Development Cor-poration. MR

Tel-el-Kebir, battle of (13 Sept. 1882), was a decisive defeat of the Egyptian army under the nationalist leader Arabi Pasha by a small British force commanded by Sir Garnet Wolseley. The battle was followed by the surrender of Cairo citadel (to 150 British soldiers) and the occupation of EGYPT; Wolseley (1833–1913) was promoted general and created a peer. SHS

Templars, the military order of knights, sergeants and chaplains foun-ded c. 1118 by Hugh de Payens, with headquarters in the temple area of Jerusalem, had as its primary objec-tive the protection of pilgrims on the road from the coast to Jerusalem. The T., who wore a red cross on a white ground, adopted a form of the Cistercian rule in 1128, when the order received papal confirmation. By the mid-12th century the order had been endowed with properties through-out western Christendom: individual houses or preceptories were grouped into regions or *langues,* but the government was highly centralized, all members owing direct obedience to the grand master. The Old Temple in London was the head house in England from c. 1128 until its replace-ment by the New Temple in 1184. The earliest English foundations, e.g. Shipley (Sussex), Cowley (Oxon.) and Cressing (Essex), date from the reigns of Henry I and Stephen; by the early 14th century the T. possessed some 50 houses in England. Two of them served as hospitals, but the majority were centres for managing and farm-ing the T.' estates and for recruiting; they had few resident members, usually only the preceptor and one or two others. There were only 165 T. in England in 1308, when the English revenues of the order amounted to £4,720 a year. The T. rendered valuable service to the crown as ban-kers, and the master of the Temple was frequently summoned to Parlia-ment.

Although the T. were not as unpopular in England as in France, Edward II followed papal directions and had them arrested and their property seized in Jan. 1308. Special commissions, including papal inquisitors, subsequently investigated the frightful accusations against the knights. Their sufferings were not as terrible as in France, but sufficient evidence of guilt was obtained, often under torture, to make pope Clement V dissolve the order in 1312. Its property was conferred on the HOS-PITALLERS, but some was evidently disposed of to the profit of Edward II and his friends.   RFW

Tenth and Fifteenth, see MOVABLES.

Test Act (1) (1673), passed by the CAVALIER PARLIAMENT and directed against Roman Catholics, broke up the CABAL but also affected Protestant NONCONFORMISTS. All holders of civil and military offices had to be communicants of the Anglican Church, repudiate transubstantiation and take the oaths of ALLEGIANCE and SUPRE-MACY. (HALES'S CASE, TOLERATION ACTS.)

(2) (1678), was passed after the POPISH PLOT excluding all Roman Catholics, except the duke of York, from both houses of Parliament.

(3) (Scotland, 1681). All state and municipal officials had to declare their belief in the Protestant faith, but the addition of conflicting clauses by the court party produced the resignation of 80 episcopal clergy and the president of the court of session. IHE

Testa de Neville, see FEES, BOOK OF.

Tettenhall, battle of (in Staffordshire, 5 Aug. 910). The English under king Edward the Elder won a decisive victory over the Northumbrian DANES of the kingdom of YORK, who could henceforward do nothing to check the reconquest of all England south of the Humber by the king of WESSEX.   CFS

Teutonic Conquest of Britain, carried out by ANGLES, JUTES, SAXONS and, possibly, FRISIANS. Although Teutonic attacks by sea and land had been increasing since the 3rd century A.D., later literary tradition dates the beginning of the T.c. to 449 when Hengest and his followers, settled in KENT as FOEDERATI, turned to conquest on their own account. Saxon groups attacked on the south coast and the Thames estuary in the late 5th and early 6th centuries and established the nuclei of the kingdoms of SUSSEX, WESSEX, MIDDLESEX and ESSEX. These southern invaders were loosely joined under Ælle of Sussex, the first BRETWALDA. For nearly two generations after their defeat by the Britons at the battle of Mons BADONICUS they did not advance west of later Hampshire, but this pause may have been due to consolidating gains already won rather than to the severity of their defeat. The conquest of the midlands is not recorded in literary sources: it began probably in the later 5th century, mainly via the rivers of the Wash and Humber, and resulted in the establishment of the kingdoms of EAST ANGLIA, MERCIA, the MIDDLE ANGLES and, possibly, DEIRA. The settlement of the north was originally a coastal settlement of the mid-6th century and resulted in the setting up of the kingdom of BERNICIA. By the mid-6th century the invaders held not much more than the eastern third of the country; but by the early 7th century a fresh surge forward had taken them to the Irish Sea, the Bristol Channel and, apparently, the Firth of Forth. This split the remaining Britons into 3 separate groups. Those of the south-west (Devon and Cornwall) were finally conquered in the 9th century; but elsewhere the permanent limits of T.c. were the Firth of Forth and the approximate line of OFFA'S DYKE. The T.c. differed from the other conquests of historic time, the ROMAN and the NORMAN, in the length of time it took, in being a general settlement of people rather than a military conquest, and in resulting in a fundamental change in all aspects of life in the territory conquered. But the actual conquest was carried out by kings and their WAR-

BANDS, not by a general movement of settlers. CFS

Tewkesbury, battle of (4 May 1471), a decisive YORKIST victory in the wars of the ROSES which assured Edward IV's retention of the throne. Despite the news of BARNET, Queen Margaret and her son Edward made a last effort on behalf of Henry VI, crossing from France, raising the LANCASTRIANS of the south-west and making for Wales. Edward IV was swiftly in pursuit; Margaret failed to cross the Severn at Gloucester, held for Edward, and was finally overtaken at T. Prince Edward, the only son of Henry VI, was killed, and a dozen Lancastrian leaders were either killed or captured and executed. Queen Margaret was captured shortly afterwards. RFW

Thegn (O.E.: one who serves), replaced during the 9th century the word GESITH. T.s held land in return for service and their status was hereditary. Various tenurial arrangements were made between t.s and their lords, and the general tendency in later Old English times was towards greater dependence and lowering of economic standards, encouraged in part by the absence of primogeniture. But such did not affect their aristocratic status for the poorest t. had a WERGILD of 1,200*s*. or, in NORTHUMBRIA, 2,000 *thrymsas*. Their influence in society depended largely on the importance of their lords; thus the king's t.s, in direct personal relationship with the ruler, were the most important. Their duties consisted of attendance on the king, attendance at the Witenagemot (WITAN), military service, to which they brought their own followers, and duties in central and local administration. In the 11th century it was held that a king's t. was one who had a specific duty in the king's court and possessed a church, kitchen, bell house, fortified dwelling and an estate assessed at 5 HIDES. The heirs of a deceased king's t. had to pay a large HERIOT to the king before they could succeed to their inheritance. They held their lands by CHARTER and in judicial matters were responsible to the king alone. Their importance was somewhat lessened by the introduction of HOUSECARLES, but it was the Norman conquest that severely reduced their powers and status, and the term died out soon after. The term mass-t. was frequently used in O.E. times to describe a priest. CFS

Third Penny, originated before the Norman conquest, when the EARL was the local representative. He received as maintenance a third of the judicial profits of the shire (COUNTY) COURT and of customary payments from the boroughs within his area. The t.p. survived the conquest but gradually lapsed. PMB

Thorough, the name given to the methods of government associated with Laud and Strafford, especially to the latter's administration of Ireland (1632–9). It signified strong, orderly and efficient rule and devotion to the service of king and state, but was based on corruption and tyrannical use of the PREROGATIVE. At this time the words 'thorough' and 'through' were interchangeable. IHE

Three Resolutions, see ELEVEN YEARS' TYRANNY.

Throckmorton Plot (1583). Francis T., an intermediary between Mary Queen of Scots and her agent Morgan, suspected by Walsingham's agents, was arrested and tortured and revealed the existence of a projected invasion. The duke of Guise was to command a force sent by Parma from the Netherlands, and, reinforced by English Catholic exiles, they were to place Mary on the English throne. T. was executed and Mendoza, the Spanish ambassador, was sent home (1584). IHE

Tibet. In 1774 Warren Hastings sent a mission to the regent of T. and established friendly relations. No definite agreements, however, were concluded for over a century. When T. was on the point of becoming a Russian protectorate, Lord Curzon sent an armed mission under Col. Younghusband to Lhasa (1904), and a convention opened 3 Tibetan markets for Indian trade. Several attempts between 1906 and 1920 to achieve a permanent settlement of the international status of T. foundered on Chinese intransigence. T.'s incorporation by force in the Chinese People's Republic (1950) has been acknowledged *de facto* by India but not by Great Britain.   SHS

Ticonderoga, battle of (8 July 1758), a British defeat in the Anglo-French struggle in North America during the SEVEN YEARS' WAR. As part of the plan to conquer CANADA the British took Louisbourg (July) and occupied Fort DUQUESNE (Nov.), but Abercrombie's senseless though gallant frontal attacks on Montcalm's entrenchments at T. were repulsed with heavy losses. Fort T. was subsequently abandoned by the French (26 July 1759) in the face of Amherst's advance.   IHE

Tinchebrai, battle of (28 Sept. 1106), fought between Henry I and his eldest brother Robert 'Curthose' for the duchy of NORMANDY. On the death of William the Conqueror in 1087 his dominions were divided as he had desired, the duchy of NORMANDY passing to his eldest son, Robert, and the kingdom of England to his second son, William Rufus. The arrangement satisfied neither. By 1091 William had occupied Normandy east of the river Seine, and in 1096 Robert mortgaged the duchy to his brother to raise money for the First CRUSADE. By the time of Robert's return in the autumn of 1100 William had been killed in the NEW FOREST and had been succeeded by his younger brother Henry. A serious rebellion in favour of Robert broke out in both England and Normandy, but by the treaty of Alton (1101) Robert recognized Henry as king of England and himself retained Normandy. Henry however, once firmly established in England, embarked on the conquest of the duchy and achieved his object in the three campaigns of 1104, 1105 and 1106. Robert was defeated and captured by Henry

at T. and was imprisoned until his death in 1134. England and Normandy were reunited under Henry I, but his possession of Normandy became secure only after his victory at BRÉMULE.   RFW

Tithe, one-tenth of the increase of all living things to be given to the church. Until the 9th century it was voluntary although encouraged, and could be given to support any form of religious activity. From the reign of Edgar (959–75) it was made compulsory and the recipient was to be the old MINSTER, unless a lord had built a church with a graveyard when the t. was to be divided 2 : 1. After the Norman conquest lords were allowed comparative freedom with their DEMESNE t., a large proportion of which was granted to monasteries. From the 10th century t. became an important element in the income of the PARISH priest, and a source of constant conflict between priest and people.   CFS

With the progressive appropriation of parochial t.s by monasteries, cathedrals and bishops in pre-Reformation Britain, rectors were replaced by vicars who were usually given the small t.s, the great or rectorial t.s being retained by the appropriators. After the DISSOLUTION impropriations created further financial difficulties for the church and with the rise of the Puritans payment of t. became an increasing grievance (especially with Quakers from the 1650s). T. was retained during the Protectorate in spite of its attempted abolition by BAREBONE'S PARLIAMENT (1653), and was again an important political issue immediately before the Restoration. In the 17th and 18th centuries t. was a deterrent to improving landlords, and INCLOSURES were first opposed by t. owners who feared loss of income. Commutation began before 1600 and the clergy were the losers in a world of rising prices but much had taken place before the T. Commutation Act of 1836 (see T. REDEMPTION COMMISSION).

T.s or teinds were retained by the Church of Scotland after the Reformation and revenue problems were eventually settled by the Church of Scotland Properties and Endowments Act (1925).

In Ireland the payment of t. to the minority Church of Ireland was an especial grievance to Roman Catholics, shared by the Presbyterians of Ulster. Resentment showed itself by acts of terrorism from the 1760s with the rise of the WHITEBOYS. After the T. war of the 1830s the T. Commutation Act (1838) substituted a rent charge fixed at 75% of the original t.   IHE

Tithe Redemption Commission. Discontent over the payment of tithes increased by movements for inclosure and the consequent apportionment of responsibility. The first national attempt to commute all tithes to a single rentcharge was adopted in 1836, and tithe commissioners were appointed to administer it. Their work was much concerned with inclosure, and in 1882 their functions were merged with the Copyhold and Inclosure Commissioners into the new Lands Commissioners, absorbed by the Board of Agriculture in 1889. Tithe rentcharges, however, caused continuing discontent, and acts of 1936 and 1951 commuted them to a lump sum redeemable by instalments up to A.D. 2000, and the T.R.C. was appointed to administer the plan. On 1 Apr. 1960 the T.R.C. was dissolved and its functions transferred to the T.R. Office of the Board of INLAND REVENUE.   PMB; MR

Tithing, a group of ten men, first mentioned in the law code of king Cnut (1017–35) when it was laid down that each free man over the age of 12 years should be in a t. By putting responsibility on the group the good behaviour, attendance at court etc. of its members could be better secured. The concept of the t. probably originated in the 10th century, and from it developed the FRANKPLEDGE system.   CFS

Tobago was discovered by Columbus in 1498, successively claimed or occupied by Spain, the Netherlands (1632) and Courland (1654–83), de-

clared neutral in 1684 and frequently changed hands between France and Britain (1762–81, 1793–1802) until it was finally ceded to Britain in 1814. In 1889 T. was separated from the WINDWARD ISLANDS and attached to TRINIDAD. T. fits best Robinson Crusoe's imaginary island.   SHS

Togoland was declared a German protectorate on 5 July 1884. Treaties with Britain (1890, 1899) and France (1897) delimitated the frontiers with Gold Coast and Dahomey. On 29 Aug. 1914 T. surrendered to Nigerian, Gold Coast and French troops and on 30 Sept. 1920 was divided between Britain and France, both being placed under League of Nations MANDATE and, in 1946, under United Nations TRUSTEESHIP. The British portion was administered by the GOLD COAST with which it was amalgamated on becoming independent GHANA (6 March 1957).   SHS

Toleration Acts. As a result of their attitude to the GLORIOUS REVOLUTION a T.A. (1689) was passed allowing Protestant NONCONFORMISTS their own places of worship, teachers and preachers, subject to certain oaths and declarations. Further relief came from the lapsing of the LICENSING ACT in 1695 and the repeal of the SCHISM and OCCASIONAL CONFORMITY ACTS (1718). The TEST and CORPORATION ACTS were repealed in 1828 but annual Indemnity Acts had been passed since 1727. Non-Trinitarians secured toleration in 1812. Saville's Act (1778) and the Catholic Relief Act (1791) gave freedom of worship and education to Roman Catholics, followed by political CATHOLIC EMANCIPATION (1829). JEWS gained relief by acts of 1846, 1851 and 1858. Atheists were admitted to Parliament in 1888.   IHE

Toll, the right to levy certain dues, later used to describe the dues themselves. In boroughs etc. t.s were a widespread form of local taxation, levied on sales, at markets, for the upkeep of bridges, roads etc.: they were paid both by townsmen and incomers. Freedom from t., granted either to an individual or to a community by the king or a liberty holder, was much prized as an aid to freer trading. PMB

Toll and Team. These words are first found amplifying a grant of private jurisdiction in the reign of Edward the Confessor, but the processes they imply are earlier. TOLL gave the grantee power to exact a payment on sales of livestock, goods etc. within his estate, and team the power to hold a court where the proper possession of such goods could be proved. PMB

Tolpuddle martyrs (1834) were the subject of the best-known incident in the early history of TRADE UNIONS. Six agricultural labourers (led by George Loveless) had combined to resist wage reductions. With the connivance of Melbourne (home secretary) they were sentenced to 7 years transportation on a trumped-up charge of administering illegal oaths. The government feared a recurrence of the agricultural insurrection of 1831. After continuous agitation the T.M. were pardoned (1836); one returned to T., the others emigrated to Canada.

T.U.C., *Book of the Martyrs of Tolpuddle* (1934). MLH

Tonga or **Friendly Islands,** the ancient seat of a highly civilized race which in the 13th century ruled over SAMOA and FIJI, was discovered by Tasman in 1643 and visited by Cook in 1773 and 1777. From 1822 Methodist missionaries converted the whole population to Christianity. An independent kingdom was established in 1845 and declared neutral by the great powers in 1886. An Anglo-German agreement of 14 Nov. 1899 led to the proclamation of a British protectorate on 18 May 1900. In 1875 King George Tupou I granted a constitution with privy council, cabinet government, legislature and independent judiciary. His granddaughter, Queen Salote, on 26 Aug. 1958 concluded a treaty which gave her complete internal and extensive external

autonomy while preserving British protection. A new treaty was effected on 30 May 1968. SHS; IHE

Tories, originally denoting Irish Roman Catholic bandits, the term was applied to the Abhorrers during the struggle over the EXCLUSION BILLS in the reign of Charles II. Supporters of NON-RESISTANCE, they upheld the hereditary succession and the PREROGATIVE. Supporting the privileges of the CHURCH OF ENGLAND and opposing toleration of NONCONFORMISTS and Roman CATHOLICS, they acquiesced in the GLORIOUS REVOLUTION of 1688. Some extremists championed the JACOBITES at the time of the HANOVERIAN SUCCESSION and this resulted in their exclusion from office in the reigns of George I (1714–27) and George II (1727–60). They ceased to be an organized opposition but remained the church party when official society was Whig. The younger Pitt, although he never called himself a Tory, re-created the party from diverse sources including courtiers, ex-Whigs and KING'S FRIENDS with a more liberal programme than their opponents. Opposition to the ideas of the French Revolution of 1789 gave them a similar advantage to that enjoyed by the WHIGS after 1714, but as a result they became reactionary, failing to appreciate the needs and problems of post-Waterloo Britain; their opposition to Parliamentary REFORM brought defeat in 1830. In the next decade the T. began to be called the Conservative Party and for a long time the older name came to be associated with reaction. The two terms are now used indiscriminately. IHE

Torres Vedras, see PENINSULAR WAR.

Tractarianism, see OXFORD MOVEMENT.

Toulouse, battle of (10 April 1814), was the last battle of the PENINSULAR WAR. Soult had retreated to T. on the Garonne. By skilful engineering Wellington crossed the wide river and attacked the commanding Calvinet ridge, $\frac{1}{2}$ mile north of the city. A premature assault by the Spanish was beaten but at length British troops under Sir W. (Lord) Beresford gained the height and Soult abandoned T.

MLH

Towton, battle of (29 March (Palm Sunday) 1461), was the largest and most fiercely contested action in the wars of the ROSES. After the DEPOSITION of Henry VI the Lancastrian army had withdrawn to the north. Edward IV followed, forced the crossing of the Aire at Ferrybridge on 28 March and encountered the main Lancastrian forces, perhaps 20,000 strong, at T., three miles from Tadcaster. Despite their superiority in numbers the LANCASTRIANS were eventually routed after a ten-hour battle in a snowstorm, with especially heavy casualties among the northern lords. Edward captured York and secured the north, and returned to London for his coronation on 28 June while Henry VI and Queen Margaret took refuge in Scotland.

RFW

Trade, Board of, originated in the first colonial period. Committees of T. were sporadically appointed from 1622 onwards: the Committee for T. and Plantations set up in 1650 was replaced at the Restoration by 2 councils, one for T., one for colonies. These were re-united in 1695 and so remained until 1768, when colonial affairs were finally separated from trade. A board, replacing PRIVY COUNCIL committees, was set up in 1786, giving the department, whose head came to be called president, its final form. Of the department's early duties, negotiation of commercial treaties, colonial affairs, import and export regulation, some still remain. Now primarily concerned with all aspects of t., including merchant shipping and civil aviation, the board has at various periods been concerned with technical education, mines, fisheries, railways, company regulation, industrial disputes, labour exchanges etc., the majority now administered by new, specialist departments.

PMB; MR

Trade Unions were a product of the INDUSTRIAL REVOLUTION. In the 18th century local clubs of skilled craftsmen developed in urban areas. They were liable to repression first by statutes relative to particular trades or by action at common law, then by the COMBINATION ACTS (1799, 1800). After their repeal (1824) there followed development of t.u. in textiles and mines and the first unsuccessful efforts to organize nationally; fear of Owen's Grand National Consolidated T.U. (1833) was a factor in repression, a notable example of which created the TOLPUDDLE MARTYRS (1834). With relief of trade depression in the late 1840s t.u. became stronger in organization and finance, and became less local. The Amalgamated Society of Engineers (1851) served as a model for national u. of skilled workers; in these friendly benefits were particularly important.

In the 1860s t.u. cooperated first locally (London Trades Council, 1860) then nationally (annual T.U. congresses from 1868) to exert political pressure for labour law reform, in which they were helped by enfranchisement of unionists by the REFORM ACT (1867). This resulted in the T.U. Act (1871), granting legal status and giving advantage to t.u. registering as FRIENDLY SOCIETIES; and the Conspiracy and Protection of Property Act (1875), substantially amending the Criminal Law Amendment Act (1871) which had limited strike action and forbidden peaceful picketing (legalized in 1859). After 1871 there was more recognition of t.u. by employers and a growth of local negotiating machinery.

A lengthy period of depression (1874–87) was followed by a quick expansion of t.u., the cardinal feature of which was combination of unskilled workers (e.g. in the docks, railways, agriculture); the success of the 1889 London dock strike accelerated the process. The new t.u. had a more militant policy than those of the skilled and were more socialist in outlook; a movement began to form a working-class party in Parliament (INDE-

PENDENT LABOUR PARTY, 1893). By demonstrating the legal insecurity of t.u. the TAFF VALE case (1901) persuaded the T.U.C. to support independent representation in what became the LABOUR PARTY. This judgment's effects were reversed by the Trade Disputes Act (1906) which put t.u. in a privileged position of immunity from liability in tort. The T.U. Act (1913), reversing the OSBORNE JUDGMENT, legalized the political levy (from which a member could contract out). In the years before the First World War there was a further sharp rise in membership (2·5m. in 1910, 4·1m. in 1914), occurring disproportionately amongst the new u. of the unskilled; amalgamations became more frequent. Increasing labour unrest was evidenced by large-scale strikes, partly under the influence of syndicalism.

After the war industrial relations remained bad despite further development of negotiating machinery and culminated in the GENERAL STRIKE (1926). Its failure was a heavy blow to the t.u. movement; the t.u. did not regain their 1926 membership (5·2m.) for 10 years. The Trade Disputes and T.U. Act (1927) declared general strikes illegal, restricted the right to picket and substituted contracting into for contracting out of the political levy. It was repealed by the Labour government in 1946. The report of the Donovan Committee (1968) was followed in 1969 by the introduction of legislation intended to curb unofficial strikes. Since the Second World War the process of amalgamation has continued. In 1965 there were 580 registered t.u. (735 in 1951) with a membership of 10·2m.; 247 had under 500 members but the 18 largest (each over 100,000) had a total of 6·9m. members.   MLH

Trafalgar, battle of (21 Oct. 1805), Nelson's victory over the combined French and Spanish fleets, the last great naval action in sail. When Napoleon's plans for the invasion of England were frustrated, he ordered Admiral Villeneuve to the Mediter-ranean for an attack on Naples. Villeneuve left Cadiz (19 Oct.) with 33 ships of the line. When the British fleet of 27 ships found them some 10 miles off Cape T., Villeneuve turned about and headed north in a single ragged line. Nelson attacked from the west in two parallel columns, leading the weather line of 12 ships himself, the lee division of 15 ships acting independently under Admiral Collingwood. The Franco-Spanish fleet was cut in two. No British ship was lost but Nelson was killed. The enemy lost 18 ships and British sea supremacy was secure for a hundred years. IHE

Trailbaston, (Norman-French, a man with a club). During Edward I's and Edward II's wars outbursts of lawlessness, particularly armed robbery, occurred in England. In the 1290s inquiries into vagrancy were irregularly commissioned. In 1305 t. justices on five circuits were appointed to deal with all felonies and trespasses committed since 1297. Similar commissions were issued in 1314, and KING'S BENCH heard some t. cases. Such pleas were abolished in 1344, jurisdiction over like offences passing to JUSTICES OF THE PEACE.   PMB

Train-bands, originated under an order of Elizabeth I (1573) that a 'convenient number' in every county levied under commissions of ARRAY were to be sorted in bands and trained. Never adequately disciplined or trained, the t.b. were summoned by Charles I against the Scots in 1639 and both sides endeavoured to use them in the CIVIL WAR (MILITIA BILL). They were not prepared to leave their localities and only the London t.b. proved of value.   IHE

Transjordan, the country east of the river Jordan, was on 25 April 1920 created a British MANDATED TERRITORY under the Hashimite amir Abdullah ibn Hussein and on 25 May 1923 separated administratively from PALESTINE. In 1925 the port of Aqaba was acquired from Saudi Arabia. The army (Arab Legion), from 1931 organized by (Sir) John Glubb, became the most efficient Arab force. On 22 March 1946 T. was recognized as an independent sovereign state; the amir assumed the title of king (25 May) and changed the name of the country to JORDAN (17 June). SHS

Transport, Ministry of. Merchant shipping and railways were originally the responsibility of the Board of TRADE. Between 1917 and 1921 and again in 1939 responsibility for merchant shipping passed to a M. of Shipping; a M. of T. was established in 1918 to oversee roadbuilding, railway amalgamations, etc.: the two were amalgamated in 1941 as the M. of War T. This became the M. of T. again in 1946. In 1953 the department was amalgamated with the M. of Civil Aviation, founded in 1946 to administer civil aviation, hitherto an AIR MINISTRY responsibility. In Oct. 1959 responsibility for civil aviation was transferred to the M. of AVIATION, and in Feb. 1965 responsibility for merchant shipping returned to the Board of Trade. The Ministry's work now covers roadbuilding, road licensing and safety, and road and rail transport. In Oct. 1969 the Minister of T. became a subordinate of the Secretary of State for LOCAL GOVERNMENT AND REGIONAL PLANNING.

PMB; MR

Transportation Act (1774), one of the INTOLERABLE ACTS. British officials accused of capital offences in MASSACHUSETTS committed in the course of duty (e.g. suppressing riots) could be removed to other colonies or England for trial. IHE

Transvaal. The territory between the rivers Vaal and Limpopo was occupied by some 20,000 Boers from the CAPE during the GREAT TREK of 1836–7, joined by Boers from NATAL after 1846. The republic set up in 1852 was recognized by Britain in the SAND RIVER CONVENTION; but in 1853 broke up into the South African Republic and the republics of Leydenburg, Utrecht and Zoutpansberg, the latter rejoining the South African

Republic in 1857–60. President Pretorius (1853–71) in 1857 invaded the ORANGE FREE STATE and 1860–3 was the president of both republics. In the 1860s further secessions were prevented by Commandant Paul Kruger, but the state church split in three irreconcilable denominations. The *volksraad* (parliament) connived at the annexation by the governor of Natal in 1877; but the population rose in Dec. 1880 and after severe defeats at LAINGS'S NEK and MAJUBA HILL Britain maintained only a vague suzerainty (PRETORIA CONVENTION, 1881). Certain reservations about foreign and native affairs were waived in the London convention of 27 Feb. 1884.

The discovery of gold on the Witwatersrand in 1884–6, together with the diamond finds in the Orange Free State and Griqualand West, brought about the industrial revolution of South Africa and, by employing African labour, destroyed tribal life. Industrialization, symbolized in the rapid growth of Johannesburg (founded 1886), was accompanied by much graft, nepotism, bribery and lawlessness under the corrupt administration of President Kruger (1883–1900). The country, where by 1895 the ratio of uitlanders to burghers had become 7 : 3, would inevitably have fallen under British rule, but for the ill-advised JAMESON RAID of Dec. 1895. It caused the resignation from office of Cecil Rhodes and the collapse of his policy of reconciling Boer and Briton, black and white, and secured the re-election of the discredited Kruger who now deliberately aimed at a showdown with Britain. His ultimatum of 10 Oct. 1899 unleashed the SOUTH AFRICAN WAR. The peace of VEREENIGING (1902) transformed T. into a British colony. After the restoration of responsible government (1907) it joined the UNION OF SOUTH AFRICA in 1910. SHS

Travancore, allied itself to the EAST INDIA COMPANY in 1784 and on 1 July 1947 formed a union with Cochin which in 1959 was merged in KERALA.

SHS

Treason, appeal of, a novel and irregular procedure employed first by the opponents of Richard II for the destruction of the king's friends, and later by Richard himself against his enemies (lords APPELLANT, MERCILESS PARLIAMENT). The appellants laid before the king in parliament articles detailing acts of the accused alleged to constitute treason—the definition of the statute of TREASONS (1352) being ignored. The lords temporal investigated the articles and pronounced judgment.   RFW

Treasons, statute of (1352), defined what crimes should constitute high treason, viz. to 'compass or imagine' the death of the king, the queen or their eldest son and heir; to violate the queen or the king's eldest unmarried daughter or the wife of the heir to the throne; to make war against the king or to adhere to his enemies within his realm; to give aid or comfort to the king's enemies either within the realm or elsewhere; to counterfeit the king's seals or money or to import false money; and to kill the chancellor, the treasurer or any of the king's justices 'being in their place doing their offices'. The s. distinguished high from petty treason and declared that other grave crimes should be treated as felony or trespass; uncertain cases should be referred to the king in parliament. Clear definition of treason was desirable in view of the severity of the penalties—ESCHEAT of the traitor's property to the king as well as death—and of the many condemnations of the troubled 1320s. The s. has remained the essential foundation of the English law of treason.   RFW

Treasurer. One of the many chamberlains in the post-Norman-conquest household achieved supremacy over the Winchester treasury, becoming known first as t.-chamberlain then, by the early 12th century, as t. Simultaneously the EXCHEQUER developed, with the t. at its head, presiding at its sessions and receiving royal financial instructions. Throughout the medieval and Tudor periods the t. was a high officer of state and the king's intimate councillor. In the Tudor period he became known as lord t. The office lapsed in 1714 when, after nearly a century of experiment, its powers were permanently entrusted to the TREASURY board.   PMB

Treasury. In Elizabeth I's reign, notably during Lord Burghley's term of office, the Lord Treasurer withdrew from the EXCHEQUER. In 1653 the office was first put in commission as the T. Board which by 1660 had acquired its own staff, administering newer sources of finance. From 1714 onwards lords commissioners of the T. have regularly been appointed: only in the mid-19th century, after the abolition of the Exchequer, did the T. become a ministerial department under the CHANCELLOR OF THE EXCHEQUER, though the lords commissioners still exercise some formal powers. Few of the T.'s powers are statutory, but derive from its close connexion with the government of the day: the PRIME MINISTER is its first lord and the government Whips are lords commissioners. Responsibility for economic affairs and planning passed (1964–9) to the Department of ECONOMIC AFFAIRS; responsibility for the payment and management of the civil service passed on 1 Nov. 1968 to the CIVIL SERVICE DEPARTMENT.

                            PMB; MR

Treasury Notes. £1 and 10s. notes issued by the TREASURY from 1914 until 1928 when they were replaced by BANK OF ENGLAND notes.   IHE

Treasury Solicitor, an office dating from at least 1655 when the t.s.'s duties were chiefly to attend king's counsel in revenue cases. Treasury business remained his pre-occupation until 1842, when his services as legal adviser and solicitor were first made available to other government departments. From 1685 to 1696 the T.S. was responsible also for political and censorship prosecutions, a duty revived 1884–1908, when the office was combined with that of Public Prosecutor. Since 1876 the T.S. has acted as PROCURATOR-GENERAL.   PMB

Treaty, a solemn agreement between two or more sovereign powers whether kings or elected representatives. The term is occasionally misapplied, e.g. to the t. of Leake 1318 between the earl of Lancaster and the MIDDLE PARTY. A t. is valid only after ratifications, generally letters patent, have been exchanged. Medieval t.s were often proclaimed, e.g. Anglo-French t.s in Gascony by the senschal, a procedure made unnecessary by modern means of communication. PMB

Trek, see GREAT TREK.

Trengganu, see UNFEDERATED MALAY STATES.

Trent case (1861). Early in the American civil war, on 8 Nov. 1861, Captain Wilkes of the U.S.S. *San Jacinto* seized two Confederate envoys, James Mason and John Slidell, with their secretaries from the British mail steamer T., which was one day out from Havana. Public opinion was inflamed on both sides of the Atlantic. The Prime Minister Lord Palmerston reworded his original, ultimatum-like dispatch at the Prince Consort's suggestion, giving the U.S. government the chance to disown the action of Captain Wilkes. Troops were sent to Canada and the fleet ordered to readiness. However, the envoys were released, though without apology, and reached London (Jan. 1862) where they were coldly received by the foreign secretary, Lord Russell. IHE

Trial by Battle, a defence against criminal charges introduced as an alternative to the ORDEAL at the Norman conquest and later extended to civil cases, notably under the writ of RIGHT. Battle was first waged in court then fought before a judge on an appointed day: in criminal cases the parties fought in person, including APPROVERS; in civil cases champions were used. The procedure declined in importance with new legal practices but battle was waged as late as 1817, leading to its abolition in 1819. PMB

Tribal Hidage, a record of the number of HIDES belonging to each PRO-VINCIA in MERCIA and among the MIDDLE ANGLES and to each kingdom south of the Humber. The oldest surviving manuscript is of the late 9th century, but the information applies to the late 7th or 8th century. It was probably compiled to enable Mercian kings to assess the dues owed them; and it is of very great importance for the information it gives concerning ancient units of local government. CFS

Triennial Act (1641) was passed by the LONG PARLIAMENT making provisions to ensure that Parliament met at least every three years, thus preventing the possibility of another ELEVEN YEARS' TYRANNY. The Act was repealed in 1664 by another T.A. Parliament was to meet at least once in three years but no provision was made for its enforcement if the king chose to disregard it. Charles II held no Parliament between 1681 and 1685. Therefore the T.A. of 1694 was passed to ensure that Parliament met every 3 years and did not last more than 3 years. This stipulation was set aside by the SEPTENNIAL ACT. IHE

Triers and Ejectors. The INSTRUMENT OF GOVERNMENT (1653) protected the puritan clergy and secured their revenues. Cromwell appointed a commission of 35 Triers drawn from Presbyterians, BAPTISTS and INDEPENDENTS to approve clergy to be appointed by private patrons (20 Mar. 1654). Local commissions of Ejectors were formed (28 Aug.) to remove all 'scandalous, ignorant and insufficient' clergy and schoolmasters. They condemned the use of the Prayer Book as well as immorality but overall they acted tolerantly. IHE

Trinidad was discovered by Columbus on 31 July 1498 and annexed for Spain but actually occupied only in 1592. Sir Walter Raleigh in 1595 raided the island which in the 17th–18th centuries was a base of the buccaneers. The Spanish crown admitted Roman Catholic settlers, chiefly French, from 1783 by which time the original Carib population had virtually died out. The Spanish governor surrendered T.

to Rear-Admiral Henry Harvey and General Sir Ralph Abercromby on 18 Feb. 1797; the cession was confirmed by the treaty of AMIENS (1802). The abolition of slavery in 1834 led to a large-scale immigration of East Indians whose descendants now form nearly half the population. In 1889 TOBAGO was administratively united with T. On 27 March/22 April 1941 defence bases on T. were leased to the U.S.A. for 99 years.

A legislative council was set up in 1831; complete internal self-government was granted in 1956. T. joined The WEST INDIES in 1958 but opted out of it in 1962 and thereby caused the break-up of the federation. On 31 Aug. 1962 T. and Tobago became an independent member of the COMMONWEALTH.   SHS

Trinity House, Corporation of (Tower Hill, London), the principal pilotage authority of the United Kingdom; also controlling the lighting and marking of the coastline and certain maritime charities. It is managed by nine master mariners and one senior officer of the Royal Navy as active Elder Brethren, chosen from the ranks of Younger Brethren. In 1512 the gild of mariners and lodesmen of Deptford Strond, Kent, sought a charter from Henry VIII to practise pilotage and encourage the arts of navigation. Its pilotage powers were strengthened in 1604 and ultimately defined in 1913 (Pilotage Act). T.H. was empowered to set up beacons and marks (1566) and acquired the Lord High Admiral's rights of buoyage and beaconage in 1594. Private lighthouses, encouraged by patents of James I, were bought out by T.H. under an Act of 1836, and its lighting and marking duties defined in 1894. The corporation settled in the City in 1670 (Water Lane) moving to Tower Hill in 1795.
IHE

Trinoda Necessitas ('threefold obligation'), frequently used as a technical term by historians to cover the three public services in Old English times of work on bridges and BURHS, and FYRD service. There is no con-
N

temporary justification for the use of the term, and *trinoda* is a misreading of *trimoda*. However, these services did form a special group and exemption from them was rarely granted. CFS

Trinovantes, a non-Belgic (BELGAE) tribe in the area of Essex and S. Suffolk. They were under pressure from the CATUVELLAUNI and so favoured Julius Caesar when he attacked the latter in 54 B.C. Early in the 1st century A.D. they were conquered by the Catuvellauni and in 43 by the Romans. The COLONIA of Camulodunum (Colchester) was established in their territory, and it was probably the loss of land to this that drove them to join the revolt of the ICENI in 61. Possibly they did not become a CIVITAS but were administered from Colchester. This, until c. 100, was also the administrative centre for all ROMAN BRITAIN.   CFS

Triple Alliance (1) (1668), between England, the Netherlands and Sweden to check the aggressions of Louis XIV of France, causing him to make peace with Spain while retaining his conquests in the Netherlands. It was destroyed by the treaty of DOVER (1670).

(2) (1717), between Great Britain, France and the Netherlands against Spain. France was to expel the Old Pretender, demolish the fortifications of Mardyke and DUNKIRK in return for guarantees of the French succession.

(3) (1788), between Great Britain, Prussia and the Netherlands for defence and maintenance of the status quo. It successfully settled the Baltic conflict (1788–90), restored Austria's hold on the Netherlands (1790), supported Britain's claim to NOOTKA SOUND against Spain (1790) and ended Austria's war with Turkey (1791). Diverging aims drove Britain and Prussia apart in 1792.   IHE

Tripura. This ancient Hindu state, formerly ruled by Maharajahs joined INDIA in Oct. 1947 and became a Union Territory on 1 Sept. 1956.
IHE

Tristan da Cunha, the only inhabited island of a group of 4 islands, named after a Portuguese admiral who discovered it in 1506. Used by the Americans as a naval base in the war of 1812–14, it was annexed by Great Britain and made a dependency of CAPE COLONY from which it was transferred to ST HELENA in 1938. An island council was set up in 1932. As H.M.S. *Atlantic Isle* (commissioned in 1942) T. is an important meteorological and radio station.

The sudden outbreak of a volcano, believed to be extinct, in Oct. 1961 made necessary the complete evacuation of the population, which however returned in 1963.   SHS

Troyes, treaty of (21 May 1420), between Charles VI of France and Henry V of England, was the result of Henry's military successes and, more directly, of his alliance with Philip the Good, duke of Burgundy. Henry was to marry Charles's daughter Catherine —and did so on 2 June—and was declared heir to, and regent of, the kingdom of France which Charles was to retain for his lifetime. No union of England and France was provided for, however. The dauphin (later Charles VII), disinherited by the treaty to which he was not a party, still held half of France, and little progress was made towards its conquest. While the treaty may be regarded as the high water mark of English fortunes in the HUNDRED YEARS' WAR, it is unlikely that it could ever have been fully enforced. Henry's early death (1422) and the eventual breakdown of the Anglo-Burgundian alliance made its failure certain.   RFW

Trucial States, see PERSIAN GULF.

Truck Act (1831) was passed to curtail the t. system, by which workers were paid partly in goods or in tokens valid only at tommy-shops in which employers had an interest. The wages of specified 'artificers' were to be paid wholly in coin, domestic servants being excepted. Amendments of 1887 widened the scope to include all manual workers (special provision being made regarding those in agriculture), of 1896 regulated deductions for bad work etc. and of 1960 (in force, 1963) authorized payment by cheque.   MLH

Trust territories, the former 'B' and 'C' MANDATED TERRITORIES of the LEAGUE OF NATIONS, which in 1945 were placed under the trusteeship council of the UNITED NATIONS (art. 77 of the charter). Of the COMMONWEALTH t.t., TOGOLAND was united with GHANA in 1957, the CAMEROONS with NIGERIA and the (ex-French) Cameroon republic in 1961, and Western SAMOA became independent in 1962. The Union of South Africa refused to place SOUTH WEST AFRICA under the trusteeship system and virtually incorporated the territory in 1949.   SHS

Tudors traced their descent to ancient Welsh royalty through Ednyfed ap Cynwrig (†1246), seneschal of GWYNEDD. In return for his services his descendants held land by privileged tenure free of all dues other than military service. The name derived from his great-great-grandson, Tudur (†c. 1367); and the eldest line, T. of Penmynydd, continued as obscure squires in Anglesey until the 17th century. One of Tudor's sons, Maredudd, ESCHEATOR of Anglesey before 1392, was father to Owain (†1461), the first to take the style of T., who entered Henry V's household and c. 1429 clandestinely married Henry's widow, Catherine. Their sons were Edmund (†1456), created earl of Richmond 1452–3, and Jasper (†1495), earl of Pembroke, principal mentor to his nephew, Henry, 2nd earl of Richmond, during his exile in Brittany (1471–85) and created duke of Bedford by him after BOSWORTH. Henry VII was the posthumous son of Edmund by Margaret BEAUFORT, inheritrix to the LANCASTRIAN claim to the throne. His triumph was regarded by his fellow-countrymen, on whose support he had heavily relied, as vindication of ancient messianic prophecies of the ultimate restoration of a prince of Welsh blood to the throne of Britain. The dynasty was continued by Henry VII's only surviving son, Henry VIII (1509–47), and Henry VIII's three legitimate children, Edward VI (1547–53), Mary I (1553–8) and Elizabeth I (1558–1603), all of whom died without issue.   GW

Tufa, a battle-standard of late Roman times. Bede (†735) tells that Edwin king of NORTHUMBRIA (617–32) had one carried before him. The name was anglicized to *thuuf*.   CFS

Tun, Old English: enclosure, the meaning being extended to include a large isolated farm or a village. It is the commonest element in English place-names. Its derivative, town, was later used to describe an urban community, but this usage is never found in O.E. times.   CFS

Tunnage and Poundage, subsidies of separate origin but, from 1350, granted together. T., a payment per tun of wine imported, appeared as a custom in the 12th century, but from 1350 was granted nationally as a SUBSIDY. P. originated in the 13th century as a custom of 3*d.* per £ of the value of all imported and exported goods. From 1415 the subsidies were granted to sovereigns for life, though Charles I's collection of them without previous parliamentary consent became a major political issue.   PMB

Turkey Company, see LEVANT COMPANY.

Turks and Caicos Islands. The T.I. were occupied from BERMUDA in 1678 for their valuable salt deposits and annexed to the BAHAMAS in 1804. The C.I. were settled by loyalists from GEORGIA in the 1790s and administered from the Bahamas. In 1848 the T. and C.I. were constituted a presidency under the governor of JAMAICA and 1873–1962 a dependency of Jamaica and in 1962 a CROWN COLONY.   SHS; IHE

Turnham Green, see EDGEHILL.

Turnpike. In Tudor times the maintenance of the highway was a parish obligation but roads continued to deteriorate. The first T. Act (1663) gave the justices of 3 counties powers to set up t.s (gates) and charge tolls on traffic for road improvement. From the early 18th century local companies as t. trusts were given similar control over short stretches of road by private acts of Parliament. These trusts increased rapidly between 1750 and 1770 and a General T. Act was passed in 1773 to facilitate their establishment. Never controlling the greater part of the highway and mostly in debt, they had effected great improvements by 1790 making faster coach traffic possible. From 1888 county councils assumed responsibility for main roads and the t. trusts were wound up between 1865 and 1895.   IHE

Tynwald, Court of (*thingvöllr*, Old Norse 'land assembly'), the governing body of the Isle of MAN, consisting of the governor, council and House of KEYS.   SHS

Tyrone's Revolt, see O'NEILL'S REVOLT (1594–1603).

Uganda, claimed by Germany in 1885, was ceded to the British EAST AFRICA COMPANY in 1890 by the HELIGOLAND treaty, pacified by Capt. Lugard (1891–2) and transferred to the crown in 1894. The most important territories are the kingdom of Buganda under a *kabaka* and the smaller kingdoms of Bunyoro, Ankole and Toro; each of them has a *lukiko* (assembly) of chiefs and elected members. Executive and legislative councils were introduced in 1920, ministerial government in 1955. On 9 Oct. 1962 U. became an independent member of the COMMONWEALTH. On 24 Feb. 1966 the Prime Minister suspended the constitution and U. became a republic on 7 Sept. 1967 with a new constitution vesting executive power in the president. U. is a member of the East African Community.   SHS; IHE

Ulnage, see AULNAGE.

Ulster, see BARONETCY; IRELAND, CONQUEST OF; IRELAND, PARTITION

OF; IRISH REBELLION; O'NEILL'S RE-
VOLT; PLANTATION OF IRELAND.

Undertakers (1614). James I's need
for money made him decide to summon Parliament and arrangements
were made in the localities by his
supporters to influence the elections.
These U. promised to secure the
return of members favourable to the
court but met with little success. The
king's responsibility in this is uncertain (ADDLED PARLIAMENT).

In the 18th century U. were magnates or borough-mongers who monopolized political power in Ireland.
They undertook to manage parliament
and executive through nominees,
secure supplies and maintain public
order in return for control of patronage.   IHE

Unfederated Malay States, became
British protectorates in 1885 (JOHORE),
1888 (BRUNEI), 1907 (PERLIS), 1909
(KEDAH, Kelantan, Trengganu). On
10 March 1909 Siam transferred to
Great Britain its rights of suzerainty
over the 4 last-named states. All of
them, except Brunei, joined the
Union (Federation) of MALAYA in
1946.   SHS

Uniformity, Act of (1) (1549), enforced the use of the first BOOK OF
COMMON PRAYER. Penalties were
comparatively mild and directed
against the clergy.

(2) (1552), enforced the use of the
second BOOK OF COMMON PRAYER and
imposed more stringent penalties and
fines on RECUSANTS for non-attendance
at church.

(3) (1559), promoted by Parliament
not the church, restored the second
BOOK OF COMMON PRAYER with minor
changes after the MARIAN REACTION.

(4) (1662), the second act of the
CLARENDON CODE, enforced the use of
the revised BOOK OF COMMON PRAYER.
All dissenting clergy were to be deprived, clergy and teachers were to be
episcopally ordained, abjure the
COVENANT and take the oath of NON-
RESISTANCE; schoolmasters and tutors
were to be licensed by bishops. About

2,000 ejections resulted, creating a
lasting division between churchmen
and NONCONFORMISTS. Protestant dissenters were largely relieved by the
TOLERATION ACT (1689) and Roman
Catholics by acts of 1791 and 1829.

(5) (Ireland, 1666), regulated the
holding of benefices similarly to the
English act of 1662.   IHE

Union, England–Scotland. Anglo-
Scottish relations entered a new stage
when James VI of Scotland became
James I of England (1603) but his
attempts to promote closer unity failed
(POST-NATI). The temporary union
effected by Cromwell (1654) did not
survive the Restoration. After the
GLORIOUS REVOLUTION of 1688–9
Scotland became the main centre of
the JACOBITES and relations between
the two countries deteriorated after
GLENCOE (1692) and the failure of the
DARIEN SCHEME (1698–9). The Scots
passed an Act of Security (1703) which
did not bind them to accept the Protestant succession provided for by the
English Act of SETTLEMENT (1701). At
this critical stage constructive states-
manship prevailed and union was
achieved by English and Scottish acts
of 1707. The Scottish judicial system
and Presbyterian church were safeguarded and 16 peers and 45 M.P.s
represented Scotland in the Parliament of Great Britain.   IHE

Union, England–Wales. Following
the reinvigoration of the COUNCIL OF
THE MARCHES in 1534–5, the u. of
England and WALES was brought
about by a series of acts, 1536–43, of
which the two most important were
27 Henry VIII, c. 26, and 34 and 35,
c. 26. Having first provided for the
creation of justices of the peace, this
legislation incorporated the whole of
Wales into England and gave the
Welsh denizen rights. It abolished the
MARCHES, enlarged the existing Welsh
counties and English border counties,
and created the new ones of Denbigh,
Montgomery, Radnor, Brecon, and
Monmouth. English law and the
administrative machinery and officers
of English shires were established

throughout Wales, and English was made the language of administration and justice. Provision was made for the parliamentary representation of Wales, the Council of the Marches was given a statutory basis, and a court of great sessions set up, together with quarter sessions and minor courts. From the standpoint of law and government, the U. was on the whole a striking success, but its effects on language and culture were unfortunate.   GW

Union, Great Britain–Ireland (1801–1922). After the IRISH REBELLION (1798) Pitt decided that a solution of the Irish problem, essential for the prosecution of the FRENCH REVOLUTIONARY WAR, might be found only in legislative u. GRATTAN'S PARLIAMENT was persuaded by bribery to abolish itself. By the Act of U. (1800, effective 1 Jan. 1801) the 'United Kingdom' Parliament included 4 Irish spiritual peers (sitting by rotation each session), 28 IRISH REPRESENTATIVE PEERS and 100 Irish M.P.s. The established Churches were united. Financial terms, the fairness of which remains a matter of opinion, allowed of a united exchequer and national debt by 1817; free trade was established though some protection was afforded to Ireland's advantage. Pitt realized that CATHOLIC EMANCIPATION might be granted with more safety by a united Parliament and intended that this should immediately follow u.; tacit promises to this effect helped to create Irish support. He was baulked by dissension in the cabinet and the king's refusal to countenance any such measure. Failure of the u. brought about the movement for HOME RULE and ultimately IRISH PARTITION (1920–2).   MLH

Unionists, see CONSERVATIVE PARTY; LIBERAL PARTY.

Union of South Africa was first suggested by Sir George Grey, governor of Cape colony (1854–61), as a federation of the CAPE, NATAL, ORANGE FREE STATE and Kaffraria, but

opposed by the colonial office which recalled Grey. The federation scheme sponsored by Lord Carnarvon as colonial secretary (1874–8) was turned down by the Cape which did not want to assume fresh responsibilities, Orange Free State and TRANSVAAL which feared the dominance of the Cape, and favoured only by Natal. The customs union of 1889 combined the Cape, Orange, Natal, BASUTOLAND and BECHUANALAND, but not Transvaal. After the SOUTH AFRICAN WAR Lord Milner as governor of the Cape and High Commissioner for South Africa (the offices having been combined since 1872) maintained that, after economic reconstruction, racial equality between the British, Boers and Bantu should be established before restoring self-government to the Boer territories. However, the Liberal government recalled Milner and granted responsible government to the Transvaal (6 Dec. 1906) and Orange (5 June 1907) colonies. A national convention, convened on 12 Oct. 1908, worked out a unitary constitution (against the wishes of Natal) which outwardly satisfied Boers and Britons by making Pretoria the administrative capital and Cape Town the seat of the legislature, by adopting a bicameral legislature, by entrenching the franchise of Africans in Cape province and the equality of the English and Afrikaans languages. In reality, the constitution not only expressly left unrepresented the Bantu, four-fifths of the population, but secured a permanent Boer majority in parliament by making allowance for gerrymandering the constituencies and packing the senate, thus paving the way for the one-party rule of the irreconcilable nationalists.

The U. came into being on 31 May 1910 and under the guidance of Botha (1910–19) and Smuts (1919–24, 1939–48) played an honourable role on the battlefields of the two world wars and in the councils of the COMMONWEALTH, the LEAGUE OF NATIONS and the UNITED NATIONS. However, the Nationalist party (founded 1912) kept alive Afrikaner nationalism, anti-

British feeling and republican sentiments. A rebellion of some pro-
German Boer generals in 1914 was
quickly suppressed by Botha and the
attempt of the pro-Nazi wing of the
Nationalists to keep the U. neutral in
1939 was scotched by Smuts. However, the Nationalists gained parliamentary control in 1924–39 and from
1948, every time on a minority of
votes.

The Mines and Works Act, 1926,
started the policy of APARTHEID by
barring the Bantu from all skilled
occupations. In 1936 the Cape Africans were disfranchised in violation of
the entrenched clause. SOUTH-WEST
AFRICA was incorporated in 1949 in
violation of the MANDATE agreement.
Further laws and ordinances, ostensibly for the 'suppression of Com-
munism', completed the police state.
The opposition of most churches
and universities to religious and educational apartheid was disregarded.
The English-speaking whites were
gradually removed from the public
services. The Dutch-born and Ger-
man-trained premier Verwoerd in
1960 obtained a plebiscite in favour of
a republic (from 31 May 1961) and on
15 March 1961 withdrew his government from the Commonwealth. SHS

Unitarians first appeared in England
after the REFORMATION and grew in
numbers during the COMMONWEALTH
and PROTECTORATE, although their
doctrines were regarded as heretical.
They were excluded from toleration
under the HUMBLE PETITION AND
ADVICE (1657) and the TOLERATION
ACT (1689). Their thought influenced
BAPTISTS and Presbyterians. After
their exclusion by the Dissenters' conference at Salter's Hall, London
(1719), they formed separate chapels
and absorbed most of the English
Presbyterians.

Originally U. were Christians who
denied the existence of the Trinity
and, in the late 18th century, noted
for their radical tendencies. Modern
U. support no formal dogma and
number agnostics and humanists
among their members. IHE

Unite, a gold coin (value 20s.) also
called a broad, from its size, was struck
by James I in 1604 instead of the
sovereign. The name derived from
the UNION of England and Scotland.
It was replaced by the GUINEA in
1663. IHE

United Empire Loyalists. The
title officially bestowed in 1789 on
those colonial loyalists or Tories who
after 1783 left the U.S.A. for CANADA
largely to avoid persecution from the
victorious republicans. They constituted a strong anti-American influence and established themselves
mainly in Upper Canada (ONTARIO),
NEW BRUNSWICK and PRINCE EDWARD
ISLAND. The Canada Constitutional
Act of 1791 was a direct consequence
of this migration. IHE

United Irishmen, see IRISH REBEL-
LION (1798).

United Nations, the successor of the
LEAGUE OF NATIONS, was prepared in
1944 by the United States, the
United Kingdom, the Soviet Union
and China; their proposals were
amended and endorsed by the 'U.N.
conference on international organization' held in San Francisco in April–
June 1945. The charter, largely the
work of Jan Smuts (1870–1950), was
signed on 26 June 1945 by 50 nations.
The U.N. came formally into existence
on 24 Oct. 1945; its headquarters is in
New York City. The United Kingdom
is one of the 5 permanent members of
the security council; all member states
of the British Commonwealth have
joined the U.N., which in 1969 comprised 126 members. SHS

United Provinces, see UTTAR PRA-
DESH.

Universities. The u. of Oxford and
Cambridge were, like the early continental u., spontaneous growths
produced by the 12th-century revival
of learning. Both belonged to the
northern or Parisian type, the 'university of masters'; neither grew out of
schools associated with religious
houses or cathedrals. In view of the
celebrity of some English cathedral

schools the location of u. at Oxford
and Cambridge seems surprising. It
is likely that scholars first came to
Oxford because its religious houses—
St Frideswide's priory, Oseney abbey
and the college of St George in the
castle—were already places of learning; that they came in increasing
numbers was due to the presence of
some famous English and foreign
teachers, Oxford's central position,
its accessibility by road and river, and
its distance from its diocesan's seat at
Lincoln. Political difficulties under
Henry II may have diverted to Oxford
students who would otherwise have
gone to Paris. By the end of the 12th
century Oxford was established as a
studium generale, having the higher
faculties of theology, canon law and
civil law as well as that of arts. There
may have been schools at Cambridge
in the late 12th century, but the
university probably came into existence only after 1209, when, following
a clash between townsmen and scholars
in Oxford, some of the latter migrated
to Cambridge.

Scholars from the temporarily
dispersed university of Paris were
invited by Henry III in 1229, and in
the course of the 13th century both u.
received repeated marks of royal and
papal favour. The Dominicans came
to Oxford in 1221 and to Cambridge
by 1238; the Franciscans to Oxford in
1224 and to Cambridge in 1225.
Their coming encouraged theological
studies, and Cambridge had its faculty
of theology by 1250. In 1318, at
Edward II's request, pope John XXII
formally recognized Cambridge as a
studium generale (which it had been in
practice for half a century) and conferred on its graduates the right to
teach throughout Christendom (the
jus ubique docendi).

At the beginning of the 13th century
the head of Oxford university appears
to have been the *magister scholarum*,
possibly appointed with the bishop of
Lincoln's permission. In 1214 papal
legatine ordinances provided for the
appointment of a chancellor by the
bishop. The 13th and 14th centuries
witnessed the steady growth of the
university's privileges, its control over
the government of the town and its
immunity from all external authority.
The bishops of Lincoln periodically
attempted to assert their authority, in
particular their right to confirm the
university's election of its chancellor.
Bulls of pope Urban V in 1367 and
1370 finally extinguished this right.
The archbishops of Canterbury
claimed, but seldom exercised, the
right of visitation—never admitted by
the university. Oxford had no written
statutes until the 1250s, observing a
body of customs largely based on those
of Paris. By the 14th century its
constitution had settled down in the
form it retained until 1636. The
chancellor, elected by the regent
(teaching) masters of all faculties,
presided over convocation and congregation, and normally held office for
two years. Non-resident chancellors,
with influence at court, were elected
from 1458 onwards, but not until 1549
were elections of vice-chancellors
regulated by statute. The proctors,
first mentioned in 1248, were originally
the representatives of the northern and
southern 'nations' into which students
were divided, the northerners including Scots, and the southerners Irish
and Welsh. The nations were abolished in 1274 after Oxford had been
disturbed by bloody fights, but the
proctors remained as the executive
officers of the faculty of arts, elected
annually by its regent masters, and
responsible for good order in the
whole university. Convocation, first
mentioned in 1252, the legislative
assembly of the university, was composed of the regents and non-regents
of all faculties; congregation, composed
of the regent masters only, dealt with
routine administration; and the 'black
congregation', of regents in arts only,
met for the preliminary discussion of
proposed legislation but appears to
have fallen into disuse in the late 15th
century. Voting in convocation was
by faculties—numbering five in the
14th century with the inclusion of
medicine—and the whole body of non-
regents. From 1320 a majority had to
consist of at least three faculties, in-

cluding the faculty of arts, and a majority of the non-regents.

The constitutional history of medieval Cambridge is less well recorded. There the regents in arts formed congregation, the deliberative and legislative assembly, which elected the chancellor (first mentioned in 1226) and the proctors or rectors (first mentioned in 1275). Gradually the non-regents claimed a share in university government. A deputy- or vice-chancellor was appointed as early as 1412, but the office was not regularly filled until after 1471, with the election of absentee chancellors. Cambridge had the same faculties as Oxford, though in both u. the faculty of medicine was never large. Although the chancellor acquired almost exclusive jurisdiction over the university in the 14th century, he remained under the supervisory authority of the bishop of Ely, achieving complete independence only in 1432–3.

The u. suffered similar internal disturbances in the 13th and 14th centuries. Faction fights of northerners and southerners were sometimes followed by secessions, e.g. from Cambridge to Northampton in 1261, and from Oxford to STAMFORD in 1334. There were disputes between both u. and the friars in their midst, who were viewed with jealousy and suspicion by the faculties of arts. Attempts to limit the numbers and powers of the theological faculties ended in settlements, 1313–20 at Oxford and 1366 at Cambridge, which made some concessions to the friars but secured the continued supremacy of arts. The increasing subordination of the towns to the u. made for strained relations which frequently deteriorated to a state of war between town and gown. At Oxford, the worst outbreak of violence was the 'great slaughter' of scholars by townsmen on St Scholastica's day 1355, while at Cambridge in 1381 the PEASANTS' REVOLT took the local form of an attack on the university, involving much looting, wanton destruction and the burning of the university's charters and deeds. The ultimate result of both

affrays was the tightening by the crown of the u.' control of municipal government, the chancellors eventually wielding greater power than any other heads of medieval u.

With few buildings of their own in the middle ages, the u. made frequent use of churches and of buildings hired from religious houses. Oxford received its own congregation house and library from bishop Cobham of Worcester in 1320. Its divinity school was built from 1423 to about 1483; Duke Humphrey's library in the room above it was completed in 1490, and a school of canon law in 1491. Cambridge had a divinity school by 1400, and the university library, in existence by 1438, received a new building from Archbishop Rotherham by 1475.

It is unlikely that the number of scholars at Oxford ever exceeded 3,000—perhaps half as many as at Paris or Bologna: in the 15th century numbers declined to under 1,000. Always smaller than Oxford, Cambridge increased in popularity in the 15th century, possibly owing to Oxford's associations with the LOLLARDS: even so, numbers probably never exceeded 1,000. The great majority of students were originally housed in lodgings rented from townsmen or from religious houses. Masters who rented lodgings became responsible as principals of 'halls' in Oxford, 'hostels' in Cambridge, for the teaching and discipline of the inmates. Gradually the u. brought the halls and hostels under their control: an Oxford statute of c. 1413 required all students to live either in colleges or in halls under their principals. The number of Oxford halls declined sharply from about 70 in the mid-15th century to a dozen or so in 1534. Many had been acquired by the colleges while others were abandoned —the result partly of recurrent outbreaks of plague, partly of a general decline from which Oxford recovered only in the 16th century. In Cambridge the two-dozen or so hostels mostly passed into the possession of colleges, who appointed 'external principals', and were eventually absorbed or deserted: all had gone by 1540. Regular clergy at both u. were accommodated either in houses of their own orders or at monastic colleges founded from the late 13th century onwards. Benedictines, for instance, could go to Gloucester Hall, founded at Oxford in 1287, or to a Cambridge hostel, founded in 1428 and later called Buckingham College.

The earliest secular colleges were University College (1249), Balliol (1260–82) and Merton (1264) at Oxford, and Peterhouse (1284) at Cambridge. Surviving foundations of the 14th and 15th centuries are, at Oxford, Exeter (1314), Oriel (1324–6), Queen's (1341), New College (1379), Lincoln (1427), All Souls (1438) and Magdalen (1458); and at Cambridge, Clare (1326), Pembroke (1347), Gonville (1348), Trinity Hall (1350), Corpus Christi (1352), King's (1441), Queens' (1448), St Catherine's (1473) and Jesus (1496). The names commemorate royal foundation or patronage, foundation by bishops or noble families, royal ministers like Henry III's chancellor, Walter de Merton, and the Cambridge gildsmen who founded Corpus Christi College. College foundation continued during the Tudor period: at Oxford, Brasenose (1509), Corpus Christi (1517), Cardinal College, forerunner of Christ Church (1525), Trinity (1554), St John's (1555), Jesus (1571); at Cambridge, Christ's (1505), St John's (1511), Magdalene (1542), Trinity, from medieval halls (1546), Emmanuel (1584), Sidney Sussex (1596). Under James I, Wadham and Pembroke Colleges were founded at Oxford and in 1602 the Bodleian Library was built there. Since the purging of Oxford of lollardy both u. had been orthodox and, especially at Oxford, there was resistance to the 'new learning' of the early 16th century where the so-called Trojans opposed the teaching of Greek. But during the 16th century the trivium and quadrivium were replaced with dialectic, rhetoric, mathematics, philosophy, civil law, theology, medicine, Greek

and Hebrew as subjects for study. Although most of the men of learning of 16th- and 17th-century England had attended u. and although both produced good individual scholars, academic standards were generally low. This was partly due to the increasing number of young noblemen few of whom desired to graduate, and whose presence emphasized the growing difference between rich and poor students. There was also the steady growth of college control of teaching and discipline at the expense of the u., and obligatory residence for bachelors desiring to become masters was abolished. The religious changes of the REFORMATION involved the u. in politics. Both in 1533 pronounced Henry VIII's divorce to be valid, and the government kept control of opinion by means of chancellors who throughout the century were men in high official position. This control was necessary as the u. produced the ecclesiastics on whom the working of the religious settlement largely depended. Both u. were given new statutes —Cambridge in 1570, Oxford in 1636 —which remained in force until the 19th century. Both u. were royalist during the CIVIL WAR; and Oxford was the king's headquarters for 4 years, contributing liberally to his cause. Many fellows were ejected for refusing to take the COVENANT and the test imposed following the execution of Charles I. Trouble occurred at both u. under James II (1685–8) due to his high-handed pro-catholic policy, but despite this Oxford showed marked JACOBITE sympathies in the earlier 18th century. During the 18th and earlier 19th centuries both produced individual scholars of distinction but general change was slow in the face of academic conservatism, and educational standards were inferior to those of the dissenting academies or the Scottish u. This was also the period of greatest social differentiation among undergraduates with the two extremes of the gentleman commoners and the sizars or servitors. But professorships of history were introduced into both under George I, mathematics and natural sciences slowly gained ground, and by 1800 written examinations had succeeded disputations as the method for awarding degrees. Acts of Parliament in 1854 and 1856 freed admissions and degrees from religious tests. In 1871 the University Tests Act freed all lay posts in U. or constituent colleges from religious tests, and in 1877 the U. of Oxford and Cambridge Act revised their statutes, favouring the u. as distinct from the colleges. From this time the range of studies and of post-graduate work steadily increased. The last third of the 19th century saw the admission of married fellows and the establishment of women's colleges—Newnham and Girton at Cambridge; Lady Margaret Hall, Somerville, St Hugh's and St Hilda's at Oxford—although women students were not accepted as full members of the u. until well into the 20th century. New English u. were established during the 19th century. Durham (1832) was in 1852 associated with the college at Newcastle. London (1836) was formed from University and King's colleges there, but until 1900 was no more than an examining body. It has now 17 constituent 'schools' and 10 'institutes', including that of historical research (1921). In 1858 London degree examinations were opened to anyone applying to sit and they were taken by students at local colleges, soon known as university colleges, the earliest being Mason College Birmingham and Owen's College Manchester. In 1884 this last was joined with colleges at Liverpool and Leeds to form Victoria University, but later Manchester, Liverpool (1903) and Leeds (1904) became separate u.; Birmingham received its charter in 1900, Sheffield in 1905 and Bristol in 1909. Between the two world wars Reading and after the second world war Nottingham, Exeter, Hull, Southampton and Leicester became u. The first new foundation after 1945 was that of North Stafford; by 1963 the u. of Sussex, York and East Anglia were under development, and before 1970 there also came into being Aston, Bath, Bradford, Brunel,

City (these two in London), Essex, Kent, Lancaster, Loughborough, Newcastle (by separation from Durham), Salford, Surrey and Warwick. There is also the Open University where teaching is done by television and correspondence. All u. are now non-sectarian and open to men and women equally. The first government grant towards u. finance was in 1889, and by 1962 the bulk of all u. income came from the treasury via the University Grants Committee.

The u. of Scotland are St Andrews (1411), Glasgow (1453), Aberdeen (1494) and Edinburgh (1585). Added since 1960 are Dundee (by separation from St Andrews), Heriot-Watt (in Edinburgh), Stirling and Strathclyde. In Northern Ireland is Queen's university, Belfast (1845, u. status 1908) and, since 1960, Ulster. The university of Wales, a federation of the colleges at Aberystwyth, Bangor and Cardiff, was formed in 1893; Swansea joined it in 1920, and St David's College, Lampeter, is now associated with it.

The u., via examination boards, are the responsible authorities for the public examinations formerly known as school and higher school certificate, now as ordinary and advanced levels of the general certificate of education.
RFW; CFS

Unlearned Parliament (Oct. 1404), the second parliament of the year, held at Coventry, and so called because Henry IV, hoping for a more amenable assembly than earlier parliaments, directed the sheriffs not to return any members who had studied or practised law. The U.P. is notable for a proposed resumption of alienated crown lands and revenues, and for an experiment with a combined income and property tax, both aimed at relieving Henry's extreme financial necessity in the face of foreign wars, internal revolts and the GLYN DŴR REBELLION.   RFW

Upper Canada, see ONTARIO.

Urn Culture, a culture of the middle BRONZE AGE of c. 1400–c. 800 B.C. Its namo io dorivod from tho largo burial urns used for the ashes of the dead. It extended, with local variations, over much of Britain; and was essentially a development within the island, assimilating with the earlier FOOD-VESSEL CULTURE. It saw the continued improvement of bronze technology and the development of spears and stabbing swords. Barley was added to cereal crops although the main emphasis was still on stock rearing. Linen and wool were used as clothing materials. The change to cremation and few grave goods shows a change in religious belief, but the reasons for this are not evident. From c. 1100 the bronze industry appears to have been reorganized with a commercial aristocracy of itinerant bronze-smiths responsible for manufacture and distribution. Techniques also improved and ideas from the European mainland produced new forms, including the double-edged sword. In the north the u.c.s continued for many centuries after their supersession in the south by the DEVEREL-RIMBURY and similar cultures.   CFS

Ushant, see GLORIOUS FIRST OF JUNE.

Usury was condemned as a sin by the medieval church. Nevertheless both church and king frequently borrowed large sums from JEWS and ITALIAN BANKERS. U. was at first dealt with by the ECCLESIASTICAL COURTS which still punished offenders in the reign of James I. Interest of 10% was legally permitted between 1545 and 1552 and again after 1571 and it was fixed at 8% in 1625, reduced to 6% under the Commonwealth and to 5% in 1714. The BANK OF ENGLAND was exempted from this limitation in 1833 and the u. laws (except those affecting pawnbroking) were abolished in 1854.   IHE

Utfangenetheof, see INFANGENE-THEOF.

Utrecht, peace of (1713), terminated the war of the SPANISH SUCCESSION between France and Spain on the one hand, Great Britain, the Netherlands, Savoy, Portugal and Prussia on the

othor. Grcat Britain obtaincd from France (11 April) the recognition of the GUELPH dynasty and the abandonment of the STEWARTS, the cession of the HUDSON BAY territory, ACADIA and NEWFOUNDLAND; and from Spain (13 June) the ASIENTO and other commercial concessions and the cession of GIBRALTAR and MINORCA. Further peace treaties were concluded between France and the emperor (Rastatt, 7 March 1714) and empire (Baden, 7 Sept. 1714), Spain and the Netherlands (Utrecht, 26 June 1714) and Portugal (Madrid, 6 Feb. 1715). SHS

Utrum Assize, born of the 12th-century conflict between lay and church courts, its form derived directly from the Constitutions of CLARENDON (1164). The jurors were asked, whether the land which N. parson of the church claims as free alms of his church against R. is the lay fee of R. or an ecclesiastical fee. As the lay courts won superiority the assize changed its character: originally extended to all tenants in FRANKALMOIN, 100 years after its inception it was restricted to the claims of parish priests, who had no corporate existence like bishoprics or religious houses, against laymen, and it became known as the parson's writ of RIGHT.

PMB

Uttar Pradesh, since 24 Jan. 1950 the name of the United Provinces, which in 1935 had replaced the name of United Provinces of Agra and Oudh, formerly (from 1902) called North-West Province and Oudh.

The country was conquered by Babur in 1525. Agra, the favourite residence of many Mogul rulers, was together with DELHI captured by the EAST INDIA COMPANY in 1803, and placed under the BENGAL presidency. The division of Agra, created in 1834, was separated from Bengal in 1836 as the North-West Province and combined with Oudh in 1877.

Oudh in 1724 gained its virtual independence from the Mogul empire of which its greatest ruler, Shuja-ud-daulah, was the vizir (1754–75). Clive in 1765 and Hastings in 1773 befriended the nawab whom they supported against the emperor, the MARATHAS and the Afghans, in return for an annual tribute and the admission of a British garrison. The relations between Oudh and the Company after Shuja-ud-daulah's death form an inglorious chapter in British history. The corrupt administration and the mounting arrears of the tribute gave the pretext for increased political pressure and financial extortions. Hastings brutally forced Shuja-ud-daulah's widow and mother to surrender their immense private property (1782); Wellesley deprived the nawab of half his territory (1801) and turned Oudh into a 'protected state' without checking misgovernment; the unfortunate country was formally annexed by Dalhousie on 13 Feb. 1856 and the last nawab deported. This unjustified action largely contributed to the outbreak of the mutiny, and long afterwards unrest prevailed in Oudh.

In 1947 three feudatory states, including Benares, were merged in U.P. SHS

Uxbridge negotiations (Jan.–Feb. 1645), were meetings between Charles I's commissioners and those appointed by Parliament and the Scots to discuss the essentially Scottish treaty of U. This proposed a permanent commission chosen by Parliament to control the army and navy, an ecclesiastical settlement in accordance with the COVENANT, Parliament to control foreign relations and have a free hand in Ireland, and proscription of leading royalists. Charles was not prepared to abandon the church or his friends and the U.n. ended (22 Feb.). IHE

Vagabonds were first dealt with by an act of 1349 forbidding them alms, and another of 1388 providing for their return to their birthplace. The unemployed and incorrigible, often wandering in gangs, became an increasing problem in Tudor times and were dealt with by the J.P.s after 1501. In 1531 a distinction was made between the impotent and the ablebodied, the latter being subjected to

brutal punishments (loss of an ear, 1536; branding and enslavement for 2 years, 1547). The Elizabethan acts were consolidated in 1597 and 1601 but vagrancy remained and transportation was added to the punishments in 1603. Branding ceased in 1713, the Acts of 1822 and 1824 repealed previous legislation. After 1834 rogues and v. were dealt with under the POOR LAWS. IHE

Valor Ecclesiasticus, a valuation of all benefices in England and Wales compiled from 1534 onwards, following the statute which gave all first fruits and tenths to the crown. The title covers both original returns and two volumes of transcripts, known as the *Liber Regis*, which superseded the TAXATION OF NICHOLAS IV as the basis for ecclesiastical taxation. Bacon's *Liber Regis* (1786) follows the same pattern, giving also contemporary patrons. PMB

Valuation of Norwich (1254), a comprehensive assessment of church property in the provinces of Canterbury and York made under the direction of Walter Suffield, bishop of Norwich. The v., which covered both spiritualities and temporalities, was a preliminary to the collection of the clerical tenth, originally granted to Henry III for three years by Innocent IV in 1250 for his projected crusade, but soon known as 'the Sicilian tenth' —its proceeds being devoted to the SICILIAN BUSINESS. The V. of N. was superseded in 1291 by the TAXATION OF NICHOLAS IV, but its surviving parts remain a most valuable source for the history of the 13th-century church.

W. E. Lunt, *The V. of N.* (1926). RFW

Vancouver Island, see BRITISH COLUMBIA.

Van Diemen's Land, see TASMANIA.

Vavassor, a term for a vassal, widespread in feudal Europe. In Normandy it had a special meaning, a freeman with less land than a baron but with some military obligations.

This definition was brought to England, and in DOMESDAY the name was applied to small free-holders in the Scandinavian areas and elsewhere. As the barons grew in wealth and power so the v.'s status rose, and the title lapsed in favour of knight; the 100s. RELIEF for a knight's fee, insisted on in MAGNA CARTA, was adopted from the early-12th-century v.'s relief.   PMB

Venice Company, see LEVANT COMPANY.

Venner's Rising, see FIFTH MONARCHY MEN.

Verderer, see FORESTS.

Vereeniging, peace of (31 May 1902), between Great Britain, the South African Republic (TRANSVAAL) and the ORANGE FREE STATE ended the SOUTH AFRICAN WAR. The Boer republics reluctantly accepted British sovereignty with the promise of eventual self-government. No extension of the franchise to natives was to be considered until after the introduction of self-government and Dutch language rights were safeguarded. £3m. sterling was given towards reconstruction as well as generous loans free of interest for 2 years. Insistence on British sovereignty made possible the UNION OF SOUTH AFRICA.   IHE

Verge, Court of the, see MARSHALSEA.

Vermont, the last of the NEW ENGLAND territories to become a separate colony. The region was first visited by the French under Champlain (1609) but the first permanent settlement was made by the English at Fort Dummer (1724), soon followed by the Dutch at Pownal. After the conquest of CANADA (1760) there was a steady influx from CONNECTICUT and MASSACHUSETTS, and substantial grants of land were made by the governor of NEW HAMPSHIRE. These awards were challenged by NEW YORK which was given control of the territory by the crown (1764). New York's rejection of the New Hampshire grants (1770)

was successfully resisted by Ethan Allen and the Green Mountain Boys of western V. In 1777 they declared their independence as New Connecticut but soon changed the name to V.   IHE

Vernacular. Norman-French was used in private speech and correspondence after the Norman conquest, and from the 13th century onwards in government for documents under the PRIVY SEAL etc. and for oral legal proceedings. By the mid-15th century it was archaic, and when in 1487 English was used for statutes, Norman-French survived only in archaic ceremonial and legal formulae. A bilingual English–French Act (Carriage by air) was passed in 1961.

Anglo-Saxon, the language of pre-conquest England, passing through unknown stages re-appeared as English in the 14th century. In 1362 it was allowed in the courts for oral and EQUITY proceedings. Its triumph over Norman-French is marked by poets: Gower wrote in both, but Chaucer and Langland, his contemporaries, in English alone. Though increasingly used in government, English did not entirely supersede LATIN as the documentary language until 1733.   PMB

Verneuil, battle of (17 Aug. 1424), was, next to AGINCOURT, the greatest English victory in the 15th-century phase of the HUNDRED YEARS' WAR. A Franco-Scottish army of about 15,000, which threatened English-held Normandy, was defeated by 8,000–9,000 men under John, duke of Bedford. Of over 7,000 enemy casualties the great majority were Scots, including their leaders, the earls of Buchan and Douglas. With the southern borders of Normandy secured Bedford was able to proceed with the conquest of MAINE.   RFW

Versailles, treaty of (3 Sept. 1783), ended the American War of Independence and the maritime war with France, Spain and the Netherlands. The independence of the U.S.A. was recognized. There was a mutual restoration of conquests between Britain and France, except that France gained TOBAGO, Senegal and the right to fortify DUNKIRK. Spain recovered FLORIDA and MINORCA from Britain. The Netherlands made peace (20 May 1784), ceding Negapatam to Britain.

IHE

Versailles, treaty of (1919), between the allied powers and Germany ended WORLD WAR I. In the prior discussions Lloyd George occupied a moderating position between Clemenceau (France), who negotiated expertly for security at any cost to Germany, and Wilson (U.S.A.), whose humane naivety was unaccompanied by experience of European affairs. The resulting compromise was aimed to prevent Germany from ever again becoming a great power. Major terms of the 440 articles, presented by ultimatum, included cession by Germany of Alsace-Lorraine to France; Eupen-Malmédy to Belgium; West Prussia, Posen and, after a plebiscite, part of Upper Silesia to Poland thus creating the 'corridor' (Danzig being under international control); part of northern Schleswig after a plebiscite to Denmark; and all colonies as MANDATED TERRITORIES of the LEAGUE OF NATIONS, the 'covenant' of which formed the first section of the treaty. The Rhine area was demilitarized for 50 km east of the river and was to be occupied for up to 15 years (British troops evacuated in 1926, French in 1930). The Saar was internationalized with a plebiscite after 15 years (resulting in re-incorporation in Germany, 1935), France administering the area and having the use of its coalfields. Germany's union with the Austrian republic (*anschluss*) was forbidden. Germany was allowed a volunteer army of 100,000 without modern equipment and a small navy and merchant marine, but most of these clauses were quickly evaded (partly with the assistance of the Soviet Union). In the discussions on reparation Lloyd George was handicapped by promises given in the 'COUPON'

ELECTION but in any case preferred the harsh views of W. M. Hughes, prime minister of Australia, to the sober opinion of Keynes. The 'war guilt' clause imposed responsibility on Germany and her allies for all allied loss and damage; the size of reparation was referred to a commission which in 1921 fixed the economically impossible sum of £6,600m., of which the British share was to be 22%. This amount was successively scaled down; when finally abolished (1932) about £1,000m. had been paid but Germany had received loans of about £3,000m.

The t. of V. was signed on 28 June 1919 and came into force on 10 Jan. 1920; it was not ratified by the U.S.A.

MLH

Vestiarian Controversy, concerning clerical vestments, began under Edward VI and became acute when Hooper refused to be consecrated at Gloucester in surplice and rochet (1550). It flared up again in 1559 when the ornaments rubric of the BOOK OF COMMON PRAYER retained those in use in the second year of the reign of Edward VI. Puritans denounced the simplest vestments as the livery of antichrist. Parker's ADVERTISEMENTS (1566) ordered conformity in the use of vestments. Enforcement led to deprivations and the growth of puritan agitation against EPISCOPACY.

IHE

Victoria was colonized in 1834 by free settlers from TASMANIA, after the failure of earlier attempts (1803, 1825) to establish a colony with convicts from NEW SOUTH WALES. In 1837 the capital of Melbourne was founded, and in 1851 V. was separated from New South Wales, with representative government. In the same year gold was discovered at Ballarat and Bendigo, and the population jumped within ten years from 70,000 to 500,000. In 1855 V. was granted responsible government. It was the first Australian state to introduce old-age pensions (18 Jan. 1901). It joined the Commonwealth of AUSTRALIA on its creation, 1 Jan. 1901.

SHS

Victoria Cross, a bronze Maltese cross, inscribed *For Valour*, with a crimson ribbon, was instituted on 29 Jan. 1856 as a reward for conspicuous bravery in war. It was the first decoration that could be awarded to all ranks of all the services, including Indian soldiers (1911) and nurses (1920). Each holder of the V.C. receives a tax-free annuity of £100, regardless of need. The V.C. is worn before all other decorations. Surviving recipients numbered about 290 in 1963.   SHS

Vienna Congress (1 Oct. 1814–9 June 1815) was convened by the Austrian chancellor Metternich to settle the affairs of Europe after the FRENCH REVOLUTIONARY AND NAPOLEONIC WARS. It was attended by representatives of nearly every power, but never met in full conference except for the signing of the 'final act' on 9 June 1815. Its work was achieved by committees and in informal meetings at banquets, dances, receptions etc. which also largely took the place of modern press conferences. The British plenipotentiaries were Viscount Castlereagh, the foreign secretary, the earl of Clancarty and, later, Wellington. Their chief aim was the restoration of the balance of power in Europe and the security of the sea- and land-routes to India: both these aims, already incorporated in the first peace of PARIS, were achieved.

Britain retained HANOVER (now raised to a kingdom and enlarged by East Frisia, Hildesheim, Osnabrück and several enclaves) and thus a vote in the diet of the German Confederation. The Netherlands (enlarged by Belgium and Luxembourg), Switzerland (recovering Geneva, Neufchâtel, the Valais and the bishopric of Basel), Savoy-Sardinia (enlarged by Genoa) and Prussia and Bavaria (both established on the left bank of the Rhine) were to contain France. On the other hand, the revival of Poland as a bulwark against Russia proved impossible. Russia, insisting on the acquisition of Poland, and Prussia, claiming the whole of Saxony, were even prepared to go to war against England and

Austria which thereupon concluded an alliance with France (3 Jan.). Unity was restored only by Napoleon's return from Elba: Russia was given 'Congress Poland' (3 May) and Prussia was compensated with parts of Saxony, Westphalia and the Rhineland.

Britain successfully opposed Metternich's scheme for an Italian league under Austrian protectorate but supported the creation of the German Confederation (8 June) which was placed under the guarantee of the great powers, as was the neutrality of Switzerland. A declaration against the SLAVE-TRADE (8 Feb.) proposed by Britain, and the regulation of the precedence and classification of diplomatic representatives (which is still in force) were successful by-products of the congress, which gave Europe a political stability lasting until its overthrow by Bismarck and Cavour.   SHS

Vikings, a term formerly applied generally to northerners who sought fortune overseas by trade or plunder, but now limited to DANES, NORWEGIANS and Swedes who raided overseas between the later 8th and mid-11th centuries. The original meaning of the word is uncertain. No part of the British Isles was the exclusive preserve of any one of these races, and all three were likely to be represented in any raiding force. But Danes predominated in the attacks on and settlement of the eastern half of England; Norwegians in the Scottish Islands and Caithness and Sutherland; both Danes and Norwegians in Ireland and the secondary settlements from there into western Scotland and north-western England. The Swedes played a very minor part in attacks on England. The first recorded Viking attacks against the British Isles took place during the last decade of the 8th century, and thereafter ravaging became intense. The Isle of MAN was occupied at the end of the 8th century; the Orkneys, Shetlands and Hebrides in the early 9th century; the settlement in Ireland began c. 830; in England c. 874; in

Caithness and Sutherland about the beginning of the 10th century. CFS

Villa, a farm-complex in ROMAN BRITAIN c onsisting of owner's dwelling, dependants' quarters, farm buildings and land. Villas varied considerably, but the better had, in the owner's dwelling, mosaic floors, bath suites and hot-air heating. The land was worked by COLONI; and in some cases villas were industrial centres. The concept, although not the luxury, was known to the BELGAE. There was no continuity with the medieval MANOR.

CFS

Villein, the unfree though not slave peasant of the middle ages. Personally bound to his lord, he provided, in return for his holding, services and dues which could be commuted to rents though the v. himself obtained freedom only by escape, entering the church or MANUMISSION. The v.'s relations with his fellows and his lord were ordered by customary law. His status varied: the growth and extension of COMMON LAW destroyed many varied pre-conquest relationships, transmuting them into common villeinage, but at times of agricultural difficulty the v.'s status rose.

In England, the south-east March, lowland Scotland and the Irish PALE v.s belonged to a MANOR, working the DEMESNE. They were the largest class, though less numerous in Scandinavian areas. Their personal services were heavy: commutation began in the 12th century, but fluctuated with intensive working of demesnes. As the lord's personal chattels v.s and their kin could be sold or granted away, with no protection from common law but proof of villeinage, except on ancient demesne. Instead, the v. formed part of and was judged by the manorial court according to the custom of the manor, together with freemen who chose to hold in villeinage. Labour shortages, particularly after the BLACK DEATH, helped the English v. gain a personal interest in his land, changing him into a COPYHOLDER though still owing certain services. This last vestige of unfree tenure in England lasted until the 1922 and 1924 Property Acts.

In North and West WALES and the south-west March bondmen, proportionally less numerous than in England except in predominantly arable areas, lived either in a *maerdref*, demesne vill, or a *tir-cyfrif*, manorial vill, providing labour for the prince or lord of the COMMOTE. A third class of vill, of free arable holdings, *gwelyau*, granted to bondmen arose in north Wales in the 12th and 13th centuries. Owing bond services, such tenants had rights of succession similar to tenants of the contemporary free *gwelyau*. Normally held by the prince, bond vills were occasionally granted to freemen or the church. Commutation began in the 13th century, and the English conquest substituted one lord for another. The Welsh bondman was excluded, like his English counterpart, from the newly-introduced common law. As in England the number of bondmen steadily decreased, and rents assessed on vills became increasingly burdensome. Bond tenure was abolished in north Wales by Henry VII's charters, but in the south lingered on into the 16th century.

In Ireland before the English conquest the v.s, *betaghs* (food-providers), within their *baile* paid tribute to their lord in return for a lease of cattle. In areas where English customs took root, this system was incorporated into manors. At first only *betaghs* were excluded, as unfree, from common law, but by slow stages, ending in the statutes of KILKENNY 1366, all native Irish were reduced by exclusion to v. status at law, to be formally readmitted only by the Irish Parliament of 1613. PMB

Vimeiro, battle of (21 Aug. 1808), the first major battle of the PENINSULAR WAR. Wellesley's 17,000 men, occupying two ridges and a hill overlooking Maceira Bay (where reinforcements were expected) were unsuccessfully attacked by 13,000 French under Junot. Wellesley was unable to follow up his victory by a march on Lisbon since he was superseded by the inexperienced Sir Harry Burrard. MLH

Vindhya Pradesh was created on 4 April 1948 a 'B-state' under the maharaja of Rewa as rajpramukh, through the union of 35 Baghelkand and Bundhelkand states, formerly under the Central India Agency. On 25 Jan. 1950, 10 states were ceded to UTTAR PRADESH and MADHYA BHARAT, and V.P. was reconstituted a 'C-state' under a lieutenant-governor. On 1 Nov. 1956 V.P. was merged in Madhya Pradesh.   SHS

Virgate, or yardland, a quarter of a HIDE or carucate.   CFS

Virginia, so called by Raleigh in honour of Queen Elizabeth I, was until the 17th century the name applied to the whole east coast of North America south of Cape Breton. Thus Ralegh's V. colony (1584–90) was established in the present NORTH CAROLINA. The first permanent English colony was founded by the LONDON COMPANY (1607), and the V. COMPANY (1609–32) saw the colony through its early difficulties. During the 'starving time' (1609–10) it was held together by Captain John Smith, and the strict discipline enforced by Sir Thomas Dale and Sir Thomas Gates between 1611 and 1616 secured its survival. By 1616 tobacco was being exported, and from 1619 negro slaves as well as indentured whites were used on the plantations. V. became a royal colony in 1624. Governor Berkeley repudiated the COMMONWEALTH but V. submitted to the Parliamentary commissioners in 1652. Berkeley resumed his post in 1660 and unsuccessfully protested against the NAVIGATION ACT which permitted the export of tobacco to England only. V. strenuously opposed the AMERICAN IMPORT DUTIES ACT and supported non-importation. Its representatives took the lead in the first Continental Congress and the Virginian George Washington was given command of the American Continental Army.   IHE

Virginia Company (1609–32) was a development of the LONDON COMPANY with governmental functions. The treasurer and council in London ap-

pointed a series of able, if despotic, governors who restored discipline in VIRGINIA after initial hardships and disasters. Communal working was in force from 1609 to 1616 and personal emigration or £12 10s. was the entitlement to one share. John Rolfe's development of tobacco curing greatly contributed to the colony's ultimate success and a general assembly was first summoned in Jamestown in 1619. Internal dissension and economic difficulties caused the V.C. to lose its charter to the crown in 1624. It struggled on as a trading concern until final bankruptcy (1632).   IHE

Virgin Islands, discovered by Columbus in 1493, were from about 1625 occupied by Dutch and English buccaneers. After the Dutch had been expelled (1666) the V.I., comprising Tortola, Virgin Gorda, Anegada and numerous small islands, were constituted a presidency of the LEEWARD ISLANDS. The British V.I. did not join the federation of the West Indies in 1958.

Of the present V.I. of the U.S.A., St Thomas was acquired by Denmark in 1666, St Croix was fought over by the Dutch, English, Spaniards and French until in 1733 bought by Denmark; St John was occupied by Denmark in 1684. This group was occupied by the British in 1801 and 1807–15 and sold by Denmark to the U.S.A. in 1917.   SHS

Viscount (Latin *vicecomes*), literally one acting as a deputy of a count or EARL. It became a style of NOBILITY in the mid-15th century, the first creation being by letters patent. In earlier medieval England *vicecomes* gained a specialized meaning as the Latin rendering of the word SHERIFF.
                                            CFS

Vitoria, battle of (21 June 1813), a great strategic success of Wellington's final campaign in Spain during the PENINSULAR WAR. Speedily crossing León he turned the French defence line on the Ebro by marching through the mountains north of Burgos. He advanced on the armies of Joseph and

O

Jourdain in the Zadorra valley before they could be joined by that of Clausel. Graham cut the Bayonne road and assaulted from the north-east, whilst three other columns attacked from the heights on a wide front. Although their casualties were not large (over 8,000 out of 66,000 engaged) the French lost their artillery, transport and much booty; allied casualties were 5,000 out of about 79,000.   MLH

Vote of No Addresses (17 Jan. 1648). The LONG PARLIAMENT, realizing some agreement had been reached between Charles I and the Scots, passed this vote declaring they would make no more proposals to the king. The COMMITTEE OF BOTH KINGDOMS was dissolved, but in September Parliament re-opened negotiations with the king and repealed the V. of No A. This signified little as power lay with the army.   IHE

Wager of Law or compurgation, found in the earliest Anglo-Saxon laws, required 12 or more OATH-HELPERS to swear to the validity of an accused's sworn statement. It was adopted into the COMMON LAW as a defence both in criminal and civil pleas, and also widely used in church courts. There were local variations, e.g. in London the 'great law' required 36 oath-helpers and in homicide cases the failure of one meant hanging for the accused. W. of l. was retained in certain actions until 1833.   PMB

Waitangi, treaty of (6 Feb. 1840), concluded by Capt. William Hobson as lieutenant-governor of NEW ZEA-LAND on behalf of the British government with 46 Maori chiefs, established British sovereignty, granted the MAORI all the rights of British subjects and guaranteed them the possession of their lands which were to be sold only to the crown. Disregard of the landed-property rights led to the MAORI WARS. The treaty of W. is still in force.   SHS

Wakefield, battle of (30 Dec. 1460), brought the LANCASTRIANS near to victory in the wars of the ROSES.

Although Richard duke of York had in November been accepted as Henry VI's heir-apparent and protector of the realm, the Lancastrians were still strong, especially in the north, and likely to attempt the reversal of the settlement. Attempting to reduce the north with insufficient forces, York was besieged in Sandal castle, outside W., by the joint northern and western Lancastrian armies under the earl of Northumberland and the duke of Somerset. Risking a pitched battle, York was overwhelmed and killed.   RFW

Walcheren expedition (1809), intended as a diversion to help the Austrians after their re-entry into the NAPOLEONIC WARS (Apr. 1809), but did not sail until 28 July, three weeks after Austria's defeat at Wagram (6 July). This major force of about 100 ships, carrying 40,000 men commanded by the earl of Chatham, was primarily designed against Antwerp, but, after landing on W. (30 July), time was wasted capturing Flushing (16 Aug.) and the French fleet escaped to Antwerp, which was soon strongly reinforced. Chatham returned to England (14 Sept.), leaving 15,000 men on the fever-ridden island of W. The remnant was withdrawn on 24 Dec. Marred by indecision, dissension and lack of medical preparations, the W.e. was an inglorious failure.   IHE

Wales. The indigenous name of the country is Cymru (from a Brythonic root *Combrog-, 'of the same land'); 'Wales' deriving from Old English 'wealas', meaning 'foreigners', 'Celts'. W. came into being as a separate country early in the 7th century as the result of the battles of DYRHAM and CHESTER, when its people became permanently cut off from uninterrupted land communication with fellow Brythonic speakers in the west and the north. A tribal and pastoral society, divided up into kingdoms hostile to one another and the Anglo-Saxons, it nonetheless preserved its political independence and its WELSH LAWS until the Norman conquest. After *c.* 1070 it was increasingly penetrated by MARCHER LORDS who absorbed the territory and regalian rights of Welsh rulers and created a series of quasi-sovereign lordships in the MARCHES. The CELTIC CHURCH in Wales was also extensively re-organized along Roman lines. In the 12th century native dynasties in GWYNEDD, POWYS and DEHEU-BARTH halted the tide of conquest and established their right to an independent existence while acknowledging the overlordship of the crown. The success of the rulers of 13th-century Gwynedd in creating a unified feudal state over much of Wales provoked more drastic retaliation by Edward I. His extinction of political independence in 1282–3 left W. divided between the PRINCIPALITY and the Marches until 1536. During this time the Welsh retained their own language and many of their customs, and their literary culture flourished as never before or since. But in the same period profound social and economic changes, brought about by the EDWARDIAN CONQUEST, war, slump, plague and the GLYN DŴR REBELLION led to the disintegration of the feudal manor and the tribal *gwely*. Out of the débris emerged a new class of gentry who made use of the wars of the ROSES and the confusion of English politics to consolidate their position. Most were firm in their support for Henry TUDOR, whose victory was regarded as the fulfilment of national destiny. By 1536 Welsh loyalty and desire for a 'new deal', combined with the state's need for greater stability and uniformity of government, produced a successful Act of UNION. The Reformation, imposed from above by the state, was accepted without overt opposition, and the Welsh BIBLE and Prayer Book began a new era in the religious life of W. These translations were also the strongest influences in preserving the Welsh language and revivifying literature in face of a marked decline in traditional bardic culture. The gentry in Tudor and Stewart W. responded eagerly to the new opportunities for building and consolidating estates and for acquiring political and administrative authority. In the conflicts of the 17th century the claims of Parliament and Puritanism met with little support from them or the masses. By the 18th century the size of the average estate had greatly increased and the number of small or middling squires was correspondingly reduced, leaving a much wider gap between a now-anglicized upper class and the mass of the people. The persistence of Dissenters and the activity of the WELSH TRUST, S.P.C.K., and CIRCULATING SCHOOLS made W. ripe for far-reaching religious change. The success of Welsh METHODISM and its impetus to older sects had by the 19th century completely overturned the balance between the Established Church and Dissent and provided new foci for social and cultural life as well as religious worship. Industrial developments brought still profounder changes. The small-scale activity begun in Tudor times was transformed by the INDUSTRIAL REVOLUTION. From *c.* 1760 and especially during the years 1793–1815 iron ore and coal deposits, together with copper smelting, were intensively exploited in the South W. coalfield, and to a lesser extent in the north, along with slate, copper, and woollen cloth. Many canals were constructed and harbour facilities improved. Following a post-1815 slump, the growth of the coal industry from the 1830s onwards, under the stimulus of world demand and improved transport by rail and steamship, was phenomenal. By 1900 the south W. coalfield had become the world's most important coalfield and the Bristol Channel its busiest waterway. Steel and tinplate works had also become heavily concentrated in the area. The structure of Welsh society became transformed. The over-population of the country-side, which had led to the REBECCA RIOTS, was relieved by mass emigration, overseas and to the industrial areas. In the latter, towns tended to be small, and the characteristic pattern was that of villages strung out along narrow valleys in ungainly and cramped terraces. Housing and labour conditions were usually harsh, and relations between masters and men were at best sternly patriarchal, at worst brutally tyrannical. Troops had to be called out against rioting workers, notably at Merthyr (1831), Newport (CHARTIST rising, 1839) and Tonypandy (1911). Yet economic change created new opportunities and paved the way for cultural and political transformation. A vigorous Welsh press reinforced the efforts of the SUNDAY SCHOOLS to satisfy the Nonconformist hunger for edification, religious and secular. It became the organ of an intense radicalism which after 1868 produced a monolithic Liberal vote. A Liberalism deeply tinged with national consciousness, it secured a national educational system, university, library and museum, and brought about WELSH DISESTABLISHMENT. Trade unions mitigated the worst evils of working hours, and the growth of organized sport and entertainment lightened leisure hours, rugby football becoming almost a religion. After 1918 this pattern was much disrupted. The concentration of industrial eggs into the baskets of coal and steel led to acute depression and large-scale emigration in the 1920s and '30s, though since 1939 Welsh industry has become considerably diversified. Except in the rural areas, with their sharply-dropping populations, Liberals were ousted by Labour. The spread of English, already noticeable long before 1914, was accelerated by popular education, newspapers and the media of mass entertainment. Pillars of Victorian society—chapel, EISTEDDFOD and vernacular press—cracked ominously. Yet there has also been a renaissance in Welsh and Anglo-Welsh culture and a continued awareness of national identity in many directions, e.g. recognition of Cardiff as the capital, devolution of authority by government offices, and the creation of Welsh-language schools.

R. T. Jenkins and W. Rees, *Bibliography of Welsh History* (rev. ed. 1962). GW

Wallingford, see WINCHESTER, treaty of.

Walton ordinances (1338), issued by Edward III at Walton-on-the-Naze (Essex) before embarking for the Low Countries, made special arrangements for the administration of England and the raising of revenues during his absence. The W.o. marked an important step in the rise of the keeper of the PRIVY SEAL, which was to be used to authenticate royal directions from abroad. The financial o. proved particularly unpopular and were withdrawn in 1340. RFW

Wandiwash, battle of (22 Jan. 1760), south-west of Madras, was won by Sir Eyre Coote (1726–83) over the French under the Irishman, Count Lally (1702–66), who a year later also surrendered PONDICHERRY. Both events secured the British position in the Carnatic. SHS

Wapentake, derived from Old Norse *vápnatak*, the brandishing of weapons at a meeting as a signal of approval. In England the term was applied to a territorial subdivision of a county. W.s occurred where Danish influence was strong: Derbyshire, Leicestershire, Lincolnshire, Nottinghamshire (FIVE BOROUGHS), and the North and West Ridings of Yorkshire. Its function was identical with that of the HUNDRED, by which name it was occasionally known. In addition w. in the first four counties above were subdivided into smaller units also known, confusingly, as hundreds. CFS

Warband, the fighting men that accompanied a king or chief during the period of the TEUTONIC CONQUEST. No details are known concerning recruitment etc., but a large w. could contain hundreds if not thousands of men, and the directing element in it, under the leader, was the COMITATUS. It was these w.s that effected the actual conquest. CFS

Wardrobe. As the EXCHEQUER passed out of court, a financial department was required for the king's itinerant household. The first expedient adopted was the CHAMBER but, in Henry III's reign, the w. under its keeper came to dominate household

finance, receiving cash or credit from
the Exchequer or those accounting
there, with little Exchequer control
over it except in the audit of accounts;
by 1258 it had so developed that the
barons demanded that all revenue
should pass through the Exchequer.
Nevertheless the w. continued to
develop: under Edward I it reached
its height, organizing the finance,
transport and victualling not only of
the household but also of the armies in
the many wars in Gascony, Wales,
Flanders and Scotland, with the
PRIVY SEAL for its departmental seal,
and a body of highly skilled clerks.
Thereafter it declined, becoming a
more rigid department, attacked by
Edward II's baronial opposition and
increasingly subject to the Exchequer.
Though temporarily superseded by
the Chamber, the w. for some centuries remained the centre of household finance as well as a repository for
clothes and, in part of the Tower of
London, of armoury and arms, but it
never regained its importance of
Edward I's time.   PMB

Wards and Liveries, Court of.
Henry VII and Henry VIII increased
their personal, CHAMBER, revenue by
strictly enforcing their feudal rights of
WARDSHIP etc. They inquired into all
lands held in chief of the crown, and by
such measures as the Statute of Uses
(1535) prevented diminution of the
crown's rights. Henry VII appointed
masters of his wards and local officers:
law suits arising were heard before
counsel learned in the law. Henry VIII
brought increasing formality, establishing the court's machinery in
1519–20 and giving it statutory powers,
jurisdiction and a seal in 1540. Increasingly unpopular, the court continued until 1645–6 when, under
parliamentary pressure, it was abolished: the abolition was confirmed at
the Restoration.   PMB

Wardship and Marriage, incidents
of feudal tenure. W. developed with
the rules of descent: the lands of a
minor heir of a tenant-in-chief remained in the king's hand until he
came of age, a boy at 21, a girl at 14.

Frequently the w. was sold to the
highest bidder, who could abuse his
trust. Marriage of the heir generally
went with the w., while all tenants'-
in-chief widows were in the king's
gift. MAGNA CARTA regulated abuses
by forbidding the wasting of inheritances, unsuitable marriages or the
compulsion of widows to marry.
These incidents, found at all levels of
feudal tenure, persisted, to be rigorously enforced by the court of WARDS
AND LIVERIES.   PMB

War of 1812, see AMERICAN WAR OF
1812.

War Office, originally the office of
the Secretary-at-War, whose predecessor appeared in 1642 in both
royalist and parliamentary armies.
At first a subordinate official as the
secretary of the Commander-in-Chief,
from 1666 he rose in status, almost to
that of a SECRETARY OF STATE, advising the sovereign, ordering troop
movements and assuming parliamentary responsibility for military
finance. His position declined from
1794 onwards when a Secretary of
State for War (and the Colonies, 1801–
54) was appointed. From 1855 the
offices of Secretary-at-W. and Secretary of State for W. were united in
the same person, and in 1863 the
former was abolished. As a result of
reforms in 1855 and 1870 the Secretary of State for W. assumed control
at the W.O. of all army affairs, his
governmental duties being combined
with various military powers taken
over from the Board of ORDNANCE,
from the Commander-in-Chief, from
the Commissariat Department of the
TREASURY and from the Board of
General Officers, whose main duty
had been to approve samples of army
uniforms. From 1904 he was advised
on military matters by the ARMY
COUNCIL. On 1 Apr. 1964 the W.O.
was absorbed in the unified Ministry
of DEFENCE.   MR

War of Independence, see AMERI-
CAN REVOLUTION.

Warrant, in origin a 'guarantee': thus
in law A. granting land to B. could be

called on to guarantee B.'s title should it be challenged. The additional stronger meaning of authorization was early adopted, e.g. in proceedings QUO WARRANTO, in w.s for payments of money, affixing the GREAT SEAL etc., and has been widely used. In each case the agent is indemnified, 'guaranteed', against the consequences of his actions, provided his w. is good and sufficient. PMB

Washington treaties (1921–2), resulting from the W. conference (12 Nov. 1921–6 Feb. 1922) called by the U.S.A. to discuss armament limitation and Pacific and Far Eastern matters and attended by the U.S.A., the British Empire, Japan, France, Italy, the Netherlands, Portugal, China and Belgium.

(1) The four-power treaty (13 Dec. 1921) between the U.S.A., the British Empire, France and Japan, agreeing to respect each other's insular possessions in the Pacific, destroyed the Anglo-Japanese alliance (1902) to the satisfaction of the Dominions and the U.S.A.

(2) The five-power treaty or W. treaty (6 Feb. 1922) on naval armaments between the U.S.A., the British Empire, Japan, France and Italy, fixing their respective strength of capital ships in a ratio of approximately 5 : 5 : 3 : 1.75 : 1.75. Further limitations were placed on aircraft carriers, ship tonnage, calibre of guns etc. Thus Great Britain conceded naval parity to the U.S.A. and Japan acquired superiority in the N.W. Pacific.

(3) The nine-power treaty (6 Feb. 1922) between all participants to respect the integrity of China. This was broken by the Japanese attack on Manchuria (1931). IHE

Watch and Ward, the responsibility of a settlement for its own safety. Henry III in 1233, 1242 and 1254, times of difficulty, issued writs of w. and w., requiring guards to be set in each township etc. The system was made permanent by the Statute of WINCHESTER 1285 which laid down

that each settlement should appoint a number of watchmen proportionate to its size to watch from dusk to dawn and to arrest strangers. The statute was repealed only in 1827. PMB

Waterloo, battle of (18 June 1815), the crowning victory ending the FRENCH REVOLUTIONARY AND NAPOLEONIC WARS, was fought 10 miles south of Brussels against Napoleon's 72,000 men by the British–German–Dutch army under Wellington (some 67,000 strong) with the last-minute support of 2 Prussian corps under Blücher. The French were weakened by their losses at QUATRE-BRAS and the despatch of a corps against the Prussians whom Napoleon believed to be retreating eastward after their defeat at Ligny (16 June); but Napoleon's defeat was brought about by inexplicably delaying his attack until 11.30 a.m. and his reluctance to throw in his élite troops (6.30 p.m.) as well as the stubborn resistance of the Nassau and Brunswick contingents at Hougoumont, the Dutch at La Haye-Sainte and the British at Papelotte and La Haye. The Prussian thrust in the French rear at Plancenoit and the final advance of the British Guards under Wellington's personal leadership were decisive. The allies lost 22,000 men, the French 36,000; the energetic pursuit eventually left Napoleon with only 2,000 men. SHS

Watling Street, a ROMAN ROAD on the line Dover – Canterbury – London – St Albans – Dunstable – Towcester – High Cross – Wall – Wroxeter. The road from Chester via Wroxeter to Chepstow has the same name; also sections of road in the north. The name is O.E. *Wæclingastræt*, the road leading to Wæclingaceaster (St Albans). In the late 9th century it was mentioned in the boundary agreement delimiting English and DANISH territory. (KING'S PEACE.) CFS

Watson's Plot, see BYE PLOT.

Wedmore, a village near Axbridge, Somerset, where at the end of June 878 Guthrum the leader of the DANES put off the baptismal dress he had assumed when baptized a week earlier at Aller near ATHELNEY. He and his leading men had agreed to accept baptism when they surrendered to Alfred king of WESSEX after their defeat at the battle of EDINGTON. It is probable that Alfred and Guthrum came to some agreement at W., but the so-called treaty of W. is in fact the agreement reached between them, probably in 885/6, after further hostilities.   CFS

Weihaiwei, port of the Shantung peninsula, was leased by Great Britain from China in 1898 for a period synchronous with the lease of Port Arthur to Russia (or, after 1905, to Japan). W. was restored unconditionally to China on 1 Oct. 1930.   SHS

Welsh Disestablishment. The adoption of Nonconformity by an overwhelming majority of the Welsh in the 19th century led to a profound religious cleavage which became intensified by political and economic differences. Among a small minority of Nonconformist radicals a demand for d. emerged in the 1830s. But it was not until the sweeping Welsh Liberal victory in the 1868 election, the Irish D. Act (1869) and the intensification of agrarian depression that the issue really came to life. Against a background of the bitterest politico-religious controversy ever known in Wales, bills for d. were unsuccessful as long as Gladstone, who opposed them, was alive. The Liberal ministry of 1905, following a royal commission (1906) which returned 74% of Welsh Protestant church members as Nonconformists, introduced a bill, twice rejected by the Lords, which became law in 1914. This disestablished and partly disendowed the church, secularizing ancient endowments to the value of £4m. to be applied for cultural and charitable purposes. The Welsh Church Temporalities Act (1919) authorized the payment of £1m. to the church. On 31 March 1920 the Church in Wales came into existence, separated from the province of Canterbury, with its own archbishop and an independent constitution. It included the four ancient Welsh dioceses of Bangor, Llandaff, St Asaph and St David's and, later, two new ones—Monmouth (1921) and Swansea and Brecon (1923).   GW

Welsh Laws were first promulgated by Hywel the Good (*c.* 910–*c.* 950) according to a tradition which, pruned of its accretions, may be authentic. 70–80 MSS are extant, of which half were written in the medieval period. The earliest Latin text (Peniarth MS. 28) is ascribed to *c.* 1175–1200, and the earliest Welsh text (Peniarth MS. 29), the Black Book of Chirk, to *c.* 1200; but it seems more likely that Welsh was the original language of the laws. Three groups of medieval versions survive, at one time mistakenly equated with territorial divisions, but now usually associated with the lawyers thought to be chiefly responsible for compiling them—Iorwerth, Blegywryd and Cyfnerth. Modified and adapted by professional jurists to meet changing circumstances, W.l. partially survived the Norman conquest and the statute of RHUDDLAN, especially in south-west WALES, where it retained considerable vitality. It was not finally abrogated until the Act of UNION.   GW

Welsh Nationalism, see PLAID CYMRU.

Welsh Office. In 1951 the additional title of Minister for W. Affairs was conferred on the Home Secretary and in Jan. 1957 transferred to the Minister of HOUSING AND LOCAL GOVERNMENT. In Oct. 1964 a SECRETARY OF STATE for Wales, with a separate W.O., was appointed to take over executive responsibility in Wales for functions previously carried out by the Ministry of Housing and Local Government and to have oversight within Wales of national policy in the spheres of agriculture, education, health, labour, planning, trade and transport.   MR

Welsh Trust, established in 1674 by an ejected London Puritan minister, Thomas Gouge, was a voluntary charitable organization, supported by

Anglicans and Dissenters, which was active until 1681. It financed the publication in Welsh of religious literature, especially Bibles; but its main aim was to found charity schools in which some 1,600–2,000 children were taught annually. It paved the way for the S.P.C.K. which, between 1699 and 1737, founded 95 schools in Wales. GW

Wergild, the compensation paid to the kin of the murdered by the murderer or his kin. Successive codes of Anglo-Saxon laws laid down the price of each free man (*wer*). In WESSEX it was 200 shillings for a CEORL and 1,200 shillings for a *gesith* or THEGN. W. marked an advance from the primitive blood-feud and characterized the period when kings attempted to see justice done to the kin rather than deal with the crime itself. As royal authority grew and new social groups replaced the kin, w. declined in importance. It survived the Norman conquest only in the small portion of the MURDER FINE allotted to the slain's kin. PMB

Wessex. The recorded founders of the kingdom of the West SAXONS are Cerdic and Cynric who landed, apparently at the beginning of the 6th century, in the area of Southampton Water. They joined with or conquered a group of early settlers on the middle Thames who had come, probably, overland from the Wash. The nucleus of W. was thus the area of the later Berkshire and Hampshire. In the reign of Ceawlin (†*c.* 593) expansion took place into Wiltshire, the lower Severn valley and north of the Thames, but the second and third of these areas were taken by the kings of MERCIA. During the 7th and early 8th centuries the West Saxons extended their power over the later Dorset, Somerset and Devon; and in the early 9th century Cornwall was conquered. The CONVERSION of W. to Christiantity took place in the mid-7th century. During much of the 7th century W. was not among the more important kingdoms: it was ruled by a number of kings at the same time; the king of Mercia ex-

tended his power to the south of the Thames, and gave the Isle of Wight and southern Hampshire to the king of SUSSEX. The merciless military activity of Cædwalla (683–8) restored the situation, and he even exercised power in SURREY and KENT. His successor, Ine, regained the territory to the south of the Thames and temporarily controlled Sussex, Surrey and London. For much of the 8th century, however, W. was dominated by the kings of Mercia; but the reign of Egbert (802–39), who had been an exile at Charlemagne's court, saw the rise of W. to predominance among English kingdoms. The defeat of Mercia at the battle of ELLANDUNE (825) led to the incorporation of Kent, Sussex, Surrey and ESSEX. In 829 Egbert made himself direct ruler of the Mercians, and the Northumbrians made a nominal submission; but he could not maintain this position, and Mercia regained its independence. The DANES had already begun their attacks on England, and the Danish invasion that began in 865 resulted in the disappearance of all English rulers except the king of W.; and king Alfred (871–99) was recognized as ruler of all Englishmen outside the areas occupied by the Danes. The reconquest of these Danish areas under Alfred's son, Edward the Elder (899–924), resulted in the kings of W. becoming kings of all England and in the disappearance of W. as a separate kingdom. The area retained its identity until the Norman period as the area in which West Saxon law was administered and as an earldom. In the 11th century king Cnut made Godwine earl of W. His son succeeded to the earldom and became king of England as Harold II in 1066; with his death the earldom ceased. W. as a sentimental concept was developed by Thomas Hardy in the 19th century, and he set the scenes of his novels there. CFS

Wessex Culture, a BRONZE-AGE culture in southern Britain that flourished *c.* 1600–*c.* 1400 B.C. It developed from BEAKER CULTURES, native and imported, and the BATTLE-AXE CULTURE which seems to have provided the ruling aristocracy. The wealth of this society was due to its position on a major trade route between Ireland, a main centre of bronze manufacture, and western Europe. Its civilization, mainly an elaboration of the Beaker culture, was marked by far-flung trading contacts extending from the Baltic to the eastern Mediterranean. Characteristic are individual burials with lavish grave goods. The main advance was in bronze technology where improved methods of founding facilitated the development of more effective weapons, although flint still had wide use. Linen and woollen clothing were worn. This culture was responsible for the major reconstruction that produced STONEHENGE III. After *c.* 1400 it was gradually replaced by a native development, the URN CULTURE, where there is no evidence of aristocratic predominance.   CFS

West Bengal, see BENGAL.

Western Australia, visited by vessels of the Dutch East India company from 1616, was named New Holland by Tasman in 1644. Their reports and those of William Dampier (1688, 1699) considered the country as unsuitable for colonization. In 1791 Capt. George Vancouver took formal possession of the southern shore and in 1801–2 Capt. Matthew Flinders made a detailed survey for the admiralty; at his suggestion the continent was named Australia in 1814. To forestall an occupation by the French (whose expeditions, from 1792, have left traces in various place-names) the governor of NEW SOUTH WALES on 25 Dec. 1826 established the first settlement at King George Sound and on 2 May 1829 Capt. Fremantle founded the Swan River Settlement. Nominated executive and legislative councils were set up in 1832 and the first shipment of wool was sent to England in 1834, but the colony remained the most backward part of Australia until nearly the end of the century. Because of the labour shortage W.A. petitioned for the introduction of convicts in 1849; their trans-

portation ceased only in 1868 owing to the opposition of the other Australian colonies; the last penal settlement was disbanded in 1886. Representative government was inaugurated in 1870 and responsible government in 1890. The discovery of goldfields in 1885 and especially 1892–3 caused a rush of immigration which reached its peak in 1896. W.A. has remained the biggest gold-producer of Australia, but the spectacular development of agriculture from 1903 (though hampered by frequent floods and droughts) has stabilized her economy. W.A. joined the Commonwealth of AUSTRALIA on its creation, 1 Jan. 1901, but a referendum held in 1934 voted for secession and the establishment of a separate dominion, which, however, was rejected by the British House of Commons.   SHS

Western Pacific High Commission was created in 1877 as the supreme administration of the British islands not under the jurisdiction of AUSTRALIA and NEW ZEALAND and excepting FIJI. The principal groups are the GILBERT AND ELLICE ISLANDS colony, the British SOLOMON ISLANDS protectorate, the NEW HEBRIDES condominium and PITCAIRN.   SHS

Western Rebellion (1549) was provoked by some class feeling against the gentry but essentially by resistance to the new Prayer Book first used on Whit Sunday. The first outbreak was at Sampford Courtenay (9 June) and the movement spread rapidly. Bodmin was the centre of the Cornish rising and the rebels took Plymouth and joined the men of Devon. Exeter was besieged throughout July, but Lord Russell defeated the rebels at Clyst Heath (5 Aug.) and routed the remnant at Sampford Courtenay (17 Aug.).
                                                         IHE

Western Samoa, see SAMOA.

West Indies, The, originally named 'British Caribbean Federation' in the British Caribbean (Federation) Act, 1956, was a federation of the islands of ANTIGUA, BARBADOS, DOMINICA, GRENADA, JAMAICA, MONTSERRAT, ST

KITTS–NEVIS–ANGUILLA, ST LUCIA, ST VINCENT, TRINIDAD and TOBAGO, i.e. all British possessions in the Caribbean except the VIRGIN ISLANDS. The federation was formed on 1 Aug. 1957 and officially established on 3 Jan. 1958, with its capital in Trinidad. The constitution provided for a governor-general, a senate of 19 members and a house of representatives of 45 members. Cabinet government was introduced on 16 Aug. 1960. It was hoped that BRITISH GUIANA and BRITISH HONDURAS would eventually join the federation; but on 19 Sept. 1961 Jamaica and on 1 Feb. 1962 Trinidad opted out. The loss of the two richest islands made the federation unviable, and the British government therefore dissolved it (18 April 1962). Barbados became independent in 1966. The common regional organizations (university, court of appeal, Caribbean Free Trade Area, etc.) are maintained by the West Indies Associated States (Antigua, Dominica, Grenada, St Kitts–Nevis–Anguilla, St Lucia, St Vincent) formed in 1967 in free association with the United Kingdom. SHS; IHE

Westminister, provisions of, see PROVISIONS.

Westminster, first statute of (1275), a miscellaneous collection of enactments, opening with a prohibition against abuse of monastic hospitality, regulating replevin, reprisals, wreck and officials' malpractices, but principally concerned with criminal matters, notably the introduction of compulsory jury trial. Those refusing a jury were to be committed to a *prison forte et dure*. This became corrupted to *peine forte et dure*, and the punishment was made harsher, involving pressing between boards of the accused until he accepted a jury or died. This was abolished in 1772, when refusal to plead was made equivalent to a conviction. Since 1827 a plea of 'not guilty' has been entered for anyone refusing to plead. PMB; MR

Westminster, second statute of (1285), a series of provisions covering many fields of law, among which *de donis conditionalibus*, gave, after judicial extension, rise to entails, another curbed collusive actions, NISI PRIUS laid the foundation of modern judicial visitations, *elegit* (perhaps based on a Jewish practice) allowed creditors to have debtors' chattels and hold half their lands until settlement, *in consimili casu* led to the extension of actions designed for one case to another, and also laid down penalties for untrustworthy accountants. PMB

Westminster, third statute of (1290), see QUIA EMPTORES and QUO WARRANTO.

Westminster, statute of (11 Dec. 1931), gave legal substance to the definition of dominion status agreed at the 1926 IMPERIAL CONFERENCE, which declared the U.K. and Dominions 'autonomous communities ... equal in status, in no way subordinate one to another.' The S. of W. made the parliaments of CANADA, AUSTRALIA, NEW ZEALAND, UNION OF SOUTH AFRICA, IRISH FREE STATE and NEWFOUNDLAND independent of U.K. legislative control. Henceforth they could repeal U.K. statutes concerning themselves whilst the U.K. parliament was denied power to extend legislation to them without their consent. Constitutional change in Canada, Australia and New Zealand still required U.K. legislation. The U.K. and Canada ratified the S. of W. in 1931, Australia in 1942 and New Zealand in 1947. MLH

Westminster, treaty of (1153), see WINCHESTER.

Westminster Assembly (1643–9), convened by the LONG PARLIAMENT, consisted of 30 laymen and 120 clergy to make a religious settlement in conjunction with Parliament. It drew up the Calvinistic Westminster Confession of Faith and Catechisms and replaced the Prayer Book by the Directory. Predominantly Presbyterian, there was a small opposition from ERASTIANS and INDEPENDENTS. The ascendancy of the army and the Independents after 1649 largely nulli-

fied the attempt to establish PRESBY-
TERIANISM.   IHE

Whigs, originally denoting Scottish
horse-drovers, later applied to Scottish
Presbyterian rebels and finally, at the
time of the EXCLUSION BILLS, as an
abusive term to the COUNTRY PARTY
under Shaftesbury, the PETITIONERS
of 1679. Organized at first from their
headquarters at the Green Ribbon
Club, they drew support from the
aristocracy and from the trading and
City of London interests, upholding
parliamentary supremacy and toleration for nonconformists. The GLORI-
OUS REVOLUTION of 1688 was mainly
their triumph, and the Whig JUNTO
formed a powerful group in the reigns
of William III and Anne. United in
opposition to the JACOBITES, they
secured the HANOVERIAN SUCCESSION
and, as the TORIES were suspected of
disloyalty, enjoyed a monopoly of
power until the accession of George
III. In the 18th century they were not
organized as a party in the modern
sense and consisted largely of personal
groups contending for power among
themselves, kept together by friendship and patronage rather than policies
and principles. They were eclipsed by
the new toryism of the younger Pitt
from 1783 and after the French
Revolution many became Tories.
They began to recover unity by supporting abolition of SLAVERY and
Roman CATHOLIC EMANCIPATION, and
triumphed in 1830 as champions of
Parliamentary REFORM. Between 1830
and 1841 they effected some major
reforms and were eventually strengthened by Peel's followers after the
Tory split of 1846. With the advent of
more radical policies the name Liberal
had by 1868 superseded that of W.
                                              IHE

Whitby, Synod of (663), was summoned by Oswiu, king of NORTHUM-
BRIA, to decide between Roman and
Celtic practice in determining the
date of EASTER. The real problem,
however, was the weakening of the
power of Christianity in England
through the existence of two differing
sets of practice and outlook. Although
the SCOTTISH CHURCH was superficially
more powerful in England, the prestige
of Rome proved decisive. In strict
fact the decision in favour of Rome
applied only to Northumbria and to
one point at dispute, but Roman
practice on all points was speedily
adopted in all Teutonic kingdoms;
and during the course of a century the
Welsh, Irish and Scottish churches
followed suit. This decision linked
England fully with the main line of
the church in western Europe.   CFS

Whiteboys. Long standing grievances against tithes, rack-renting and
inclosures caused the rise of these
Irish Catholic peasant societies in
Munster in the 1760s. Temporarily
suppressed by legislation and military
action, they again terrorized southern
Ireland from 1786 until after the
rebellion of 1798. From the 1820s
peasant evictions led to the reappear-
ance of similar secret terrorist associations called Whitefeet, Blackfeet,
Molly Maguires etc.   IHE

White Ship (25 Nov. 1120). The
W.S., bound from Normandy to England with some 300 passengers, was
wrecked off Barfleur with great loss of
life. Among the many Anglo-Norman
nobles drowned was King Henry I's
only legitimate son, William. This
led to the disputed succession between
Maud and Stephen, daughter and
nephew of Henry I, and the ensuing
ANARCHY after Henry's death in 1135.
                                              RFW

Whitgift's Articles (1583) were
issued soon after his appointment to
the see of Canterbury with the intent
of disciplining the Puritan clergy who
were compelled to accept the royal
SUPREMACY in matters ecclesiastical,
the BOOK OF COMMON PRAYER and
the 39 ARTICLES. Rules on clerical
dress were also enforced. The court of
HIGH COMMISSION was employed to
these ends and many Puritans were
deprived. The unofficial presbyterian
organization was destroyed, which
might have undermined the Anglican
Church from within.   IHE

Wilkes' Case, see GENERAL WARRANTS.

Will, Tenancy at, the tenure of a man holding his land by no fixed agreement and for no fixed period, but solely at the pleasure of his lord. Though such lands were not heritable, their tenants were comparatively free. Medieval t. at w. was relatively uncommon, but it spread with the breakdown of manorial structures and the changing law in tenancy. Grants at will were, however, regularly used by kings to reward servants, without complete alienation. Though largely replaced by fixed terms, t. at w. still survives.   PMB

Wills. The history of testamentary disposition of goods and lands is complicated. W. of goods were from Old English times made, for to die intestate was a disgrace. Such w. were circumscribed by custom, e.g. the wife's due portion; wives could not make them without husband's consent; VILLEINS might make them, but their lords could seize their goods before probate. W. of lands were at first uncommon, barred by rigid customs and laws of inheritance, but became more common with the growth of freehold. Anglo-Saxon w. were vague settlements: in the 13th century executors began to be appointed to whom the deceased in theory conveyed his goods for distribution, satisfying legal conveyancing theories and giving the will something of its modern form. Probate was the church courts' concern for many centuries, but the COMMON LAW impinged on it, dealing with executors' misdemeanours, rationalizing the decaying church courts by its influence, attacking them together with other special courts. They survived into the 19th century: then a mass of probate jurisdictions, from the metropolitans to the lords of manors, depending on the value and distribution of the estate, was swept away. The lay probate court was established in 1857, now forming part of the PROBATE, ADMIRALTY AND DIVORCE DIVISION of the Supreme Court.   PMB

Winchelsea, naval battle off (29 Aug. 1350), known as *Les Espagnols sur Mer*. The English fleet, commanded by Edward III and based on Dover, intercepted a Spanish fleet under Don Carlos de la Carda as it passed from Sluys into the Channel. The Spanish fleet was destroyed after a desperate action, characterized by the grappling and boarding tactics of the middle ages, in which the English ships suffered severely.   RFW

Winchester, rout of (14 Sept. 1141). The Empress Maud besieged Wolvesey castle in W., held for King Stephen, in Aug. 1141. With the arrival of royalist relieving forces the besiegers found themselves besieged in their turn. Their withdrawal from an untenable position became a rout, in the course of which Maud's principal supporter, Robert, earl of Gloucester, was captured at Stockbridge. King Stephen, a prisoner since the battle of LINCOLN, was released by Maud in exchange for Robert. Although the r. of W. brought the wars of the ANARCHY no nearer a conclusion, it marked the end of Maud's best opportunity to secure the throne for herself.   RFW

Winchester, statute of (1285), issued by Edward I, brought together and expanded many regulations for maintaining peace and good order, laying down remedies against harbouring felons and concealing crimes, instituting regular WATCH AND WARD, incorporating the assize of ARMS, forbidding the hearing of pleas on a Sunday and the holding of fairs and markets in churchyards. At first enforced by the SHERIFF, then by keepers and JUSTICES OF THE PEACE, the statute remained in force until 1827.   PMB

Winchester, treaty of (6 Nov. 1153), which ended the ANARCHY, was agreed upon at W. and formally ratified at Westminster in December; hence its alternative name of the treaty of Westminster (sometimes also called, erroneously, the treaty of Wallingford). As King Stephen's eldest son and designated successor, Eustace, had died in Aug. 1153, Stephen now formally made Henry of Anjou, son of the Empress Maud, his heir and successor to the kingdom of England, but Stephen was to retain the throne as long as he lived. From Henry the kingdom was to descend to his heirs, and some compensatory provision was made for Stephen's second son William, earl of Surrey. Both parties undertook to dismiss their troops and to destroy ADULTERINE CASTLES. Stephen died on 25 Oct. 1154, and Henry duly succeeded to the throne as Henry II, the first sovereign of the house of PLANTAGENET.   RFW

Windmill Hill Culture, see NEOLITHIC.

Window Tax, imposed in 1696 to defray the expense of replacing the clipped and damaged coinage, took the place of the HEARTH TAX. The younger Pitt greatly increased it in 1782 and 1797. Houses with fewer than 7 windows were exempted in 1792 and fewer than 8 in 1825. It was reduced in 1823 and replaced in 1851 by an extension of the house duty (first imposed 1798). Scotland was exempted under the terms of the Act of UNION (1707). Houses were designed and windows blocked to avoid it.   IHE

Windsor, the name of the royal house and family as well as of all male descendants of Queen Victoria who are of British nationality, was assumed by King George V on 17 July 1917, in place of the designation of Saxe-Coburg-Gotha deriving from the Prince Consort Albert (1819–61). The name was altered on 8 Feb. 1960 to Mountbatten-Windsor for the descendants of Queen Elizabeth II other than those entitled to the styles of royal highness, prince and princess.
,SHS

Windsor, assize of, see GRAND ASSIZE.

Windsor, treaty of (1175), recognized Rory O'Connor as high-king of those parts of IRELAND not yet under English rule, in return for the promise of an annual tribute to Henry II.

However, Rory (d. 1198) never exercised effective authority outside Connaught, nor did the treaty restrain the English from further conquests at the expense of native rulers.   RFW

Windward Islands, were declared neutral in 1748 but passed under British rule in 1763. They were federated in 1763–7 (GRENADA, ST VINCENT, DOMINICA, TOBAGO), and in 1833 (without Dominica) placed under a single governor while keeping their distinct administrations. In 1838 ST LUCIA was added, in 1875 BARBADOS was separated, in 1889 Tobago was attached to TRINIDAD, in 1940 Dominica was re-transferred from the LEEWARD ISLANDS. The W.I. joined the WEST INDIES federation in 1958 and were federated with the Leeward Islands in 1960.   SHS

Winwæd, battle of (655), was fought on an unidentified river near Leeds, Yorks, between the BERNICIANS under king Oswiu and a composite force of MERCIANS under king Penda, a few EAST ANGLES under their king, and Britons under a number of princes. The king of DEIRA, Penda's ally, did not take part. Oswiu was victorious, and Penda and the king of East Anglia were killed.   CFS

Witan, Old English *wita* (plural *witan,* genitive *witena*) originally meant 'one who knows' but later acquired the specialized meaning of king's councillor. By the 11th century the plural *witan* was at times used in the sense of the king's council, but not until later is the term *witenagemot* found. Each kingdom originally had its own assembly, derived from the COMITATUS of the ruler; but these disappeared as kingdoms lost their independence, re-appearing only in times of crisis. From the earlier 10th century there was generally one assembly (MOOT) for the whole land. Membership was virtually confined to higher ecclesiastics and laymen, including king's THEGNS, and there is no evidence of any popular element. It had no fixed time or place of meeting. It was not concerned with routine administration but its advice and consent were sought for foreign affairs, legislation, the imposition of GELD, the calling out of the FYRD, grants by CHARTER, ecclesiastical changes etc., and it decided judicial matters where important men were concerned. It elected the new king although this was a formality where the succession was straightforward. After 1066 it developed into the *commune concilium*. The term *witan* could also be used for lesser formal assemblies such as the governing bodies of towns (*burhwitan*) etc. CFS

Witchcraft, long a popular belief, was subjected to active persecution in Tudor England when an act of 1542 condemned it as a felony. Causing death by w. became a capital offence in 1563. In the same year a Scottish act imposed the death penalty for w. and sorcery. James I, a firm believer in witches, encouraged witch-hunting and the law of 1603 inflicted death for invoking evil spirits. Witch-hunting reached its peak under Presbyterian influence in the 1640s. Persecution was renewed at the Restoration but declined after the 1670s. The last trial for w. in England was in 1712 and the last execution in Scotland in 1722. English and Scottish w. laws were repealed in 1736. IHE

Wite, a penal fine in Old English times paid to the king or other public authority for disturbing the peace, failing to obey royal commands etc. It was a payment additional to any due to an injured individual (WERGILD). CFS

Witnesses. The origin of w. either in law or to transactions lies in the age of small communities, perpetuated in the MANOR, TITHING etc., where each man knew the other's business. In early COMMON LAW this knowledge was tapped by requiring 2 w., one who saw, the other who heard. With the advent of the jury system w. declined in importance until, in the 16th century, the JURY shed the pretence of special knowledge. By an Act of 1563 plaintiffs' w. could be compelled to attend, but the defence could not compel w. or have them sworn until 1702: the modern expert witness is a long way from the early Common law. W. to transactions, found in the early Anglo-Saxon laws, gave some guarantee to each party before the age of written titles. Such transactions often took place in a court and the whole court would testify. As written titles grew the function of w. changed. By the 13th century they had become guarantors, not necessarily present when the transaction was completed: in modern times this change has been reversed. Nevertheless, whether the w. were present or not, the witness lists of medieval charters etc. are good guides both to the date of the document and to the associates and staff of the grantor. PMB

Women's franchise, see REFORM ACT (4); SUFFRAGETTE MOVEMENT.

Woods, Forests and Land Revenue, see CROWN ESTATE COMMISSIONERS.

Wood's Halfpence. The need of small coins in Ireland led to the grant of a patent to the Duchess of Kendal, George I's mistress, for the issue of copper coins (1722). She sold it to William Wood for £10,000. The Irish Parliament objected vehemently, arguing that the excessive amount of copper Wood planned to introduce would lead to the country being drained of its small stock of gold and silver. Swift's *Drapier's Letters* (1724) roused the whole country against the scheme and Walpole was forced to withdraw the patent (1725). IHE

Woodstock, Treaty of, was concluded on 30 Apr. 1247 between Henry III and princes Owain and Llywelyn ap Gruffydd of GWYNEDD, by which the latter were recognized as rightful rulers of Gwynedd above Conway but abandoned their claims to territory and homage elsewhere in north WALES. GW

Woollen and Worsted Industry. Until the 19th century the manufacture of woollen and worsted cloth was England's premier industry. Both fabrics were of very early origin, but

the coarser worsteds tended to predominate in rural industry and to
displace woollens in the 17th century.
New fabrics were gradually added,
notably the 'new draperies', lighter
cloths of finer quality which were
introduced by immigrants to the East
Anglian towns in the 16th century; and
the proliferation of mixed cloths
eventually blurred the old distinction between woollens and worsteds.
Woollen yarn was spun in the home,
often by women, and technical improvement was continuous. From
the 16th century onwards the spinning
wheel steadily replaced the distaff,
and in the 18th century Hargreaves'
spinning jenny (1767) and Crompton's
mule (1776) greatly increased the rate
of production. Weaving, a more
specialized task and principally a man's
trade, also made technical advance,
culminating in Kay's flying shuttle
(1733) and Cartwright's power loom
(1785). The application of these inventions in the late 18th and early 19th
centuries did not permanently reduce
employment in the industry, although
the ruin of the handloom weavers in
the 1820s by the power loom remains
the classic case of technological unemployment.

The financing and organization of
production was on a capitalistic basis
from early days. The various methods
employed are usually known as the
domestic system, a system whereby
production was carried on at home,
but where the producer was effectively
an employee of a clothier or merchant
who supplied the raw materials, the
credit and the marketing facilities for
the finished product. Unlike the
COTTON INDUSTRY, woollen production
was not concentrated in factories until
quite late, although the use of steam
power based on coal made this necessary by 1850. The industry was
widespread geographically until the
19th century, and its fortunes were
always closely bound up with English
agriculture. There had been an urban
industry since the 12th century in
eastern England and rural industry
developed in many areas from the mid-
13th century. In the 14th and 15th

centuries rural industry advanced at
the expense of the towns due to
demand for water power for the fulling
mills and freedom from the urban
gilds. Although the East Anglian
towns revived with the 'new draperies',
the countryside continued to produce
most of the coarser cloths and the
industry was not fully urbanized until
the growth of factories during the
INDUSTRIAL REVOLUTION. In the 17th
century the south-eastern counties and
the Midlands declined as areas of
production, and the West Country and
East Anglia followed in the 18th century. By 1860 woollen cloth production was concentrated in the West
Riding of Yorkshire.

Sheep farming expanded steadily
after the Norman conquest, especially
under enterprising landlords such as
the Cistercians in the 12th century.
Until the 14th century much wool was
exported, chiefly to Flanders and
Italy, and the staple system was developed to control and protect this major
source of wealth. But from the 1380s
the demand for wool by the new cloth
industry increased and wool exports
declined thereafter, prohibited by
James I and, in 1660, by statute. In
the 18th century additional supplies
had to be obtained from Spain,
Silesia and Saxony, and in the 19th
century from Australia.

The marketing of cloth in the middle
ages was handled to a great extent
through the STAPLE towns and by the
Italian and HANSE merchants. These
foreigners were slowly ousted by the
MERCHANTS ADVENTURERS and by the
end of the 16th century cloth exports
were in the hands of various English
companies. Until the late 17th century
most cloth was exported unfinished to
be dyed etc. in Flanders, but gradually
other types of cloth were developed
for new and expanding markets such
as the Mediterranean. Despite severe
recessions in the 1560s and 1620s
cloth exports continued to diversify
and expand, and as the chief exporter
the industry received strong government protection. The export of Irish
woollen cloth, except to England, was
prohibited (1699) and the Calico Act

(1721) attempted to end the competition from imported Indian calicoes. In fact it only encouraged the growth of an Indian textile printing industry. Despite the competition from other fabrics and other countries, however, the supremacy of the woollen industry was not shaken until the development of the cotton industry at the end of the 18th century. IHE; RBG

Worcester, battle of (3 Sept. 1651). After DUNBAR and the capture of Edinburgh Cromwell advanced on Perth, designedly leaving the way to the south open. Charles II crossed the border and established himself at W. but few English joined the invaders. Cromwell closed in with a superiority of nearly three to one and the Scots were beaten back into the city with disastrous losses. This was Cromwell's 'crowning mercy'. Monck completed the conquest of Scotland and Charles II escaped to France. IHE

Worcester, pact of (12 Dec. 1264). A number of MARCHER LORDS led by Roger Mortimer, taken prisoners by the MONTFORTIANS at LEWES but released because of the danger of Welsh attacks, proved a constant menace to the government of Simon de Montfort. Failing to honour an agreement made in August at Montgomery to surrender the royal castles and Montfortian prisoners they held, the Marchers were eventually compelled by military force to accept the pact of W. Simon de Montfort was to receive the western possessions of Henry III's son, Edward, including the palatinate of Chester, while the Marchers promised to go into exile in Ireland for a year and a day. This promise was never fulfilled, and the Marchers eventually played a major part in De Montfort's final overthrow at EVESHAM. RFW

Worcester, treaty of (March 1218), ended hostilities between the regency government of Henry III and Llywelyn ab Iorwerth of GWYNEDD, who, allying with the opponents of King John and his son in the BARONS' WARS, had made himself ruler of the greater part of Wales. Llywelyn did homage to Henry III but, to secure peace and an opportunity for recovery, the English had to allow him to retain his conquests and in particular royal lands in south Wales—nominally as the king's lieutenant. RFW

Workhouse, as a means of providing relief for the able-bodied poor by setting them to work, has its origins in the houses of correction designed for VAGABONDS under the POOR LAW Act of 1601, but it essentially dates from 1696 when Bristol Corporation promoted an act of Parliament for such an establishment. Other towns and parishes followed suit and a general permissive W. Act was passed (1723); it denied relief to those refusing to enter until modified by GILBERT'S ACT (1782) and the SPEENHAMLAND SYSTEM (1795–6). The w., so vividly portrayed by Charles Dickens in *Oliver Twist* (1838), again became the central feature of Poor Law relief in 1834. IHE

Works, Ministry of, see Public BUILDINGS AND WORKS.

World War I (1914–18) had its origin in the reaction of the other great powers to the aspiration of the German Empire after 1871 to predominate in European and world affairs. The effect of this was to divide the powers into two camps. While Germany formed with Austria–Hungary (1879) and Italy (1882) the military but defensive Triple Alliance, France joined with Russia (1893) and, less formally and later, with Britain (ENTENTE CORDIALE, 1904) in a diplomatic Triple Entente. Provocations such as the German design on Morocco (1911) and the Austrian annexation of Bosnia (1908) hardened the division between the two blocs and rapid armament increased international tension; Britain in particular feared Germany's great increase in naval strength since 1898. The war was caused proximately by insurgent nationalism in the Balkans, where the interests of Austria–Hungary and Russia were irreconcilable. Austria–

Hungary, whose position was weakened by Serbia's gains in the Balkan war of 1912–13, took the alleged complicity of the Serbian government in the murder, at Sarajevo (Bosnia) on 28 June 1914, of Francis Ferdinand, heir to her thrones, as pretext, with Germany's prior approval, for declaration of war (28 July). Russia, who dared not let Austria's influence spread in the direction of the Straits, mobilized in Serbia's support (29–30 July). The German government, dominated by the general staff, declared war on Russia (1 Aug.) and, in furtherance of the Schlieffen plan for prior swift victory in the west, on France (3 Aug.). These events left Britain hesitant; her moral obligation to France was recognized by the foreign secretary, Sir Edward Grey, but did not unite the Liberal government in favour of war. Germany's violation of Belgian neutrality (4 Aug.) was decisive; an ultimatum to desist expired at 11 p.m. on that day. Japan joined the allies immediately and Italy in May 1915; Turkey allied with Germany in Nov. 1914 and Bulgaria did so in Oct. 1915.

For the first two years Britain's contribution was mainly naval. A vigorous open blockade was instituted, and sea-borne trade and troop movements were maintained. Lone German raiders were rounded up and the German China squadron, after CORONEL (Nov. 1914), was defeated at the FALKLAND ISLANDS (Dec.). With the aid of the Dominions and Japan most of the German colonies (CAMEROONS, TOGOLAND, SOUTH-WEST AFRICA, NEW GUINEA, SAMOA) were quickly overrun; only in TANGANYIKA was resistance prolonged. Until the U-boats became dangerous in 1917 Britain had complete command of the seas. Only at JUTLAND (May 1916) was supremacy challenged by the full German fleet.

On land France quickly became the principal battleground for Britain. The HALDANE REFORMS had ensured that an efficient expeditionary force was immediately available. The 90,000 men under Sir John French were in action at MONS (23 Aug.) but became involved in the retreat of the French armies before Moltke's wheeling thrust through Belgium and south towards the Seine. After helping to stabilize the line by counter-attacking over the Marne (7–9 Sept.) the B.E.F. withstood, at the first battle of YPRES (Oct.–Nov.), the German attempt to reach the Channel ports. By the end of 1914 a static defence line, of which the British held only 21 miles, extended from the Belgian coast to Switzerland.

In 1915 an attempt to break this stale-mate was made in the GALLIPOLI CAMPAIGN (April 1915–Jan. 1916) but mishandling led to failure. On the western front the British army, reinforced but handicapped by shortage of ammunition, indecisively fought at Neuve-Chapelle (March), 'second YPRES' (April–May), Festubert (May) and in the allied September offensive (Loos) after which Haig succeeded French in command. Meanwhile the Central Powers had directed their effort to the eastern front, occupying Poland and most of Lithuania; Serbia was overcome; a substantial allied force arrived at Salonika (Oct.) too late to be effective. For three years an army, which in 1917 included 200,000 British troops, was locked up in a strategically useless Macedonian campaign. This and the MESOPOTAMIAN CAMPAIGN against the Turks strained shipping resources.

Although the French already had 2m. casualties (the British ½m.) a large offensive on the western front was planned for 1916. This was forestalled by the Germans who heavily assaulted the French at Verdun (Feb.–July). To relieve the situation Haig felt obliged to open the battle of the SOMME (July–Oct.) before his large reinforcements were fully ready. Again there was no decision but the battle was later recognized by the Germans to be the real turning-point of the war, both morally and materially, for they lost the great advantage they till then had in the survival of trained soldiers.

Criticism of Liberal leadership in

Britain began in the spring of 1915 when the munitions shortage became known. Asquith, giving way to Conservative pressure, formed a coalition in July; Churchill left the Admiralty where since 1912 he had performed as sterling a service as had Haldane for the army, and Lloyd George became minister of munitions. This government introduced general conscription in May 1916 but it was not properly applied until 1918 (and not at all in Ireland where the EASTER RISING had taken place). The death of Kitchener (June 1916), a difficult colleague as war minister but one with prestige at large, further weakened Asquith's position. In Dec. 1916 he withdrew under pressure from the premiership in favour of Lloyd George (who had succeeded Kitchener at the war office). Aspects of Lloyd George's conduct of the war are open to criticism—e.g. his refusal to reinforce Haig to the limit—but his forcefulness gave the country confidence in its ability to win.

Both sides tried to achieve a decision in 1917. In Jan. Germany resorted to unrestricted submarine warfare, calculating on Britain's submission before the U.S.A.'s inevitable intervention became effective. The U.S.A. declared war on 2 April, in which month allied shipping losses rose to 870,000 tons and Britain had only 6 weeks stock of food. By the end of the year, however, the danger was almost mastered with the adoption, at Lloyd George's insistence, of the convoy system. On the western front the new French commander, Nivelle, scrapped Joffre's plans for attrition warfare in favour of one smashing blow. In spite of the German withdrawal to the Hindenburg (Siegfried) line Haig had limited success on the Arras front (April) capturing Vimy Ridge, but Nivelle's all-important attack in Champagne did not break through. This failure with heavy loss led to mutinies in the French armies and the replacement of Nivelle by Pétain. The full weight of the offensive had then to be taken by Haig in Flanders at the third battle of

YPRES (July–Nov.). A British penetration at Cambrai (Nov.) when tanks were used with effect could not be exploited since reserves had been sent to the Italian front after the defeat of Caporetto. Meanwhile in the east the Russian offensive following the March revolution collapsed and in Dec. the new Bolshevik government sued for peace (treaty of Brest–Litovsk, 3 March 1918). An attempt to save the situation was made by the MURMANSK–ARCHANGEL EXPEDITION.

In 1918 it was vital for Germany to use the numerical superiority resulting from no longer fighting on two major fronts to achieve quick victory in France before U.S. troops could arrive in force and before the increasingly severe naval blockade completed German economic disruption. Ludendorff first attacked the Scarpe–Oise sector (21 March) driving the British back almost to Amiens, then turned to Flanders attacking the British astride the Lys (9 April); here he gained much ground but could not break through to the Channel ports. In the crisis Foch was appointed 'coordinator' (26 March) and allied general-in-chief (14 April). Next the Germans attacked further south over the Aisne (27 May) and drove a deep salient to the Marne at Château Thierry. But by now the German lines were fully extended; shortage of men and material was being felt. An effort to widen the salient failed, allowing Foch to make an important counter-attack which wiped out the bulge (second battle of the Marne, 15 July–6 Aug.). Haig followed by an offensive in front of Amiens (8 Aug.) which by mid-Sept. had pushed the Germans back to the Hindenburg line. Attacks everywhere made progress; in the south Pershing's American army was engaged in the St Mihiel salient near Verdun. The final concerted assault started in late Sept., the brunt being taken again on the British front where Haig broke the Hindenburg defences between St Quentin and Cambrai. With the whole front from Ypres to Verdun in movement the Germans had no chance of rallying. First overtures for peace were made on 4 Oct.; by 11 Nov. when an armistice was signed the allies had recaptured western Belgium and almost all French territory.

Events in other theatres were also moving fast against the Central Powers. In Italy the Austro-Hungarian army was defeated at Vittorio-Veneto (Oct.) and capitulated 3 Nov. In Palestine a British army under Allenby which had captured Jerusalem (Dec. 1917) crushingly defeated the Turks at Megiddo (Sept. 1918) and captured Damascus and Aleppo; success there and in Mesopotamia led to a Turkish armistice on 31 Oct. In Macedonia an allied breakthrough towards the Danube was followed by the capitulation of Bulgaria (30 Sept.).

As a result of the Paris peace conference the treaty of VERSAILLES was signed by Germany (28 June 1919), that of St Germain by Austria (10 Sept. 1919), that of Trianon by Hungary (20 June 1920), that of Neuilly by Bulgaria (27 Nov. 1919) and those of Sèvres (10 Aug. 1920) and Lausanne (24 July 1923) with Turkey.

British Empire casualties were 996,230 killed and died (including navy losses, 33,361) and 2,289,860 wounded.   MLH

World War II. Its underlying causes may be sought in the compromise terms of the treaty of VERSAILLES and in the failure of the great powers to use effectively the admittedly imperfect machinery of the LEAGUE OF NATIONS, but responsibility for its outbreak rests squarely on Nazi Germany. At a staff conference in Nov. 1937 Hitler favoured gaining 'living space' in Europe by war in 1938 or 1939. Austria fell in March 1938. When the MUNICH AGREEMENT of Sept. had been followed by annexation of the rest of Czechoslovakia (March 1939), Poland, to whom Britain and France gave guarantees (31 March), became the next objective. At another conference in

May 1939 Hitler proposed to attack and accepted the probability of a general war in the west. Almost to the end he hoped to keep Britain neutral; this was a motive for the Hitler–Stalin pact (23 Aug.). Although an Anglo-Polish alliance had been signed 5 days before, on 1 Sept. the onslaught on Poland was launched. British and French ultimatums to withdraw expired 11 a.m. and 5 p.m., 3 Sept. The allies could not help; Warsaw surrendered 27 Sept. and by the end of the month occupation by Germany and Russia was complete. German forces were then concentrated in the west.

Denmark and Norway were invaded on 9 April 1940. Denmark did not resist and in Norway the Germans quickly took Oslo and the chief ports. Small allied forces (first intended for operations in Scandinavia and Finland—attacked by Russia in Nov.— and to interrupt iron-ore supplies to Germany) landed near Trondheim in central Norway and near Narvik in the north. Terrain and climate were difficult whilst frequent change of strategic plan created muddle, but the deciding factor in withdrawal from the Trondheim area (2–3 May) was lack of air cover; and from Narvik (8 June), events in France. Disappointment led to a Commons censure motion (7–8 May) when 33 government supporters voted for it and 60 abstained. This lack of confidence persuaded Chamberlain to resign and Churchill, who had been First Lord of the Admiralty since outbreak of war, became Prime Minister of a coalition government on 10 May. On the same day the German *Blitzkrieg* in the west opened with the invasion of Belgium and Holland.

The British Expeditionary Force (394,000 men; 10 divisions) under Lord Gort advanced with the allied left wing into Belgium, but the Germans broke through over the Meuse in the Ardennes to Amiens and the coast, thus cutting off the Belgian army, the B.E.F. and the French 1st Army from the main French forces. Weygand, who succeeded Gamelin as supreme commander (20 May), could not close a widening gap and, when Belgian collapse was imminent, the British government ordered evacuation of Gort's troops (26 May), accomplished by the navy at DUNKIRK (29 May–4 June). B.E.F. losses were 68,000. Pétain for France signed an armistice with Germany on 22 June and with Italy (which had declared war on Britain and France, 11 June) on 24 June.

As in World War I naval supremacy was vital to Britain's survival. Blockade and the convoy system operated immediately, but the navy had to contend with the U-boat, the surface raider, magnetic and acoustic mines and the bomber. British naval losses in Norway were proportionately less serious than the German but disconcerting after the fall of France and the entry of Italy; the position was somewhat alleviated by the 'destroyer deal' with the U.S.A. (Sept.). Possession of continental ports from Biscay to North Cape gave Germany an all but decisive advantage in the 'battle of the Atlantic' (and later in the Arctic).

After the fall of France Churchill rallied Britain to face immediate threat of invasion, but Hitler's plans were postponed when the battle of BRITAIN (Aug.–Oct. 1940) failed to yield command of the air, which alone could have nullified temporarily British control of the Channel; and by Dec. Hitler was thinking of invading Russia in May 1941. In the Mediterranean the position was critical. Loss of French support seemed to imply such Italian naval preponderance that naval withdrawal (as in 1798) was discussed. The Navy's confidence in its superiority was vindicated by the naval air attack at Taranto (Nov. 1940) and by the battle of Cape MATAPAN (March 1941). The decision to reinforce Egypt and Malta was made in Aug. 1940. In Dec. Wavell counter-attacked the Italians, who had moved into Egypt in Sept., and reached Benghazi (6 Feb.) capturing 113,000 troops, but a precipitate retreat was made to the Egyptian frontier (a garrison being left in Tobruk) in face of the newly-arrived *Afrika corps* under Rommel. For in March Wavell's command had been depleted when 62,000 men under Sir H. M. Wilson had been sent to Greece; she had routed the Italian invaders but was threatened by Germany. The sanguine object of the expedition was to stabilize a Balkan front. Hitler, having made arrangements with Rumania and Bulgaria, opened his offensive on 6 April against Yugoslavia and Greece. Resistance crumbled and Wilson's force was evacuated by the end of the month. Its participation was justified more on political than on military grounds. Large-scale air invasion of Crete (20 May) was followed by evacuation of 18,000 men under Maj.-Gen. (Lord) Freyberg (out of 32,000 on the island), naval losses being most severe. In June, one precious month behind schedule, Hitler turned on Russia, achieving surprise in spite of prior warnings from Britain. By Oct. the Germans were in occupation of a large area from besieged Leningrad to Rostov and had pushed a salient almost to Moscow, which was saved by a counter-attack in Dec.

During the first months of 1941 Wavell had successfully undertaken campaigns in SOMALILAND and Abyssinia (capture of Addis Ababa, 5 April). In order that any necessary relief might be given to Turkey, a pro-German government was dislodged in Iraq (April) and Syria and Lebanon were captured from Vichy France (Jan.–June). In Nov. Wavell's successor, Auchinleck, once more attacked Rommel and, after the fierce battle of Sidi Rezegh, reoccupied Cyrenaica. Then the centre of interest switched dramatically to the Far East with Japan's attack on Pearl Harbor (7 Dec.). With the U.S. fleet crippled, the Japanese were able to use their aircraft carriers and amphibious forces to terrible effect against troops untrained in jungle warfare. So extended were Britain's naval commitments that only recently had she sent, as a political gesture, two capital ships, *Prince of Wales* and *Repulse*, to Singapore; with no air cover both were sunk. Japan's occupation of Indo-China and Siam provided a base for invasion of Malaya (8 Dec.) defended by 3 divisions; without adequate sea and air support they were pushed down the peninsula on to Singapore which surrendered (15 Feb. 1942) with the loss of 85,000 men. Loss of sea-power and Japanese attack into lower Burma made Rangoon untenable; Sir H. (Lord) Alexander fought a skilful retreat into Assam. Simultaneous attacks had meanwhile been made on U.S. territories (surrender of the Philippines, April–May 1942) and the Netherlands East Indies (Sumatra, Java, parts of New Guinea). By April the Japanese were supreme in the South Pacific and Indian Ocean. India and Australia were both threatened, as was the Cape sea-route to safeguard which an allied force occupied Madagascar. But this was the height of Japanese success, for attempts on Port Moresby (New Guinea) and Hawaii were abandoned after the Coral Sea (May) and Midway (June), two ultimately decisive naval–air battles.

Despite America's entry into the war with Germany (11 Dec. 1941)— and the close Anglo-American co-operation which was immediately established on the highest level in the Combined Chiefs of Staff Committee —in the first months of 1942 reverses continued. Malta was temporarily neutralized and the eastern Mediterranean for the moment lost. Rommel, reinforced, swiftly pushed back the 8th Army to El Gazala (Jan.) and, capturing Tobruk (21 June), to El Alamein, 60 miles from Alexandria. In the Atlantic shipping losses increased alarmingly (585 ships of over 3m. tons in the first 6 months of 1942) owing to early U.S. preference for patrol rather than convoy and to heavy commitments in the Arctic where convoys to Russia had to be protected against the remaining German capital ships now in Norwegian waters. The navy, repeatedly switching its depleted forces between Arctic,

Atlantic and Mediterranean, was stretched to its limits. This led to some questioning of the emphasis in resource being placed on R.A.F. Bomber Command's strategic offensive against Germany at the expense of Coastal Command's patent need of aircraft for escort in mid-Atlantic. A further crisis in the Atlantic occurred at the beginning of 1943; in March danger to Britain's survival was as great as in April 1917. But the position was quickly altered during the summer (in July 37 U-boats were sunk), partly as a result of the introduction of escort carriers—a permanent improvement emphasized by the agreement (Oct. 1943) for use of the Portuguese Azores.

Churchill and Roosevelt agreed (Jan. 1942) that, as U.S. potential came into play, victory over Germany rather than over Japan should have top priority. At first a 'second front' to relieve Russia in 1942 was considered; but at British insistence this plan was postponed in favour of driving the Axis from North Africa by a dual thrust, thus preparing for invasion of Southern Europe. In Oct. 1942 the 8th Army, reinforced, re-equipped and under the leadership of Montgomery, attacked Rommel at El ALAMEIN, drove him along the coast through Tripoli (23 Jan. 1943), assaulted the Mareth Line (21 March) and advanced north into Tunisia. An Anglo-U.S. expeditionary force under Eisenhower landed, 8 Nov. 1942, at Casablanca, Oran and Algiers, Vichy French resistance being minimized by collaboration with Adm. Darlan. Advancing into Tunisia 1st Army (Lt.-Gen. Sir K. Anderson) and American II Corps were faced by a German army greatly reinforced from the air. With Alexander as group commander in Tunisia, an assault on the Axis perimeter (6 May) led to occupation the next day of Tunis and Bizerta and surrender of 248,000 German and Italian troops (12 May).

A second and in scale much larger turning point in the war occurred in Russia at the same time as Alamein. The immense German offensive of the summer of 1942, directed at the Caucasian oilfields and across the Don to the Volga, was contained at Stalingrad and just failed to reach Grozny. In counter-attacks the Russians were able to punch out the Don salient and eliminate Paulus's 6th Army before Stalingrad (Jan. 1943). This was the important start to the successful offensives of 1943 and 1944.

In Jan. 1943 a cross-Channel invasion of France was again postponed in favour of Mediterranean operations. Under Eisenhower's supreme command, Alexander's army group (Montgomery's 8th Army and U.S. 5th Army) landed on Sicily (10 July 1943) and occupied the island in 38 days. But naval and air superiority did not prevent evacuation of 100,000 Axis troops to the Italian mainland. The Italian campaign which followed was subordinated to the plan (*Overlord*) for the invasion of N.W. France from the U.K. (timed for May 1944) and was made dependent upon its requirements for men and materials; its object, and the object of operations planned for the Balkans (Dodecanese) and southern France, was to contain the necessary number of divisions to enable *Overlord* to succeed. 8th Army moved across the Messina straits on 3 Sept. and 5th Army landed at Salerno (9 Sept.), 150 miles nearer Naples. Although the Italians had collapsed (fall of Mussolini, 25 July; armistice, 3 Sept.) a German front was established and 5th Army encountered strong opposition. Joined by Montgomery, progress was slow to the 'winter line' dominated by Monte Cassino. At this point 7 divisions were returned to U.K. Fierce fighting in the first months of 1944, in spite of a bridgehead precariously established at Anzio (Jan.), delayed the capture of Rome until 4 June. Rapid progress was now made to the Gothic line (Spezia to Rimini) assaulted in August. In difficult terrain and weather and with his force seriously depleted by the 'strategically useless' diversion into southern France, Alexander made advances but could gain no decisive advantage before

winter. In 1945 victory was quickly obtained. The assault being renewed in April, 8th Army broke through to Ferrara and 5th Army reached the Po north of Bologna. The capture of Verona split the German army. Trieste fell, 2 May, and on the same day the German army surrendered. That the object of the Italian campaign was triumphantly achieved is evidenced by the fact that in the summer of 1944 it was tying down 55 German divisions.

Preceded by an air offensive which paralysed the German air force and disrupted communications, the British 2nd Army and U.S. 1st Army, under supreme command of Eisenhower, landed in the Baie de la Seine (6 June 1944): on D-day nearly 160,000 men were landed; by 2 July, 1 m. Montgomery was essentially successful in his plan to draw and hold German armour on the left flank by a sustained British offensive through Caen, thus allowing U.S. forces on the right to isolate Cherbourg and develop a wheeling movement to the Seine. The U.S. breakout from St Lô came on 25 July and by mid-August had reached Angers and Nantes in the south and Orleans and Chartres in the east; an envelopment by British 2nd Army and Canadian 1st Army from the north and U.S. 1st and 3rd Armies from the south closed the Falaise–Argentan pocket with heavy German loss (including 344 tanks). Paris was liberated on 25 August. With German armies in full retreat, British and Canadians raced through Flanders into Belgium (Amiens, 31 Aug.; Brussels, 3 Sept.) whilst U.S. armies (including a U.S.–French army which had advanced up the Rhône, having landed in southern France, 15 Aug.) were on the Meuse and Moselle. On 23 Aug. Montgomery had proposed to Eisenhower a plan for a single powerful thrust against the Ruhr through the Pas de Calais, which might end the war in 1944. Then, as later, Eisenhower favoured advance on a broad front, but Montgomery was enabled to attempt a crossing of the lower Rhine with airborne assistance, and Army reached airborne forces at Nijmegen (20 Sept.) but could not relieve ARNHEM until too late. Failure thus to outflank the Siegfried Line, together with German control of the Scheldt (making Antwerp unusable) and checks to U.S. 1st and 3rd Armies dispelled hope of victory before winter. Now Hitler, who was 'backseat-driving' throughout the campaign in France, determined on a final offensive; on 16 Dec. he ordered an attack in the Ardennes, lightly held by U.S. 1st Army; a salient ('the bulge') was pushed almost to the Meuse, but Montgomery's brilliant tactics, the heroism of the American soldiers and German lack of petrol dictated a retreat (7 Jan. 1945). Whilst post-war arrangements were being made at YALTA (Feb.) the final allied offensive began. With the Russians on the Oder in the east, on the western front the Germans were pressed back to and over the Rhine; Montgomery's 21st Army Group crossed at Wesel (23 March) with airborne support and encircled the Ruhr.

Eisenhower, disregarding political considerations, left Berlin, Prague and Vienna to the Russians; such was American preponderance in the field that Churchill's protests went unheeded. After crossing the Elbe, Montgomery accepted surrender of German forces in north-west Germany, Holland and Denmark at Lüneburg Heath (4 May). General capitulation on behalf of Dönitz, Hitler's successor, was signed at Reims (7 May) and ratified in Berlin on 9 May.

The R.A.F. made a great contribution to victory over Germany in several ways: in the battle of Britain, in the battle of the Atlantic, in creating the conditions in which invasion of Normandy could succeed, in close support of the armies and not least in the strategic bombing of Germany. The building of Bomber Command (from Feb. 1942 commanded by Sir A. Harris) to an active strength of 1,600 aircraft by April 1945 absorbed a high proportion of the nation's resources, at the expense of other vitally needed materials. Hopelessly inadequate in 1939, not until 1942 were limitations of equipment and method realized. Precision attack gave place to area bombing; radar and the Pathfinder force were introduced. But in the application of strategic bombing there were misconceptions, disagreements and mistakes, for no effective precedent for this type of warfare existed. The results of area bombing on industrial production were not as great as anticipated; nor were moral effects (although 593,000 Germans were killed in aerial attack, compared with 61,000 U.K. civilians in German air-raids). The bombing of Germany became a cardinal feature of allied strategy in 1943, but until 1944 the German fighter force prevented the attack being pressed home with the concentration necessary for success, while in the later stages of the war the calls upon the command (in particular against the oil industry and transport) were so diverse that the general strategic offensive could not be fully staged. On Bomber Command operations 47,268 aircrew were killed.

Burma was the principal British theatre of war against Japan. In Aug. 1943 Lord (Louis) Mountbatten was appointed supreme commander, S.E. Asia, and Lt.-Gen. (Sir) W. Slim, commander of 14th Army. In the absence of amphibious forces conquest of Burma had to be through Assam or China, entailing a long and tedious campaign with dependence for supplies on air support. At the beginning of 1944 the American Gen. Stilwell advanced with his Chinese army upon Myitkyina in the north (aided by Wingate's Chindits behind the enemy lines) while British forces attacked in Arakan and towards central Burma. The Japanese reacted violently but their failure in Arakan, at Kohima and Imphal allowed 14th Army to take the offensive (Aug. 1944). Mandalay was captured (21 March 1945) after the Irrawaddy had been crossed north of the city, and the river was also crossed in force 100 miles to the south where an advance was made to Meiktila (5 March), held against heavy counter-attack. The Japanese withdrew and there developed a race to reach Rangoon (300 miles to the south) before the monsoon—the supply position was eased by success of the campaign in Arakan. In the event the city was occupied (2 May) by a division seaborne from Akyab. Mountbatten then planned to attack Singapore in Sept., but by then the war was over.

In the Pacific the Americans parried the danger to Australia by striking at Guadalcanal in the Solomons (Aug. 1942); a lengthy sea, land and air battle established U.S. naval superiority and enabled a strategy based on sea-power to be pursued. In 1943 New Guinea and New Britain were largely cleared. Attacks were launched on the Aleutians, and on the Marshall, Gilbert and Caroline Islands. The invasion of the Philippines produced the greatest naval battle of the war, Leyte Gulf (23–26 Oct. 1944), where the main fleet of Japan was decisively defeated. Manila was liberated (Feb. 1945) and the Philippines freed by June; the same month Okinawa was captured. In May and June Australian forces landed in North Borneo. Plans for invasion of Japan, in which British forces were to participate, were forestalled by the atomic-bombing of Hiroshima and Nagasaki (6, 9 Aug.) which compelled the Japanese government to surrender (14 Aug.).

Casualties to U.K. forces in W.W.II amounted to 340,672 killed and missing (Navy, 51,578; Army, 177,850; R.A.F., 76,342; Merchant Navy, 34,903). Similar figures for other parts of the Commonwealth total about 147,000.   MLH

Writ, Anglo-Saxon *gewrit*, Latin *breve*. Though owing much to continental models in origin, the development of the w., an administrative letter authenticated by WITNESSES and a SEAL, into a flexible and all-pervading instrument of government is a peculiarly English achievement. Writs were used at least as early as Alfred's reign. Their language was then VERNACULAR: after the Norman conquest the Anglo-Saxon phrases were translated into LATIN and the use of the w. constantly extended. Three main types emerged: letters close, ephemeral documents directed to one or more named persons, for administrative, judicial etc. purposes; letters patent, more permanent documents addressed to all who should see them and used for licences, commissions etc., and the CHARTER, a further development of letters patent addressed to all future readers as well as present, which replaced the cumbersome solemn diploma of Old English times. The types of w. evolved by the royal clerks had a profound influence on non-royal correspondence, and the w. was copied abroad, e.g. in Norway. See also CLOSE ROLLS; CONGÉ D'ELIRE; COUNTY COURT; CURSITORS; ENTRY, WRIT OF; HABEAS CORPUS; PATENT ROLLS; PETTY BAG OFFICE; PROHIBITION, WRITS OF; QUO WARRANTO; RIGHT, WRIT OF.   PMB

Wyatt's Rebellion (Jan.–Feb. 1554) was an attempt to promote Protestantism and prevent the unpopular marriage between Queen Mary and Philip II of Spain. Leaving Maidstone with his Kentish followers, Wyatt was checked at London Bridge. He crossed the Thames at Kingston and marched to Ludgate where he abandoned his cause as hopeless. The ringleaders and many others were executed, including the Lady Jane Grey and her husband, Lord Guildford Dudley, who were not involved. Elizabeth was sent to the Tower. IHE

Wycliffites, see LOLLARDS.

Yalta conference (4–11 Feb. 1945) was the most politically important of the WORLD WAR II meetings between allied heads of government. At Tehran (Nov. 1943) decisions were mainly military; by the time of the POTSDAM CONFERENCE the iron curtain had fallen; but at Y. post-war roles had still to be formulated.

Agreement was reached on 'the complete disarmament, demilitarization and dismemberment' of Germany; at Churchill's insistence, France was given an occupation zone and a seat on the high commission; the Morgenthau plan for 'pasturalization' of Germany was tacitly dropped, and reparations were referred to a commission with $20,000m. as a basis for discussion (Britain dissenting from this figure). Poland took up more time than any other topic, both Britain and Russia being vitally concerned; Stalin argued from strength since he was in military occupation. Churchill agreed to recognize a broader-based Lublin government instead of that exiled in London, pending 'free and unfettered elections as soon as possible'; this compromise evaded the real issue, as Russia required a friendly Polish government, which could not result from a free election. The Curzon line was recognized as Poland's boundary with Russia. An American draft 'declaration on liberated Europe' calling, *inter alia*, for 'earliest establishment through elections of governments responsive to the will of the was people' passed without comment.

Roosevelt was less concerned with Europe than with furthering the UNITED NATIONS and securing Russian entry into the Far Eastern war; moreover, he had faith in Stalin and distrusted 'British imperialism'. A compromise formula (with disastrous lack of definition) on voting in the Security Council was accompanied by agreement that Russia should have three seats in the General Assembly. On the Far East Roosevelt and Stalin drew up a secret protocol by which the latter promised to declare war on Japan 2 or 3 months after the German war ended, in return for preservation of the *status quo* in Outer Mongolia and cession of certain rights and territories lost after the Russo-Japanese War (1904–5); although Chinese interests were involved, Chiang Kai-Shek was not consulted.

With the German war still to be won and victory over Japan an estimated 18 months further off, the paramount necessity at Y. was continuance of the grand alliance. Divergencies of out-

look were not probed, facts were not faced.   MLH

Ye, see RUNES.

Year Books, notes of cases, principally of oral proceedings, compiled for the use of the legal profession. As the COMMON LAW developed, the Y.B. changed: at first they seem to have been collections attached to legal treatises, then they laid stress on the technical prowess of serjeants and judges, finally, as the law of precedent developed, becoming embryo law reports. The series ended in 1535, but was immediately replaced by the early printed reports, continuing to this day as the law reports of important and leading cases.   PMB

Yeomen of the Guard, at first a royal bodyguard of 50 scarlet-uniformed men established at Henry VII's coronation (30 Oct. 1485). Henry VIII had 600 Y. at the FIELD OF CLOTH OF GOLD (1520). Since the GUNPOWDER PLOT (1605) they have searched the vaults of Parliament. Their strength was fixed at 100 by Charles II in 1669. Their nickname 'Beefeaters' is attested first in 1645. They last accompanied the king on the battlefield at DETTINGEN (1743) and are now a ceremonial force which includes the Y. Warders of the Tower of London.
                                                     IHE

Yoke, a quarter of a SULUNG.   CFS

York, a Danish kingdom (DANES), established by Halfdan in 876 and occupying approximately the area of the former kingdom of DEIRA. Very little is known of its history, but its kings soon became Christian. In 909 it was attacked by an English army, and in 910 the power of these Northumbrian Danes was broken by king Edward of WESSEX at the battle of TETTENHALL. With their weakened power they were unable to resist the NORWEGIAN invaders from Ireland who crossed the Pennines and, in 919, set up the Norse kingdom of Y. In 920 their leader submitted to king Edward, and in 927 king Athelstan, his son, drove out the Norse king and destroyed the defences of Y. Norse kings reigned there again 940–4, 947 and 949–54. The last king, Eric Bloodaxe, died fighting at STAINMORE (954) and the kingdom came to an end. The area became a SHIRE, but its Scandinavian division into RIDINGS was continued.   CFS

York, statute of (1322), made in the parliament which assembled at York on 2 May, completed Edward II's triumph over the Lords ORDAINERS. While all statutes made by the king and his ancestors were to remain in force, the ORDINANCES of 1311 were entirely repealed. The attention of historians has been largely directed, however, at certain additional clauses of the s. of Y., viz. that in future any ordinances or provisions made by the king's subjects concerning the royal power or 'against the estate of the king . . . or of the crown' shall be of no effect; when necessary, establishments touching these matters shall be made by the king in parliament, with the assent of the prelates, earls and barons and 'the commonalty of the realm, as has been hitherto accustomed'. It is unlikely that the introduction of any new method of legislation was intended or that an attempt was being made to ensure that constitutional issues should be dealt with primarily by parliament. Since it is doubtful whether 'the commonalty of the realm' was intended to mean 'the commons in parliament', it is unwise to attach great significance to the statute in the history of the place and powers of the Commons. The main intention of Edward II and his supporters was probably to ensure against any further activity by surviving Ordainers. RFW

York, treaty of (Sept. 1237), helped to stabilize the Anglo-Scottish frontier on the line of the Tweed, the Cheviots and the Solway, although in places the border remained ill-defined. Alexander II of Scots, who had supported the baronial opponents of King John and Henry III and revived the Scottish claim to Northumberland, Cumberland and Westmorland, gave up his claim and received lands in Northumberland and Cumberland which he was to hold of Henry III and which were to remain parts of England. Although other important problems, such as the feudal relationship between the kings, were not tackled, the treaty was followed by half a century of unusually peaceful relations between the kingdoms.   RFW

Yorkists. (1) the kings of the house of York, i.e. Edward IV (1461–83), temporarily deposed during the RE-ADEPTION of Henry VI (1470–1); his elder son Edward V, never crowned, and deposed by his uncle, Richard, duke of Gloucester, who then reigned as Richard III (1483–5) until his death at the battle of BOSWORTH. Richard had been predeceased by his only legitimate son, Edward, while Edward IV's sons, Edward V and Richard, duke of York, appear to have been murdered in 1483 (PRINCES IN THE TOWER). Under Henry VII the pretender Perkin Warbeck (executed 1499) claimed to be Richard of York and was proclaimed as Richard IV by his followers. Another impostor, Lambert Simnel, captured by Henry VII in 1487, had been crowned as Edward VI in Dublin, and claimed to be Edward, earl of Warwick, son of George, duke of Clarence, Edward IV's brother (executed 1478). The real Edward, earl of Warwick, the last of the direct male line of York, was executed by Henry VII in 1499. The marriage of Henry VII to Elizabeth, elder daughter of Edward IV, helped to consolidate the TUDOR dynasty by making it represent both Lancaster and York. But there were many other representatives of York: the Courtenays, Poles and De la Poles, descendants of Edward IV's younger daughter Catherine; of Margaret, daughter of Clarence; and of Edward IV's sister Elizabeth: for these, Yorkist blood was a dangerous, and frequently fatal, legacy.

(2) The supporters of Richard, duke of York (†1460), and of his sons, Edward IV and Richard III, against Henry VI and the LANCASTRIANS in the wars of the ROSES. After Richard

III's death at Bosworth, Yorkist sympathies found outlets in rebellions against Henry VII and support of pretenders. After 1497, however, Henry was not in serious danger, and his imprisonment in 1506 of Edmund de la Pole, earl of Suffolk, removed the most likely leader of the disaffected.   RFW

Yorktown, surrender at (19 Oct. 1781), the decisive event in the American War of Independence. After hard-fought campaigns in the Carolinas (1780–1) the British under Cornwallis entered Virginia and established themselves at Y. near the entrance of the Chesapeake (2 Aug.). Supported by French naval forces, Washington and his French allies, advanced southwards. The English fleet was beaten off in the Chesapeake (5 Sept.) and the land forces began the siege of Y. (30 Sept.). Cornwallis failed to break out and finally surrendered to forces that were preponderantly French. This disaster re-awakened Parliamentary opposition to the war and marked the end of British efforts to subdue the Americans.   IHE

Young Ireland, a group of intellectual nationalists, founded in 1841, which disseminated its idealist views in the *Nation* newspaper. Its leaders drew patriotic inspiration from the Gaelic past and from Mazzini's Young Italy society. After the famine, the 1848 revolution in France excited members to insurrection which, with little or no support, completely failed, half-armed peasants under W. Smith O'Brien, M.P. for Co. Limerick, being dispersed at Ballingarry, Co. Tipperary (July 1848).   MLH

Young Wales or *Cymru Fydd* ('Future Wales'), was a nationalist movement founded in 1886 by Welsh Liberals, in imitation of Young Italy and Young Ireland. It embraced cultural and social aspirations as well as Home Rule. Despite a short spell of prosperity during 1892–5, when the Liberal majority of 40 in the Commons included 32 Welsh members, it

was dead before 1900 from inadequate leadership, personal rivalries, the Liberal defeat of 1895 and public indifference in Wales to political nationalism.   GW

Ypres, battles of in WORLD WAR I. **(1)** (12 Oct.–22 Nov. 1914), the German attempt to reach the Channel ports during the 'race to the sea' following stabilization of the allied defensive line at the Marne. The Germans made three attacks: on the whole front from the sea at Nieuport to La Bassée, held by the Belgian army, French troops, and the B.E.F. under Sir J. French (20 Oct.); south of Y. between Messines and Gheluvet (with the capture of Messines ridge), the brunt being taken by Haig's I Corps and Allenby's cavalry (31 Oct.); astride the Menin road against I Corps and II Corps (Smith-Dorrien) in an effort to capture Y. (11 Nov.). In each case the Germans nearly broke through, or did so but were stopped by reserves. British casualties were over 50,000.

(2) (22 April–25 May 1915). The Y. salient, held by 5 British and 2 French divisions was attacked by 11 German divisions. French withdrawal on the north side when faced with chlorine gas (used for the first time) necessitated a British retreat before Y., for recommending which Smith-Dorrien was replaced by Plumer in command of 2nd Army; desperate fighting ensued on the Frezenberg ridge (8–14 May). The Y. salient was reduced to a flat curve 2 miles from the town and overlooked by a ridge to the east. British casualties: 59,000.

(3) (31 July–10 Nov. 1917), a British offensive aimed at the Belgian ports; it was prolonged, at Pétain's entreaty, to draw German attention from the French armies, mutinous after Nivelle's failure. The first attack, mainly by Gough's 5th Army, gained little ground. The next major attack (20 Sept.) was planned by Plumer of 2nd Army to go forward in short stages; by 4 Oct. the crest of Y. ridge was gained. Despite deteriorating weather Haig decided to continue; in the battles for Passchendaele (taken 6 Nov.) most of the Y. ridge was taken, but lack of air support and the terrible state of the ground, which prevented use of tanks, made for heavy casualties. British losses were 245,000; German, considerably more. MLH

Yukon Territory was, following the discovery of gold (1896), carved out of the Canadian NORTHWEST TERRITORIES in June 1898 and constituted a separate territory under a commissioner, now assisted by an elected council.

SHS; IHE

Zambia (from *Zambesi*). The name adopted in 1964 when NORTHERN RHODESIA became an independent republic within the COMMONWEALTH. It incorporates the former British Protectorate of Barotseland. IHE

Zanzibar, inhabited by Bantu who were converted to Islam in the 10th century, became a Portuguese base in 1503 and was *c.* 1700 conquered by the Arabs from MUSCAT AND OMAN. In 1832 the imam of Oman established his capital at Z. and by 1837 brought under his control the islands of Z. and Pemba and the coast of EAST AFRICA. From the mid-18th century Z. was the biggest slave-market of the Arab world, but from 1822 the sultans co-operated with the British in gradually extirpating it. In 1861 Z. was declared independent of Oman by an arbitration of the governor-general of India. From 1849 when the Hamburg merchant, William O'Swald, established a trade factory in Z., German economic influence became paramount; in Aug. 1885 German warships forced the sultan to acknowledge German overlordship. In 1886–9 he relinquished his claims south of Cape Delgado to Portugal; between Cape Delgado and Vanga to Germany (TANGANYIKA); and north of Vanga to the British EAST AFRICA COMPANY (KENYA). By the HELIGOLAND treaty of 1 July 1890 Z. was placed under British protection; it was transferred from the foreign to the colonial office in 1914. Executive and legislative councils were set up in 1926, a privy council in 1956, and parliamentary government was introduced in 1961. On 24 June 1963 Z. achieved internal self-government and on 9 Dec. became an independent member of the Commonwealth. On 12 Jan. 1964 the sultanate was overthrown and Z. was declared a people's republic. In Apr. this joined with Tanganyika to form the United Republic of Tanganyika and Z.— renamed TANZANIA, 29 Oct.

Z. is the greatest supplier in the world of cloves which have been cultivated in Z. since 1818 and constitute more than half of her exports.

SHS; IHE

Zeebrugge raid (23 Apr. 1918), the gallant but only partially successful naval operation conducted by Vice-Adm. Sir Roger Keyes to render the U-boat base at Bruges inoperative. The attacks on the mole, railway viaduct and canal at Z. largely succeeded and block-ships were sunk but the attempt at Ostend (repeated on 9–10 May) failed. This St George's day raid made by a force of 146 small vessels had but temporary effects on U-boat activities. IHE

Zeven monastery, N.E. of Bremen, where on 8 Sept. 1757 the Duke of Cumberland, after the defeat of HASTENBECK, signed a convention by which he disarmed and dissolved his army and abandoned HANOVER and Brunswick to the French. George II relieved his son of his command and the Newcastle-Pitt government repudiated the convention and continued the SEVEN YEARS' WAR by the side of Frederick II of Prussia. SHS

Zinoviev letter (1924), advocating preparation for armed revolution, purported to be addressed by Z. and other members of the presidium of the Communist International to the British Communist Party. Issued (25 Oct.) 4 days before the general election by the Foreign Office, whose protest to the Soviet government seemed to certify authenticity, it increased disquiet aroused by the Anglo-Soviet treaty awaiting ratification. The Z.l.'s effect on the election was probably to confirm an already certain Conservative majority. The Liberal party was the main loser in the election, but about 100 of its candidates had stood down to ensure a united front against socialism. The Z.l. was established as a forgery in 1966.   MLH

Zululand, a powerful Bantu kingdom, established by Chaka (1818), reduced by the Boers (1840) and dissolved after the war of 1879, was annexed by Britain in 1888 and joined to NATAL on 30 Dec. 1897.   SHS

Zulu war (1879). The prime cause of the British annexation of the TRANS-VAAL (1877) was its weakness in the event of Zulu attack thereby endangering NATAL. The British high commissioner, Sir Bartle Frere, after making a favourable boundary award to the Zulus, ordered Cetewayo, their king, to disband his impis. On refusal British troops invaded ZULULAND to meet with disaster at Isandhlwana (Jan.). Natal was saved from invasion by a courageous stand at Rorke's Drift; the Prince Imperial of France, serving with the British forces, was killed in a skirmish, but the Zulu power was destroyed at Ulundi (July). The removal of the Zulu threat precipitated the first SOUTH AFRICAN WAR (1880-1).   IHE